# The Art of Return

# THE ART OF RETURN

## THE SIXTIES & CONTEMPORARY CULTURE

The University of
Chicago Press
Chicago and London

JAMES MEYER

The University of Chicago Press, Chicago 60637
The University of Chicago Press, Ltd., London

Published 2019
Printed in China

28 27 26 25 24 23 22 21 20 19    1 2 3 4 5

ISBN-13: 978-0-226-52155-8 (cloth)
ISBN-13: 978-0-226-62014-5 (e-book)
DOI: https://doi.org/10.7208/chicago/9780226620145.001.0001

This publication is made possible in part by the Andy Warhol Foundation for the Visual Arts.

The Andy Warhol Foundation for the Visual Arts


Library of Congress Cataloging-in-Publication Data

Names: Meyer, James Sampson, 1962– author.
Title: The art of return : the sixties and contemporary culture / James Meyer.
Description: Chicago : The University of Chicago Press, 2019. | Includes bibliographical references and index.
Identifiers: LCCN 2019014805 | ISBN 9780226521558 (cloth : alk. paper) | ISBN 9780226620145 (e-book)
Subjects: LCSH: Art, American—20th century. | Nineteen sixties. | United States—Civilization—1945–
Classification: LCC N6512 .M479 2019 | DDC 709.73/0904—dc23
LC record available at https://lccn.loc.gov/2019014805

♾ This paper meets the requirements of ANSI/NISO Z39.48-1992 (Permanence of Paper).

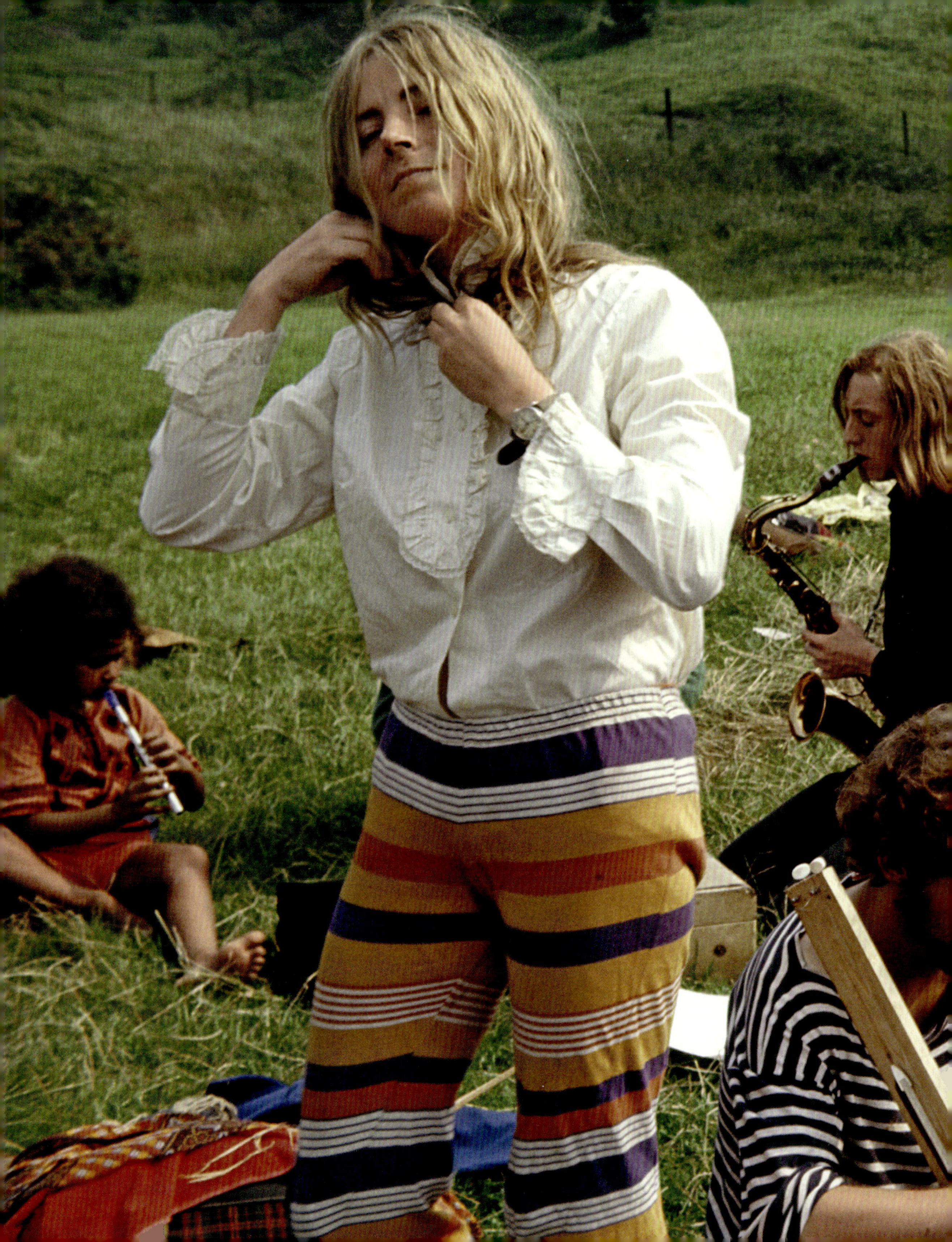

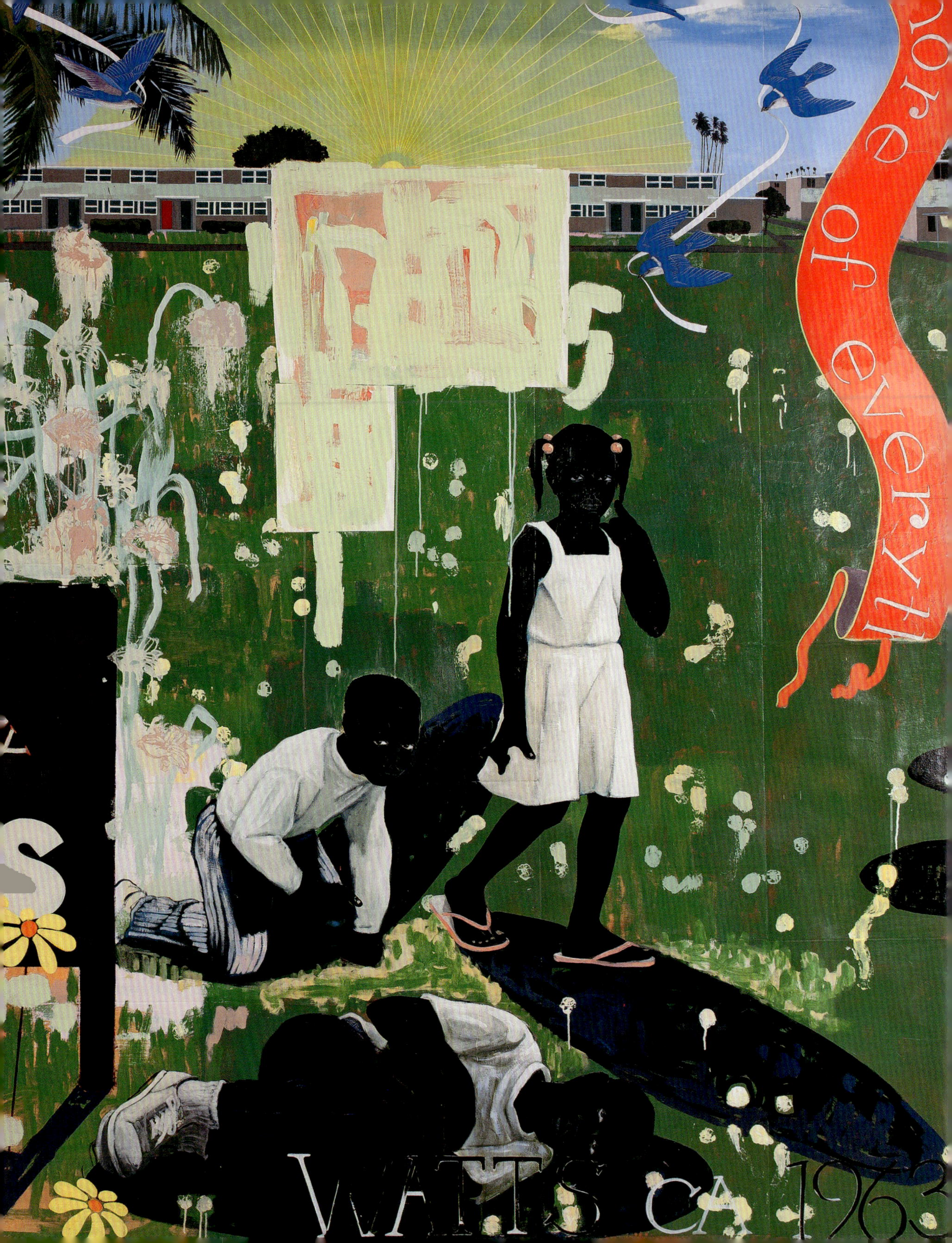
WATTS CA 1963

**To Charlotte Meyer and Harry Cooper**

**The obscure awareness of these moments, these places, perhaps more than anything else, confers on childhood memories a quality that makes them at once as evanescent and as alluringly tormenting as half-forgotten dreams.**

Walter Benjamin, *A Berlin Chronicle*

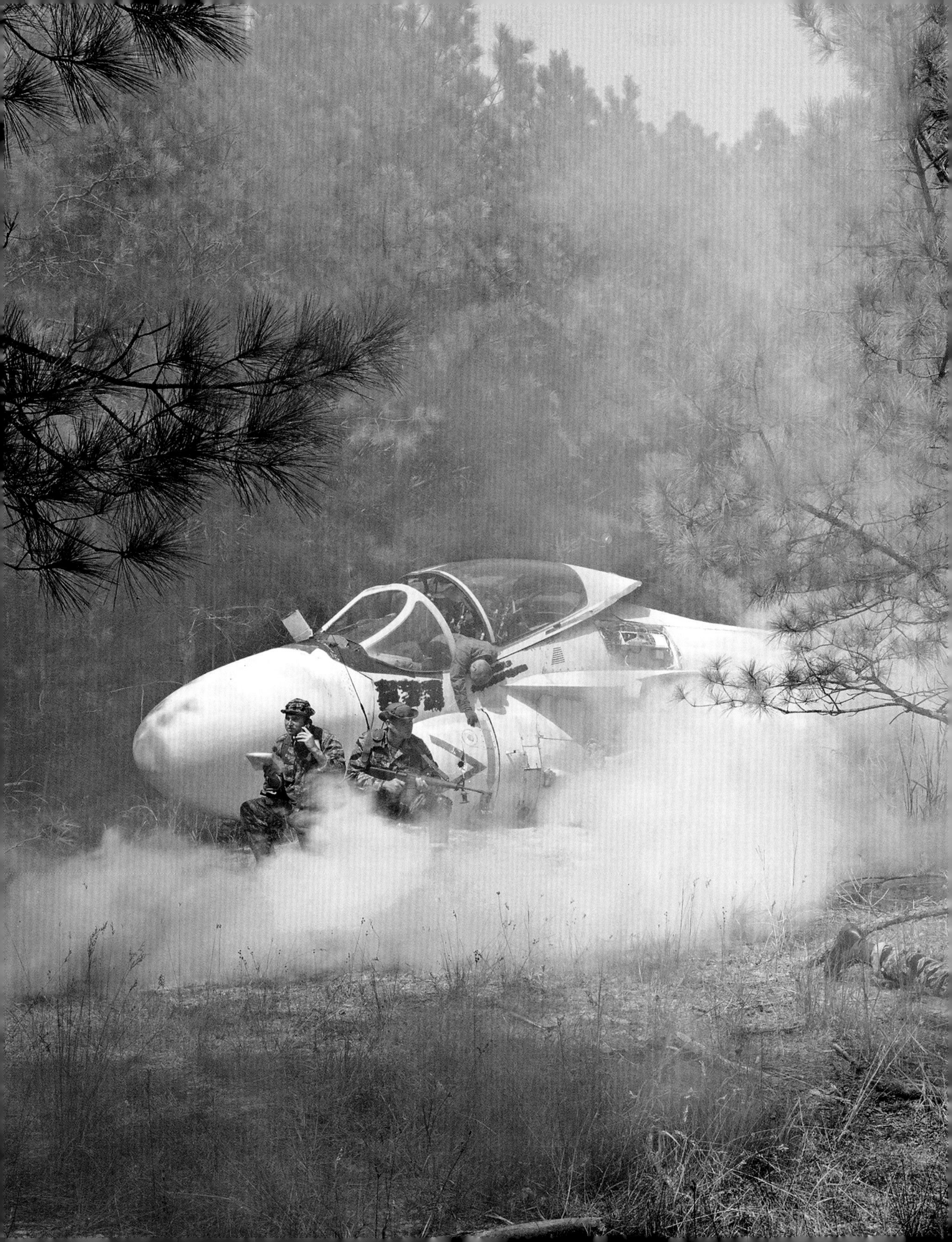

# CONTENTS

# INTRODUCTION

August 1971. The Summer of Love has finally arrived on Martha's Vineyard. When it comes, it hits hard. A mania for nude swimming and sunbathing has overtaken the beaches. Men and women retreat to the dunes to make love and frolic in the pools of melted clay that collect below the great cliffs of Aquinnah, from which they emerge covered head to toe in oily gray gunk, primeval beings for an afternoon.

That summer James Taylor performs for free in a meadow across from an old white church. My mother, quietly curious about these bacchanalian goings-on, so foreign to our suburban way of life, has brought me along with the stated intention of tracking down my teenage brothers, who have been seduced by the new ethos of hedonism and openness and who often disappear down the beach and to mysterious parties, away from our prying. They are nowhere to be found. And so we sit down in the brilliant summer night in a sweet cloud of marijuana and listen to Sweet Baby James's earnest ballads.

The Summer of Love is the Summer of the Road. People of all ages crowd the island lanes, thumbing for rides. A friend and I, determined to prove our independence, have hatched a secret plan to journey to the large town at the opposite end of the island entirely through our own efforts. We walk many minutes to the main road and stick out our thumbs as others do.

I am nine years old.

Drivers take pity on us, and we reach the town without fuss. I cannot recall how we spent those precious hours. The return journey doesn't go so well. Cars and trucks zoom past, indifferent to our plight, maddeningly empty of passengers. The afternoon shadows are growing long, my legs are fatigued, we are miles from home. Now we hear a sputtering sound, a shift of gears. An old VW microbus slows to a halt.

"Come on in!"

The person who welcomes us has shoulder-length hair, a blond beard, and penetrating gray eyes. He looks as I imagine Jesus looked. We scamper inside the swinging side door and find places to sit. The other passengers are teenage girls and young women in sarongs and flower dresses. With their untamed hair and golden tans, with their bare feet and earthy scents, they look like the members of some ancient, barbaric tribe. To my child's eyes they look magnificent. What a thrill to find myself among the sort of young people my father objects to for reasons I don't quite understand. To find myself in a bus of hippies.

The engine struggles as the driver switches gears, and the microbus lumbers uphill. The ride seems to take forever. The vehicle stops—"Come on in!"—and stops again. It stops in villages, in front of dirt roads, it stops in the middle of nowhere. Jesus *always* has room. Eventually nine or ten bodies squeeze inside the stuffy van.

I am glad I am small. I can still crawl beneath the corner table behind the large sofa in my parents' living room where no one will notice me; I can slither through the panes of open windows, and skip on the boulders of the harbor jetty without falling. Sailboats barely tilt when I step aboard. Squeezed in the side seat of the microbus, I scarcely take up any room (my twig limbs brush up against the bronzed legs and arms of my companions). Slowly my excitement dwindles. The pace of our progress is so lethargic I think only of home.

Then I begin to see, as we let off another passenger and welcome yet another, that there's a *logic* to this arrangement. With each stop, each greeting, Jesus is making a point that even a child can understand. The ride is not your usual hitchhike pickup but a moral lesson, an idea.

We're all in this together.
There are no hierarchies.
Together, we move forward.
No matter how long it takes.

Nobody hitchhikes on the island anymore. The hippies, the nudists, the couples having sex in the open air have vanished. The sun worshipers grew old. Their taut bodies became flabby, their once-supple skin wrinkled and spotted; gray hair dappled the men's chests; the women's legs became marbled with varicose veins. The couples now wear floppy bathing suits and carry umbrellas to protect them from the sun's harsh rays. Assisted by adult children and grandchildren, they struggle up dunes they once climbed with ease. Or they have disappeared from the beach completely. My impressions of that euphoric time remain, vivid and impossibly distant, as if the experiences that deposited these images in the deepest recesses of my memory were absorbed by a different version of myself, by someone from another time, by somebody else.

We are woven into history whether we realize it or not. An event as ordinary as my childhood hitchhiking adventure could only have happened in a particular place and moment. My experience with the bearded young driver, who generously picked up two unaccompanied young boys and took them home, is of another time. I did not know, until researching this book, that my turn in the microbus had a name: it was known as a Free Ride, a type of travel sharing more or less invented by a collective in San Francisco, the Diggers, who ferried passengers in buses without charge. Nor did I know that the widespread popularity of the VW microbus and Bug, the emblematic cars of the Sixties, had been instigated by a highly successful marketing campaign that constructed these automobiles as "countercultural."[1] By the early Seventies the fashions and mores of the Haight-Ashbury and East Village had migrated to the farms of Vermont and the tawny beaches of the Vineyard, upending Yankee traditions of restraint and self-reliance. And then—it is hard to pinpoint just when—it was over.

We live through blocks of time, periods. As children, especially, we are porous to an era without understanding that our experiences are historical, that what we take to be a given, unmovable reality, an eternal present, will not last in its current arrangement for much longer. We do not know this then. We do not yet understand that the encounters we take to be so personally and uniquely *ours* are only possible there and then. That they do not repeat. As children, we are imprinted with images of situations and events; we absorb these impressions with a rapt attentiveness, a completeness that surpasses our understanding of what is really going on. And because we do not entirely comprehend the few searing impressions we are able to hold onto as new memories crowd out the older ones, these images, fascinating rebuses, hold onto us, trail us, dog us. Eventually, we identify with these images. They come to define who we think we are. The time that marks us irreparably is the time when we are very young.

Our perceptions of a previous era and the present exist in parallax. A given past appears distant or meaningful in relation to our present course, as the contours of our own moment assume some sort of definition. So it was during the final weeks leading up to the 2004 U.S. presidential election, as I installed a show I had organized on that subject at a gallery in New York.[2] In October 2004, the catastrophic events of September 11, 2001, were a painful recent memory in that city. The U.S.-led invasion of Iraq was a year and a half old. The appalling abuses of captives at Abu Ghraib prison had just been exposed. Analogies between the Iraq and Vietnam Wars were constantly posed during an election that at times felt like a referendum on the Sixties itineraries of the Baby Boomer candidates who had been young then: a bellicose president who, having avoided service in Vietnam, had ordered the Iraq invasion under false premises, and a decorated Vietnam veteran who joined the antiwar movement in 1970 and was now the target of a smear campaign by some of his former comrades, the so-called Swift Boat Veterans for Truth.[3] Some thirty years after the fall of Saigon, the great fissures of the previous era—between the counterculture and New Left, on one hand, and President Richard Nixon's anticommunist "Silent Majority," on the other—resurfaced as an insuperable divide between "Blue" and "Red" voters.

The artist Martha Rosler appeared at the gallery with two cardboard packages. Unsealing the mats, she removed a pair of photomontages. *Election (Lynndie)* depicts the American soldier Lynndie England at Abu Ghraib with her infamous leash. England stands in an up-to-the-minute "gourmet" kitchen of stainless steel appliances, dark wood cabinets, and white marble countertops (fig. 0.1). Hanging on racks and scattered on counters are cooking and shelter magazines, their attractive covers replaced with gruesome depictions of torture, such as the infamous silhouette of a hooded Ali Shallal receiving electrical shocks, which Rosler has arranged serially throughout the room to emphasize the unspeakable inhumanity of that image and to suggest, through the technique of repetition, the numbness of the contemporary subject who is bombarded by such representations; and a clipping of a hapless editorial from the *New York Times* exhorting "concerned citizens" to help ensure that the imminent election will be "honest and fair." Behind a kitchen sink, dishwasher, and electric mixer (those reassuring emblems of middle-class domesticity), behind a wall of picture windows, are black-and-white panoramas of Iraqi streets. A car bursts into flames. Nearby, a raging fire consumes an apartment house. Clouds of smoke block out the sky. Day is night in Baghdad, in Fallujah. Men look on helplessly at the destruction.

The second of Rosler's pair, *Amputee (Election II)*, depicts an apocalyptic hotel suite at night (fig. 0.2). A spotlight illuminates cheap carpeting. On a flat-screen TV President George Bush and his brother, Florida governor Jeb Bush, chortle and guffaw as Jeb slaps his arms around the president's shoulders. A shirtless vet walks away from this rebarbative image of fraternal hilarity, his prosthetic leg a grim reminder of a war that has taken the limbs of a great many American servicemen and women, as the city beyond the picture windows goes up in flames.[4]

With these works Rosler resumed her practice of photomontage, a medium originally explored in her *House Beautiful: Bringing the War Home* series (1967–72), reprising this technique in order to defy yet another ill-fated war. Infusing a "Sixties" format with contemporary imagery, Rosler

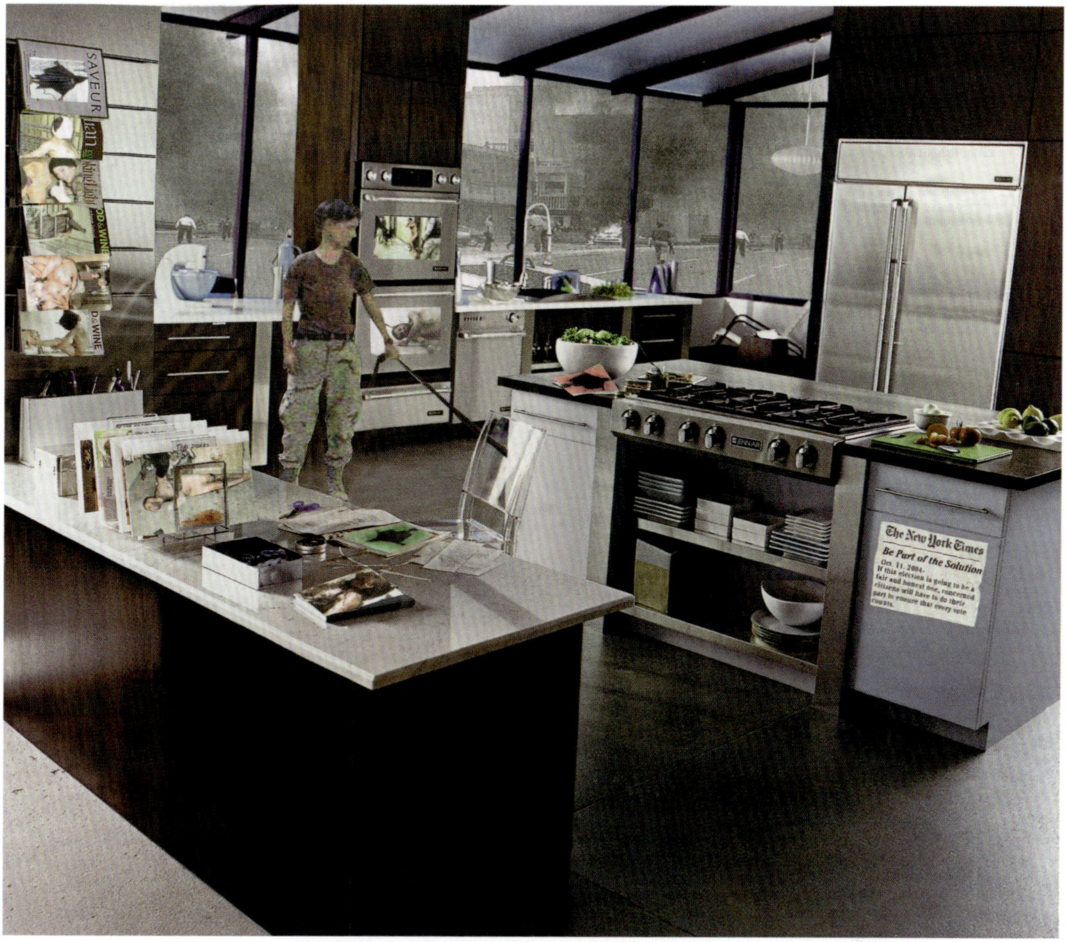


**Fig. 0.1.** Martha Rosler, *Election (Lynndie)*, 2004. From the series *House Beautiful: Bringing the War Home, New Series.* Photomontage. © Martha Rosler. Courtesy of the artist and Mitchell-Innes & Nash, New York.

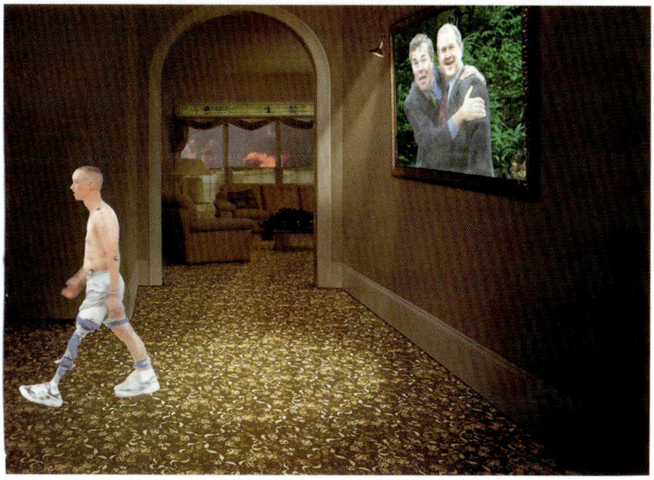

**Fig. 0.2.** Martha Rosler, *Amputee (Election II)*, 2004. From the series *House Beautiful: Bringing the War Home, New Series.* Photomontage. © Martha Rosler. Courtesy of the artist and Mitchell-Innes & Nash, New York.

staged a structure of comparison between the Indochina and Iraq incursions, illuminating the sharp differences and uncanny continuities between the wars and the periods they defined. The wounded figure in *Tron (Amputee)* (fig. 0.3) recurs in *Amputee (Election II)*, where the GI's modern metal prosthesis has replaced Tron's bandaged stump: though distinct in sex, ethnicity, and temporal and geographical location, the white male soldier sent into battle in Iraq and the Vietnamese civilian are equally the casualties of a misbegotten U.S. foreign policy. And where in Rosler's *Red Stripe Kitchen* male draftees "invade" a bright-hued suburban kitchen of late Sixties vintage (fig. 0.4), in *Election (Lynndie)* the protagonist is a woman soldier of the modern volunteer army established by President Nixon in 1973 that put an end to the widely disliked draft, quelling antiwar dissent. The working-class dominatrix supplants the traditionally gendered, wasp-waisted, middle-class homemakers of Rosler's *Cleaning the Drapes* and *Vacuuming Pop Art* from the first series. One kind of labor replaces another: in lieu of the housewife's tasks and efforts through a strict regime of dieting and styling to achieve womanly perfection (critiqued in Betty Friedan's *The Feminist Mystique* [1962] and other Second Wave salvos) England gleefully engages in the "masculine" activity of torture, her gender marshaled as an added humiliation for male captives raised in Muslim societies. The achievement of some measure of equality in the armed forces made possible by feminism sustains the war apparatus "after" feminism, Rosler's work implies. In the infernal corridors and torture chambers of Abu Ghraib gender itself was deployed as a technique of abuse.

The second *Bringing the War Home* series was not warmly embraced. The new photomontages baffled viewers unpersuaded by Rosler's reuse of a signal format of her early work; they dismissed her project and other manifestations of Sixties return in contemporary culture as revivalist, "academic," and so on. Reviewing an exhibit of these works, critic Jerry Saltz observed:

> Many younger artists, critics, and curators are fetishizing the Sixties, transforming the period into a deformed cult, a fantasy religion, a hip brand, and a crippling disease. A generation is caught in a Freudian death spiral and seems unable to escape the ridiculous idea that in order for art to be political it has to hark back to the talismanic hippie era—that it must create a revolution.... Many things happened during the Sixties, but the period is no more significant, better, or more "political" than today.[5]

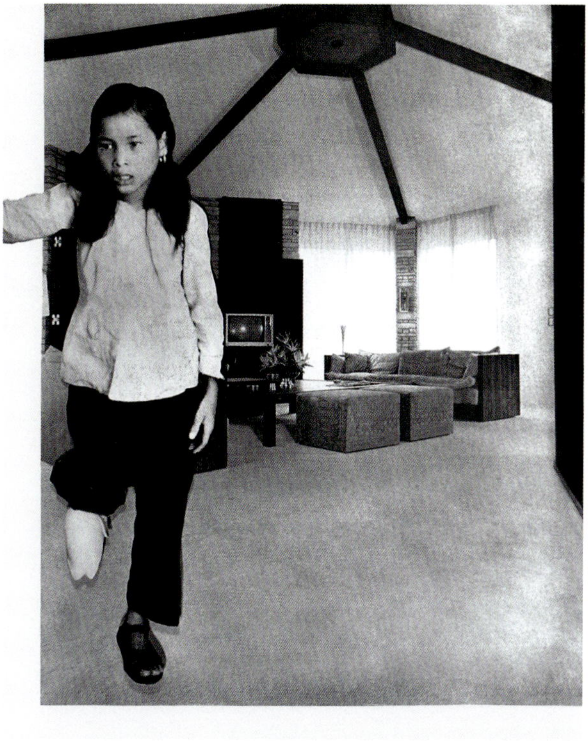

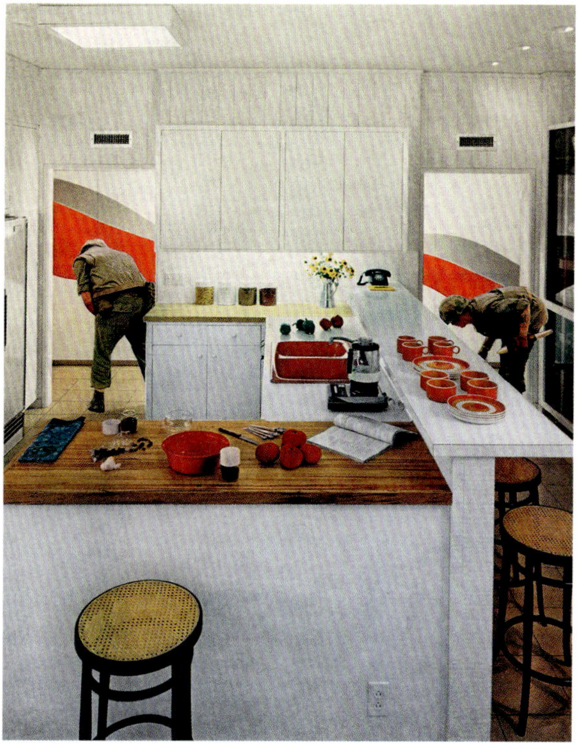

**Fig. 0.3.** Martha Rosler, *Tron (Amputee)*, c. 1967–72. From the series *House Beautiful: Bringing the War Home.* © Martha Rosler. Courtesy of the artist and Mitchell-Innes & Nash, New York.

**Fig. 0.4.** Martha Rosler, *Red Stripe Kitchen*, c. 1967–72. From the series *House Beautiful: Bringing the War Home.* Photomontage. © Martha Rosler. Courtesy of the artist and Mitchell-Innes & Nash, New York.

This book is about a broad cohort of artists, filmmakers, writers, and academics who are compelled to reexamine the Sixties and Seventies in their work, and whose fascination with the history, politics, and culture of that era is no "cult" or "disease" but a mnemonic and historical pursuit impelled by a gripping curiosity. For if our perceptions of a previous time and our moment are inextricably linked, comparisons between the Vietnam and Iraq Wars, the civil rights and Black Lives Matter movements, or between the Watergate and "Russiagate" scandals (to name the more obvious alignments) position the period encompassing the late Fifties, Sixties, and Seventies, described here as the long Sixties, as a recurring topos and origin. To insist that aesthetic practice turn its back on *that* past—a past that occupies a pivotal place in our collective memory—is to affirm a blinkered presentism. It speaks of a critical failure to come to terms with the centrality of the operations of history and memory in aesthetic and literary practice in recent decades. Precisely by returning *to* the long Sixties, we desanctify that era; we perceive its messy, historical character. Returning, we trouble the nostalgic fantasy that one time is "more significant, better" than any other.

As the Sixties pulls away from us, another "Sixties" projects forward, returns. It has returned repeatedly, and always differently, since the historical Sixties came to an end. And so we often find ourselves *returning to* this not-too-distant past as we attempt to define our own moment, the time we are in. *Return of/return to*: our discussion is located in the transversal space denoted by a slash, where the pulsions of history and memory meet and cross.

Why do the Sixties matter? Why so fabled? A half-century on, that era appears to us as a crux, a beginning. The Sixties, I argue in this book, constitute both the conclusion of modernism and its memory, the memory of the futurist dream of being-new. The last period of world revolution appears to us as a monumental past that feels timely *as* it becomes remote, yet is recent enough that many people remember it. The ambiguous nature of the not-so-distant past—a time that is both and equally history and memory—is a central preoccupation of this book. And so the hermeneutics of history enter our discussion: Reinhardt Koselleck's concept of historical time (history as overlap and return); Hannah Arendt's theory of revolutionary time; and Nietzsche's triadic scheme of historical narration ("monumental," "antiquarian," and "critical" histories). The literature on memory, known as memory studies, is also fundamental to this project, and we will often consult the writings of Walter Benjamin, Pierre Nora, Richard Terdiman, Dominick LaCapra, and Charles Meier, as well as psychoanalytic accounts of memory including traumatic recollection.

Between memory and history: the Sixties rub up against the contemporary in a perpetual imperfect tense. Writings on the period tend to divide between the firsthand accounts of the memoirist (who was "there") and the putatively "objective" third-person narrations of the historian/archivist: the recollections of "Boomers," on one hand, and the more distanced depictions of those who scarcely remember the Sixties, or not at all, on the other. With a few exceptions, most of the practitioners I discuss were born during the long Sixties. My research points up the fallacy of the Baby Boomer demographic of the census takers and marketers, which would have us believe that the subjective experiences of persons born from 1946 to 1964 are somehow equivalent or comparable, and that the experiences of individuals born during the Sixties and Seventies are not. I attempt to present a more precise description of late or post-Boomer sensibility, as expressed in the artworks and writings examined in this book.[6]

One need not have been born during a period to identify with it, to want to reconstruct or reimagine it: the period that concerns us is of compelling interest to younger artists and writers. Yet a central concern of this book is the peculiar generational identity of those who were born during that era or in its wake. The progeny of the last revolutionary period throughout much of the world were imprinted with the memory of a time of radical political and cultural imagination, and profound, even traumatic turbulence. The classical generation theory of Dilthey and Mannheim will lead us to the contemporary accounts of Nora and Terdiman, who argue that the generation in the modern sense emerges in the period encompassing the French Revolution (modernity's cataclysmic eruption) and Napoleon's rise and downfall. The mnemonic weight of those events is so immense that it defines, indeed creates, the generation as an idea. As revolution became a world principle, young people who came to maturity in the aftermath of these convulsions were imprinted with the imagery of a momentous period they barely glimpsed or missed outright.

The impulse to revisit the time of earliest memory increases as we enter midlife. Sixties children are not unique in this regard. What I am calling the Sixties return is an expression of *contemporary* sensibility. The practices that interest me emerged in response to the virulent denunciations of the Sixties by conservative politicians, pundits, and critics during the culture wars—the period of the Nineties and Aughts that also witnessed a new mobility and the rise of digital technologies and the internet. My discussion reflects these shifts of placement and technique. We will move between the fiction and memoir of Sixties return; documentary photos and films, and works that enlist analog and digital formats interchangeably; installations, sculptures, paintings; and reenactment, a performance of exacting replication of a historical event or speech described here as "doubling." Felix Gmelin's remake of a revolutionary student film of 1968; the respeakings of Sixties-era speeches by Mark Tribe and the collective BLW; the director John Malpede's reenactment of Robert Kennedy's 1968 "Poverty Tour" in eastern Kentucky; Vik Muniz's reproductions from memory of Sixties press photos; Nancy Davenport's and Matthew Buckingham's photos, and Nathan Hill's fictional depiction of campuses that witnessed protest; Wu Shanzhuan's remakes of Maoist simple character posters and reenactments of Red Guard humiliations; Jiang Ji-Li's memoir of her childhood in Cultural Revolution–era Shanghai; Cai Guo-Qiang's reproductions of a famous work of Maoist propaganda, *Rent Collection Courtyard*; Anri Sala's interrogation of his mother about her political activities in Seventies Albania; the "returns" to Vietnam of writer Nam Lê and photographer An-My Lê; Zarina Bhimji's cinematic meditation on her family's expulsion from Uganda in 1972; and Luke Fowler's archaeology of the radical London-based Scratch Orchestra: all these are among the projects examined in part 1, which explores the interpenetrating borders of history and memory, of pastness and recentness on a global scale, and the themes of "Sixties children" and Sixties topographies (definitions of the period as decadal, "long," or reducible to the pivotal year of 1968).

The narrative spans my lifetime, literally. A diachronic thread runs through these pages, twining my own recollections and the myriad "returns" of others. Where part 1 recalls episodes of my childhood, part 2 brings the reader into my adulthood and middle age, and the shifting perceptions of the long Sixties arising at different moments. I describe my attraction to the work and persona of Robert Smithson, and the enduring afterlife of the ephemeral sculptural forms of an artist who died tragically at thirty-five, an event that has shadowed the reception of his work ever since, folding his "life" and art upon one another in complex ways that are not easily disentangled; and the practices of such artists as Renée Green, Sam Durant, Mike Nelson, Tacita Dean, Jeremy Millar, Tom Burr, and Seth Price, who have continued, inverted, and displaced the formats of Smithson's work. To my thinking, this "Smithson return" has much to do with an implicit association of the artist and his work with the Romantic tropes of the ruin and the artist-genius who dying prematurely leaves behind a legacy of absence and longing as we imagine what might have been. My discussion examines the desire of the historian of the recent past to have known the subjects he or she writes about, impelled by a fantasy of complete archival knowledge or mastery. My inspirations here are Henry James's novella *The Aspern Papers* (1888), an unflinching examination of the scholarly impulse; a split-screen film by Amy Granat and Drew Heitzler, loosely based on Goethe's *The Sorrows of Young Werther*; and the gorgeous funereal sculptural ensembles of Banks Violette.

Smithson's dialectical system tethers the ephemeral and enduring, forgetting and remembrance, the entropic and monumental. We recall his ephemeral works and those of his contemporaries long after their ruination. They are "monuments" because they inspire us to remember them, even though their makers may not have imagined these projects would endure as long as they have. But entropy is more than a material process for Smithson; it implies *social* decay. Where the compass of part 1 is transnational, part 2 examines a construct of the United States during and since the Sixties as a society in decline, as entropic. *Partially Buried Woodshed* (1970), an earthwork that Smithson made at Kent State University in Ohio, came to be associated with the notorious massacre of that year. The Kent tragedy came to exemplify the "bad" Sixties in the United States, a Sixties that conservatives equate with an unraveling of cultural and moral "authority," a Pandora's Box we need to close. The obverse of this Sixties is an era fondly recalled on the Left as a time of widespread activism and aesthetic daring, the Sixties of the antiwar, civil rights, feminist, LGBTQ, and environmentalist movements and the counterculture—a "good" Sixties. The artworks I consider by Green, Durant, and Nelson dismantle this Manichean arrangement, revealing the "two Sixties" to be mutually imbricated, two sides of the same coin. And though the paradigm of the two Sixties has played out in very particular ways elsewhere (in France and Germany, for example) the focus of part 2 is the rise of the stark political and cultural divide between "Red" and "Blue" states and voters that remains fundamental in current descriptions of the American polity and nation-state.

Part 2 addresses the affective character of our fascination with a past that we barely glimpsed, or missed—the feeling known to us as nostalgia. Nostalgia, the third and final mode of return examined in this book (after the discussion of history and memory in part 1), is the desire to revisit the time of childhood as we grow older. One might claim that many of the practices discussed in this book—and this book itself, too—were impelled by nostalgic longing. The theoretical writings of Jean Starobinski and Susan Stewart; novels by Jennifer Egan, Dana Spiotta, and Rachel Kushner; and a video installation by Seth Price have inspired my attempt to flesh out the definition and character of this powerful form of mnemonic attachment.

Yet the intention of this study is antinostalgic. Like the artists and writers who inspired my research, I am concerned to retrieve the memory of a period that functions in the Left imaginary as the "last" era of social justice on a broad scale, a ground zero of progressive politics. But I am absolutely convinced that the memory of the Sixties will serve us only insofar as we historicize—and criticize—that storied time. The aim is to retrieve a Sixties we neither glorify nor dismiss; a Sixties of contradiction; a Sixties we can historicize and judge, as Nietzsche would have us do.

Part 3, the book's concluding section, turns to Kerry James Marshall's *Mementos* series (1998–2003), a meditation on the presence and weight of civil rights memory for African Americans, as publicly marked by the events surrounding the fiftieth anniversary of the 1963 March on Washington for Jobs and Freedom, held in 2013. During the present era of resurgent activism in the United States catalyzed by the Black Lives Matter movement, the memory of the era of civil rights and black nationalism remains timely as past horrors seem to repeat themselves. The lesson of Marshall's installation is a Nietzschian one: as the weight of a monumental past increases it becomes more and more necessary to let go of memory and nostalgia, to forget. With the slippage of the Sixties into a past that feels ever more distant as the demands of the present increase comes the eventual waning of the Sixties return.

•

What is the form of this book, a work that braids historical and personal memory? My previous scholarship enlisted the techniques of "proper" history to define a historical art movement, willing a recent past into a farther, definite past.[7] If the driving concerns of that inquiry were *what* and *how*, the central question of this essay is *why*: why do the Sixties return, and why do we return to that time? What is the desire of the artist or writer or scholar who revisits a period that precedes his or her full cognizance?

The locations of Sixties memory are infinite. Just as this book moves backward and forward temporally, it moves sideways from one site of Sixties eventfulness to another. We will find ourselves in the Rathaus Square in West Berlin during the visit of the Shah and Empress of Iran in 1967; in a schoolyard in Shanghai in 1966 at the height of Cultural Revolution fervor; in the corridor of a classroom building at the University of Wisconsin blocked with the bodies of antiwar protesters; in a pine forest in Virginia with Vietnam War reenactors, and in the passenger hall at the decaying Entebbe Airport, where we are witnesses to the fleecing and deportation of Uganda's South Asian citizens some thirty years before. This book explores a generational set of interests, yet it reveals that generations are local formations, as generation theory holds: our experiences of the same time are particular, endless—and ultimately incomparable. Though transnational in reach, the book cannot claim to present a truly global analysis. A reflection of the taste, interests, and experiences of its author, whose many "identities" and identifications inform this text in ways he may not entirely perceive, this account is admittedly partial and incomplete.

Walter Benjamin described his essay "Berlin Childhood around 1900," a text we will often turn to, as an attempt to "inoculate" himself against the pangs of nostalgia for a place and time that were irretrievably lost to him. He returned imaginatively, in writing, to the streets and parks of his childhood that he could not visit in actuality. Rather than tell the "story of his life," the ambition of the memoirist, his essay periodizes the material and social circumstances of his upper-middle-class Jewish boyhood in the imperial city. The narrator who describes the places and objects of his youth is a witness to their existence. Yet Benjamin himself almost disappears.

This book began as an attempt to make sense of those obdurate impressions of childhood that appear strange to me even now. What has emerged is not a self-portrait but its antidote, a countermemoir:

the narrator or "I" of this book is one of many such rememberers engaged in a generational act of self-examination. I wrote the book as an antidote not only to the nostalgia that has haunted me since that time, but also to our own culture of balmy presentism, of infinite self-regard, of navel-gazing memoirs and reality TV shows, of narcissistic selfies and personal webpages documenting our lives for public consumption and trumpeting our achievements. Returning—returning as I understand it—we learn that the experiences we imagine to be exclusively *ours* are woven into history, tethered to place, as if by a force of inevitability. Returning, we begin to perceive the historical nature of subjectivity itself—our embeddedness *in* time.

# PART 1
# THE SIXTIES RETURN

**I delight in a palpable imaginable *visitable* past—in the nearer distances and the clearer mysteries, the marks and signs of a world we may reach over to as by making a long arm we grasp an object at the other end of our own table. The table is the one, the common expanse, and where we lean, so stretching, we find it firm and continuous. That, to my imagination, is the past most fragrant of all, or of almost all, the poetry of the thing outlived and lost and gone, and yet in which the precious element of closeness, telling so of connections but tasting so of differences, remains appreciable.**

Henry James, preface to the New York edition of *The Aspern Papers*

What can one period mean to another? Under what circumstances does a previous time become meaningful, useful even, and the past no longer appear to us as merely past? What are the forms of these animations, the mechanisms of these returns?

T. J. Clark has referred to modernism as our antiquity.[1] The version of modernism he describes in *Farewell to an Idea* projects a view of history as a forward motion, a process that we can steer and mold. The modernism Clark describes supposes that we can cast off a burdensome past, invent new forms, wipe the slate clean. It promises that we can *be* new. This belief system is now so ossified we can barely understand it, Clark says. The modernist future is a dead future, one whose logic we cannot even begin to grasp. Clark's account is a cautionary tale, a tissue of contradictions. Utopic dreams yield dystopic outcomes. Formal innovation and cooptation are inextricably linked. Modernism fails. Again and again. From Jean-Louis David's Paris of Year 2, to El Lissitzky's Vitebsk, to Jackson Pollock's Manhattan, the modernist ideals of social improvement and unfettered freedom are ruthlessly betrayed.

Yet the slow decline of modernism as a viable aesthetic principle does not foreclose the *future* as an idea.[2] To speak of the future entails that we consider the recent past, the past that bleeds into our moment. Narratives of the present are historical narratives, genealogies of the contemporary. Matthew Arnold once described the condition of being modern as an "impatient irritation of mind" in the face of the "immense, moving, confused spectacle" we call the present. Being modern requires a comparative awareness: we are "delivered" from our self-absorption, our myopia, and our sheer perplexity, the poet says, when we consider other cultures and eras. When we *compare*. Arranging two events in our minds allows us to perceive their difference—the distinction between a current state of affairs and a prior condition. The moment we are in—Arnold's "confused spectacle"—is a little less confusing.[3]

Theories of modernism and postmodernism, for all their refinements and differences, typically compare a current moment to an earlier time, a generic "past." Where futuristic modernism, the modernism of Friedrich

Nietzsche and T. J. Clark, negates the past as burden, as something we need to forget, a second version of modernism (associated with T. S. Eliot and Clement Greenberg) is a narrative of continuity, of tradition. The most salient contemporary works of art and literature invite comparison with older monuments. The rare innovator, the "individual talent," is capable of expressing emotions in ways previously unexpressed. The old languages will not do.[4] But rather than transgress the medium's proprieties, as the avant-gardist (a Marcel Duchamp or John Cage) attempts to do, the modernist poet or painter brings the medium forward another step by eschewing established formal norms. Modernism "*continues* the past without gap or break" by *not* repeating what came before.[5]

Postmodernism repudiated the historicism of the second modernism while mourning the utopic imagination of the first. It rephrased newness as *post*-ness. Once-radical innovations, such as the grid and monochrome canvas, were now perceived as preexistent, repeatable, no longer new.[6] The postmodernist work could only speak of its belatedness, its status as supplement, as copy, as allegory.[7] The work was never "present" to a viewer as the modernist artwork was claimed to be.[8] Its temporal character was far more ambivalent. Douglas Crimp describes the paradoxical nature of the exemplary postmodernist work, the "Picture," as "both present and remote." A viewer does not necessarily remember the original image (the particular movie that may have inspired a Cindy Sherman *Film Still*, for example). He or she remembers its *having been present*, which is to say its absence. A distance has been established between the time of viewing and another moment, prior yet uncertain, evoked by the Picture.[9]

Futurist modernism, historicist modernism, postmodernism: the seminal aesthetic theories of the last century were narratives of *time*. The contentious debates between critics associated with these paradigms typically addressed how works of art and writing come to terms with the past—and how this "past" exerts a tenacious hold on the present. And, in fact, the representation of the past, the imagination of history, has reemerged as a contemporary preoccupation. The histories of indigenous peoples; the court of Henry VIII; the Middle Passage of slaves from Africa to the Americas; the colonial cloth trade; a text by the eighteenth-century feminist Mary Wollstonecraft; a coal strike in Thatcher's Britain: artists and writers explore these and other histories. In a time that is often described as presentist and temporally ambiguous, practitioners rifle the past opportunistically to illuminate a present condition. Reimagining history, they ask what the past means to us now.[10]

Now, there is no past more *present* during our time than the Sixties.[11] If modernism is our "antiquity," then the Sixties is indubitably our modernism—or what stands for it at present. The Sixties is our modernism, I argue in this book, because the Sixties represents the memory of modernism and earlier modernities, the memory of the fantasy that we can "be new." That we can invent new forms, wipe the slate clean. That we can build a more just society. Futuristic modernism did not seem so ancient then. Utopic longings were not so easily dismissed. The Cultural Revolution was the memory of the People's Revolution, the counterculture the memory of older utopic communities, the "neo" avant-garde the memory of the historical avant-garde.[12] During the Sixties the imagination was constantly spoken about, lauded, molded into a politics. ("All power to the imagination!" the students of Paris declared to the world during the "Events" of May 1968.) What we call the Sixties is the last time the imagination was so enunciated, so celebrated, the last time it seemed as if "everything was possible," as Fredric Jameson once observed.[13]

What was this "everything," what made it possible? A new economic order came into place then, Jameson suggests in a classic argument, an order he defines as a transition from one phase of capitalist and technological innovation to another. During the long Sixties—a period roughly spanning the mid-Fifties to the late Seventies, and on which we will have much to say—the industrial economy of high modernity evolved into a nuclear, televisual, and digital order. Advanced capitalism, postindustrial society, consumer culture, the media age: that era has many names.[14]

Jameson's Sixties is the most theorized we have—a structuralist mapping of "levels" emerging simultaneously around the globe.[15] His account is richly dialectical. On one hand, the Sixties represent a toppling of authority, a revival of the Enlightenment dream of universal freedom, a dream of being new. Globalization was then a fantasy of universal socialism, of Marxist totality, incredible as that now seems. "The globalization of revolutionary forces is the most important task of the whole historical period that we live in," the leader of the German New Left, Rudi Dutschke, declared then.[16] But hegemonic forces were equally at play. Colonialism mutated into neocolonialism; multinational corporations penetrated Third World economies; the Green Revolution opened up new markets; the U.S. military-industrial complex competed with the Soviet Union for Cold War dominance.[17] The long Sixties ushered in new forms and experiences of mediation, an infiltration of the televisual and digital into psychic life, a depletion of the somatic. And it catalyzed awareness of domestic and global injustices, a longing for new freedoms and bodily pleasures and alternative lifestyles. The new economy generated middle-class affluence, the necessary precondition for the repudiation of this "System" by young people.[18] The counterculture that emerged then "was grounded paradoxically not in the failure, but in the *success* of a high industrial economy."[19] To write or research or make art about the Sixties is to confront an era of extreme paradoxes, of irreconcilable contradictions. We are grappling with them still.

## Sixties Children

The Sixties is both distant and near. It is our future past, for it imagines, and spectacularly fails to imagine, this moment, however we would describe it. The Sixties is a crux, a tectonic shift in politics and culture. It is modernism's apogee and conclusion, its final bow; and it is the beginning of the time we are in.[20] And so the meaning of the Sixties is fiercely contested. Some would leave behind a period they experienced—to forget what they remember. They view the ideologies they embraced, the choices they made then, with skepticism or even contempt.[21] They have turned the page—a long time ago—and chasten us to embrace our presentness. To move on, get on with it. If we can't "be new," we can at least be contemporary.[22] Others view that time nostalgically. They remember what happened—they were "there." And they inveigle the rest of us (who were not "there") to remember, too. Remember the March on Washington. Remember Stonewall. Remember feminism. Remember May. Remember Vietnam. Remembering the Sixties helps us imagine that change is still possible. Sixty-eight, most iconic of Sixties years, is thus proposed as an imaginary "space for thinking, describing, and theorizing social change in the present tense."[23]

Others (the numbers grow ever larger) don't understand what all the fuss is about. They have no memories of the Sixties or Seventies nor cherish their parents' memories of that time. That era feels as ancient to them as modernism; Angela Davis is "almost as remote" a figure to this cohort as Emma Goldman.[24] And there are others who have heard "too much." Who are burdened with secondhand memory. Who remember their parents' memories, their professors' memories. Who have heard about the glory days, the daring exploits of the Sixty-eighters. Who are reminded that they live in an era of diminished expectations—a dull time. And they are weary of these comparisons.[25]

There are others who recall that time vaguely. Who barely remember—but cannot forget. Who remain fascinated by those random images that remain, inexplicably, from that tumultuous era, secreted in the depths of memory. Sixties children, I call them. One need not have been born during a period to harbor a feeling for it, to identify with it, to be marked by it. "We do not necessarily belong to the generation to which the dates of our birth consign us," historian Pierre Nora has written.[26] Nora's claim—that we often identify with a past era, or with a generation that is not properly "ours"—is complicated when this past is relatively recent, when

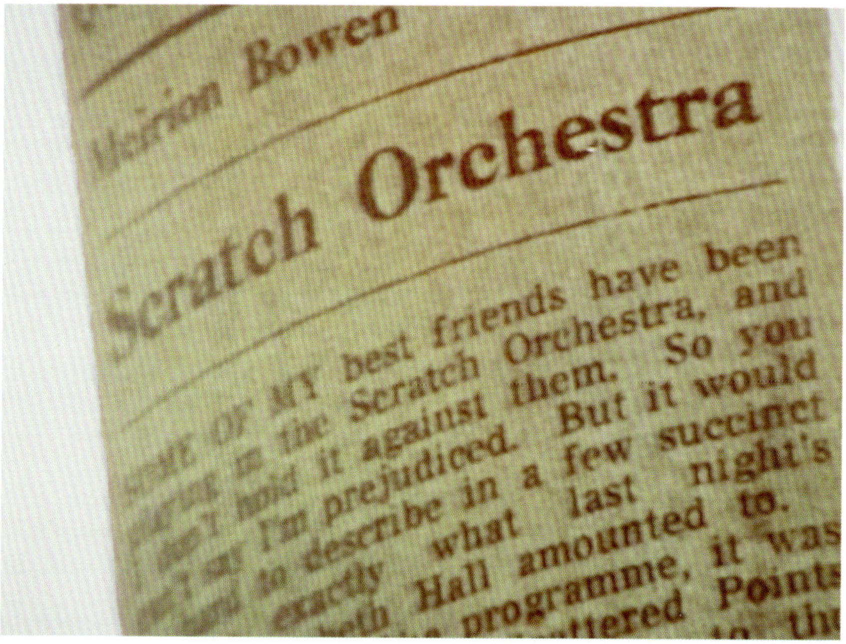


**Fig. 1.1.** Luke Fowler, *Pilgrimage from Scattered Points* (still), 2006. DVD, color and black-and-white, sound. 45 minutes. Courtesy of the artist and The Modern Institute / Toby Webster, Ltd., Glasgow.

it brushes up against the contemporary, when it impacts us in ways we don't entirely grasp. The Sixties is recent history, after all, and certainly momentous. It remains insistently *present* even as it feels more historical, more foreign, with every passing year. It returns—and we return *to* that time. And so many practices of return were developed by artists and writers born during the long Sixties, whose earliest memories date to that period, or who were born in its aftermath.[27] Children of the Sixties. How did the upheavals of that era affect them before they were aware of what was happening? Who are they?

We catch a glimpse of them in *Pilgrimage from Scattered Points* (2006), a film and photo installation by Luke Fowler (fig. 1.1). Fowler revisits the history of the Scratch Orchestra, the anarchic musical ensemble co-founded by British composer Cornelius Cardew in 1969. Some of the Scratch members were trained musicians; many were not. Scratch arrangements were based on graphic notations and verbal instructions instead of traditional lined scores and compositional principles. Intended to precipitate new modes of listening and cognition, these works typically met with incomprehension. The orchestra's *Popular Classics* were discordant riffs on cherished melodies. Cardew's *The Great Learning* (a choral work based on Ezra Pound's translation of Confucius) lasted six hours, trying the patience of even the most intrepid listeners.

During the summer of 1970 the orchestra toured Cornwall and Wales; the following year they traveled north to Newcastle. Forsaking the respectability of white tie and traditional concert venues, the members performed in ordinary dress in village halls, train stations, shopping centers, and public parks. Rather than stay in hotels, they slept outdoors.[28] A Romantic idea of childhood informed Scratch theory and practice:

> The experience of the Scratch Orchestra, at least in its first two years (its Golden Age) now seems like a second childhood. This feeling is not merely due to such Scratch phenomena as a craze for snake whistles, but the emphasis on *doing* without bothering about the how or why. Everything—a sound, a sight, an action, no matter how "ordinary"—was held, with child-like wonder, to be an amazing experience.[29]

Cardew composed his *Schooltime Compositions* (1968) to be performed "as though it had been played by a child," and he welcomed children in Scratch activities.[30] In a photograph recovered by Fowler during his

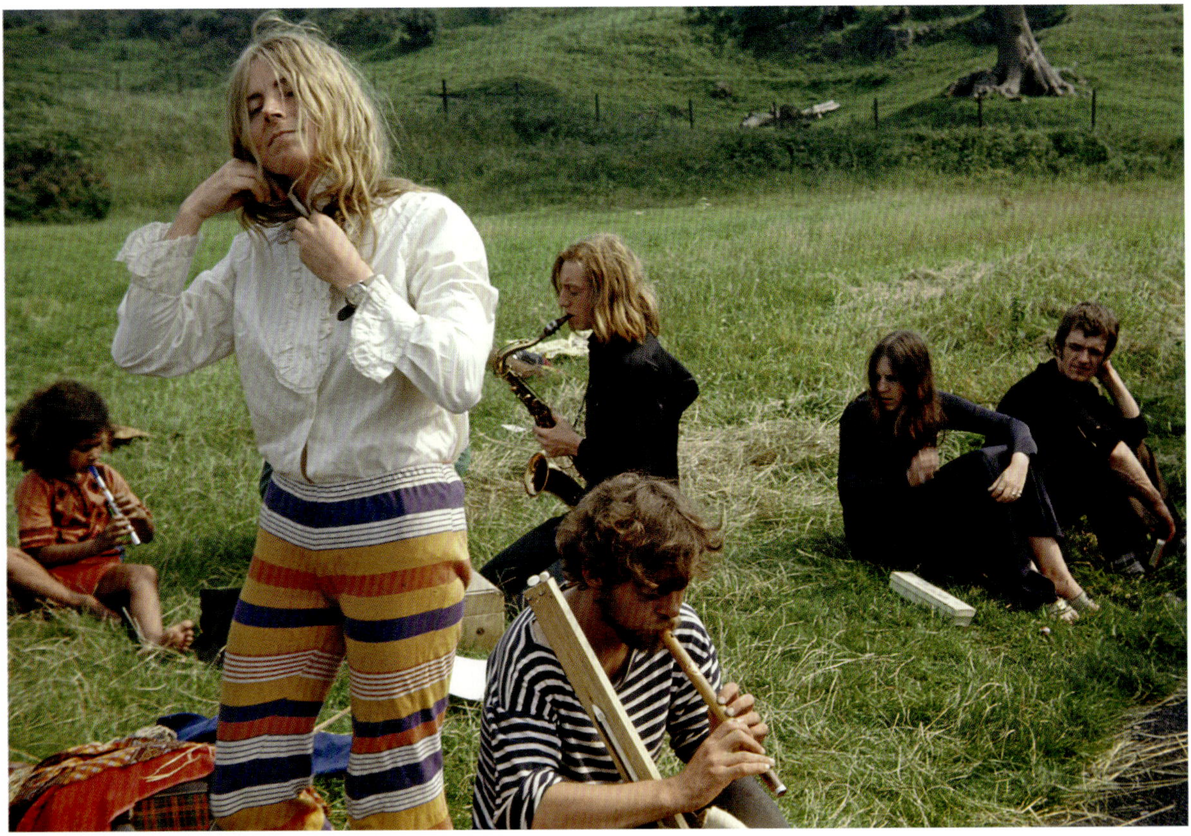

**Fig. 1.2.** Luke Fowler, Digital reprint of a photograph by Alec Hill. Birgit Burckhardt (center), Seba Phombeah (left), Hugh Shrapnell (whistle), Greg Bright (sax), and Diane Jackman (background). North East Tour, 1971, 2006. C-print. Courtesy of the artist and The Modern Institute / Toby Webster, Ltd., Glasgow.

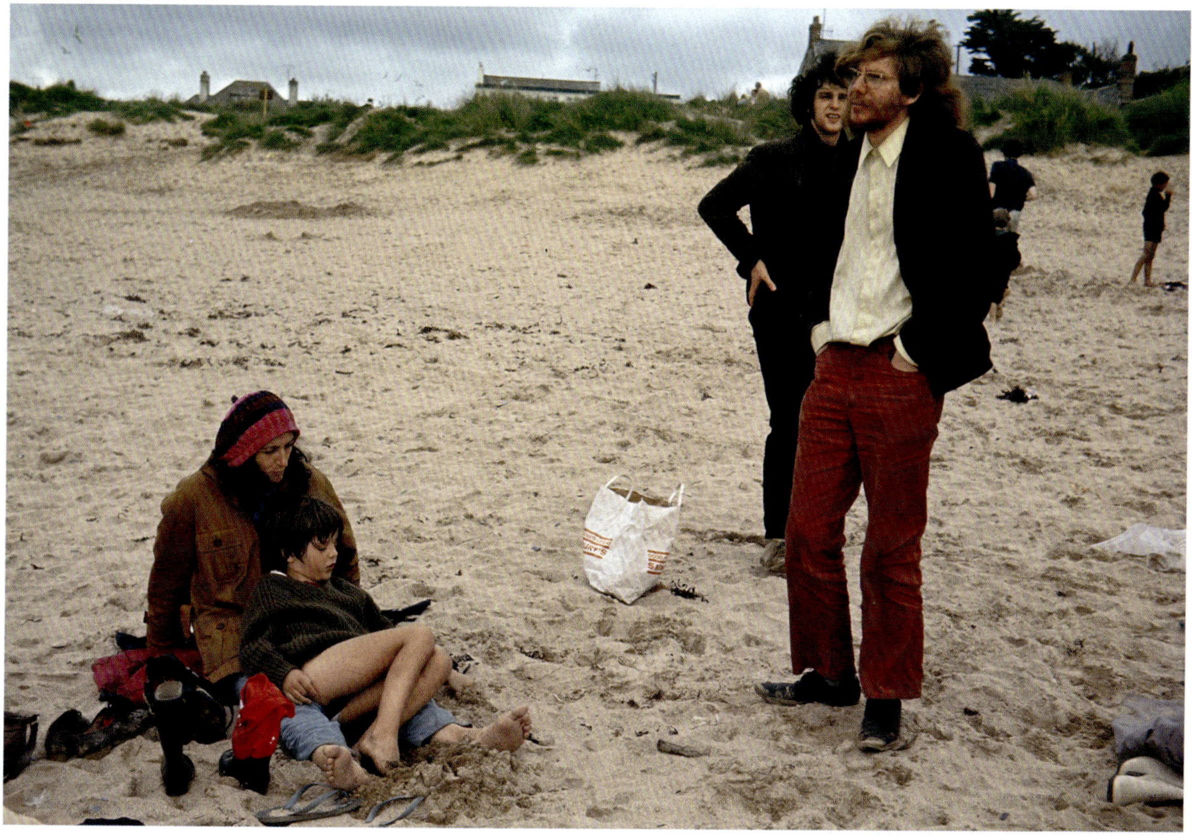

**Fig. 1.3.** Luke Fowler, Digital reprint of a photograph by Alec Hill. Michael Chant and Carole Finer holding Horace Cardew on the beach in Cornwall. Village Halls Tour, 1970, 2006. C-print. Courtesy of the artist and The Modern Institute / Toby Webster, Ltd., Glasgow.

research, a girl sits in a field playing a child's recorder with musicians in their teens and twenties (fig. 1.2). Another photo depicts a boy of five on a beach in Cornwall. He lies in the lap of a woman who, it turns out, is not his mother. The boy is Horace Cardew, Cornelius's younger son (fig. 1.3).

Scratch children enjoyed a great deal more freedom than the offspring of more conventional parents. Cardew believed that children should not be confined or condescended to; "he treated [them] as equals."[31] His biographer, John Tilbury, describes how Horace and his brother were permitted to run around these campsites "with pagan energy and bliss."[32] There were down moments, too. In the photograph, the Cornish sky is overcast, the afternoon chilly. The woman who looks after the boy, orchestra member Carol Finer, wears a knit cap and coat. Horace digs his heels impatiently in the sand and looks away. They are passing the time. *Waiting.* The progeny of revolutionaries must be patient. They endure unusual situations, extreme situations, that other children do not.[33] As children, they have no other choice.

The theme of Sixties children is also explored in Felix Gmelin's two-channel video *Sound and Vision* (2005; fig. 1.4). One video is a clip from a Swedish sex education film produced in 1970.[34] A teenage boy and girl stand bravely at the head of an elementary school classroom, undressed. They are on display; yet they are invisible to the students who sit in front of them. (Close-ups reveal that the children are blind.) At a teacher's prompting a young girl runs her fingers down the youth's chest, and then his stomach. She touches his penis and squeezes his testicles (fig. 1.5). The boy next to her places his hands on the young woman's breasts and examines her pubis. A new style of teaching has replaced book learning and rote memorization in Sweden during the early Seventies. Knowledge is gained through sensual experience, blindness overcome by touch. This is the lesson the children are being taught. It is hard to imagine these pedagogical methods being used now. The teacher who guides the girl's hand to the young man's penis, a wedding band displayed on this woman's finger, is a shocking sight to contemporary eyes. How liberated, how foreign, it all seems.

The adjacent video shown by Felix Gmelin was actually made by the artist's father (fig. 1.6). Otto F. Gmelin (1931–95) was a professor and media theorist who wrote about television, psychoanalysis, children's education, and feminism; he also made videos.[35] The videotape, which Otto completed in 1984, features the two of them. Otto holds up a series of

**Fig. 1.4.** Felix Gmelin, *Sound and Vision*, 2005. High-resolution video, 3-minute loop. Installation view from Berlin Biennial 4, 2006, "Of Mice and Men," curated by Maurizio Cattelan, Massimiliano Gioni, and Ali Subotnick. Photograph: KW Institute for Contemporary Art, Berlin, and the Berlin Biennale for Contemporary Art. Courtesy of Felix Gmelin.

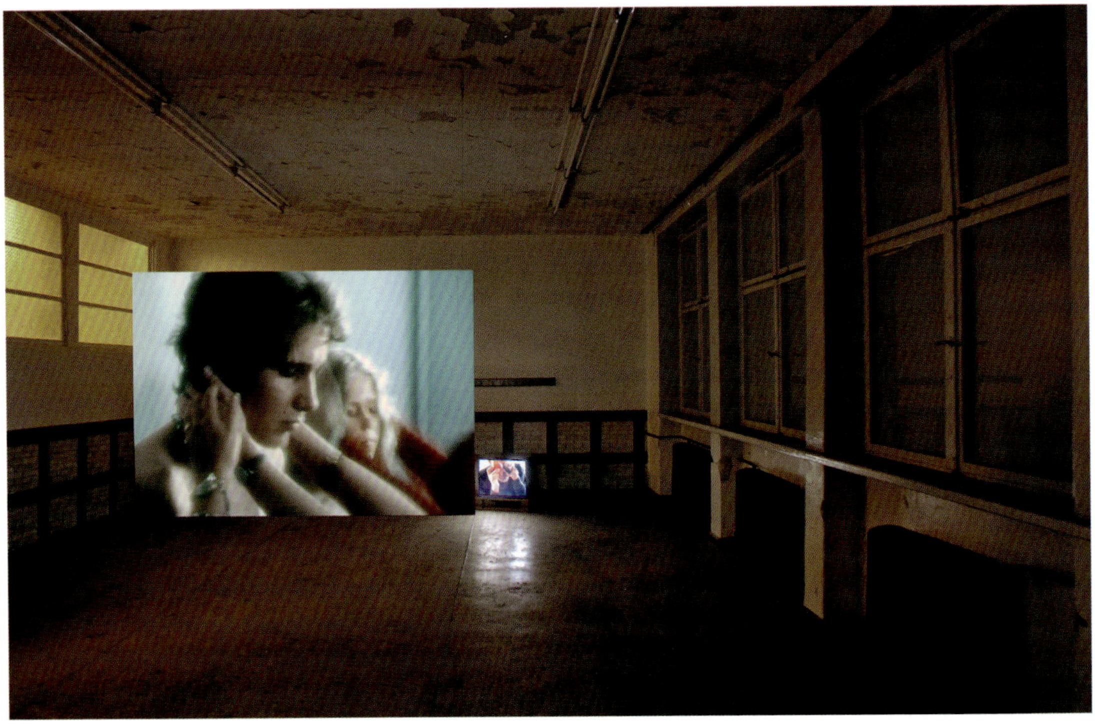

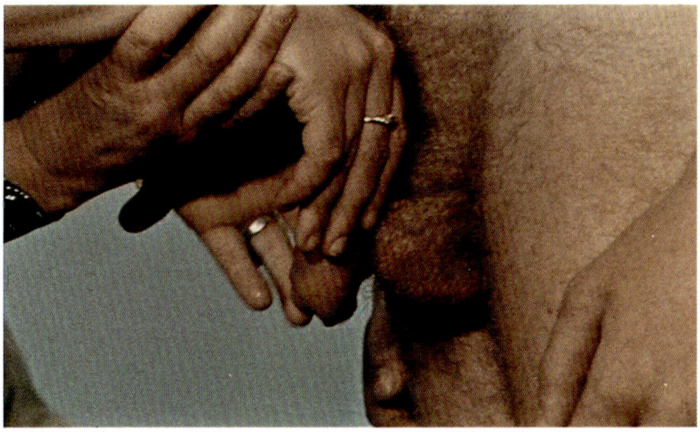

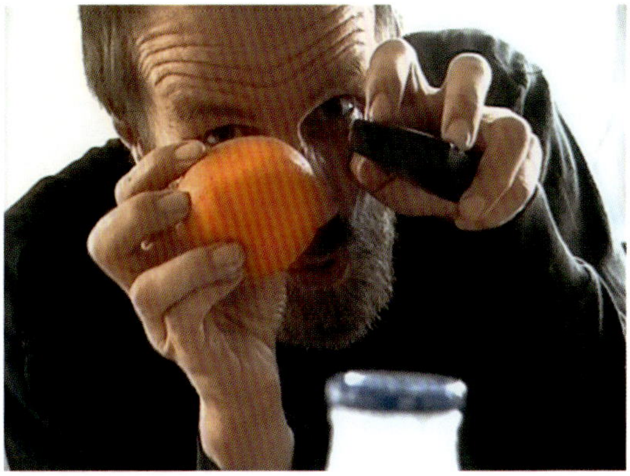

**Fig. 1.5.** Felix Gmelin, *Sound and Vision*, 2005. High-resolution video, 3-minute loop. Screen shot. Courtesy of Felix Gmelin.

**Fig. 1.6.** Felix Gmelin, *Sound and Vision*, 2005. High-resolution video, 3-minute loop. Screen shot of Otto F. Gmelin, late 1980s. Courtesy of Felix Gmelin.

objects: an orange, a candlestick, a banana peel, a black-and-white photo, a children's book. Each of these things elicits a different sound. Otto grunts, he whistles. His facial features contort. A water bottle elicits a hiss, an apple a piercing scream. These objects are inanimate, passive. We take them for granted much of the time. Otto animates these things, gives them voices. He makes them "speak." Why has Felix combined Otto's tape with the sex education film? Where the teacher helps her students "see" by combining touch and sound with linguistic mastery, Otto detaches things from their ordinary names. He invents a strange new language of objects; he causes the ordinary associations of these things to melt away.

Otto's experiment has another focus: Felix. Just as our perception alternates between the sex education film and Otto's video, within the video our gaze moves between the father and the son. Otto's work is a record of his language game—and of Felix's reactions. It's a portrait of *them*. With each scream, each whistle, Otto demands Felix's attention. He demands it relentlessly. Felix was twenty-two when Otto made the video. He smiles sheepishly at each noise. He is amiable; he is used to this kind of thing. He dutifully watches his father's synesthetic experiment as he steals glances at a book. But reading is impossible this afternoon. The interruptions keep coming. Otto holds up another object, and another. He grunts, he screams. He whistles. Felix looks up. Otto wants Felix to see these things in a different way—*his*.

Where Felix Gmelin, in *Sound and Vision*, explores the dissociation of things and their names, Anri Sala, in his film *Intervista (Finding the Words)* (1998) sets out to recover words that have been emptied of significance.[36] And where Gmelin examines the lasting influence of his father's personality and aesthetic views, Sala investigates his mother's past, a history unknown to him when it was happening, one that resurfaces later, by chance.

A young film student (Sala himself) discovers a sealed box during a move. Inside he finds a reel of 16 mm film wrapped in a paper bag. The black-and-white film depicts a public event in a large hall. The audience clap enthusiastically, in slow motion, as several men and women file onstage. The event is followed by an interview with a buoyant young woman, a prominent presence onstage; she breaks into laughter at the end of the exchange. There is no sound (fig. 1.7).

Back to the present. A woman with glasses has the settled features, the cropped hairstyle, of a person in middle age. Sala puts a videotape in a VCR. The film we have just seen plays on the monitor. "*Quelle surprise!*" the woman laughs. "It's from the time I was a militant." [More laughter.]

We learn that the film depicts a Communist Youth Congress meeting in Tirana, Albania, in 1977. The crowd applauds wildly as an older man, the dictator Enver Hoxha, takes center stage.[37] He puts his arm around the young woman's neck with avuncular affection as they exchange pleasantries. The interview comes on, and we realize that the woman in the film and the woman watching her are the same person: the artist's mother.

Valdet Sala was thirty-two then, Anri a small boy. She doesn't remember the interview or recall what she said then. *Intervista* records Sala's extraordinary efforts to recover his mother's lost words. In order to reconstruct the interview, he conducts several others. He locates the man who interviewed his mother in 1977, who informs him the audiotape is probably lost. He tracks down an elderly couple in a run-down building who had been friends with Valdet then. Their apartment is sparsely furnished, with peeling walls, a far cry from his mother's comfortable home. Liri and Todi Lubanja had been leaders of the Youth Union, the group gathered in the auditorium. Why do they not appear in the party film, Sala asks. "It was after our expulsion," Liri confesses. They were in prison by then.[38]

Sala visits a school for children with hearing and speaking disabilities. He shows the film to two women who attempt to lip-read his mother's remarks. Pencils in hand, they reconstruct the interview word by word. We watch Valdet watch the dubbed version (fig. 1.8). The words appear onscreen. Young people must "unite under the guardianship of the Marxist-Leninist party" to "join the struggle against imperialism," the young woman says confidently. The older Valdet is perplexed. Then she is angry. ("It's gibberish!") Pointing at the TV monitor, Sala ventriloquizes the old, dead words. The son instructs the mother: the Maoist jargon is hers. Sala forces Valdet to come to terms with a nearly forgotten self. The young woman who stood onstage with Hoxha no longer exists. Sala restores her voice, retrieves her from forgetting. He recalls who his mother was then, what she believed—and so do we.

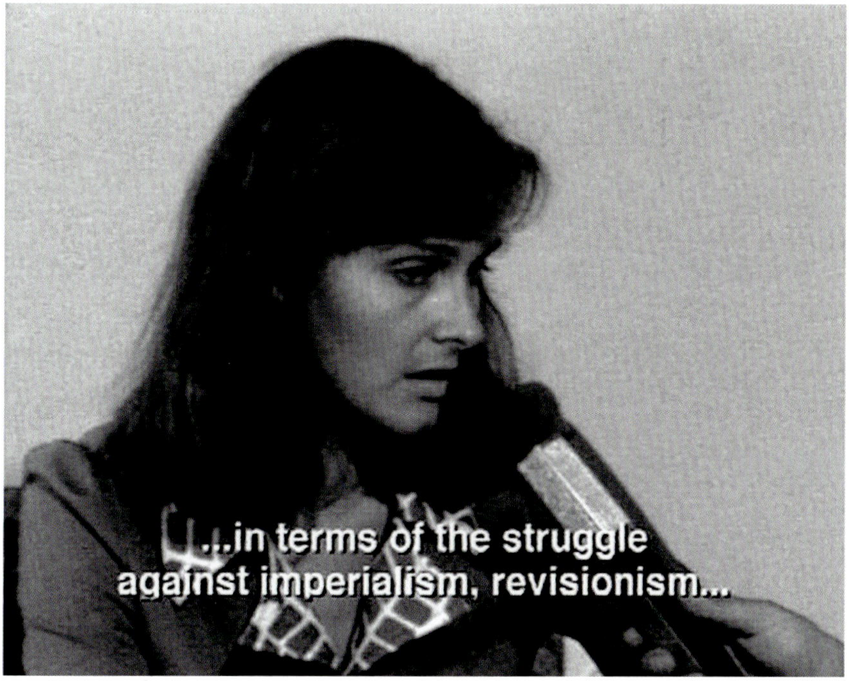


**Fig. 1.7.** Anri Sala, *Intervista (Finding the Words)*, 1998. Single-channel video and stereo sound. 26′00″. Still. Courtesy of Idéale Audience International, Paris; Galerie Chantal Crousel, Paris; Galerie Esther Schipper, Berlin; Galerie Rüdiger Schöttle, Munich; and Marian Goodman Gallery, New York/Paris.

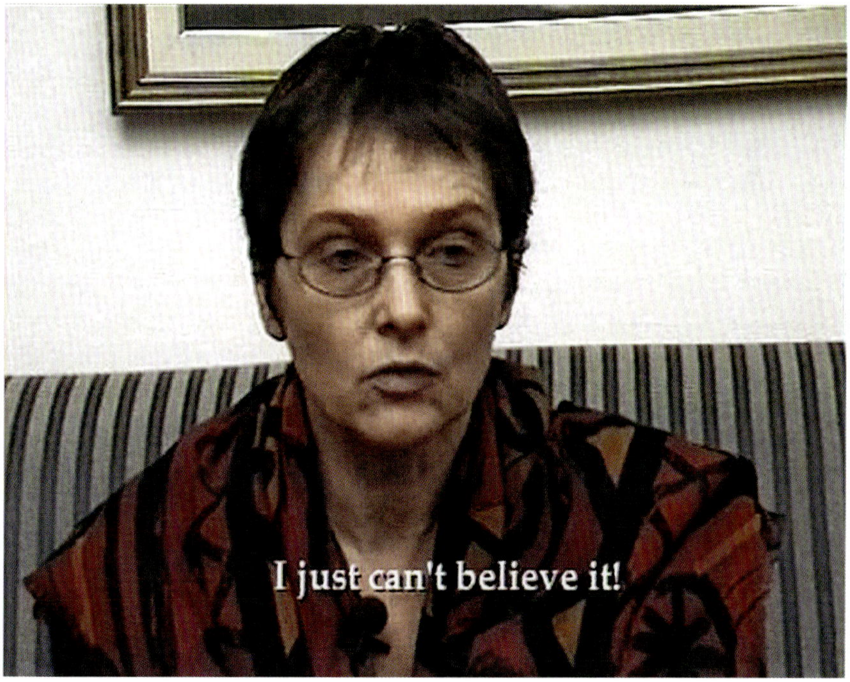


**Fig. 1.8.** Anri Sala, *Intervista (Finding the Words)*, 1998. Single-channel video and stereo sound. 26′00″. Still. Courtesy of Idéale Audience International, Paris; Galerie Chantal Crousel, Paris; Galerie Esther Schipper, Berlin; Galerie Rüdiger Schöttle, Munich; and Marian Goodman Gallery, New York/Paris.

•

In my final example, Nam Lê's story "Love and Honor and Pity and Pride and Compassion and Sacrifice," we are confronted with yet another parent's past that the child knows little about. A father has sought out his son after a long absence.[39] The narrator, Lê's alter ego, is a graduate student at the celebrated Iowa Writers Workshop. He is awakened by the doorbell one morning. His father has journeyed a long distance. Although the visit was arranged, the father has arrived too early, which is to say, unexpectedly. They have not seen one another in years; their conversation is strained. The narrator has few happy memories of this man from childhood. He remembers only his deprivations ("No personal phone calls. No female friends.") and his harsh discipline ("He knew how to cane me twenty times and leave one black-red welt.").

They are "Vietnamese boat people," the father explains to a homeless man they meet on the riverbank in Iowa City. As the story unfolds we begin to see what this means. A "before" is always just beneath the surface of their interactions. That past can still be heard in the sharp staccato sound of the author's (and narrator's) name. "To my father there was no other name—only mine [Nam], and he had named me after the homeland he had given up."

There is no other name—and no time other than a past that precedes Nam's memory, a past that can't be named. He remembers an evening when he was a boy and allowed to stay up late with his father's friends. Drunk on cheap beer, the men trade stories of war. The father tells a story the narrator has never heard before. A story about a battle, of hiding in a bunker. Of being forced out of the family home by U.S. soldiers and marched to the outskirts of their village. Of being forced into a ditch.

> I didn't understand it. My sister didn't even cry. People were now shouting, "No VC, no VC," but the Americans just frowned and spat and laughed. One of them said something, then some of them started pushing us into the ditch. It was half full of muddy water. My mother jumped in and lifted my sisters down.

A story of gunshots, of the father's mother taking bullets to protect him, her body falling onto his (her body "kept jumping for a long time"). He lay still for a long time until the men and the helicopters left, his own body just a body in a pile of bodies "dark and wet and warm and sweet." A story of infamy: Nam's father grew up in the village of Tu Cung, "later known to the Americans as My Lai."

Flash to the present. The narrator is having trouble completing assignments in his fiction class. He is uncertain what exactly to write *about.* "How can you have writer's block?" a classmate asks incredulously. "Just write a story about Vietnam." "Ethnic" literature is "hot," his professor remarks. *Write about what you know.*

He knows about his father, knows more than he wants to know. Initially unwelcome in Iowa City, the father has become a welcome presence, for he has given the narrator a subject. The son presses the father to finish his story so he can finish *his* story. The father complies. He describes how after the massacre he was conscripted into the South Vietnamese army. How, after the war ended, he was interned in a Viet Cong reeducation camp. (To prove the point, he demonstrates the tortures he underwent, appearing to the narrator "a skinny old man in Tantric poses . . . faintly preposterous"). He recalls escaping to Australia with his wife and the baby Nam on a fishing boat, a journey few survived.

Nam has extracted his father's testimony. He can see the past more clearly now—a past that precedes memory yet affects him in ways he may not even know. Seemingly cured of writer's block, he knocks out a story on an old typewriter, a device as dated as the story he summons from its keys. He has made the past useful, mastered it. He has scored history. He even dares to fantasize that this will be *good* for his father. Telling his story, his father will feel a deep sense of relief, the son imagines. He will have begun to let go of the trauma, work it through. As the narrator confides in the reader, his narcissistic investment in all this becomes clear:

> He would read it, with his book-learned English, and he would recognize himself in a new way. He would recognize me. He would see how powerful was his experience, how valuable his suffering—how I had made it speak for more than itself. He would be pleased with me.

The narrator puts the story on his desk. When he wakes up from a long sleep, his father is nowhere to be seen. He has disappeared with the manuscript, the only hard copy that exists. The son eventually finds him on the riverbank with the homeless man he befriended days earlier, a person as rootless as Nam's father. It is winter. Their breath hangs in the frigid air like smoke. The meandering river is sheathed in ice. The men are warming themselves in front of a gasoline drum filled with flames. The father's hands are empty. He has destroyed his (his and Nam's) story. "The ashes, given body by the wind, floated away. . . ."

The ashes scatter; the memory remains. The father was fourteen years old when Charlie Company came to the village—a boy. Nam, the narrator of the story we read, was not at My Lai. He never heard the barking orders of the Americans, the deafening noise of the helicopters. He doesn't recall his family's perilous crossing of the South China Sea. He was an infant then. He was there—and not there. The child of a Sixties child, he has received this history secondhand. And only yesterday, only after he asked questions. Only after his father disclosed what happened. That time has more of an impact on them than they can possibly know.

What happened to these children? How did the upheavals of that era affect them—affect them before they were born (in the cases of Fowler and Lê) or *while* they were children, in the instance of Sala? Why do they return now? But what is it to "return"?

Allow me to make a grammatical distinction, the difference between two prepositions, two ideas—what I will call the *return of* and *return to.* I will speak about the Sixties as an effect—the impact of one period on another. The "return of" describes a pulsion of history, the process by which a previous era becomes resonant in a later time—our time. "Return to" is something we *do.* Practices of return are acts of salvage—the often elaborate efforts of scholars to imagine an event they did not see, of performers to respeak a speech they never heard, of artists and writers to revisit a place of childhood, to remember the not-quite-forgotten sounds, sensations, and textures of a time they barely glimpsed or missed. To "return" is to grasp that *we* are historical, to locate ourselves in relation to a past that feels urgently present.

Who is the one who returns? What does he or she hope to accomplish? In *A Berlin Chronicle*, the first version of his *Berlin Childhood around 1900*, Walter Benjamin describes memory as a form of excavation. The rememberer is for Benjamin a "digger" (*ein Gräber*) who explores the loam of faintest memory, who scatters this mnemonic deposit as a digger "turns over soil" in his spade. The rememberer, he observes, is not afraid to "return again and again to the same matter" (*immer wieder auf einen und denselben Sachverhalt zurückzukommen*).[40] The German *Zurückzukommen* means "to return, to come back." That is what the rememberer does. Not content with the initial find, the quick discovery barely concealed in the topsoil, he seeks a deeper knowledge. Benjamin's digger is an archaeologist of his past, a detective of his childhood. He "returns to the scene of the crime."[41] Driven to reconstruct what happened, he consults his memories and the memories of others "who were there." The "return to" is thus the retrieval of a past that is not entirely past, a history that has not concluded. It is the rediscovery of the time when our parents were active, when *they* were young, and when we perceived the world and the events swarming around us through their eyes.[42] The era that redefined the idea of youth for the late twentieth century remains even now an archetypal image of youth, of how to *be* young. That time is finished. Even those who remember know this.

Yet the Sixties don't go quietly. That era relinquishes its hold reluctantly. As the historical Sixties recedes, another "Sixties" dominates our imaginations: a Sixties that returns even in Sixties exhaustion and forgetting, in Sixties kitsch and satire. This Sixties is hopelessly dated, and comical—and insistent. In his memoir *A Heartbreaking Work of Staggering Genius* (2000), Dave Eggers describes the adventures of some recent college graduates who have moved to San Francisco at the height of the dot-com boom. Ambitious young journalists, they start a magazine for other "twentysomethings."[43] Eggers is anxious to distinguish himself and his peers from the legendary Sixty-eighters. And yet "Generation X" lacks a sense of purpose, a cause. "We have a hard time finding the fire in the belly for such things.... All we really want is for no one to have a boring life, to be impressive, so we can be impressed."[44]

The young editors are desperate to stand out—and desperate not to be bored. To promote their fledgling venture, they instinctively rifle the grab bag of hip Sixties imagery. They emulate the free-spirited behavior made famous during the Summer of Love. For the cover photo of the debut issue, they run down a frigid Pacific beach in the nude, holding hands, modern-day streakers, hippies for an afternoon:

> It's like the Sixties! Look! Look, we say to one another, at the imbalances, the glaring flaws of the world, aghast, amazed. Look how things are! Look at how, for instance, there are all these homeless people.... Look at how high rents are! Look at how the banks charge these hidden fees when you use their ATMs![45]

In Eggers's satirical universe the Sixties are another absurdity. The Sixties are absurd because they represent a kind of meaningfulness, an earnest purposefulness, that no longer rings true. The Sixties are over, and have been for a long time. Still they reach for it. Eggers and his friends have flocked to the Bay Area as an earlier generation did. They have gathered in San Francisco and Berkeley and Oakland because that is what young people are supposed to do. They remember another time without knowing much about it. To be new, they ventriloquize the most stereotypical Sixties forms.

Historian Reinhardt Koselleck describes this phenomenon as the "future past." A future past is the mnemonic reverberation of one period in another—the "return of." There is no one continuous time, no single history, says Koselleck—only times. Each era has a temporal rhythm, a velocity, and thus a "horizon of expectation"—the anticipation of its return at a future date.[46] It exceeds its historical moment, the time of its first occurrence. It foretells its becoming meaningful at a later date. The moment of return is unpredictable, and historical in each instance. As I wrote this book, the Sixties "returned" again and again, differently and unexpectedly.[47] Koselleck describes this temporality of loops and repetitions, of anticipation and recollection, as "historical time," and he opposes this to "natural time." "Natural time" flows linearly from one point to another. Measurable, cyclical, divided into hours, days, seasons, years, this is the "time" we think we know, the timeline we consult in our fitful efforts to map out our lives. "Natural time" is diachronic, the time of the chronicle. One event follows another in an order we can easily grasp. We organize the major events of human history by reference to this linear timeline. This, we imagine, is the way events "really" happened at a particular moment, "the way it really was" (*wie es eigentlich gewesen*, as the nineteenth-century historian Leopold von Ranke famously put it).[48] "Historical time" is less certain. There is no history "as it was," Koselleck insists, only the representation of the past *as* past. "Historical time"—the time theorized by Koselleck—refutes a linear temporality. It does not begin at a definite point or come to a definite end. Its path is circuitous and proleptic. The future lies within *its* future, its "horizon of expectation." For Koselleck, it is as if eras have a kind of volition, entering and exiting the vast sweep of history, appearing and reappearing like actors on a stage. Periods overlap with other periods. Eras cross. A "future past" is a period's hermeneutical future—the *meaning* of one time for another.[49] So there is the Sixties of "natural time," a Sixties of specific duration, a Sixties that came to an end. This Sixties is becoming more distant with every passing year. Then there is the "Sixties" that comes after the historical Sixties, that returns: this is our subject.

## Topography of the Sixties

To be sure, "natural time" is more ambiguous than it appears. We know that something happened after the fact, and so our perception of time is narrational. Describing what occurred, we transform a perplexing jumble of incidents and facts into a flow of events, a story.[50] Histories of the Sixties are stories of that time. Each suggests a different Sixties—a particular comprehension of what happened then, shaping how "what happened" came to be understood for decades to come. Three chronologies (three stories) dominate depictions of that time. Let us map these topographies: I refer to them here as the *decadal Sixties*, the *long Sixties*, and *Sixty-eight*.

The decadal Sixties has precise parameters; it begins promptly on January 1, 1960, and concludes on December 31, 1969. Kerry James Marshall represents this Sixties in his painting *Memento V* (fig. 1.9), the last of his *Souvenirs* canvases on the theme of civil rights memory, which I turn to later in this book. Marshall paints the number of each year between the slats of a silver-glitter curtain drawn shut by an angel of memory—an African American woman with translucent wings. He counts the decadal Sixties year by year. Viewers of Marshall's painting recite these cardinal numbers one by one (1960, 1961, 1962, 1963 . . .).

Counting the Sixties, we wonder what exactly the "Sixties" is, and what a decade is. The decade posits the illusion that time unfolds decimally, that we can divide history into ten-year increments. It brings eternity down to human scale. We divide eternity into millennia, and millennia into centuries, and centuries into tidy installments of ten years. We think of our own lives along these lines. We tell ourselves that we live through decades, and from one decade to another (I was such-and-such a person in my twenties, this other person in my forties, and so on). But this schema, which seems so intuitive, becomes less credible the longer we stare at these numbers. For Marshall has stenciled these figures in a Sixties-vintage font onto the collaged surface, rotating them ninety degrees and wedging them between the shimmering silvery slats on the left and right sides of the image, splitting the "Sixties" in half. He *estranges* the "Sixties," puts it on its side and slices it in two. And so we perceive the fractal logic of this decadal scheme. We define decades in relation to smaller temporal increments (individual years) and larger ones (entire centuries), and to *other decades*: there is no Sixties without the "Gay" Nineties, the "Roaring" Twenties, the "Silent" Fifties, and so on.[51]

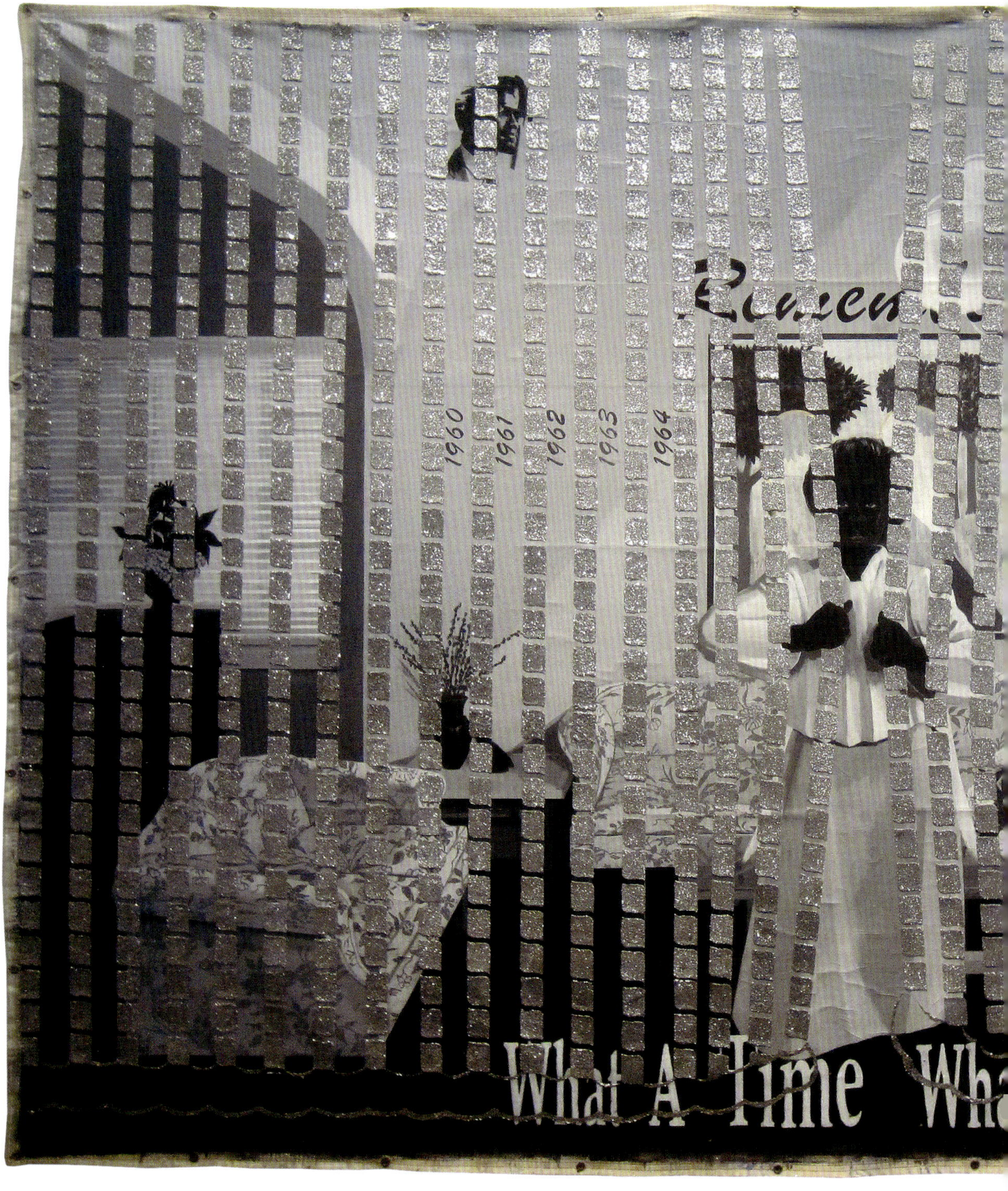
1960
1961
1962
1963
1964
What A Time

**Fig. 1.9.** Kerry James Marshall, *Memento V*, 2003. Acrylic and glitter on paper adhered to unstretched canvas banner. Nelson-Atkins Museum, Kansas City, Missouri. © Kerry James Marshall. Courtesy of the artist and Jack Shainman Gallery, New York.

The decadal Sixties affords a certain knowledge. The most "natural" Sixties is the most obvious; it almost seems not to be a representation. Here is the Sixties we know best, the Sixties "itself." The television series *Mad Men* has been deservedly praised for its fine-tuned reconstruction of the period's design and the patriarchal, racist, and homophobic attitudes prevalent then.[52] The show's vaunted historical fidelity is secured by the mimicry of a decadal logic that viewers perceive as truthful. Beginning during the spring of 1960—the Kennedy-Nixon election looms in the background—the series traces the fortunes of a Madison Avenue advertising agency and the men and women who work there. Changes in decor, fashions, hairstyles, in music and personal morality convey the impression of a meticulously drawn illusionism. This obsessive attention to period detail inspires the fantasy that we have stepped back into a Cheeveresque world of leisurely martini lunches and lit cigars, of sweater girls and off-color remarks. Here, we imagine, is the Sixties "as it was." As *Mad Men* also reveals, the decadal Sixties is a teleological Sixties, replete with the "beginnings and endings . . . turning points and climaxes" that allow us to arrange events into a sequence, to see connections between them, to think of history as a narrative, as Arthur Danto has described.[53] Events follow one another with seeming inevitability, as if they "had" to happen as they did and in the order in which they happened. (A period or event "makes sense" once it can be turned into a story, Danto suggests.) The Sixties declension narrative—a Sixties that is always getting worse—is arguably the most rehearsed story of all.[54] This Sixties is emblematically American; it leads from 1960 to 1969, from Camelot to Altamont, from the marble steps of the Lincoln Memorial to the bloodstained balcony of a Memphis motel. High-minded ideals wither. Political leaders and entertainers die young and in tragic circumstances. The thoughtful tactics of civil disobedience cede to violence and anarchy. There will be more to say about this "bad" Sixties in part 2.

Now, the long Sixties. This "Sixties" dips deep into the Fifties and extends into the Seventies; its contours are broad, its duration imprecise.[55] *Brown v. Board of Education*, the Birmingham bus boycott, the Cuban revolution, and independence movements in Algeria, Ghana, Cameroon, and other African nation-states are beginnings. The Kent State massacre, the murders of Israeli athletes at the Munich Olympics, the Watergate scandal, the fall of Saigon, the U.S. Bicentennial, the death of Mao Zedong and fall of the Gang of Four in 1976, the violent "German Autumn" of 1977, and the elections of British prime minister Margaret Thatcher and U.S. president Ronald Reagan in 1979 have all been proposed as endings of this elongated "Sixties." Where the decadal Sixties has strict boundaries, the contours of the long Sixties are open-ended and subjective. (We each have different ideas as to when the era begins and concludes.)[56] Yet like the decadal Sixties, the long Sixties is an ideological notion. It represents an assault on power, the principle that ordinary citizens are capable of asserting their rights against the most insurmountable odds (*participatory democracy*, the New Left called it). During this approximately twenty-five-year period old regimes of oppression—colonialism, segregation, patriarchy, and heteronormativity—were challenged or collapsed outright. And so the long Sixties has come to represent an ideal of social justice whose promise remains perpetually deferred, forever unfulfilled.[57] And it stands for other disruptions: the sexual revolution (catalyzed by the FDA's approval of Enovid, "the Pill," in 1960), an environmentalist revolution (the founding of Earth Day and the Green movement), a musical revolution (the rise of folk, rock, and funk), and an aesthetic revolution (a revival of avant-garde formats, such as the readymade and monochrome, and the emergence of neo-Dada and pop, minimalism, conceptualism, land art, and identity-based tendencies). Careening into the mid- and late Seventies, the long Sixties is a Sixties that refuses to end, a post-Sixties "Sixties." It stands for the extension of Sixties disturbances beyond that era, and right-wing initiatives to contain and suppress them.

And what of Sixty-eight? The most emblematic of Sixties years has inspired a voluminous literature of its own. The events of those twelve months unfolded with a dizzying celerity. January brought the Tet offensive (the incursion of Viet Cong forces into Saigon); March, the massacre at My Lai (not revealed until 1969); April, the assassination of Martin Luther King Jr. in Memphis, the shooting of Rudi Dutschke in Berlin, and the student occupation of Columbia University. May brought a national student and factory strike in France (the "Events of May") and the toppling of De Gaulle's Fifth Republic; June, the assassination of Robert Kennedy, and the shooting of Andy Warhol by Valerie Solanas; July, no less than four attempts to hijack commercial airliners by pro-Cuban and pro-Palestinian guerrillas, and the founding of the American Indian Movement in Minneapolis; August, the Soviet invasion of Prague and the disastrous Democratic Convention in Chicago; September, the first feminist protest against the Miss America Pageant; October, the Tlateloco massacre in Mexico City (some two hundred students murdered by the Ordaz regime). How can we think these events together? Did they trigger one another in a catalytic motion, as the Arab Spring of 2011 appeared to do? Or did they occur discretely? Does Sixty-eight usher in an unprecedented global awareness, as some historians claim? Or does this presumption of Sixty-eight's salience in recent world history reinforce a Westernist view of a Sixties that unfolded principally in the West?[58]

Sixty-eight is the crux of most Sixties narratives. The decadal and long Sixties converge here. This is the period's climax, the year that points backward and forward to other years of world historical significance (1789, 1830, 1848, 1917, 1928, 1989, 2001). It represents an "event" whose impact is still playing out.[59] Sixty-eight stands for the idea of the Sixties as a *revolutionary* era, and for the generation that led the way, the generation that came to understand itself as a generation then and is named for it. And so Sixty-eight is a trigger of Sixties media memory, of Sixties anniversaries and denunciations. Every ten years former activists are invited to dilate on their youthful involvements. Film series are staged, exhibitions mounted. Academic and mass market journals organize special issues on the theme.[60] But Sixty-eight also stands for the collapse of the Sixties, the end of utopia. It represents a new fractiousness in politics, a Spenglerian decline, a descent into entropy. It marks the slippage of a "good" Sixties into a "bad" Sixties of unbridled mayhem. A single year has come to stand as a synecdoche for an entire period. Sixty-eight is the culmination of the Sixties as epoch and idea—and the beginning of the end.

## After the Revolution

> **"It was a huge miscalculation. A huge mistake."**
> **"At least you did something. What a world that must have been where ordinary people actually did things. Things that affected, however tangentially, history."**
>
> Dana Spiotta, *Eat the Document*

Earlier I spoke of a widespread impulse to mine the past in art and literary practice. The long Sixties, a Sixties broadly limned, inspires a great many of these projects. Why does this period compel us to understand what happened then? Why do we return?

The more a time is experienced as new, the greater its demands on the future, Koselleck observes.[61] The revolutionary moment is the emblematic *modern* moment. The modern concept of revolution enacts a rupture with an earlier, Copernican model—revolution conceived as a cyclical motion, as the restoration of a previous state (*revolvere*, "to roll back, to unroll").[62] With the French Revolution the modern definition of revolution comes into being. The fall of the Bastille was not a "revolt" that could be put down, the Duc de la Rochefoucauld-Liancourt informed the incredulous King Louis XVI: it was a *revolution*. "Revolution" now suggests an "irresistible" movement, "beyond human power to arrest it" (Hannah Arendt).[63] It implies an "increasingly positive sense of progress" (Raymond Williams).[64] History is henceforth conceived as a unary process, a world movement, in the writings of Hegel and Marx, futurist modernism's lodestars. As the long Sixties began to wane, evolutionary models of progress lost their explanatory force. Postmodernist theorists and neoconservative thinkers alike spoke of the "end" of Enlightenment narratives and ideologies, the obsolescence of revolution as an idea.[65] Yet during the Sixties the memory of the dream of "being new" remained extremely potent. Koselleck wrote in 1969:

> It almost seems that the word "revolution" itself possesses such revolutionary power that it is constantly extending itself to include every last element on our globe. . . . What is there in the world that could not be revolutionized—and what is there in our time that is not open to revolutionary effects?[66]

"Revolution" still meant something then; it still "possesse[d] revolutionary power." Nowhere was this truer than in the West German university and in the extraparliamentary circles in West Berlin, where the ideas of

Mao Zedong, Herbert Marcuse, and Che Guevara had enormous currency. Yet Koselleck's text reveals an underlying skepticism.[67] For Koselleck describes revolution as a *recurring* figure. As repetition. Revolution had become fashionable during the late Sixties, "an empty formula, flogged to death by the most diverse groups."[68] Koselleck was highly dubious that history could unfold as linearly as the New Left imagined it did. The ubiquity of revolutionary thought gave the theorist pause. How promiscuously this word was used then! How it was bandied about! The word whose etymology Arendt had traced with such confidence and such precision just a few years before had come to mean less and less.

Events exist in "historical time," Koselleck suggests. They mean differently from one era to another, from the moment of first happening to the moment of return. Or they lose their resonance. (Their "velocity" has run out.) The revolution is *the* archetypal future past, the past that keeps returning. *This* is when everything changed; *this* moment precipitates what follows; *this* is History. The revolution signifies these things. It demands *to be remembered*. It refuses to be forgotten. And so the generations that follow are compelled to understand how that moment continues to shape their own, for better or worse.

In the writings of the Restoration period in France we are confronted with the mnemonic traces of a disruptive recent past, Richard Terdiman has argued.[69] In Alfred de Musset's novel *The Confession of a Child of the Century* (1836), the narrator, a young man named Octave, describes his contemporaries as an "ardent, pale, nervous generation." These "sons of the Empire and grandsons of the Revolution" are captivated by the memory of a "before."[70] They are revolutionary only in their imaginations, a "revolutionary generation deferred."[71] The Revolution of 1830, "their" revolution, merely succeeded in replacing one monarch with another, the king of France with the king of the French. (As one observer remarked: "There has not been a revolution. There has been but a simple change in the person of the Chief of the State.")[72] Nothing has changed. Nothing, it seems, will change.

The members of this generation lack a sense of purpose, a *cause*. No urgent tasks await them. They had been groomed to become soldiers, yet the war was over before they could join it; raised to become heroes, the battles they would have fought had already been fought.[73] The present is an inscrutable morass, a troubled sea, "vague and floating," a "something" that feels like nothing, a *je ne sais quoi*.[74] It is their time; yet this moment is indifferent to their efforts to mold it. "The star of the future is loath to rise," Musset writes.[75] The "children of the century" are haunted by memories of childhood—images of their fathers, Napoleon's soldiers, magnificent in gold-braided uniforms and mounted on steeds. They recall their grandparents' harrowing tales of the Revolution. They remember the Convention and Terror without having witnessed them personally. "There was something in that word liberty that made their hearts beat with the memory of a terrible past and the hope of a glorious future."[76]

Octave and his contemporaries are burdened with the memory of a monumental past. The weight of this mnemonic affliction is so ponderous that it affects their ability to act in the here and now, and to imagine a future of their own design. Crucially, Musset defines this malaise as a generational problem. The recollection of a glorious "before" binds the members of the generation of 1830 to one another, defines them *as* a generation. It is part of what it meant to be a young person in France then. The "memory crisis" that develops during the July Monarchy (1830–48) does not end with the generation of Musset. It *begins* then, Terdiman claims—and remains a recurring topos of modernity ever since.[77] What I am calling the "Sixties return" can be conceived along these lines. The fascination with the Sixties is the hyperawareness of a "before," a time that appears far more momentous than ours; it is the memory of the generation of Sixty-eight and the modern idea of the generation as such.

The concept of the generation has long preoccupied sociologists and cultural historians.[78] What constitutes a generation is notoriously difficult to pin down, yet a brief detour into these debates is necessary, not least because the generation is a defining principle of the Sixties, an essential reference of Bob Dylan and the Who, of Margaret Mead and Charles Reich alike, and so the generation informs the art of Sixties return as both subject matter and structure.[79] These practices explore the idea of contemporaneity, of being born during and living through a period; they ask what a generation is. How is memory transferred, distorted, and lost from one era and generation to the next? What role could Sixties memory play in a progressive politics now?[80]

I take from this literature certain claims. A generation is both historical and local. (Location, the *place* where we experience history, is a major concern both of generation theory and of this book.) Other factors affect our perceptions of the time that defines us generationally. Persons of the same approximate age, born in the same country, and of comparable economic background and education are said to have absorbed similar "impressions." In other words, they share a sensibility, a point of view. Their experiences are arguably quite similar.[81] A generation is the result of influences absorbed during youth, the period of maximum impressionability according to Wilhelm Dilthey, whose speculations predate the early developmental theory of Freud. ("Those who receive the same impressions during their formative years form a generation.")[82] Classical accounts of the generation valorize the idea of an authentic, firsthand memory—Dilthey's "imprint."

The early impression is the key to understanding how a shift in attitude or a new aesthetic has come about. Karl Mannheim develops this distinction between personally acquired and appropriated memory, the memory "I take from someone else." Only the firsthand memory, the sociologist insists—the "knowledge I have personally gained in real situations"—has true staying power. Only firsthand memory binds together the members of a generation; the memory of others matters far less.[83]

Pierre Nora complicates this equation of the generation and firsthand memory. He questions Dilthey's notion of the early imprint, the singular "impression" that stamps each of us with the same world view, the same ideas.[84] Generational memory is less the recollection of a common experience, Nora suggests, than the compulsive recollection of a time that *precedes* one's birth, a time that is *not* one's own. What the members of a generation share is the recollection of a momentous past—typically recent—next to which the present feels unmonumental and bland. "The Revolution for the romantics . . . World War II for postwar generations; the [French] Revolution again . . . for the generation of Sixty-Eight. . . . Generational memory is stocked with remembrances not so much of what its members have experienced as of what they have *not* experienced."[85]

A generation's memory is an attachment to a past that is not properly their own. It is a longing for firsthand, "authentic" memory, for *experience*. It is the gnawing sense that others have lived in historical times, that *they* have made history, that we cannot be so influential. The generation and revolution are contemporaneous notions, braided together by the operations of memory. In Nora's topology the memory of a close community, such as a village or ethnic group—a *milieu*—is shared between generations. The generation as we know it is the product of the modernity that the French Revolution sets in motion: it is what Nora calls *un lieu de mémoire*, a place where memory resides and from which the rememberer is estranged. The *lieu*, the monument, obliges future generations to remember this event. For Nora, the notion of the generation in the West is a kind of monument. Each generation is under a compulsion to remember the "first" generation to carry forth the memory of the generation of 1789 in its own "revolutionary" behavior.[86] From 1789 to 1968 the idea that a new generation had emerged as history's torchbearer was repeatedly rehearsed.[87] At the end of the Sixties the generation of Sixty-eight surfaced as an avatar of revolutionary memory, exemplifying the structural momentum that reemerged then:

> There is a revolution coming. . . . It will originate with the individual and with culture, and it will change the political structure only as its final act. . . . Its ultimate creation will be a new and enduring wholeness

and beauty—a renewed relationship of man to himself, to other men, to society, to nature, and to the land. This is the revolution of the new generation.[88]

How do we read this breathless passage, the opening lines of Charles Reich's 1970 manifesto *The Greening of America*? Reich's words are dated, to say the least. It is hard to conceive that a book could dare to espouse a "revolution" anymore, much less become a bestseller in the United States, as *The Greening of America* did. It is hard to imagine a book mattering as *The Greening of America* mattered then. The book was "the talk of the Nation," the jacket boasts. It caused "a storm of controversy." And so on.

Reich did hit a nerve. I remember distinctly an exchange between my father and my older brother, a teenager then. We were seated at the round table in my mother's kitchen, a white Formica disk edged in black. I felt at ease in a black Eames chair. My feet, swinging under the table, didn't reach the floor.

Every evening we watched the *CBS Evening News*. Our meals were accompanied by reports of war. Icons of U.S. and Viet Cong flags flashed onto the slightly convex TV screen—a black-and-white set, already antiquated then. The numbers next to the flags were often in the three digits. Walter Cronkite, the "Most Trusted Man in America," recited these figures nightly, his voice a sonorous baritone. The digits on the screen represented lives that had been extinguished that very day, a concept we children, having absorbed this information for as long as we could remember, had long taken for granted. This was the news. Our news.

My father turned on the television, the signal for dinner to begin. The national broadcast came on at six-thirty, following the local news report or *McHale's Navy* or *Hogan's Heroes*, World War II sitcoms that my father, who had served in the Pacific, found entertaining. (Later in the evening we watched more serious fare: *The World at War*, a documentary history of that conflagration, which loomed large in my parents' recollections, and a reminder to all of us that the Shoah that had taken the lives of so many family members—an aunt, three uncles and countless in-laws, children and grandchildren—had happened not so long ago.) By the time my mother cleared the soup bowls and salad plates, images of rice fields, of remote villages, of anonymous faces beneath conical hats came into view. A platter of roast chicken or brisket appeared on the white table with the black edge. The whirring sounds of helicopters and the voices of reporters interrupted our strained efforts at conversation.

My brother held up a paperback. The title was printed in bright green letters in an inviting font on a white cover. The words *The Greening of America* evoked in my child's mind the idea of a verdant nation, a healthy America; I was taken aback when my father became agitated and condemned the little white book. My brother, the object of this torrent, fell silent. How could a mere book aggravate my father so very much, I wondered.

The United States was in a state of crisis, Reich claimed—no understatement in a year that saw the invasion of Cambodia and the Kent State shootings, and the riots catalyzed by these events. A professor at Yale Law School and a disciple of such Leftist social theorists as Herbert Marcuse and Jacques Ellul, Reich criticized the generation that had fought in World War II and had come to power in the period after the war. Its members were leaders in government and industry, in academia and the professions, yet the values of rationality and efficiency they esteemed had led them on a destructive path. These "good men" embodied the bureaucratic mentality that had precipitated the irrational cycle of violence in Southeast Asia and at home, as represented by the two- and three-digit numbers and pictures and sounds of helicopters and soldiers, of protests and riots, that appeared on the black-and-white TV night after night. Reich examined this troubling contradiction. America's problems were so intractable that reform would do little to solve them. A more drastic transformation of society was called for. Where did this future lie?

Young people were the harbingers of the new mentality.[89] "Technocracy's children," the new generation had turned their backs on the System. Teenagers and twentysomethings believed in the power of community (as expressed in their music, their festivals, their communal structures of living); were environmentally aware; and they welcomed the altered perceptions of psychedelic drugs. This "greening" of the nation's youth would change America for the better. The World War II generation embodied the old mentality whose dominance was ending, as Dylan proclaimed:

> Come mothers and fathers
> Throughout the land
> And don't criticize
> What you can't understand
> Your sons and your daughters
> Are beyond your command
> Your old road is rapidly agin'
> Please get out of the new one if you can't lend your hand
> For the times they are a-changin'[90]

And now the generational transition that Reich proposed was enacted before my eyes as my father angrily denounced and my brother haplessly defended the author's claims.

A revolution was coming. The new mindset was phasing out the old. So Reich believed. Practices of return revisit these astonishing claims, retrieving the memory of a submerged and allegedly obsolete radicalism. *The Greening of America* is sweeping, relentless, so sure of itself. Its revolutionary rhetoric is futuristic, its technophobia uninflected. Reich's condemnation of his stodgy peers is absolute; his speculations are of their moment. Yet his adamant belief in young people, in his students' ability to change the status quo, is moving to read; his critiques of American society remain remarkably valid.[91] How dated is *The Greening of America*? Extremely. And not in the least.

It is often said that we live in an era of mindless conformity. This, too, is not a new claim.[92] What interests me is how this sense of powerlessness has been widely felt and spoken about since the early Nineties, with notable interruptions,[93] and how that awareness has inspired nostalgia for moments of resistance, the Sixties especially. The postwar boom economy in the West fostered middle-class prosperity and an explosion in the number of college students relatively untouched by financial concerns; this, and the requirement of the draft, were ripe conditions for the rise of the antiwar movement in the United States, as I noted earlier.[94] During the 2000s, other social and economic forces—global integration and recession, job scarcity, and the maintenance of a volunteer military in the United States—quelled campus dissent. After an initial round of protests, resistance to the Iraq invasion abated. A second campus-based antiwar movement never emerged. The Sixties did *not* return. Young people were reproached for their "docile behavior," their compliance with authority, their quietude, by Boomers filled with the memory of their own resistance to the Vietnam War.[95] However sanctimonious, such criticisms spoke of the frustration and fear felt by progressives during the period after September 11, 2001, when the Bush and Blair regimes invaded Iraq on false pretense and installed a series of domestic suppressions in the name of state security.[96] Yet the paternalist tone of such reproaches betrayed a sclerotic nostalgia—nostalgia for a previous era of political enunciation, the sense of collective belonging that mattered so deeply and was poignantly expressed in the music then. Nostalgia for a Left that no longer existed. Nostalgia for their own youthful exertions.[97]

Nostalgia is an attachment to a previous time, a pining for a past or origin that is impossible to reach, a desire that can never be sated, that is always deferred. It entices us to gaze backward—to turn our attention away from the reality in front of us. Nostalgia has its uses. My own slender memories of that time instigated this book's writing; I set about this research to understand the nature of such longing. I concluded that the most trenchant practices of return view that emotion, and Sixties

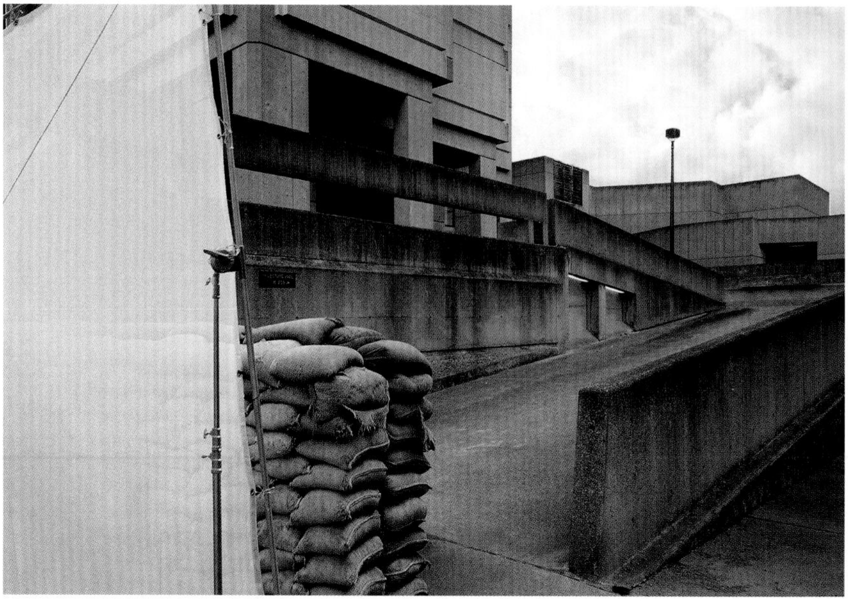

**Fig. 1.10.** Nancy Davenport, *Humanities*, 2004. C-print. Courtesy of Nancy Davenport.

nostalgia in particular, with deep skepticism: the "good old radical days" were not always what they seem.

Consider *Campus* (2004), a photographic project by Nancy Davenport. In order to take these photos, Davenport visited colleges and universities that became hotbeds of antiwar activity during the Sixties. Completed in 2004, her project establishes a structure of comparison between two periods defined by U.S. military aggression and two generations of young people—the Boomers and "Millennials." The plush interiors, mega-gyms, IT labs, and branded food courts of the contemporary campus are strikingly absent from these depictions, as are the students themselves. Davenport trains her camera on the campus of the Sixties and Seventies, or what is left of it. Images of bleak concrete façades, classrooms, and plazas designed in the Brutalist style favored by architects and administrators then, her photos evoke memories of a faded radicalism. Quadrangles that once overflowed with protesters are empty. Auditoriums where teach-ins were held sit vacant. The Ross classroom building at Toronto's York University depicted in *Humanities* is as impenetrable as Kafka's castle (fig. 1.10). A tarp partially blocks the windowless façade. Cement walls edge out the drab sky. Piles of sandbags impede a student's entrance into this temple of knowledge.

Where Davenport depicts the Sixties campus in its current entropic state, Nathan Hill's *The Nix* (2016) describes the Brutalist environment at its apogee. Hill's novel of Sixties return centers on the dynamic of an aging Boomer and the now middle-aged son she abandoned when he was a boy. Beginning in 2011, the narrative fluctuates between that moment and 1988, 2004, and 1968. Hill eventually returns the narrator (and reader) imaginatively to Chicago in August 1968. Reconstructing what happened to his mother during that fateful summer, the narrator, Samuel, discovers the answer to the recalcitrant riddle of his emotional life.[98]

The eighteen-year-old Faye Andresen arrives at the University of Illinois, Chicago Circle, to begin her freshman year. She soon realizes that the campus that had appeared so appealingly modern in the brochures is "impossible to navigate." The elevated concrete walkway traversing the campus casts long shadows, alienating students who take this path from their classmates who walk underneath it. The stairwells in the M. C. Escher–like Behavioral Sciences Building lead to landings where other stairwells intersect, "all of them identical looking." Based on the geometric principles of field theory, this structure had been designed to disrupt conventional architecture's "tyranny of the square" with its layout, a bewildering pattern of octagons inset with circles. Like the campus itself, the difficult-to-navigate building was conceived as an environment for innovative thinking, a place of fresh perceptions. Out with the old. Out with the *square*:

> Why this was better, philosophically, than a square, the brochures never explained. But Faye could guess: A square was old, traditional, antique, and therefore bad. It seemed to Faye the worst thing on this campus, for both the students and the buildings, was to be *square*.[99]

The perplexing architecture of the Sixties is no hindrance to activism, but rather, Hill suggests, its necessary setting. Rejecting the square and "squareness," the Brutalist campus incites revolutionary feeling. Faye and her classmates soon find themselves in downtown Chicago, caught up in the convulsive protest in Grant Park outside the Democratic Convention, one of the most violent events of that violent year.[100] She never recovers. After experiencing a terrible accident during that event, Faye drops out of school, returns to her Iowa hometown, marries her high school boyfriend, and has a son. She abandons her dreams to invent a new life for herself. Years later she leaves her family without a word. At the origin of Samuel's eventual abandonment is the unspoken trauma of Sixty-eight.

Davenport's images of Sixties campuses are as vivid and well imagined as Hill's fictional depiction of Chicago Circle. Natural details—reflections of clouds in windows, the rust stains of mullions—cohabit with staged ones, such as the piles of antiwar leaflets placed by the artist on an empty terrace in *Library* (fig. 1.11). The flyers flutter across the De Chirico-esque plaza in a fictive wind, diminishing in size thanks to Davenport's wide-angle-lens camera and deft manipulation of the Photoshop cursor. The tiny white specks at the far end of the plaza suggest a perspectival illusionism so exacting and precise as to expose the sheer artifice of the image, reminding us that we are looking not at a direct transcription of an actual place but at a *picture* where two eras rub up against one another uneasily. STOP WAR, a sheet reads. ANSWER—the acronym of the antiwar coalition founded after September 11th—says another. The flyers scatter across the terrace, disseminating their pacifist message—to whom? There is nobody here to read them.

Now Davenport takes us inside these structures. The TV monitor in *Classroom #1* is a reminder that video art is another Sixties form (fig. 1.12).[101] Davenport took this exposure in Yale's Art and Architecture Building, whose floors of varied heights, atrium, and striated concrete walls were the last word in architectural innovation when Paul Rudolph completed this structure in 1963. Once controversial, Rudolph's design is now canonical. Brutalism no longer shocks or disturbs. The classroom in Davenport's photo is vaguely carceral; the walls have darkened with

**Fig. 1.11.** Nancy Davenport, *Library*, 2004. C-print. Courtesy of Nancy Davenport.

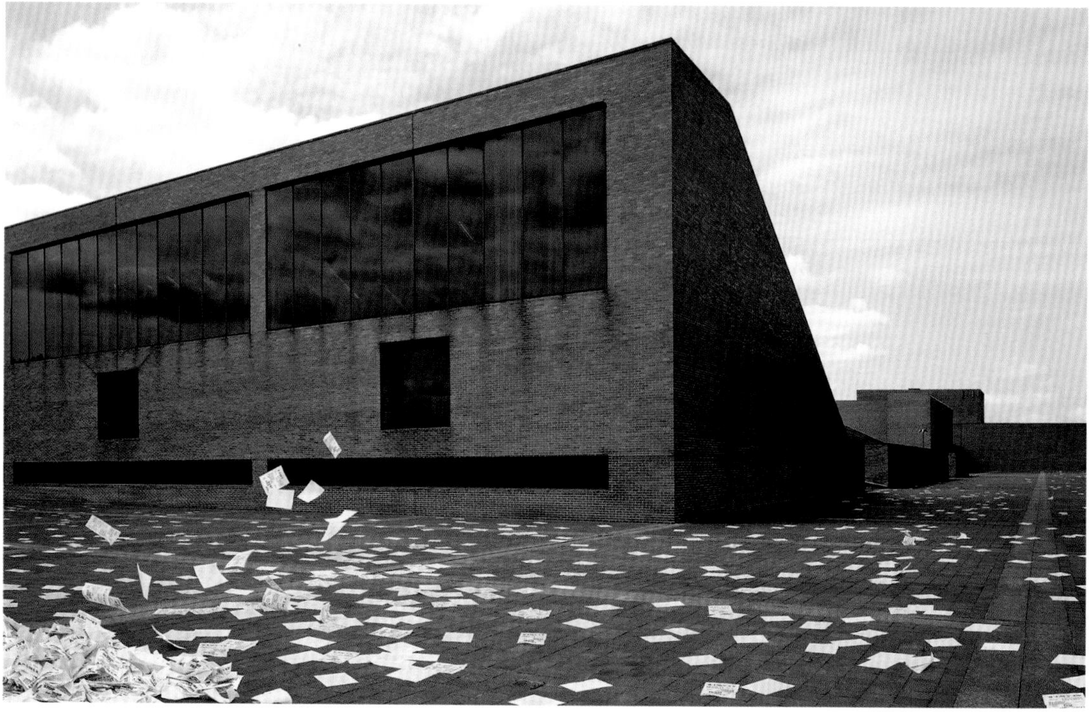

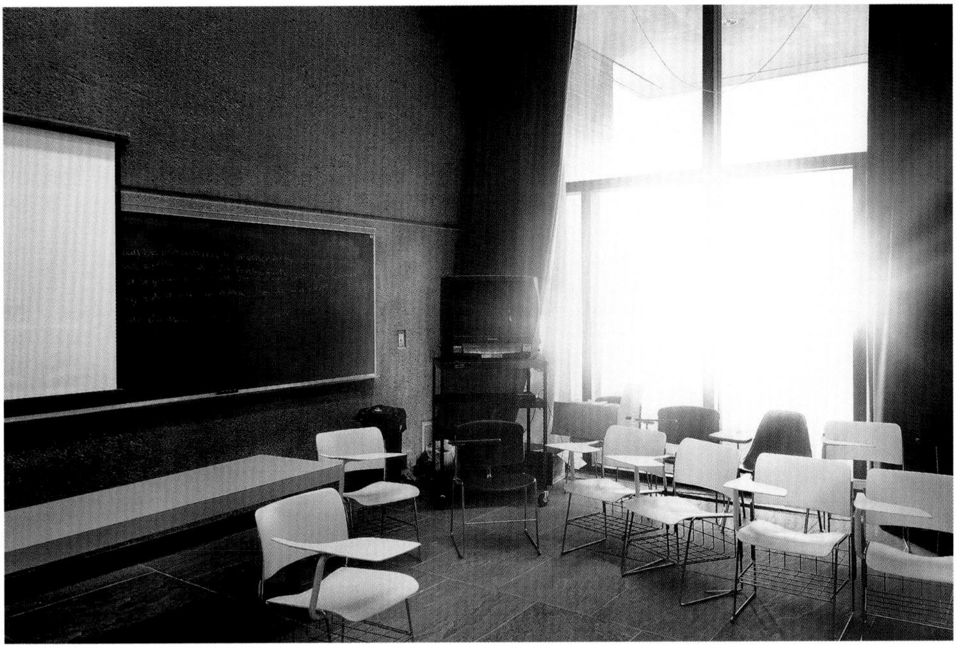

**Fig. 1.12.** Nancy Davenport, *Classroom #1*, 2004. C-print. Courtesy of Nancy Davenport.

soot. A gloomy light pours in. The DVD cart is an odd presence (or was when Davenport took this picture, before file-sharing and streaming made this technology obsolete). The Sixties are getting old; young people recall that era's battles and dreams less and less.

Davenport captures this Sixties forgetting. Ostentatiously drab, her *Campus* photos give visual form to the empty feeling of Musset's *je ne sais quoi*—a numb presentness, a general exhaustion, an incapacity to imagine anything else. The bland titles of these works evoke deadened emotions, a foreboding banality. *Administration* depicts a concrete- and brick-clad building at night (fig. 1.13). The lights inside illuminate newspapers taped to the clerestory windows. The nondescript structure is Taylor Hall at Kent State University, home to the university's journalism school and location of the shootings during the infamous antiwar protest of May 4, 1970. Davenport does not disclose where she took this picture. Her depiction of the site of the massacre at night doesn't elicit the kinds of emotions that historical images of the protest do. We have no way of knowing that four undergraduates were murdered just a few feet from where Davenport took the exposure, or that scores of their classmates hid behind the concrete piers just above the camera, where they barely escaped with their lives. Davenport offers no such clues. Her photos are cold pictures, images of indifference.

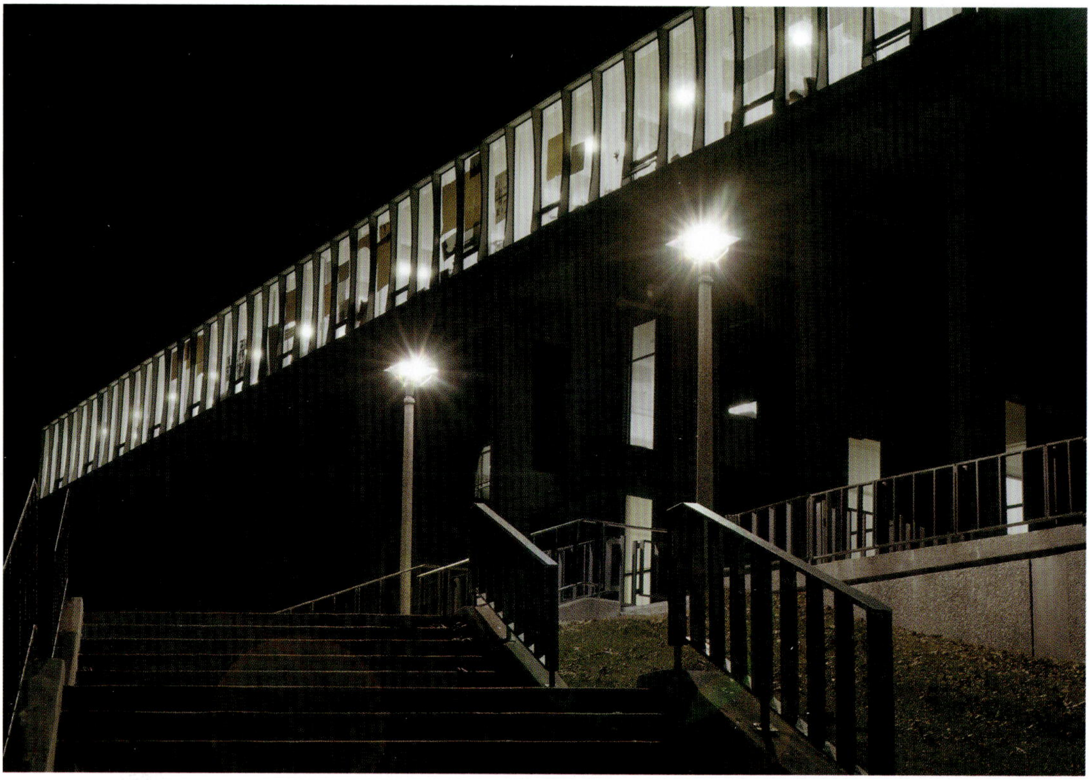

**Fig. 1.13.** Nancy Davenport, *Administration*, 2004. C-print. Courtesy of Nancy Davenport.

They do not prescribe what we should remember about May 4th or even that we *should* remember. They don't seem to "express" anything at all.

Matthew Buckingham's installation *Will Someone Please Explain It to Me, I've Just Become a Radical* (2008) focuses on a single campus. A clipping from the *Wisconsin State Journal*, "76 Hurt in UW Rioting; Campus Strike Results," informs us that a demonstration against the Dow Chemical Company took place at the University of Wisconsin, Madison, on October 18, 1967. A second article describes a battle that occurred in Vietnam the same day ("Planes Hit Haiphong Again after Fierce Aerial Dogfight"). The specificity of Buckingham's investigation is important. We are reminded that a major corporation, Dow Chemical, was a leading manufacturer of napalm then. A jelly-like substance developed in the manufacture of waxes and oils, napalm creates firebombs when combined with petroleum. Under the direction of the U.S. Department of Defense, Dow's scientists developed a "superior" formula, combining resin polystyrene with conventional napalm to enhance its flammability and adhesive quality. Dropped from the sky by American pilots, the compound reached temperatures of 1,500– 2,200°F upon explosion. At the moment of exposure the burning substance clung tenaciously to its victims, causing their flesh to melt.

In January 1967 graphic photographs of children with life-threatening burns appeared in the Leftist magazine *Ramparts*.[102] The sight of these photographs inspired Martin Luther King Jr. to denounce the war in a speech connecting the violence in Southeast Asia perpetrated by America's "strange liberators" to civil rights struggles at home.[103] At Madison the outrage festered over the spring and summer. That October students mounted a protest against the presence of Dow recruiters on campus. The university had seemed a benign entity to students fortunate enough to enroll there. A public institution, it made higher education broadly accessible. It had appeared to be a force for good. In truth, the university was a player in the detested war, students noted. A graduate could end up working for the manufacturer of napalm and Agent Orange.[104] A less fortunate individual, who was not a student and thus was ineligible for draft deferment, could end up using these chemicals on other human beings. The protesters were determined to expose these connections.

That morning some three hundred young people crowded into Madison's Commerce Building to confront the recruiter. Inspired by the nonviolent tactics of civil rights protest, the students sat down in the building's main corridor to derail the interviewing process; within a few hours the president of the university called in the police. The responders, mainly traffic cops and off-duty officers untrained in riot control, broke down the glass doors and marched down the hallway in a rampage.

Nightsticks battered heads and torsos. Faces and hands became sticky with blood. The hard granite floors and tiled walls ricocheted with screams. A crowd of some two thousand watched in disgust as their battered classmates stumbled outdoors onto Commerce Plaza, and the seriously wounded were carried out on stretchers. The most aggressive observers hurled bricks and rocks at the police. Some raised their arms in a fascist salute. *"Sieg Heil!"* they screamed. *"Sieg Heil!"*[105]

A photograph from the campus newspaper records this moment (fig. 1.14). A group of young people stand at the entrance to the classroom where the recruiter sat. The protesters in front of them, whom we cannot see, are being attacked. We see this plainly in the students' faces. They are *next*.

A girl ducks for cover, her arm caught in the strap of her handbag. The tall boy next to her reaches for the hand of a female friend (he will successfully escape the crowded corridor),[106] while another young man with a shock of black hair and thick-framed glasses gapes at the violence. Another boy pulls a sheepskin coat around his shoulders, preparing for the worst. (He will be clubbed mercilessly.)[107] Who is the boy with the mustache, whose face has been outlined in black by the dangling cord of the camera's

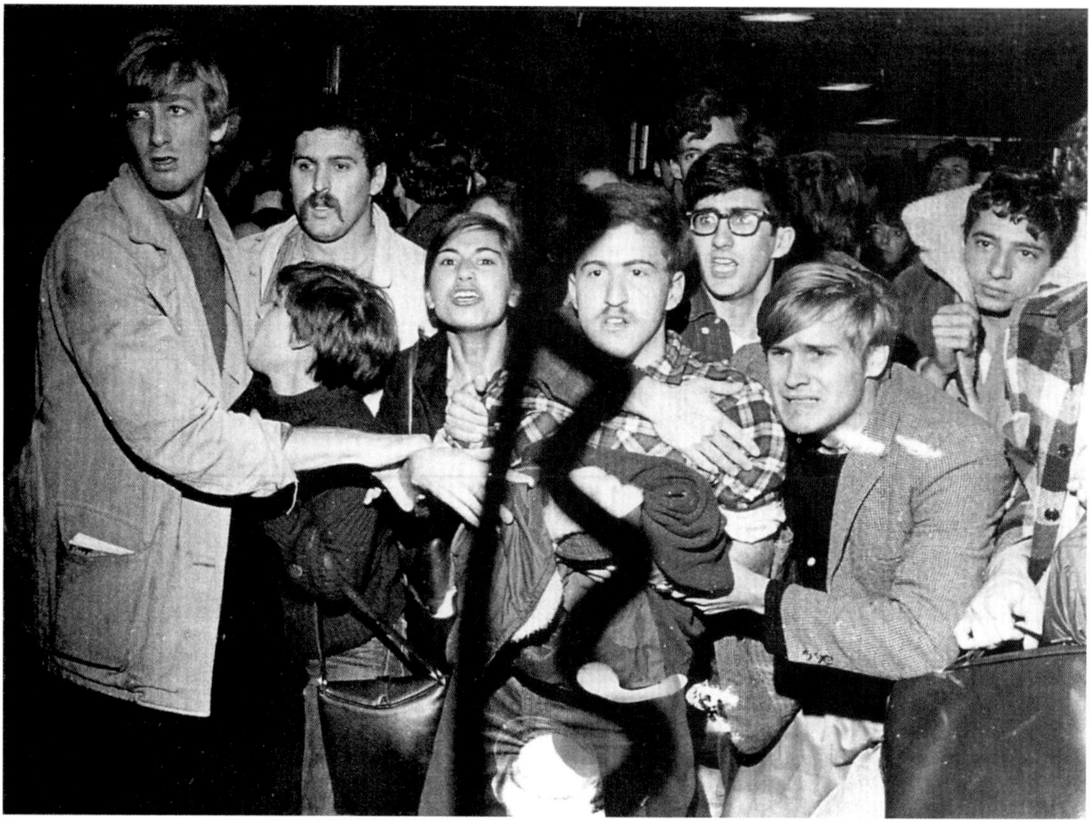

**Fig. 1.14.** Matthew Buckingham, *Will Someone Please Explain It to Me, I've Just Become a Radical*, 2008. Photograph. Courtesy of Matthew Buckingham.

flash, who clutches a sweater in self-defense? Who is his friend with parted hair who grimaces at the spectacle, who pulls the mustached boy away from the mayhem? They touch one another intimately as lovers do.

Open displays of feeling between men were exceedingly rare then, as they are now. There would have been little if any recognition for this couple, if these men were a couple.[108] It is the fall of 1967. The first anti-homophobic protest in the United States was staged by the Daughters of Bilitis and the Mattachine Society two years earlier.[109] Stonewall is a good year and a half away. Contempt for gay people is a widely accepted sentiment. The term *homophobia* has not yet been coined. The previous June CBS broached this forbidden subject on broadcast television for the first time. The program was called *The Homosexuals*; its portrayal of gay life could not have been more bleak.[110] The reporter, Mike Wallace, interviews psychiatric experts who define homosexuality as an "illness." Closeted men describe their experiences. (Lesbians never even enter Wallace's presentation: as yet, homosexuality can only be described as a male affliction.) We hear these men but do not see their faces, veiled in darkness or kept safely outside the camera's reach. The men are criminals in the eyes of the law. They remain anonymous.

A married man laments his loveless marriage. A teenager on a date with his girlfriend is arrested for soliciting another man in a public bathroom. (The camera accompanies him as he is handcuffed and driven to jail.) A proudly "out" man describes his attraction to other men without a hint of guilt. The program's one positive note, he provides a modicum of "balance" to the devastating report.

What future awaits the homosexual? On this point Wallace is clear. He is a "displaced person," "an outsider." Society will never welcome him. Happiness will forever elude him. The homosexual is an urban dweller, a creature of the night. The camera pans to a city street, black sky. The headlights of passing cars pierce the darkness. This anonymous urban scene is the backdrop of Wallace's portentous remarks. A drawing of an effete gentleman with slicked-back hair, a stereotypical "homosexual," appears with the credits.

During the Dow protest two boys held one another. The sight of imminent violence catalyzed this disclosure of an intimacy that could not under ordinary circumstances be revealed. A touch that must be hidden. Then the officers lurched forward with their batons, and the group captured in this remarkable image dispersed. Two young men held one another. One protected the other. Is this a glimpse of something new? Could it be that the unscalable wall of homophobia of the McCarthy years is beginning to crumble ever so slightly? That there was *cause* for "the growing concern about homosexuals," as Wallace sternly warned the viewers of his program?

*The Sixties is the beginning of the time we are in.* The image of the students rediscovered by Matthew Buckingham is a glimpse of transition. It depicts a moment when everything is being questioned. Everything. ("Everything had changed. Everything was different now," a former student recalled.)[111] The Dow protest was a tipping point, one of many then. The Sixties is a rapid succession of such events, one precipitating the other. Extraordinary events. Historic events. The tempo is rushed, impatient, revolutionary. ("Your old road is rapidly agin' / Please get out of the new one if you can't lend your hand": Dylan again.) At Madison the spectacle of the battered students stumbling onto Commerce Plaza activated classmates who had thought precious little about Vietnam. "I'm a radical!" a young woman shouted at a teach-in on the campus that evening. "I don't know what it means, but will someone please explain it to me? I've just become a radical!"[112]

There are moments in our lives when we are shorn of habitual ways of thinking, of doing things. Our sense of ourselves has suddenly changed. We think of ourselves not as individual atoms but in relation to others.

We understand that we are part of a community—a polity. We find ourselves taking up a cause. These sentiments were sorely lacking in 2008, when Buckingham exhibited this work, and the protest movements of the long Sixties and the identity and AIDS activist politics of the early Nineties loomed large as models of possibility.[113] His work recalls a Sixties antiwar protest during a later war that inspired little resistance after an initial outburst of dissent. Unlike Davenport, Buckingham doesn't bother to enhance the shots digitally. In the tried-and-true method of Sixties photo-conceptualism, he shows what his camera finds. His images eschew mediation. And where Davenport does not specify the locations in *Campus*, Buckingham explicitly sites his project, temporally and locationally, exhibiting a reproduction of the clipping from the *Wisconsin State Journal* describing the protest and that day's air battle in Vietnam (fig. 1.15). He makes us aware of a history we otherwise would not know.

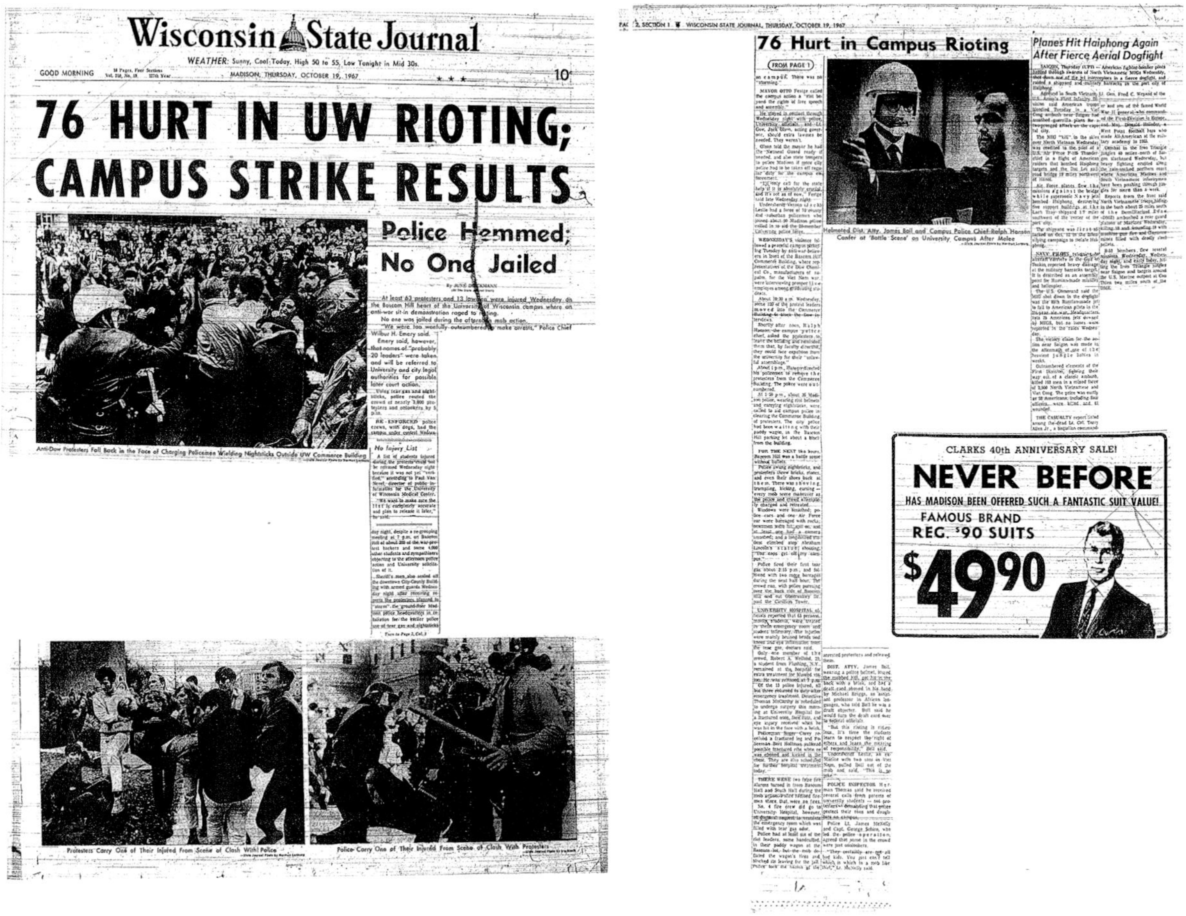

Wisconsin State Journal

WEATHER: Sunny, Cool Today. High 50 to 55, Low Tonight in Mid 30s.

GOOD MORNING — MADISON, THURSDAY, OCTOBER 19, 1967 — 10¢

# 76 HURT IN UW RIOTING; CAMPUS STRIKE RESULTS

## Police Hemmed; No One Jailed

At least 63 protesters and 13 lawmen were injured Wednesday in the Bascom Hill heart of the University of Wisconsin campus where an anti-war sit-in demonstration raged to rioting.

No one was jailed during the afternoon mob action.

Anti-Dow Protesters Fall Back in the Face of Charging Policemen Wielding Nightsticks Outside UW Commerce Building

Protesters Carry One of Their Injured From Scene of Clash With Police

Police Carry One of Their Injured From Scene of Clash With Protesters

2, SECTION 1 WISCONSIN STATE JOURNAL, THURSDAY, OCTOBER 19, 1967

## 76 Hurt in Campus Rioting

(FROM PAGE 1)

Helmeted Dist. Atty. James Boll and Campus Police Chief Ralph Hanson Confer at 'Battle Scene' on University Campus After Melee

## Planes Hit Haiphong Again After Fierce Aerial Dogfight



**Fig. 1.15.** Matthew Buckingham, *Will Someone Please Explain It to Me, I've Just Become a Radical*, 2008. Photograph of *Wisconsin State Journal*, October 19, 1967. Courtesy of Matthew Buckingham.

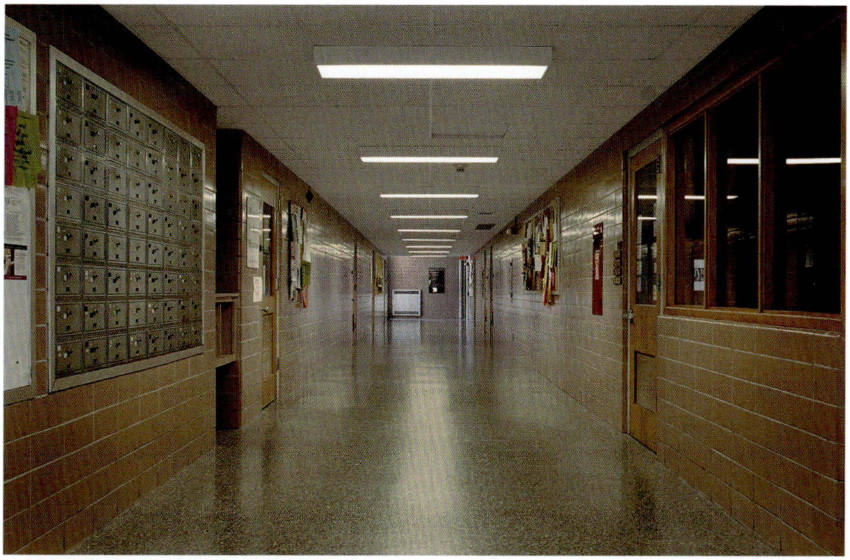

**Fig. 1.16.** Matthew Buckingham, *Will Someone Please Explain It to Me, I've Just Become a Radical*, 2008. Color photograph. Courtesy of Matthew Buckingham.

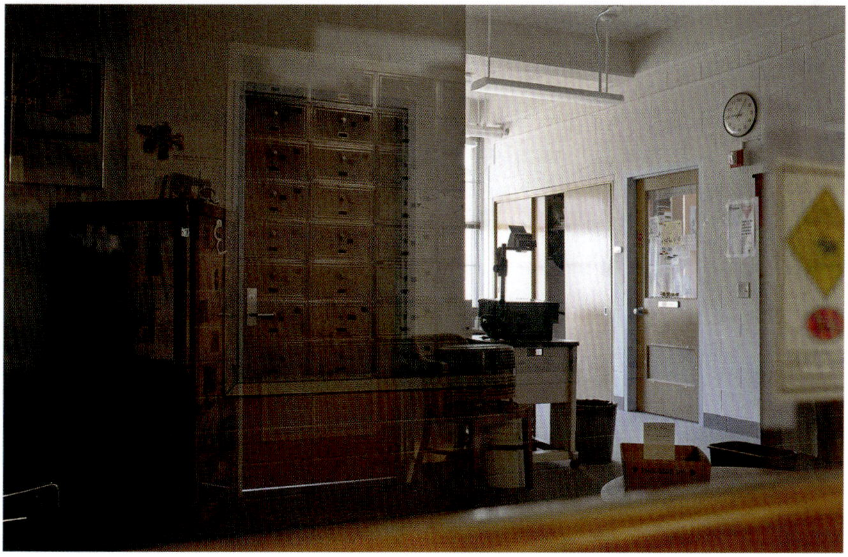

**Fig. 1.17.** Matthew Buckingham, *Will Someone Please Explain It to Me, I've Just Become a Radical*, 2008. Color photograph. Courtesy of Matthew Buckingham.

He *remembers* the Dow action—and asks us to remember it. *Here* is the hallway where the students sat down that October morning (fig. 1.16). *Here* is the classroom where the recruiter sat (fig. 1.17). *Here* are the stairwells and restrooms where the protesters hid to escape the officers' batons.

Buckingham combines two types of information: the clippings from the local newspaper and a press shot from the student newspaper, *The Daily Cardinal*, and his own photos.[114] Physically the former Commerce Building appears unchanged. The salmon-tiled walls and large-paned windows in the central corridor are vintage details. The lighting fixtures and occasional chair or paper towel dispenser are distinctly contemporary. A comparison between two eras is established. As Buckingham notes, the former business school, now Ingraham Hall, houses programs that were founded in the wake of the Dow action in the late Sixties and Seventies, when women and students of color demanded the establishment of a multicultural curriculum. A single act of defiance unleashed a new era of activism, transforming the university in ways the young protesters could scarcely have imagined.[115]

The questions they raised remain. Everything has changed. And not much.[116] "The process of return is a tactic of defamiliarization that makes it possible to critique the current moment," Buckingham observes.[117] His stay in Madison as a visiting professor eventuated in a work that addressed the diminished state of antiwar dissent during the period after September 11, 2001, when the War on Terror filled the economic and ideological void left by the end of the Cold War and precipitated a war and war economy propagated in its name.[118] As Buckingham notes, Richard ("Dick") and Lynn Cheney were graduate students at the university in 1967. Of the protesters Dick Cheney later recalled:

> They were a distraction. They were disruptive. You didn't get caught up with the issue that people were protesting or demonstrating against. There were a lot of us who felt, "This is a pain in the neck. I've got to get to class."[119]

Buckingham's work revolves around two protagonists: Cheney, who avoided the draft on five occasions,[120] and the anonymous student who was so enraged by what happened that she was transformed into a "radical." Representing the antipodes of Sixties ideology in the United States, his pairing of the student activist and the politician is a structure of comparison—one that reiterates the work's thematic focus on two eras and two wars. While we may never know what happened to the young radical, the career of Cheney would be written in bold script. A chief architect of the Iraq invasion and Patriot Act, and an advocate of "justified" torture, the future U.S. vice president and chief executive of Halliburton would straddle the post-Vietnam reconfiguration of U.S. power in pivotal roles, emerging as the very avatar of the security state. I interpret the title of Buckingham's project as profoundly ironic. There are no "radicals" in his photographs, no protest signs, no groups of students with joined hands, and no lovers. No hints of movement or noise. The corridors and stairwells of Ingraham Hall are empty. It is *silence*, ultimately—a silence literal and metaphorical—that Buckingham and Davenport depict.

## The Double: Return and Reenactment

In the film I now want to consider, a young man steps up to a podium. An iconic form, the Washington Monument, towers above (fig. 1.18). The afternoon is bright and breezy, and the American flags that encircle the monument flutter merrily in the wind. Gaggles of tourists walk around the obelisk, indifferent to the goings-on below—the small audience of listeners and the speaker who asks:

> What kind of system is it that justifies the United States or any other country seizing the destinies of the Vietnamese people and using them callously for its own power? . . . We must *name* that system. We must name it, describe it, analyze it, understand it and change it.[121]

Paul Potter, the twenty-five-year-old president of Students for a Democratic Society (SDS), delivered these famous remarks at this very place during the first major protest against the Vietnam War in 1965.[122] However, this version of Potter's speech is unmistakably contemporary. The projected image we encounter in a gallery, or the download we watch online, has the crisp contours and vivid coloration of digital video. The speaker is not Potter but an actor. The performance is one of a series of respoken New Left speeches known as *The Port Huron Project*, organized in 2006–8 by Mark Tribe.[123]

To reenact is to repeat, to double, and it could be claimed that reenactment, a medium that came into prominence at the turn of the millennium, is a reprise of postmodernist tactics of appropriation.[124] Reenactment, or "doubling" as I want to call it, is the restaging of a prior event at a later moment—the reanimation of a speech, performance, or film. Reenactment is a technique of recollection, a scaffolding for historical thought. The re-creation of an event or respeaking of a talk forces us to hold two points in time or eras simultaneously in our minds. This is not an easy thing to do. As we experience a reenactment, we become conscious of the temporal delay, the distinction, between a past moment that has been retrieved for our awareness and *this* moment, the time we are in. We begin to perceive the present in relation to another time; we begin to think historically. And so reenactment has emerged as a central preoccupation of artists and filmmakers exploring questions of historical memory, including Sixties memory.[125]

The double is not a forgery but an overt replica. Its resemblance to what it copies, to the "original," causes us to perceive its replicated nature—that

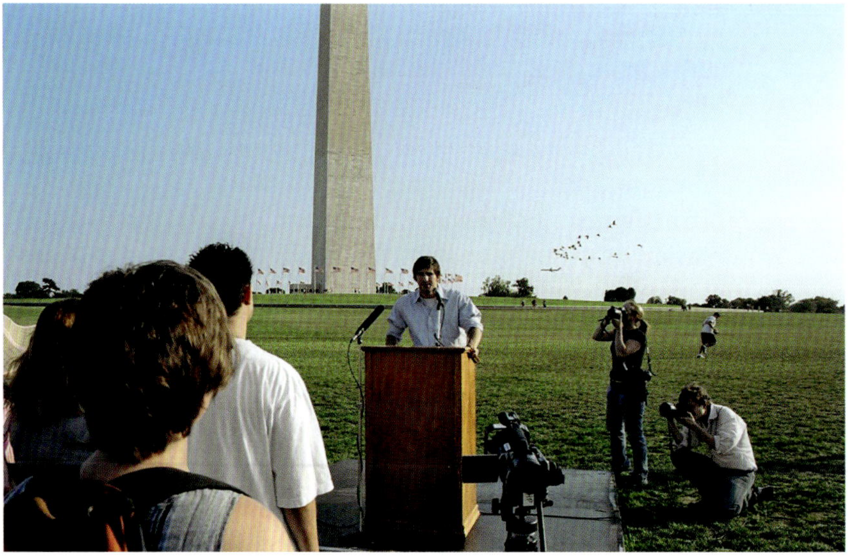

**Fig. 1.18.** Mark Tribe, *The Port Huron Project: We Must Name the System: Paul Potter 1965/2007*, Washington, DC, 2007. Photograph: Brendan Polmer. Courtesy of Mark Tribe.

it is not the same. The reenactments that concern us in this book do not create the illusion of pastness, the fiction that we have "returned." They expose their anachronistic nature, their artifice; they cause us to perceive that they repeat. The differences between the versions are important, for difference is the engine of signification, as Ferdinand de Saussure, the founder of semiology, the study of signs, famously observed.[126] To perceive difference is to *compare*—to name a thing with this word, and this other thing with another. Comparison makes it possible to articulate the differences between things and their names.

The juxtaposition of two seemingly identical terms, of like with like, reduces difference to a bare minimum. Juxtaposed, two syllables or phonemes that sound alike begin to mean something. As Claude Lévi-Strauss and Roman Jakobson noted, a baby's random utterances become speech when she assigns the second syllable a role distinct from the first. A doubled syllable is distinguished from "a potentially limitless series of identical sounds"—in a word, babble.[127] A single /pa/ or /ma/ is nonsensical at first, as is a sequence of repeated utterances (pa/pa/pa/pa). Only the second phoneme (pa/pa) confers meaning. Now the first syllable has become meaningful: what was once nonsense has become a unit of speech. Together, the two syllables form a word.[128] Doubling is the pivotal moment when a child has begun to take possession of language, when she is capable of making meaning—a primal instance of language's use (what Saussure calls *parole*) in the mastery of language as a system (*langue*). Difference is revealed at the phonemic level as the nonequivalence of two syllables that sound identical. There hardly seems to be a distinction between these sounds, and yet there is.

Reenactment is a kind of doubling. It makes us keenly aware of the difference between an event and its restaging. The second version "*emphasizes* the meaningful intention of the first."[129] As Roland Barthes noted in a different context, the double is a "fabrication of a world which resembles the primary one, not in order to copy it but to render it intelligible." (Barthes's celebrated description of structuralism as an activity that finds meaning in the "little enough" between "two objects" or "two tenses" could well serve as a definition of reenactment.)[130] One of Lévi-Strauss's central claims in *The Raw and the Cooked* is that myths involve doubling. The retelling of a primary story introduces a "meta-" or secondary plane of understanding to the first, allowing us to compare them. Lévi-Strauss calls this analytic technique "mythic thought," for myth is a form of thought, he insists. His account of the Bororo legend of South America, the myth that inspired his analytic approach, concerns the different versions of that story. There is not one Bororo myth but *two*. The second is a retelling of the first.[131] In reenactment, an action or speech repeated is emphasized; it has been selected from all the other speeches and events that the artist could have "remade" but chose not to. Repeated, it has become meaningful. We are made aware of an event, an entire history, that we may not have thought much about or even known of.[132]

As we listen to the speech, as we observe the speaker's gestures, we become acutely aware of a temporal fissure *within* the reenactment. Reenactment dramatizes the temporal delay embedded in the semiological sign—the deferral constitutive of acts of speech.[133] The double is "the two-step that banishes the unitary condition of the moment, that creates *within* the moment an experience of fission," Rosalind Krauss has written. Reenactment makes explicit the temporal nature of the double.[134] It sets up the illusion that we have "returned" in order to disrupt the fantasy of historical presence, Ranke's "the way it really was." For reenactment stages repetition in and *as* time, stretches out time, gives it volume. Watching a reenactment, we fantasize for a passing instant that we have been touched by the past. That we are "there." The fantasy doesn't last: the nagging awareness that the event at which we are present is a copy of a prior one causes us to perceive the temporal divide between the "primary" occurrence and its contemporary rehearsal. Before the remake the event inhabited a more nebulous past (it was simply "in the past"). To hold two moments in our awareness is to grasp that the past never repeats itself in exactly the same way. I would further suggest that we perceive this distinction most acutely in those reenactments that most exactingly resemble the primary event—that most ostentatiously reveal the logic of the double. The more similar the replication is to the "original," the more glaring is its dissimilitude. Likeness reveals *un*likeness. Precisely because "everything is so much the same, one becomes acutely aware of the differences."[135]

Consider Mary Kelly's *WLM Demo Remix*, a work included in the artist's installation *Love Songs* (2005–7). Kelly's work consists of two projected images that appear nearly the same (fig. 1.19). The first depicts a 2005 remake of a staged women's liberation march (WLM) of 1970, the focus of the second image. The 1970 march commemorated the fiftieth anniversary of the passage of the Nineteenth Amendment of the U.S. Constitution, which granted women suffrage. The image of the reenactment dissolves over the course of ninety seconds, which is to say slowly, into the archival shot of the 1970 event. "Natural," diachronic time has been reversed. As the earlier event comes into visibility, the reenactment fades—yet not entirely. The older image does not replace the contemporary one. The visual confusion caused by this arrangement is the result of this palimp-

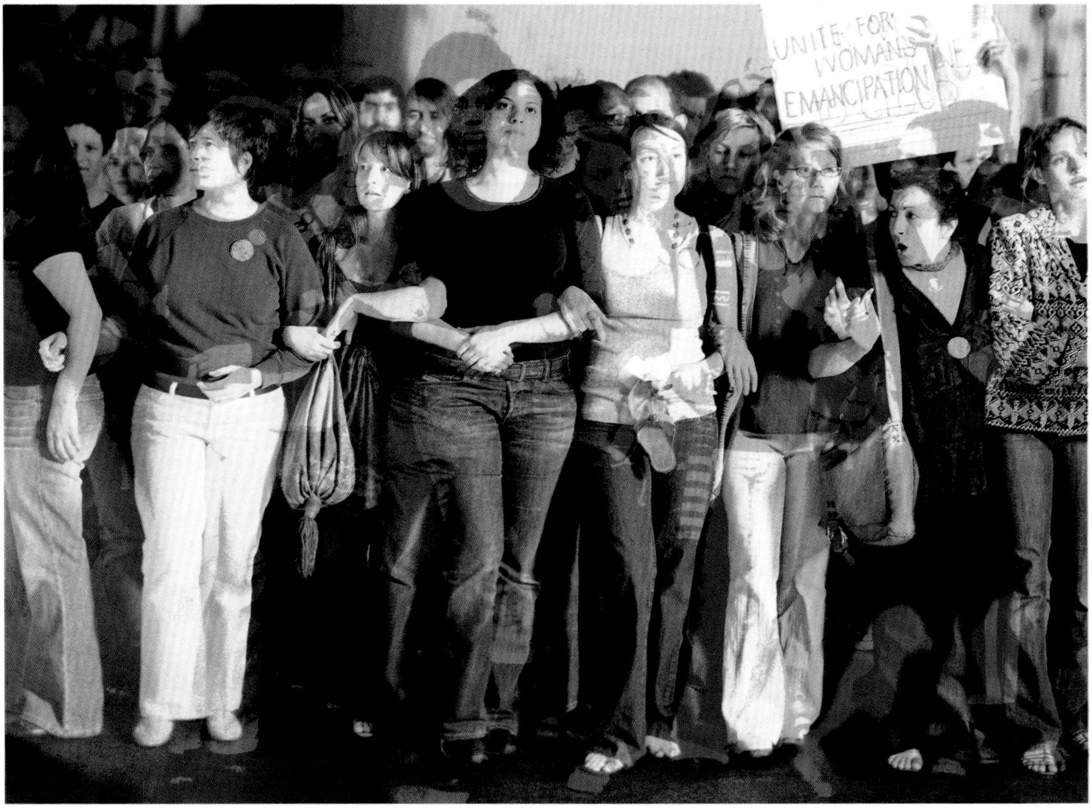


**Fig. 1.19.** Mary Kelly, *WLM Demo Remix*, 2005. 90-second black-and-white film loop. Dimensions variable. Installation view of *Love Songs* at Neue Galerie, Documenta 12, Kassel, Germany, 2007. Photograph: David Familian. © Mary Kelly. Courtesy of Mary Kelly and Mitchell-Innes & Nash, New York.

sest of faces and bodies, of bizarrely similar self-presentations. Both groups of women don T-shirts and hip-hugger jeans, and they wear their hair in the natural styles of the early Seventies.[136] Gazing at Kelly's projection, it is indeed a challenge to say for certain which women are historical and which are contemporary, who are the Second Wave feminists and who the reenactors.

The loop concludes. The reenactment alone fills the screen. The image of the historical event has bled into the image of its re-creation, and the work starts all over again. Mixing and remixing, Kelly's work is never still.[137] The contemporary "march" doesn't follow the first chronologically, as we might assume. The copy *precedes* the original. The work is dizzyingly simulacral, which is not "a simple imitation," as Gilles Deleuze observed. The simulacrum is precisely "the act by which the very idea of a model or privileged position" of the primary instance is "challenged and overturned."[138] The reenactment is thus the scrim through which the historical image comes into visibility; it both veils the prior event and *allows it to be seen*. It does so as a copy. As repetition. *WLM Remix* establishes the Second Wave as a point of origin and comparison for contemporary feminism, even as it "challenges" the iconic status, the priority, of Seventies feminism as an irretrievably monumental past—a time of immense gains for women, never to be recaptured. It subtly undercuts nostalgia for that time—a nostalgia that might preclude feminist action in the present tense.

A second work in the *Love Songs* sequence, *Multi-Story House* (2007), explores these questions in three dimensions. A viewer's body is the vehicle of that cognition (fig. 1.20). A gabled structure evokes the feminist group project *Womanhouse* (1972) and other works of Seventies art that transformed the home, emblem of domesticity and women's confinement, into a site of consciousness raising and collaboration.[139] In *WLM Demo Remix*, it was noted, a blending of two projected images that appear alike and unalike forces us to compare two eras of feminist politics and generations (feminist "mothers" and "daughters.") Kelly's "house" is both a sign and an object, a feminist icon and sculpture. It is something to look at, walk around—and something to read.[140] It refers obliquely to the geometric vocabulary of Sixties Minimalism, yet it disrupts the strictly somatic encounter of works by artists like Donald Judd and Robert Morris, which attempted to purge reference and meaning from the work of art.[141] For Kelly covers the exterior and interior of her sculpture with *writing*. The translucent Perspex panels of the sculpture's exterior are emblazoned with texts arranged in no particular order. There is no one way to read the remarks etched into the milky white panels:

> My mother was a feminist, so yeah, I read *Our Bodies, Ourselves* when I was eight.
>
> I love my birthday—May '68. But I wish my parents had been part of something like the German student movement. Now, in my way, I'm trying to be more revolutionary.
>
> Second wave, third wave, missed everything. I went through puberty in Saudi Arabia. There wasn't even a first wave yet.

The letters are incisions, cuts. They are lit from behind. The texts—each and every one of them a memory—are both translucent and transparent, legible and opaque. Kelly solicits two forms of attention at once. We read and peer through these remarks to the sculpture's interior at the same time, and catch a glimpse of other viewers standing inside the "house" who are, at that moment, reading a second arrangement of inscriptions and looking back at us. Eventually we join them. Stepping inside this stuffy space (warmed by white fluorescent lamps encased in a transparent floor and by our bodies) we read more "stories":

> You didn't speak for others.
>
> Everyone had a voice.
>
> Men on the left said it was about mobilizing women for the "main struggle," but we told them, to hell with that, our demands are important too.

The recollections of Kelly's peers are powerful, and unfailingly positive:

> I was part of the left, but from '69 on, women's liberation was the main thing. We lived together and we helped each other. It was the strongest community I've ever experienced.

Placing the collective memories of her generation of feminists on public view, Kelly recalls another, younger self, who was actively involved in the movement during the Seventies.[142] And she explores another generation's perceptions of that time—the views of women who were born while or after that history was being made.[143] The memories of some center upon a feminist mother and a feminist discourse encountered when they were children ("I read *Our Bodies, Ourselves* when I was eight"). Others have no such recollections. "I wish my parents had been part of something," one

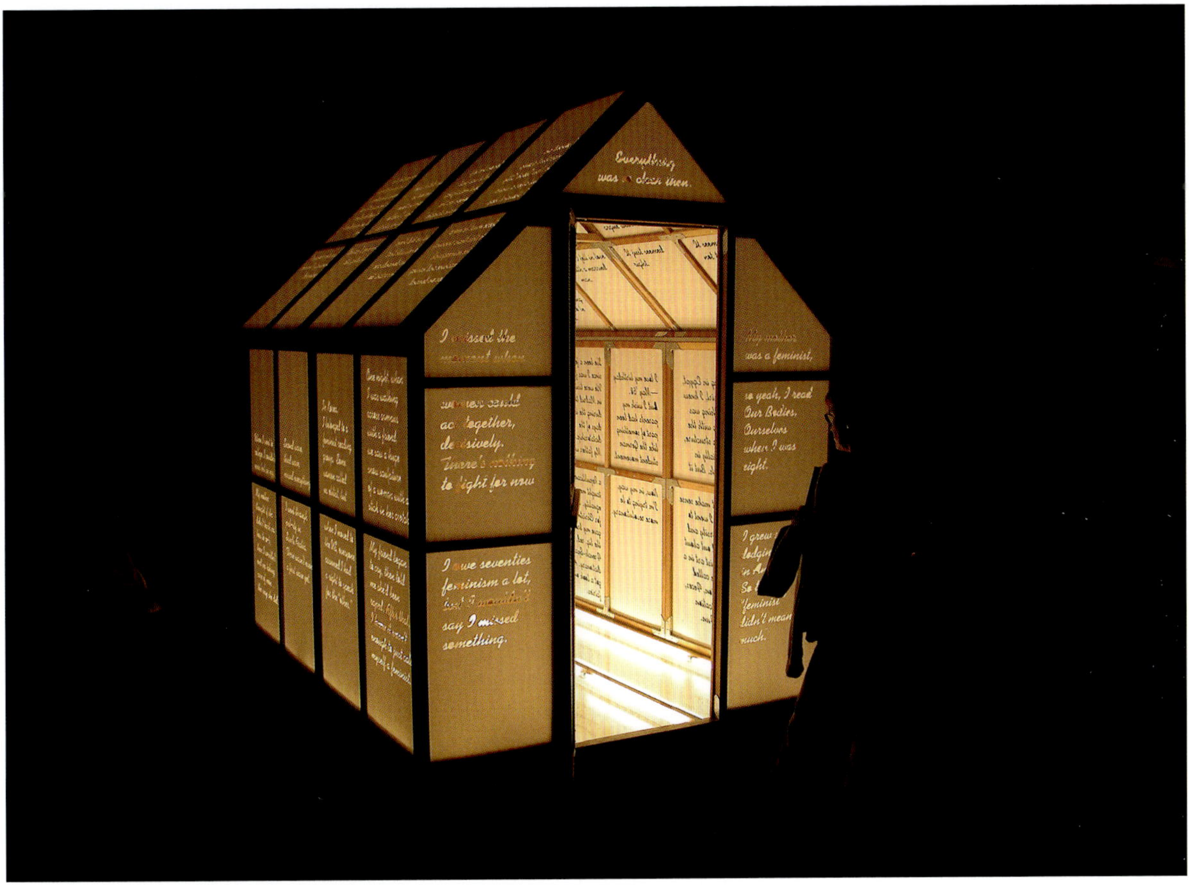


**Fig. 1.20.** Mary Kelly and Ray Barrie, *Multi-Story House*, 2007. Wooden frame, cast acrylic panels, plate glass floor, fluorescent light. Installation view of *Love Songs* at Neue Galerie, Documenta 12, Kassel, Germany, 2007. Photograph: David Familian. © Mary Kelly. Courtesy of Mary Kelly and Mitchell-Innes & Nash, New York.

woman remarks ruefully. "Second wave, third wave, missed everything," laments another.

Where the memories of the first generation suggest a strong solidarity, those of the younger cohort betray a lack of mutual identification. *Multi-Story House* stages these inter- and intra-generational dissonances in volumetric space. It reveals itself—its crossing of feminist voices and histories—in time to viewers who move inside and outside and around it, who experience it *as sculpture*. From the exterior we read the memories of Kelly's peers backward. Inside, the memories of the younger women are inverted. The polyvocal "stories" never resolve into a univocal narrative of feminist progress.[144]

*Love Songs* only poses questions. Can we still speak of feminism as a movement in the twenty-first century? What happened to the sense of community the older women speak about? What has feminism achieved since then, and for whom? (Some of the younger women point to a dearth of feminist progress internationally and to the relative privilege of Western white women who were, and are, in a position to criticize patriarchy: "I went through puberty in Saudi Arabia. There wasn't even a first wave yet"; "I grew up dodging bullets in Angola. So the term 'feminist' didn't mean much.") How do the older feminists look back at their earlier involvements? How does Kelly? Do the upbeat memories we read in the sculpture's cozy interior coincide with her memories? Do these women speak for her? Do the younger women? It would be simple enough to interpret *Love Songs* as a love letter or homage to a lamented solidarity, a *mouvement perdu*. It is far less resolved than that. Kelly interrogates this longing for a lost community, a "before." She keeps nostalgia at bay. Ultimately, the concern of her project is the unresolved status of feminism itself: its unfinished business, its becomingness, its future.[145]

I suggested earlier that reenactments incite us to "see time." As the words are respoken we imagine we hear the tonality of another era, its aural textures; we hear the sound of pastness. Reenactment sets up this illusion of historical transparency knowingly. We know very well that this is a performance, and that the speaker is a performer. We know that the "event" is happening *right now*, in the present tense. Reenactment—reenactment in the critical sense—rejects the fantasy of return, the nostalgic's dream of time travel. Respoken, the words lurch forward in time, meet us in our time, if words can do such a thing. Words that had been spoken to others are spoken to us. They have been reanimated. We listen. But now we notice that they are old words, referring to past events and to wars that ended some time ago. We hear the names of people who are no longer alive. The person whose words are spoken may no longer be living: we are reminded of this, too.[146]

Reenactment reveals the "obvious" fact that historical eras are nonidentical, distinct. The reconstruction of an event causes the initial version to appear even more distant, *more past*, and ultimately *strange*, as the past inevitably seems to the historian. The event appears *both* familiar and remote, in a word, uncanny.[147] The strangeness of this encounter is especially apparent when the reenactment is "reenacted." In his 2008 restaging of an antiwar speech presented by Stokely Carmichael, the co-founder of the Student Non-Violent Coordinating Committee (SNCC), in Dag Hammerskjöld Plaza at the United Nations in 1967, Mark Tribe commissioned two different performers to respeak the activist's remarks. The actors interpreted Carmichael's speech and appearance in distinctive ways.[148] The dramatic difference in their self-presentations—one performer wore a button-down, oxford-cloth shirt and slacks, similar to what Carmichael

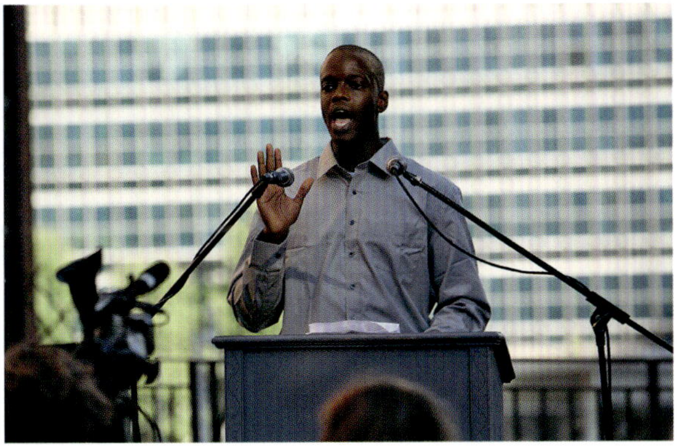

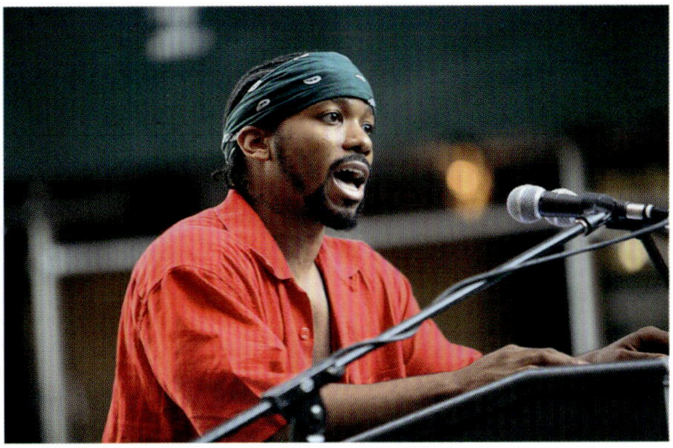

**Fig. 1.21a and 1.21b.** Mark Tribe, *The Port Huron Project: Let Another World Be Born: Stokely Carmichael, 1967/2008,* New York, 2008. Two performances. Photographs: Meghan Boudreau. Courtesy of Mark Tribe.

wore, the other an Afro with a headband, beard, and open shirt evocative of Black Panther dress[149]—reminded viewers that we were witnessing two versions of a prior event, a double of a double (fig. 1.21a, b). The heavy presence of cameras and mikes in front of the podium and among the audience underscored the awareness that the performances were made to be recorded, to exist in a perpetual future tense. The audience gathered in a park in midtown Manhattan that day would now be replaced by a potentially limitless audience of spectators who could view the filmed performance as a projected image in an installation or as a video feed on Tribe's website, where it could be reexperienced at will.[150]

Doubling, I suggested, is a marker of difference: the more we concentrate our attention on two noises that sound alike, or two things that appear alike, the more unalike they seem. To hear a historical speech *in situ*, reenacted in real time, is one experience; to replay it on a video or computer screen another. The "actual" reenactment requires our presence. Being present, we are brought imaginatively closer to the historical moment. The recital of Carmichael's fiery speech twice magnified the brilliance of his oratory:

> The draft is white people sending black people to make war on yellow people in order to defend the land they stole from red people.[151]

As the audience listened to the same words respoken by two performers with unique styles of presentation, the differences between the moment when Carmichael spoke and the present were set into relief. Just as Potter's reference to "Negroes from Mississippi and Alabama" in Tribe's respeaking of his speech sounded strange to contemporary ears, Carmichael's denunciations of the much-hated military draft of the Vietnam era dated his remarks.[152] More striking, perhaps, was how *undated* these speeches seemed. Listening to Potter's searing analysis of President Lyndon Johnson's *casus belli*—

> The president says that we are defending freedom in Vietnam. Whose freedom? . . . Perhaps what the president means when he speaks of freedom is the freedom of the American people—[153]

the crowd gathered at the Washington Monument experienced a sense of *déjà vu*. Just as President Johnson rationalized the war in Indochina as a defense of "freedom" abroad in order to secure "freedom" at home, as Potter noted, President George W. Bush enlisted this very rhetoric some forty years later to justify yet another misbegotten war:

> The greatest weapon in the arsenal of democracy is the desire for liberty. . . . And when that hard work is done and the critics of today recede from memory, the cause of freedom will be stronger, a vital region will be brighter, and the American people will be safer.[154]

Wars are rhetorical productions, legitimated by words. Potter's "Name the System" speech related the Vietnam War to the language of U.S. constitutionalism, wherein the Enlightenment values of freedom and liberty are marshaled in support of a sovereignty defined as "radically democratic within an open and continuous space of expansion," an imperialist project.[155] Tribe's re-presentation of Potter's speech examines how the classical American rhetoric of freedom and democracy has all too frequently been put in the service of less high-minded goals. Respoken in 2007, Johnson's argument sounded queasily familiar. The listener of Tribe's reenactments was jolted from a slumberous presentism: one could hear the susurrations of still older eras and more distant wars: rather than a "second Vietnam," the Iraq War could be perceived within the long history of American expansionism reaching back to the early years of the Republic.

The Sixties is rightly celebrated for its glorious oratory and orators. The inaugural addresses of presidents John Kennedy and Patrice Lumumba; the "I Have a Dream" speech of Martin Luther King Jr.; the moving testimonial of voting rights activist Fannie Lou Hamer at the 1964 Democratic Convention in Atlantic City; Mario Savio's "Operation of the Machine" remarks during the Berkeley Free Speech movement; and Malcolm X's seminal "The Ballot or the Bullet" speech of the same year are typically encountered as sound bites in documentaries, or as texts on the page. Reading the words they spoke, we imagine that we can hear the speaker's voice and the rapturous applause that he or she invoked. Yet a mortal air clings to these words if the speaker died violently, as many of these individuals did—and even if they did not. The respeaker invites us to remember the *speaker*, a person who is no longer here to speak. For what purpose?

In his *Robert F. Kennedy Performance Project (RFK in EKY)* (2004)—to my thinking a masterpiece of the genre—theater director and performer John Malpede reconstructed Senator Robert Kennedy's "Poverty Tour" of southeastern Kentucky in February 1968.[156] Malpede and a battery of collaborators associated with the Los Angeles Poverty Department acting ensemble returned to each of the towns and hamlets that Kennedy had visited. They reenacted the field hearings that the senator conducted, the speeches he gave, and his appearances in private homes, schoolhouses, and at a strip mine (figs. 1.22, 1.23).[157] Attired in period dress per Malpede's instructions, residents of these communities respoke the remarks of Kennedy and local politicians, and the citizens he met, and participated as extras and audience members. Some of the reenactors read a parent's comments. A few respoke their own words.[158] The themes of wealth distribution, children's hunger, and educational inequality raised in 1968 received a second airing during a period of escalating disparities of wealth and antitax fervor in advance of the Tea Party "revolt" of the 2010s, when the social welfare programs of the New Deal and Great Society came under assault.

The act of return in this instance entailed a journey to the places Kennedy had visited, and the involvement of individuals who remembered his

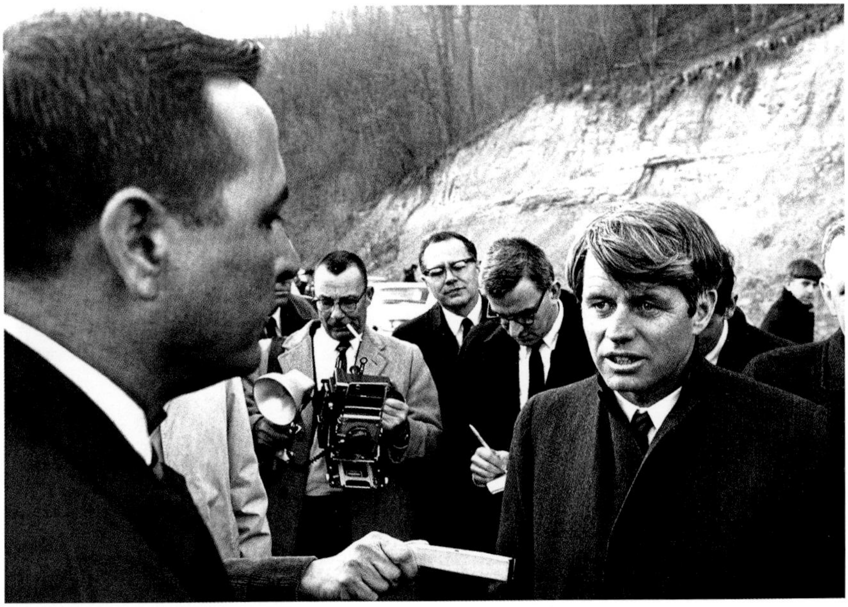

**Fig. 1.22.** Robert Kennedy visiting the strip mine at Yellow Creek, Kentucky, in 1968. Berea College Special Collections and Archives, Berea, KY.

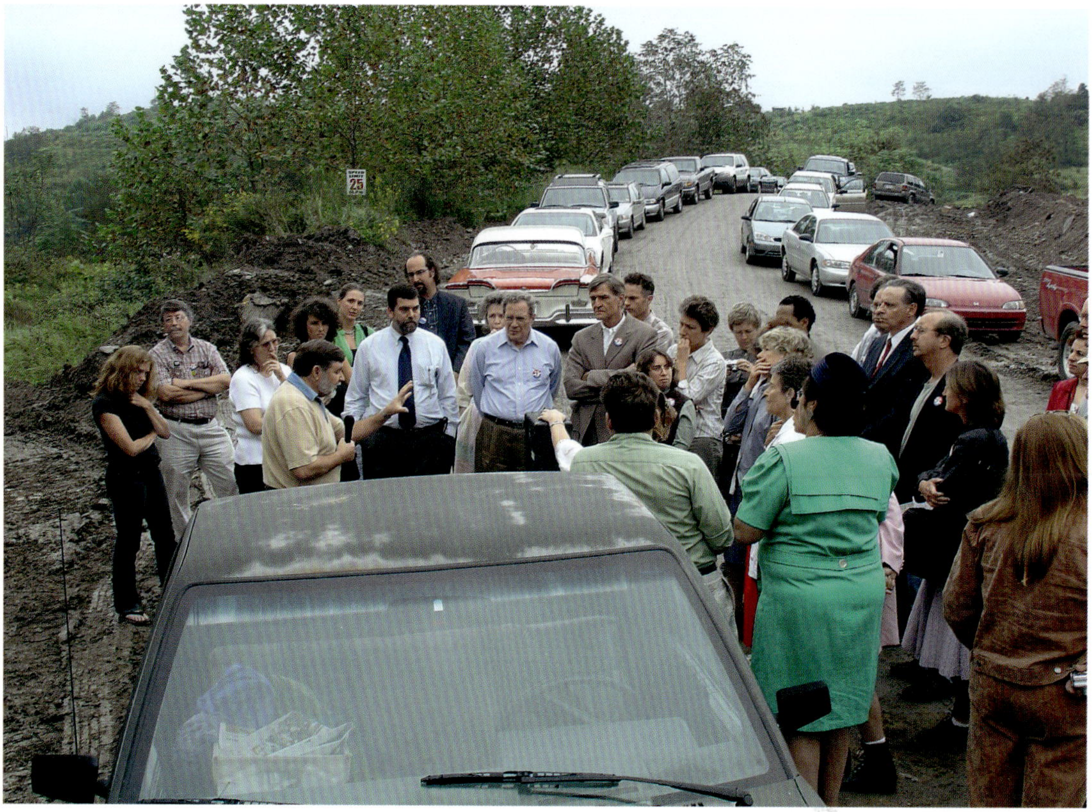


**Fig. 1.23.** Los Angeles Poverty Department, *Robert F. Kennedy Performance Project (RFK in EKY)*, 2004. Reenactment at Yellow Creek, Kentucky, strip mine, 2004. Photograph: Carmela Castrejon. Courtesy of John Malpede and Henriëtte Brouwers.

tour first- and secondhand. Not unlike Tribe's *Port Huron Project* respeakings, Malpede's project drew much of its impact from its siting, and from the participation of individuals with strong personal and mnemonic connections to these re-creations. Another project I want to consider, *Queen Mother Moore at Greenhaven Federal Prison* (2007–8), a series of respeakings by the collective BLW (Rozalinda Borcila, Sarah Lewison, and Julie Wyman) eschewed this rigorous structure. The members of BLW restaged a historical speech far from its original setting and without the participation of firsthand rememberers.

Civil rights activist Audley E. "Queen Mother" Moore spoke to an audience of largely African American men at Greenhaven Federal Prison in upstate New York in 1973. At a time when the number of incarcerated black men, never greater, had become a national scandal, BLW's retrieval of Moore's remarks had an unusual salience. A backward glance to the black nationalist and prisoners' rights movements of the Sixties and Seventies, *Queen Mother Moore at Greenhaven Federal Prison* recalled yet another speech and an even earlier era of black politics, the famous lecture delivered by United Negro Improvement Association (UNIA) founder Marcus Garvey at the Longshoreman's Hall in New Orleans in 1922. Moore recalls how a white lynch mob had threatened to assassinate Garvey in order to prevent him from speaking. The audience in the Longshoreman's Hall grew impatient; eventually they were filled with rage. Moore describes the dramatic moment when Garvey finally appeared at the auditorium: "Everybody's gun came out, and this is what they said, 'Speak, Garvey speak! Speak, Garvey!' with the guns in their hands."[159]

Moore was seventy-five years old in 1973. She had sat in the audience at the Longshoreman's Hall fifty-one years earlier. Inspired by Garvey's words, she moved to New York to join his UNIA and embarked on a career as a black rights advocate. The memory of Garvey's speech—and of the successful efforts of the audience members to assert their constitutional right to free assembly—is Moore's. The respeaker of her talk summons the memory of a memory, or two memories, at once: Moore's speech to the inmates of Greenhaven, many of whom came from Attica Prison, the site of the notoriously lethal riot of two years earlier, and Garvey's speech at the Longshoreman's Hall. Garvey and his audience "speak" *through* Moore, as Moore "speaks" *through* her reenactors: a history of black resistance to white silencing is recalled as a history of speech.

Respeaking is not commemoration, the conscientious, administered remembrance that Pierre Nora describes as *un lieu de mémoire*, the memory we are obliged to remember. The aim is to critique the values and beliefs of a prior era, or conversely, to reignite a prior moment of intensity. Reenactors are interested in the possibility of attracting listeners distracted by mediated forms of absorption, who yearn for the experience of *presence*; and they are interested in the ways that acts of listening are capable of inciting speech. "We want to know how we might be called to speak. In what ways might the actions of others enable us to speak?" BLW write. In what ways can a work of art rekindle the Sixties desire for *participatory democracy*, as it was called then—to "give people the opportunity and the courage to listen, speak, and act as free citizens in a true democracy"?[160] The mode of address in *Queen Mother Moore at Greenhaven Federal Prison* shifts from the first to the second person plural, from "we" to "you." "In what ways can *you* no longer be silent?" Borcila, Lewison, and Wyman ask.[161] I would add: how can an artwork inspire speech? Respeaking is a purposeful mimicry, an assumed eloquence. Speaking another person's speech, a performer listens to herself speaking. She hears what speech sounds like, is herself a speaker. (The ancient study of rhetoric instilled in the student the *confidence* to speak.) Reenactments like BLW's catalyze exchanges of voices and identities, slippages from "I" or "we" to "you." Distinctions between the roles of artist, performer, and audience member blur productively.

Tribe, Malpede, and Mary Kelly set up the illusion of "return" in order to arrange past and present into a comparison. Both Tribe and Malpede re-enacted the events in the locations where they originally occurred and asked performers to appear in period dress. Tribe went a step further, enlisting actors of the same ethnic or racial background as the historical speaker. A white male actor recited Potter's speech. Performers of African descent respoke Carmichael's. A black actress in a mourning hat, dress, and pearl necklace presented a speech delivered by Coretta Scott King in Central Park a month after King's assassination. A Latino actor respoke a speech given by César Chavez in a park in Los Angeles in 1971. Such performances allow us to "return" imaginatively, while their overt theatricality (established by the presence of cameras and mikes) undercuts nostalgia. They force us to think two eras together, I have claimed. Yet performances so meticulous set up the illusion of a timeless, transparent identity bound to locality, foreclosing identifications across ethnic and gendered lines. They bring us back to the Sixties and, with regard to our political identities, leave us there.[162]

Less meticulous, *Queen Mother Moore at Greenhaven Federal Prison* elicits unexpected identifications. In the filmed version of this work, created at Pilot Chicago in 2006, the artists read Moore's speech out loud. Unlike Tribe's trained actors, Borcila, Lewison, and Wyman struggle to ventriloquize Moore's words. The film's final sequence is a montage of Moore's recitation next to the tape of their respeakings (fig. 1.24). Compared to Moore's extraordinarily moving performance, the rising cadences and inflections of her voice evoking the deep oral tradition of the black church, the artists' recitations fall flat, implying the limitations of identification with persons of another gender or ethnicity, or individuals of another era. Their attempt to "return" is a failure—which is exactly the point.

Another version of *Queen Mother Moore at Greenhaven Federal Prison*, produced in collaboration with San Francisco's City Studio Art Education Project in 2008, suggested another approach. Rather than foreclose identification, the San Francisco event facilitated multiple acts of speech and identifications. BLW invited a cohort of high school students to recite Moore's talk.[163] With this displacement the project changed dramatically: now the reenactment was less a "performance" than a pedagogical activity. Both actors and audience members, the reenactors came to know Moore's speech far more intimately than if they had passively watched it recited by a professional. As the teenagers took their places behind the podium, BLW projected a slide of Moore speaking to the Greenhaven inmates onto a screen and flooded the lectern in a raking light (fig. 1.25). The projected image of Moore, the speaker's silhouette, and the actual speaker made up a single tableau.[164] As the student read Moore's inspiring remarks, two eras overlapped. Different generations "spoke" to one another. This meticulous

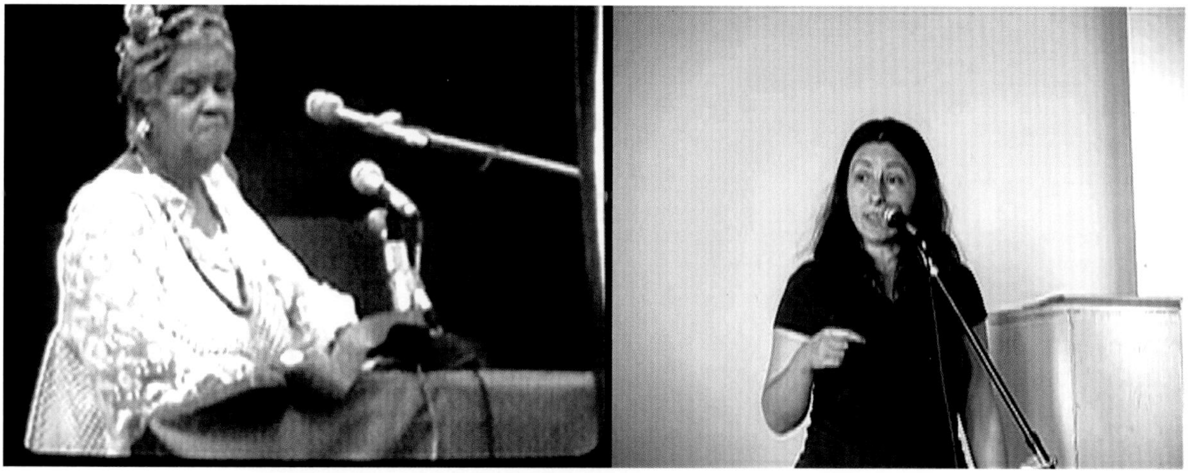

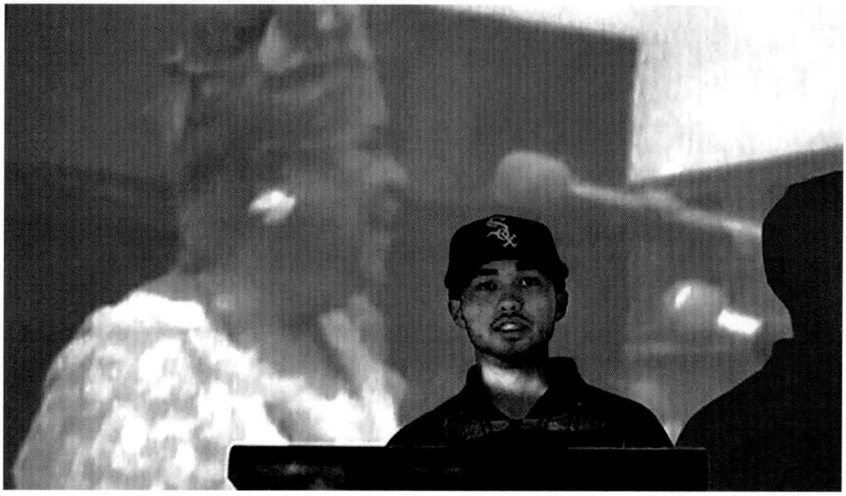

**Fig. 1.24.** BLW (Rozalinda Borcila, Sarah Lewison, Julie Wyman), *Queen Mother Moore at Greenhaven Federal Prison*, 2007–8. Courtesy of BLW (Rozalinda Borcila, Sarah Lewison, Julie Wyman).

**Fig. 1.25.** BLW (Rozalinda Borcila, Sarah Lewison, Julie Wyman) in collaboration with City Studio Art Education Project, *Queen Mother Moore at Greenhaven Federal Prison*, 2008. Courtesy of BLW (Rozalinda Borcila, Sarah Lewison, Julie Wyman).

disposition of images and bodies positioned the reenactor as both the medium and the receiver of Moore's message: her shadow "listened" to the words she respoke. Speaking and hearing Moore's words, the participants could identify with the elderly woman on the screen and with their classmates at the lectern.

Reenactment is a kind of collage, a doubling of one element by another. A voice becomes audible in another's. Moore "appears" with her youthful reenactors, who stand before *their* silhouettes. We listen to Moore's speech, to Potter's, to Carmichael's.... At the moment of return the past dilates, fills the room, touching us. We *feel* it. But now the performer has no more words to recite. The speech has come to an end. The moment is over. The past closes shut like the folds of an accordion.

## "A No Man's Land of Time"

**It is difficult to reach 1972.**
**It feels like being pushed to the edge.**

Zarina Bhimji

The notion of "return of" suggests an archaeological model of time.[165] It projects a vision of human history as a succession of discrete eras, not unlike those excavations that cause us to perceive a city's past as a geological stratum or layering of time zones and cultures. The slices don't blend in a continuous narrative: time doesn't "flow." In his "Theses on the Philosophy of History," Walter Benjamin contemptuously refers to the idea of history as a continuous, unfolding narrative as "the whore called 'Once upon a time.'" The scholar who writes history so confidently recounts events in a hallowed tone "like the beads of a rosary."[166] What Benjamin finds so offensive about this approach, otherwise known as historicism, is its supposition that history is inevitable, that things happened as they were "meant" to. With historicism, the narrator cedes control of the past to the powerful. ("Empathy with the victor invariably benefits the rulers.")[167] The historicist tells *their* stories, narrates their exploits—and so ignores the histories of the oppressed.

Benjamin's model is discontinuous; he refutes the dangerous belief that things are as they have always been and as they should be. His theory of history is dialectical and Marxist. Past events are force fields with subsequent effects. Histories cross. Latent in an earlier time is an unfulfilled present possibility, a radical promise. Benjamin calls this untapped potentiality *Jetztzeit*, the "time of the now." A previous era feels timely to us—urgently so. It returns *in* the present. For Benjamin, "the time of the now" means something more than a present that is *merely* now (*Gegenwart*), a fleeting moment disconnected from the past and the future.[168] *Jetztzeit* is imbricated in both the past and the future. It is both a mystical and a revolutionary concept, the "Messianic potential of the present."[169] "The time of the now" places a heavy responsibility on the historian. History's suppressed promise will only be ignited—will only return—if we seize hold of it. *Jetztzeit*, the *return of*, implies an *active* remembrance, a *return to*.[170] To Robespierre "ancient Rome was a past charged with the time of now which *he* blasted out of the continuum of history," Benjamin writes.[171] Robespierre appropriated this image of the republic for present-day use. For Benjamin, history is *in*cautious, daring, a political act. The historical materialist (as the critic described himself) intervenes in its narration. He writes history "against the grain," "blasting" a "specific era" out of the homogeneous past.[172] As he observes elsewhere: "In order for a part of the past to be touched by the present instant, *there must be no continuity between them*."[173] The present and past cross only if there is enough distance between them. Only when an earlier moment is truly over can it "return."

The gap between two points in time is thus a negative substance. It defines the first moment as a "before"—a time of interest to us now. And it defines the moment of awareness of this past's possibility (the moment of "return") as a time in itself. The first moment happened; it was. Its tense is the preterite, the *passé simple*. It is knowably past, over and done with. According to Benjamin, the Paris of the early nineteenth century, the Paris of the shopping arcades, the Paris of the dandy and of Baudelaire, had formed a "constellation" with his own moment. The two eras could be thought together. The historian who rejects historicism "grasps the constellation which his own era has formed with a definite earlier one."[174] For Benjamin, a reverberation existed between this outmoded, this forgotten Paris, and the Paris he knew—the Paris of the Twenties and Thirties. The city of the arcades became timely again once it was seen as historical. In this faraway, forgotten Paris, glimpses of modernity in its inchoate form could be perceived. The decaying commodities, out-of-date fashions, and passé architectural forms that inspired his unfinished *Arcades Project* were the material evidence of this research. The scholar who perceives these linkages—these "dialectical images," Benjamin called them—sees history in a flash and makes connections between times. Blasting a vein of disturbance out of the sedimented layers of pastness, he or she unsettles the status quo.[175]

Yet to speak merely of "return" when we are discussing a past as recent as the Sixties, as I have attempted to do, risks overshooting the mark. After all, the long Sixties is not really "ancient," and it is by no means obscure. Millions of its inhabitants are still alive. We remember that era firsthand, secondhand. Movies, TV series, documentaries, and books ask us to remember it. The long Sixties remains insistently *current*. It refuses to be forgotten. Practices of return demonstrate this again and again.

What sort of past is a *recent* past? The contours of recentness are imprecise, its tense "imperfect" (from Latin *imperfectus*, "unfinished"). The recent past is subjective (a past that may seem "recent" to me may not seem so to you). It overlaps with a present that is slipping away, on the verge of becoming past. And so the recent past occupies an unstable epistemological ground, a "no man's land of time," as historian E. J. Hobsbawm once called it. The recent past, he adds, is "by far the hardest part of history for historians, or anyone else for that matter, to grasp."[176]

Much has been written about the distinction between history and memory—about these respective ideas of pastness and the relative preeminence of one or the other in academic and public discourse. Memory studies (also known as the "memory boom" or "memory crisis") developed in the wake of the "historians' controversy" in West Germany during the Eighties and of the discussions of Holocaust memory and memorialization that continue to this day.[177] The rise of this disciplinary field posed a challenge to proper history—its lingering positivism, its claim that we can make sense of a past only if it is remote. The far past, it was long assumed, is more friendly to empirical study. It can be analyzed more objectively than a near past whose effects are still felt, a past in which we still live.

Memory does not shy away from the past that proper history shunted to the margins. For the object of memory is a past that impinges on the present, that has not yet played out. Terdiman describes the memory crisis in postrevolutionary France as the incapacity of a generation to absorb a past that looms so large it staves off the future. The memory boom of the last forty years has been characterized in remarkably similar terms. "The surfeit of memory is a sign not of historical confidence but of a retreat from transformative politics," a loss of a "future orientation," the historian Charles Meier has written. We are *burdened* with memory, memory theorists claim, because there is far too much of it.[178]

Now the Sixties exerts a particular hold. It incites nostalgia—and memories that are hardly so pleasurable. The mnemonic "surfeit" that memory theorists speak about is typically occasioned by traumatic events—the memory of a reality so disturbing we cannot master it. The long Sixties witnessed the deaths by violence of millions of individuals in Indochina and Indonesia; the brutalities of Cultural Revolution China and postcolonial Africa (Nigeria, Biafra, Uganda, Algeria, Congo); forced disappearances of thousands of people in Brazil, Argentina, Guatemala, and Chile; and countless riots, bombings, hijackings, terrorist attacks, and assassinations. Practices of return examine these troubled histories. Many of these endeavors were inspired by journeys—literal returns—to places of traumatic recollection.[179] The projects of two artists who were forcibly exiled from their homelands, the Ugandan British filmmaker Zarina Bhimji and the Vietnamese American photographer An-My Lê, have inspired my discussion.

Zarina Bhimji was born in Mbarara, the capital of the Ankole kingdom in western Uganda, in 1963. Her birth coincided with Uganda's transition from a British Protectorate to an independent state a year earlier.[180] During the Sixties and Seventies, when Bhimji was a girl, Uganda descended into violence as it transitioned into a postcolonial state.[181] Fredric Jameson's important insight that the long Sixties unleashes liberation and domination in equal measures globally is nowhere truer than in Uganda, where the troubled regime of postindependence dictator Milton Obote (1962–71) was followed by Idi Amin's reign of terror (1971–79) and by a second Obote administration even bloodier than Amin's (1980–85). More than a million people lost their lives then. As art historian Sidney Littlefield Kasfir has memorably observed, in Uganda during this period "the Nile at times ran red with blood, corpses piled up in the Mabira Forest, and so many thousands of bodies were dumped into Lake Victoria that commercial fishing all but ceased."[182]

"It is difficult to reach 1972," Bhimji says.[183] This is the challenge that Bhimji set for herself as she conceived her twenty-five-minute film *Out of Blue* (2002). *Out of Blue* addresses a notorious event of Amin's reign. A year and a half after taking power, the dictator made a series of announcements aimed at the destruction of the country's South Asian population. The first "Asians" had migrated from western India and Pakistan as indentured laborers on the railroad as the British empire expanded into East Africa. Others followed. They oversaw mining and farming operations; became shopkeepers, tailors, tradespeople, and bankers; and they operated as middlemen between the white rulers and native Ugandans. The Asians had remained aloof, Amin said in an infamous radio speech on August 10, 1972. They had discriminated against their black neighbors; their control of the economy exceeded their number. It was time for them to go.[184]

Amin claimed that the idea of the expulsion came to him in a dream. It was Allah's wish, he said. In truth, antipathy toward the Asian community had been growing for some time.[185] Nor was the concept of expulsion new to Uganda.[186] By scapegoating this minority, Amin, who came from the historically marginal north, strengthened his tenuous grip on power; his redistribution of the assets of the Asian minority proved to be extremely popular with other Ugandans.[187] The Asian Ugandan writer Mahmood Mamdani recalls that time:

> Every evening at eight o'clock all sat glued to their televisions sets, if they owned one; if not they turned on the radio. A new tune signaled the beginning of the news. The lyrics went: "Farewell Asians, farewell Asians, you have milked the economy for too long."[188]

At first only noncitizens were forced into exile. Soon enough the entire population of some seventy-five thousand individuals was deported.[189] An atmosphere of fear spread through the South Asian community. Gunshots rang out over the cities and countryside. Rumors circulated of arrests and shootings.[190] Many of the exiles were robbed and beaten by

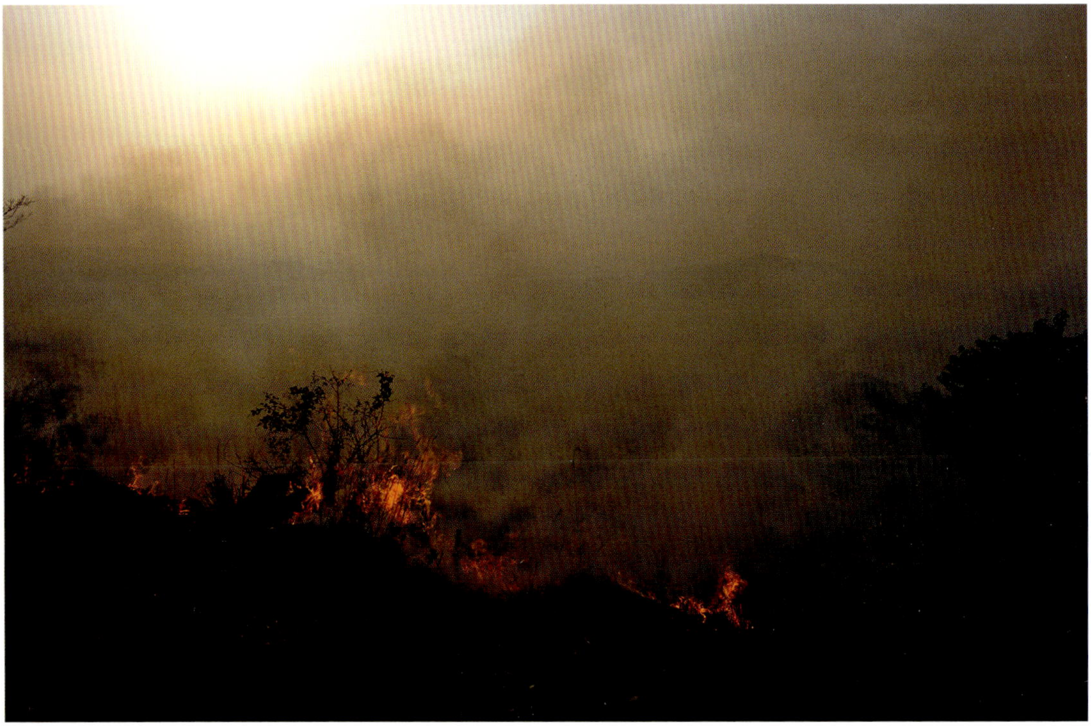

**Fig. 1.26.** Zarina Bhimji, *Out of Blue*, 2002. Screen grab. Super 16 mm color film, DVD transfer, single-screen installation with sound. Courtesy of Zarina Bhimji.

the police at roadblocks on the way to Entebbe Airport. Gathering in the departure lounge at Entebbe, they waited for flights to London and other destinations, their futures uncertain.

Bhimji followed her family to England in 1974. Returning to Uganda some twenty-five years later, she took photographs of her native country.[191] Returning a second time with a film crew, she shot *Out of Blue*.

The opening shot is a pan of a lush valley bathed in mist, illuminated by a pale orange sun. The cries of birds and buzzing noises of insects evoke a world coming to life, an unsullied, Edenic Africa. A woman sings a Sufi chant, her voice soaring as the melody ascends. Slowly, these dulcet sounds dissolve into human screams and radio announcements. A man with a British accent mentions a date, November 17, 1972. (Amin "nationalized" the country's property and expelled its British residents three months after exiling the Asians.) A plant catches fire, and now a tree. Within seconds a hillside is ablaze. Drained of color, the sun disappears in a cloud of smoke (fig. 1.26).

Smoke dissolves to sunlight, movement to stasis. An exterior shot of a barracks. Inside, the floors of a long room are lined with heaps of linen. Clothes dry on a string. A sheet billows in the breeze. Men's voices.

A prison cell. Another cell, and another. The shots of these bleak rooms begin at the top of a barred window and proceed downward. Bhimji often shoots this way. Repeated, these downward pans plunge viewers into darkness. The buzzing of insects, evocative of organic life in the opening shot, seems menacing here, evoking mental impressions of flies swarming on roadkill or bodies, and human beings too weak or indifferent to brush them away. The filthy walls are caked with the names and initials of former inmates. Whispers. A man behind bars is barely visible. Is he inside the cell, or is the camera, where we imaginatively stand?

A shelf cluttered with mugs and bowls. A hall lit in a raking light. A rack of guns. Men's shadows fall on these rifles. The guns are animated by these moving silhouettes, these jerking traces. Outside, a sinister courtyard with high walls surmounted by barbed wire—a place of execution, for sure.

From the deathly claustrophobia of the prison to a city street. But the city is dead, too. Inside a courtyard, the camera is high up underneath the ceiling, as if a viewer's head had been shoved into this tight space. Old shoes hang in a window. We hear a child crying. Coal embers burn to the rat-a-tat-tat of gun shots. Then the patter of rain. The rapid breath of a woman shivering.

An empty room, a puddle. Bhimji's interiors are never clean. The elements have invaded, causing things to decay, to fester, to smell. On the outside, the buildings are formal, colonial, official-looking. Their black windows are sockets without eyes. In the courtyard, a peep of chickens, clucking, wandering. Rain dissolves to sunlight. Tombstones bake in the blazing heat. Names chiseled in English and Indian script. The old headstones lean at odd angles. Ruins of a lost world.

Propeller sounds. An airport control tower. The doorways have no doors. The camera pans from the top of this structure to the ground: *ENTEBBE, 3789 FEET*, the letters say.[192] Inside, the camera surveys the empty passengers lounge where the refugees waited for their flights. Sounds of a crowd. Dust balls tremble on the windowpanes. Spiders scamper on the broken glass, consuming their prey in delicate mouthfuls.

Asphalt shimmering in the heat. The camera points down at the rushing runway. Airborne, the beholder spies a village at the edge of water, a composition of turbid browns and chalky whites. The village is at the edge of Lake Victoria, named for the sovereign whose empire brought Bhimji's father to this land of green hills. There is only water and sky now, only blue. Entebbe: a place of return is again a place of departure.

Mamdani drafted his memoir *From Citizen to Refugee: Uganda Asians Come to Britain* shortly after his arrival in London. He completed it "in haste," he writes. There seemed no more urgent task than to describe the terror he and his family felt in Uganda and their cold reception in England. Mamdani documents the patronizing behavior and stinginess of their hosts, and the racist remarks and threats he witnessed or heard about. (The Ugandan Asians were subject to a double form of racism: forced from their homeland because they weren't "black," they were unwelcome in Britain because they weren't "white.") The history he describes was inarguably "recent." He penned his memoir to protest these injuries and to record his memories while they were still fresh.[193]

When Bhimji screened *Out of Blue* in 2001, the expulsion had largely been forgotten.[194] The distinctive cultural identity of the Ugandan Asians had been brutally erased. The challenge this posed was immense. How does a filmmaker who experienced that event address this subject cinematically? How does she "reach 1972"? For starters, Bhimji eschews the documentarian's methods. Her film has no narrator or running text, and provides little information guiding our understanding of what we're looking at. There is little or no action apart from the opening and closing shots. Human beings are all but invisible. Nor is the film conventionally autobiographical. A viewer never learns whether the city streets and houses in *Out of Blue* were known to Bhimji as a girl. Images and sounds are experienced *as* images and sounds.[195]

The title of her subsequent film, *Yellow Patch* (2011), expresses this formalist intention succinctly. The title recalls Proust's description of the "small patch of yellow wall" (*petit pan de mur jaune*) in Vermeer's *View of Delft*, a passage of canvas so well painted "that it was, if one looked at it by itself, like some priceless specimen of Chinese art, of a beauty that was sufficient in itself."[196] The yellow patch represents a formal perfection so consummate and contained it can stand "by itself." It is sufficient as paint, as color, as form. The brushwork that Vermeer has laid down in this small section of canvas is so exquisitely wrought, the motif (most likely the roof behind the city's Rotterdam Gate) is very much beside the point. The yellow patch is far more than what it depicts. And it is nearly impossible to achieve.[197]

Bhimji's films are beautiful, certainly. They aspire to the state of "abstraction" that she has spoken about. ("My work is not about actual fact, description. It is about abstraction.")[198] But her cinema transcends the ample visual pleasure it affords. The places and landscapes she films "have been punctured and scratched by so much."[199] The past, terrible and ever present, inhabits these barracks and hopeless jail cells. It clings to these valleys, these old tombstones. One can begin to "reach 1972" through suggestion, evocation. For there are experiences that we are unable to master, memories that keep returning. Images and sounds can on their own terms point to something opposite to beauty, whose nature is also to evade depiction.

Freud describes trauma as a precipitous and rapid increase of "unpleasure" so enormous that the ego's protective shield is broken. The psyche is "flooded with large amounts of stimulus" it cannot bind and dispose of.[200] The problem of trauma is not that we have fantasized the event but, to the contrary, that the trauma occurred. It happened. "It is indeed the truth of the traumatic experience that forms the center of its psychopathology. It is not a pathology of falsehood or displacement of meaning, but of history itself."[201] Trauma is a species of memory that eludes narration. Initially imprinted as "sensations or feeling states," traumatic recollections are not transcribable.[202] And so traumatic memories resurface unbidden, as sensations that elude description.[203]

Bhimji embeds memory in historical time, the time of overlaps and returns. Her trilogy moves ever backward. Where *Out of Blue*, the first of the films, marks the tragic ending of nearly a century of Asian Ugandan history, *Yellow Patch* extends Bhimji's archaeology to the origins of that community in western India in the late nineteenth century, when Britain acquired possession of Kenya and Uganda during the so-called scramble for Africa. The thread of familial memory brings Bhimji to the arid plains of Kutch, where her mother was born, and to a lavish, abandoned house in southern Gujarat, the region where her father grew up. It brings her to the Princess Dock at Mumbai, and to the port at Mandvi, from which thousands of Indians and Pakistanis migrated to Kenya and Uganda as Britain expanded its empire, Bhimji's father among them. It brings her to the edge of the Arabian Sea.[204] The final film in this trilogy, *Jangbar* (2012–15), crosses over to East Africa and onto the Uganda Railway, whose construction between Mombasa and Kisumu, Kenya, at the turn of the last century resulted in the deaths of some twenty-five hundred Asian laborers.

The Sixties is the memory of modernism and of earlier modernities, I argued. Bhimji's trilogy is an archaeology of colonial modernity. *Jangbar* follows the tracks of a half-abandoned railway created during the last great era of global expansion. *Yellow Patch* depicts the records hall at the Princess Dock, a nerve center of British colonial trade during the Victorian era. Shots of trading desks and shelves loaded with musty stacks of long-forgotten transactions culminate in a pan of a crumbling marble statue (fig. 1.27). Half of the figure's face is missing. The orb she holds in her palm has cracked. Yet the creased, deep eyes and dainty crown are unmistakably those of the queen-empress in whose name Britain's colonial aggressions were made.

In fact, many practices of return reach back to prior moments of modernity that well precede the Sixties, we have seen. Kelly's reenactment of a 1970 feminist action evokes the suffragist marches of the early twentieth century.[205] BLW's recitations of Moore's prison talk recall Marcus Garvey's

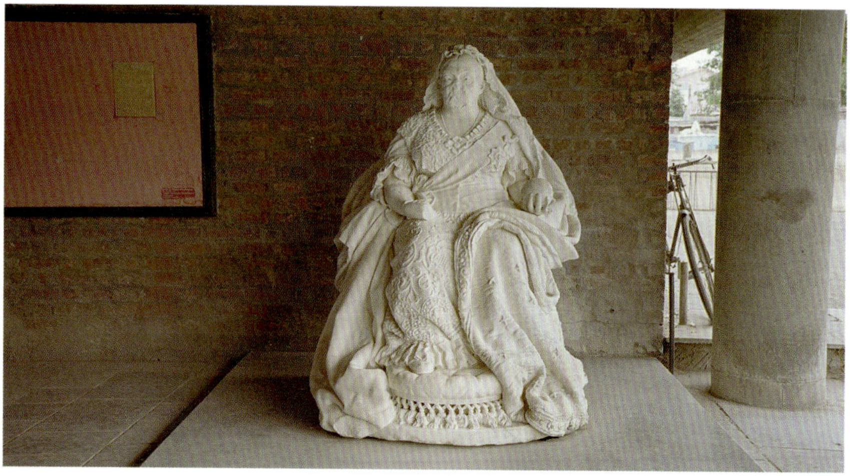

**Fig. 1.27.** Zarina Bhimji, *Yellow Patch*, 2011. Screen grab. 35 mm color film, HD transfer, single-screen installation with Dolby 5.1 surround. Courtesy of Zarina Bhimji.

peroration of a half-century earlier, contextualizing both speeches within the long history of black struggle. The memory of the Sixties inspires reckonings with more remote pasts, and nowhere more urgently than in Africa. Postcolonial situations such as Amin's reign of terror cannot be approached otherwise. Filled with the violent traces of both the colonial and precolonial past, postcolonies are entrapped in these "hydra-headed" temporal "entanglements," theorist Achille Mbembe has written. "As an age, the postcolony encloses multiple *durées* made up of discontinuities, reversals, inertias, and swings that overlay one another, interpenetrate one another, and envelope one another."[206] Is it any wonder that Bhimji did not conclude her meditation on the expulsion with *Out of Blue*? That this film was only the *beginning* of her excavation? In order to "reach 1972," in order to come to some understanding of the defining event of her childhood, she seems to have understood that it was not enough to revisit that moment, the time of postcolonial transition, in isolation. It was necessary to return to India, and then to Zanzibar and Kenya, in order to retrace the itineraries of her parents and the South Asian migrations that anticipated her birth. One "return" led to another—from Uganda to Gujarat and Mumbai; from India to Zanzibar and the half-abandoned railroad stations on the "Lunatic Line" east of Mombasa, whose construction cost so many South Asian workers their lives.[207] The year 1972 led to 1885, 1885 to the 1920s. Bhimji's familial archaeology dilated and deepened. One film became three. Fifteen years later the project was finished; there were no more returns.

An-My Lê was born in Saigon in 1960. In 1975, she went into exile with her family when the government of South Vietnam collapsed. After studying in the United States and working in France, the artist returned to her homeland during the mid-Nineties, when diplomatic relations between the socialist state and her adopted country were formally reestablished. These visits yielded Lê's inaugural work, the book *Viêt Nam* (1994–98).

Lê shot the photos in *Viêt Nam* with a five-by-seven-inch tripod camera, a device capable of achieving extremely slow shutter speeds and, accordingly, of capturing the most minute details and slightest movements.[208] The images imply a loose narrative. Shots of primeval jungle, of villages and farms, many of them captured with wide-angle lenses, cede to depictions of urban streets and modern apartment blocks. The Vietnam to which Lê returned was both unchanged and starkly different from the country she was forced to leave decades before. On one hand, a family of farmers poses in front of their chicken farm in the Mekong Delta, an image pastoral and timeless (fig. 1.28). On the other, billboards crowd the riverfront in Lê's depiction of Ho Chi Minh City, where the signs and logos of computer and cellphone manufacturers and breweries create a fortress-like barrier along the banks of the Saigon River (fig. 1.29). The men in the traditional dinghy in the foreground are out of scale and out of place. More than two decades after the Americans were forced out by the communists, multinational corporations, some of them based in the United States, have reclaimed the southern capital.

"The question of war was not central to the photographs I made in Vietnam," Lê has remarked.[209] How do we interpret this claim? The war is not the stated *subject* of these works. There are no pictures of places of obvious notoriety, such as the killing ditch at My Lai or the road to Trang Bang, where, in the famous photograph of 1972, the local children fled naked from their homes down a lonely road, their skin severely burned from a napalm bombing. The places that Lê photographed were suffused with war memories nevertheless. Her photograph of the place called Soc Son depicts an old house. The ancient columns and carved capitals are highly detailed, as one would expect in the work of a photographer who apprenticed with the Compagnons du Devoir du Tour de France, the architectural guild responsible for the construction and care of medieval monuments in France.[210] We look out at a pond, a field, at distant mountains. We take in this pleasant scene. And then we focus on the house: the wall is scarred with graffiti and pockmarked with bullet holes.

In Lê's photograph of another village, Son Tây, the tidy rows of cabbage and cucumbers are interrupted by berms overrun with ivy (fig. 1.30). Whitewashed buildings with thatched roofs and electrical towers press down on the horizon. A typical Vietnamese hamlet, like any other: so Son

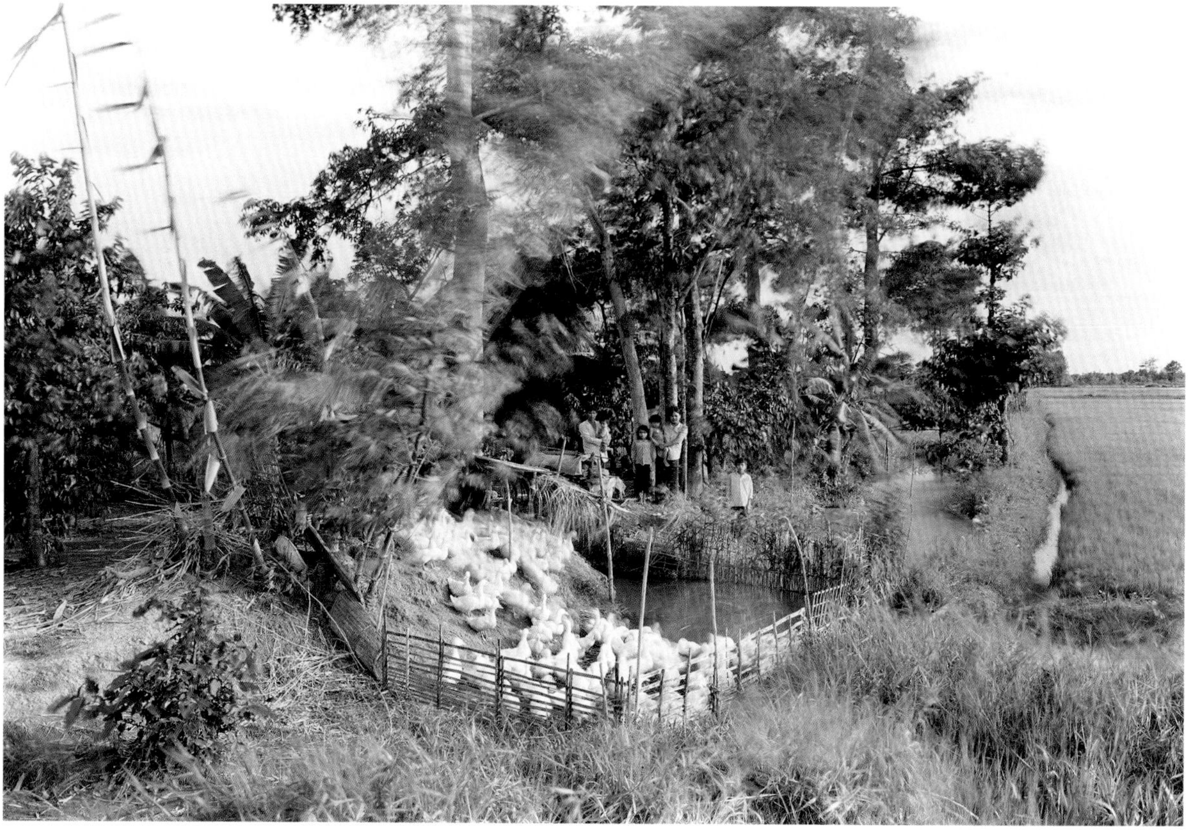

Fig. 1.28. An-My Lê, *Untitled, Mekong Delta*, 1994. Gelatin silver print. © An-My Lê.

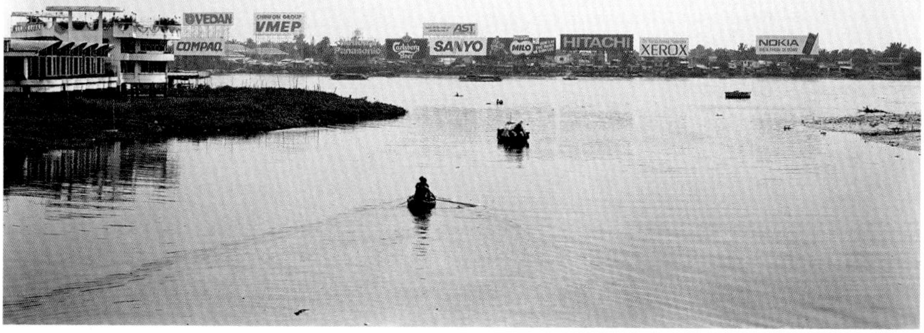


Fig. 1.29. An-My Lê, *Untitled, Ho Chi Minh City*, 1995. Gelatin silver print. © An-My Lê.

Tây appears. Yet the place-name is faintly familiar; it turns out that Son Tây is *not* ordinary. During the Sixties these walls contained an infamous prisoner of war camp, one of several in North Vietnam. American prisoners were interned here. They lived on a subsistence diet in filthy conditions, and experienced torture. On November 21, 1970, U.S. Special Forces invaded the camp to rescue the sixty captives with the hope of boosting troop morale and improving public opinion of the war, which was then at a low ebb.[211] Unfortunately, the Pentagon's intelligence report was out of date: the captives had already been moved to another location. The raid yielded no rescues, but resulted in scores of North Vietnamese casualties.

I wonder that Lê did not depict Son Tây deliberately; that she pictured *this* village, as opposed to all the other villages in Vietnam, without knowing that Americans were imprisoned in this place, and that an army of Hughies descended on these fields that night to save them.[212] Other places she photographed do not have the historical weight of Son Tây. Less obviously memorable, these locations are also steeped in memory. In Lê's photo of Lao Bao a meadow has burst into flames. The presence

**Fig. 1.30.** An-My Lê, *Untitled, Son Tây*, 1998. Gelatin silver print. © An-My Lê.

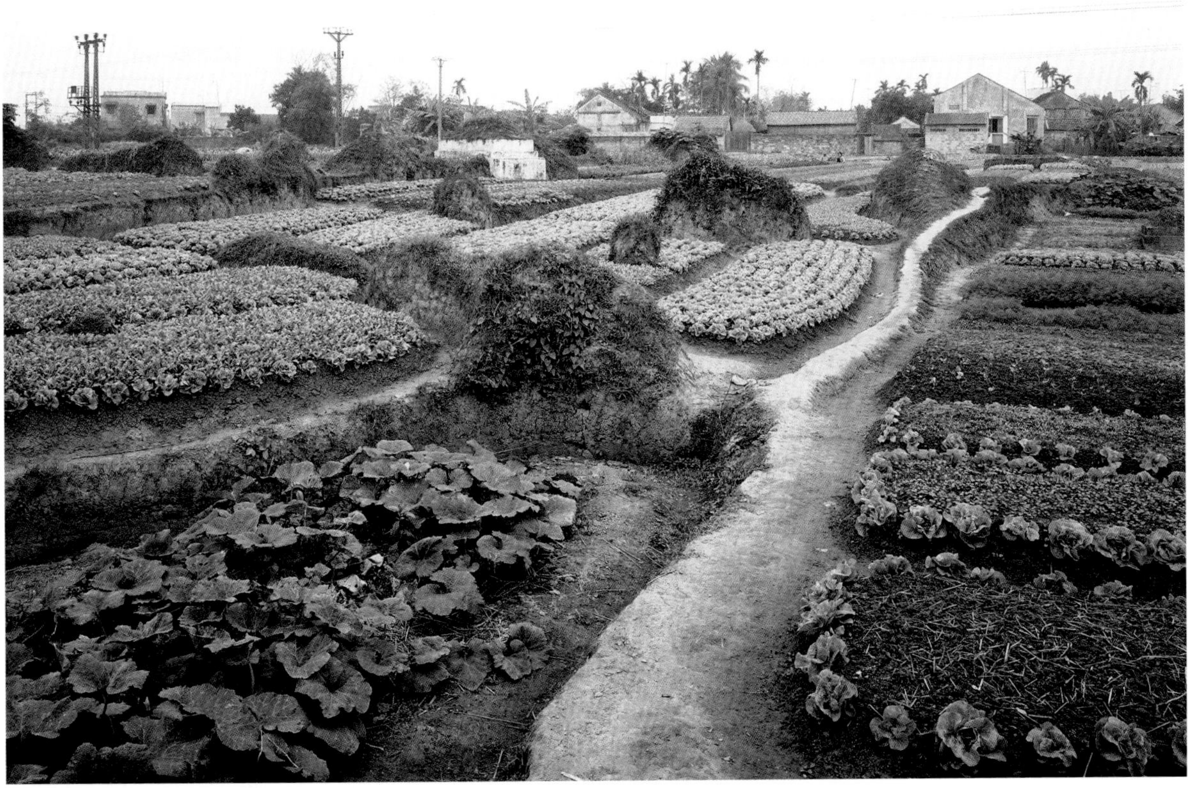

of a bystander on a riverbank does nothing to explain the source of the fire. Lê's image of the hamlet called Tien Phuong centers on a young boy with a slingshot. The boy perches on a low stone wall and stretches his entire body as he holds up the weapon. The man behind the child who walks toward the camera is out of focus, zombie-like. A woman, identifiable only by the top of her head, hides behind an enclosure where she appears to have disrobed. The boy takes aim at a target hidden in the branches of an old tree: a bird is about to fall dead at his feet.

In Lê's photo of Ho Chi Minh City, kites dip and swerve above a field (fig. 1.31). These wind-borne toys are also blurry, their motion arrested, and it would be easy to mistake them for predatory birds or bombers, and the clouds of dust hovering above the ground as evidence of recently exploded shells. There is something unsettling about this image of a park, too—the low horizon, the queasy focus, the portentous and finely tuned modulations of gray. Is it possible to depict Ho Chi Minh City now without evoking Saigon *then*—the Saigon of April 30, 1975, when the capital was conquered, and mobs of frightened South Vietnamese scrambled onto the roof of the American embassy to escape in Chinooks and Sea Knights? Lê recalls that time obliquely. She depicts a crowd of pleasure seekers on a day off. The relaxed demeanors of these men and boys suggest there is nothing to worry about. And there *is* nothing to worry about. Most of the kite flyers—teenagers and men in their early twenties—don't personally remember what happened. And so "what happened" then may or may not mean very much. The war is in the past. It is old news, a mythic time. "They listen to our stories as if they were fairy tales. They did not witness it. They don't believe it," an older woman, a survivor of that era, remarks in Dinh Q. Lê's three-channel video projection *The Farmers and the Helicopters* (2006), yet another meditation on the war, its memory and forgetting.[213]

*They did not witness it. They don't believe it.* It would be reasonable to interpret the image of kite flyers as an anodyne depiction of leisure. It would be reasonable to view this field as a field like any other. But I cannot look at these kites as kites, this field as just any field. I cannot look at Lê's picture of Lao Bao without thinking of all the riverbanks that burned then. And I cannot look at her poignant *Untitled, Mekong Delta, 1994* without thoughts of Viet Cong guerrillas or Swift boats suddenly disrupting the halcyon scene, and shooting the poultry farmer and his family—a fantasy triggered, in my imagination, by the blurry smear of scattering chickens and the formal arrangement of the figures, the mother and father and children who line up in a row. The war is a long time ago. Stories of what happened then are as fanciful as "fairy tales." Yet the memory of violence

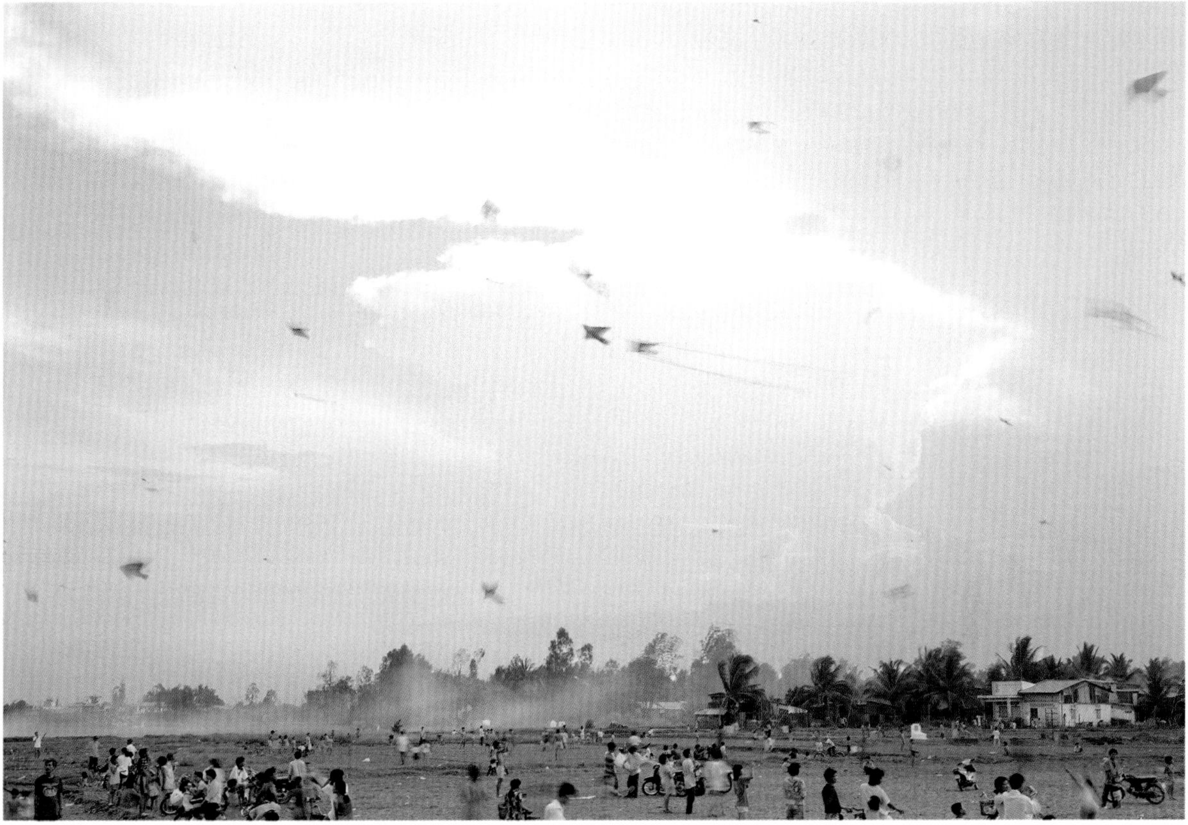

**Fig. 1.31.** An-My Lê, *Untitled, Ho Chi Minh City*, 1998. Gelatin silver print. © An-My Lê.

is everywhere in Lê's pictures, at least *to me*, even if Lê did not necessarily intend to conjure it. A place is never what it seems.

Lê inverted the techniques of *Viêt Nam* in her next project, *Small Wars* (1999–2002). Where in *Viêt Nam* the traumatic past is a constant, hidden presence, *Small Wars* is an explicit "depiction" of war, with an important twist, as will be seen. Soldiers huddle under tents and lie on cots. An infantryman reads a letter from home. A campfire burns in darkness. A young man has removed his helmet and put down his rifle; he appears well fed and at ease. There are images of battle, too. A lone soldier dressed in camouflage walks through a field on a mission. Men point their rifles at unseen targets. A grenade detonates in a meadow. Shells explode in a stream. Flames crackle in the dark.

In *Rescue* (1999–2002), a fighter plane has just landed (fig. 1.32). A soldier scrambles out of the cockpit as his comrade speaks into a walkie-talkie. The others crouch with rifles, on the lookout for enemy soldiers.

The air chokes with fumes. A rescue mission, it would seem. Lê's composition is symmetrical, arranged—a bit too much so. The pilots stand in the center of the image, the sentries to the left and right. Where *Viêt Nam* depicts actual places of historical eventfulness or situations that evoke sensations of unease, *Small Wars* is all artifice. The costumes and haircuts are vintage, as are the guns and airplane. The pine forest in which these "battles" play out, a private property in rural Virginia, is a long distance from the jungles and rice fields of Indochina. The soldiers are not enlisted men but reenactors. The woman who crouches behind a dune, who prepares to shoot the unsuspecting GIs in the middle distance? This "sniper" is none other than Lê herself (fig. 1.33).

Lê places herself in the picture. She joins the others—white men in their thirties, forties, and fifties—in this theater of war memory. By participating in these events, she confounds a bias in the critical literature on reenactment. There are, we are told, two kinds of reenactment: a critical practice, typically produced by an artist or historian, that illuminates the conditions of its fabrication, that makes explicit its illusionism (a "Brechtian" reenactment; I have described the projects of Tribe, Malpede, and BLW along these lines); and the allegedly unreflective activity of the hobbyist—the Civil War reenactor, the Renaissance Faire-goer, and the like (an "unconscious" reenactment). The art of Lê questions this simplistic opposition (and implicit class division) of "smart" and "naive" techniques of anamnesis.[214] Her practice straddles these genres of historical performativity. She developed *Small Wars* after making contact with a closed circle of Vietnam War reenactors. The men involved in these activities re-create specific battles with scrupulous accuracy. Lê participated in these events over the course of several years, taking on different characters drawn from the charged iconography of Vietnam War cinematic depiction. She played a "Kit Carson" scout who betrays her Viet Cong comrades when she informs the Americans of their whereabouts. And she played a "sniper girl," the solitary guerrilla who remains in a village stocked with booby traps and ends up shooting a platoon of GIs until she is apprehended and cruelly executed (the plot line of Stanley Kubrick's film *Full Metal Jacket*, in fact). The Vietnamese woman is "the ultimate Gook, different from the American soldier through race, culture, language, and gender. She is the complete and threatening object of both rapacious desire and murderous fear, the embodiment of the whole mysterious, enticing, forbidding, and dangerous country of Vietnam," Viet Thanh Nguyen has written.[215] Just as Lê performed some of these stereotypical archetypes of Vietnamese womanhood during their pretend war games, her collaborators reenacted the roles of GIs who were sent into battle, often against their will, in a faraway land where they were brought into contact with a culture and

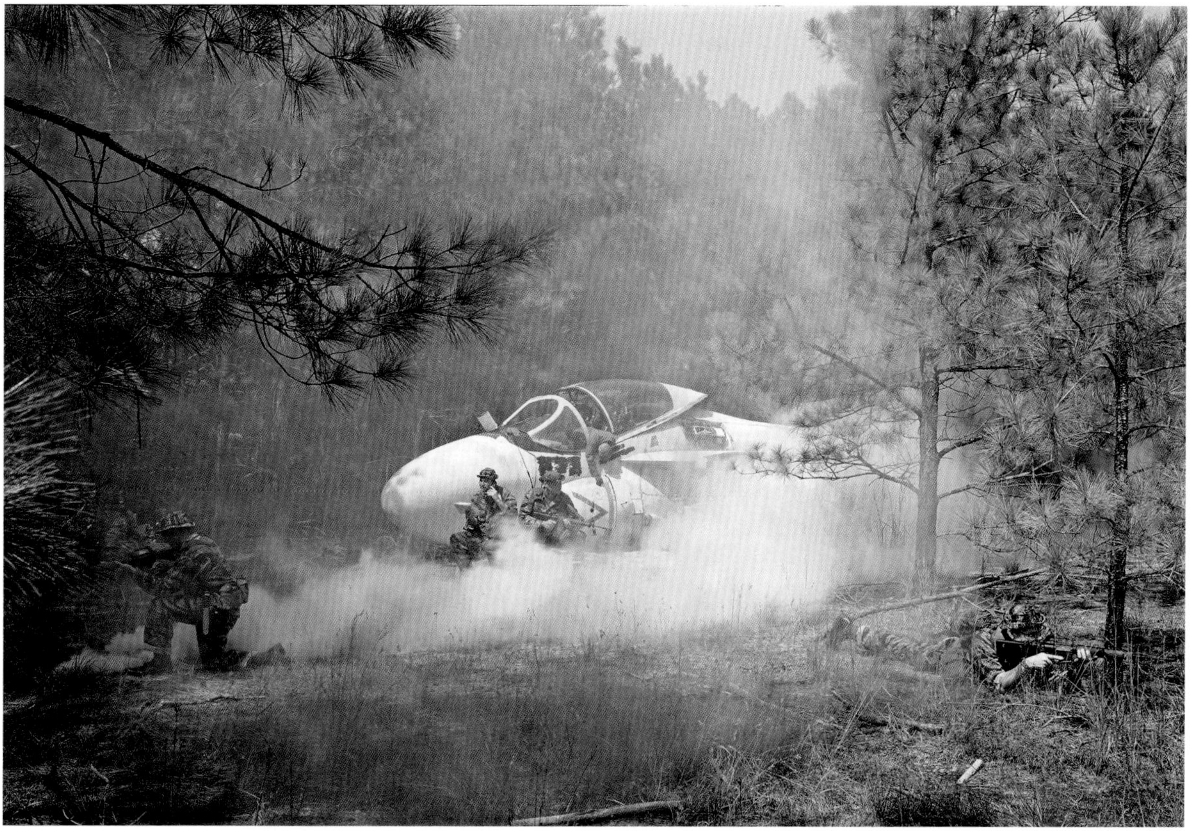

**Fig. 1.32.** An-My Lê, *Rescue*, 1999–2002. Gelatin silver print. © An-My Lê.

**Fig. 1.33.** An-My Lê, *Sniper I*, 1999–2002. Gelatin silver print. © An-My Lê.

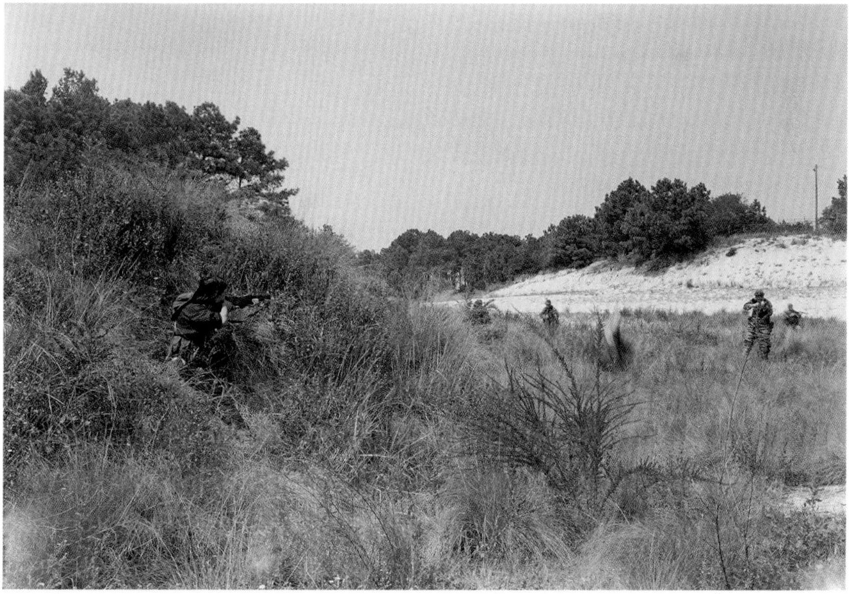

with people who were foreign to them and to whom *they* were foreign. The binary identities and identifications upon which the Vietnam conflict hinged and that cost so many lives were made perspicuous during these reenactments—reified so they could be *seen*. As she became more involved in these activities, Lê, the sole woman participant and the only person of Vietnamese descent, came to identify with these men who, like herself, had a personal interest in reimagining a cataclysmic event that had affected them in various ways.[216] I like to think that the men who fought in these "small wars" came to identify with Lê, too.

A conflation of memory with violence has long animated memory aesthetics, which initially focused on survivor testimony and representations of traumatic events, such as the Shoah. Critics have conceived of return as *Nachträglichkeit*, Freud's "return of the repressed"—the suppression, displacement, and repetition of psychic content too disturbing for integration.[217] Many practices of return explore troubling memories, and may be discussed along these lines; they perform the "arduous task of *Durcharbeiten*," or "working through," the painstaking reexamination and overcoming of resistances to trauma.[218] Arduous indeed. Bhimji and An-My Lê journeyed to the homelands from which they had been exiled as children. They developed photographic and cinematic forms that were capable of evoking the mnemonic residue of a violence that had burrowed into the very soil and buildings they depict; by returning to these places (places they had once been or never been) they explored, through the techniques of art, suppressed and forgotten feelings of fear and displacement.

In his story "Love and Honor and Pity and Pride and Compassion and Sacrifice," his portrait of the My Lai massacre survivor and his son, Nam Lê traced the reverberations of a violent history passed between generations, a trauma one or two steps removed.[219] The narrator's attempt to tell his father's story that precedes and encompasses his own life (and that ends with a perilous boat trip across the sea that he and his parents barely survived) results in the physical destruction of the story and, what is more, its salvation. The unique hard copy, burned on the shores of the icy Iowa River, is "saved" for posterity in a secondary narrative: the story of the son's attempt to write his father's past, the story that we read. Lê evokes a recentness so disturbing it can *never* be "worked through." The narrator's memories of his father's memories of My Lai and the North Vietnamese internment camps and the boat trip affect him in ways that he is only beginning to comprehend.[220]

And yet a traumatological conception of "return" that has long dominated theories of memory and memory aesthetics after the Shoah does not always serve a discussion of Sixties memory.[221] A Sixties defined perforce as "traumatic" is a pathologized recentness from which we have yet to recover, may never recover. The hugely influential role of mass media in shaping how the events of that era were transmitted and received has been much noted.[222] Television transmitted powerful images of contemporary events *as they were happening*; our memories of that time are bound up with these depictions. A Sixties that "won't go away" is a replayed Sixties, a Sixties that returns as representation, as image: I take this to be a central concern of Vik Muniz's remarkable series *Memory Renderings: The Best of Life* (1989–2000).

To prepare these works, Muniz made sketches of photos published in *The Best of Life*, an album of iconic images published in the news magazine *Life* during the mid-twentieth century. Most of these pictures date to the long Sixties: the three-year-old John Kennedy, Jr., saluting his father's funeral caisson (1963); a South Vietnamese general unloading a pistol in the temple of a Viet Cong prisoner (1968; fig. 1.34); Neil Armstrong walking on the moon (1969); the severely burned Kim Phúc escaping the napalm attack at Trang Bang (1972); or the teenager Mary Ann Vecchio kneeling next to the corpse of Jeffrey Miller at Kent State (1970; fig. 1.35). Muniz sketched these images from memory without consulting the originals. He then photographed each drawing and printed the resulting exposure through a halftone screen. His *Memory Renderings* are digital images of drawings of photos, made from memory, printed in the halftone dot technique of the original press reproductions. Muniz evokes a type of memory that is neither first- nor secondhand but simulacral, the memory not of something real but of a representation, the very definition of memory according to Aristotle. The philosopher describes our capacity to remember as the retention of an "impressed affection":

> When one remembers, is it this impressed affection that he remembers, or is it the objective thing from which this was derived? . . . For when one actually remembers, this impression is what he contemplates, and this is what he perceives.[223]

During the Sixties, press images circulated across media and national borders, depositing such "impressions." As a boy living in Saõ Paulo, Muniz absorbed these images. He became interested in these photos many years later when he came upon a copy of *The Best of Life* in a garage sale in Chicago. After making several attempts to work with the photos, he ended up losing the book. Only then—only when he was forced to remember these representations—was he able to conceive the elaborately mediated technique of the *Memory Renderings*.[224] The images that he depicts evoke

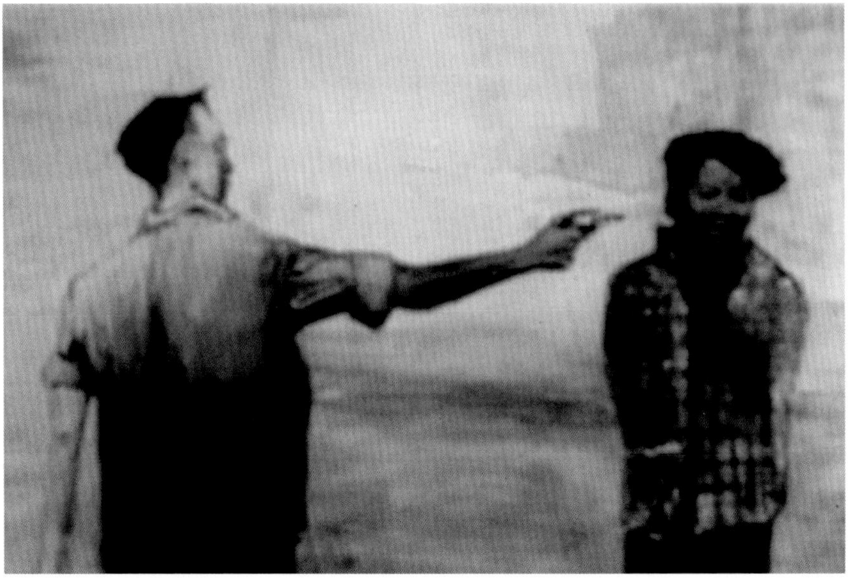

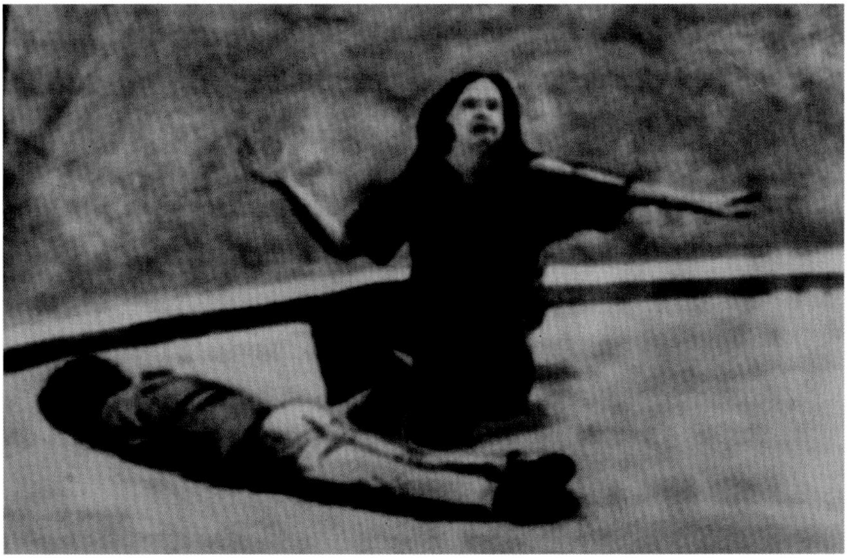

**Fig. 1.34.** Vik Muniz, *Memory Rendering of Saigon Execution of Viet Cong Suspect* (from *The Best of Life*), 1989–2000. Gelatin silver print. Art © Vik Muniz / Licensed by VAGA, New York.

**Fig. 1.35.** Vik Muniz, *Memory Rendering of Kent State Shooting* (from *The Best of Life*), 1989–2000. Gelatin silver print. Art © Vik Muniz / Licensed by VAGA, New York.

a mass consciousness centered on the American Cold War imperium, an American "Sixties." That the Brazilian-born artist could recall these impressions vividly—so vividly that he could depict them from memory with such acuity—is a testament to the ways that dominant media images infiltrate and shape our historical awareness, how they lodge themselves inside our consciousness and never disappear.[225]

Where Muniz, in the *Memory Renderings*, presses highly familiar press photos through a sieve of manual and digital filtration, An-My Lê takes analog exposures of places steeped in memory. Lê's works don't point to a single event or atrocity as Muniz's do. Her photos are condensations of firsthand memories of the war and its mass depiction. ("My photographs could be as much about my memory of GIs walking down Tu Do Street in Saigon as an echo of the depiction of the Air Cavalry machos in *Apocalypse Now*.") Lê explores these transactions of personal and media recollection. There is, she says, the "actual" Vietnam, the Vietnam that she has literally returned to and depicts in her eponymous series, the Vietnam she remembers; and there is another "Vietnam," the *Vietnam of the mind* as she has described it, an imaginary place and time re-created in the pine forests of rural Virginia with her fellow reenactors: the "Vietnam" of *Small Wars*. Practices of return like Lê's and Muniz's blur rigid distinctions between "history" and "memory." More precisely, they examine the different versions of veracity implied by these narratological forms.[226] In other words, they ask what "recentness" is—the knowability and limits of our understanding of a period that many people remember, a time that is at the same time receding ever further into the past.

The long Sixties is a particularly contested recentness. The editors of *The Sixties without Apology*, a prescient investigation of these questions published by the journal *Social Text*, observed in 1984:

> Visions of history play an enormous—if incalculable—role in people's political practice in the present; and this all the more when the interpretation in question is a matter, not of "attitudes" toward a bygone age . . . but rather of people's immediate past. What you finally decide to think the Sixties was is one of the forms in which you affirm or repudiate a part of your own life.[227]

During the Eighties the Sixties was indeed recent. The long Sixties had just ended; it was "people's immediate past." The memories were personal. The "you" to whom the editors directed their remarks was a collective "we." The reader was imagined to be a fellow Sixties veteran and the same age, reasonable assumptions at the time.[228]

*The Sixties without Apology* is an apologia for a generation: the "Sixty-eighters." The editors defend their youthful involvements, their Leftist commitments. They defend the "Sixties." Whether one affirmed or denounced the Sixties mattered then, not only because the history being scrutinized was their own. The story one told about this quite recent past mattered during the Reagan-Thatcher era, when the radical social and cultural transformations of the long Sixties came under fire. *The Sixties without Apology* is not sentimental; its approach is antinostalgic. At a time when the Sixties was so near, scholarly analysis appeared the strongest defense against denunciations of the gains that had been made and conservative attempts to repeal them.

The process of Sixties historicization thus began at the moment the long Sixties ended, at the very moment something like "the Sixties" was beginning to be perceived as such, as an era that had passed. *The Sixties without Apology* marks that awareness. Starting in the Nineties, new generations of scholars began to imagine and reconstruct events (or situations or works of art) they hadn't witnessed or seen.[229] They took the process of historicization another step, enlisting the historian's tools of archival research and historical narration to the writing of the recent past. The field of contemporary art history, for example, emerged as an investigation of a recent past—the long Sixties and the neo-avant-garde tendencies that emerged then. Practices heretofore perceived as "contemporary" came to be perceived as "historical."

An extreme version of this historicizing impulse—this ambition to write the Sixties into and as the past—finds expression in the Rankean claim of one scholar that "history is what happened," as if "history" were more impartial and more accurate a narrational form than memory; as if the distinction between "history" and "memory" that memory studies has long challenged was perfectly clear.[230] To assert that "history is what happened" is to assume that the "Sixties" is over and done with, a corpse we cannot revive. It involves a denial of the idea of historical time, of history as overlap and return, as a dynamic force, as variously imagined by Benjamin, Koselleck, and Nietzsche; and it ignores the relative recentness of the long Sixties and the centrality of memory and mediation in that era's voluminous depiction.

One need not agree with such assertions to note a historical turn in contemporary studies—the accounts of scholars who were uninvolved in the histories they write. A generation is bound together by "remembrances not so much of what its members have experienced as of *what they have not experienced*," Nora insists.[231] The editors of the journal *The Sixties* (founded in 2008) speak of their fascination for a past "that is not properly our own." Too young to have witnessed or participated in the events they describe, the journal's editors claim an "affinity" with a period they barely glimpsed or did not see. "Ourselves born between 1964 and 1970, we were too young to have been fully in the thrall of the Sixties, but just old enough to know that we missed something big."[232] In the statement "we missed something big," the dilemma and desire of the contemporary historian is clearly expressed. This gnawing sense of belatedness inspires us to take charge of the history we did not experience; it goads us to understand what happened—to reconstruct, reimagine, and *retell* the long Sixties. As historians, we recount the events of that time omnisciently; our voices do not intrude in the telling; as if by scholarly instinct, we enlist the tenses of pastness, the preterite and pluperfect ("it was," "it had been"). The grammatical devices of classical narrative serve us well.[233] We arrange facts and interpretations into stories that have the feeling of objectivity, of finitude, of *having happened*. We will things and events and people into a prior time, even if this "past" is imperfect, incomplete, brushing up against the present moment. We transform a past within the reach of many people's memory into "proper" history. As we historicize, we draw a strict line between "now" and "then." We suppress our subjectivities—memories of things we may have seen or heard about. Memories of events we watched on television without understanding what they were, memories that exist as a kind of sediment in the pit of our awareness. The account is confidently historical, compellingly "objective." All is past. Such, at least, was the intention of my previous work on that era—and the point of departure for this book.[234]

## Judging the Sixties

**As a child, you accept what adults do.**

Bettina Röhl

Practices of return explore such ambiguities. If the aim of the contemporary historian is to transform fugitive memories into historical narratives, the artists and writers who inspired this study dwell stubbornly in the interstices of history and memory, the murky "no man's land of time" earlier described as recentness. Rather than ask "what happened," they ask *why* this era still affects us, and what it means to us now. And they do not hesitate to judge that storied time.

Consider another work by Felix Gmelin. *Farbtest, Die Rote Fahne II* (*Color Test, The Red Flag II*; 2002) is a projection of two films side by side (fig. 1.36). Two projectors hang a few feet in front of a wall. The images they screen are identical in dimension—each is the size of a sheet of paper—and it seems at first sight that the films are the same. The scenario is straightforward enough. A young person runs down an urban street carrying a bright red flag. After a few minutes he relinquishes his charge to another runner, who hands it to another, and so on. We watch as the two marathons unfold.

The shot is steady, perspectival. Our eyes flicker back and forth between the films—the silent, doubled images of runners and traffic and the street. As we watch the films, we struggle to hold the images together in our

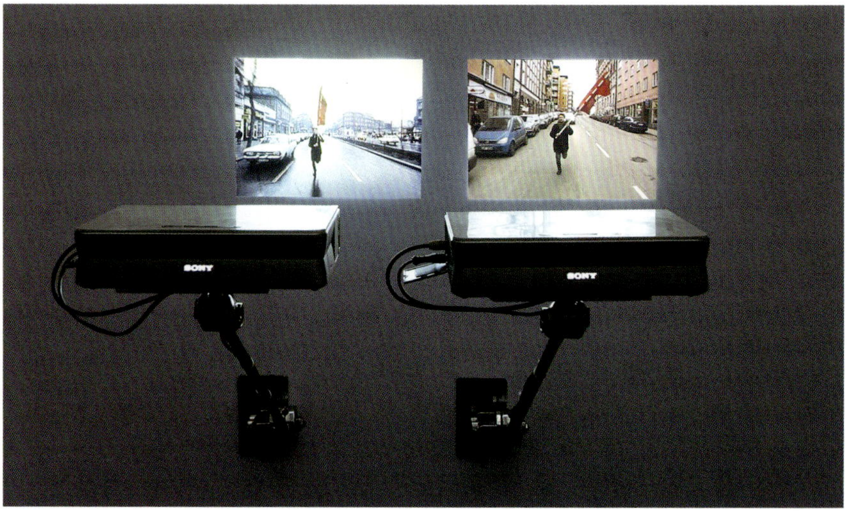

**Fig. 1.36.** Felix Gmelin, *Farbtest, Die Rote Fahne II (Color Test, The Red Flag II)*, 2002. After Gerd Conradt's *Farbtest, Die Rote Fahne*, 1968. 2-channel video installation with 2 small projections 22 × 30 cm, 2 small LCD-projectors and 2 manipulated Manfrotto stands. Silent. 12 minutes. Installation at Portikus, Frankfurt, 2005. Courtesy of Felix Gmelin.

minds. Vision is divided, split, between the moving pictures. As our eyes move restlessly from one runner to the other (from left to right and from right to left) we "hear" the honking horns of automobiles, the sirens of police cars, and the screeching sounds of heavy trucks coming to a halt.

Now we notice that the films are not the same: that it is raining in one and overcast in the other (droplets of rainwater cling to the lens of the first camera); that the left film has the luscious grain of celluloid, the right, the sharp contours of digital imaging; that the films are not synchronized (when one runner comes to a halt, his counterpart stops slightly before, or later); that they were filmed in different locations and probably different moments in time (we see old Volkswagens and Daimlers in one film, contemporary models in the other); that even the hairstyles are distinct (unkempt in the first film, postpunk in the second), as are the runners: while the performers in the first film are exclusively male, in the second film young women also carry the flag.

We are near the end. The pace quickens. On the left a man with a shag of blond hair enters a public square and runs inside an important building. Minutes later another figure storms onto the balcony above the main entrance, where he waves the flag triumphantly and drapes it over the railing as the camera zooms in (fig. 1.37). Bystanders gawk at the incendiary action. A man points at the camera accusatorily and scolds the cinematographer. How angry he seems!

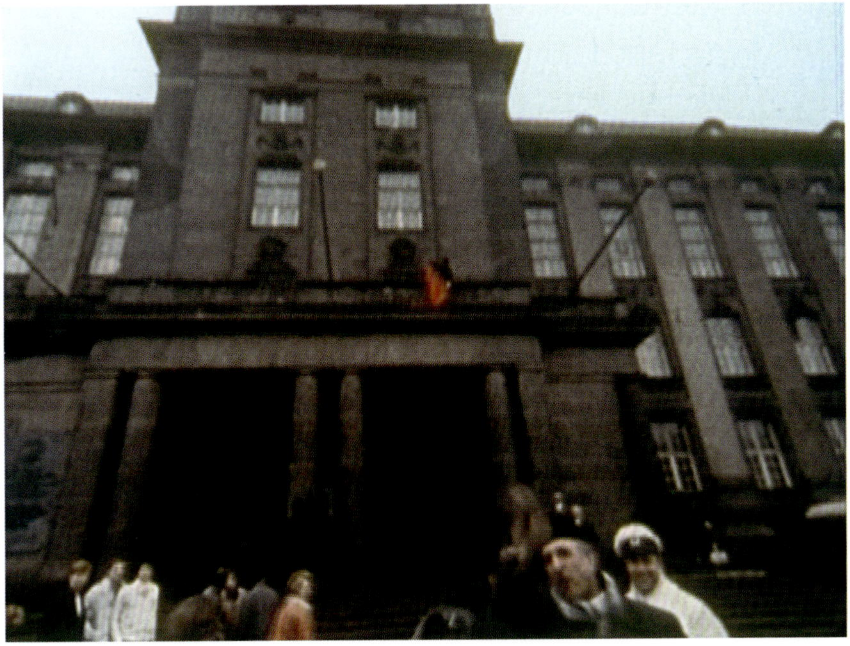

**Fig. 1.37.** Felix Gmelin, *Farbtest, Die Rote Fahne II (Color Test, The Red Flag II)*, 2002. After Gerd Conradt's *Farbtest, Die Rote Fahne*, 1968. Screen capture: Schöneberg Rathaus, Berlin, 1968. Courtesy of Felix Gmelin.

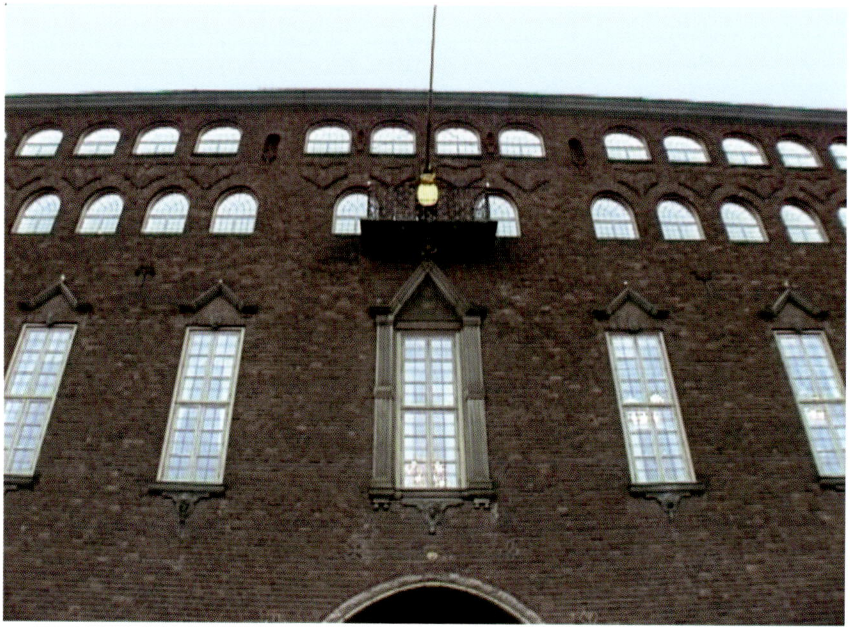

**Fig. 1.38.** Felix Gmelin, *Farbtest, Die Rote Fahne II (Color Test, The Red Flag II)*, 2002. After Gerd Conradt's *Farbtest, Die Rote Fahne*, 1968. Screen capture: Stockholm City Hall, 2002. Courtesy of Felix Gmelin.

In the film on the right, a bearded man runs into another public building, and the camera zooms in yet again. This time the balcony above the entrance remains empty (fig. 1.38). The city square is deserted. A solitary jogger runs past the camera unaware that a film is being made. *Nothing happens.*

*Die Rote Fahne* is a 16 mm film shot in West Berlin in 1968 by Gerd Conradt. The digital film at right is a restaging of *Die Rote Fahne* by Felix Gmelin in Stockholm in 2002. Together the two films are challenging to see, which is exactly the point. The sliver of white wall dividing the images forces us to look at both of them separately and together at the same time. Together the projected images constitute a single work of two parts—a double. The double is a retelling of a story, a rewriting of a primary narrative, according to Lévi-Strauss. By repeating a story, a narrator puts the first version and the second into a kind of relief. The internal structures of each of the narratives, and their differences, are made perspicuous. Gmelin forces viewers to compare two highly similar, yet ultimately dissimilar, events. For what purpose?

Gmelin inherited the archive of his father in 2001. Otto F. Gmelin—the man in Felix's *Sound and Vision*, who made ordinary objects "speak"—had died several years before.[235] At the end of the Sixties Otto Gmelin was a professor of media theory at the Deutsche Film- und Fernsehakademie Berlin (DFFB), where Conradt and the cast and crew of *Die Rote*

*Fahne* were students.[236] In 2002, the younger Gmelin encountered Conradt at a screening of Conradt's film *Starbuck Holger Meins* (2002), a reflection on the life and death of the Red Army Faction (RAF) leader Holger Meins; Felix learned that Conradt and Meins had both been students of his father. After being shown the original *Die Rote Fahne* by Conradt, Gmelin decided to reenact the flag run, enlisting his own students at Konstfack in Stockholm to perform the relay—a productive and fascinating choice.[237]

Before turning to Gmelin's project, we do well to recall the historical setting of Conradt's filmed performance. What did it mean to run through the streets of West Berlin with a red flag in 1968, and to wave this provocatively from the balcony of the Schöneberg Rathaus, the city hall of the blockaded city? How does Gmelin's work shape a contemporary perception of that place and time?

The Sixties in West Germany is remembered as a period of extraordinary consequence in Left narratives—an era of quasi-mythic events and personalities. The story, told many times, goes something like this.[238] A feeling of confidence was widely shared among the thousands of young people who moved to West Berlin in the years after the construction of the wall in 1961, an "unbelievable sense that a new beginning was underway."[239] This was not to last. The escalating suppressions of the Federal Republic of Germany (BRD) precipitated a hardening of emotions and political attitudes, as new arrivals adapted to the deteriorating climate described by one observer as a "permanent state of emergency."[240] The "Sixties" lasted a very long time in West Germany, as long as anywhere, in no small measure due to the activities of the RAF, the radical left-wing organization that turned to terrorism in opposition to state power, imperialism, and the Vietnam War (its bombings of federal and U.S. army bases, its cruel assassinations, its publicity campaigns); then the capture of its most prominent members in 1972 and, in the years following, their horrendous imprisonment and deaths. Three events in October 1977—the alleged group suicide by leaders Johannes Baader, Jan-Carl Raspe, and Gudrun Ensslin at Stammheim Prison, the kidnapping and murder of businessman and former SS officer Hanns-Martin Schleyer by a younger cohort of RAF members, and the hijacking of a Lufthansa plane by the Popular Front for the Liberation of Palestine in support of the Stammheim prisoners—became known as *Deutscher Herbst*, or German Autumn.[241] The rise of Helmut Kohl's Christian Democratic Union in 1982 announced a rightward turn (*Wende*) in West German politics that occurred within a broader context of Sixties repudiation in the West.

Historians link the rise of the German New Left to the emergence of the Außerparlamentarische Opposition (Extra-Parliamentary Opposition, or APO) and a revived Sozialistischer Deutscher Studentenbund (German

Socialist Student Federation, also known as SDS), which emerged in direct opposition to the conservative "Grand Coalition" government of Chancellor Kurt Georg Kiesinger.[242] The Kiesinger regime was then in the process of establishing New Emergency Laws (*Notstandgesetze*) that were eventually ratified on May 30, 1968. The New Emergency Laws were particularly alarming to the APO and SDS, as Hitler had seized power in this very manner thirty-five years earlier. Moreover, Kiesinger was himself a former Nazi, like so many prominent figures in the Federal Republic (he had been an assistant to Goebbels, no less).[243] Last but by no means least, the Kiesinger government actively supported the Vietnam War, allowing its NATO ally, the United States, to maintain military bases on German soil to protect its border with the Communist East. The local presence of American bombers and munitions enraged antiwar activists, who placarded West Berlin with posters denouncing the war as early as February 1966.[244] In April 1967, members of the collective Kommune I hatched a plan to throw custard pies at U.S. vice president Hubert Humphrey during a state visit (the plan came to naught).[245]

The state visit by the Shah and empress of Iran that June was a catalytic event. Activists plastered around the city "Wanted for Murder" posters with the dictator's portrait and organized a symposium enumerating his crimes. In response to a flattering profile of the empress in a society magazine, the gifted journalist Ulrike Meinhof published her "Open Letter to Farah Diba," a withering account of the poverty, hunger, and illiteracy of the Iranian people, the government's torture and murder of dissidents, and the Shah's embezzlement of billions of dollars in aid since his restoration to power by a U.S.-led coup.[246] On June 2, 1967, the Shah and Shahbanu were welcomed by the mayor at the Schöneberg Rathaus, the very location of President Kennedy's "Ich Bin ein Berliner" speech and the culminating scene of *Die Rote Fahne*. Unlike the ecstatic reception of the charismatic American president four years earlier on June 26, 1963, the arrival of the Pahlavis was met with fervent resistance. Anonymous in paper masks with caricatures of the Shah and empress (who saw their own faces represented as U.S. "puppets" glaring back at them across the plaza), the most aggressive protesters threw bags of paint and tomatoes at the Rathaus entrance. At one point, an egg sullied the shoe of one of the Shah's goons, the CIA- and MOSSAD-trained SAVAK (the Farsi acronym for "Organization for National Security and Intelligence of the Nation") and these men proceeded to whack the protesters with wooden staves as the German police watched.[247]

That evening a crowd of several thousand gathered across the street from the State Opera, where the guests were to attend a command performance of *The Magic Flute*. Tomatoes and insults were hurled as the imperial couple and dignitaries hurried inside. A caravan of ambulances suddenly appeared, disgorging swarms of the Shah's men. The SAVAK now began to assault protesters and bystanders with truncheons, with the active assistance of the West Berlin police, who wielded clubs and water hoses against the crowd. Trapped between barriers facing the Bismarck Strasse and the sidewalk, and at both ends, the protesters and observers were unable to escape the punishing jets of water and the severely administered beatings—a "liver sausage" technique of crowd control, as the police chief proudly described it. ("The left end stinks [so] we had to cut in the middle to take off the end."[248]) Next came Operation Foxhunt, the hunting down and abuse of protesters in the streets surrounding the opera. A twenty-six-year-old comparative literature student named Benno Ohnesorg was cornered in a parking lot on the Krumme Strasse. A plainclothes policeman approached the young man and shot him in the head, execution style.[249]

Ohnesorg died instantly. Henceforth June 2 was an infamous day. The APO had its first martyr. Thousands of people marched behind the slain young man's coffin through the streets of Berlin. A New Left was reborn in West Germany.

Lines were irreparably drawn, enemies identified and condemned. The Federal Republic had been exposed for what it was, young people said—an authoritarian state, a republic in name only, tainted by a criminal past it had yet to acknowledge. Its fascist character had been decisively revealed. Protest had proved futile, deadly even, against a state and a police force controlled by former Nazis. A young woman sobbed uncontrollably at an SDS meeting the next day, drops of mascara running down her cheeks. Her name was Gudrun Ensslin. Her remarks became famous: "This is the Auschwitz generation! You cannot argue with the people who made Auschwitz! They have weapons and we haven't. We must arm ourselves!"[250]

Autumn witnessed more protests, the following spring an escalation of violence. Activists organized a "tribunal" of the detested Springer Company, whose newspapers blamed the protesters for Ohnesorg's death. Much like the *enquêtes* (inquests) of structures of authority then being held by Maoists in Paris, the hearing was a presentation of data and research.[251] Participants analyzed Springer's monopolistic control of the press, its programmatic bias against the Left, its inciting of conflict. A few weeks later a Vietnam Congress at the Frei Universität attracted Leftist activists from around the world.[252] Standing on the stage of the university's great auditorium beneath a Viet Cong flag and a quotation from Che Guevara, the charismatic SDS leader Rudi Dutschke spoke of a "global revolution" against Western imperialism.[253] Two delegates from the American Student Non-Violent Coordinating Committee (SNCC) described the Vietnam War and the subordination of African Americans as inextricably linked. Refuting the Gandhian principles of nonviolence embraced by Martin Luther King Jr. encoded in the organization's name, Dale Smith and Ray Robinson espoused the militant views of Malcolm X, declaring that armed resistance was an acceptable, even necessary, response to state-sanctioned violence.[254]

Six weeks later, on the night of April 2, 1968, Ensslin, Baader, and two comrades set off firebombs in two department stores in Frankfurt. During their defense trial the future RAF leaders spoke of their intention to awaken the German public from its somnambulist consumerism and "indifference [*Gleichgültigkeit*] [to] the genocide in Vietnam."[255] They were sent to prison nevertheless. Nine days later, an addled house painter named Josef Bachmann, inspired by incendiary reports in the Springer newspaper *Bild*, approached Dutschke outside the SDS offices on Berlin's Kurfürstendamm and shot him three times. That evening Dutschke's supporters attacked Springer headquarters and trucks as Dutschke lay in the hospital fighting for his life; these "Easter protests" went on for days. The militant views of Smith and Robinson found resonance in Ulrike Meinhof's article "From Protest to Resistance," published in the Left journal *konkret* that May. After Ohnesorg's murder, protesters "set Springer newspapers on fire. This time they tried to prevent their distribution," Meinhof wrote. "In February, there was an amusing film about the production of Molotov cocktails; this time there were real fires."[256] Two years later, Meinhof demonstrated what exactly "resistance" meant when she secretly joined the RAF and participated in Baader's escape from prison; a guard was killed in the scuffle.[257] She was a fugitive now, one of the guerrilla's most prominent members (the RAF was renamed the Baader-Meinhof Gang by the government and press). Her mugshot appeared with those of her comrades on news reports and on "most wanted" posters as the group committed crimes of an increasingly savage nature.

Conradt filmed *Die Rote Fahne* on January 17, 1968, just before the Vietnam Congress and the bombing of the Frankfurt department stores and the Easter protests. How do we situate his film in this tumultuous sequence of events? Who was its intended audience? Even more, why did Gmelin remake this work in another city, in Stockholm, some thirty-five years after Conradt staged the initial version?

Look again at *Die Rote Fahne*. Consider its imagery, its orchestration. (The formal choices that Conradt made then are pivotal for any claims we could put forth as to its current meaningfulness.) Consider the serial

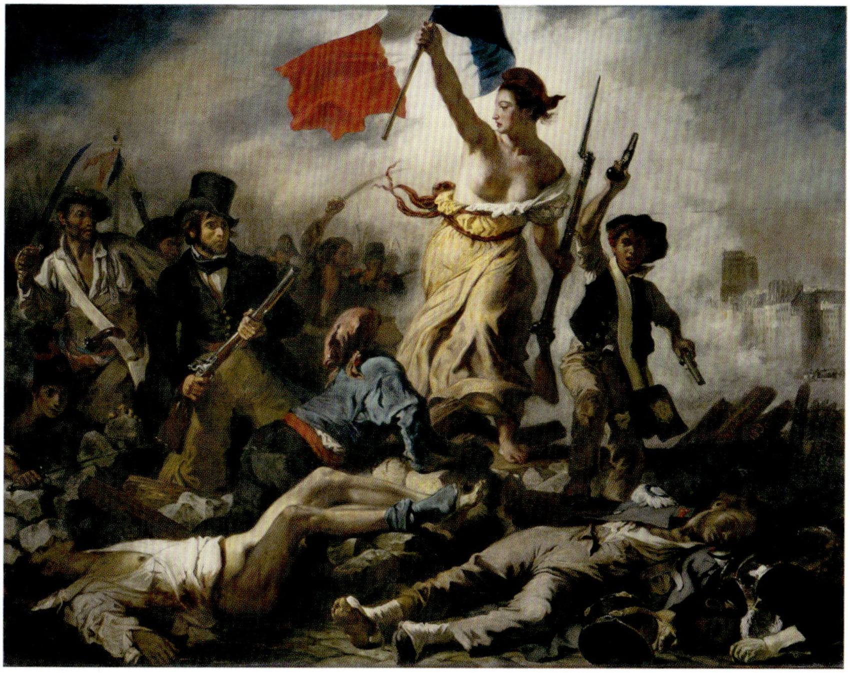

**Fig. 1.39.** Eugène Delacroix, *Liberty Leading the People*, 1830. Oil on canvas. Musée du Louvre. Photograph: Erich Lessing, Art Resource/New York.

formation of the runners, as one replaces another; the narrative conceit of the relay, which escalates in speed and dramatic effect as the penultimate runner approaches the Rathaus Square and the final runner bursts onto the balcony and waves the flag furiously. Consider the film's historical sources: Eadweard Muybridge's protocinematic motion studies of athletes and animals that record a bodily action in several frames, or those early films of Andy Warhol where the sitters perform the most mundane activities, such as eating a mushroom or brushing their teeth, facing the camera as Conradt's runners do. Conradt fuses these photographic and cinematic formats with the ancient iconography of victory (Nike figures, Olympians) and a modern vocabulary of revolutionary depiction based on these prototypes.[258] In the pivotal work of that genre, Delacroix's *Liberty Leading the People* (1830), the flag bearer is the cynosure. Marianne strides past the bodies of royalist soldiers and revolutionaries, holding up the tricolor for all to see (fig. 1.39).

Revolution is irresistible, Arendt tells us. The revolution will happen, and soon. Revolution denotes movement, a forward motion. The revolutionary is a *restless* body. Delacroix gives form to this impatient temporality. A *petit bourgeois*, his face modeled on the artist's, rushes ahead with a rifle. A working-class boy brandishes pistols. And Liberty herself: her gait is strong, her gaze purposeful, her breasts, democracy's nurture, blush with youth. Conradt marshals this tried-and-true iconography. He knows what revolution is supposed to look like. His runners run toward the seat of government they are about to overtake.

Like Delacroix's revolutionaries, Conradt's runners are young—terribly young. He depicts the "last" revolutionary generation in the West, the last generation of young people who could still believe that they ran in history's advance. A more modest effort than Jean-Luc Godard's *La Chinoise* (1967), that feature-length portrait of a *groupuscule* of French Maoists, *Die Rote Fahne* gives visual expression to the radical imaginary of the Sixties, Jameson's "everything was possible." And like Godard, Conradt implies that this generation *would make* this "everything" possible. The revolution is their revolution. Conradt's film gives cinematic form to this modernist idea—the revolution invented and reinvented by previous generations. *Die Rote Fahne* depicts a collectivity, a body politic. It fosters a generational "structure of feeling."[259] The runners are in this together: the relay format indicates this very clearly. As the last of the flag bearers unfurls the red cloth over the balcony, a new generation announces its presence.

In *Die Rote Fahne*, the imagery of revolution and that of generation conjoin. A moving image of moving bodies, of running and revolution, the film depicts the generation as an abstraction, as an idea. Conradt portrays a *particular* generation, the "Sixty-eighters," who would theoretically be emboldened to collective action after seeing the staged relay. I take this to be the film's historical meaning. In fact, *Die Rote Fahne* was not universally admired within the radicalized milieu of the DFFB. For some of Conradt's classmates the film did not go far enough.[260] It did not advocate the full-throated "resistance" that SNCC members Smith and Robinson spoke about, and that Meinhof would claim had become an absolute necessity. Indeed, Conradt's flag relay must have appeared slightly anodyne in comparison with Holger Meins's agitprop film *Herstellung eines Molotow-Cocktails (How to Make a Molotov Cocktail)*, the work Meinhof mentions that inspired viewers to attack Springer headquarters with homemade bombs, and Gmelin's father to blow up a car.[261] It does not hit so hard as Harun Farocki's *Nicht löschbares Feuer (Inextinguishable Fire)* (1969), an exposé of the Dow Chemical Company depicting napalm's noxious effects on a rat. *Die Rote Fahne* does not encourage a viewer to perform violent acts. It does not analyze a war economy based on a division of labor so alienating that Farocki's Dow technicians fail to realize they're making napalm. Neither an agitprop work nor a critique of the military-industrial complex, *Die Rote Fahne* is something else: a film that compels us to look at it decades after Conradt completed it. A work of its time, the flag run exceeds its moment. Why are we drawn to this film so many years later? What is the nature of its attraction—its romantic imagery, its youthful cast, its formal closure? (The race comes to a satisfying conclusion, as Muybridge's photo sequences of athletes do.) What might the red flag have meant to those disgruntled onlookers in the Rathaus Square, much less to Conradt and the other runners? What could it mean to us now?

At the time, *Die Rote Fahne* caused a small ruckus at best. The director and cast were suspended from DFFB. Gmelin's father resigned from his teaching post in solidarity with the students. Conradt had secured permission from the city authorities to shoot *Die Rote Fahne*, and had even been granted permission to film the "traffic situation" from the Rathaus balcony. The act of occupying the balcony politically was a step too far. Unfurling the red flag in such a public space was an incendiary act. The Schöneberg town hall, the ground zero of the West German *polis*, is a mere three miles from Checkpoint Charlie, the notorious gate to East Berlin. Draped on the Rathaus balcony, the scarlet flag exposed this uneasy proximity. (The onlookers do not hide their exasperation. The man who approaches the camera has a threatening mien.) The invasion of the city hall by the final runner made explicit the tenuous status of West Berlin itself, surrounded as it was by the socialist Democratic Republic of Germany (DDR) during a period of heightened Cold War *froideur*. (The spring of 1968 is Prague Spring.)[262] The red flag was a blunt reference to this threatening neighbor. And it evoked another reference less familiar to the taxi drivers and bystanders in the Rathaus Square, yet very much present in the minds of the runners themselves. The red flag pointed above all to China, and to the person and ideology of Mao Zedong.

During the late Sixties and Seventies the idea of revolution was entwined with a dream of China. To many young Leftists in the West and around the world, Maoism appeared as a refreshing antidote to the calcified Marxist-Leninism of the Soviet Union and its European satellites.[263] Formally severing its ties to Moscow in response to Khrushchev's "revisionism" in 1960–62, China presented itself as an authentic beacon of revolution grounded in the concerns of the peasantry and the Third World; it stood at the forefront of the battle against "Western imperialism" that Dutschke spoke about.[264] And where the Soviet Union was ruled by the gray men of the Politburo, the People's Republic was led by a *bona fide* revolutionary hero, Chairman Mao, under whose direction China was undergoing a "cultural" revolution at that very moment: a second "revolution" that promised to fulfill the sweeping aims of the first.

The Cultural Revolution appealed greatly to Western radicals, for it overturned two cornerstones of Enlightenment aesthetics that had heretofore seemed antipodal—the Kantian principle of aesthetic autonomy and the Marxian model of base and superstructure that subordinates culture to base.[265] Mao described culture (*wenhua*) as a "consciousness" (*yishi*), and synthetically as "cultural consciousness" (*wenhua yishi*).[266] "Culture" so conceived was neither separate from society nor a Plekhanovian reflection of base or class. As *consciousness*, a mental state of being, Maoist "culture" occupies our thoughts and shapes our values, transforming society from the individual outward. The inculcation of *wenhua yishi* involved a constant exercise of mental hygiene—a rigorous, at times dangerous practice known as self-criticism. Only a daily ablution of "old ideas, old culture, old customs, old habit" (the Four Olds, they were called) would stem the tide of revisionism that hindered revolutionary progress. The *Quotations from Chairman Mao Tsetung* (the *Little Red Book*) is filled with metaphors of cleanliness. "We should check our complacency and constantly criticize our shortcomings, just as we should wash our faces or sweep the floor every day to remove the dirt and keep them clean."[267]

An application of "Mao Zedong thought" to daily life, the Cultural Revolution entailed a drastic simplification of Mao's more abstruse arguments. The epigrams collected in the *Quotations from Chairman Mao Tsetung* afford a reduced understanding of Maoist dialectics, which imbues opposite terms with an internal contradiction—a contradiction that inhabits everything and animates it in contradiction to other things.[268] The *Quotations* offered a theory of absolute difference eviscerated of dialectical complexity—contradiction without contradiction. "Whoever sides with the revolutionary people is a revolutionary. Whoever sides with imperialism, feudalism, and bureaucrat-capitalism is a counter-revolutionary."[269] And so on. It was this Maoism—a Maoism of simple slogans, of Manichean oppositions—that appealed to many young Leftists in the West.[270] Farocki, who made a propaganda film celebrating the *Quotations*, recalled:

> It [was] slightly alienating that funny sentences from China simplify the world. The history of German leftist theory has to do with Adorno, with the most complex ideas and sentences, where even the simplest thing is embedded in long clauses. Then suddenly comes a biblical tone making politics so simple. You know it can't be so simple. Yet at first it appealed to me and others as poetry.[271]

How irresistible it seemed. Maoism, the "wind from the East," became fashionable in radical Left circles in the West as China plummeted into a state of terror. *China Pictorial* and other propaganda magazines presented glowing depictions of revolutionary activities while occluding from view the fear and abuse experienced by many Chinese at the explicit command of the ruthless, aging Chairman. What mattered was not the real China, it was said, but the China "in our heads."[272]

There will be more to say about the effects of this traumatic past on Chinese artists and writers later in this book. Gmelin's *Farbtest, Die Rote Fahne II* retrieves the memory of Western Maoism, this dream of China. This fantasy was orientalist: unlike the traditional orientalism that views the East as culturally inferior, by a logic of inversion Western radicals and intellectuals embraced a different kind of orientalism, or Third World-ism, centered on the model of China and the cult of Mao.[273] Red was, of course, the very symbol of the Cultural Revolution itself, the ubiquitous hue of the great banners displayed during the mass rallies in Tiananmen Square and of simple character posters. It was the color of revolutionary clothing accessories—the armbands of Red Guards and the kerchiefs worn by elementary school students. And so it was in Berlin, where the red flag was an instantly recognizable sign of Left dissent: during a rally in support of the "custard pie" conspirators in 1967, some one thousand protesters carried them.[274]

The identity of the final runner in *Die Rote Fahne* is notable in this regard. He is Holger Meins, the director of *Herstellung eines Molotow-Cocktails*. Then a promising film student and close colleague of Conradt and Farocki, Meins eventually emerged as a leader of the RAF along with Meinhof, Ensslin, and Baader, the stoic "Starbuck" of that ill-fated crew.[275] Viciously beaten by the state police from head to toe upon his capture in 1972, Meins was placed in the *Toter Trakt*, or dead zone, of Wittlich Prison, where twenty-four-hour camera surveillance, fluorescent lighting, constant searches, and a loss of contact with other human beings left prisoners in a state of extreme disorientation.[276] Eventually Meins joined his RAF comrades in other prisons in a series of hunger strikes to protest these conditions.[277] To refuse to eat was to "resist" in the only way he could. This final act of renunciation, carried out for fifty-four days with the most concerted application, resulted in the indignity of being force-fed.[278] Slowly, deliberately, Meins starved himself. At the time of his death on November 9, 1974, at thirty-three, the six-foot, two-inch filmmaker weighed a mere eighty-six pounds, his elegant, handsome person reduced to a grotesque shell. The athletic runner of Conradt's film is the physical opposite of the corpse in the gruesome photos taken at Meins's deathbed, a near-skeleton with hollowed-out eyes, bloated sternum, contorted limbs, and Rasputin beard—an image so horrible it is impossible to forget once we have glimpsed it.[279] Meins had sculpted his body into a very different body by the end. The "Aryan" had become a *Muselmann*, the concentration camp victim tortured and starved to death by his Nazi persecutors, a person who is no longer a human being, or even a corpse, but a humanoid, a *Figur*.[280] And in making his body this body, a body that was no longer exactly human, he had fashioned himself into an image of Auschwitz, of Treblinka, of Belzec, a body that enunciated in the most explicit terms possible a direct link between the democratic Federal Republic and its direct antecedent, the Third Reich. *Dieser mann "expresste" den Deutschen Staat* ("This man 'expressed' the German state"), as one poster put it, a depiction of Meins's corpse next to a photo of an emaciated concentration camp survivor.[281] Meins had become another martyr to the cause, like Ohnesorg, murdered, it was alleged, by the fascist state.[282] His death marked an apogee of positive feeling toward the Baader-Meinhof among liberals and socialists in the BRD before the horrendous turn of events of the German Autumn.

Meins's participation in *Die Rote Fahne* is adventitious yet significant. A revenant, barely visible, he is extraordinarily *present* in the film. On the Rathaus balcony he is hidden from view by the flag he unfurls and drapes, the flag that flutters in front of his animated body, the flag he so believes in. He embraces the scarlet cloth. His somatic identification with the red flag is complete. (Meins was a fanatical reader of Mao.)[283] It is Meins who carries the flag to its final destination, who brings it farther than the other runners, who crosses the fault line into a full-throated resistance when he screens *Herstellung eines Molotow-Cocktails* and crosses another line still, a point of no return, when he joins the guerrilla. To speak of Meins in this context forces us to shift our analysis from the seemingly firm soil of history to the unstable ground of recentness. My thinking here is prompted by a remark of the younger Gmelin, who recalls: "Ulrike Meinhof and Holger Meins were in my parents' apartment. I had their smoke in me." He adds: "I didn't know what was going on."[284]

This recollection is partial, fragmentary. Gmelin's memory is triggered by the memory of a smell, an exchange of breath. They were in the same room once. They occupied the same space. The others are historical figures now. Their lives and deaths have come to represent a kind of Leftist extremity, a belief system that no longer makes sense. They turned to acts of violence to protest a world they found unjust, and died young seeing through their perfervid vision.

Let us return to that evening. Gmelin's parents have guests. Everyone is smoking. Perhaps they're drinking wine or tumblers of vodka. Maybe they're passing a joint. They're becoming tipsy or stoned. Vinyl records spin on the stereo. A boy of six or seven is looking up at the adults. He has come to fetch his mother; he tugs her arm; he wears long cotton pajamas with slipper feet. The lanky young man has shoulder-length hair, a quiet intensity. The woman chain-smokes nervously (an ashtray fills up with the butts of her extinguished cigarettes). She speaks passionately about matters beyond the boy's comprehension. The father listens, responds. He directs the flow of conversation. The young man speaks rarely. The visitors say goodnight, and the boy and his mother retreat to the child's bedroom. The boy falls asleep in minutes. The conversation and drinking continue as the LPs drop onto the record player and the apartment fills up with smoke.

This is the encounter as I imagine it. The memory is Gmelin's—my reconstruction of his memory. The memory of the lanky man, and the woman who chain-smoked and talked and talked. The memory of the young, bearded Otto—the man we see in *Die Rote Fahne*. The memory of Gmelin's mother as a young mother. The memory of their lives in Berlin before they decamped to Sweden, the location of the future flag run.[285] The memory of people who have been endlessly written about and transformed into movie characters. The memory of people who are no longer alive. People whom few living persons remember. Above all, the memory of not understanding, "not knowing [what's] going on."[286]

Benjamin describes memory as a "cautious probing," a turning of the shovel in rich deposits. Rare and precious, these half-forgotten images of childhood (*Bilder*) reveal themselves slowly, and with tenacious effort.[287] It took Benjamin several drafts to arrive at a "final" version of his memoir in 1938, yet even this remained unfinished, as if the exile's inability to visit his native city in actuality were mirrored in his struggles to return there *in writing* (return is haunted by the gnawing sense of its impossibility). Yet Benjamin's memoir is not nostalgic, Susan Buck-Morss reminds us.[288] Initially inspired by a bout of homesickness, his memoir is an attempt at self-immunization, a homeopathic treatment against this malady, as it became painfully apparent that the critic would never again see his hometown.[289] His Berlin text is not autobiography in the conventional sense—a divulgation of feelings once felt, an arrangement of events in a sequential narrative. Autobiography is dependent on "sequence and what makes up the continuous flow of life," Benjamin writes. Like historicism, the "once upon a time" form of history he finds so distasteful, autobiography presumes that the author can arrange the disparate events of his or her life into a coherent order. It supposes that a person's life "makes sense," adds up—that it can be *explained*.

Benjamin is a countermemoirist; his text is historically ambitious and personally modest. Benjamin does not presume to recount the "story" of his life; his study of his childhood lacks a firm beginning and ending. From one draft to another, whole sections were added or cut, embroidered and edited down. There is no one story, no right version, only drafts awaiting revision.[290] Images (*Bilder*) and glimpses of moments (*Augenblicken*) stand resolutely as themselves, disconnected. Benjamin was part of these situations; he walked in the same park or occupied the same room. His gesture entails a withdrawal of the "I" from the scene of action: the self in his Berlin essay is a fragmented mirror, reflecting things and situations, and at the same time embedded in these things. As for Proust, his favorite author, the memories that count, that return in writing, are often those of objects or perceptions—the kitchen larder with its forbidden treats, the oval brooch with the large yellow gemstone that his mother wore on special occasions, or the vegetal pattern of the family porcelain upon which he focused his gaze during the "battles" that raged around the dining table; or even the distinctive way the moon, penetrating the windows of his bedroom, illuminated the washing basins and jugs on his nightstand, transforming this most familiar of spaces into an alien place, a "terrain so deceptively illuminated" it appeared to exist on an "alternate earth."[291] "Evanescent and alluringly tormenting," these images are concealed in "ever-new" places and buried in "ever-deeper" mnemonic deposits. Benjamin looked for them and kept looking for them as he rewrote his text. An *active* remembrance, the "dark happiness" of digging itself: this is the core of the matter.[292]

Recentness is a fugitive quarry. Returning to the Berlin of 1900, Benjamin depicts a city that fewer and fewer people remember. A Berlin of temporal layers: beneath the imperial city of his childhood is the city of his parents' earliest recollections (the Berlin of Wilhelm I), and the city of his grandparents' memories (the Berlin of Friedrich Wilhelm III and IV). The entire nineteenth century permeates Benjamin's descriptions of the turn-of-the-century metropolis. (Recall the critic's irresistible remark: "Like a mollusk in its shell I had my abode in the nineteenth century, which now lies hollow before me like an empty shell. I listen to it.")[293] Buried along with these earlier Berlins is another history: in his descriptions of the lake in the Tiergarten, of the shopping trips to the chic boutiques and department stores frequented by his mother, of the strict Kaiser Friedrich School he attended and disliked, we have a compelling portrait of the German Jewish upper-middle class from which Benjamin emerged, a community on the precipice of annihilation. At the center of this account is the bourgeois domesticity of the family home.[294]

The most striking details that Benjamin shares are personal, familial—such as the "species of things" that cluttered his grandmother's capacious flat on the Blumeshof (shelves of knickknacks, overstuffed ottomans) and the collection of postcards he received during her peripatetic travels (he credits his own wanderlust to this "enterprising lady"), or the distinctive slap of his mother's knife on the rolls she buttered every morning for his father's lunch, or the imagined raps of the gavel that lay on this gentleman's desk, the anticipation of which evoked in his child's mind his father's work in an auction house and his role in the grown-up world of affairs. There are less agreeable memories, too—such as the night his parents locked themselves in a bedroom in their country house to escape a gang of burglars, or the time his mother demanded that he "do her bidding" if he hoped to go out to the opera one evening. Although the memory of that particular performance of *William Tell* faded a long time ago, the feeling of "violated trust" associated with it has never left him. Even in middle age, even as he mourns his mother's death, the critic cannot bring himself to forgive her that imposing demand, a betrayal too painful to describe.[295]

Parents and grandparents are conspicuous presences in the art of return, I have claimed. Works that are not obviously "about" a parent invariably *are*. Mothers and fathers are filmed and written about, interviewed and researched. They are the sphinxlike repositories of memory, the reluctant prey of grown-up children who badger them for information as they track down the hidden traces of their subjectivities. The narrator of Lê's "Love and Honor and Pity and Pride and Compassion and Sacrifice" interviews his father to make sense of their estrangement, only to learn that he is a child survivor of My Lai and a Viet Cong "reeducation" camp. Sala interrogates his mother about her participation in a propaganda film he discovers accidentally, uncovering a history she has kept to herself and confronting her about it. The narrator of Hill's *The Nix* investigates his mother's traumatic experiences as a college student during the tumultuous Chicago protests in 1968 in order to make sense of the mother's abandonment of him as a boy—an event that would result in a life of romantic and professional failures. In Dana Spiotta's novel of Sixties return, *Eat the Document* (2006), a work I discuss in part 2, a woman who was once a member of a Weather Underground–like collective, whose members killed an innocent man, eventually confesses her identity to her son. In a corollary plot, the young female protagonist discovers that the genial owner of a progressive bookstore in Seattle was a member of the same radical group and this woman's former lover.[296]

The parents and parental figures in these works are mysterious figures with mysterious pasts. As these narratives progress, an artist or writer or character recovers a history that he or she dimly knew with immense bearing on his or her present life. The Sixties is by no means over; it is only beginning to be narrated and understood. The life itineraries of the older generation, the choices they made then, are reconstructed and examined—and judged.

Which leads us again to *Farbtest, Die Rote Fahne II*. In his reenactment of Conradt's film Gmelin cast himself among the runners. Gmelin appears twice in his film, early on and near the conclusion. During the

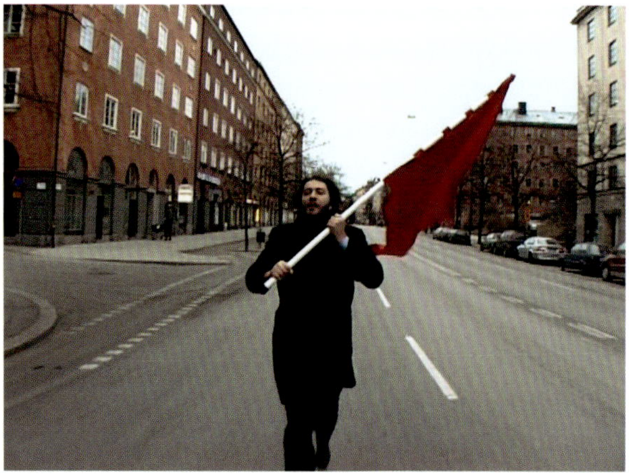

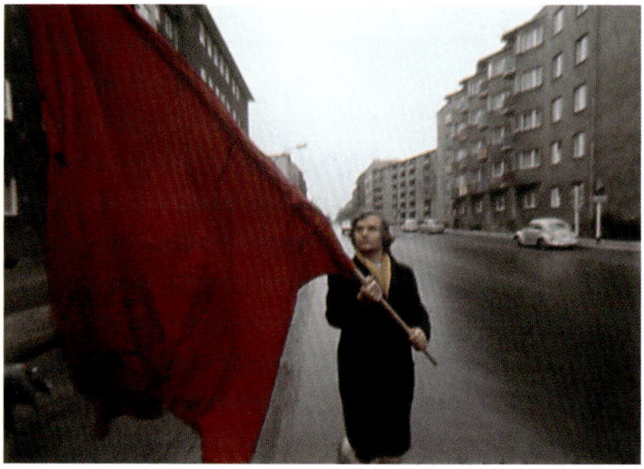

**Fig. 1.40a and 1.40b.** Felix Gmelin, *Farbtest, Die Rote Fahne II (Color Test, The Red Flag II)*, 2002. After Gerd Conradt's *Farbtest, Die Rote Fahne*, 1968. Screen captures of Felix Gmelin, 2002, and Gerd Conradt, 1968. Courtesy of Felix Gmelin.

penultimate scene of the flag relay, he and Conradt (the runner with the shoulder-length blonde hair) run into the Stockholm and Schöneberg city halls, respectively. The directors jog "next" to one another (fig. 1.40 a and b). Now we notice that Otto F. Gmelin makes two entrances in *Die Rote Fahne*. A man of more mature aspect than the other participants, with russet beard and long coat, he is the first of the runners in Conradt's film. During his second appearance he takes the flag from another young man who wears a mustache and hands it off to Conradt, who runs into the Rathaus Square. In other words, Otto appears in front of Felix in Felix's work. The father runs *before* the son (fig. 1.41).

What is at stake in Gmelin's remake of Conradt's flag relay, after all? Why did he include the video of Otto "making things speak" in *Sound and Vision*? As I will now suggest, Gmelin's works depicting his father (and we shall consider others) are not entirely concerned with Otto. Just as Benjamin's meditations on Berlin evoke a more remote history, the period of his parents and grandparents, Gmelin's works centered on the compelling figure of Otto and his students disinter the memory of a prior generation, a further past. The return to one era leads to yet another.

The Sixty-eight generation in West Germany is referred to as the *Nachgeborenen*, a word that suggests "those who were born during or after" the Third Reich. It is also known as the *Zweite* (second) generation. The psychic drama of the *Nachgeborenen* has been described in a language of ambivalence—as a "double bind." The double bind is the psychic effect of a contradictory injunction, of mixed messages. It suggests the state of confusion, the mental paralysis, of a child who both identifies with and is unable to identify with parents who deliver these conflicting messages.[297] The parents of the Sixty-eighters—the "first" generation—passively accepted the National Socialist project or joined outright. Having

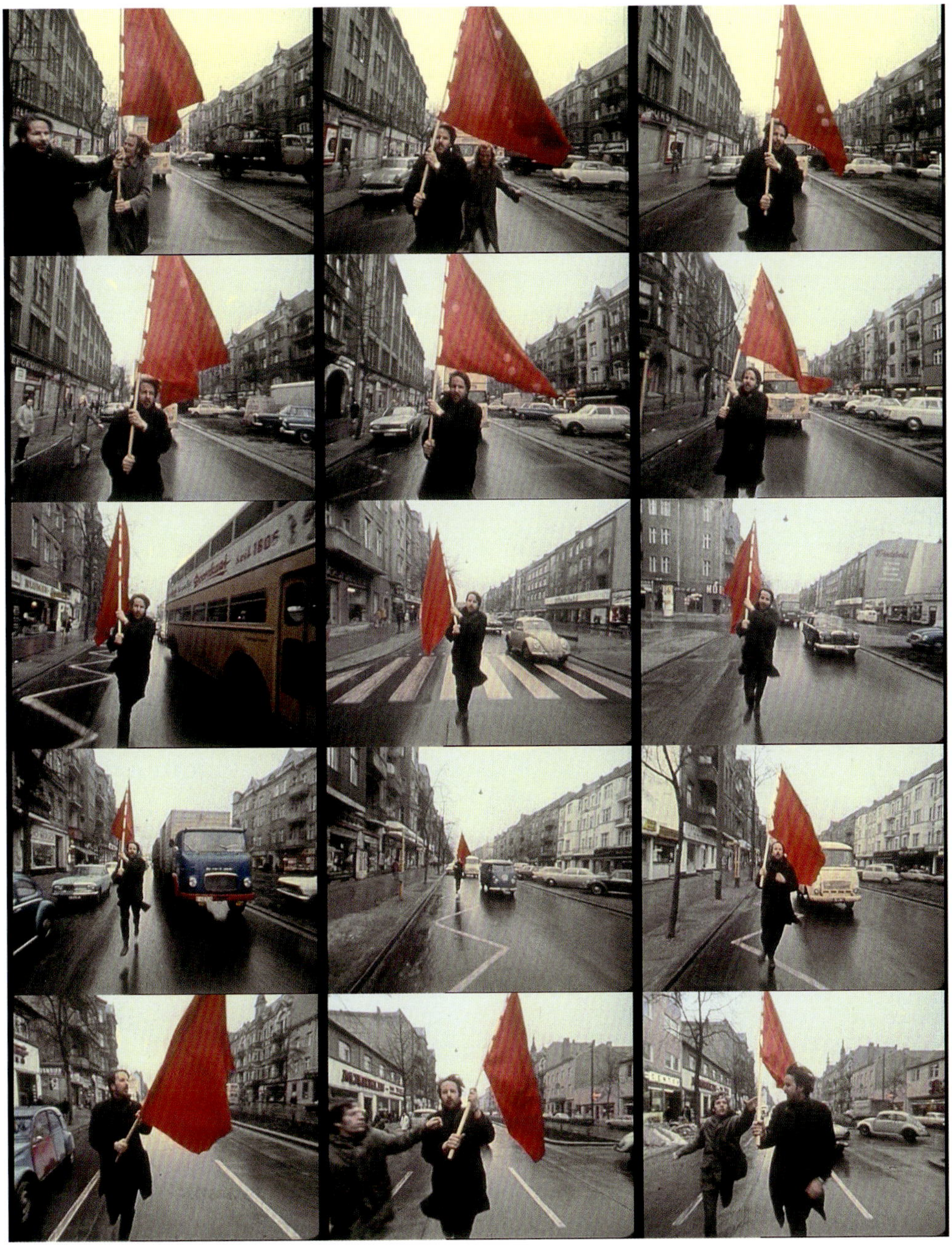

**Fig. 1.41.** Felix Gmelin, *Farbtest, Die Rote Fahne II (Color Test, The Red Flag II)*, 2002. After Gerd Conradt's *Farbtest, Die Rote Fahne*, 1968. Screen capture of Otto F. Gmelin, 1968. Courtesy of Felix Gmelin.

survived the firebombings and deprivations of the war's final months and the sting of defeat, they experienced a severe melancholia centered on the loss of the symbolic father, the Führer.[298] As a consequence, an unspoken sorrow haunted the postwar German family. The recent past was a criminal past, implicating the fathers and mothers. It could not be spoken about. Beneath the trappings of normalcy—the regimen of fine manners, impeccable hygiene, and strict morality—was a history that could not be named. The *Nachgeborenen* came to understand themselves as a generation bound together not by longing for a "before" but a deep revulsion for a repugnant recentness. As critic Michael Schneider recalled (I quote his remarks at length):

> The majority of the men and women who belong to my generation know little more about the former political lives of their parents and close family members and their experiences during the Third Reich than they know what life was like during the Stone Age.... Only in 1968, the year in which many of the sons and daughters of the bourgeoisie were awakened to political consciousness, did they understand the peculiar faces which had accompanied their daydreams.... It was as if the ghosts of their fathers had suddenly appeared before them in Nazi uniforms, and their living fathers, with whom they had sat down at the supper table for twenty years, had been indicted in the most horrible collective crime committed by any generation during this century.[299]

Schneider describes the horrific "chance discoveries" of his contemporaries: snapshots of parents sunbathing in the nude on a beach decorated with Nazi banners; a portrait of someone's father in a "snappy" SS uniform; a toy car found in the back drawer of a desk inscribed with the words "SS-wedding"; the dawning awareness of a friend that his father, an eminent attorney, as a young man had authored a legal article on the "concept" of "race" in *Mein Kampf*.[300]

An unmourned trauma incited the protest activity of the Sixty-eight generation and their more extreme efforts of disavowal—highly critical memoirs of parents (a genre that came to be known as *Vaterliteratur*, or "father literature") and the brutalities of the RAF.[301] Anguished by the memory of a crime, this "Hamlet" generation made it their most somber duty to expose a scandalous past their parents desperately tried to forget. Schneider describes the efforts of his peers to sabotage the "rules and prohibitions" of their elders.[302] In *Traktat* (1967), a film by Michael Makritsch, the basis of Felix Gmelin's work *Manifesto* (2010–11), Otto

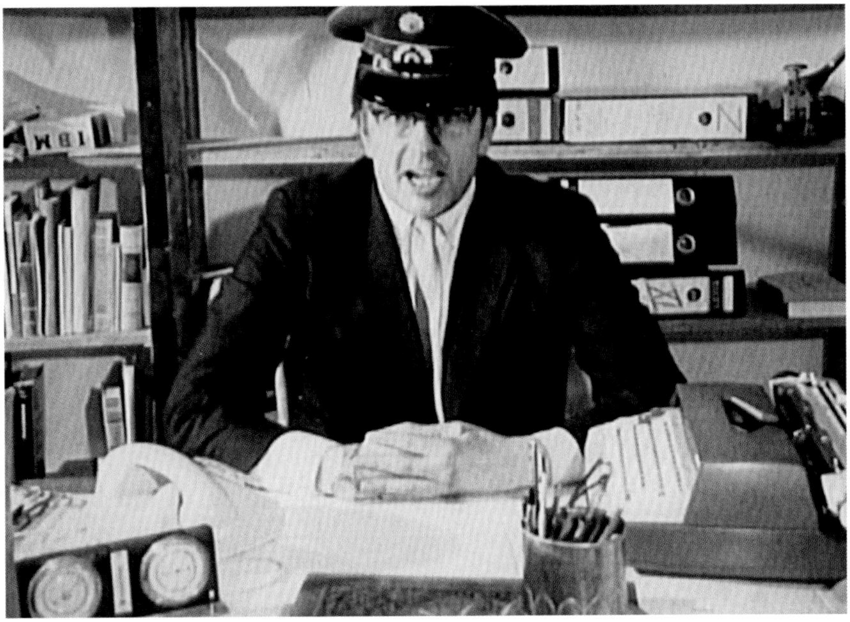

**Fig. 1.42.** Felix Gmelin, *Manifesto*, 2010–11. Single-channel video with sound, 8′06″. After Michael Makritsch, *Traktat über die Verträglichkeit einer Pflanze* (Treatise on the Tolerability of a Plant), 1967. 16 mm film. Still of Otto F. Gmelin. Courtesy of Felix Gmelin.

F. Gmelin does exactly this. He plays a business clerk, a policeman, a priest, a professor, changing hats and altering the intonation of his voice as he switches between these roles (fig. 1.42). Otto mimics the speech of state, clerical, and academic authority. The guttural German of his policeman invokes the barking commands of the SS officer. His pompous professor garbles the refined German of Goethe and Schiller. Uttering these harsh and preposterous remarks out loud, Otto exorcises the Nazi personality that allegedly lurked within each and every German (the "Hitler within you," Meinhof called it).[303] Born in 1931, Otto was not a "Sixty-eighter" properly speaking; his childhood memories of Hitler's Germany were real. Much like Meinhof, who was born in 1933, he strongly identified with the younger activists who took to the streets during the late Sixties, as we have seen. Apparently, Otto had his own demons to contend with: by giving voice to this Germanic subjectivity, perhaps he sought to expose the wartime complicity of his own father (whose company had flourished during the war) or yet another family member with whom he shared the same name and even the same initials, another Otto F. Gmelin, a party-approved novelist who achieved some renown during the Nazi era.[304]

The offspring of the *Nachgeborenen*, also known as the "third" generation, became inscribed in this "chain of negative dependencies."[305] The fate of Sixties children in West Germany is a gripping subject.

The offspring of the most radicalized figures suffered from the extreme self-absorption of parents consumed with their political activities and the pursuit of sexual freedom. (The moral attitude of the RAF member was that of a revolutionary "who must sever all connection with her origins and burn all her bridges behind her," a historian of the movement observes.)[306] We read of the anonymous baby that Baader fathered, and of Felix Ensslin, son of Gudrun and author Bernward Vesper, both abandoned when their parents took on new partners and went underground.[307] We read of Bettina and Regine Röhl, the twin daughters of Meinhof and publisher Klaus Rainer Röhl: how their lives were turned upside down after their mother divorced the philandering Röhl, forsaking the bourgeois comforts of a villa in Hamburg for an apartment in Berlin; how they often arrived at school late (Meinhof being more involved with her journalism and her efforts to help troubled children than with her daughters' education); how they disliked the cruel Baader, who moved into their apartment with Ensslin; and how Meinhof, in one of the most bizarre episodes in the history of the RAF, had the girls kidnapped with the aim of relocating them to an orphanage in a Palestinian refugee camp, where they were to receive instruction in revolutionary ideology, and where, had their mother's plan succeeded, their may have lost their lives.[308] We read of Meinhof's conflicted views of motherhood (the "politically active woman ... is disarmed with her children") and how she was often attacked by Ensslin and Baader for her maternal feelings; how she was denounced as a "bad mother" in the right-wing press, which had previously described her as mad.[309] Then the deep misery of her final years: solitary confinement in the *Toter Trakt* at Cologne-Ossendorf for months on end; the final visits with the twins; her decision to break off contact with them after her reunion with Ensslin in 1974; and her death on the second Sunday of May 1976—Mother's Day. "Letters were returned unopened. Visits were no longer desired," Bettina Röhl has recalled. "It was a completely silent second break-up. And it was once and for all."[310] The history that Röhl retrieves is steeped in memory—her own. As she states very clearly, once their mother chose to remove her and her sister from their "little lives" in Hamburg, once they were kidnapped at their mother's bidding, their identities changed forever. They were no longer "just somebody's daughters." They had entered the grim annals of the RAF; they were victims of Baader-Meinhof. History was done *to them*. "As children we didn't really know the reason why [we were kidnapped] but we didn't ask," she explains in Shane O'Sullivan's documentary film *Children of the Revolution* (2010). "As a child, you accept what adults do."[311]

*Retornare*, in Latin, means "to turn back" or "go back." As Röhl, a journalist, has courageously attempted to do.[312] Her parents are the principal focus of her research; she conceives her project as a critical revision of previous narratives of the RAF, "the RAF myth and the myth of Ulrike Meinhof."[313] Her book *So macht Kommunismus Spass! Ulrike Meinhof, Klaus Rainer Röhl und die Akte Konkret* (Making Communism Fun: Ulrike Meinhof, Klaus Rainer Röhl and the Konkret Files; 2006) recounts the meeting of her parents, committed communists; their propaganda activity and marriage; and the history of their left-wing magazine *konkret* and Meinhof's journalistic career before she joined the RAF—the period that precedes and encompasses Röhl's childhood.[314] And she assesses her parents' choices and compromises. Röhl deflates, in particular, the image of her mother as radical "icon," a martyr to justice—Meinhof as a New Left Joan of Arc.[315] The Stasi archive is her ally. Röhl explores its obscure corridors, rifles once-forbidden files, discloses her parents' most closely held secrets: their membership in the West German Communist Party (KPD) and the covert funding of *konkret* by the East German propaganda ministry, a funding stream sufficiently lavish to support her parents' "extremely comfortable right-wing lifestyles," as she drily describes it.[316] She refutes her parents' politics and exposes their hypocrisies. Her liberal democratic views are the diametrical opposite of Meinhof's Leftist anarchism in particular. In a curious outburst, Röhl defends the Federal Republic, the RAF's detested "great white whale"—the government that detained and jailed her mother ("The Federal Republic of Germany, or West Germany ... was by far the best possible state on German soil at that moment").[317] The tone of these denunciations is furious, utterly self-convinced—and uncannily familiar. Despite her strenuous efforts to distance herself from Meinhof, when I read Röhl's prosecutions I cannot fail to hear the authoritarian cadences of Meinhof's propagandistic journalism, as if Röhl is forever condemned to speak her mother's tongue, ventriloquize her speech.

Like Röhl, Gmelin is of this third generation. He also confronts the history his parents and their contemporaries made, yet his practice is far more ambivalent. In his installation *Ambiguous Gestures* (2009), a video projector surmounts a stack of fruit boxes.[318] Paintings and C-prints by Felix surround a small moving image projected onto the wall, yet another video made by Otto (fig. 1.43). The video reveals Gmelin's father and a female companion reclining nude on a bed stacked with unstretched canvases. They squeeze tubes of oil paint on one another; from time to time they press their bodies into the canvas and make love. When the sheet is imprinted with traces of their bodies Otto removes it from the stack and stores it in a cabinet, and the lovers begin again.

Gmelin has spoken of his "embarrassment" upon discovering this video among Otto's belongings.[319] Still he asks us, his viewers, to watch this odd tape. He positions us as Otto's voyeurs—and we are curious and slightly

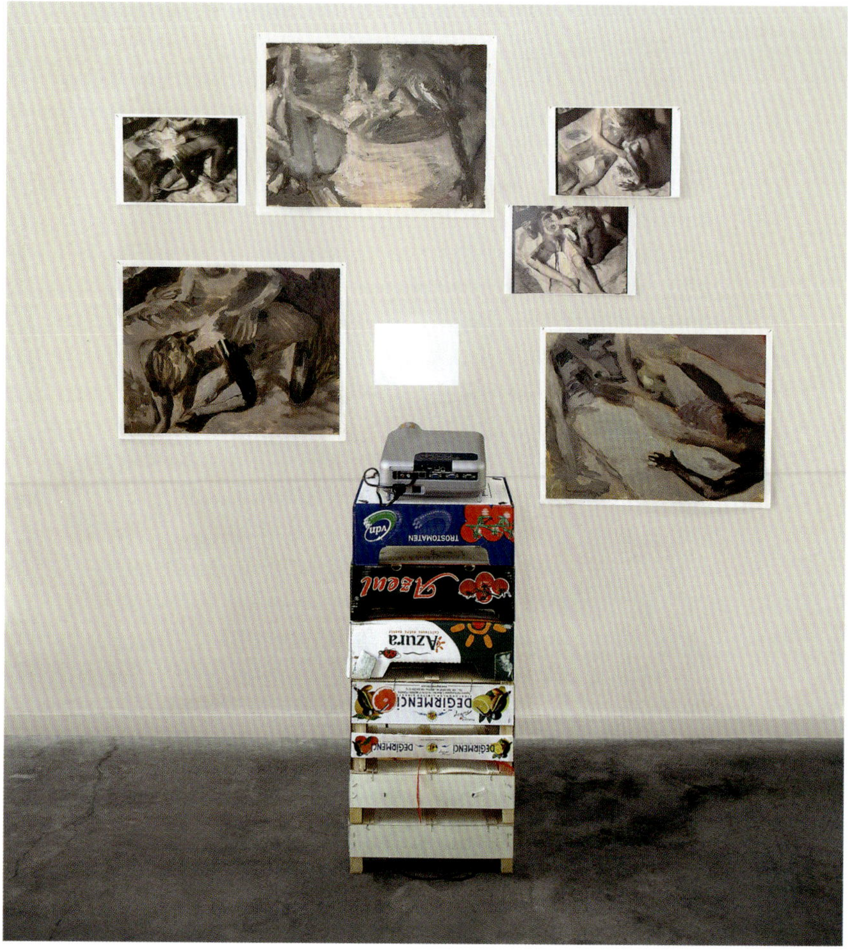

**Fig. 1.43.** Felix Gmelin, *Ambiguous Gestures*, 2004–9. Multimedia installation including tree oil paintings on polyester, tree C-prints on paper, a 45-minute single-channel DVD-video, and 5 fruit boxes in wood and cardboard. Courtesy of Felix Gmelin.

embarrassed. We observe his middle-aged father cavorting with this much younger woman whose face we never see. Felix appropriates Otto's private endeavors—revises his videos, re-presents them, and arguably *completes* them—quite possibly against his father's wishes. He exposes Otto's protuding belly, his thin arms, his genitalia, reveals his nakedness, the penultimate filial crime. ("And Noah awoke from his wine, and knew what his youngest son [Ham] had done unto him.")[320] But Gmelin's project eludes a strictly oedipal reading. In Felix's works about Otto we are confronted with the image of a man who seeks fresh sensations and ways of seeing, who has made it his life's work to challenge the status quo, and patriarchy in particular.[321] Gmelin's works about his father are admiring, critical, and perplexed all at once—"ambiguous," indeed. Above all, they reveal an indescribable sorrow: by integrating Otto's films into his own projects and exposing them to public view, Gmelin saves his father's efforts from oblivion, prevents their forgetting, not unlike the mourner who holds on to a loved one's favorite hat or coat long after its utility has run its course, as if this object, this relic, could keep his or her memory alive for a little longer. Yet *Ambiguous Gestures* is more than an act of salvage. Recall the canvases and C-prints framing Otto's video, paintings and reproduction of paintings based on stills of the tape we see. Not content simply to *present* the video, Gmelin *records* these intimate scenes in the language of painterly gesture. He limns the lovers' heads and limbs, reconstructs their poses (kneeling, embracing, lying down), covers these figures in brushstrokes of tan and pink and royal blue (fig. 1.44). He *paints* Otto and his lover, as they painted one another—an operation I can only describe as extraordinarily tender. Tracing these blurry figures with his hands and brushes, Gmelin inscribes his own body into this act of mnemonic retrieval. He remembers Otto, and asks us to remember him.

To return: to go back to a place after a period of absence. To look around, to gather souvenirs. To reminisce. To recall. To mourn.[322]

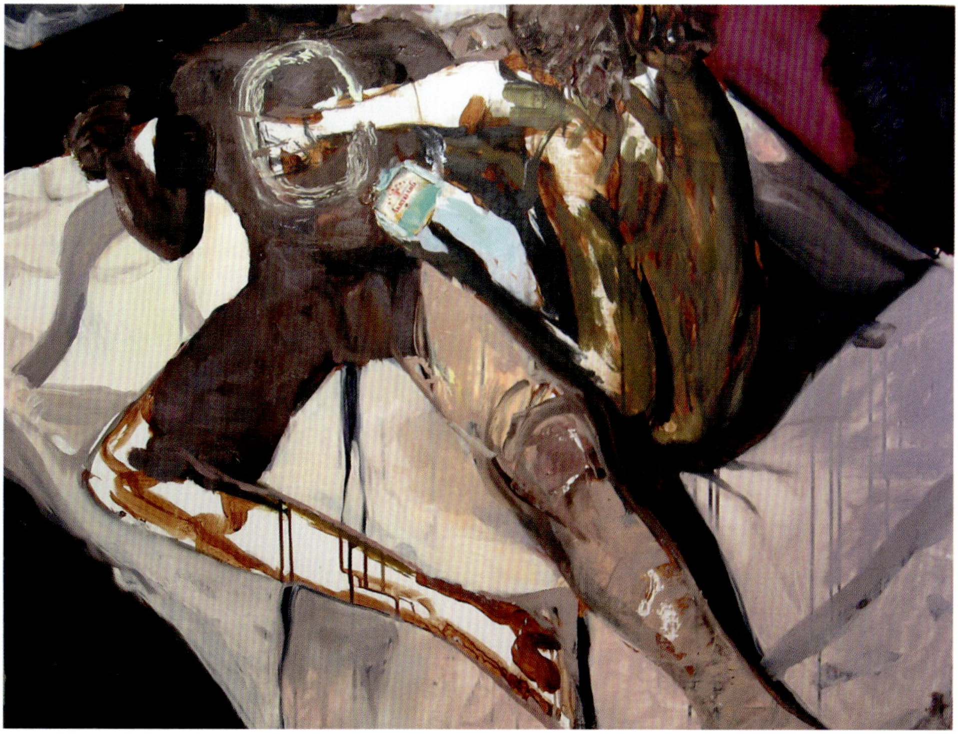

**Fig. 1.44.** Felix Gmelin, *Film Stills 1.4*, 2004. From the series *Ambiguous Gestures*. Oil on canvas. Courtesy of Felix Gmelin.

Which brings us again to Berlin, to Sixty-eight. Death—a death that comes early and needlessly—is a recurring figure of the long Sixties. Narratives of the German New Left are inescapably narratives of death. The movement coalesces in the hours after Ohnesorg's murder, and escalates after Dutschke is shot (he eventually died from the complications of his injuries from the madman's bullets). The bombings, shootouts, murders, and suicides associated with the RAF, culminating in the grotesque events of October 1977, complete the story. The children of the Sixty-eighters are the inheritors of a grim history; they interrogate their parents' uncompromising views and choices. They historicize Sixty-eight and question its mythologies. Their practices are critical history as Nietzsche described it. Let us briefly examine this idea as we conclude this discussion.

The late nineteenth century suffered from the sort of mnemonic overload that contemporary memory theorists speak about. "We are all suffering from a malignant historical fever," Nietzsche announces in *On the Use and Abuse of History for Life* (1874), the second of his *Untimely Meditations*.[323] The historical "fever" that he describes was endemic during the 1870s and 1880s, when the puffed-up mansards of Second Empire style, the absurd turrets and confectionary traceries of the neo-Gothic, the intricate terracotta of Queen Anne, and the rusticated profiles of the neo-Romanesque blurred architectural vocabularies. The philosopher never bothers to distinguish history and memory: for Nietzsche these terms are thoroughly intertwined. History *is* recollection; the capacity to remember allows us to think of ourselves historically. History is not empirical knowledge, however—a set of facts to be assembled into an "objective" narrative. Nietzsche rejects Ranke's command to describe "things as they were." His concern is how history can benefit or imperil the living, its "uses" and "abuses" for us, now.

Animals live in a perpetual present. They lack a sense of history; we envy them the contentment this allegedly brings. Our awareness that time is ever slipping away causes us to suffer. We cannot learn to forget, even if we wanted to. We "[hang] on to the past," Nietzsche writes—and the past hangs on to us. History is a "chain" we can't unload. We are never able to live entirely in a moment, for during that instant we recall a *prior* instant. The "return of," for Nietzsche, is disquieting, a haunting. "The moment that is here and done ... returns like a specter to trouble the quiet of a later moment."[324] Nietzsche does not deprecate history outright, but rather an insalubrious relationship to the past. When memory exerts too strong a hold (as memory theorists claim it does now), all we can do is remember.

The chain weighs us down. Memory depletes our vitality, impedes our ability to act. And so we must, at times, try to forget. ("There is a right time to forget as well as [a] right time to remember.")[325]

History is a burden, but it is something we need. The historical sense has its advantages (*Nutzen*). Nietzsche distinguishes three interpretive approaches, three ways that history can assist us. Monumental history, a history of great men and women (*Übermenschen*), incites us to recall the heroic deeds of an earlier time and those who performed them. An admiration for a monumental past allows us to imagine that we can achieve important things in our turn. Change is possible—and we can bring it about.[326] Nietzsche calls the second history "antiquarian." The historian so described is a "mad collector" of artifacts who breathes a "moldy air." Hidden away in the archive, in the bowels of the museum, the antiquarian knows how to preserve life but not how to create it. He is so engaged in this obsessive activity that he is unable to arrange these artifacts into a meaningful order, a usable past.[327] He suffers from that "indolence of the heart" that Benjamin ascribes to the historicist who is so impressed with what others have done that he is unable to do anything himself.[328] About the third type Nietzsche has this to say:

> Man must have the strength to break up the past, and apply it, too, in order to live. He must bring the past to the bar of judgment, interrogate it remorselessly, and finally condemn it.[329]

Critical history is an expression of the life-impulse. It investigates the past "remorselessly" and judges the evidence. The critical impulse *tears down* the past. ("The same life that needs forgetfulness sometimes needs its destruction.") One could well describe the third type of history as revolutionary, as modernist. The critical historian is a ruthless character, who thinks nothing of putting a "knife" to the "roots" of a past that is no longer useful.[330]

It seems that Nietzsche favors the third history. An expression of the life-force, critical history is violent forgetting; it is the revolutionary dream of "being new." Active forgetting is what futurist modernism did. And so Nietzsche has been blamed for modernism's worst excesses, as if it were but a simple step from *On the Use and Abuse of History for Life* to F. T. Marinetti's "Futurist Manifesto," that savage expression of contempt for everything that is old.[331] Yet as Nietzsche, most brilliant of aphorists, insists: "A leaf is continually dropping out of the volume of time and fluttering away—and suddenly it flutters back into the man's lap."[332] His metaphor of time as a book, and of a moment as a leaf that drifts away only to return unbidden and disturbing, is a time that is impossible to hold onto and just as impossible to forget. History so construed is a Faulknerian web of crimes and misdemeanors passed from one period to another, and from one generation to another. "As we are merely the resultant of previous generations, we are also the resultant of their errors, passions, and crimes."[333]

Each of these concepts is relative; each has its benefits and costs. Monumental history reminds us that we can achieve greatness, yet it diminishes the present. Antiquarian history is both a spirit of reverence and an unhealthy fixation on the fragmentary, the artifact, the ruin. Critical history disrupts our fixation on the past. Without this impulse, nothing new or original can come about. ("No artist will paint his picture, no general will win his battle.")[334] But critical history is blind to itself, for it falsely imagines that we can extricate ourselves from the influence of earlier eras and generations; the past does not release its hold so willingly.[335]

We need all three kinds of history, Nietzsche says: a proper combination yields a past that we can use. Many practices of return strike a Nietzschian balance among these models.[336] The art of Gmelin, for example, conceives the Sixties as monumental history, a time when "everything was possible," and as antiquarian history (his inheritance of Otto's archive prompted his current work).[337] But the critical impulse also animates Gmelin's practice as he interrogates the mythologies around Sixty-eight. The slightly bored affect of the runners in the second film, the absence of a public in the closing shot, the disappearance of the flag behind the Stockholm city hall: as we compare this version of the run with the earlier one, we begin to grasp the profound differences between the Sixties and the contemporary, and the beginning of a difference between the time of the reenactment and time of the work's projection. The "present" depicted in the second film (the year 2002, when the second film was made) already seems slightly distant. Already the post–September 11 era is starting to feel like a "recent past." Already a *Farbtest* (*Rote Fahne III*) has been made (reenacted by Conradt in Venice in 2003), a *Farbtest IV* (by Conradt in Sulmona, Italy, in 2007), a *Farbtest V* (Hong Kong, 2007), a *Farbtest VI* (Berlin, 2007), and a *Farbtest VII* (Beijing, 2008).[338] Each remake marks another "present" that looks back to the "original" moment from a new (or same) place. The red flag means differently depending on where and when it is carried. And each new flag run anticipates another. *Die Rote Fahne* is always *about to be remade*; it anticipates its revival at a later date. (This is its "horizon of expectation," as Koselleck would say.) And with each refrain *Die Rote Fahne* retrieves the memory of the first run, of the first runners, of Sixty-eight and the Sixty-eighters, the generation who believed the revolution was just around the corner.

Yet the revolution did not come. The world did not change as Otto Gmelin, Meins, and Meinhof and their contemporaries imagined it would.

It did not yield to their radical wills. Even the most cherished countercultural values, the most extreme aleatory techniques, could be appropriated by the System they vigilantly opposed.[339] Once-radical works would take on other meanings as others performed them and exhibited them, and as they entered the canons of art history and the spectacular environs of the contemporary museum.[340]

A generation reexamines the time of childhood. A not-so-recent past is represented without illusion and nostalgia. Old videos and home movies are put on public display. The archive is rifled, its contents exposed. The evidence is presented. The Sixties return to be judged.

## Red Scarf Children

> ***Fluttering Red Flag* . . . red, a (rectangular) piece of solidified "blood" . . . I want people to look at it (think of it) as though looking at boiling water (boiling blood) from a great distance.**
>
> Wu Shanzhuan, "On the Space of Performance, Installation and Object"

Felix Gmelin's *Farbtest, Die Rote Fahne II* recovers a faded fantasy of the Sixties Left, a Western dream of China so remote we struggle to remember it. How have Chinese artists reimagined China then, a China awash in Maoist flags and banners and copies of the *Little Red Book*—a Red Ocean, as it was called? What are the Sixties for them?

Recent histories of the Sixties propose a "kaleidoscopic" view of that era. They attempt to map within a single volume a Sixties that unfolded on every continent and in every nation-state all at once, a Sixties of many different parts, each worthy of our attention. Like Jules Verne's Phineas Fogg, the reader of these accounts is propelled in a breathless circumnavigation of the globe circa 1968.[341] Yet the Sixties and its cartographies are complicated when we turn to China. The decadal Sixties, for example—a Sixties that begins in American accounts with the election of President Kennedy in 1960—is less resonant in a country whose history is blocked out in temporal increments equated with particular leaders and sweeping social policies. The Great Leap Forward (1958–61), Mao's catastrophic effort to collectivize and industrialize agriculture, resulted in the deaths of millions; lasting a miserable three years, it is reckoned a "period" unto itself. Sixty-eight, the seminal Sixties year in the West, is less momentous in China than 1966, when the Cultural Revolution began, and 1976, when the Gang of Four, the oligarchy led by Mao's last wife, Jiang Qing, fell out of favor. It may be that China has no "Sixties" in the Western sense, even as the figure of "China" is pivotal to the Sixties imaginary in the West. In fact, the avant-gardist ethos so prevalent elsewhere during this period only erupts in China after Mao's death and the Gang of Four's downfall.[342] Triggered by Deng Xiaoping's market reforms (1982–87), the heady period of democratization leading up to the Tiananmen Square protest and massacre of June 1989 is *the* pivotal era of countercultural activity in modern China. The Eighties—an era of retrenchment in the West—are arguably China's "Sixties."[343]

The Cultural Revolution was a revolution nevertheless, a major convulsion reaching across every sector of Chinese society. Conceived as a reenactment and fulfillment of the revolution of 1949 and previous efforts of modernization, it expressed a particularly Chinese ambition to achieve a state of "total modernity" dating to the founding of the modern Chinese state by Sun Yat-Sen in 1912—the achievement of a "new nation rather than a new epoch," as art historian Gao Minglu has described it.[344] The modernist impulse to transform society from the ground up was expressed in the language of Chinese nationalism. With the advent of this second revolution, the Chinese mind (*yishi*) would be transformed; the old values, the Four Olds, would wither away; the humiliations of colonialism and the gross inequities of the imperial and bourgeois past would be laid to rest. China would indeed "be new."

The Cultural Revolution had a shattering effect on aesthetic and literary practice. Scar art (*shanghen meishu*), a sentimentalized depiction of traumatic incidents in a Socialist Realist format by Chen Conglin and Gao Xiaohua; the placid still lives and landscapes of the "No Name" artists that quietly refute Socialist Realist conventions; the subversive little wood carvings of Wang Keping that deform Mao's iconic face into caricature; the "Political Pop" paintings of Wang Guangyi and Yu Youhan; the Conceptual (*guannian yishu*) activities of Xu Bing, Gu Wenda, and Wu Shanzhuan: all of these emerged during the decade and a half after Mao's death. It has been claimed that the post–Cultural Revolution era is also now in the past, as artists turn their attention to the remarkable changes that China has undergone in recent decades (its transformation into the world's second-largest economy; its breathtaking urbanization; the migration of millions of people to the new megalopolises; an erasure of traditional customs, artifacts, and spaces more sweeping than even the Cultural Revolution was capable of). And yet the memory of that strange time, the most tumultuous of modern China, remains vivid. Perhaps the Cultural Revolution has not so much "returned" as a subject matter of aesthetic and literary practice as it has remained a central reference *ever since*, slipping into history and becoming meaningful all over again, never ceasing to return.[345]

Classical theories of the generation are parochial, nation-based. Dilthey's Romantics share a sensibility, a point of view. Their mutual identification has not only to do with being born at around the same time and living through the same period. They share a cultural and linguistic identity, and a geographical identity.[346] In other words, what I have called the Sixties return cannot be understood apart from its spatial contours, the *locations* of Sixties experience and recollection: the practice of return is inextricably bound to place.

We have considered several. The Vietnam of An-My Lê (the country she visits as an adult and the "Vietnam of the mind" she re-creates in Virginia with her fellow reenactors); the Communist Albania of Sala's childhood; the Scratch Orchestra's peregrinations documented by Fowler; the massacre site of My Lai that haunts the narrative of Lê's "Love and Honor and Pity and Pride and Compassion and Sacrifice"; the college campuses documented by Davenport and Buckingham, and imagined by Hill; the Uganda recalled by Bhimji, and the Berlin of the Sixty-eight generation retrieved by Gmelin; the suburban kitchen in Massachusetts where my family watched nightly reports of body counts, riots, and protests: each of these "returns" is mediated by the imaginative recollections of the artist or writer who, whether or not he or she occupied these spatial and temporal coordinates, has attempted to retrace them, to walk backward, knowing full well that the destination he or she seeks is unpredictable if not unreachable, that there is no returning.

Children born into the Cultural Revolution grew up in the kind of circumscribed milieu that generation theorists consider fundamental to generation formation: a pre-internet and largely pre-television China of tightly closed borders, a China that subjected its citizens to the techniques of constant and relentless indoctrination. They were imbued from earliest memory with the memory of *another* generation and time more monumental than their own, the crucibles of generational identification according to Nora. Consider this passage from Jiang Ji-Li's memoir of that time, *Red Scarf Girl* (1997):

> My friends and I had grown up with the stories of the brave revolutionaries who had saved China.... We had often been sorry that we were too young to have fought with Chairman Mao against the Japanese invaders, who tried to conquer China; against the dictator Chiang Kai-shek, who ruthlessly oppressed the Chinese people; and against the American aggressors in Korea. We had missed our chance to become national heroes by helping our motherland.[347]

They were a belated generation; they had "missed [their] chance." The red scarves they wore—the scarves that identified them as a generation—were "precious" emblems, "soaked in the blood" of the revolutionary generation's martyrs."[348]

The red scarf—a sort of miniaturized, wearable red flag—interpellated the wearer in Maoist semiology. It projected the image of the Red Scarf Child *to* the child who knotted it around her throat, who perceived her own face in the mirror framed in a burst of vermilion. ("When I wore the red scarf for the first time, I constantly admired the red floating in front of my chest.")[349] The red scarf instilled revolutionary *yishi* (consciousness) in the

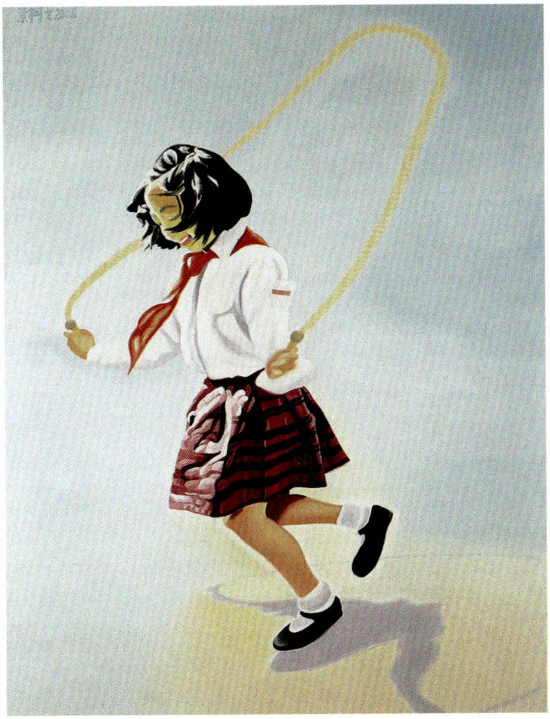

**Fig. 1.45.** Jing Kewen, *Dream 2006, #11*, 2006. Oil on canvas. Courtesy of Jing Kewen.

wearer, and a sense of indebtedness: Red Scarf children (or preteen Red Successors or teenage Red Guards) had missed the 1949 revolution, and were often reminded of that unfortunate fact, reminded of all they owed Mao and his comrades, who had saved China from its many enemies (the Japanese, Americans, capitalists, landlords, elitists). The Cultural Revolution answered and exploited a generational longing, a profound feeling of lack. It presented new opportunities for heroic action and new forms of excitement (now they could feel like "real revolutionaries"). Smashing the Four Olds was "a new battle, and an important one."[350]

Children and young people occupied a pivotal role in the Maoist imaginary, as the term "Red Successor" suggests. The successor is one who comes after. Who succeeds. Who *inherits*. The Red Successor carried the asymptotic project of revolution forward another step. The idea of the "successor" expressed a generational logic in the modern sense, a Marxian imminence; it invoked a future within reach yet always deferred.

What was the existence of the Red Scarf Child? Consider the *Dream Paintings* (2003 and ongoing) by the Beijing-based painter Jing Kewen (fig. 1.45). On the face of it, Jing's works reveal a palpable nostalgia for China during or preceding his childhood in Xian (Jing was born in 1965). Derived from snapshots and albums scavenged in flea markets, many of these works depict children at play, soldiers, or sitters in official dress—the sort of clothes a person posing for a portrait might wear. The excesses of the period are absent from these halcyon depictions. Jing depicts a buttoned-up, orderly China, a China unified in patriotic solidarity behind the deified Mao, a China that "works."

The opening pages of Jiang Ji-Li's *Red Scarf Girl* capture that moment. It is the spring of 1966. The Cultural Revolution has just been launched. A teenage Red Guard has recently returned to Shanghai from a pilgrimage to Beijing, where she and many other young people have been ferried on government trains to "make revolutionary contacts" and attend rallies. An audience has gathered to listen in a factory cafeteria, the twelve-year-old Jiang Ji-Li among them. The young woman wears a belted army uniform and a red armband. She stands on a dais beneath a banner inscribed in red characters: CHAIRMAN MAO AND THE RED GUARDS: THEIR HEARTS ARE ONE.

She recalls how, shortly after their arrival in the capital, she hears a rumor that Chairman Mao will make an appearance in Tiananmen Square, and hurries there. Others have heard this rumor. Within a few hours hundreds of thousands of students have gathered in the great plaza. The young woman waits until the evening; spends the night there. She waits until the end of the next day. Then, a deafening cheer: Mao Zedong has finally appeared on the balcony of Tiananmen, the Gate of Heavenly Peace. Her voice quivers as she describes what happened next:

> He was right in front of me, up on top of the gate, waving to us. I was crying so much that I could hardly see anything else, but I could see him shining in his army uniform. And then, out of all the comrades in the square, he looked at me! He looked straight at me![351]

At the time, anyone who had the chance to see Chairman Mao in the flesh was reckoned "the happiest person in the world," Jiang Ji-Li writes. The young woman's description of that experience is so affecting that Jiang and the others break into tears.

The *Dream* paintings of Jing Kewen conjure this beatific state of mind. Many of the figures wear red scarves. Young soldiers pose awkwardly in their starched green uniforms. Two girls of middle school age, sisters perhaps, paddle a boat in a lake. A six-year-old skips rope. Her scarf encircles her neck and dangles on the diagonal in front. The luminous yellow rope rises up into the atmosphere. Absorbed in the pleasurable repeated motion of this activity, the jumping girl floats in the dreamy ether.

In *Dream 2007, Number 7* (fig. 1.46) three young women pose for an unseen photographer at a tourist site, likely the Gate of Divine Power

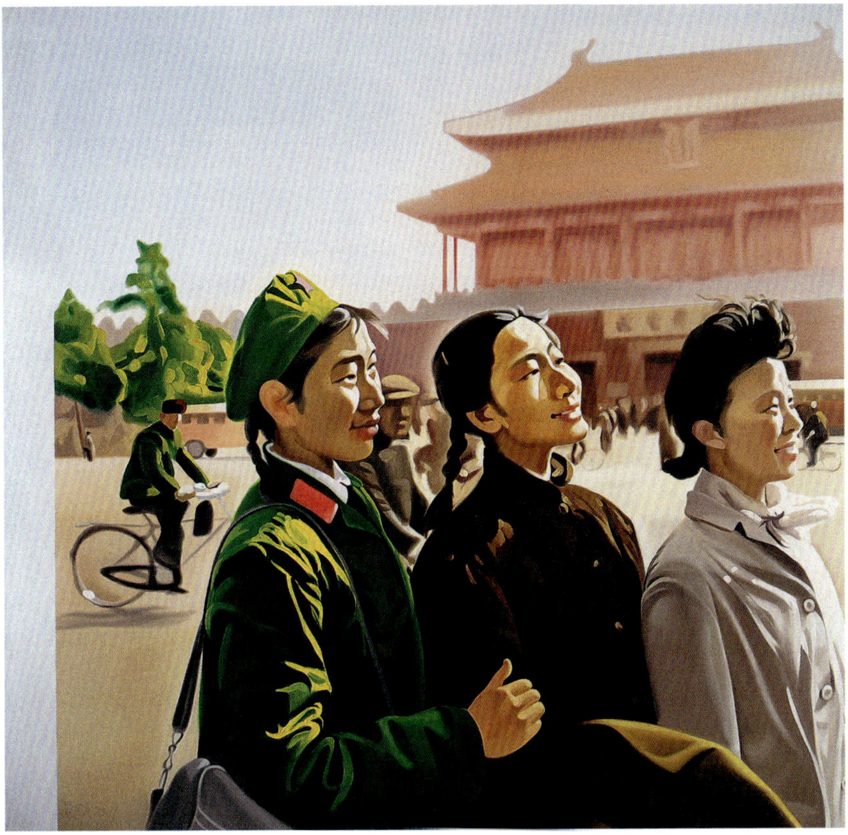

**Fig. 1.46.** Jing Kewen, *Dream 2007, #7*, 2007. Oil on canvas. Courtesy of Jing Kewen.

at the north entrance to the Forbidden City. The first of the friends is dressed in a soldier's uniform, the second in the brown garb of a peasant, the third in the gray jacket of a factory employee. Together they represent the three types of workers often depicted in propaganda then summarized by the formula *gong, nong, bing* (worker, peasant, soldier). Inspired, like Jing's other works, by a found photograph, the painting evokes in a viewer's mind the real women who posed for the exposure and the possible circumstances of their visit (perhaps they were on holiday from a provincial city, or attending a party-organized event). At the same time, an informed spectator—a Chinese person of a certain age—necessarily perceives these women as *types*, or embodiments, of a class-based subjectivity (as *gong, nong, bing*). The tonal atmosphere is ethereal here, too. Jing's China is typically lit by a warm afternoon sun. Shifts of value are exaggerated, on the verge of chiaroscuro. The folds of the soldier's uniform are contrasting tones of black, chartreuse, and daffodil yellow. The flesh tones of the women's faces bleed into white.

How they smile! Jing's figures invariably do. In fact, they smile *constantly*. Wide-eyed, their teeth exposed, their lips stretched, even contorted, into the same expression, they look more or less identical. Like the creepy laughing men who populate the canvases of Jing's contemporaries Yue Minjun, Geng Jianyi, and Fang Lijun, these young women can hardly be told apart.[352] It is ultimately undecidable whether Jing's works express a longing for this previous China, a China unified in patriotic ardor and collective purpose (which could not be more different from the current regime of privatization and crony capitalism), or whether these bizarre images are critical depictions of brainwashed youth; whether they mourn the loss of an obsolete system of thought and behavior that now exists only in memory, or look back at the Maoist era with horror. The interest of Jing's art, for me, is the instability of its point of view, its bizarre euphoria, its ambivalence.[353]

Other Chinese practices are unreservedly critical, such as Jiang Ji-Li's *Red Scarf Girl* and other memoirs penned by scions of "black" families that document in crushing detail the abuses that they and their families endured. Jiang describes the initial state of elation during the spring of 1966, when Mao announced the second revolution's coming. A crowd pulls down and destroys the sign of Shanghai's Great Prosperity Market to denounce the capitalist overtones of the store's name. "They stamped, bounced, and jumped with excitement.... We all laughed," Jiang Ji-Li writes.[354]

A subsequent scene hints at what is to come. Teenagers known as student inspectors, charged with enforcing the new values, accost a stylish young man on the street whose "bourgeois" appearance is incompatible with the new values. These enforcers measure the width of the man's trousers (too narrow) and denounce his fashionable two-toned shoes (too pointy). Eventually they cut up his pants with a pair of scissors and slice his shoes apart. "His handsome face blushed scarlet, then turned pale. A few times he bit his lips.... He stood on the sidewalk, awkward and humiliated, trouser legs flapping around his ankles, socks falling down.... Our eyes met. Immediately he turned away."[355]

The noose closes tighter. The grandmother of Jiang Ji-Li's best friend, the widow of a landlord, jumps to her death from her apartment. Herself revealed to be a landlord's granddaughter, Jiang is barred from becoming a Red Successor and is put through a "struggle session" by classmates jealous of her academic success. Her parents' home is raided by Red Guards, their belongings confiscated and destroyed. Her elegant grandmother spends her days in a public park, terrified of being discovered and abused. Her father, a professional actor, is tortured at his theater. Many Cultural Revolution memoirs follow a similar narrative arc: relative stability before May 1966; the mania of the early days; descent into violence; lives

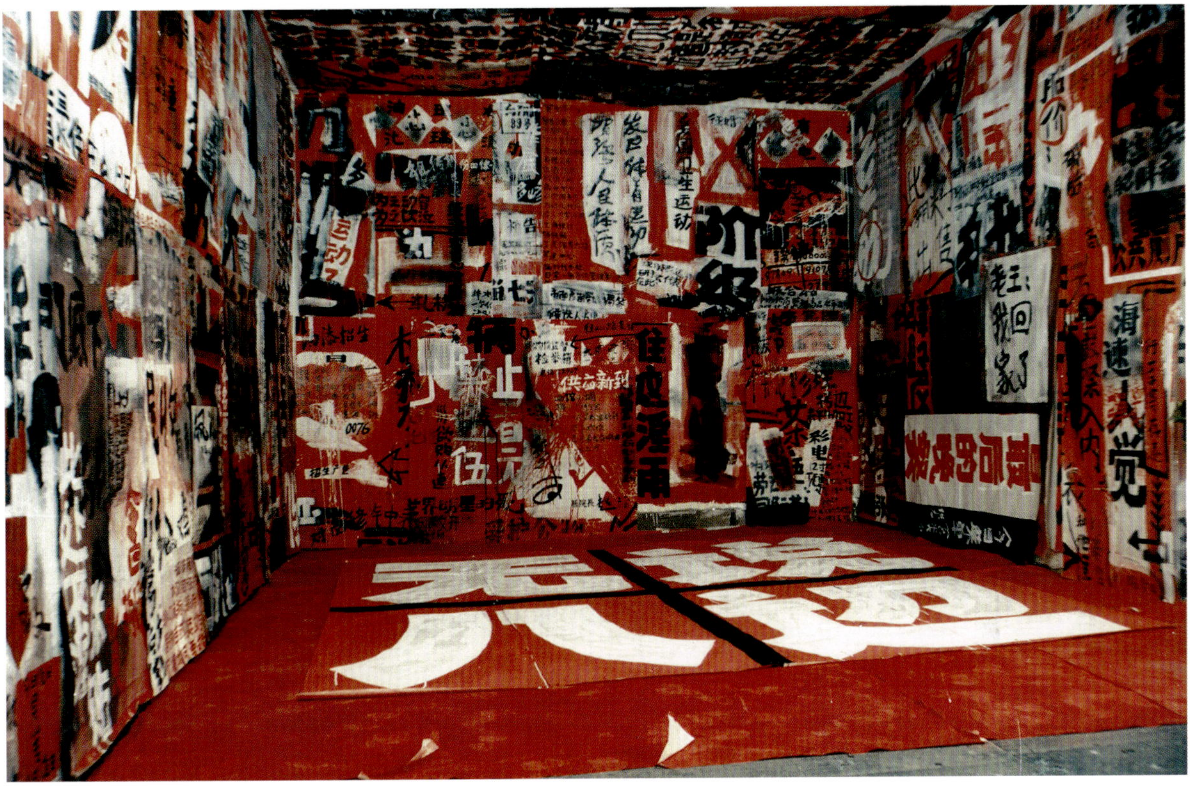

**Fig. 1.47.** Wu Shanzhuan, *Red Character: Big Character Posters*, Zhoushan, 1987. Courtesy of Wu Shanzhuan Archive at Asia Art Archive.

completely overturned, followed by emigration to the West. In books like Jiang's *Red Scarf Girl*, Moying Li's *Snow Falling in Spring*, and Da Chen's *China's Son*, and in the art practices of Wu Shanzhuan, Shao Yinong, and Mu Chen to which I will now turn, we are confronted with the delirium and terror and strangeness of truly revolutionary situations.[356]

I begin with *Red Humor*, a remarkable sequence of installations and events orchestrated by Wu Shanzhuan in 1986–88. In the most significant of these presentations, *Red Characters: Big Character Posters* (1987), Wu covered every surface of a studio space with posters painted in red, black, and white boldface characters (fig. 1.47). Executed a mere eleven years after the Cultural Revolution ended, the arrangement instantly evoked to a beholder the simple character posters, or *dazibao*, that had once covered the walls of China's public edifices and festooned the nation's streets.

Many of these texts were found phrases discovered by Wu and various friends and acquaintances in Zhoushan, a port located on an archipelago in Zhejiang Province on the East China Sea. At Wu's invitation, these participants (among them laborers, fishermen, and fellow artists) selected and wrote down the phrases of their choosing, an important detail, as we shall see. Wu plastered these sheets all over the room, even covering the ceiling and floor with these ersatz posters. Here and there a viewer glimpsed revolutionary maxims ("Exercise in strengths for class struggle," "To struggle with selfishness and to criticize revisionism") and the paired statements "Develop sports/athletic movement" and "Strengthen people's health," which hung side by side as they usually did in Mao's China.

During the Cultural Revolution such posters were ubiquitous. In Wu Shanzhuan's little room, however, these uplifting messages almost disappeared in a sea of messages—ads for wonton soup and steamed turtle fish, and for a house painting service; traffic signs ("You will be fined for crossing the street during a red light," "Passing forbidden"), nautical signs ("Watch shore ahead"), public announcements ("Notice: This afternoon no water"), and private communications ("Old Wang: I'm returning home"). Other posters contained Buddhist sutras and quotations of classical Chinese poetry, the title of a famous Western artwork (Leonardo's *The Last Supper*), and, last but not least, an amusing description of the artist, who had apparently decamped from Zhoushan, abandoning his artwork ("Looking for missing person: Wu Shanzhuan, male . . . long dark hair, wearing glasses, slightly dizzy").[357]

*Red Characters: Big Character Posters* is an emblematic work of the Conceptual (*guannian yishu*) vein of the '85 avant-garde, along with Xu Bing's installation *A Book from the Sky* (1989) and Gu Wenda's *Pseudo-Characters* paintings (1986). In the practices of these artists the rigid system of representation that arose during the Cultural Revolution was regurgitated, inverted, decontextualized, and, it has been claimed, purged of significance altogether. Wu's *dazibao* room marked the withering presence of the simple character poster as Deng's economic policies dramatically reshaped Chinese society, where commercial solicitations competed with and crowded out revolutionary messages. The poster "Seeking marriage" hung next to the Maoist exhortation "Patriotism and sanitation movement." The white-lettered text "Today's menu," rotated ninety degrees and placed next to the floor, appeared below the title of Leonardo's fresco, itself written in red characters and rotated ninety degrees. Inserted into this visual cacophony even the simple public announcement "Notice: This afternoon no water" made no sense.[358] No single register of meaning (political, commercial, personal, "high" or "low") prevailed over any other.[359] Nor any *voice*. (Who is the "I" who informs "Old Wang" that he or she is returning home? Who is looking for the missing artist?) Nor any reader. (To whom are these appeals addressed? to Old Wang? to consumers, diners, pedestrians? To everyone and no one.)

Wu painted four oversized white characters on large sheets of paper covered in red paint and placed the sheets on the floor. Thick black stripes divided the characters, stressing their autonomy as signs. Together they spelled *wushuobadao* (or *hushuobadao*), a phrase that means "Nonsense" or, more rudely, "Bullshit."[360] Stated somewhat differently, the characters declared that they did "not mean anything" or—a slightly different reading—that there was no reader capable of interpreting them.[361]

During the Cultural Revolution the Chinese language was made to speak in a single authoritative voice. The simple character poster communicated its message unequivocally. Wu caused the *dazibao*, the ultimate expression of that semantic reduction, to mean "nothing." More precisely, it had become a sign of its meaninglessness—a contradiction in itself. For the characters that spell *wushuobadao* successfully communicate the "sense" of nonsense, of jabberwocky. The four enlarged letters inform a viewer that they do not mean, and this causes the notion of nonsense itself to seem nonsensical. *Wushuobadao* makes just enough sense for us to "get it." Once we do, this phrase is no longer truly nonsense but a statement of the idea of nonsense, which, paradoxically, makes sense.

*Wushuobadao* yields an open-ended chain of questions without simple answers. What is alleged to make no sense? (the characters? the posters? everything at once?) Who is suggesting this? Wu? Do the enlarged characters on which a viewer stands reveal this "intention?" Why does Wu *revoke* the cornucopia of meanings suggested by these ads, epigrams, titles, messages, citations, and street directions? Why insist that none of it means anything?

To declare the Chinese character null and void after its extreme instrumentalization was an impossible task, which takes nothing away from the efforts of artists like Wu Shanzhuan, Xu Bing, and Gu Wenda to do exactly this, quite consciously: the various manipulations of the Chinese character in their works mimicked the textual interruptions of historical *dazibao*. Wu and his contemporaries have made pseudo-*dazibao* (or pseudo-characters, in the instance of Xu Bing) to "deconstruct" the simple character and criticize the Cultural Revolution's hijacking of the Chinese script. Each of these artists took a distinct approach.[362] Wu, for one, attempted to invent a different language outright—an alphabet of "red deficit characters." The red deficit character (*chizi*) stands both for "red" (*hong*) and "empty" (*kui kong*). It implies that the color red and its cognates (China, Mao, the Cultural Revolution, the red flag, and so on) have become meaningless signs, empty characters. But Wu does not stop there. He complicates this argument; he makes the paradox "red is empty" paradoxical.[363] The red deficit character is one "whose *literal* meaning has been deficited."[364] The character's ordinary meaning has been reduced. But rather than meaning "nothing," it means *less* than it once meant. It is the remainder of a process of subtraction, the meanings that are left over after its "red" meaning has been withdrawn. "Deficiting" the red character is thus an additive process (yet another paradox). Once the character undergoes this procedure, it is able to "exist comfortably as itself." It is no longer merely "red." It can mean other things—lots of things.

Wu's deficit character parodies Mao's simplified character. The reductive processes of each resemble one another yet produce diametrically opposite results. The classical Chinese script is bewilderingly complex, comprising some forty-nine thousand characters; its usage had been the province of the Mandarin elite (the English adjective "mandarin" implies "an ornate complexity of language.") During the Cultural Revolution the government attempted to establish a ground zero of language, a Chinese cleansed of Four Olds associations, a Chinese so aggressively legible it could be read instantly and by anyone. The designs of characters changed constantly as leaders searched for an elusive holy grail, an ever *simpler* script.[365] Wu has attempted to restore the semantic fulsomeness of the Chinese script by "deficiting" these characters even more. Subtraction, he discovered—the removal of a character's ordinary meaning—could have a converse effect. By withdrawing the *dazibao*'s normative associations, he undermined the closed system of representation in which every character was made to serve an ideological function. His maritime surroundings inspired him: in lieu of Mao's "red ocean" Wu envisioned a "silent ocean" of language, substituting a famous nautical metaphor of the Cultural Revolution with one I interpret as its negation. Unlike a restricted sea of "red" language, where every signifier refers to Maoist principles in a tautological loop, the silent "ocean" of Wu is porous, without borders, "formless," and "genderless," the artist once observed. It "accepts . . . anything" from "absolutely everyone." Anyone may contribute to it. And it is never full.[366]

The Zhoushan display of *Red Characters: Big Character Posters* established a temporal distance between its moment and the revolutionary recent past. Bromides such as "Exercise in strengths for class struggle" and "To struggle with selfishness and to criticize revisionism" appeared dated, if not absurd, by the end of the Eighties: already the Cultural Revolution felt remote.[367] But Wu's installation was equally a meditation on recentness, a time so slippery and borderless we have trouble defining it. By spatializing this encounter three-dimensionally—literally immersing the body in a claustrophobic environment of enlarged simple characters—Wu forced the few viewers who were lucky enough to see his installation into a mnemonic confrontation with a China literally papered over in edifying and hortatory messages, a China they remembered all too well.

"Red is for our memories," Wu has written.[368] His poster room was indeed a theater of memory. In the Zhoushan *dazibao* room, recollections of a disturbing recentness, including traumatic memories, could be revisited and confronted. As suggested, Wu invited people he knew to contribute texts to this project; other signs were found in Zhoushan's streets. He asked his collaborators to make posters of these phrases, which he included in the installation. Drawing ersatz *dazibao* in their own hands, they no doubt remembered making real *dazibao*, as teenagers and schoolchildren were forced to do during the late Sixties and early Seventies.

Nowhere did *dazibao* have a more powerful presence than in elementary and middle schools. Traditional pedagogical methods being deemed as Four Olds, the making of simple character posters was a party-approved alternative to classical instruction, and the very surfaces of schools became stages of revolutionary articulation. Posters put on display one day were frequently replaced by others the next. Entire corridors and courtyards were papered over with *dazibao*. In the yard of Jiang Ji-Li's Shanghai middle school, posters "hung like flowers" from tree branches. "Long ropes strung across the playground were covered with still more *dazibao*, looking like laundry hung out to dry."[369] In Xining, a city in the mountainous Qinghai-Tibet Plateau where the photographer Shao Yinong grew up, simple character posters crowded the walls of the school next to his parents' apartment. Eventually they reached as high as Shao's second-floor window. ("If I stretched out my hand I could easily touch them.")[370] *Red Characters: Big Character Posters* evoked the tactility of the *dazibao* and its arresting visuality. In Wu's Zhoushan presentation, the simple script migrated from the wall to the ceiling, and even to the floor, and to the surfaces of common things.[371]

"Rolls of white paper, dozens of brushes, and many bottles of red and black ink were brought into the classroom," Jiang Ji-Li recalls. She adds: "Teachers were nowhere to be seen."[372] Teachers and professors were among the principal targets of *dazibao,* as Jiang suggests. The aim of these attacks was to single out instructors who had allegedly polluted students' minds with "bourgeois" thoughts and consumerist longing. One did not learn to write then simply to achieve linguistic competence: one mastered the Chinese script in order to criticize, to denounce.

I am fascinated by a photograph of the Zhoushan installation in which Wu appears (fig. 1.48). The simple characters on the floor are so large that the crouching artist seems almost childlike in comparison. (The character he kneels on, *shuo*, means "to say" or "to speak.") Wu evokes a streetscape covered in slogans and denunciations, a world papered over in harsh language. The simple character poster exerted a cognitive and psychological domination on adults and children alike. It was a form of semantic violence, and a perpetrator of violence. From the beginning the *dazibao* was a platform for *ad hominem* attacks, like the notorious sweater knitted by Dickens's Madame Defarge, inscribed with the names of her

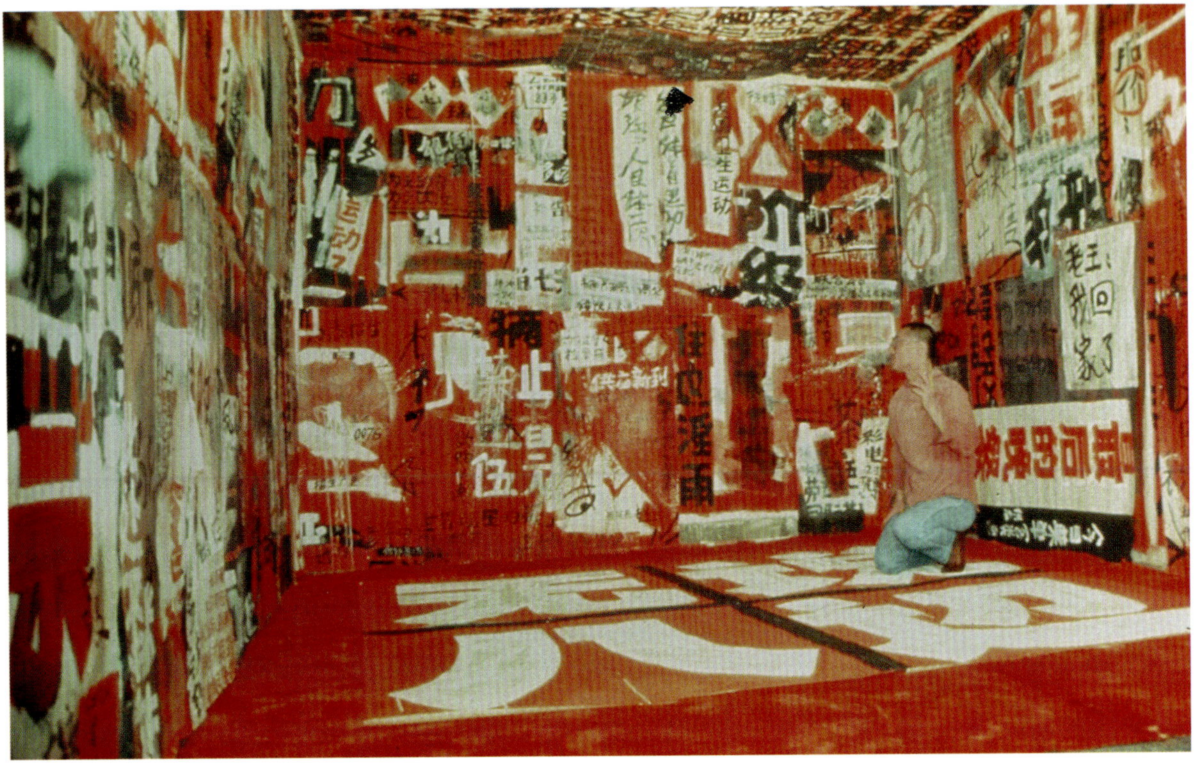

**Fig. 1.48.** Wu Shanzhuan, *Red Character: Big Character Posters*, Zhoushan, 1987. Courtesy of Wu Shanzhuan and Asian Art Museum, San Francisco.

enemies.[373] In the worst instances, and there were many, a person's name was written upside down in red and crossed out with a large X. With a simple turn of phrase or inversion of characters the person's ideological commitments were questioned, his or her life placed at risk. By the time one saw someone's name treated so disrespectfully it was likely he or she was dead. "If you wanted to kill somebody, you did it not by gun but by brush," recalls Xu Bing, whose father, a distinguished historian, lost his position at Beijing University during this period. (The young Xu eventually became an adept maker of *dazibao* to atone for his "black" background.)[374]

Workers pointed fingers at coworkers, neighbors at neighbors. Children condemned other children. Arriving at school one day, Jiang Ji-Li and her classmates are instructed to criticize their teachers. She writes down their names on a sheet; she considers whether any of them opposed the party or Chairman Mao. She cannot denounce any of them, and she pays a price for her integrity. A few days later a *dazibao* is displayed at the playground. The large red characters had the appearance of "blood." The poster imputes an improper sexual relationship between an older male teacher "and his favorite student, Jiang Ji-Li."

> I suddenly felt dizzy. Relationship? Me? A relationship with a male teacher? The whole world faded before my eyes.... A shaft of evening sunlight flashed on my name. The characters danced before my eyes, growing larger and redder, swallowing me up.[375]

The condemned were brought to assembly halls and public squares for struggle sessions, where they were forced to wear dunce caps painted with calumnious characters and shame necklaces of large wooden beads. Signs attesting to their crimes were hung around their necks.[376] A few decades later, Wu Shanzhuan and his collaborators reenacted the sadomasochistic subject-positions of those dreaded rituals. By playing both "red" and "black" characters, the artist and the other performers caricatured this Manicheistic system; in so doing, they revealed the capricious nature of identity itself in Maoist society, where a person once held in favor could easily and suddenly become a figure of opprobrium, fighting for his or her life.

In preparation for his performance *Windy Red Flags—Oath* (1987), for example, Wu created a phony revolutionary meeting hall hung with red flags and fake *dazibao*. He played a new party member taking an oath of allegiance beneath a red flag in one performance, and a local party chairman giving a speech in yet another. Inversely, in *Windy Red Flags—Violent Criticism*, he appeared as a revisionist "ox ghost" or "snake demon" being interrogated by Red Guards, bent over in humiliation, his arms bound behind his back. Eventually his character confessed to his "crimes" (fig. 1.49).[377] The Cultural Revolution did not seem far away after all. Wu, who

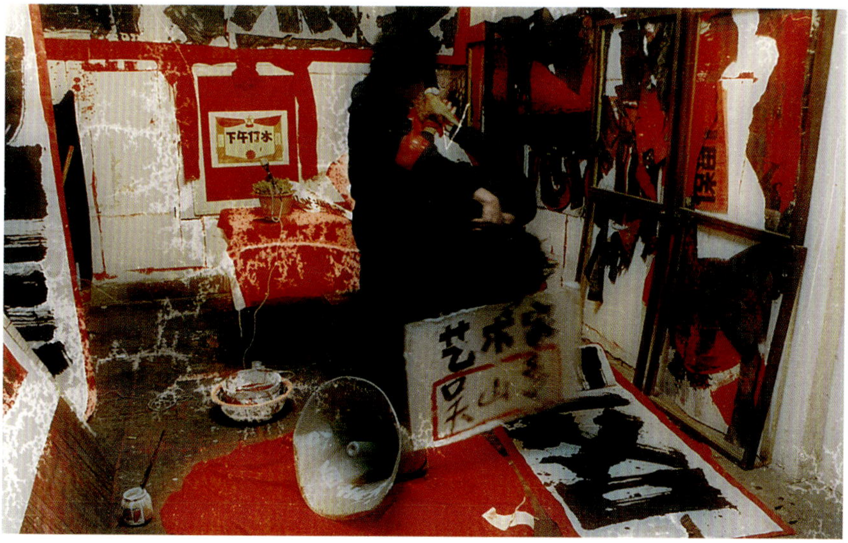


**Fig. 1.49.** Wu Shanzhuan, *Windy Red Flags—Violent Criticism*, Zhoushan, 1987. Courtesy of Wu Shanzhuan Archive at Asia Art Archive.

was born in 1960, remembered it. The other performers remembered it. Visitors to his studio remembered it. *Red Humor*—the poster room and its related installations and performances—began the process of historicizing the era of the *dazibao*, even as it incited recollections of a violent recentness that remained uncomfortably close.

*Red Humor* was very much of its time. What is the fate of these works as the Cultural Revolution becomes increasingly distant? Are they doomed to obsolescence, like the *dazibao* that Wu remade, parodied, and recontextualized in his Zhoushan project?

Consider the subsequent fortunes of Wu's installation. Following its initial presentation in 1987, *Red Characters: Big Character Posters* underwent a severe alteration after Wu emigrated to the West, like so many other artists of his generation, in response to the massacre of pro-democracy protesters during the notorious "June 4th incident." He presented a second version of *Red Characters: Big Character Posters* in a traveling exhibition in the United States.[378] Wu mounted the original posters that he had managed to save onto long scrolls and added new material. The version that he exhibited at the Asia Art Museum in San Francisco in 1999 consisted of two of these scrolls mounted in discrete registers on three walls (fig. 1.50). Where at Zhoushan Chinese characters plastered every available surface, in the San Francisco presentation portions of wall and the ceiling were left bare, and a carpeted floor replaced the four oversized characters. White walls and track lighting enhanced the elegance of the arrangement. The anarchic, unbridled messiness of the original version was no longer in evidence.

A white wooden plaque printed with black letters (such as one often saw at the entrances to hospitals or official buildings during and after the Cultural Revolution) announced the work's title. A second plaque bore the bland, talismanic text *This Afternoon No Water*. The characters of this announcement appeared stitched in yellow on a red cloth attached to the wall, disrupting the strict red, black, and white palette of the Zhoushan work. Additional texts—such as the phrase "Tear down"—located the work in a different "present," circa 1999, alluding to the policy of aggressive urbanization instigated under China's latest leader, Jiang Zemin, whose wanton destruction of old buildings throughout China proved as effective an erasure of the past as anything Mao envisioned. Wu introduced other new elements in San Francisco: a selection of ceramics decorated with simple characters arranged on a pedestal and a pile of posters with multicolored ads stacked on the floor, yet another departure from the revolutionary palette of the first version.

The traveling installation *Red Humor* was less compelling than the original, in part because the artist was not always present to install it.[379]

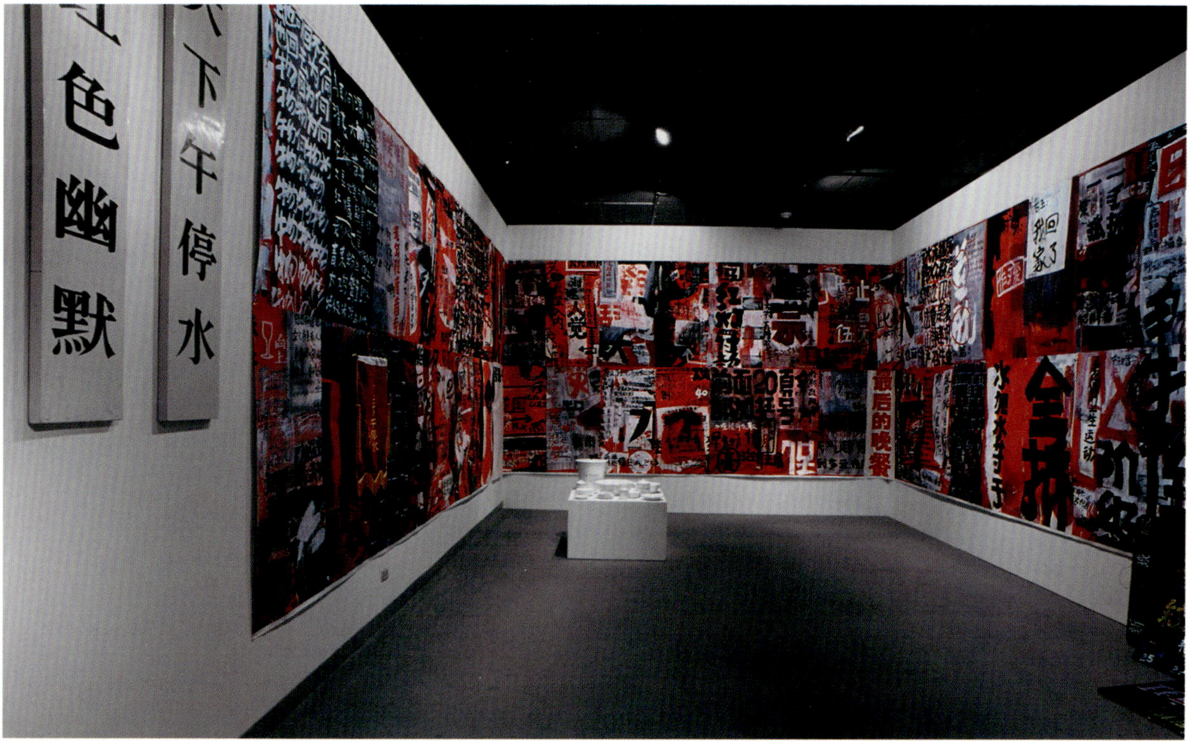


**Fig. 1.50.** Wu Shanzhuan, *Red Character: Big Character Posters*, installed at Asian Art Museum, San Francisco, 1999. Courtesy of Wu Shanzhuan and Asian Art Museum, San Francisco.

Transferred from China to North America more than a decade after Wu made it, from the private space of his studio, where it was experienced by an intimate circle of friends and collaborators, to an institutional setting, the *dazibao* room had in effect become a different work, one that embodied not one era but several: the periods of Mao, Deng, and Jiang (the Cultural Revolution, the Eighties, and the millennial present, respectively). *Red Humor* now spoke not only of the period of Wu's childhood, the era of Cultural Revolution euphoria and terror, but also of the artist's exilic existence. The original version had become a period piece, an artifact of a now-defunct Chinese avant-garde (repressed at home, globally dispersed) and the democracy movement led by Wu's contemporaries, so viciously suppressed at Tiananmen Square.

•

> A colleague of my mother's once took me to a criticism meeting in an assembly hall that was crowded with people.... On the stage were people wearing boards around their necks and tall pointed hats, resembling rocket launchers; some were standing and some were kneeling. I did not know what was going on.[380]

*I did not know what was going on*, the photographer Shao Yinong remarks of the struggle session he witnessed as a boy in Xinghai—the unsettling memory of people on a stage standing and kneeling, wearing signboards and tall pointed hats. *I didn't know what was going on*, Gmelin observes of his boyhood encounter with Meinhof and Meins in his parents' smoke-filled apartment in Berlin. I myself didn't know how to read a photo of a girl kneeling behind a boy lying on the ground, an image, I later learned, of the student protester Jeffrey Miller shot dead by the National Guard at Kent State University, one of several distant memories, mere snapshots, that have never left me, and which, never fading entirely, instigated the writing of this book. (I consider this image in part 2.) We often go to great lengths to understand impressions such as these, glimpses of something not understood, events that elude our comprehension. Practices of return disinter these half-buried recollections, uncover what was partially hidden. They arrange these images into a narrative, a work of art, a composition. The "return to" is the search for a form, the aesthetic embodiment of a memory that won't go away.

In the case of Shao Yinong, the mental image of that criticism session in Xining would catalyze the artist's rigorous investigation of an obsolete architectural form, the assembly hall, the setting of that unforgettable tableau. To research their photographic series *Assembly Halls* (*Da litang*) (2002–6), Shao and his collaborator Mu Chen reconstructed the itineraries of *Geming Dachuanlian*, the travels undertaken by teenagers to sites of revolutionary significance during the Cultural Revolution.[381] Just as John Malpede reimagined Robert Kennedy's Poverty Tour in eastern Kentucky, stopping at every town and hamlet visited by the senator and his entourage, so too Mu and Shao walked in the footsteps of Red Guards in Jiangxi, Shanxi, Fujian, and Guizhou provinces, documenting the hundreds of assembly halls they came upon during these trips. Their research lasted three years. Shot with wide-angle lenses from the deepest point in these interiors, these exposures recall Hiroshi Sugimoto's frontal depictions of old movie theaters and Bernd and Hilla Becher's taxonomic images of historical building types; yet Shao and Mu's photos examine a specifically Chinese architectural form, one indissociably linked with a traumatic recent past. They returned to places they had never been that felt strangely familiar; places that induced a queasy sensation of *déjà vu* ("The discovery of the assembly hall arouses thoughts of a new empty space—a memory of a familiar, yet unknown space").[382]

The artists' recollections of that time are distinct, reflecting the temporal and geographical specificity of their upbringings. If Shao (born in 1961) witnessed the most violent phase of revolutionary activity in a remote northwest province (recall his image of "people wearing boards around

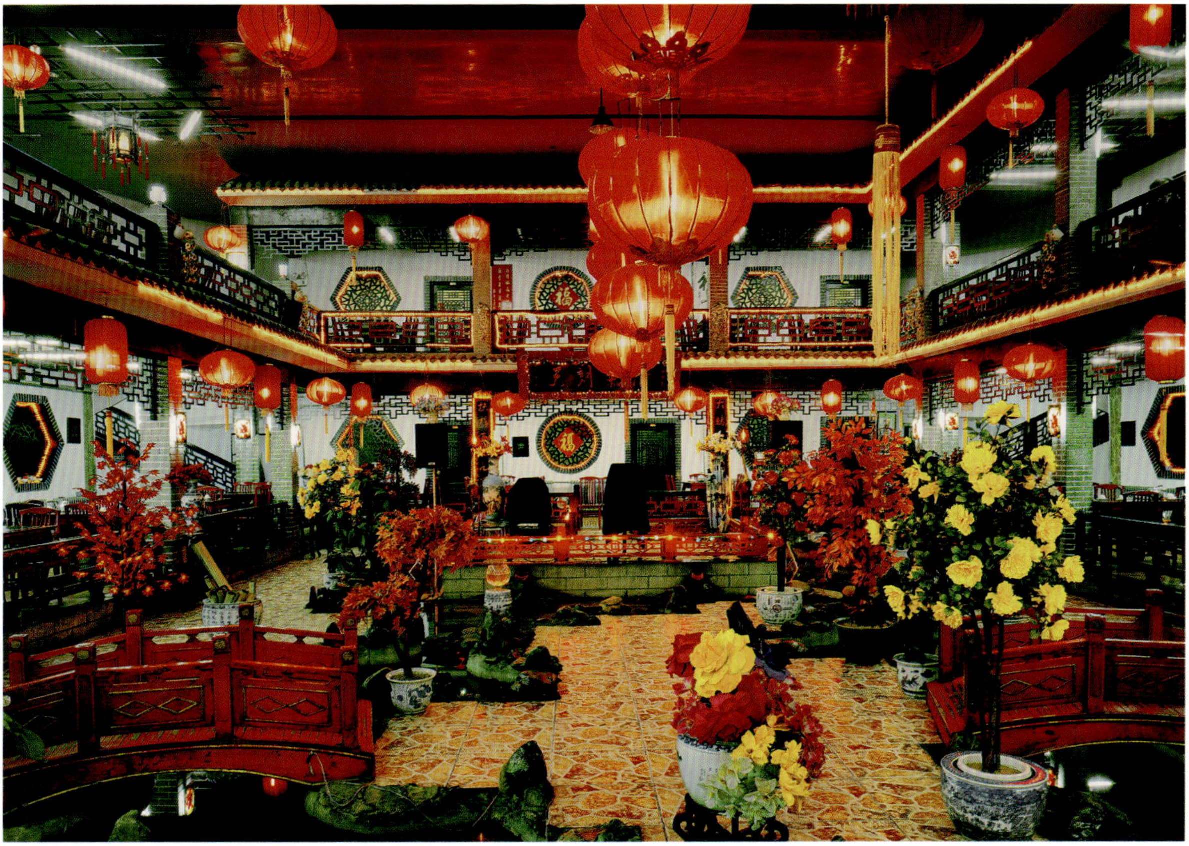

**Fig. 1.51.** Shao Yinong and Mu Chen, *Assembly Halls*: *Xiaoqiao*, 2002–6. C-print. Courtesy of Shao Yinong and Mu Chen.

their necks and tall pointed hats"), Mu, who was born in 1970 and enjoyed the relative privileges of an army officer's daughter, remembers the assembly hall in her hometown in Liaoning Province as a place of entertainment, where movies were screened and plays were staged. She recalls also the carnivalesque atmosphere of revolutionary spectacles—the clamor of gongs and drums, and streets sprinkled with heaps of confetti—and following these colorful processions on foot.[383]

Shao and Mu's photos of assembly halls document the various fates of these gathering places. One former hall was now a dusty warehouse littered with sandbags, another a cattle depot strewn with hay, another a Buddhist temple, a particular irony (traditional religion was considered Four Olds during the Cultural Revolution). Others had been transformed beyond recognition: the assembly hall at Tongji was now a banal lecture hall fitted with plastic yellow seats and a projection screen, the hall at Xiaoqiao a gaudy restaurant fitted up in faux imperial decor with red paper lanterns and phony bridges and goldfish ponds (fig. 1.51).

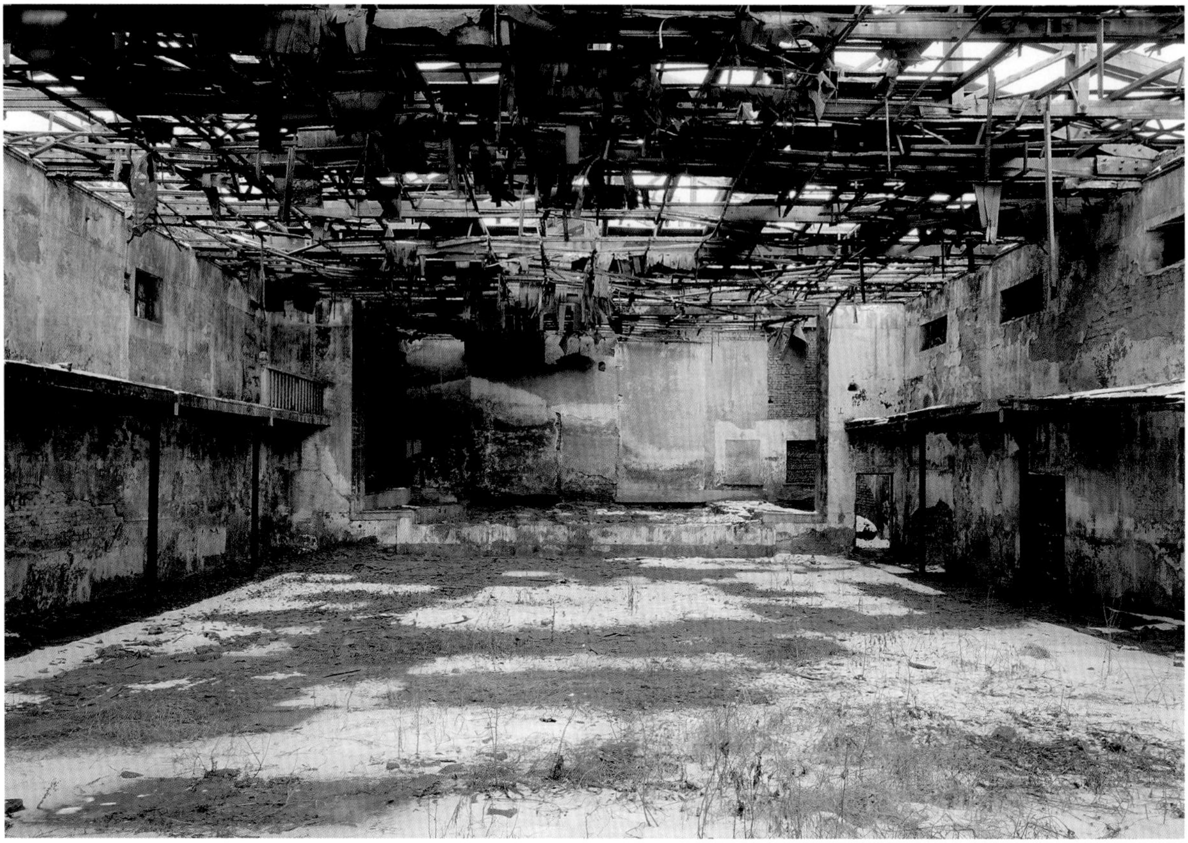

**Fig. 1.52.** Shao Yinong and Mu Chen, *Assembly Halls: Shengli*, 2002–6. C-print. Courtesy of Shao Yinong and Mu Chen.

Most of these buildings were razed not long after Shao and Mu visited them. The exposures they took are in many instances the final records of these felled structures.[384] Printed in highly saturated tones and scaled to our bodies, these images capture something of the experience of actually standing inside these haunted spaces, these places on the verge of erasure. The roof of the assembly hall at Shengli has completely fallen apart, exposing the interior to the harsh weather of northern China (fig. 1.52). We can almost smell the dankness of this abandoned hall, feel the chilly temperature, and looking down, perceive the fine white plaster powder clinging to our shoes. On the wall to our left, the red characters of Maoist injunctions fade into illegibility.

Our eyes drift down the chalky pavement to a raised area, the remnant of a stage. We imagine the cheers and screams of the audiences who gathered here, who watched party-approved films and model operas depicting "black" and "red" characters, where the latter invariably vanquished the former. Then, the real-life dramas: people with heads bent in shame and wearing dunce caps. The shouts of party officials and Red Guards bearing weapons. The catcalls of neighbors and colleagues. The interrogations, the abuse. The confessions of the unlucky.

Reenactment establishes the fiction that we can "see" the mechanisms of historical time. At its most effective, it inspires us to perceive, if only for a moment, our historicity—that we exist in and *through* time. It does this by establishing two moments in a relation, a temporal symmetry: at the moment of "return" we are brought closer to the prior time and distanced from it all at once. The respeakings of Mark Tribe, of John Malpede, and BLW, and the projections of Mary Kelly and Felix Gmelin cause us to imagine that we can hold two points in time (or entire periods!) in our minds simultaneously—an astonishing mental feat. The actor who recites Paul Potter's "Name the System" speech takes the same amount of time as Potter did, more or less; the Washington Monument stands behind the respeaker as it did behind the original speaker in 1965. A viewer of Tribe's video of that event perceives that his reenactment and the historical speech are not the same.

The work I will now describe, Cai Guo-Qiang's *Venice's Rent Collection Courtyard* (1999) is also a reenactment, one that transforms a masterwork of Cultural Revolution art into an event, a performance. Yet Cai's project complicates the model of temporal symmetry or doubling examined earlier in this book. As we experience the making of this work, the sort of comparative arrangement that causes a perception of simultaneity, of return—the sense that a previous era speaks to our own—yields to a vertiginous perception of history, of time as an endless layering of times. The past summoned by Cai's artwork doesn't feel "recent" or timely, but, like the strange, halcyon world of Jing Kewen's paintings, increasingly alien and distant.

Allow me to recall the origins of Cai's project. In 1964, the faculty of the Sichuan Fine Arts Institute created a sculptural ensemble of extraordinary ambition in the former manor house of Liu Wencai, a wealthy landlord during the prerevolutionary period in Dayi County in Sichuan Province. In his "Talks at the Yenan Forum on Literature and Art," Mao argues that artists and writers who wish to serve the revolution must remold their ideology by living with the peasants they aspire to represent. Living where they live, working as they do, listening to their stories, the painters and poets would begin to understand the class struggle experienced by these farmers: only then could they imbue their work with "proletarian feeling."[385]

The Cultural Revolution named this concept *Xiaxiang* (Down to the Countryside movement). The Sichuan professors took this principle to heart. They left their studios in Chongqing for rural Anren, where they lived among the local inhabitants and recorded their recollections of the injustices and abuses of feudal life under the dreaded Liu, a patron of the Kuomintang. They began to conceive a monumental work that could adequately capture this infamous past. Drawing on the traditional methods of Buddhist sculptors, they built the figures out of clay mixed with straw applied to wooden armatures, allowing each layer to dry slowly until the sculptures hardened; as a finishing touch, they added a preservative coating and placed black marbles in the figures' faces, another ancient technique. They now arranged the sculptures in the very courtyard where Liu and his men had collected usurious rents from the many tenants who had tilled the thousands of *mu* under the landlord's control.[386]

The original *Rent Collection Courtyard* was a Socialist Realist depiction, scrupulously detailed, of class types and class conflict. It comprised an impressive 114 life-size figures divided into six narrative groups, each staged where the event depicted had occurred. As visitors proceeded from one tableau to the next, they experienced a growing empathy for the peasants, an identification with their class position, and a mounting indignation.

In the opening scene malnourished farmers arrive with wheelbarrows and baskets overflowing with grain. Enormous sacks weigh down their bent backs. Liu's henchmen inspect the grain for "flaws" (peasants could be whipped if their offerings did not please the inspector). Now they place the sack into a "trick winnower," a machine designed to scatter a portion of the grain onto the floor, which would be collected by Liu's goons after the farmers left. The inspector places the remaining grain into a specious scale measuring a third less than the actual amount, all but guaranteeing that the peasants will never be able to repay their debt.

An old man approaches the landlord's elegant desk. A shifty accountant reckons his account on an abacus. The peasant's grain does not cover his rent; he is in arrears; his son—the strong young man standing just behind—is surrounded by Kuomintang recruiters who conscript him against his will. Liu observes this outrage; his face is a mask of cold indifference. A string of beads dangles from his manicured fingers, an emblem of the landlord's capricious power over the indigent peasants. More horror: another old man is whipped in front of the trick winnower. A blind man cries out as his granddaughter is sold into indenture. An indebted woman is thrown into the manor's notorious dungeon, reputedly half-filled with water.[387] A young mother is ripped away from her newborn to supply fresh milk for Liu's table; her own baby will surely starve.

*Rent Collection Courtyard* drew great crowds to the manor complex at Anren when it was first put on view along with the landlord's private quarters, pleasure chambers, and granaries. The sculpture was so popular that a second set was commissioned for the Forbidden City in Beijing.[388] Deemed a masterpiece of that era, along with Liu Chunhua's *Chairman Mao en Route to Anyuan* (1967) and other iconic portraits of Mao, the ensemble generated many more copies that would be displayed in every Chinese province and in socialist countries allied with China. Among the millions of viewers who saw one of these sets was a boy in Quanzhou in Fujian Province named Cai Guo-Qiang.

*Venice's Rent Collection Courtyard* is an elaborate and meticulous—even obsessive—"return to." Invited by the curator Harald Szeemann to participate in the forty-eighth Venice Biennale in 1999, Cai traveled to Anren to examine the original ensemble.[389] ("In the Sixties, when Cai was looking at the sculptures he was still in elementary school. This time, he made a special trip to see it again.")[390] Like the assembly hall photographers Shao Yinong and Mu Chen, he "returned" to a place he had never been in an effort to come to terms with a gripping memory of childhood: the recollection of viewing the Quanzhou set some thirty years earlier, a key moment of his indoctrination in Cultural Revolution ideology before he could fully grasp who and what the sculpture was meant to represent.

My claim that period memory is locational—that our recollections of the same time are contingent and distinct—is amply demonstrated by the practice of Cai, whose memories of that time depart from the disturbing accounts of Jiang Ji-Li, Xu Bing, and so many others of that generation who grew up in cities and towns where the principles of "Mao Zedong thought" were rigorously enforced. Quanzhou, a cosmopolitan port city located on the Strait of Taiwan, escaped the worst excesses of ideological enforcement. Four Olds cultural practices, including Buddhist and Taoist rites and ancestor worship, and classical painting and calligraphy, went on without interruption, albeit secretly.[391] Cai is "a *product* much more than a *victim* of his time," art historian Alexandra Munroe has aptly observed.[392] The Cultural Revolution did not persist as traumatic memory in his work; its influence was formal and political. On one hand, the imperative to "tear down" the Four Olds, to destroy the old in order to build the new, would inform Cai's aesthetic process, which examines the porous boundary between creation and destruction, making and unmaking.[393] On the other, the Cultural Revolution's dream of collectivity would remain a compelling memory as China radically transformed itself in the decades after Mao's death. In short, the art of Cai, and *Venice's Rent Collection Courtyard* in particular, explored from a Chinese optic the sorts of questions examined concurrently in T. J. Clark's *Farewell to an Idea*: the relative pressures faced by artists in communist and capitalist societies, and the various outcomes of the futuristic modernist dream of being-new (the Chinese fantasy of "total modernity," particularly). Not unlike the 1999 version of Wu's *Red Humor*, *Venice's Rent Collection Courtyard* gazed backward at the Sixties and Seventies from a measured distance; it marked a caesura between the China of Mao and the millennial China of Jiang Zemin, between a China under the grip of a rigid communist ideology yet unified by collective belief, and one that had embraced an ideology of unbridled capitalism and privatization. It forced into the open questions of Chinese artistic identity at the turn of the millennium—the divergent choices made by artists who had remained in China after the Tiananmen Square protests versus those artist-travelers who had established themselves as rising stars in a cosmopolitan circuit of exhibitions and art fairs, exemplified by none other than Cai himself.[394]

The decisions that Cai made as he reimagined the Dayi work were crucial. Rather than invite all the living Sichuan art faculty to collaborate in remaking the ensemble, he asked only the artist Long Xu Li to participate, and invited younger sculptors trained at Beijing's Central Academy of Fine Arts to assist them.[395] And just as the Sichuan artists had modified the original set for Beijing, and the Beijing set for subsequent presentations, Cai adapted the work for the cavernous galleries of Venice's Arsenale, arranging the figure groups on two levels (fig. 1.53). Cai's remake both continued and revised the principles of the historical work.[396] The Dayi set had generated numerous copies; it was, it could be argued, a work *made to be copied*. Unlike his predecessors, Cai did not allow the clay figures to harden. This decision reversed the terms of the project dramatically. Cai's version of *Rent Collection Courtyard unbuilt* itself. A viewer never perceived a *completed* work—only figures in the process of being made and in the process of falling apart (fig. 1.54). And so the experience of viewing it was quite unlike that of the historical sets. The decaying figures no longer related to one another. The scenes of mistreatment no longer made much sense. The narrative of Liu's crimes based on the peasants' testimony, carefully re-created by the Sichuan artists, could not be followed—which is not to say that Cai's version was not moving to behold.

*Venice's Rent Collection Courtyard* was less an "appropriation" of a monument of Cultural Revolution art (as it is often described) than a reenactment of the Dayi ensemble's creation, a performance.[397] A comparison was established between the time and place of the original set's making and its refabrication—a temporal symmetry. But now Cai complicated this arrangement with several hanging lanterns containing images of the Sichuan artists' sketches, which spun at different speeds.[398] Later presentations of Cai's work—such as *New York's Rent Collection Courtyard*

**Fig. 1.53.** Cai Guo-Qiang, *Venice's Rent Collection Courtyard*. Realized at Deposito Polveri, Arsenale, Venice, 1999. 108 life-sized sculptures created on site by Long Xu Li and 9 guest artisan sculptors, using 60 tons of clay, wire, and wood armature. Commissioned by 48th Venice Biennale. Photograph: Elio Montanari. Courtesy of Cai Studio.

**Fig. 1.54.** Cai Guo-Qiang, *Venice's Rent Collection Courtyard*. Realized at Deposito Polveri, Arsenale, Venice, 1999. 108 life-sized sculptures created on site by Long Xu Li and 9 guest artisan sculptors, using 60 tons of clay, wire, and wood armature. Commissioned by 48th Venice Biennale. Photograph: Elio Montanari. Courtesy of Cai Studio.

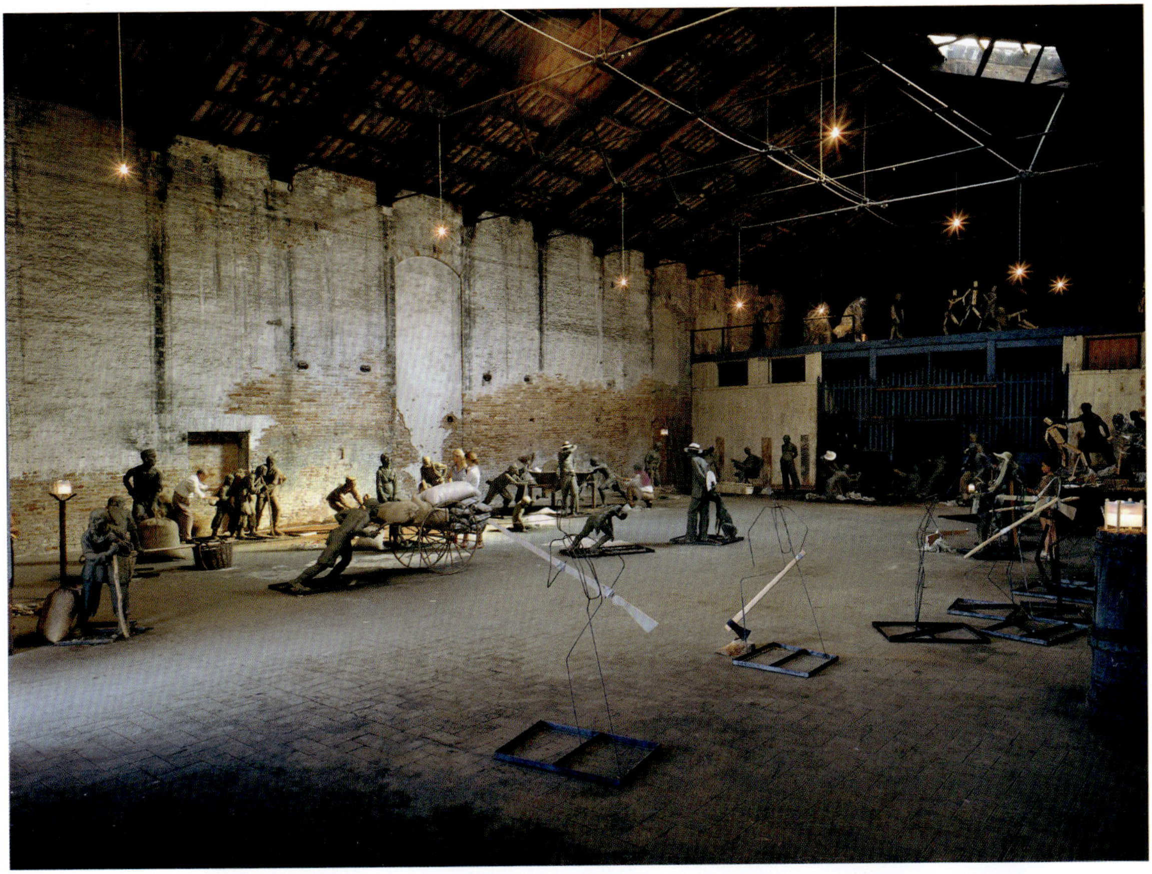

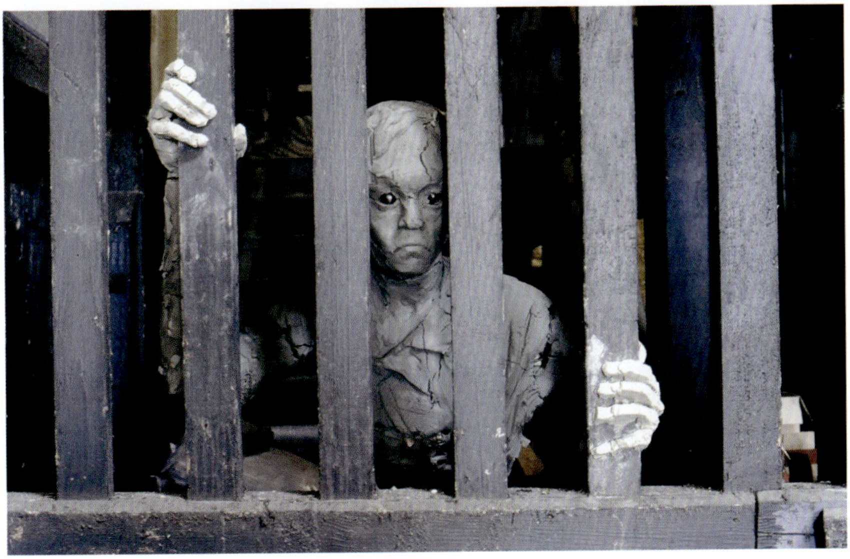

(2008) at the Guggenheim Museum and *Bilbao's Rent Collection Courtyard* at the Guggenheim Museum Bilbao (2009)—complicated this structure yet again (fig. 1.55). One lantern revealed a photo of the Sichuan work and artists, another the Venice installation, and at Bilbao, an image of the version recently installed in New York. A final lantern depicted the Bilbao exhibit in which I stood.

Cai's project was additive, forever incomplete. Not unlike the original *Rent Collection Courtyard*, which yielded copies throughout China and beyond, the Venice set was succeeded by other versions pointing to one another in a vectored manner. The Dayi set was a site-specific work made for the courtyard where the events occurred: the six *tableaux* were physically bound to their setting. But once the historical *Rent Collection Courtyard* was remade (and remade again and again), once it traveled throughout China and on to North Korea, North Vietnam, and Albania, it was transformed into a "mobile site" sculpture, a work of many parts pointing to one another in a spatiotemporal loop.[399] Cai embedded traces of his own earlier versions (and the many historical versions) into each new one: the sense of temporal simultaneity caused by other reenactments described in this book fragmented into a perception of time as multilayered and recursive. Entering *Bilbao's Rent Collection Courtyard*, I found myself surrounded by artists hard at work on sculptures of meticulous execution that were being completed or already coming apart. A memory of all the prior *Rent Collection Courtyards*, beginning with the 1965 "original," the Bilbao version was becoming a memory of itself.

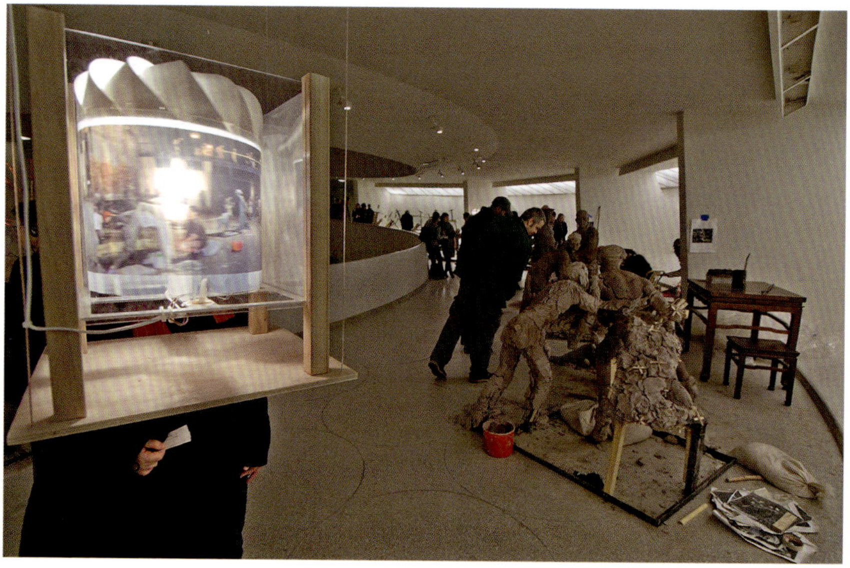

**Fig. 1.55.** Cai Guo-Qiang, *New York's Rent Collection Courtyard*. Realized at Solomon R. Guggenheim Museum, New York, February 2008. 72 life-sized sculptures created on site by Long Xu Li and 8 guest artisan sculptors, using clay, wire, and wood armature, and other props and tools for sculpture, spinning night lamps, facsimile photocopies of documents and photographs related to *Rent Collection Courtyard* (dated 1965). Photograph: Hiro Ihara. Courtesy of Cai Studio.

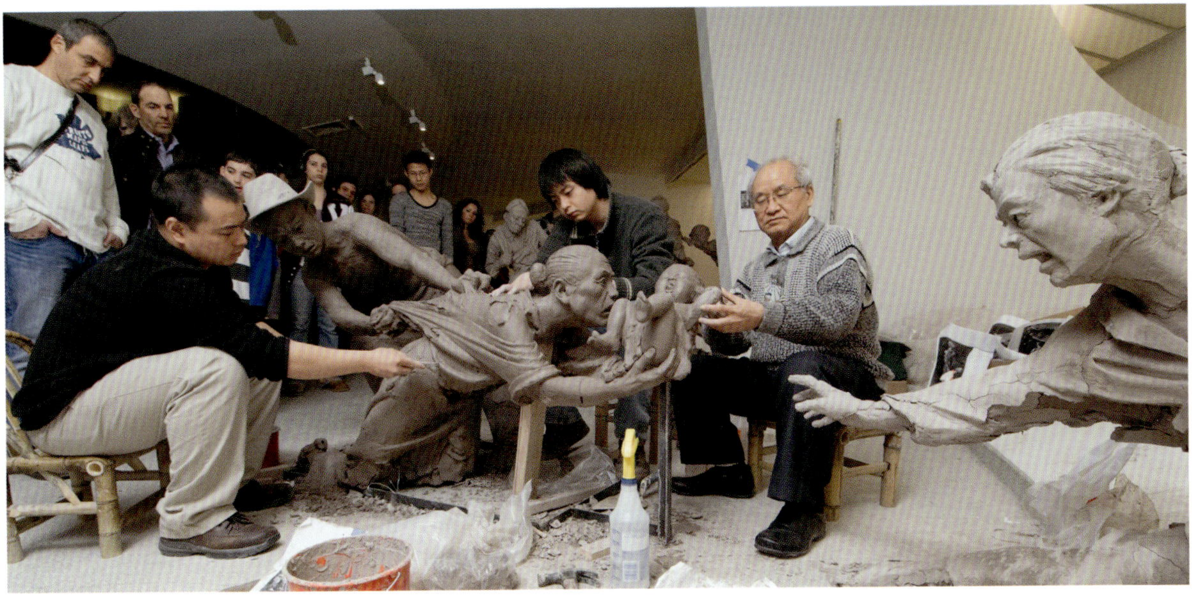

**Fig. 1.56.** Cai Guo-Qiang, *New York's Rent Collection Courtyard*. Realized at Solomon R. Guggenheim Museum, New York, February 2008. 72 life-sized sculptures created on site by Long Xu Li and 8 guest artisan sculptors, using clay, wire, and wood armature, and other props and tools for sculpture, spinning night lamps, facsimile photocopies of documents, and photographs related to *Rent Collection Courtyard* (dated 1965). Photograph: Hiro Ihara. Courtesy of Cai Studio.

Look at Cai and the others making a work they'll never complete. Look at the half-finished figures held together by flimsy sticks and wires—all that is left of limbs and necks. Look at their cracked faces, their peeling skin, their eyes protruding from hollow sockets. The marbles may drop at any moment. . . .

Look at the sheets of paper dumped on the floor like garbage, photocopied images of the Dayi set consulted by Cai and his collaborators. Look at the haughty Liu at his imposing desk, and at his heartless accountant with his ledger and abacus. Look at the old man who begs the callous landlord not to send his son into battle.

Look at the old woman with sunken cheeks whose daughter has been taken from her. The infant in her arms is crumbling. A crack rips the baby's face in two. It has no feet. Eventually the old woman will have nothing to hold, and her body will also collapse into dust. The figure she beseeches is missing. She reaches out to nothing (fig. 1.56).

During the Cultural Revolution these sculptures induced tears of recognition with stunning success—the response that Mao called "revolutionary feeling." The large audiences who saw the copies of *Rent Collection Courtyard* exhibited then could recall similar stories from their own lives or the lives of others, or from the books they read or the movies and model operas they saw.

Cai's *Rent Collection Courtyard* is affecting in ways the Sichuan artists did not necessarily intend. The sculptures that surround me are visions of entropy, intimations of death. Their faces are pockmarked, drying up; their mendicant gestures invade a viewer's space; their skeletal bodies are grotesque. In their twisted agony, their desiccation, Cai's figures tell a story that fails to make sense. His crumbling peasants no longer speak of revolution and utopic longings but of abandoned systems and stale ideas; and they recall a dream of collectivity, of artists joined together in a greater cause, misguided as that ambition may have turned out to be. Above all, these cracked, contorted bodies express the abiding ambivalence of Cai himself, who having absorbed the radical impulses of the Sixties in childhood emerged, decades later, as a highly successful player in a global art economy centered on the promotion of individual careers and aesthetic commodities. His *Rent Collection Courtyard* embodies such contradictions; it bears the memory of the revolution he saw with his own eyes and events he could not understand. It asks us to remember what happened in China then, even as the mnemonic traces of that cruel and momentous time are being erased.

I marvel as Cai and the others model lumps of clay into life-size sculptures. Transitional sculptures, not-quite-sculptures. Sculptures that never reach a finished state. That will soon disappear. I step on bits of clay and clay dust, and on the stacks of images of the Dayi work scattered beneath my feet. I walk among the gray phantoms.

# PART 2
# ENTROPY AS MONUMENT

**This contemporary obsession with ruins hides a nostalgia for an earlier age that had not yet lost its power to imagine other futures. . . . Yet this nostalgia persists, straining for something lost with the ending of an earlier form of modernity. The cipher of this nostalgia is the ruin.**

Andreas Huyssen, "Nostalgia for Ruins"

## The Smithson Return

A quarter-century after his death in an airplane crash in the West Texas desert, Robert Smithson reemerged as a figure of contemporary sensibility. Beginning in the Nineties, Smithson excited the sort of devotion that certain painters and poets do after their deaths. He became a figure of special interest to artists and scholars too young to have seen his works when he made them, and to have read his writings when they were first published in the pages of *Artforum*.

We had missed Smithson, but not entirely. Our acquaintance was one step removed. I met an artist who had interviewed him for her master's thesis, and befriended another who shared the memory of Smithson arguing with Carl Andre into the early morning at Max's Kansas City, and frequenting the bar's back room, where a Flavin sculpture cast a whorehouse glow on the red tablecloths and napkins and glamorous patrons—Warhol and his Superstars. Someone else pointed out the building where Smithson had lived with his wife Nancy Holt in Manhattan's meatpacking district at a time when the cobblestone streets, now lined with designer emporia, reeked of blood and rotting organs and garbage, and the crumbling piers on the river were places of crime and illicit pleasure.

These were passing glimpses, snapshots; they did not yet make up a composite image. During this period, when I began my doctoral dissertation, the long Sixties had slipped into the past. The fall of Saigon and the German Autumn had occurred just fifteen years earlier; to a young person these events felt like ancient history. Yet the more I researched that time the closer it seemed. The more I returned, it returned; the more I identified with it, the more I felt part of it. Many of Smithson's contemporaries were still alive and working then. I wrote letters to them, requested interviews. I visited their studios and houses, and took meals with them. I wrote down their remarks sedulously. I drew out their confidences.

I brought a cassette recorder along to these visits. My index finger pressed the "On" button, and the tiny wheels of brown magnetic tape turned silently, capturing the patter of our conversation. I wrote down their memories, and my memories of them, such as the recollection by an important artist of a dismissive review of his first show (he never forgave the critic), and the patronizing responses of the artist-writer Donald Judd to the work of many of his peers. (It mattered little that the individuals recalling these slights thirty years after the fact were world famous: the put-downs we experience in our youth leave a mental stain it is impossible to wash away.) And if the machine ran out of tape or was turned off at the interviewee's insistence, the taping device in my brain was very much "on." In my determination to develop my expertise, I fashioned myself into a sort of recording device, a memory machine, as if my ears were microphones and the retinas in my eyes were delicate plates coated with photosensitive emulsion. Those remarks and those images, those recollections of triumphs and slights, were stamped in my mind instantly and forever. I gathered these perceptions greedily, stuffed them in my pockets. I hoarded them like little stones.

Memories of the dead were the most precious of all. Smithson had died young. Eva Hesse and Gordon Matta-Clark had died young. As had so many others.[1] The works of these artists had become pivotal references of a burgeoning field called "contemporary art history." Many of these projects were meant to last for a short time; others had decayed beyond recognition, become ruins of their former selves. We could reconstruct these works from archival photos and reviews, but we would never *see* them as they had been seen. We would never know them for ourselves. And if the artist had died young we would never know him or her. That awareness—that we would never speak to Smithson, Hesse, or Matta-Clark, would never hear artists like Jimi Hendrix or Janis Joplin live—inspired a longing unique to the scholar of the recent past, a desire to know a person one might have known, or to experience their art new. (As Koselleck would say, our "historical times" overlapped; our "biological times" did not.) As I set out to write the history of the Minimalists and Post-Minimalists—the so-called greatest generation of American artists[2]—I came to identify not a little with the narrator of Henry James's ravishing novella *The Aspern Papers*, whose fervent desire to "know" a dead poet of a previous era has become the motivating force of his scholarship, and comes to dominate his entire existence—a mnemonic longing so intense it makes it impossible for him to live fully in his own time.

The fictional poet Jeffrey Aspern was a leading light of literary Romanticism. When James's story begins, at the end of the nineteenth century, Aspern's work is in the midst of a revival; it is "a part of the light in which we walk," the narrator, a young enthusiast, observes.[3] Aspern's death at the height of his abilities has only enhanced his reputation. He is recalled as a genius who died too soon; an aura surrounds his name. Aspern remains forever young, handsome, and gifted. He did not live long enough to lose his inspiration. He is a figure of infinite expectation, about whom one can say: "What more would he have achieved?"

James's narrator venerates Aspern, and the time when Aspern lived. The poet emerged "when the century was young"; that era appears infinitely more energetic and important than the narrator's present moment.[4] The age of Aspern is what Nietzsche calls monumental history: Aspern's talent was nourished in this fertile soil. Like Nietzsche's antiquarian who is always gazing backward, the young nostalgic of James's story pines for a period he has missed. In his effort to "know" Aspern, the scholar attempts to ingratiate himself with Aspern's aging mistress and her niece in order to procure Aspern's papers—the letters the poet wrote to her when she was young, now hidden in her desk. Yet his unscrupulous actions only catalyze the destruction of these precious letters, and the old woman's death.

When I met them, Smithson's peers had reached an advanced and (for the most part) contented middle age. They had lived long enough to develop the implications of their early work, and in many instances they had challenged the rigorous precepts and sober formality of their classic styles.[5] When I tried to imagine Smithson (the portrait of the artist in my mind was becoming clearer, more recognizable), I did not think of a historical person, as James's narrator describes Aspern, whose portrait shows a young man in a high-collared green coat and a buff waistcoat, the antiquated dress of the early nineteenth century. No: Smithson felt insistently *present* during the Nineties. His death did not seem as distant as the most famous Sixties tragedies, such as the assassinations of the Kennedys, Patrice Lumumba, and Martin Luther King Jr. It was an event that his friends still mourned. In their company, it felt as if he had died not so long ago.

On July 20, 1973, Smithson went out with a pilot and photographer in a two-propeller Beechcraft Baron to stake out the site of an earthwork at the edge of an artificial lake on a ranch outside of Amarillo. The summer afternoon was clear and bright. The desert shimmered in the heat. The whirring sound of propellers mixed with the hot air as the plane ascended.

We don't know what happened next. In my imagination one of the engines sputtered, and the pilot's attention was diverted. One of the wings dipped. At some point Smithson and the others realized what was about to happen. Then the plane rammed into a rocky hill a few hundred yards from the location where Smithson planned to build his work, and the men died instantly. The news reached New York that afternoon.[6]

March 2007. Utah. I have joined a group of tourists on a journey to the earthworks that Smithson and Holt built during the Seventies. Thousands have made this pilgrimage since Smithson completed *Spiral Jetty* and

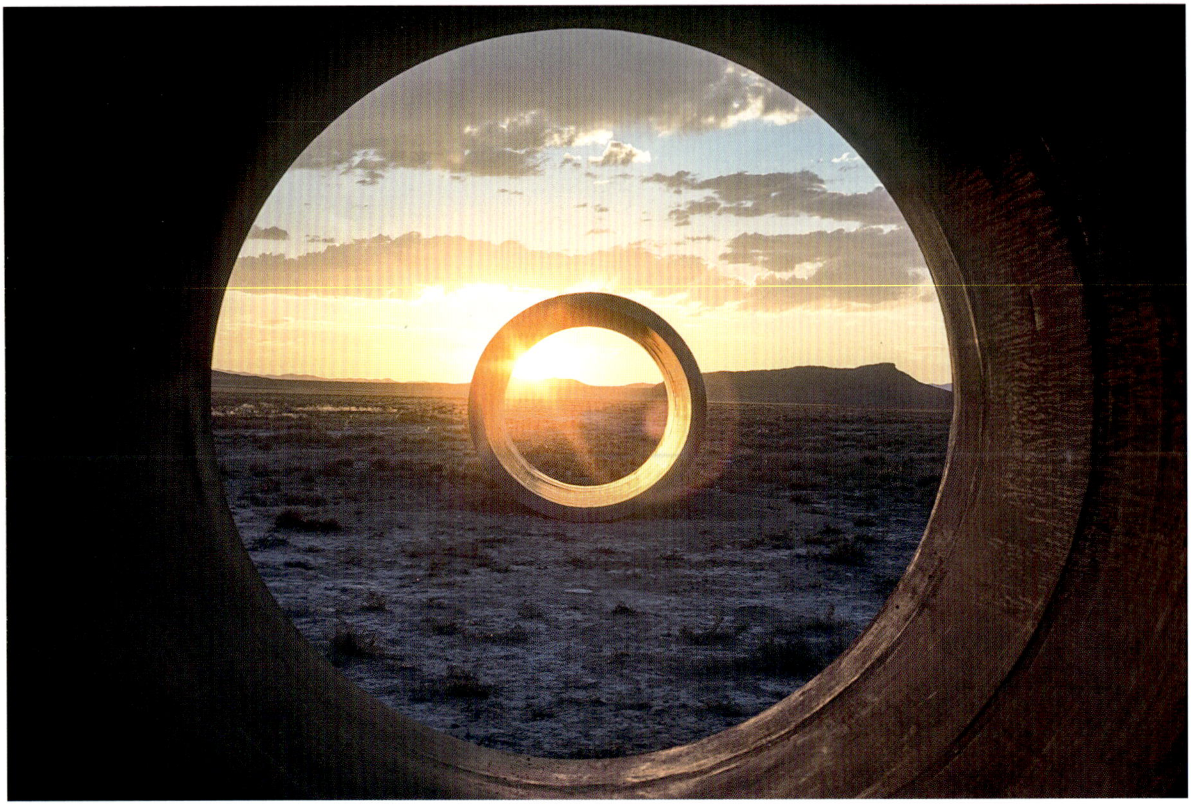

**Fig. 2.1.** Nancy Holt, *Sun Tunnels*, 1973–76. Great Basin Desert, Utah. Concrete, steel, earth. Art © Holt-Smithson Foundation / Licensed by VAGA, New York. Courtesy of Holt-Smithson Foundation.

Holt her *Sun Tunnels* on the northern and western shores of the Great Salt Lake. Our group includes artists and scholars and museum professionals. Holt is our guide.

We drive first to the Bonneville Salt Flats, the fastest surface on earth, where drag races are held and car commercials are filmed, a remnant of the enormous pluvial Lake Bonneville that covered much of what is now Utah during the Ice Age. (I grab a handful of salt; the crystals crumble in my hand.) We stop for a steak-and-potatoes dinner at the Maddox Ranch House, where Smithson and Holt often ate as he built *Spiral Jetty*, and drive past the abandoned Golden Spike Motel in Brigham City, where the artists stayed with Smithson's gallerist and patron Virginia Dwan. (A "for sale" sign hangs at the entrance. The cracked windows are boarded up.) We take a twisting dirt road north of the casino town of Wendover to a plain surrounded by mountains. In the distance we spy an arrangement of four large concrete barrels laid down in the middle of nowhere that Holt has transformed into a "somewhere": *Sun Tunnels*. We walk around and inside these gorgeous drums, and sit down (fig. 2.1). The walls of the cylinders are punctured with holes arranged in patterns evoking the constellations. Drops of sunlight quiver in the cool interiors as the earth moves.

A long drive around the lake's northern edge, past the Golden Spike Monument, and we reach Rozel Point down a dirt road rutted with rocks. The car crawls along a bluff. We fall silent as we look down at a large whorl floating in the gray water: *Spiral Jetty* (fig. 2.2). The work is hard for Holt to reach. Afflicted with bad knees, she has trouble navigating the terrain she walked with Smithson. She places her hands on my shoulders for balance as we make our way through this lunar landscape, as we edge down a plunging path slithering narrowly between black boulders. I feel the force of Holt's small body pressing on my back, the full weight of her sixty-nine years.

At the lake's edge she points uphill—"Bob drew there"—and I recall certain sketches Smithson made of the earthwork from this spot. On that summit, gazing down to the shore, he adjusted the work's size to its expansive setting, established its scale. He designed a taut spiral that sucked the lake water, shoreline, and sky into its churning shape like a

**Fig. 2.2.** Robert Smithson, *Spiral Jetty*, 1970. Great Salt Lake, Utah. Mud, salt crystals, rocks, water. Collection of Dia Art Foundation, New York. Photograph by George Steinmetz. Art © Holt-Smithson Foundation / Licensed by VAGA, New York. Courtesy of Dia Art Foundation, New York.

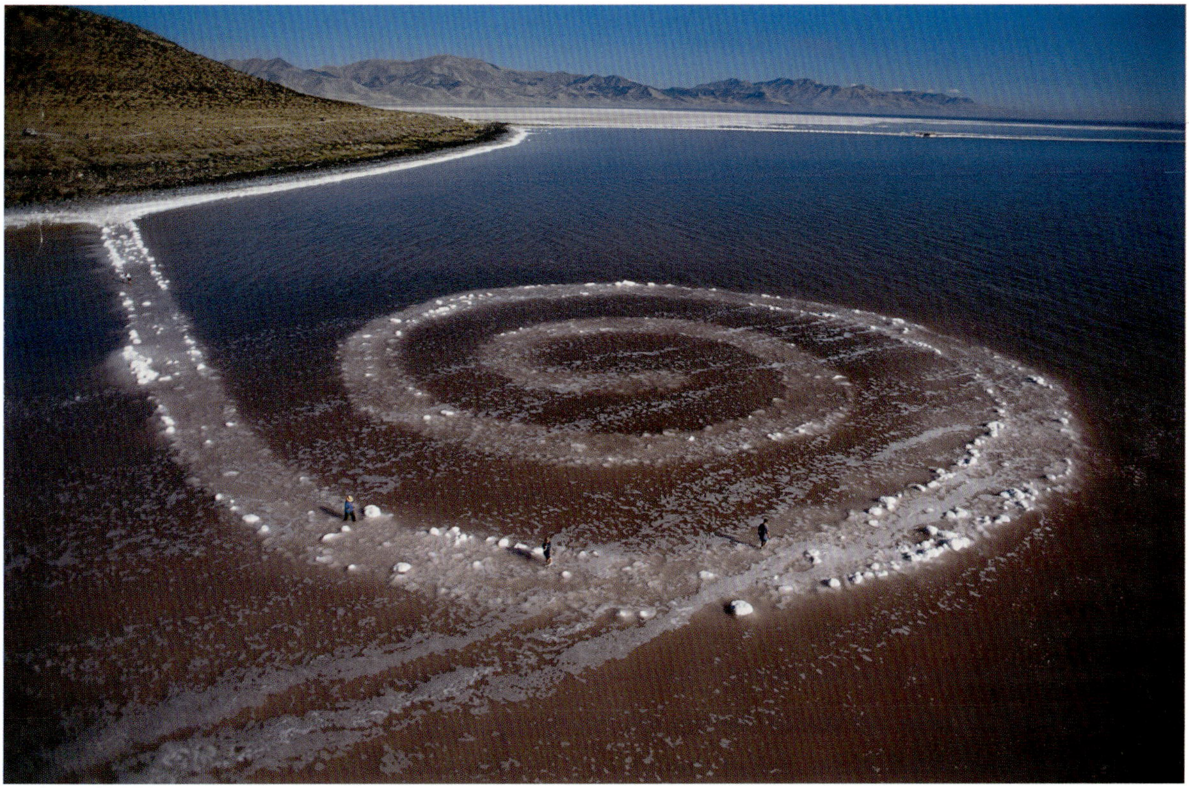

blender.[7] Inset into an environment infinitely greater than itself with which it doesn't compete, *Spiral Jetty* is not a large work by current standards of sculptural sizing. It feels relatively compact next to those gargantuan "site-specific" projects of recent years that loom over and overwhelm us, that cry out for our approval, as if by becoming larger and more costly, and more ambitious, they could hold the fickle attention of viewers grown accustomed to such spectacles.

The scale of art "depends on one's capacity to be conscious of the actualities of perception," Smithson wrote.[8] For it is the scale of *Spiral Jetty* that inspires a consciousness of ourselves as embodied beings in this place. Smithson's earthwork is exactingly poised between shore and lake and sky. Entering his sculpture, my bare feet sink into the orange sand. Water sloshes between my legs, oily and slippery. Lacy patterns of salt form on my calves.

And as I walk the length of *Spiral Jetty* I intuit a relationship between myself and the other members of our little group that I have not felt until now. They move around the watery coil and stand, as I do, at different points of its circumference like the numbers on a clock. When we have fully entered the world of Smithson's sculpture we enter a system of perception. We are not monads, isolated in ourselves, but part of the work and the place where we are as others are, and we are inseparable from them. We experience the sense of interconnectedness that the philosopher Maurice Merleau-Ponty calls Being-in-the-World. "Our own body is in the world as the heart is in the organism," Merleau-Ponty writes. "It keeps the visible spectacle constantly alive, it breathes life into it inwardly, and with it forms a system."[9]

As I move deeper into *Spiral Jetty*, this sense of placement, of contiguity, unravels like the thread on a turning spool. Reaching the end of Smithson's spiral I pivot three hundred and sixty degrees. In the middle of his work is an empty center, an absence. The eye of the storm. Standing here, I find that Smithson's work is hard to read. I *know* that the sculpture is a spiral, knew this before coming here. I have now walked it myself. But as my eyes drift along the half-submerged boulders and across the mysterious lake and horizon, the *Jetty* dissolves perceptually. It refuses to resolve into a discrete mental image, a Gestalt. Scale "operates by uncertainty," Smithson observed. "To be in the scale of the *Spiral Jetty* is to be out of it."[10] I am in the *Spiral Jetty*, and so I can't perceive it as a whole. Smithson's work yields somatic awareness—the sense that I *am* a body. It causes me to perceive, to feel, that I am *here*. But then disorientation sets in. An organized disorder. Embedded in Smithson's coil of basalt and dirt is a "surd" state (rhymes with "absurd") that undermines its structure. A surd area is a place where "logic has been suspended."[11] A place where our perception is put to the test. Arriving at the conclusion of Smithson's watery promenade, we enter a surd condition. This sense of disorientation has only grown as *Spiral Jetty*'s taut arrangement has loosened over the years and the crevices between the rocks have filled up with silt.

The *Spiral Jetty* that my companions and I encounter only somewhat resembles the *Spiral Jetty* of 1970, the work we know from photographs and from the *Spiral Jetty* film. The famous aerial shots that Smithson took from a helicopter just after the work was completed established a lasting idea of its appearance. The *Jetty* we remember has just been built. It is not the work we experience now.

As the iconic sculptures and earthworks of that era have aged our perception of them has changed, complicating previous accounts of these works.[12] A contemporary visitor's experience of *Spiral Jetty* exceeds and undermines those depictions. Visitors to Rozel Point attempt to reconcile the mental image of Smithson's aerial photos of the just-completed *Jetty* with an experience of a work that has decayed considerably, a *Jetty* that we can no longer walk on, much less run upon (as Smithson does in the final frames of his film), a *Jetty* that is no longer a jetty. His work is a bare trace of its former self—a ruin. But it is *there* nonetheless.

Holt waits for us on the shore. During our drive to Brigham City the conversation turns to Smithson. It's awkward to say "your husband" in her presence. "Smithson" sounds slightly cold. To Holt's "Bob" we say "he" and "him." We don't dare use his proper name. At some point we say "Bob," too. *Bob*. We feign intimacy with a man who died before we could meet him; we speak as if we knew Smithson. In a sense we do. We know his earthworks and nonsites, and the peculiar timbre of his voice (implacable, without modulation). We know the narrator of *Spiral Jetty* and of the slide lecture *Hotel Palenque*, who describes the architectural "features" of a broken-down motel. We know his essays and interviews. But what do we know, really? What can we know of a person we have never met?

## Two "Sixties"

The phenomenon that concerns us emerged during the Nineties,[13] and reached an apogee in the early years of the new millennium.[14] And it continues. How do we account for Smithson's contemporaneity? Why have his earthworks—all of which met the fate he prescribed for them (to decay, to no longer resemble, or barely resemble, the projects he made in his lifetime)—come to seem so memorable, so *monumental*, to use one of his favorite words? What is the connection between these Smithsons—between the historical artist and the figure of our imaginations, who inspires others to build ersatz *Partially Buried Woodsheds*, to reassemble his library, to make works he "could" have made?

Allow me to differentiate these "Smithsons." The first Smithson lived during the long Sixties. The second surfaces twenty years after his death and even more insistently during the aftermath of September 11, 2001, when America descended into a state of enmity and moral conflict unseen since the Vietnam War.[15] Smithson became timely during the second Bush administration, the era of Fallujah, Abu Ghraib, and the plunder of Baghdad, the period of Hurricane Katrina and the flooding of New Orleans, and the abandonment of that city's poorest citizens in a lawless and filthy Superdome.[16] And he remains timely during the present moment, when hurricanes and fires grow ever more frequent and wrathful, the threat of nuclear war is again spoken about, and an atavistic politics of nativism and racial discord threatens American unity. His pseudo-Piranesi-esque drawings of smoldering structures and vacant battlements, of stairs leading to nowhere, do not seem strange or visionary to ears grown accustomed to reports of climate change and color-coded security alerts, or to eyes familiar with images of melting towers and rubble-strewn streets (*Entropic Landscape*, 1970; fig. 2.3).

Smithson is an augur of disaster, a builder of "corners of hell."[17] He is entropy's bard and its prophet. ("My 'position' is one of sinking into an awareness of global squalor and futility," he remarked.)[18] Of the seminal artists of the Sixties, it is surely Smithson and Warhol who imagine most acutely the world we now inhabit.[19] The fate of advanced societies is entropic:

> The Second Law of Thermodynamics … extrapolates the range of entropy by telling us energy is more easily lost than obtained, and that in the ultimate future the whole universe will burn out and be transformed into an all-encompassing sameness. The "Blackout" that covered the Northeastern states recently may be seen as a preview of such a future.[20]

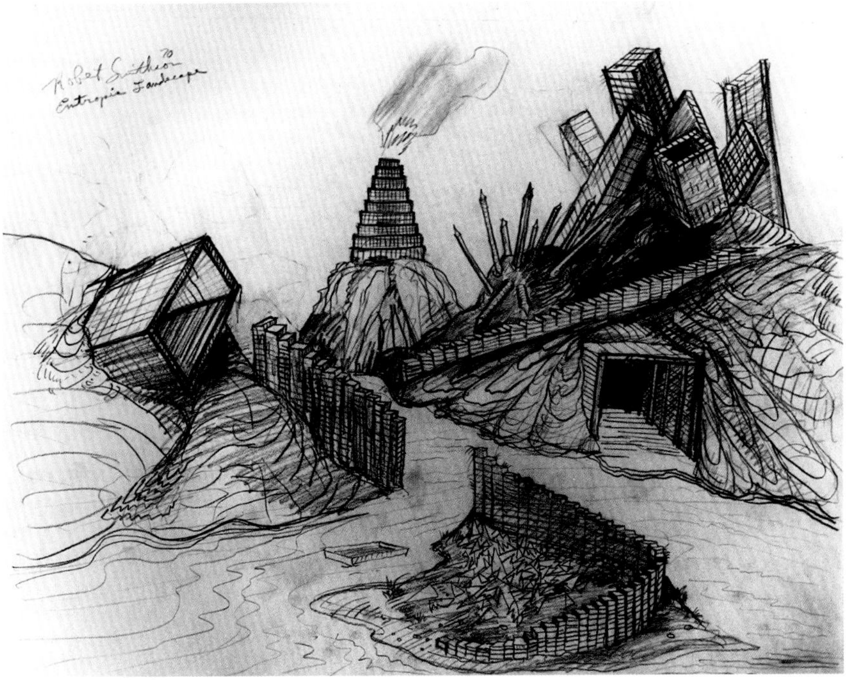

**Fig. 2.3.** Robert Smithson, *Entropic Landscape*, 1970. Pencil on paper. Collection of Richard Serra. Photograph: Robert McKeever. Art © Holt-Smithson Foundation / Licensed by VAGA, New York.

The blackout of 1965 that Smithson writes about in "Entropy and the New Monuments" (1966) left millions of North Americans without power. Normal activities were suspended. Crowds flooded the streets. A "mood of euphoria . . . swept over the darkened cities."[21] Smithson's dystopic discourse was not unique during the period after the Cuban Missile Crisis, when the threat of world annihilation did not seem farfetched.[22] Yet his equation of entropy, a physical law, and avant-garde aesthetics was highly original. Who but Smithson could claim that the geometric forms of Minimal sculptors like Donald Judd, Robert Morris, and Dan Flavin were not abstract shapes signifying nothing but "monuments" to entropy? Where traditional monuments built of marble and bronze evoked a sense of timelessness, the works of these artists (made of factory-processed plywood, metal, Perspex, and fluorescent bulbs) spoke of their origins in mass production, expressing a sense of disposability, the feeling that things don't last. "Instead of causing us to remember the past like the old monuments, the new monuments cause us to forget the future," Smithson wrote.[23]

Smithson alludes to Lévi-Strauss's famous distinction between "hot" and "cold" societies, itself inspired by the Second Law of Thermodynamics. *Entropology*, the study of the "disintegration of highly developed structures," would eventually replace anthropology, the study of man, Lévi-Strauss predicted.[24] The cold (the "primitive") society uses no more energy than it needs. Mechanical, self-generating like a clock, it maintains its equilibrium. The cold society is static, unchanging; it exists in a state of perpetual harmony; it "has no history."[25]

Its opposite, the "hot" society, resembles the steam engine described by the physicist Sadi Carnot, whose paper *Réflexions sur la puissance motrice du feu et sur les machines propres à développer cette puissance* (1824) was the first to describe the tendency of energy to dissipate. Carnot noted that in order for steam energy to be useful mechanically, it must be condensed by a cooling device. A certain amount of energy is lost in this process; this heat loss is irreversible.[26] Like the mechanical engine that inspired Carnot's speculations—the engine that loses energy in the transfer of steam from the boiler to the condenser—the "hot" social system expends more energy than it makes. It is far more sophisticated than the cold society, for it converts raw materials into forms of social organization, or "nature" into "culture," Lévi-Strauss claims.[27] It achieves a high degree of productivity; yet the immense expenditure of raw materials and human labor required to maintain the system catalyzes disequilibrium, unrest.[28]

The "hot" society is entropic. It is the social expression of the dissipation principle, otherwise known as "heat death," the claim of entropy theorists that the universe will eventually cool, that biological life will die out, that the sum amount of energy that underlies all will eventually disperse.[29] The hot society foretells its self-destruction. Then, a frigid eternity: a world devoid of human beings and history (the ultimate "cold" state of affairs), the world that Smithson first describes in "Entropy and the New Monuments" and which the Minimalist work foretells. In opposition to Marinetti's futurist dream of a society of ever-increasing speed and animation, Smithson envisions a future of infinite desolation:

> The world is slowly destroying itself. The catastrophe comes suddenly, but slowly.... But some of us have to simulate upheaval, step up the action. Sometimes we have to call on Bacchus. Excess. Madness. The End of the World.[30]

Entropic time is endless, preceding and succeeding the time of human memory. Now there is another time we must consider, the time when Smithson lived, the time that Koselleck describes as "biological." To think and write about Smithson is always to be reminded of Amarillo. Of his death. Studying Hesse, or Matta-Clark, or Bas Jan Ader also impacts how these artists and their works are perceived.[31] The reputations of these individuals have grown precipitously since the Seventies, even as many of their works have decayed or no longer physically exist. Makers of ephemeral projects, these artists have themselves become avatars of entropy.

The figure of the artist or poet who dies too soon resurfaces during the long Sixties—a period that revives the Romantic idea of blazing youth, an expenditure of the physical self in an act of supreme aesthetic daring. Smithson was highly conscious of the ways in which biography mediates how an artist's practice is interpreted and described. As he remarked about Hesse, whose death preceded his: "I think people's lives are affected by how long they live. And that creates an ambience."[32] A Romantic atmosphere surrounds this generation and the period when they lived and worked. Smithson is a major idol of this entropy cult.

The First Law of Thermodynamics holds that energy is constant. In a closed system the amount of energy remains the same. The Second Law describes what happens when the system opens up, an unbalancing. As energy disperses, entropy increases. "The energy of the universe is constant—the entropy of the universe tends toward a maximum."[33] Above all, entropy implies *change*. It shares the same root as the word "trope," a figure of speech suggesting "turn" or "transformation."[34] It suggests a mutability not only of matter but of meaning, the potential of words to alter, to signify other things. The ephemeral objects and earthworks of the Sixties and Seventies dramatized the tropological condition of the work of art, a physical and semantic alteration. Photographs taken at the moment of the works' completion locate these projects in a time we have missed. We do not "see" these works so much as we remember and reimagine them. And so they trigger the sorts of nostalgic associations that certain memories do.

Such images evoke a fantasy of the Sixties as a last (and lost) moment of avant-gardism, a time when "everything was possible." What was it like to slice a condemned house in two, as Matta-Clark did? To make concentric ice rings in a river dividing two countries, a work that melted soon after Dennis Oppenheim completed it (fig. 2.4)?[35] What drove some artists to imagine that they could achieve an art so ephemeral it could not be bought or sold, escaping the market's clutch? Some of these projects were meant to fall apart, to erase themselves. Others did not court their destruction but accepted their inevitable decay. Yet these endeavors have not disappeared. To the contrary: the more ephemeral the work, the more compelling it often appears to us now. The more abbreviated its existence, the stronger its mnemonic hold, the harder we struggle to remember it. The entropic work *lasts*. Ephemerality remains.[36]

For Smithson, this is not a contradiction. For his *is* an art of contradiction, of scissions and reversals—a dialectics without resolution.[37] He conjoins the mirror with its reflection (in his early relief *Enantiomorphic Chambers* [1965; fig. 2.5]).[38] He pairs the nonsite—a container of rocks and map—with the site where the rocks were harvested (*A Nonsite, Pine Barrens, New Jersey* [1967–68; figs. 2.6a and b]). He buries a woodshed under dirt until its central beam has cracked, launching a built thing into a process of decay (*Partially Buried Woodshed* [1970; fig. 2.7]). Each of these terms is insufficient without the other. There is not one mirror but two, no "site" without the "nonsite," no *Partially Buried Woodshed* apart from the dirt that causes its destruction. Smithson examined one of these

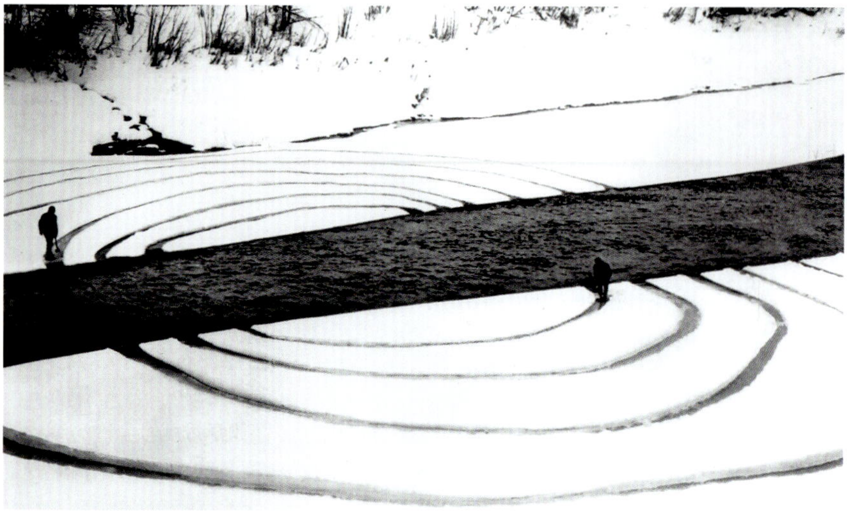

**Fig. 2.4.** Dennis Oppenheim, *Annual Rings*, 1968. USA/Canada boundary at Fort Kent, Maine, and Claire, New Brunswick. 150′ × 200′. Schemata of annual rings severed by political boundary. Time: USA, 1:30 pm; Canada, 2:30 pm. Courtesy of Dennis Oppenheim Estate.

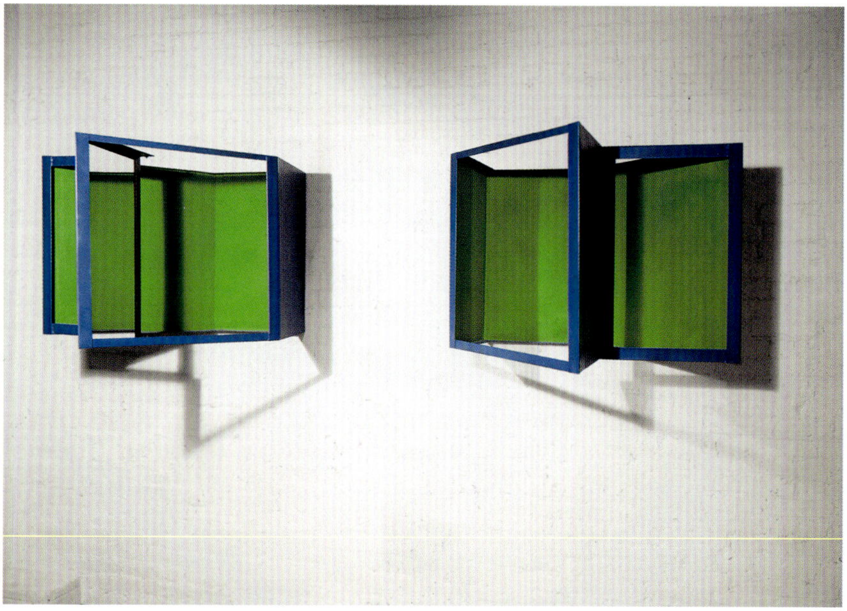

**Fig. 2.5.** Robert Smithson, *Enantiomorphic Chambers* (reconstruction), 1965/2003. Steel and mirror. 2 components. Collection of Estate of Robert Smithson. Art © Holt-Smithson Foundation / Licensed by VAGA, New York. Courtesy of James Cohan, New York.

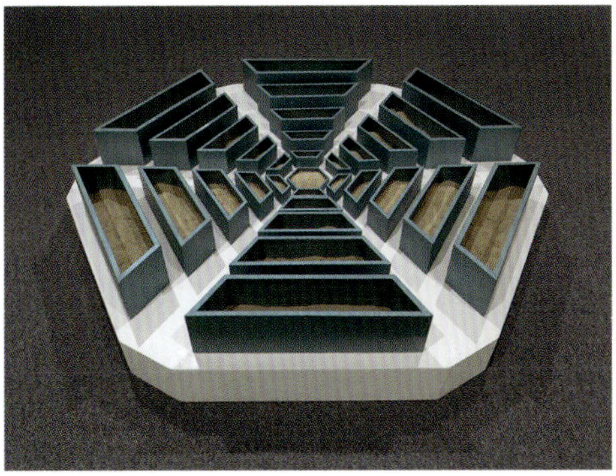

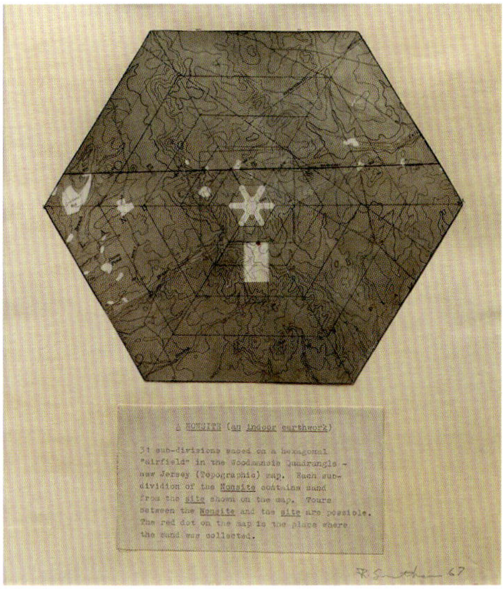


**Fig. 2.6a and 2.6b.** Robert Smithson, *A Non-Site, Pine Barrens, New Jersey*, 1967 (photostat of map); 1968 (sculpture: painted aluminum, sand, painted wood; photostat of map with typed text). National Gallery of Art, Washington, DC. Gift of Virginia Dwan. Photograph: Lee Ewing. Art © Holt-Smithson Foundation / Licensed by VAGA, New York.

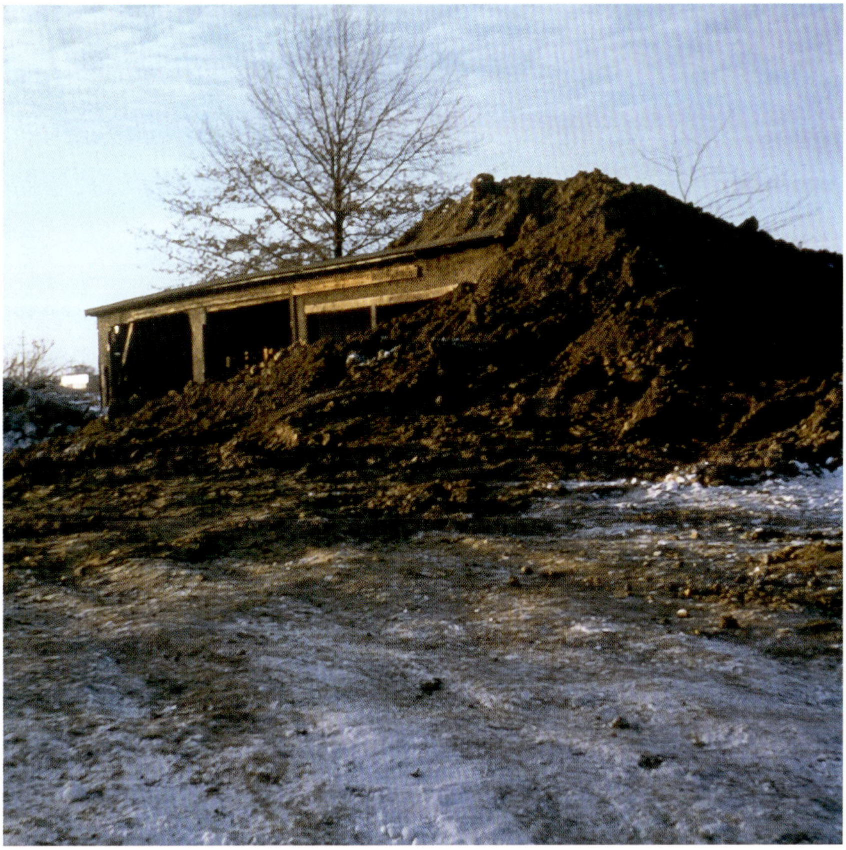

**Fig. 2.7.** Robert Smithson, *Partially Buried Woodshed,* 1970. Kent State University, Kent, Ohio, January 1970. 1 woodshed and 20 truckloads of earth. Art © Holt-Smithson Foundation / Licensed by VAGA, New York. Courtesy of James Cohan, New York.

oppositions with particular intensity. He speaks of entropy in relation to the Minimal artworks (the "monuments") of Judd, Flavin, and Morris. In every monument is its future as ruin. Even things that are meant to last succumb to the brutal law. Inversely, ephemeral things become monumental, causing us to remember them as monuments do.

Enlisting Smithson's system, we could describe a Sixties of contradictory impulses, a monumental and entropic Sixties, not one Sixties but two. The antiwar movement and Nixon's Silent Majority; the culture wars of the Eighties and Nineties; the fissure of the electorate into "red" and "blue" constituencies of recent years expose the fault lines of a peculiarly American divide that surfaced during the Sixties, locating that era at the origin of the present moment, however we describe it.[39] "If you look back on the Sixties and think there was more good than harm, you're probably a Democrat," President Bill Clinton has remarked. "If you think there was more harm than good, you're probably a Republican."[40] Many Sixties narratives follow this dualistic scheme. The "good" Sixties is monumental history, a period when everything changed, usually for the better. The rights of minorities, women, and LGBTQ people were enunciated then. The "bad" Sixties instigated a moral and cultural decline whose reverberations are still felt. In the writings of conservative intellectuals and politicians, the "Sixties" became a code name for various slippages: a disrespect for "authority," moral turpitude and slothful living, irrational thinking, and a slide in educational and aesthetic standards.[41] The bad Sixties is not strictly an invention of the Right. Historians and memoirists, many of whom were active in the New Left, describe the Sixties in a language of loss. This Sixties is not malign so much as disappointing, a Sixties that never made good on its extravagant promises, a Sixties that collapsed under the immense weight of its aspirations. This "declension narrative" is as tendentious as conservative deprecations of the Sixties.[42] In decadal narratives centered on the United States, an idealistic early Sixties convulses into its violent opposite, from President Kennedy's inaugural speech to Dallas, from the March on Washington to Memphis, from Woodstock to Altamont and Kent State. The story is powerful, and much rehearsed.[43]

"Despite a forty year remove, the tumult of the Sixties and the subsequent backlash continues to drive our political discourse," President Barack Obama has written. Born in 1961 to an interracial couple, Obama describes himself as a "pure product" of that time.[44] His first campaign drew heavily on Sixties imagery and Sixties affirmations. Endorsements of the candidate by the Kennedy family and activists from the civil rights movement constructed this child of the Sixties as the rightful bearer of the legacies of the Kennedys and Dr. Martin Luther King Jr.[45] In his campaign book *The Audacity of Hope*, Obama describes his childhood and adolescence as a passage from one Sixties to another, from the innocent, maternal Sixties of earliest memory (Obama recalls his mother's "incorrigible, sweet-natured romanticism . . . of a decidedly pre-1967 vintage") to a late Sixties and Seventies associated with "Huey Newton, the 1968 Democratic National Convention, the Saigon airlift, and the Stones at Altamont."[46] The second Sixties seduces; it distracts; it leads the teenage Barry astray. In college he questions its dangerous allure, and lets it go.

*The Audacity of Hope* is both an autobiography and a narrative of the recent past. The story goes something like this. Before the Sixties (before the "before") a politics of consensus reigned in Washington. Its apogee was the New Deal and the collective effort of winning World War II. During the Sixties a politics of moral absolutes came into place. The antiwar movement, the counterculture, and identity politics polarized voters and politicians.[47] The gains of the civil rights, feminist, and LGBTQ movements are undeniable, says Obama, yet the rigid views and staunch disagreements that arose then still fester. During the presidential elections of 2000 and 2004, the "psychodrama[s] of the Baby Boom generation" continued to play out.[48] Obama calls for a renewal of the old politics of comity, an overcoming of Sixties fractiousness, an end of the end of the Sixties—a premature prescription, as it turned out. Obama's dream of bipartisanship was quickly undermined by the rise of the Tea Party in 2010 and the politics of intransigence of the U.S. Congress that defined his tenure, while the presidency of Donald Trump has reopened the wounds of racial animus that the civil rights movement sought to heal, and an election scandal has emerged that has been much compared to Watergate, the culminating event of the bad Sixties in the United States.

In the works of art and writing discussed in this book, the paradigm of the two Sixties is made perspicuous—and ultimately dismantled. Manichean oppositions come unfastened. There is no "good" or "bad." For entropy is without judgment, amoral. The slippage of an ordered or higher state into a disordered one is inevitable and irreversible. Clocks break. Buildings age. Jetties sink. Civilizations collapse. Memory fades. There are "no periods of decline."[49] There is only entropy, and *more entropy*. Smithson's works demonstrate Carnot's fundamental insight again and again. *Partially Buried Woodshed* most of all.

## Kent, Ohio (1970)

Let us recall the making—and unmaking—of *Partially Buried Woodshed*. Smithson had initially planned to create a mudflow at Kent State University in Ohio, the future setting of the infamous uprising of May 4, 1970, that left four students dead and nine wounded, about which there will be much more to say. Demonstrating two physical laws, gravity and entropy, in their mutual inflection, the mudflow idea was generated by the *Glue Pour* that Smithson had completed in Vancouver the previous month (fig. 2.8).[50]

To execute this work, Smithson positioned a large container of glue at the crest of a hill and toppled the open drum to the ground. Performing this deceptively simple action, he revealed that liquid will dribble downhill, and that glue exposed to the air and elements will dissolve and eventually disperse. It rains often in Vancouver, and the terrain on which Smithson performed the work was a dark sludge. The orange slime glistened as it seeped into the mud. When the glue no longer poured Smithson and his collaborators left the scene. The making of *Glue Pour* was over; yet his artwork had just begun. As I imagine it, birds and small animals walked on the sticky mud in the days afterward. The gooey soil clung to their claws and paws and rubbed off onto other life forms—tree trunks and branches. When it rained, the glue thinned out. And when it rained again, and again,

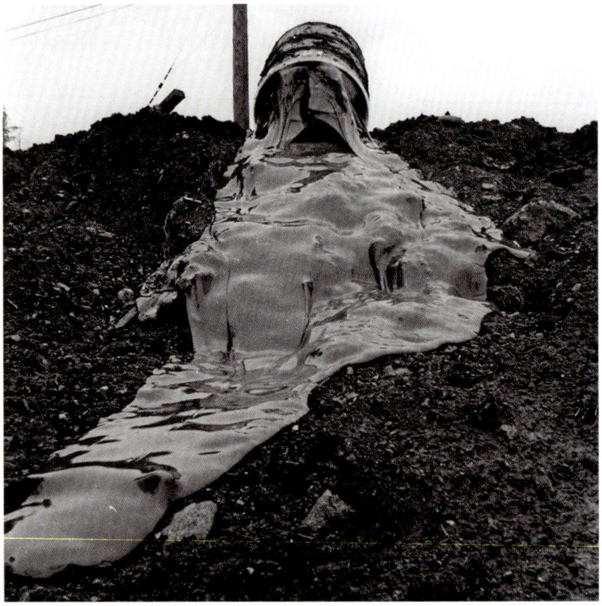

**Fig. 2.8.** Robert Smithson, *Glue Pour*, January 1969. Vancouver, British Columbia. Art © Holt-Smithson Foundation / Licensed by VAGA, New York. Courtesy of James Cohan, New York.8

all traces of Smithson's work disappeared, apart from the photos that he took of the action.[51]

*Partially Buried Woodshed* demanded a different approach. The winter of 1970 was unusually frigid in Ohio. The mud would not pour.[52] And so Smithson proposed to bury a building, an idea inspired by photos he'd seen of houses in Iceland that had been buried in volcanic ash, and by his trips to Rome and the Yucatán (at Yaxchilán he marveled at the sight of temples overgrown by "creepers and weeds").[53] Smithson looked for a structure with open windows. An old shed was located, and the idea for *Partially Buried Woodshed* took shape. The preparatory drawings he made document his thinking as he reconceived the work from pour to burial (fig. 2.9).[54] The initial sketch depicts the shed as Smithson found it. Signs of cracking mar the structure's façade, indicative of its age. The left compartment contains

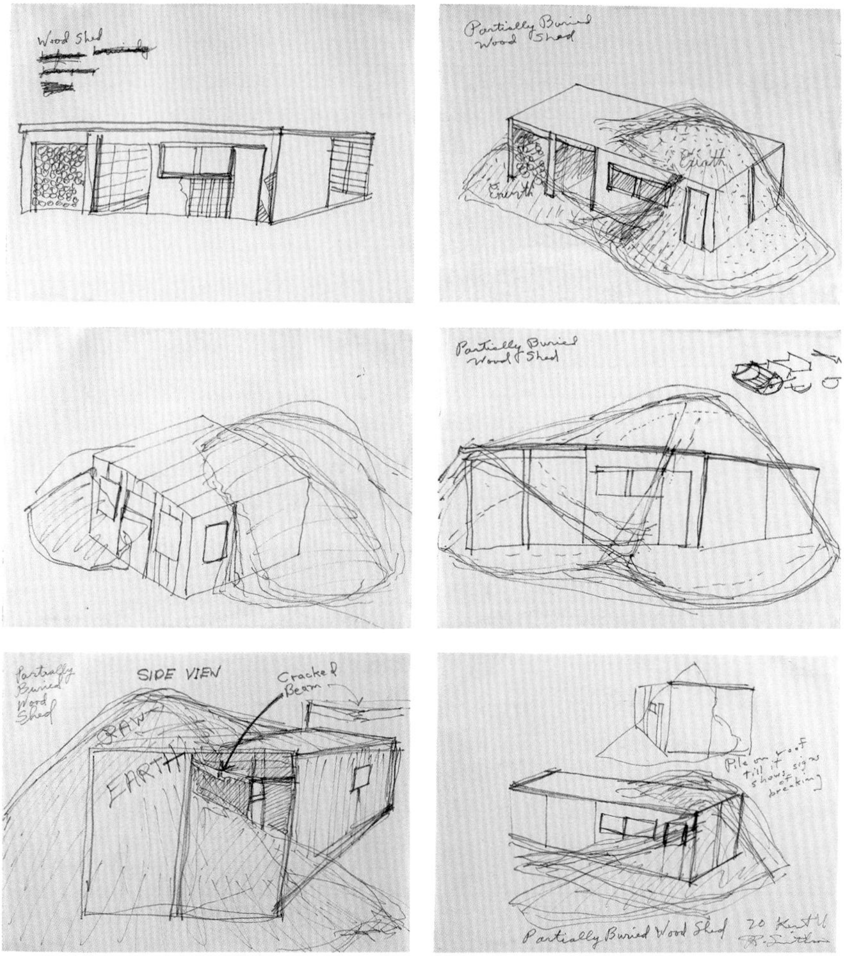


**Fig. 2.9.** Robert Smithson, *Partially Buried Woodshed*, 1970. Black felt-tip pen on 6 sheets of wove paper. National Gallery of Art, Washington, DC. Gift of the Estate of Robert Smithson and Werner H. Kramarsky. Photograph: Christina Moore. Art © Holt-Smithson Foundation / Licensed by VAGA, New York.

a stack of logs suggestive of its prior use. In the following sketches soil flows around the shed like mud, as if, at this point, Smithson imagined the project as both pour and burial. In a further drawing Smithson has arranged the dirt in two pie-shaped volumes and inserted a triangular shape in between. A backhoe retreats into the background.

A side view depicts the cracked beam in detail. The action of dumping dirt is a means to an end. What matters is the outcome of the action, the alteration of the structure. A final sketch shows the work that Smithson actually made. Earth envelops the shed, falling in a spiral arrangement from the top around the right corner where it pours into an open window. A triangular mound has piled up within.[55] Smithson has left the stack of firewood, an acknowledgment of the shed's history. What appears to have been an anarchic dirt dump was in actuality a highly calculated arrangement.

A few students, professors, and the artist Allan Kaprow accompanied Smithson that bright cold day. Bundled in coats, knitted caps, and scarves, they warmed themselves next to a fire as they watched a contractor dump load after load of dirt onto the shed with a backhoe (fig. 2.10). As the number of loads increased to the desired twenty, the sheer mass of dirt bore down on the old structure. Interior and exterior caved into one another. Distinctions between inside and outside became less defined. The cracking of the central beam was the tipping point. It launched the woodshed into a state of irremediable decay, like the fate of Humpty Dumpty, the self-satisfied and rather dim egg-shaped creature we encounter in Lewis Carroll's *Through the Looking Glass*. Humpty Dumpty interested Smithson immensely. Perched on a high, narrow wall, the fragile egg-man boasts of the White King's "assurances." Were he to fall from his precarious perch, and break, he would be put back together *exactly* as he is right now ("*The King has promised me—with his very own mouth*—to—to . . .").[56] The clever Alice knows better. She has learned the nursery rhyme by heart. She knows that Humpty Dumpty is in for a terrible shock. She knows about entropy.

Smithson knew that his *Woodshed* could not be put back together again, either. The moment the central beam breaks is the moment it becomes the just-completed *Woodshed*—the beginning of its existence as a work of art. An artwork is "a material object plus *y*," Arthur Danto notes. The *y* in this instance was Smithson's decision to bury an ordinary structure that had heretofore been of no interest—buried it until its spine cracked.[57] In destroying the shed's major structural element, Smithson divided the building's past from its future, transforming it from one category of thing to another.[58] Henceforth, it was no longer a disused woodshed but something entirely different.

Smithson completed *Partially Buried Woodshed* on January 22, 1970. His project anticipated the shootings by just three and a half months. Much

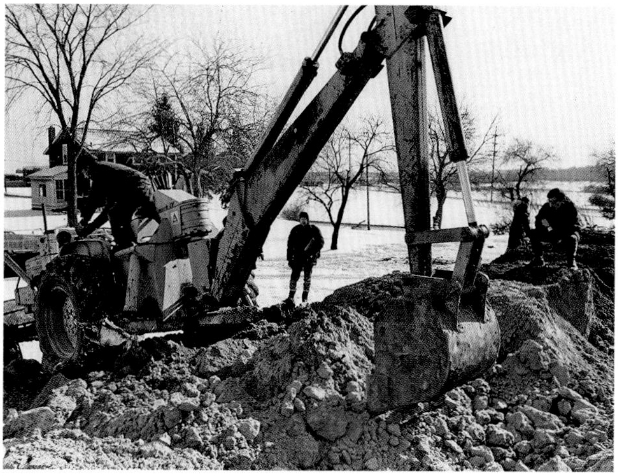

**Fig. 2.10.** Construction of *Partially Buried*, January 1970. Kent, Ohio. Photograph: Doug Moore. Robert I. Smithson, *Partially Buried Woodshed* Papers, Kent State University Libraries, Special Collections and Archives. Art © Holt-Smithson Foundation / Licensed by VAGA, New York.

has been made of this intriguing connection. Learning about the massacre in Utah, where he was busily planning *Spiral Jetty*, Smithson allegedly described the *Woodshed* as "prophetic" of the tragedy. Smithson's editor Philip Leider seconded this view, hailing the earthwork as their generation's *Guernica*.[59] It is tempting to see his work in this light. It is understandable that Smithson himself did so upon hearing the terrible news.[60] Rather than attribute a proleptic or symbolic agency to the *Woodshed* (the cracking of the beam *foretells* May 4), let us recall the actual circumstances in which his artwork came about. (One does not bury a building at a university so easily.) The Kent State campus "was alive with talk of the war—mostly antiwar" when Smithson arrived there, and so it had been for years.[61] To suggest that Smithson's earthwork predicts the massacre puts art in advance of history; it constructs the complex sequence of events that led to May 4 as a backdrop for a heroic aesthetic act. It constructs Smithson as Cassandra, as prophet. Smithson's work became part of a history that was *already* under way, and it affected that history. Yet his *Woodshed* would have meant something different had it been made on another campus or at another point in time. Had he made it a year earlier or later, or *anywhere else*, it would not have become the work it became. Smithson did bury a shed at Kent State, of all places. He made his work less than four months before the shootings. These are facts. And though no clear line of cause and effect can be drawn between these events, the relationships exist. In what follows I explore these connections, tease them out.

Let us return to that dangerous spring. The U.S. antiwar movement had grown in numbers and prominence since Paul Potter spoke to a crowd of twenty-five thousand in Washington five years earlier. The national Moratorium (Mobe) action of November 1969 attracted an estimated two million participants.[62] The newly elected president, Richard Nixon, was under intense pressure to conclude a war that had driven his predecessor, Lyndon Johnson, from office. On the advice of Secretary of Defense Melvin Laird, Nixon proposed to withdraw 150,000 GIs from Indochina, a policy known as Vietnamization. By creating the impression that the South Vietnamese were sufficiently prepared to lead the battle against the North and the Viet Cong, the administration could keep the war going, as it fully intended to do, but at a less aggressive pace.[63] The image of withdrawal was a ploy, an obfuscation. The "secret" bombings in Cambodia and Laos, which began after Nixon took office in his effort to extend the war for political advantage, were already under way.[64] For a brief while, "Vietnamization" worked. There was little reason to protest a war that was being scaled down. Criticism of the administration abated that winter; the movement appeared to be losing steam.[65]

A televised speech of April 30 changed everything. Now Nixon claimed that Cambodia harbored Viet Cong sanctuaries along its border with Vietnam, and the headquarters "for the entire Communist military operation in South Vietnam"—a total fabrication, as it turned out.[66] The lives of Americans stationed in Vietnam were "endangered," the president said. In order for Vietnamization to continue, it was necessary to invade *another* country.[67] Operation Rockcrusher was already under way when Nixon announced it. The detested war was not contracting but expanding.

Events unfolded quickly that weekend: an enormous number of protests and rampages in university towns (Kent was hardly unique); a remark by an elated Nixon at the Pentagon denouncing antiwar activists as "bums"; then the shootings at Kent State at midday Monday. A callous response to the shootings by the reviled vice president, Spiro Agnew—who compared protesters to Nazis and Klansmen and advised the public to "act accordingly"—added fuel to the fire.[68] Students responded with great fury. Protests occurred at 1,350 colleges and universities, an unprecedented event in American history. Flags were lowered to half-mast. Mock funerals were held. Teach-ins were organized. Hundreds of campuses went on strike and shut down for the rest of the school year. And then a *second* massacre occurred during a protest at Jackson State College in Jackson, Mississippi, in which two students were killed and twelve were injured by city and state police; all were African American.[69] The following weekend some one hundred thousand marchers gathered on the great lawn in front of the White House in protest. Inside the presidential mansion Nixon's drunkenness and erratic behavior were cause for alarm. During the early morning of the day of the protest the beleaguered president went out in his limousine for a spin. At the Lincoln Memorial he chatted with a group of baffled young people about the pleasures of surfing and college football. Driving on to the Capitol, he gave a speech in the deserted House of Representatives to an audience of one: his valet. Word of these antics spilled into the press. To many, it seemed as if the president of the United States was becoming unhinged.[70]

The Kent State shootings reignited the movement. Moderates who had supported the war until then joined the liberals and New Leftists in denouncing it. Rumors swirled that a general strike was imminent. Radicals spoke of revolution.[71] And there were marches *in support* of the Cambodia invasion and the Nixon administration, and physical and verbal attacks against antiwar protesters.[72] The good citizens of Kent and Ravenna, Ohio, frightened by their towns' descent into anarchy, condemned the shooting victims in a letter-writing campaign in the local newspaper. A majority of Americans agreed with them: the kids got what was coming to them.[73]

May 4, 1970, exposed a sharp divide of the American polity unseen since the Civil War; the United States, the dominant world power, appeared to be in free fall. The rhetoric of entropy permeated public and private discourse alike. America was experiencing a "physical breakdown," Mayor John Lindsay of New York remarked. "The very fabric of government was falling apart," Henry Kissinger, author of Nixon's disastrous Indochina policy, later recalled. "We're graduating into a society gone mad.... All our education will be meaningless in a nation programmed for destruction," the editors of the student newspaper at the State University of New York, Buffalo, declared.[74]

May 4 is the next step after Altamont and the Manson Family murders, the culmination of the American bad Sixties. How does an artwork, a buried woodshed, address an untenable situation? Can we speak of a *politics* of entropy, a natural law that positively ridicules human agency, the optimistic belief that we can make things better? Smithson was deeply skeptical of the modernist future, I have noted. Is it any wonder that he never joined his friends Carl Andre and Robert Morris in the left-wing Art Workers Coalition protests, that this trailblazer of land art kept the ecology movement at arm's length?[75] Lévi-Strauss's entropology is useful here. His analogy likening advanced societies to steam engines is a theory of social control, as indebted to Marx as to Carnot. The more complex the engine, the more "differentials" it contains. (In a combustion engine a differential is the gap between the boiler and condenser that allows the steam's heat to be put to use: entropy is the loss of energy that occurs in this transaction.) The "hotter" the society, the more energy it needs; the more levels of hierarchy, the more susceptible it is to malfunction. Order yields disorder.[76]

The Kent State massacre led to the temporary cessation of the most technologically advanced society in history. During the weeks after the shootings the "System" came to a grinding halt. Smithson made an artwork at the very fault line of disturbance. He made it in a place, a public university, heretofore obscure, whose name would become synonymous with the bad Sixties. Of all the works Smithson could have built at Kent, he made one that pointed to its own future as ruin. He made a work that would sag and rot and crumble. A work that appeared to foretell the shootings.

Yet when Smithson arrived at the university that January, the events of May 4 could not be predicted. Nixon's promises of withdrawal had had a pacifying effect on the school's antiwar activists, as had the long, cold winter.[77] While political activity was at a lull on the campus, the arts scene was comparatively lively. Smithson visited the university under the aegis of an avant-garde arts festival.[78] This detail is often overlooked in the literature, or simply assumed. In my view it is essential: had Smithson not been invited to Kent at that moment, the *Woodshed* would likely not have come to be. The making of his work was adventitious, but it was not random. Smithson had been planning to bury a building for some time. The opportunity now presented itself. He seized it.

The avant-garde as a vital principle is lost to us, Clark says. Yet in 1970, in this small university town, the memory of modernism remained a compelling idea, a driving principle. The Kent festival was unabashedly avant-gardist. The organizers, many of them students, were well informed. They were energetic. They sought out the most advanced practitioners they could find. And, in fact, the Kent State festival, the fifth of these events, was the most radical up to that point.[79] The artists and writers they invited were working at the limits of their chosen medium—in some instances, of medium itself. John Ashbery, author of poems of surpassing opacity, read from his new book, *The Double Dream of Spring*, a good five years before he became celebrated with the publication of *Self-Portrait with a Convex Mirror*. The composer Morton Subotnick performed electronic music, a medium he was in the process of inventing. The director John Vaccaro led a workshop on "Ridiculous" performance, a theater of camp allusions, cross-dressing, and savage humor developed with Charles Ludlam in opposition to the dominant strain of naturalism ubiquitous in American theater then and now. Days before Smithson buried the woodshed, Kaprow staged a Happening outdoors—yet another work that required the participants to face the blistering cold. In order to make this work, *Graft*, Kaprow withdrew a portion of his artist's fee and stuffed ten plastic bags with thirty one-dollar bills each. Pinning the bags to palm fronds, he instructed volunteers to climb the trees outside the student center and hang the money bags on high branches (fig. 2.11).[80] Just as the stockbrokers of Wall Street scrambled for the fistfuls of dollars that Yippie provocateur Abbie Hoffman threw to the floor of the New York Stock Exchange three years earlier (a prank inspired by Kaprow's

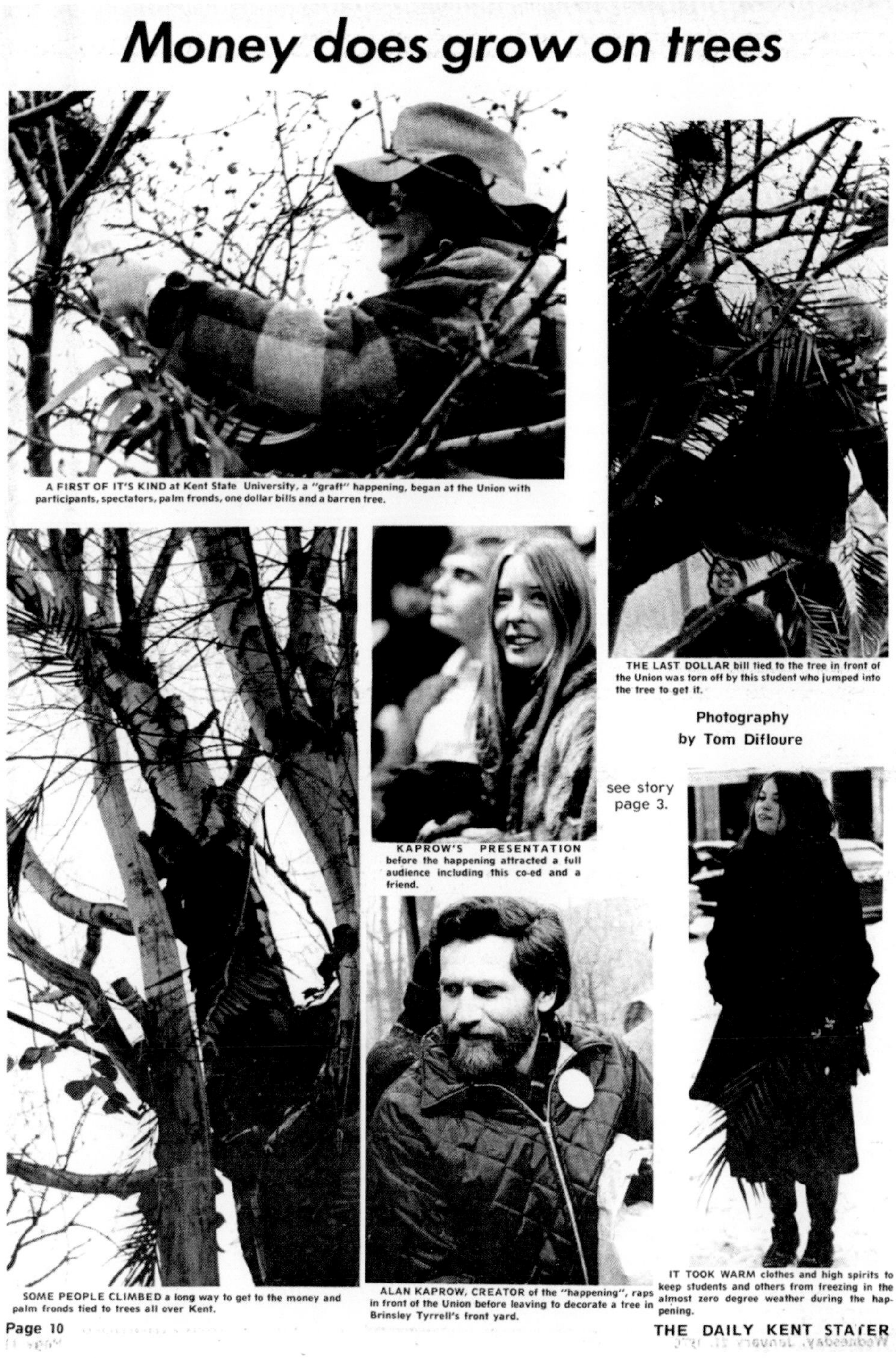

# Money does grow on trees

A FIRST OF IT'S KIND at Kent State University, a "graft" happening, began at the Union with participants, spectators, palm fronds, one dollar bills and a barren tree.

THE LAST DOLLAR bill tied to the tree in front of the Union was torn off by this student who jumped into the tree to get it.

Photography
by Tom Difloure

see story
page 3.

KAPROW'S PRESENTATION before the happening attracted a full audience including this co-ed and a friend.

SOME PEOPLE CLIMBED a long way to get to the money and palm fronds tied to trees all over Kent.

ALAN KAPROW, CREATOR of the "happening", raps in front of the Union before leaving to decorate a tree in Brinsley Tyrrell's front yard.

IT TOOK WARM clothes and high spirits to keep students and others from freezing in the almost zero degree weather during the happening.

Page 10 THE DAILY KENT STATER

**Fig. 2.11.** "Money Does Grow on Trees." *Daily Kent Stater*, January 21, 1970. Kent State University Libraries, Special Collections and Archives.

Happenings as much as it seems to have inspired Kaprow), the Kent students clambered up the tree trunks after their classmates, grabbing the money bags as soon as they could.[81]

In his keynote speech that week, critic Alan Rich lamented the "disillusionment and despair" widely felt across America then. There was no barometer more sensitive to these sentiments, he suggested, than aesthetic practice. ("The chaos of the times is reflected in the arts.")[82] The "chaos" that Rich described would find consummate expression in the earthwork that Smithson built four days later. Of all the works presented during the arts festival, Smithson's project most directly evoked the social fragmentation that Rich described. Holt once described the *Woodshed* as "intrinsically political."[83] The social implications of Smithson's work are embedded within it, intrinsic, Holt suggests—its arrangement of dirt and structure, its blending of interior and exterior, its contingency with the site. Smithson understood that no place, not even a marginal location on a campus, is neutral. Destroying a building at Kent State meant something at a time when universities had become contested sites, theaters of dissent.[84] And while the students there and elsewhere typically targeted buildings associated with administrative control, Smithson enacted a different kind of dismantling. He accomplished this by destroying something altogether insignificant: a building that had lost its utility when the farm it had been part of was converted into roads and parking lots, outbuildings and laboratories—the various dependencies of the postwar research university. The target of his *Partially Buried Woodshed* was not an important building, or even a *particular* building, but architecture *as such*—architecture as a symbolic form.

"The dream of architecture, among other things, is to escape entropy," Yve-Alain Bois has written of Smithson's work.[85] Architecture does constant battle with entropy, Bois suggests; entropy is its fiercest foe. The threat that entropy poses is more than physical, for architecture is more than just a building, a built thing, Georges Bataille insists. It represents something other, or more, than the function it serves. The idea of architecture refers to "whatever there is in an edifice that cannot be reduced to a building . . . whatever is aesthetic about it."[86] Entropy left unchecked disarticulates a building, violates it. It withdraws from the aesthetic surplus that elevates a mere building into architecture. The process of decay that every building endures not only alters how a building looks and undermines its utility; it challenges its identity *as architecture*. And so architecture resists entropy. As Bataille suggests, the storming of the Bastille, the ur-event of the revolutionary imaginary, was a seminal event in the history of the built. The destruction of the royal prison exposed something fundamental about architecture, its symbolic nature, its embodiment of hierarchy. It is in the forms of the prison, the cathedral and palace that the church and state "spea[k] to the multitudes and impos[e] silence on them," the philosopher notes.[87]

During the Sixties and Seventies this argument took on the appearance of truth. (Not for nothing was Bataille's thinking revived during the aftermath of May 1968).[88] While on university campuses military recruitment centers (ROTCs), classroom and administration buildings, and research laboratories became sites of dissent, in Washington the Pentagon and White House were the principal targets of antiwar activity. During the week after the Kent State shootings, a vast barricade of buses manned by policemen and secret service agents surrounded the White House, a building with immense symbolic weight, to fend off the thousands of young people who had gathered at the president's doorstep.

A woodshed is barely a building. Occupying the lowest rung of architecture's hierarchy of the built, it almost escapes symbolization. It is practically nothing, and means practically nothing.[89] The shed that Smithson unbuilt is the White House's diametric opposite, its extreme other. The abandoned farm building lacked windows or even a floor before Smithson buried it. Already its façade had begun to chip and crack. Now, a shed "partially buried" is even less than a working shed, if that is possible. And so it is much more. By withdrawing its already tenuous status as a building, a technique he called "dearchitecturization," Smithson elevated the sagging structure into an aesthetic object, as we have seen. He caused it to provoke, to signify; he evoked the hot society's bloated, repressive grandeur. Facilitating its slide into oblivion, Smithson caused the students and faculty to take notice of a building that no one had noticed before, and a part of the campus that was then on the university's periphery.

Interest in Smithson's work grew. Students visited it, did illicit things in it. They covered the walls with graffiti. They made it their own. That summer an anonymous vandal altered the work irreparably. The inscription *May 4 Kent 70* appeared on the lintel in white enamel paint; henceforth Smithson's work was no longer merely a "Smithson" either. Rather than prophesying the massacre, the *Woodshed* now spoke of a traumatic recentness. It was a memorial now, the first of Kent's monuments to the dead, a point I will resume.[90] And then one day in March 1975 yet another vandal doused the rotting shed with kerosene and lit a match. Fire did what earth and rain and wind could not do. Within hours only the right compartment was left standing. A landscaping crew removed the rubble.[91]

Smithson's earthwork seemed out of place, like the working shed it replaced. Still it remained. Protected by a deed of gift signed the day he

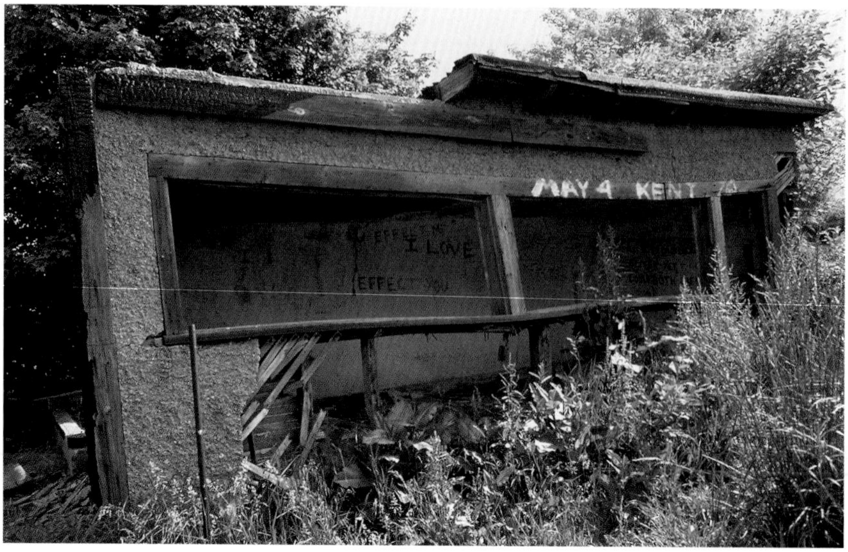


**Fig. 2.12.** Robert Smithson, *Partially Buried Woodshed*, 1970. Kent State University, Kent, Ohio. Photograph: Nancy Holt, 1975. Art © Holt-Smithson Foundation / Licensed by VAGA, New York.

completed it—a document that declared the project and its setting an artwork worthy of conservation—*Partially Buried Woodshed* was allowed to exist in a state of progressive decay (fig. 2.12).[92] As it altered, so did its surroundings; as the university built a new campus around it, Smithson's ruin, a holdover of the free-spirited arts festival and antiwar era, stood as an unwelcome reminder of the day the place-name "Kent State" became infamous. It was a jarring note on the architecturally staid campus, an irritant to administrators and campus planners alike.[93] In 1982, the left half of the remaining shed collapsed; a grounds crew cleared the remains and planted a wall of cedars around the site, hiding it from view.[94] And then one day in the winter of 1984 the last remnants of Smithson's sculpture disappeared. The unruly work was gone. Fourteen years after the artist's visit, only the foundation remained.[95]

## A Woodshed Series (1996–2004)

In 1996, Renée Green paid a visit to her parents in Cleveland, the city of her birth. Accompanied by her parents, she visited nearby Kent State University, a forty-five-minute drive from her childhood home, and walked around the campus. Green took notes and photographs, and shot reels of film documenting the trip. She eventually presented the results of her research in an installation at Pat Hearn Gallery in New York called *Partially Buried* (1996).[96]

We are greeted at the entrance by a Saarinen "Tulip" table displaying three talismanic objects: a vitrine of twenty-three paperback novels and nonfiction books by James Michener, including that author's *Kent State: What Happened and Why* (1971), the most widely read account of the massacre; a smaller vitrine containing a few shards of concrete; and an aerial shot of the campus placed on the tabletop (fig. 2.13). Michener's narrative of "what happened" at Kent begins on Saturday, May 2, 1970. A student pilot from the school's military regiment is taking a spin above the town. He notices plumes of smoke rising up from the campus and steers his plane away. The army's recruitment office (ROTC) is burning down.

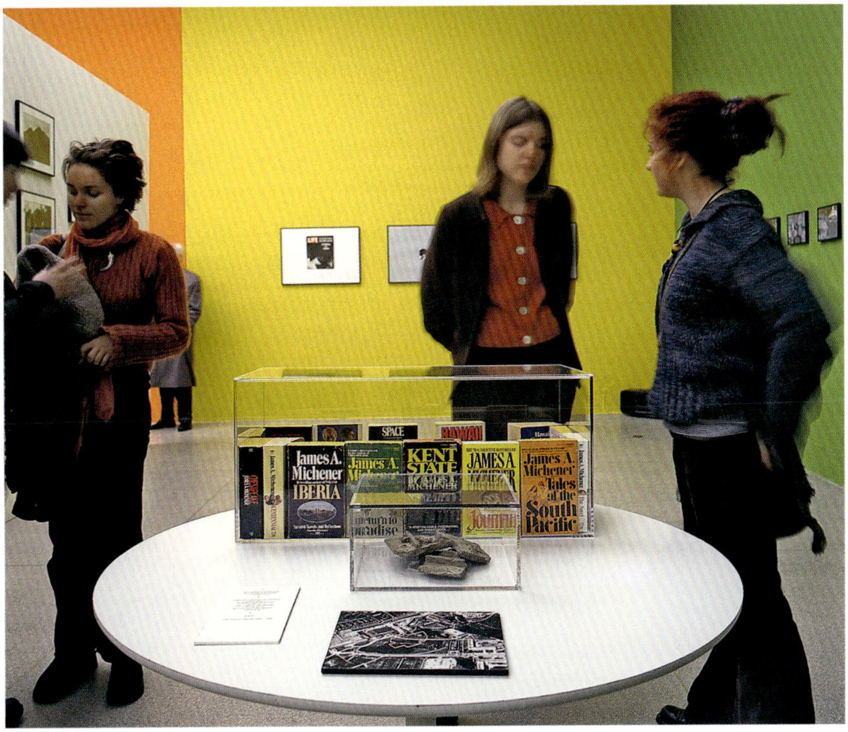


**Fig. 2.13.** Renée Green, *Partially Buried*, 1996–97. Mixed-media installation. Installation view, Vienna Secession, 1999. Image: Pez Hejduk. Courtesy of Renée Green and Free Agent Media.

Who actually set fire to this building was never established.[97] As Michener notes, the students were in a rowdy mood that weekend. A riot broke out downtown as young people exited the bars that Friday. Store windows were broken, garbage cans were set afire. The police made arrests. The recruitment office burned the next night. The mayor called the governor; the governor called up the National Guard, who took command of the campus.

On the morning of May 4, a Monday, a large crowd of students gathered in front of the torched structure to protest the guardsmen's presence. A commander read the Riot Act, and the soldiers chased the students up a knoll known as Blanket Hill. After reaching the summit, the men marched down to an athletic practice field where they were greeted with taunts and rocks. Within minutes they retook the hill. A shout was heard, and without warning the guardsmen unleashed a fusillade of sixty-seven bullets into the crowd. The gunfire lasted thirteen seconds.

A white outline is visible on the map in Green's tabletop museum. The shape spreads out across the campus like a fan. It marks the location of a gym annex that was built on the site of the infamous practice field several years after the shootings. The construction of the gym annex where the guardsmen rallied just before the massacre caused another confrontation in 1977, when activists occupied Blanket Hill in tents.[98]

Green revisits this contentious history; she evokes two "Sixties." The tent city protesters believed the confrontation with the authorities seven years earlier was a just response to an immoral war. They interpreted the construction of the annex as an erasure of that history. Michener rejected this point of view. The author of *Tales of the South Pacific*, *Hawaii*, and the other thick tomes on view, Michener freely combined the narrative techniques of fiction and nonfiction. His plots build to climaxes, his narrators are omniscient; intricate histories are homogenized into easily digestible diegeses. A moral bias skews his "nonfictional" account of the massacre.[99] Incredibly, he blames neither the guardsmen nor the public officials who ordered the soldiers to the campus but the marchers themselves. His narrative gives ample voice to the Silent Majority of Americans identified by President Nixon, who looked on activists and hippies with contempt.[100] Michener depicts two kinds of students, representatives of two "Americas". The clean-cut ROTC flyer of Aryan appearance ("six-feet-three, slight of build, with wavy blond hair . . . a good student . . . quietly patriotic") represents a traditional value system under assault. A bearded, long-haired rabble-rouser bearing the Jewish-sounding name Steve Sharoff embodies the destructive ethos that is tearing the country apart. Sharoff, a graduate student, is a maker of mayhem, a catalyst of entropy. His arrival on the campus is "a bombshell."[101] Burying the U.S.

Constitution in a public ceremony on the campus Commons that Friday, Sharoff triggers the series of events culminating in the massacre.

Michener's condemnations are not confined to male students. "Unladylike" young women also incite the author's ire. The harsh chants and uncouth speech of the Kent "girls" offended the men of G Group and A Company:

> They were hot, and angry, and disgusted at having been pinned down against the fence, infuriated by the students who challenged them, and bitterly resentful of the girls who even now trailed them up the hill, cursing and reviling them.... There was a single shot....[102]

What has Smithson's *Woodshed* to do with all this? The chunks of concrete displayed in Green's tabletop museum are remnants of the shed's foundation. Placing these relics next to Michener's books and the campus map, Green implies that May 4 and Smithson's sculpture are parallel phenomena. That we cannot understand the *Woodshed* apart from the shootings; we can only retrieve this history through Smithson's methods. For what is *Partially Buried* but an elaborate nonsite of *Partially Buried Woodshed*? Just as Smithson's containers of sand and rocks, aerial photographs, and maps allude to the places where these materials were found, Green's tabletop museum sets up comparisons between two locations (Kent, Ohio and New York) and points in time: the winter day in 1970 when Smithson buried the shed and the present moment of viewing when Green asks us to remember this other place and time.

We enter a space with walls painted olive green and beige (fig. 2.14). Black-and-white pictures cover one of these walls. Text seeps into the margins of these prints, indicating they are not vintage but rephotographs from Michener's book, pictures of pictures. The events at Kent State were copiously documented. Student journalists emerged from their classrooms in Taylor Hall, photographing the confrontation moment by moment. The most famous of these images—John Filo's shot of Mary Ann Vecchio kneeling behind the corpse of Jeffrey Miller—won the photographer a Pulitzer Prize (fig. 2.15). Filo's Vecchio wears a dark blouse and a white bandana knotted around her neck. Her jaw is agape, her hair is unruly, her arms are stretched in convulsive grief. She grasps the air, as if she's trying to reach something invisible—as if she's trying to hold onto Miller's life. His body turns away from the camera, twisting on the diagonal, floating on the pavement lit by midday sun. Miller is faceless, his head is a messy ball of hair, limp as a rag doll's. A stream of blood trickles down the sidewalk behind where Vecchio kneels.

Michener calls her "the girl with the Delacroix face" (recalling, perhaps,

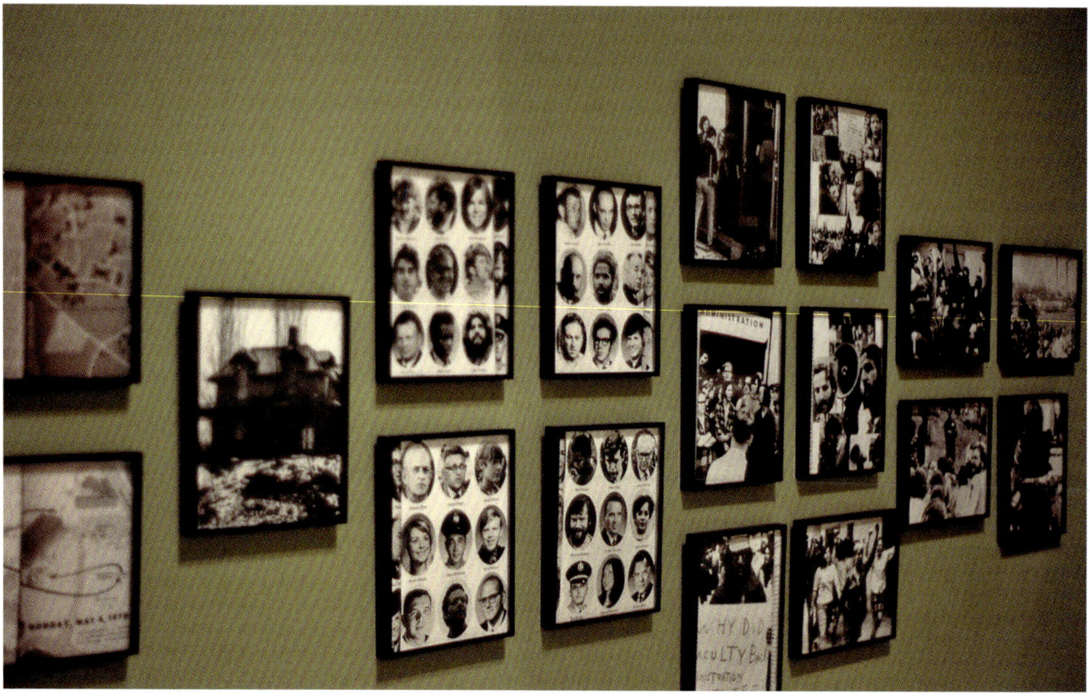

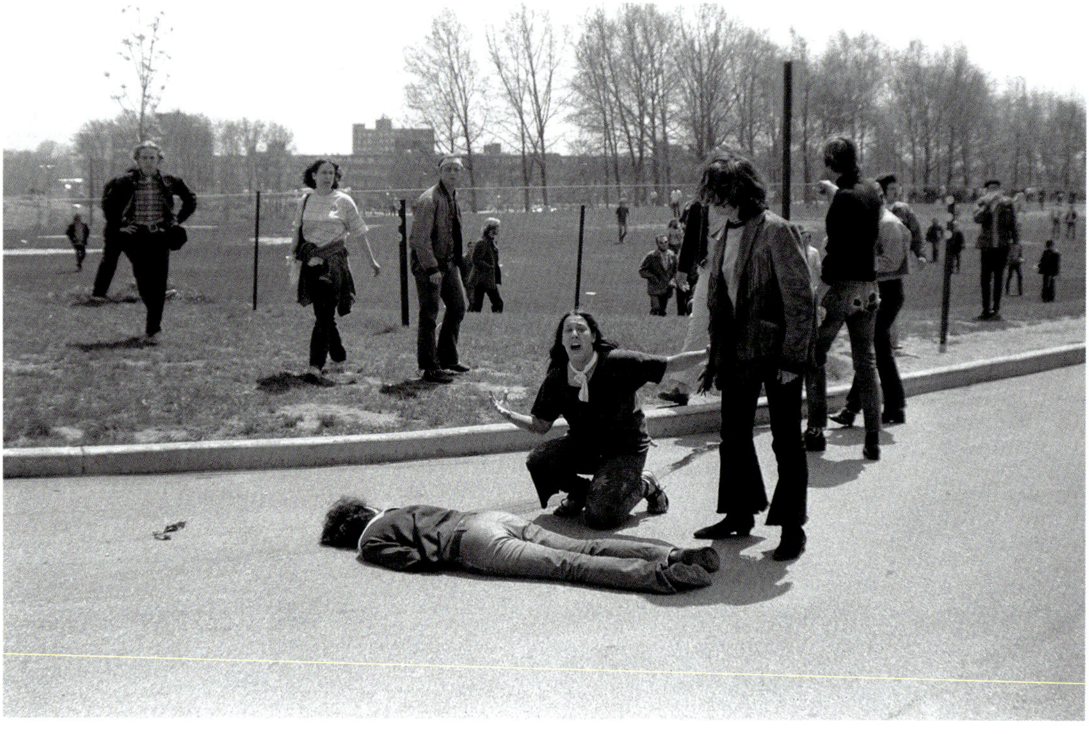

the French painter's *Massacre at Chios*), but Vecchio's expressive eyes and mouth and dramatic pose recall archetypal depictions of grief that Delacroix knew—statues of Niobe defending her children, the Niobids, as vengeful Artemis and Apollo annihilate them, and Renaissance Lamentations (depictions of the Virgin and Magdalene kneeling before the dead Christ). Part of the power of Filo's photo is that it is not staged—that it is real. At the same time, the reality it captures is mediated by images we already know. It is a picture that looks like a picture. It calls to mind a history of depiction, of tried-and-true compositions orchestrated to elicit viewers' empathy. This blending of the found and known, of the real and artificial, is the source of that image's extraordinary power.

Michener places this photo last. He locates the mysterious girl and tells us about her. He takes aim at the teenage Vecchio, topples her from Filo's pedestal. This heroine of the New Left, Michener tells us, is in fact a fourteen-year-old runaway from Florida who found herself in Kent, Ohio, because the group of hitchhikers she'd joined during her aimless travels brought her there. She threw rocks at the guardsmen not because she was against the war but because it was something to *do*. "She was doing what everyone was doing and that made it all right."[103] Vecchio exemplifies a nation that is being led astray by radicals and feckless students. She is a child of the bad Sixties, and for Michener, its very emblem.

Green omits Filo's celebrated image from her picture gallery. Removing it, she depletes its aura, its singularity, its synecdochical power. That image came to stand for everything that happened at Kent that weekend; it represented an America plummeting into the abyss. Its absence in *Partially Buried* is conspicuous (when most of us think about "Kent State," we think of Filo's photo). Green deflects our attention to other representations of that day and the events leading up to it described by Michener—such as the 1968 protest by the Black Student Union objecting to the presence of recruiters from the Oakland, California, police department (among the principal enemies of the Black Panthers) and a 1969 antiwar demonstration in the Music and Speech Building.[104] In Michener's telling one action leads to another. Activism precipitates violence. Protest incites shootings. And so he implies, again and again, that the widespread dissent on America's campuses must be suppressed. ("The radicalization of the young is proceeding at a terrifying pace and should be halted.")[105]

Green scrambles Michener's depiction, questions his authority. She arranges the images in his book in no particular order.[106] Michener's account is not an objective depiction of "what happened" but a narrative of these events, and an extremely biased one. Yet her work is not simply a critique of Michener, a dissection of his diegesis. For *Partially Buried* is also a narrative of "what happened" at Kent State, as every account of

**Fig. 2.14.** Renée Green, *Partially Buried,* 1996. Mixed-media installation. Installation view, Pat Hearn Gallery, New York, 1996. Image: Tom Warren. Courtesy of Renée Green and Free Agent Media.

**Fig. 2.15.** John Filo, *Kent State Massacre,* May 4, 1970. © John Filo. Courtesy of Getty Images.

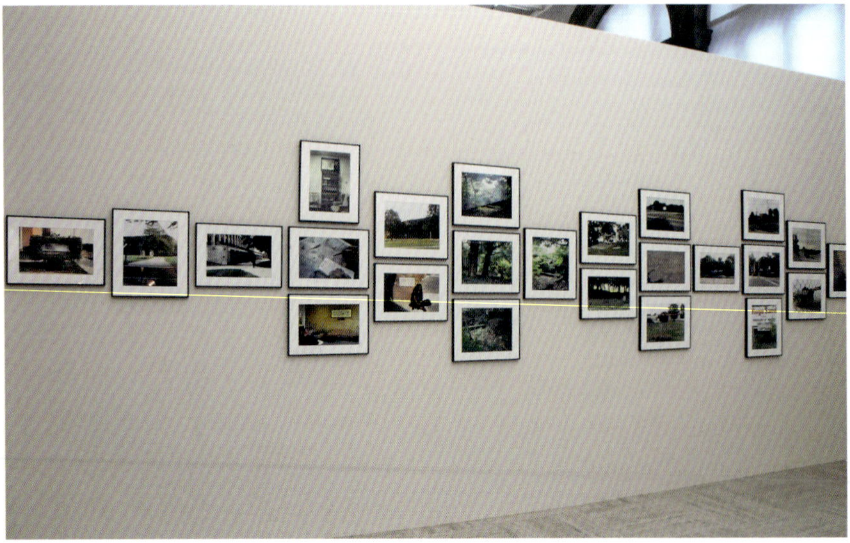

**Fig. 2.16.** Renée Green, *Partially Buried*, 1996–97. Mixed-media installation. Installation view, Musée cantonal des beaux-arts, Lausanne, 2009. Image courtesy of Renée Green and Free Agent Media.

May 4 invariably is, as much a fiction as Michener's "nonfiction." At the center of these narratives is the journalist, artist, or historian who attempts to reconstruct what occurred, who imaginatively "returns" to that fateful moment when the American system was profoundly shaken, and to the place where it all occurred.

A selection of color photos recalls her visit (fig. 2.16). Arranged, too, in no given order, are images of the town of Kent and its industrial environs (such as a crumbling barn, a cracked sidewalk, a fast-food joint, a heap of mining waste) and still photos of Green touring the locations on campus where the momentous events described by Michener occurred; and there are photos of Green visiting the site of the *Woodshed*. Close-ups, long shots, and pans, these exposures are staged, cinematic. They resemble film stills. Such images cannot fail to remind us of Smithson's magazine piece "A Tour of the Monuments of Passaic, New Jersey" (1967), itself a cinematic narrative of return. Enlisting yet another format of Smithson's, the "tour," Green unearths Smithson's earthwork and its complicated history, and—simultaneously—her own history.

Smithson takes a bus from Manhattan to Rutherford, New Jersey, the town where he grew up, and walks along the Passaic River to Passaic, the place where he was born. His article leads a reader on a tour of the rusted totems (the "monuments") of the industrial city. His text is a meditation on a hot system that is cooling—that is slowly, inevitably, winding down. A long pipe on a muddy shore pumps sludge from the river bottom to an unseen destination (*The Great Pipe Monument*, Smithson calls it, with characteristic irony). *The Fountain Monument*—six horizontal "smokestacks" embedded in the riverbank—floods the polluted water with "liquid smoke." The first of these sights is *The Bridge Monument* (fig. 2.17). As Smithson crosses the old bridge spanning the river—as he enters the surreal world of New Jersey's "glassy" air and "stale" sun—metaphors of depiction replace actual things and places. The midday sun "cinema-tize[s]" the river shore. The bridge he walks on is an "enormous photograph" of wood and steel. The muddy river beneath the bridge's pylons resembles a moving film, its imagery "a continuous blank." Photographing the bridge is like "photographing a photograph," Smithson writes. "I have been wandering in a moving picture that I couldn't quite picture."[107]

In *Partially Buried*, Green also wanders in a forest of depictions. All the photos, films, and writings about the Kent State massacre, about Smithson and his *Woodshed*, precede and mediate her journey. Green has walked into an "enormous picture" of Smithson's invention. Her visit to Kent State has been catalyzed by Smithson's journey there thirty-six years earlier.

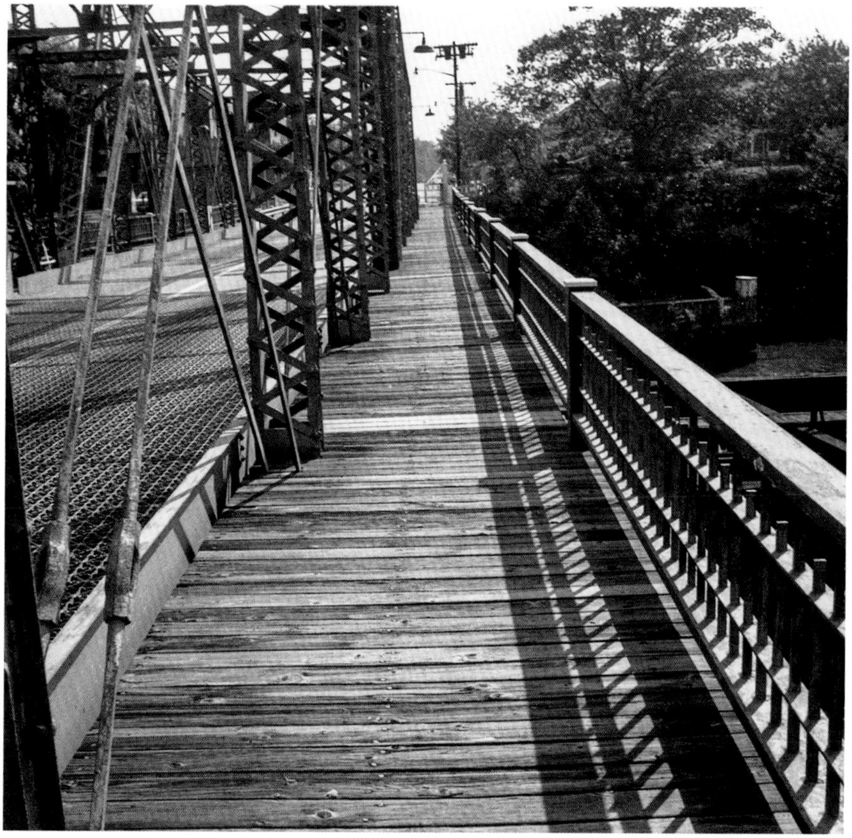

**Fig. 2.17.** Robert Smithson, *A Tour of the Monuments of Passaic, New Jersey (The Bridge Monument)*, 1967. 6 photographs and 1 cut photostat map. National Museum of Art, Architecture and Design, Oslo, Norway. Art © Holt-Smithson Foundation / Licensed by VAGA, New York. Courtesy of James Cohan, New York.

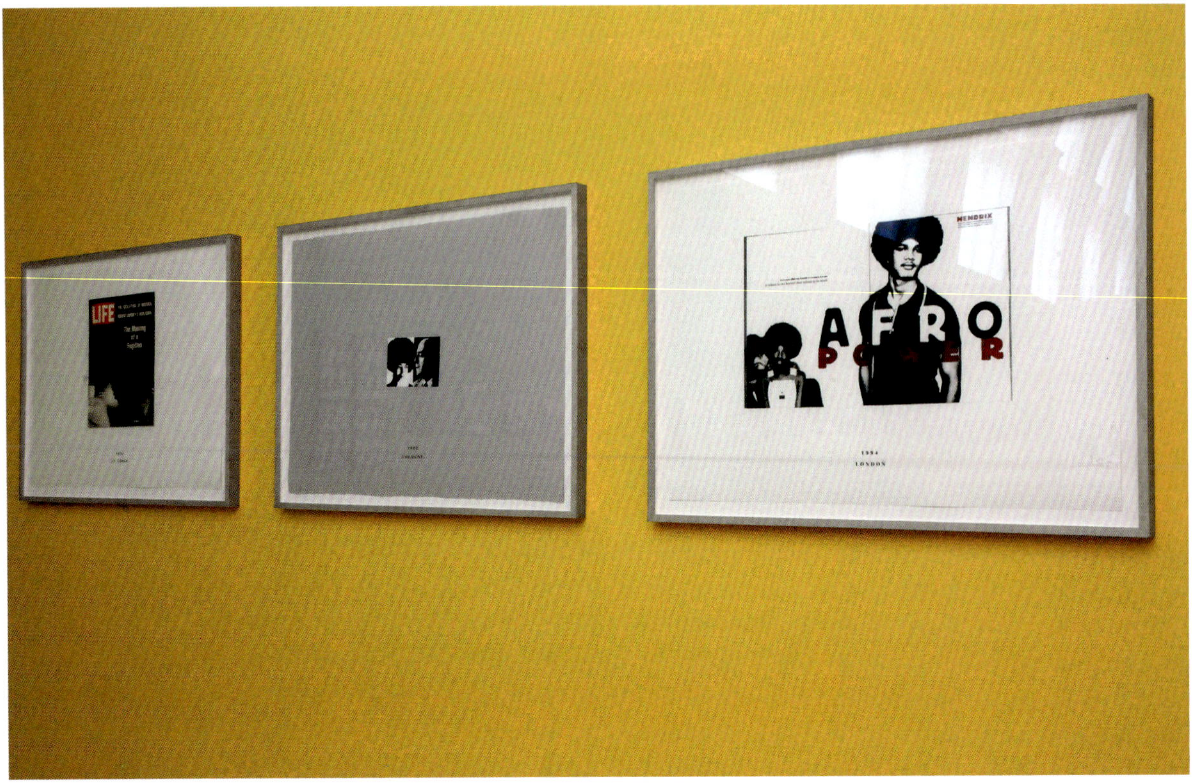


**Fig. 2.18.** Renée Green, *Partially Buried Triptych*, 1996. 3 lithographs. Image courtesy of Renée Green and Free Agent Media.

We arrive at an arrangement of three framed photo lithographs (fig. 2.18). The first of these images is the cover of the September 11, 1970, issue of *Life* magazine. It depicts the activist and political theorist Angela Davis after guns registered in Davis's name were used in a failed kidnapping that left a Marin County judge and three other people dead, and after Davis went underground ("The Making of a Fugitive: Wanted by the FBI: Angela Davis," the headline reads).[108] The middle image is a double portrait of Davis and philosopher Theodor Adorno, whose course she attended in Frankfurt in 1965–66. Juxtaposed with the incendiary *Life* cover, the diptych affords a more nuanced view of Davis as a young Frankfurt School intellectual.[109] A layout from a Nineties British fashion magazine completes the arrangement. Depicting black models in hip-huggers and natural hair (dubbed "the Hendrix" by the magazine's editors), the portfolio is a pastiche of radical Sixties and Seventies imagery. As we look from left to right, the signature "Afro" hairstyle adopted by black people in defiance of straightened "white" hair undergoes a transformation. Denatured, divorced from its historical context, the Afro has become yet another prop for marketing Sixties-nostalgic clothing and accessories. A once-potent symbol of Black Power is a degraded copy of the original, a signifier of "revolutionary glamour," of fashion with an edge.[110]

We enter a second gallery painted the color of an overripe orange. Shag and sisal carpets, paper globe lanterns, tangerine pillows, vintage furniture, a macramé wall hanging, video monitors, and a Super 8 film projector complete the arrangement (fig. 2.19). The chairs and pillows beckon us to sit down, to read and look. We peruse copies of the 1970 Kent State yearbook and 1970 *World Almanac*, and a hardcopy edition of Michener's book. More than ninety pop and R&B albums familiar to Green from childhood are displayed along a wall and are available to play.[111]

We move around the room, listening to these tracks and viewing the different monitors. *Super 8*, a short film shot in the very medium of Sixties home movies, depicts Green's childhood home and neighborhood, and her visit to Kent State.[112] Green re-presents the trip documented in the wall of "film stills" as an actual *film*, adding yet another layer of depiction, another point of view, to the expansive installation. After a few minutes, a phone rings. An unidentified man leaves a message. Green could have omitted this interruption but has chosen not to—an important detail,

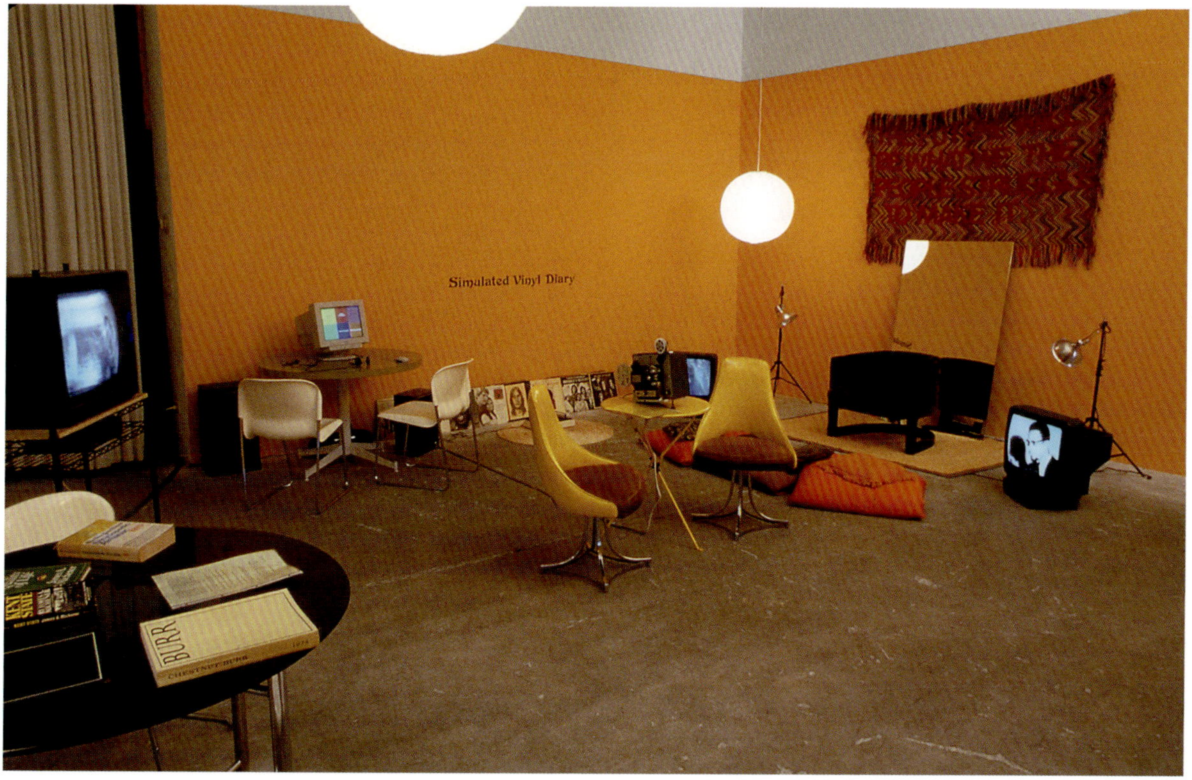


**Fig. 2.19.** Renée Green, *Partially Buried*, 1996. Mixed-media installation. Installation view, Pat Hearn Gallery, New York, 1996. Image: Tom Warren. Image courtesy of Renée Green and Free Agent Media.

in my view. The caller's voice disrupts the film's exegesis, the "story" of her "return." And so we realize that *Super 8* isn't a film, exactly, but a video of a film projected onto a screen, a work internally divided, split in two, two media folded into one. And, in fact, there are *too many* parts in *Partially Buried*, too many different media, too many ways of listening and seeing, too many images to take in, too many *things*.[113] What might at first appear a lack of formal rigor is precisely the point: there is no one "true" account of the massacre or of any event, Green implies. There are only further accounts and recollections.

So it is with Smithson, too—his life and his work. Another monitor shows an interview with Brinsley Tyrrell, the art professor who hosted Smithson during his visit, and a conversation with the journalist and curator Dorothy Shinn.[114] Shinn retells the history of *Partially Buried Woodshed*'s creation and its decay, events also recounted by Tyrrell. Shinn's account of Smithson's visit supplements Tyrrell's firsthand memories. (Shinn, who gives Green the concrete shards, is also a source of primary evidence.) Now Green entwines her work and biography with Smithson's. On a different monitor, the artist's cousins, Lonnie and Janice Turner, recall the heyday of black activism in Cleveland during the Seventies, and its decline during the Eighties and Nineties. Eventually the discussion turns to Green and her family. The protagonist of *Super 8* and the photo frieze is a *character* in a work by Green, a persona, I suggested. Green identifies her in the third person as "she." The Green who interviews the Turners speaks in the artist's voice, as an "I." There are two narrators in *Partially Buried*, two "Renée Greens," two rememberers. The second Green, who speaks in her own voice, recalls the fear she felt during the Hough riots in Cleveland in 1966, in which several African Americans lost their lives.[115] And she recalls her perplexity as a small child watching news reports of civil rights marchers being water-hosed in Birmingham, and a family trip to Georgia when she experienced the humiliations of Jim Crow firsthand:

> Hosings of black people in the South, watching it on TV and just saying, "What's going on with that? Why are they doing that?" And then us trying to make a trip to the South, when I was three, we all had to go in a caravan, we couldn't drive around and stay in any hotels, or go into any restaurants.[116]

She remembers the Kent State shootings too. The artist's mother, Gloria Constance Green, was an instructor in an experimental music course in the Music and Speech Building that spring. She drove to Kent that very morning. A running script in the video *Partially Buried* mimics the news flashes the ten-year old Green watched as she waited for her mother to return from the violent campus:

> The girl watched the news and waited anxiously, often. That's partly what she recollects of childhood. Waiting. Seeing the running text of news reporting students shot at Kent State moving across the bottom of the TV screen.

Their reunion is a dim recollection, dominated by the memory of pop songs (all of them available for us to listen to) drifting in from neighbors' houses:

> TV programs were interrupted and her mother late returning home from there. Across the street kids played Jackson Five 45s and Sly Stone. The girl smoothed her bedspread and checked for order. Finally her mother did arrive, but she can't remember now what either said.[117]

A final monitor plays an excerpt from *Underground* (1976), Emile De Antonio, Haskell Wexler, and Mary Lampson's agitprop film about the Weathermen. Michener names several members of the radical group as "regional travelers" to Kent State in the months leading up to May 4, 1970, and claims they did much to foment the massacre. "Wanted" fugitives in 1976, Kathy Boudin, William Ayers, Bernardine Dohrn, Jeff Jones, and Cathy Wilkerson, are shown in a safe house in Los Angeles through a dark scrim with the lights turned off and from behind, their backs reflected in a mirror. A facsimile of this set—a large mirror, a brown velvet chair—dominates Green's orange room. A tattered banner hangs above, emblazoned with the Weathermen slogan *The Future Will Be What the People Struggle to Make It* (fig. 2.20).

The long Sixties is the last time the modernist dream of radical newness did not seem farfetched, I have claimed. The idea of revolution did not seem altogether implausible then—at least not on the radical left, and not as late as 1976. The "Sixties" are definitely not over in the self-enclosed world of screens and mirrors presented to great dramatic effect in *Underground*. "History isn't something that happens far away and long ago," Ayers says. "History is made by people." "We want to make a revolution. We think there *has to be* a revolution," declares Dohrn. "We're professional revolutionaries," says Jones without the slightest trace of doubt.[118] "Eventually there will be a revolution," an anonymous woman remarks. "I hope I'll be around to see it." A cover of the pop song "New World Coming" closes *Underground*. As performed by activist Nina Simone, the lyrics of Barry Mann and Cynthia Weil's Aquarian anthem "New World Coming" assume an apocalyptic edge:

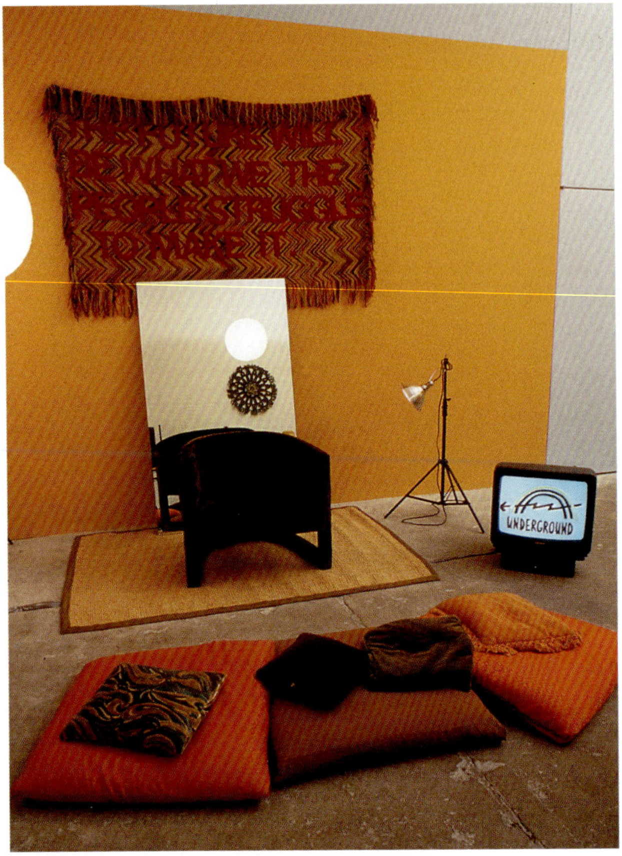


**Fig. 2.20.** Renée Green, *Partially Buried*, 1996. Mixed-media installation. Installation view, Pat Hearn Gallery, New York, 1996. Image: Tom Warren. Image courtesy of Renée Green and Free Agent Media.

> There's a new world coming
> And it's just around the bend
> There's a new world coming
> This one's about to end. . . .[119]

*There's a new world coming. This one's about to end.* A rainbow crossed with a lightning arrow, the Weathermen logo, appears as Simone sings. During the sunny era of Clintonian neoliberalism, when *Partially Buried* was first exhibited, the revolutionary rhetoric of the Seventies could not seem more strange, more remote.

As it turned out, *Partially Buried* was the first of many *Woodsheds*.[120] Sam Durant's *Partially Buried: Utopia Reflected/Dystopia Revealed* (1998) consists of two mirrors placed flat on the floor covered in loam (fig. 2.21). Durant's work evokes one of Smithson's rock-salt-and-mirror *Displace-*

*ments* of February 1969, yet not exactly.[121] For Durant has buried CD players beneath the dirt piles, a clue that we are not looking at a Smithson at all. One of the tapes projects the voice of Hugh Romney (also known as "Wavy Gravy"), speaking at Woodstock that summer. In the film *Woodstock* (1970), directed by Michael Wadleigh, Romney, a member of the collective Hog Farm, is a picture of generosity. Nobody had expected such a massive crowd. The local townspeople were unprepared for the hundreds of thousands of teenagers who poured in. When it rained, the audience was covered in mud. Romney's gravelly voice, emanating from the sod, is reassuring yet distant: "What we have here is breakfast in bed for four hundred thousand. Now, it's not gonna be steak and eggs or anything, but it's gonna be good food.... We're all feeding each other! We must be in heaven, man!"

The second soundtrack is of Altamont, the infamous concert staged by the Rolling Stones that December to capitalize on Woodstock's astonishing success. The organizers were also unprepared for the crowd of several hundred thousand that gathered on the burned hills above the Altamont Speedway in northern California. The sound system and waste facilities

**Fig. 2.21.** Sam Durant, *Partially Buried 1960s/70s Dystopia Revealed (Mick Jagger at Altamont) & Utopia Reflected (Wavy Gravy at Woodstock)*, 1998. Mirrors, dirt, audio systems. Photograph courtesy of Sam Durant.

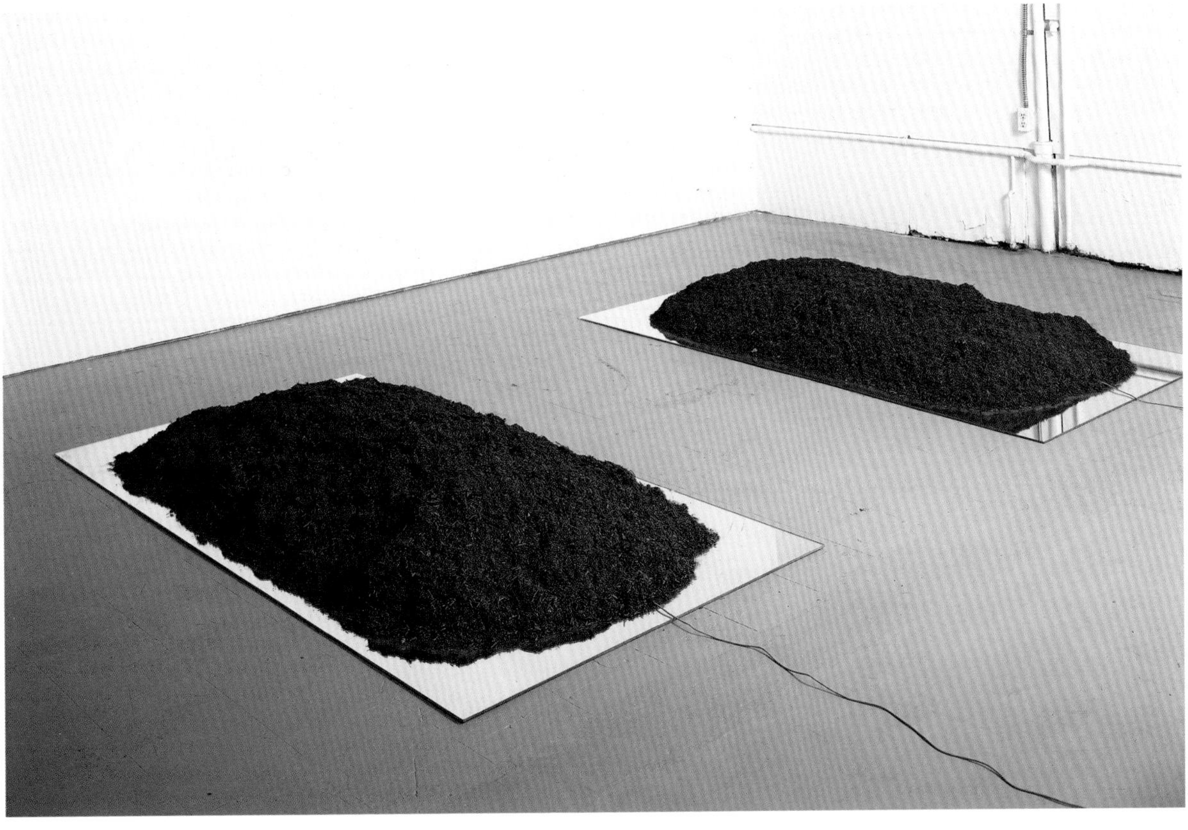

were woefully inadequate. Hits of bad acid circulated through the crowd.[122] The tape captures the festival's culminating incident, as recorded in the Maysles Brothers' film of the concert, *Gimme Shelter* (1970). The strung-out crowd is pushing aggressively toward the stage. The Hells Angels, who have been hired as bodyguards, attack the audience with sawed-off billiard cues. "Why are we fighting? Why are we fighting?" Mick Jagger cries. "Everyone—Hell's Angels, everybody, let's just *keep ourselves together*." One of the concertgoers near the stage, an eighteen-year-old black man named Meredith Hunter, wearing a lime-green suit, allegedly brandished a gun. He was immediately stabbed to death by a pugnacious Angel. Three other people died at Altamont that day. Two fans were run over in a hit-and-run incident, and yet another, high on LSD, jumped into a ditch.

Where Durant's dirt piles alluded to the *Partially Buried Woodshed* in name only, the works he exhibited in his show "Altamont" at Blum & Poe in Los Angeles referenced Smithson's work literally.[123] In contrast to the actual, decaying earthwork, Durant's *Upside Down and Backwards, Completely Unburied* is a miniature scale model of a brand-new woodshed—the woodshed the farmer built before the university acquired the site. Durant imagines the woodshed long before Smithson discovered it, untainted by age or history. Inversely, in *Reflected Upside Down and Backwards* (1999), a scale model of this "new" woodshed supports its charred twin, the *Partially Buried Woodshed* vandalized in 1975 (fig. 2.22).

Durant's works are impossibly anachronistic. His "new" shed would have antedated the shed that Smithson buried, while the burned shed postdated Smithson's visit by five years. In the first of these works, CD decks play the Rolling Stones' "Gimme Shelter," Neil Young's "Hey, My My (Into the Black)," and Nirvana's "Smells Like Teen Spirit" simultaneously. In the second, acoustic versions of Nirvana's "All Apologies" and Young's "My My, Hey Hey (Out of the Blue)" overlap in a continuous loop. Just as the voices of Wavy Gravy and Mick Jagger blurred in Durant's dirt mirrors, here the sounds of Sixties rock and Nineties grunge blend in an indiscernible din.

A subsequent work in the artist's "Altamont" sequence, *Entropy in Reverse (Gimme Shelter Backwards)* (1999), is a two-channel video of the Maysles film sped up and played backward (fig. 2.23). The project opens with the garbled sounds of Jagger singing, and a shot of a rapidly rising sun—the film's final frames. (The actual film concludes with a sunset.) Concertgoers leaving Altamont walk backward, like zombies, toward the speedway. Medics carry a body on a stretcher in reverse. A young woman bursts into tears. Her words are inscrutable; yet her grief is unmistakable. The Rolling Stones gather in the Maysles' editing room, where they watch Hunter's murder in slow motion. The knife retracts from Hunter's body into

**Fig. 2.22.** Sam Durant, *Reflected Upside Down and Backwards*, 1999. Wood, acrylic, asphalt, audio system. Photograph: Josh White. Courtesy of Sam Durant.

**Fig. 2.23.** Sam Durant, *Entropy in Reverse (Gimme Shelter Backwards)*, 1999. Video, twin-channel projection. Photograph courtesy of Sam Durant.

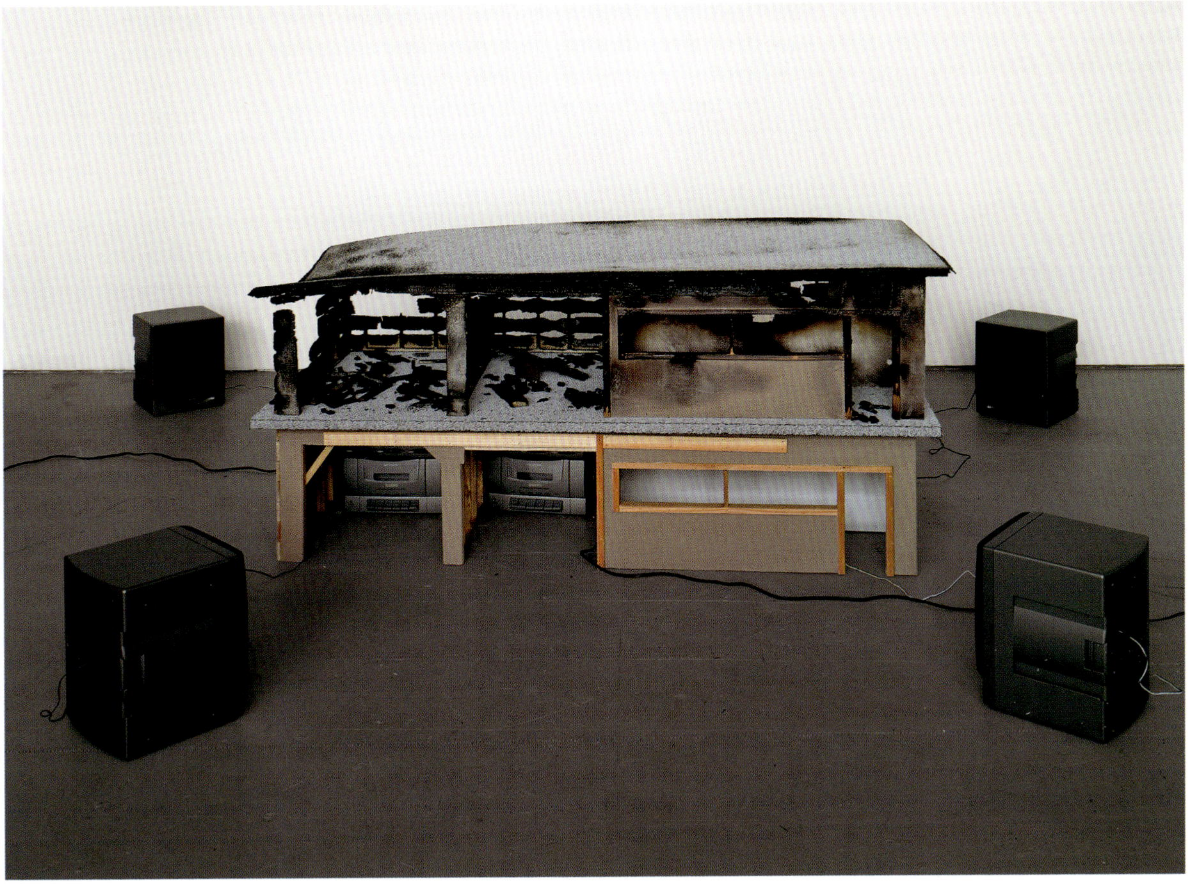

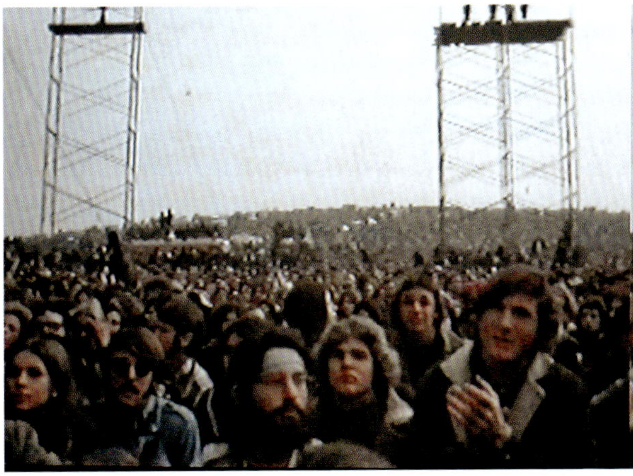

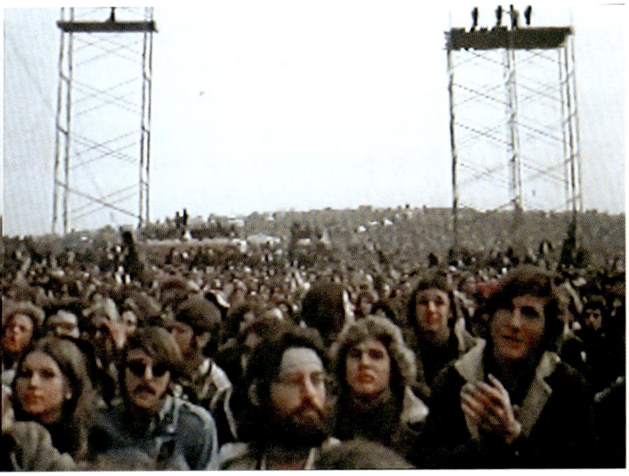

the Angel's hand. A naked woman dances in a trance in front of the stage. The Angels ride in on motorcycles, backward. The loop arrives at the beginning.

Doubled, reversed, put into fast forward, *Gimme Shelter* is no longer the film we think we know.[124] Estranged, it has become an object. We see it differently. We see it *again*. *Gimme Shelter* consolidated the view of Altamont as a turning point, a transition from one Sixties to another. It became a pivotal reference in Sixties declension narratives. Woodstock, it is often said, was utopia, Altamont dystopia. In the Catskills the counterculture triumphed, at Altamont it collapsed. Like "Kent State," the stabbing of Hunter has come to represent the end of the good Sixties. *Gimme Shelter* documents this entropic descent frame by frame.

In Todd Gitlin's remarkable memoir *The Sixties: Years of Hope, Days of Rage*, the descriptions of the ill-fated concert are reminiscent of the paintings of Bosch. Stoned fans crawl over one another to get closer to the stage. Doctors are prevented from helping people come down from bad trips. The "angels of death" beat up fans. At Altamont, observes Gitlin, "we ... witnessed the famous collectivity of a generation cracking into thousands of shards." For Gitlin, a former president of Students for a Democratic Society, the Stones concert, the Manson murders, the Weathermen bombings, the Chicago Police Department's execution of Black Panthers Fred Hampton and Mark Clark, and the Kent State massacre are of a piece. These events represent a shattering of Sixties ideals, the immolation of the counterculture under the pressure of an unnamed yet powerful entropic force.[125]

Durant's interpretation of this history is more ambivalent. His works suggest a fascination with the dreadful concert he missed. Altamont is not a firsthand memory, as for Gitlin, but a memory of *representations* of that event, the Altamont of all the photos he has seen and the articles he has read, above all, the Altamont of *Gimme Shelter*.[126] Durant gives aesthetic form to the "two Sixties." Literalizing this binary scheme sculpturally and cinematically, he unsettles Sixties declension narratives. He reverses *Gimme Shelter* and speeds it up, images the impossible. He reverses time (the time of the film's duration, visible in the left monitor, decreases as the tape moves forward) and "reverses" entropy (as the clock is turned back, the day's violent incidents are "turned around," *as if they haven't happened*). Altamont was not an aberration or betrayal of Sixties values, the works of Durant suggests, so much as the entropic fulfillment of the era's exalted expectations. For every Dr. King there was a Charles Manson, for every sweet-natured Wavy Gravy an "angel of death" clutching a knife.

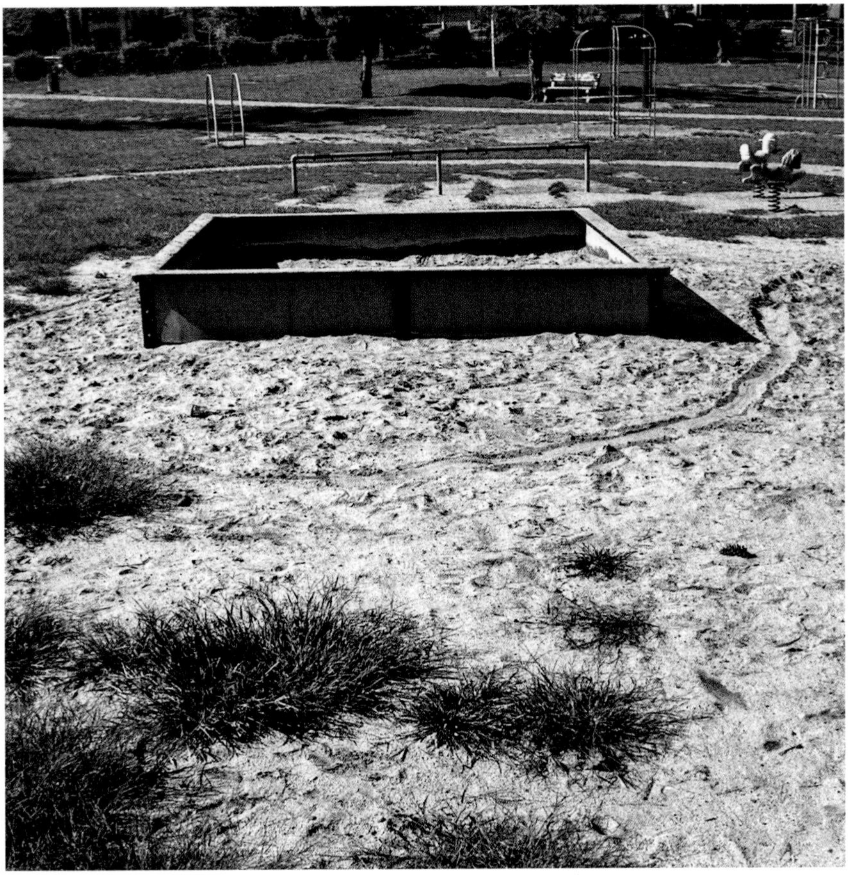

**Fig. 2.24.** Robert Smithson, *A Tour of The Monuments of Passaic, New Jersey [The Sandbox Monument]*, 1967. 6 photographs and 1 cut photostat map. National Museum of Art, Architecture and Design, Oslo, Norway. Art © Holt-Smithson Foundation / Licensed by VAGA, New York. Courtesy of James Cohan, New York.

Durant's dissection of the Woodstock/Altamont myth is a demonstration of entropy, the transition from a "pure" state into a degraded one. Rather than privilege one over another, he stages the constitutive relationship of these terms, an opposition that breaks down, inevitably.[127] Think of Smithson's description of the *Sand-Box Monument* in "The Monuments of Passaic" (fig. 2.24). One half of the sandbox is filled with white sand. The other half contains black sand. A child runs clockwise around the box until the sand becomes gray. Then she runs counterclockwise around the box and the sand becomes even grayer. The discrete halves of the box, black and white sand, have become a blurry mess. In his works inspired by *Partially Buried Woodshed*, Durant stages the collapse of two closed systems repeatedly. The result of this mixing is "unitary chaos," a chaotic sameness. Woodstock and Altamont inhabit the same entropic system. The "two Sixties" are one.[128]

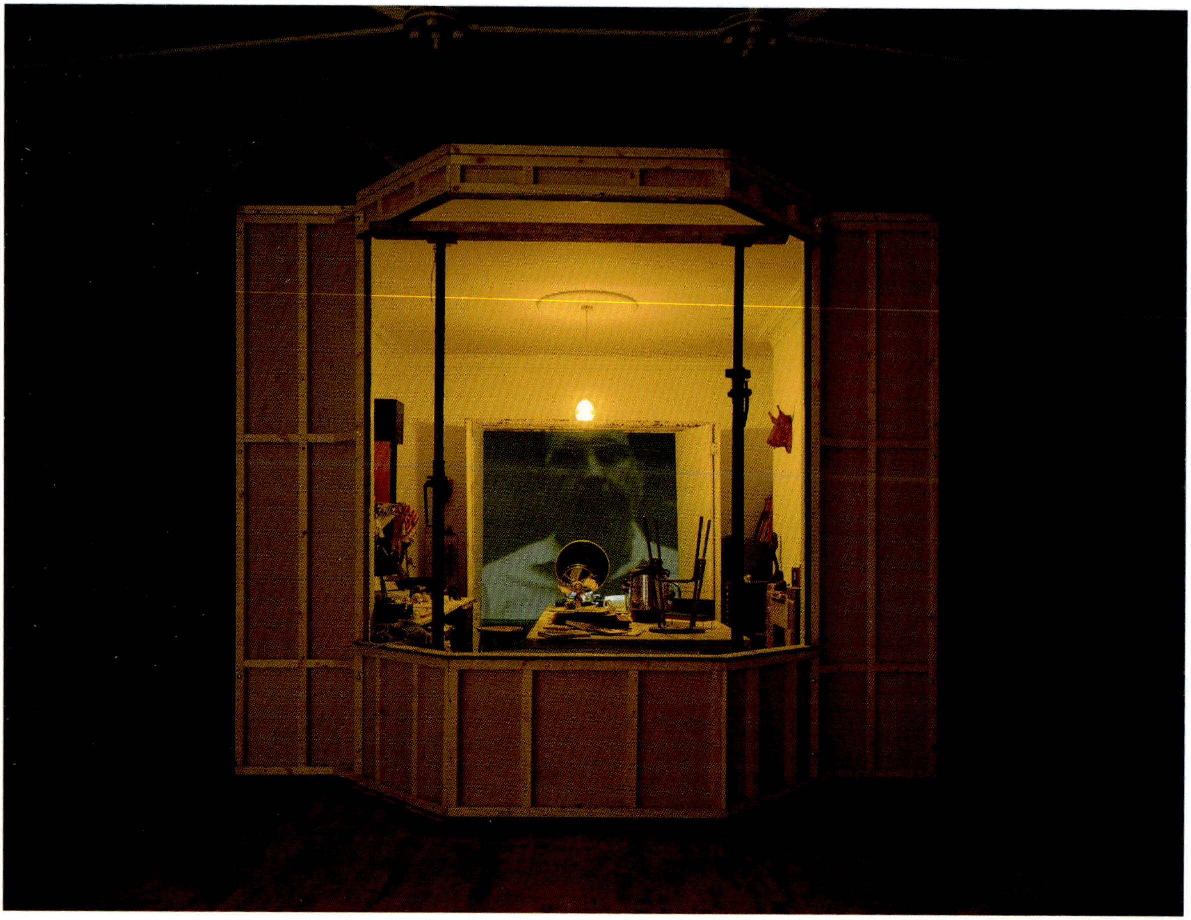

**Fig. 2.25.** Mike Nelson, *Triple Bluff Canyon (The Projection Room)*, 2004. Reconstructed studio of Mike Nelson, 1996–2004, with found video projection. Courtesy of Mike Nelson and 303 Gallery, New York; Galleria Franco Noero, Turin; Matt's Gallery, London; and neugerriemschneider, Berlin.

Now consider Mike Nelson's *Triple Bluff Canyon*, an installation presented at Modern Art Oxford in 2004. We enter a dimly lit foyer, where we encounter the closed ticket booth of a seedy movie theater.[129] Moving through a door up a stairwell, we come upon a reconstruction of Nelson's former South London studio, a room that no longer exists (fig. 2.25). A bare lightbulb creates a portentous mood. Things used and no longer useful—a coffee pot, a fan, an overturned stool, a thrift-store painting of chimpanzees, a statuette of a decapitated Virgin, a stuffed raven—crowd every available surface. The thrift-shop smell of these things permeates the gallery. On a table we spy a package addressed conspicuously in Arabic with a stamp depicting a mosque.

A film projection on a back wall. A conspiracy theorist named Jordan Maxwell is speaking with an American accent. Maxwell discusses the purported occult symbolism of U.S. government and corporate logos (the double cross of Exxon, the pentagram of the Pentagon, and so on). His ramblings are easy to dismiss. The sensible viewer knows better than to listen to this crank. Yet Maxwell's remarks, recorded in 1993, are bizarrely resonant in the age of terror, when security alerts are broadcast with the frequency of weather reports and surveillance of public spaces and private communications is increasingly common.[130] Quite unexpectedly, Maxwell's paranoiac discourse dovetails with Smithson's entropology. The visionary artist and the conspiracy theorist are both interested in the ways the threat of entropy impacts "hot" societies. "The U.S. government wants to frighten people," Maxwell says. "They want as much chaos as possible."[131] Maxwell speaks of a widespread fear of entropy and the manipulation of that emotion by the state: the looming threat of social breakdown serves to maintain social control. That is how hot systems sustain themselves. In "Entropy and the New Monuments," Smithson describes the mass jubilation occasioned by the 1965 electrical blackout in northeastern cities. The threat of social anarchy that inculcates fear in much of the populace, as Maxwell suggests, is a cause of celebration by the multitudes at the lowest rungs of the hierarchy.

Entering another door in Nelson's warren of rooms, we find ourselves in a claustrophobic wood corridor resembling a mine shaft traversing a sand-filled space. We arrive at a room lit by a single incandescent bulb (fig. 2.26). Within this strange, dark chamber, half-buried in orange sand, we discover a barrel emblazoned with the cockle shell logo of the eponymous energy conglomerate. Reversing our course, we climb another stairwell into a high open gallery, only to realize that the corridor and room we have just left is a hidden chamber of a reconstructed *Partially Buried Woodshed*, buried in the spiral counterclockwise manner of the original (fig. 2.27). Trudging in the sand, we climb Nelson's manmade dune. Inside the shed are more barrels; one of them is painted "TEXACO."

Where Green documents the fact that the *Woodshed* barely exists physically, and Durant makes it "new" and burns it, Nelson reconstructs the work that Smithson made. His work resembles the *Partially Buried Woodshed* of January 1970, the *Woodshed* we know from photographs.[132] Nelson is Smithson's restorer, his Viollet-le-Duc. His "shed" is not pristine like Durant's scale models, but a replica of the *Woodshed* of 1970, a "shed" that has *just* been buried—a "fresh" *Partially Buried Woodshed*. We imagine we are viewing a perfect copy until we notice the many adjustments that Nelson has made. The cracks on the stucco façade are not the same length or in the same location as in the original. The central pier of

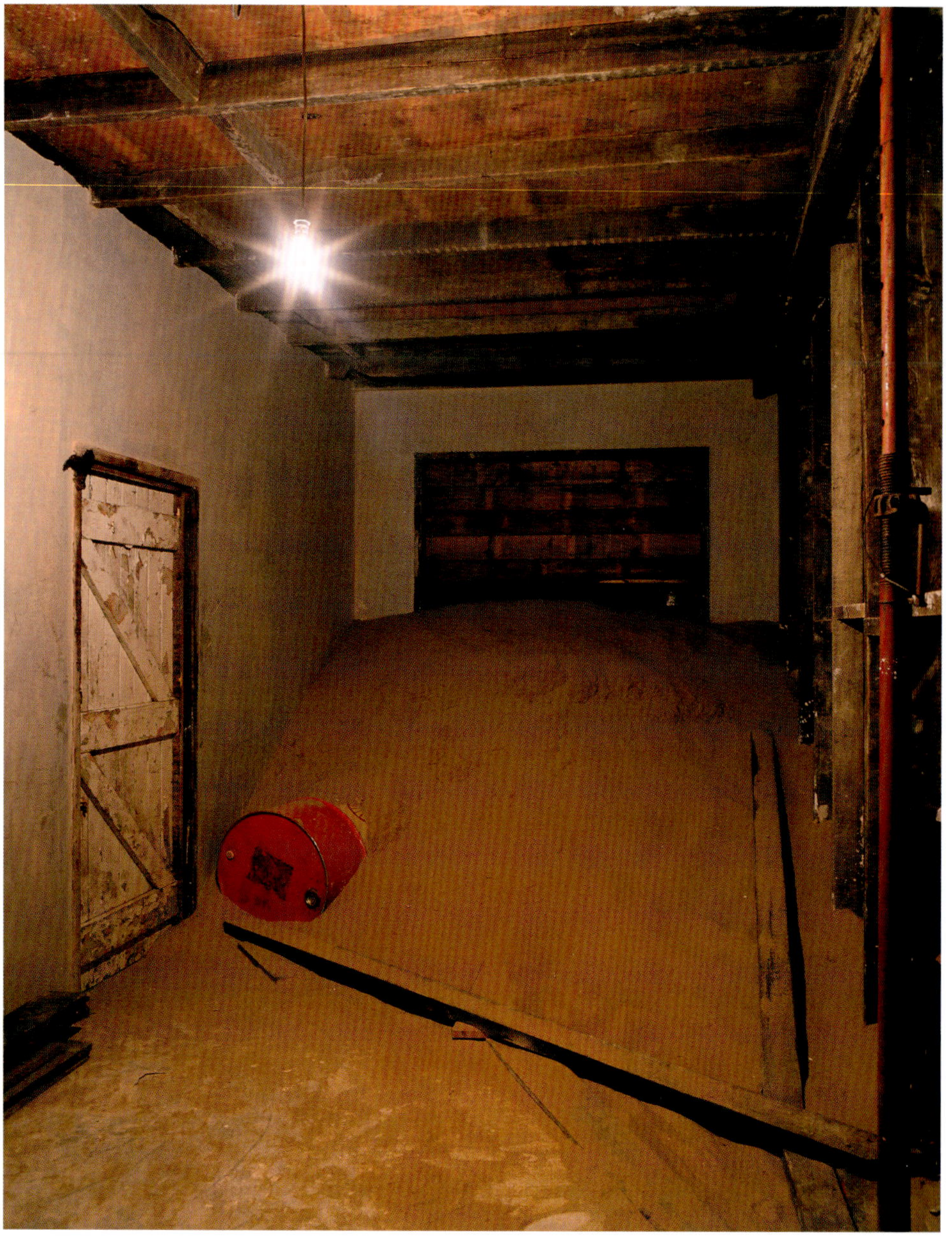

**Fig. 2.26.** Mike Nelson, *Triple Bluff Canyon*, 2004 (interior view). Built environment. Courtesy of Mike Nelson and 303 Gallery, New York; Galleria Franco Noero, Turin; Matt's Gallery, London; and neugerriemschneider, Berlin.

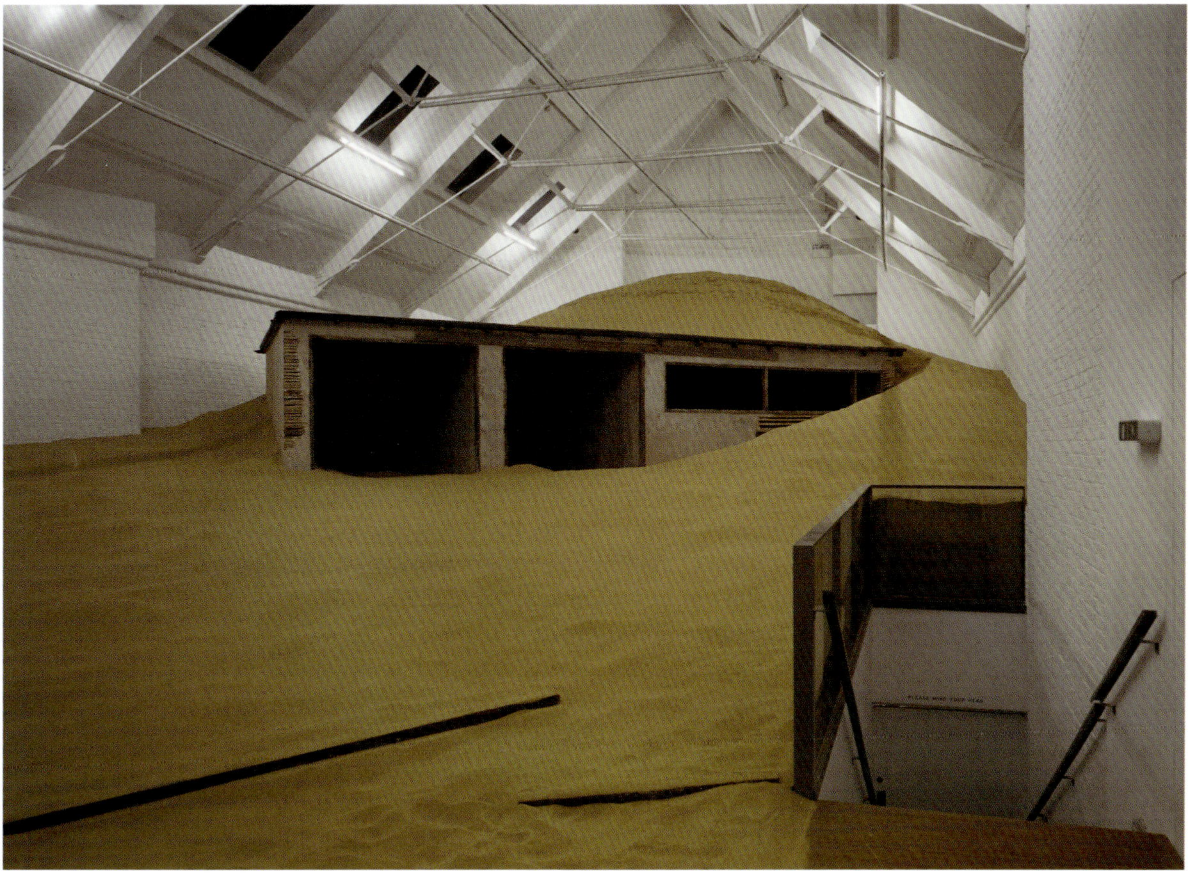

**Fig. 2.27.** Mike Nelson, *Triple Bluff Canyon*, 2004 (installation view). Built environment. Courtesy of Mike Nelson and 303 Gallery, New York; Galleria Franco Noero, Turin; Matt's Gallery, London; and neugerriemschneider, Berlin.

Nelson's construction lacks the diagonal cross-beam of Smithson's shed. Even more, Nelson has built his artwork to three-quarter scale.[133] Nelson's "Woodshed" is an inexact replica. It is neither pristine like Durant's scale model, nor is it the actual ruin discovered by Green. His work is an ersatz *nonsite* of Smithson's work of 1970, a project that no longer exists in its initial form. Reimagining Smithson's earthwork across time, Nelson perverts it, as Durant does (rendering the *Woodshed* miniature, burning it, presenting it "new"). He combines Smithson's arrangement with the contemporaneous work of another land artist (Walter De Maria's *Earth Room* [1968]), and with other works by Smithson (he pours the sand of the *Sand-Box Monument* "onto" the *Woodshed*). Nelson displaces Smithson's unruly dirt dump to the pristine modernist gallery it attempted to escape. As Smithson writes in his essay "Cultural Confinement":

> Museums, like asylums and jails, have wards and cells—in other words, neutral rooms called "galleries." A work of art when placed in a gallery loses its charge, and becomes a portable object or surface disengaged from the outside world. A vacant white room with lights is still a submission to the neutral.[134]

Nelson does not heed the lesson of Smithson's text, his Foucauldian critique of the "neutral" white cube. Replicating the *Woodshed* inside an art gallery, he contains a project that was meant to scatter and decay, betraying the older artist's intentions. He stages the fantasy that we could "return," if that were possible—that we could turn back entropy. He allows us to imagine for a moment that we are *seeing* the just-buried *Woodshed* for ourselves—and then he forecloses that desire. We are reminded, after the initial gasp of surprise, that Nelson's shed is ersatz after all. That it will be dismantled after the show comes down, far more quickly than Smithson's work was, in fact. We are reminded that his work is temporary *and* contemporary, even as Smithson's *Woodshed* endures. The entropic work flickers in and out of awareness; the idea of the *Woodshed* has far outlasted the sculpture that Smithson made.

Nelson's *Woodshed* speaks of its moment. It is the spring of 2004. The outrageous abuses of Muslim prisoners at Abu Ghraib have come to light. The British military will count seventy-five casualties in Iraq before the year is over.[135] Nelson's replica of Smithson's earthwork, buried in sand, in a hall in Oxford, England; his drums emblazoned with the logos of energy conglomerates; his package inscribed in Arabic; and his projection of Maxwell's creepy lecture locate viewers with exacting precision in the very place and time of viewing. And this establishes a structure of comparison between that situation and another place and time. Nelson's remake of an iconic artwork of the Vietnam War era exposes an absence of dissent in his own time, the hopeless failure of the Left and peace activists to mount an effective response to the U.S.–U.K. invasion of oil-rich Iraq.[136] His simulacral *Woodshed* confronted viewers' nostalgia for the Sixties and Seventies, when avant-garde works of art and activism seemed to make a difference.

## Against Nostalgia

**At least you did something. What a world that must have been where ordinary people actually did things.**

Dana Spiotta, *Eat the Document*

Why have artists felt compelled to remake *Partially Buried Woodshed*? The fact that Smithson's work became entangled in the history of the antiwar movement, an unusual feat for any artwork, is part of the story. I want now to explore what I would describe as the affective quality of the ephemeral artworks of the Sixties and Seventies—works we can only know retrospectively. The Happening, the Judson dance, the Post-Minimalist process sculpture, and the earthwork were made at *specific* moments. The time of the work's making and viewing (often but hardly always the same) was embedded in the work's form. The titles of some of these projects spoke of their duration. The viewer of Richard Serra's *Tearing Lead from 1:00–1:47* (1968; fig. 2.28), for example, was asked to imagine the action of a body, of Serra, ripping strips of lead with his metalworker's tools. The heap of metal displayed on the floor of a gallery and the work's title, a gerund, indicated that Serra himself had recently performed this action, that this had taken forty-seven minutes, and that it had taken place in this very room. Serra exhibited the strips of lead as evidence of that effort. The work and title were equivalent.

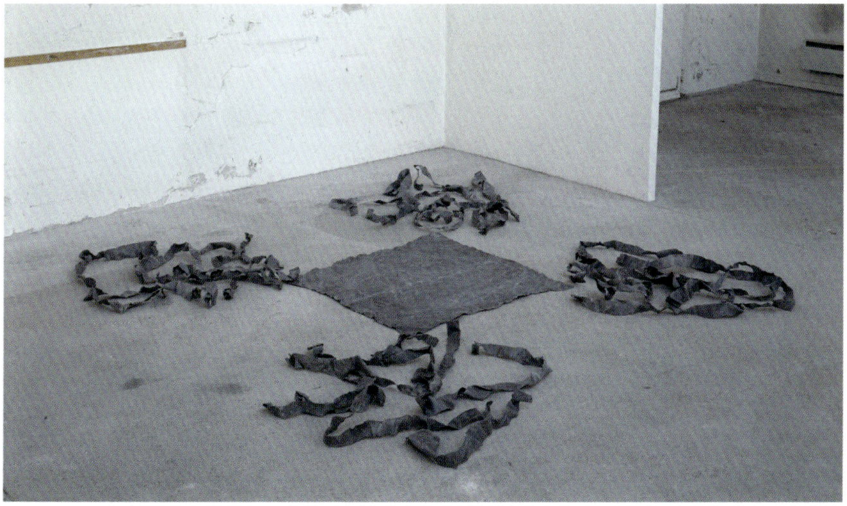

**Fig. 2.28.** Richard Serra, *Tearing Lead 1:00–1:47*, 1968. Lead. Musée national d'art moderne, Paris. © 2017 Richard Serra / Artists Rights Society (ARS), New York. © CNAC / NMAM / Dist. RMN-Grand Palais / Art Resource New York.

Yet Serra's project embodied a contradiction. An audience viewed the sculpture after it was made. An event described in the present tense was presented as an action completed. (The lead had *just* been torn.) And once Serra exhibited the work, it entered the temporal "no man's land" of the recent past. The metal refuse arranged in tatters spoke of a past moment so close to the moment of viewing as to appear invisible. A half-century later, the temporal lag between these moments, the instants of making and perception, is undeniable. Those forty-seven minutes happened a long time ago. They transpired before most viewers of works of this kind were born. And because we can no longer imagine such works as having "just" been made, we perceive them differently than did viewers who saw them new.

As the ephemeral artworks of the Sixties and Seventies age, the well-rehearsed arguments of that time—that they embody the "process" of their making, a process that unfolds in a continuous present tense—make less and less sense.[137] More and more their *pastness* is part of their meaning. These works force us to remember them, to imagine the experience of seeing them for the first time. They inspire longing for an experience we have missed. Smithson once spoke about

> nostalgia for the "pre." We have almost a rinky-dink idea of nature, Mickey Mouse, like the people of my generation have grown up in the industrial blight, and it's not like the wood side that we remember.[138]

The "pre" is Smithson's word for nostalgia, a concept he holds in obvious disdain (a "rinky-dink idea of nature, Mickey Mouse"). It suggests a longing for childhood and nature, for a lost purity. (Wordsworth: "For nature then / (The courser pleasures of my boyish days / And their glad animal movements gone by) / To me was all in all.")[139] Entropology is the science of impurity: there is no such thing as a "pure" natural state unspoiled by human labors, Smithson insists, only a universal condition of entropic becoming, of order dissolving into disorder, of difference decaying into sameness. During the late Thirties and Forties—the period when the Minimalists and Post-Minimalists grew up—the great factories and infrastructural systems of modernity were operating at full steam. "Nature" was never so unspoiled as Smithson's peers imagine. They miss the "wood side" they may never have experienced in actuality, something more likely encountered in works of art and poetry; they miss an experience they missed.

Smithson's Passaic tour leads a reader from a grainy reproduction of Samuel F. B. Morse's *Allegorical Landscape* (1835–36)—a Parnassian image of Mount Helicon and the nymph and spring Aganippe, and a setting sun—into the maw of the "hot" society that came into place as a result of such nineteenth-century technological advances as the steam engine, the railroad, and the telegraph, the last of these invented by Morse himself. (As Smithson implies, these seemingly disconnected inventions—the telegraph that recodes written communication and Morse's nostalgic depiction of a world unpolluted by modernity—are historically linked.) "The Monuments of Passaic" is fiercely antinostalgic. Smithson describes his return to the place of early childhood memory, a place he came to see as "stifling" and "suburban," and which he abandoned as soon as he could.[140] The *Sand-Box Monument* he discovers "under the dead light of the Passaic afternoon" triggers no warm recollections of boyhood games. This and the other "monuments" he encounters are the inglorious reminders of New Jersey's entropic past and future.

Entropy is without feeling, a thermodynamical process. The entropologist is not sentimental. Peering down into this pit, Smithson spies an entropic universe in miniature. The *Sand-Box Monument* affords a premonition of "infinite disintegration and forgetfulness." It is an open grave—a monument *to* entropy. "No longer were there green forests and high mountains," Smithson writes. "All that existed were millions of grains of sand, a vast deposit of bones and stones pulverized into death."[141] The *Sand-Box Monument* causes us to remember the far future, a world emptied of biological life. A site of childhood play affords a vision of catastrophe, a sight of death.

What is the "pre" for the generation of Durant, Nelson, and Green? A rolling text in *Partially Buried* asks:

> Did people have more fun then? Burying buildings with dirt, pouring glue down hills, making islands out of broken glass? Allan Kaprow gave students dollar bills to pin on trees at Kent State then. But what a question! She was alive then. Contemporary. A ten-year-old contemporary.[142]

The "pre" so described is not Smithson's wood side, a "rinky-dink idea of nature," a nature we have known intimately as children and wish we could return to as adults. In practices of return like Green's and Durant's the "pre" is an idea of *culture*. It is a fantasy of aesthetic daring—the nagging suspicion that we have come too late, that the time for such gestures is past, that the Sixties was the "last time" for that sort of thing.

Earlier I suggested that artists and writers who reflect on the Sixties and Seventies in their work betray the mnemonic excess that memory theorists attribute to postrevolutionary generations (they remember "too much.") The desire to revisit the time of childhood or a time that precedes one's birth is known to us as nostalgia.[143] Yet, rather than merely *express*

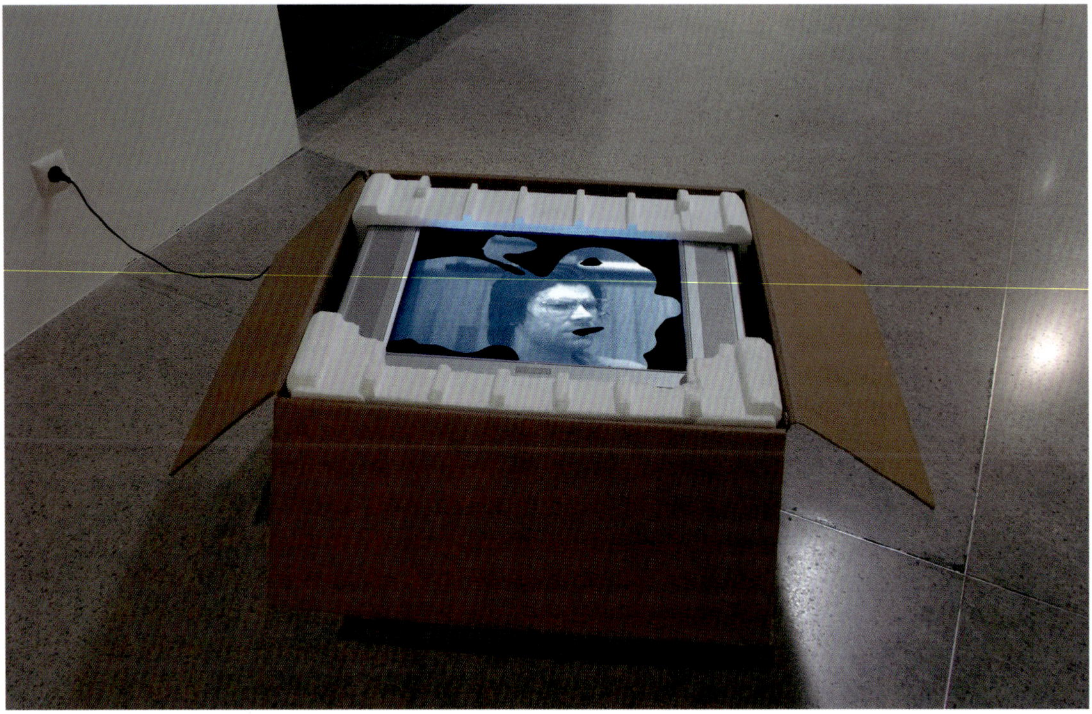

**Fig. 2.29.** Seth Price, *Digital Video Effect: "Spills,"* 2004. TV/DVD player in original packaging, video with altered footage shot by Joan Jonas c. 1970. Detail: Robert Smithson. Photograph courtesy of Seth Price.

or indulge nostalgic longing, the practices that concern us in this book ask how such feelings arise; they interrogate the nature of nostalgia as such—its historical contingency, its sources and effects. And so we will describe these works as antinostalgic.

Consider *Digital Video Effect: Spills* (2004), an installation by the artist Seth Price (fig. 2.29). A single-channel monitor rests on the floor, placed on its side in a Styrofoam-lined shipping box. A twelve-minute video plays in a recurring loop. The original tape was filmed by video artist Joan Jonas. It records a conversation between Smithson, Richard Serra, and the dealer Joseph Helman in Helman's house in St. Louis in 1970.

Price prohibits our usual experience of watching TV. The screen, which faces up, is too low to view comfortably. Instead, we bend down and kneel to watch it. Price blackens Jonas's grainy video, now digitized, with a digital "ink," occluding and revealing the speakers while referencing their works (Smithson's *Glue Pour* and Serra's *Splashing* [1968], a work that entailed pouring molten lead against a wall). The speaker inside the box is muffled, the soundtrack is uneven. The clinking of glasses and uncontrolled comments of Helman's young children interrupt the exchange. We listen carefully in order to understand the artists' and dealer's remarks.

The men are discussing site-specificity, the premise that a work be made for a single location, and only there—the underlying principle of the earthworks and site-constructions of the Seventies. A work made for a place specifically addressed a weakness of modernist sculpture, these artists claimed. Ridding itself of the pedestal of traditional sculpture and the monument's memorializing function, the sculptures of modern masters like Brancusi and Giacometti became portable. As they became nomadic objects, they could be shown anywhere. Yet they bore no connection to the places where they were installed.[144] Worse, the artist forsook control over how his or her work would be presented. ("You take a portable sculpture and put it in a garden setting—that garden setting carries with it a whole set of values that has no benefit to the artist," Smithson remarks to the others.) The generation of Post-Minimalists aimed to exert maximum authority over how their works would be sited and perceived. They dreamed of creating earthbound projects that could not be moved and sold.

Cutting-edge artworks decorate the walls of Helman's home—a Donald Judd metal relief, Robert Morris's plastic model of an earth sculpture, a Warhol *Marilyn* print. The pipe of a Serra prop sculpture is visible behind Serra. Price's virtual ooze flows and ebbs across the screen. Close-up of Marilyn: the movie star's thick eyelashes and famous lips disappear in the digital "ink." The women of the house—Helman's wife Barbara in a fashionable short skirt, a black housekeeper in a domestic's dress—observe the discussion from the kitchen above the den where the men sit. Holt stands aside at the edge of the circle. The Helmans' daughter, a girl in pigtails, pays a visit to Serra and sticks out her tongue at the camera. She then offers Jonas a piece of gum.

Smithson is speaking now. He theorizes an art that "challenges" the "site." An art that will be seen as he intends. A site-specific work is not necessarily a "good" work, Helman retorts. A trader of portable commodities, the dealer is skeptical of artworks that defy this premise. Smithson's response to Helman is defensive and self-righteous:

> I'm not making judgments about whether this is good or bad. I have the right to make my work. Nobody is going to legislate or judge what I'm doing. This whole idea of aesthetic taste is so much baloney, because it's all done on the basis of economic talent. It has nothing to do with my right to make my work.

To display Jonas's tape on its side in a shipping box, emblem of economic exchange, is to put to question the fate of site-specificity forty years later, when the moral claims of this idea sound as anachronistic as the

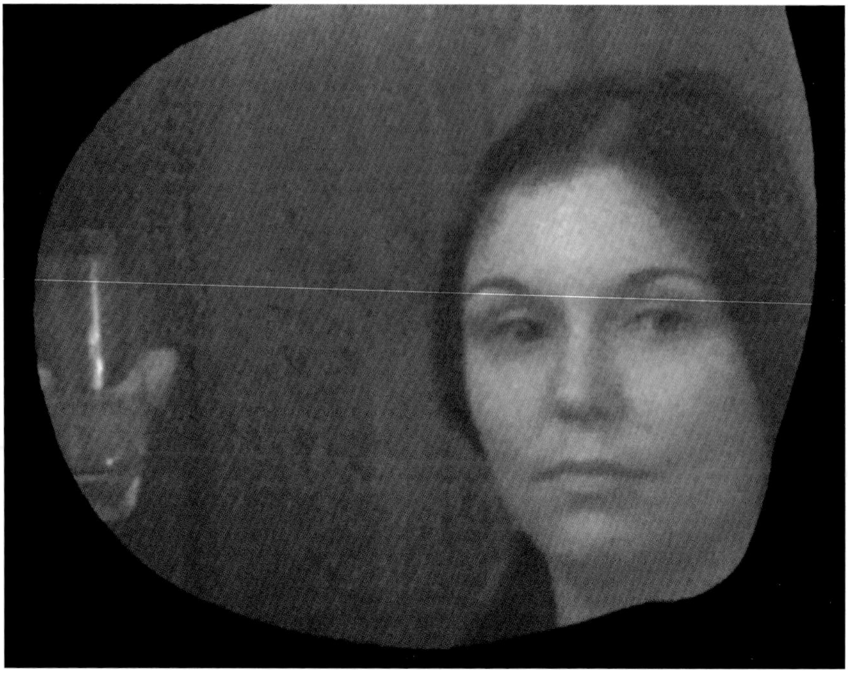

**Fig. 2.30.** Seth Price, *Digital Video Effect: "Spills,"* 2004. TV/DVD player in original packaging, video with altered footage shot by Joan Jonas c. 1970. Detail: Nancy Holt. Photo courtesy of Seth Price.

Weathermen's talk of revolution.[145] At Guggenheim Bilbao, at Tate Modern and LACMA, on the estates and foundations of today's well-heeled collectors, the site-specific project once envisioned as a refusal of the status quo has been reimagined as a sited commission of lavish production values and grandiose proportion, a form of institutional and personal branding—the ultimate trophy of the global art market. Price *sites* site-specificity. He locates this premise historically then and now, forcing us to think critically about this increasingly hollowed-out notion. His project disrupts nostalgia in another way. In the group are two significant women artists: Jonas, whom we cannot see, and Holt, both of whom would collaborate with these men.[146] At one point, black "ink" floods the screen. Holt peers through a hole in the ooze. Her lips are pursed, her expression is sphinxlike. She is a mysterious presence (fig. 2.30).

While the children chatter and scream without inhibition as the men converse, the women in the room say nothing.[147] Their silence speaks volumes about gendered codes of behavior in downtown art circles then. *The Flamethrowers* (2013), a novel by Rachel Kushner set in the New York art scene of the 1970s, examines this dynamic in detail. Kushner narrates the fledgling career and amorous fortunes of a female conceptual performance artist and gifted motorcycle racer. When we first meet her, the novel's protagonist, Reno, has developed a daring new art form involving the tracing of lines on the earth with the tires of her bike, an actual project by Michael Heizer of this period.[148] As an art student in Nevada, Reno learns about *Spiral Jetty*. After graduation she journeys to the Great Salt Lake on her motorbike to see Smithson's work. The experience is so compelling she feels emboldened to become a professional artist:

> The best ideas were often so simple, even obvious, except that no one had thought of them before. I looked at the water and the distant shore of the lake, a vast bowl of emptiness, jagged rocks, high sun, stillness. I would move to New York City.[149]

Reno arrives in New York three years after Smithson's death, in 1976. Kushner describes a downtown art scene haunted by the memory of the recent past—of works like *Spiral Jetty*, Tricia Brown's performances on Soho's roofs and façades, and Matta-Clark's striking architectural interventions. An intriguing character named Henri-Jean carries poles of painted wood wherever he goes (a reference to the Polish-Romanian artist André Cadere). In the downtown world of *The Flamethrowers* one innovation precipitates another. Artists compete with one another in a never-ending race to the finish line of art world immortality. The pressure to come up with something new is immense. "It's up here on the roofs where all the good stuff is taking place," an artist whom Reno meets informs her, alluding to Brown's urban choreography. "But actually, the roofs are somewhat last year. Gordon Matta-Clark just cut an entire house in half. It's going to be tough to beat that."[150]

The man who ponders this is a sculptor named Sandro Valera. Valera makes large, open aluminum boxes that "[shine] like liquid silver" on the stained industrial floorboards of the loft building he owns in Soho, where he displays the works of his friends in rooms each defined by a single bed (Donald Judd is the reference here). Valera is at the center of a social network of highly competitive artists and the female dealer who represents them, Helen Hellenberger. The motorcyclist becomes Valera's lover—he gives her the nickname "Reno," a name evocative of cheap casinos and Western provincialism—and she moves in with him. Reno attempts to establish herself professionally in this milieu, to no avail. Bamboozled and condescended to by Valera and his peers, and by the sexist Hellenberger, she never develops a career. Her dream of becoming an artist fades. And her personal life unravels when Reno is replaced by a pliant young woman devoid of ambition, a perfect complement to the egomaniacal sculptor. The artist-motorcyclist is "continually overrun, effaced, and silenced by the very masculine world of the novel she inhabits," Kushner observes.[151]

While the characters depicted in *The Flamethrowers* are fictional composites, the participants and observers in Price's *Video Effect: Spills* are real. Jonas's video is an archival record of an actual exchange. Placing this moving image on its side and on the floor, Price makes us look and listen. His digital "ooze" uncovers things we would not otherwise see. He causes us to *see silence*. Holt's silence. Barbara Helman's silence. The housekeeper's silence. We return to that moment. We see what it was like. Price disabuses our lingering fantasies of Seventies Soho, as Kushner does. The storied downtown New York of nonprofit spaces and cold-water lofts, of radical feminist interventions and street performances, of gloriously ephemeral and commercially unviable artworks, is revealed to have been deeply patriarchal. Who would want to return to it?

Nostalgia is an ancient emotion. Homer's account of Odysseus's longing for Ithaka, and his eventual return home, is the greatest of nostalgic narratives; the word describing how Odysseus *felt* is a modern invention. The word "nostalgia" was coined in the late seventeenth century by an Alsatian physician named Johannes Hofer to describe the malaise of soldiers billeted to foreign lands, Jean Starobinski tells us (Greek *nostos*, "return"; *algia*, "sorrow").[152] Not simply a case of homesickness (*Heimweh*), nostalgia was an illness of potentially dire consequence, the "mental disease" of the Alpine dweller displaced to the lowlands, or the English sailor conscripted to sea for years on end.

The meaning of nostalgia changed by the late eighteenth century. In the writings of Kant and Rousseau nostalgia has come to suggest a *temporal* malady—a desire to retrieve the fresh sensations of childhood. The nostalgic hopes to regain "youth itself ... an age which is forever beyond his reach," Starobinski writes.[153] Not merely the memory of one's past, nostalgia now suggests a longing for a milieu or way of life that no longer exists.

Nostalgia has to do with loss, like melancholia. Rousseau calls it a "bitter sorrow."[154] It is the desire to "return" and the baleful sense that we cannot, the awareness that return is impossible. Nostalgia is a locational maladjustment, preventing us from focusing on where or when we are. Always looking backward like Nietzsche's antiquarian ("who enfolds himself in a moldy smell"), the nostalgic finds it difficult to navigate a present reality. The most perceptive writers on the subject describe nostalgia as a chronic condition—as a disease.

Each period has a temporal rhythm, Koselleck says. Each era has a pattern. A period becomes significant or falls into obscurity according to its own rhythm or "velocity." There are few eras that inspire nostalgia like the long Sixties. Why is this so? What are we wistful *for*?

Nostalgia is the memory of a previous nostalgia, the "desire for desire," Susan Stewart writes.[155] It is a *mise-en-abyme* of longing. The object of nostalgic fantasy is an image we cannot quite grasp.[156] In *On Revolution*, Hannah Arendt observes that revolutionary moments, for all their ecstasy, are characterized by a "strange pathos of novelty, so characteristic of the modern age."[157] Arendt describes the modernist idea of "being new" as an unfulfilled passion. Modernism is the longing to *be modern*. The revolutionary imaginary is not nostalgia's opposite (revolution looks forward, nostalgia backward), but its inverse: revolution is the memory of the revolutions that precede it. We are nostalgic for the Sixties in part because the Sixties were nostalgic—nostalgic for the outmoded, the obsolete; for childhood and nature; for modernist forms of "being new."[158] *This is the first day of the rest of your life*, as the San Francisco Diggers put it so well. The future so imagined is one that we ourselves can shape. It is happening *right now*. But this future is nostalgic, a longing for older utopias. "Being new" is the dream that we can again be new.

Consider the Diggers. A collective initially made up of theatrical performers who took the name of a radical sect of seventeenth-century reformers led by Gerrard Winstanley, who appropriated unclaimed lands during the English revolutionary period (1649–50), the Diggers of the Haight-Ashbury attempted something just as improbable: to build a community based on the principle of free exchange, or *Free*, in the robust capitalist milieu of postwar northern California.[159] It all began with the Digger Stew (fig. 2.31). Distributed every afternoon for a period of time in 1966–67 in the Panhandle of Golden Gate Park, the Stew was a ritualized enactment of the moral philosophy of Free. The recipient of Free Food walked through a square wooden gate. Passing through this yellow tori—the Frame of Reference, the Diggers called it—one departed the Frame of Reality, the mind-numbing System that could "market anyone, anything, anytime," transforming human beings into passive consumers. Entering the zone of Free, one could begin to imagine a life lived outside such arrangements, an existence without private property.[160] In the Digger social economy, giver and recipient were on an equal footing. The exchange of comestibles was *not* an act of charity. The food was free "because it's yours." And so, potentially, was everything else. The many initiatives instigated by the Free Stew—the Frame of Reference store, the Free Clinic, the buses that offered Free Rides up and down Haight Street, the Free housing provided to hundreds of teenage runaways during the Summer of Love—extended the Digger principle of collective sharing to other zones

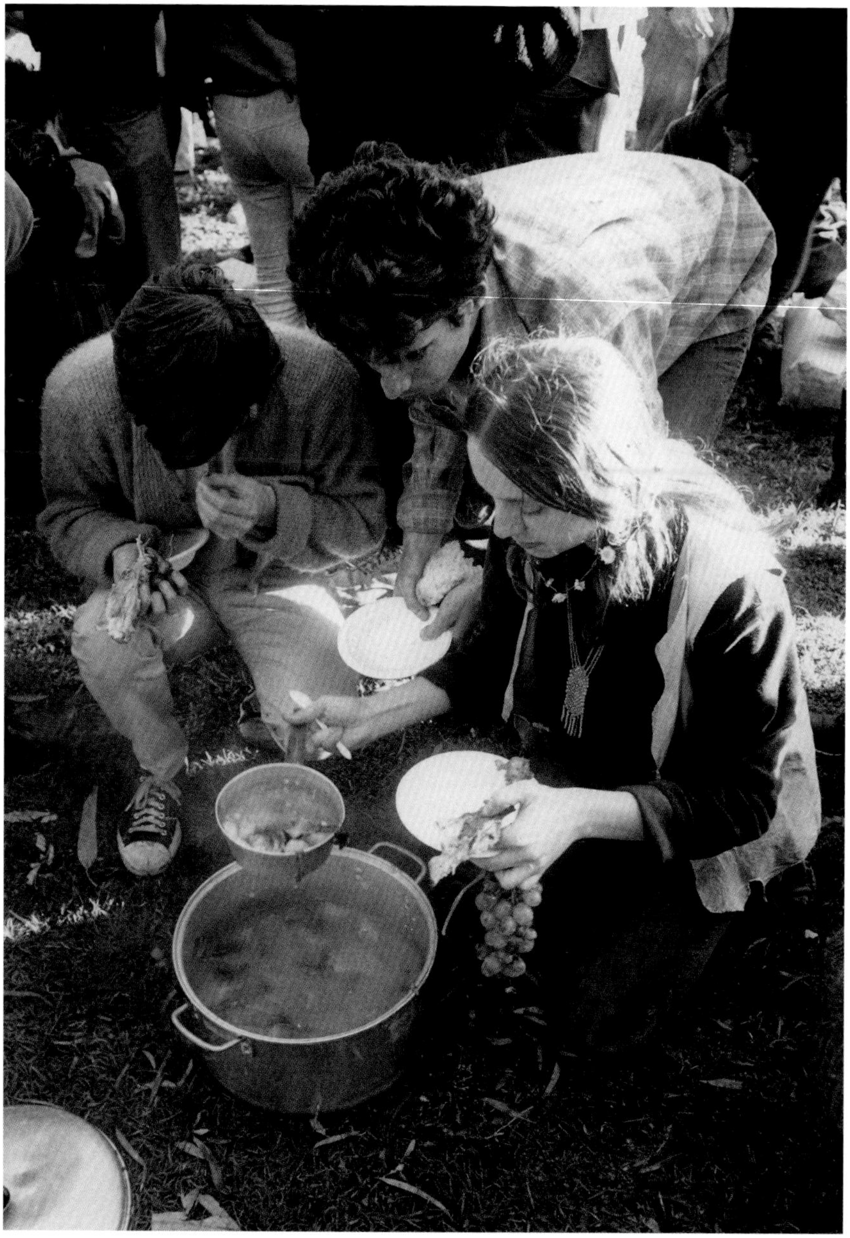

**Fig. 2.31.** *Digger Stew, Golden Gate Park, San Francisco*, c. 1966–67. Photograph: Gene Anthony. © Owned by Wolfgang's Vault, all rights reserved.

of experience and, eventually, to places far afield, as I discovered as a child hitchhiker that sun-dappled afternoon in 1971 some three thousand miles from the Haight-Ashbury. Boarding that lumbering, impossibly crowded VW microbus, I took a Free Ride. The impression left by that encounter precipitated the writing of this book.

We live by not remembering, says Nietzsche, who defines happiness as the "power of forgetting."[161] For Nietzsche suffered from the historical longing he insists we must overcome. ("I am the nursling of older ages like the Greek, and less a child of this age.")[162] We need history, the philosopher says, history in its various forms—monumental, antiquarian, critical. But to be modern, to be monumental—to achieve anything at all—we need to forget. ("Life in any true sense is absolutely impossible without forgetfulness.") We need to look ahead. The person who makes a difference "recognizes one law—*the law of that which is to be*."[163]

The counterculture attempted exactly this. It adamantly rejected the world as it had been in order to invent something new. Certainly, the imperative to "be new" was hardly new. It was a memory of previous utopias—of Winstanley's Diggers, of Bronson Alcott's Fruitlands, of William Morris's Arcadia, and so many other attempts to rebuild society from scratch.[164] Like these historical precedents, the most radical Sixties collectives understood the achievement of this state of newness, a sort of ground zero, as a refusal of material success. As failure. To "fail" in the Digger sense was to let go, drop out.[165] It meant turning one's back on the capitalist war machine, its environmental and human degradation. It meant an existence without private property lived beyond the media's pernicious reach. It meant leaving the hot society for good.

The future so imagined is a return to a lost Edenic state. Only by "failing" could one regain in adulthood that sense of "presence"—that wondrous feeling of oneness with nature—that children feel.[166] The future the counterculture imagined was Rousseauvian, nostalgic—for childhood, for the "pre."[167]

The savvy Diggers were hardly flower children; once the counterculture mushroomed into a media phenomenon, they became its most dogged critics. They perceived media's appropriation of hip references as the encroachment of the Frame of Reality on the Frame of Reference. The truth was more ambivalent; the counterculture was hardly monolithic. Where the Diggers aspired to a collective identity, signing their statements with pseudonyms, other countercultural figures, such as the Yippie personalities Abbie Hoffman and Jerry Rubin, made publicity the very focus of their activities. And the Diggers themselves were hardly anonymous. Media-savvy performers (the core figures had worked in a mime troup) they used media opportunistically to circulate their ideas, and their activities were frequently reported in the Bay Area press. The Free Meal was a daily act of generosity—and a "bold and attention grabbing move."[168]

The Human Be-In of January 14, 1967, was a major turning point for the San Francisco counterculture. Heavily advertised in the alternative newspaper, *San Francisco Oracle*, this "Gathering of the Tribes" attracted

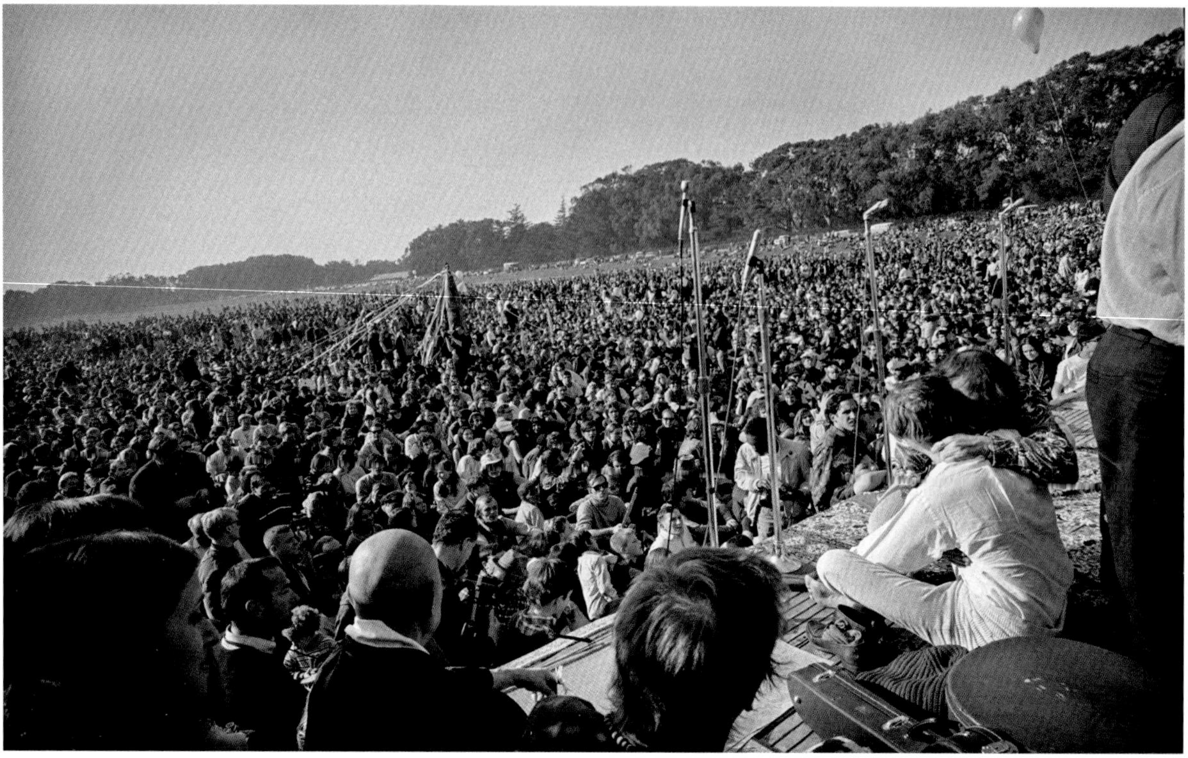

**Fig. 2.32.** *Human Be-In, Golden Gate Park, San Francisco, January 14, 1967.* © Jim Marshall Photography LLC.

some 30,000 celebrants to the Polo Field in Golden Gate Park (fig. 2.32).[169] The attendees carried blankets, bells, cymbals, and drums, and wore beads and feathers and flowers in their hair; they came with their children and pets. They listened to acid rock bands (the Grateful Dead, Jefferson Airplane) and to Beat poets (Allen Ginsberg, Gary Snyder, Lenore Kandel). They listened to the psychedelic drug advocate Timothy Leary, who exhorted the audience to "turn on, tune in, drop out" as tabs of "White Lightning" LSD made in the underground laboratory of Oswald Stanley were widely dispensed. They ate Free turkey sandwiches and fruit handed out by the Diggers, and stared in wonder as a parachutist appeared in the sky above the Polo Field and landed in the crowd.[170] As the day started to fade, Snyder took the stage and sounded a conch shell. Ginsberg, dressed in a white Khaddar suit, turned to the setting sun over the Pacific and recited prayers to Maitreya, the Buddha of Coming Love.[171]

Many aesthetic practices of this period—the Minimalist sculpture, the Happening and Judson dance, earthworks like *Spiral Jetty*—yielded a somatic awareness of oneself and others and one's surroundings, the feeling of interconnectedness that Merleau-Ponty describes as "Being-in-the-World." The Human Be-In extended this phenomenological principle to a public scale, infusing these encounters with sociopolitical meaning. Thousands of people came together that afternoon to "just be." There was a great deal at stake in this notion. To "just be" meant being with *others*. "It was the people who turned me on.... People being together, un-programmed, uncommitted, except to life itself," one participant recalled.[172] Being with others allowed one to imagine a new Frame of Reference, a greater collectivity. It would bring about the "face to face beginning of a new époque," one of the organizers claimed.[173]

In truth, the "tribes" who gathered in Golden Gate Park that day were not allowed to "just be." They were depicted in the *act of Being*. ("There was a good deal of picture-taking going on.")[174] The producers conceived the Be-In as a staging of mass co-presence, a *spectacle of Being*, an event so colorful and extraordinary it would be photographed and filmed and written about. Only by securing media's fickle attention would the event's antiwar, anticapitalist message resonate. Only by *representing* Being would this phenomenological-political principle become known beyond the Haight-Ashbury.

By any measure they succeeded. Copycat Be-Ins were held in other cities across the United States. Thousands upon thousands of teenage runaways flocked to San Francisco that July, a pilgrimage the national press dubbed the Summer of Love.[175] Yet media conjugated this collective experience of Being in the tense of recentness, as an experience that the magazine reader or TV watcher had missed.[176] And so the Be-In became an object of nostalgia more or less immediately, two years before Woodstock, the ultimate object of Sixties longing.

That fall the Diggers organized a different sort of event. On October 6, 1967, they staged a *Death of Hippie, Birth of Free* parade to "exorcise" a personage invented by the press. A notice was sent out announcing the death of Hippie, "devoted son of mass media" (fig. 2.33).[177] Hippie's "friends" were invited to attend a sunrise funeral in Buena Vista Park. Pallbearers carried a casket, filled with love beads and paraphernalia heaped upon a mannequin, down Haight Street. Others walked with funeral bouquets and held up signs. The Haight-Ashbury had had enough. Once it was transformed into a media event—the so-called Summer of Love—the counterculture was alienated from itself. Killing off Hippie was a gesture of self-definition, an act of resistance.

•

She'd missed it, she knew by the silence. Crossing the lush, foggy park, she heard nothing but the drop of condensation running from ferns and palm leaves. By the time she reached the field, the vast emptiness

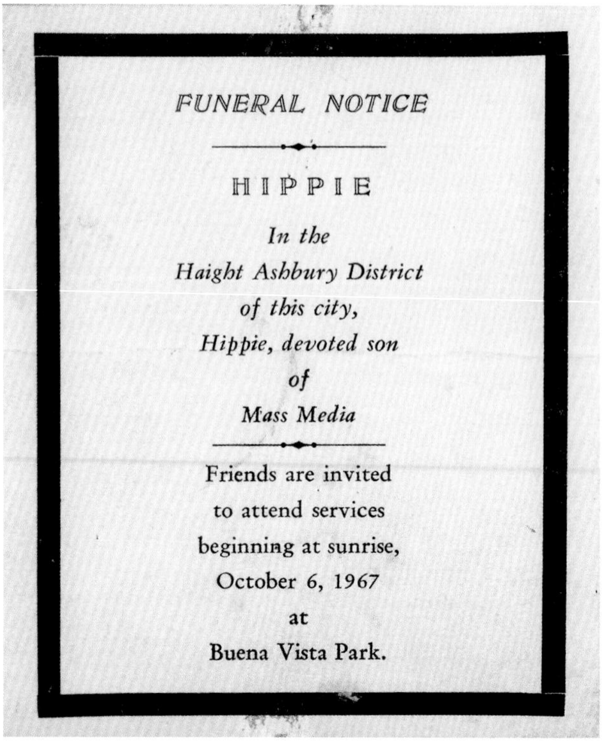


**Fig. 2.33.** Unknown artist. *Buena Vista Park, San Francisco, 10/6/67, "Funeral Notice: Hippie,"* 1967. Denver Art Museum. Collection: Partial Gift of David and Sheryl Tippit; partial purchase with Architecture, Design, and Graphics Department acquisition funds; and partial purchase from the Volunteer Endowment Fund in honor of R. Craig Miller, 2007. Photograph courtesy of Denver Art Museum.

> came as no surprise.... "Excuse me," she said. "Did I miss it?" "You did," he said.[178]

Jennifer Egan's novel *The Invisible Circus* (1995) is set in San Francisco in 1978, a place and time in transition. Phoebe O'Connor, a recent high school graduate, lives in a haze of melancholia. Her father was a Sunday painter and would-be Beatnik whose corporate job drained his creative spirit and physical well-being, according to family lore; he succumbed to an unnamed illness when she was a girl. Her older sister Faith was an antiwar activist who died in mysterious circumstances, her body discovered below a cliff in Italy's Cinque Terre in 1970.

Nostalgia and melancholia are related emotions; both the nostalgic and the melancholic are unable to come to terms with a profound loss.[179] In Phoebe, Egan has created a character in whom these emotions are completely interwoven. She mourns her father and sister constantly. And she is nostalgic for the Sixties, a period dominated by the memory of these romantic figures. Phoebe's current life is "without significance," Egan observes. Uncertain whether to attend college, she still lives with her mother in the family home. She wears Faith's hippie clothes, which don't quite fit her, and sleeps in Faith's former bedroom instead of in her own.

This room is a monument to her sister—a Sixties museum. Swaths of blue batik drape from the ceiling. Glass prisms and incense burners crowd the bookshelves. Wind chimes hang outside the window where Faith put them, their sound ripe with "the giddy unevenness of children's laughter." Newspaper clippings of the Kennedy assassination and an anti-war protest with Faith's picture cling to a bulletin board. Phoebe is the curator of this period room, this monument to Faith. Despite her efforts to maintain the bedroom, entropy has its way. The batik is a magnet for dust. The yellowed clippings crumble if touched. "There was a kind of erosion . . . a sagging and curling and fading [Phoebe] was powerless to halt."

Phoebe sets out to attend the tenth anniversary of a hippie event, the Festival of the Moons. By the time she arrives, the park is empty ("She'd missed it, she knew by the silence"). She encounters a young man who looks uncannily familiar. Faith's former boyfriend, Kyle, is a law student now. His long hair is respectably short. In his apartment the conversation drifts to the Sixties, and to Faith:

> "Sometimes I feel like she's still back there," he said. "In that time. I miss it like hell."
>
> "Me too," Phoebe said, an ache in her chest. "Even if I wasn't really there."
>
> "Sure you were there."
>
> "No, I was a kid."
>
> There was a long pause. "I wasn't there, either," Kyle said. "Not totally."

None of the characters who were "there" were there. Kyle experienced the Sixties but "never quite hit it." Faith was "there" but is no longer here. Phoebe "wasn't really there"—she was just "a kid." Kyle's confession unsettles her ("'You were there, Kyle,' she assured him."). The mnemonic presence of the recent past and of Faith are weighty indeed. After a fumbled attempt at sex Phoebe gets up and leaves.

During the seventeenth century, nostalgia was considered a disease so lethal it could kill you. Egan depicts the ravages of a nostalgia that has gone too far—a Phoebe who is not entirely "here," who sleeps so much she feels "like a zombie . . . like I can't wake up." When she places a pair of marble eggs in her eyes and lies down, the eggs resemble "coins on the eyes of the dead," Egan writes.

If the present feels unreal, her memories of childhood remain acute. She remembers a dangerous turn on a motorcycle with Faith and another boyfriend, a Hells Angel. And she remembers the night of the Invisible Circus, a raucous Happening organized by the Diggers in an old church. Faith invites a group of hippies to the family house in the middle of the night.[180] Awakened by the clamor of pots and pans and strange voices, Phoebe discovers her sister and another boyfriend, Wolf, making breakfast. Her mother's kitchen is a wonderland of candles and otherworldly visitors. To her eyes, her sister's guests—a Queen of Spades in a purple velvet gown, a magician juggling silver balls, a Mad Hatter in a top hat, and a White Witch—are a fascinating sight. Faith bends down and whispers:

> "Something is happening," she said softly. "Can you feel it?"
> "What?"
> "I don't know, but I feel it. Like this vibration underground" . . .
> "What are you talking about?" Phoebe said.
> "Everything's changing," Faith said. "Everything's going to be different."

Faith speaks grandiloquently of revolutionary time, the time that Arendt describes as "irresistible." ("This is history. You can't stop it.") An unseen force is changing everything. It is going to be "huge."

The revolution happening in their kitchen grinds to a sudden halt. Their brother Barry—a more conventional figure and foil to Faith—threatens to call the police. The strange visitors must go; Phoebe must come with him. But Phoebe wants to be part of Faith's scene, not his. She wants the magical night to go on and on. And it does. Choosing Faith's world of romance and revolution over her brother's pragmatic course, Phoebe saves the Invisible Circus. Barry leaves, defeated. The revelers climb to the roof and watch the sunrise over San Francisco. When the morning comes, the guests disperse. The Invisible Circus is already a memory.

The departure of the White Witch and Mad Hatter is the beginning of the end of the Sixties in Egan's novel. In 1978, when the narrative begins, the decadal Sixties has fallen back into the past. The long Sixties is coming to a close, even as the radical excesses of that time are still playing out (Phoebe sights a newspaper headline detailing the brutal murder of former Italian prime minister Aldo Moro by the Red Brigades).

Fewer and fewer people recall what happened then; even fewer care. At Phoebe's high school student activism is dead; the antiwar strike led by Faith ten years earlier has been forgotten. In the Haight-Ashbury tourists walk around the streets clutching maps in search of hippies and Sixties souvenirs. Nostalgics have purloined the street signs identifying the fabled intersection. The "dead center" these tourists are searching for is missing.

The long Sixties is over, yet the memory of that time exerts a psychic pressure on every character we meet. (Only the brother, Barry, embraces the present with gusto: a Silicon Valley millionaire at twenty-three, he alone embodies the Nietzschian principle of healthful forgetting.) *The Invisible Circus* is a *Bildungsroman*, a novel of self-discovery. How will Phoebe overcome nostalgia's lethal grip?

Using a small inheritance from her father she travels to Europe, where she walks in her sister's footsteps. The postcards that Faith sent home during her final journey lead the way. And like her intrepid sister, Phoebe puts herself at risk.[181] Dropping a tab of LSD in Paris, she sees a girl in a shop window who appears to be Faith. The girl beckons her to "cross over" to the other side. Faith has become Phoebe's *Doppelgänger*, her malign twin. Phoebe bangs her body hard against the window, almost shattering it. On a bridge above the Seine she hurls the postcards to the river. "Killing" her sister allows Phoebe to live. ("It was her or me, one of us had to go.") The *Doppelgänger* doesn't go easily. In her hotel room Phoebe spies "Faith" in a mirror: the ghoulish face staring back is her own.

In Munich Phoebe meets Wolf, Faith's former boyfriend—the man she danced with the night of the Invisible Circus. Pumping him for information, she eventually learns Faith's truth. "We were after something. . . . Hundreds and thousands of us, all reaching," he recalls. Wolf and Faith left San Francisco in 1970 because of the "bad feeling" in the United States. Altamont, Kent State, the Weathermen townhouse explosion: the bad Sixties settled in like a dark mist. Faith still believed; she wanted to keep going. Arriving in Paris, she and Wolf encountered other young people who were nostalgic for May 1968—the revolution of two years earlier. ("You couldn't make anything build, it was all aftermath," Wolf remarks.) Germany seemed more promising. A woman they met mentioned her friend Ulrike Meinhof, who had just gone underground, and the lovers headed to Berlin. Eventually Faith "hits it." She meets someone who knows Meinhof. Resurfacing after a long absence, she is a changed person—an errand runner for the RAF. She even carries a pistol. Her world view is all black and white: there are no grays. ("You're either with it or you're not.")

Back to the present. Phoebe and Wolf have become lovers. Her attraction to him is saturated with the imagery and sensations of childhood. The smell of the interior of his car triggers the memory of the "tart and sweet" scent of his T-shirts she'd once discovered in Faith's room. ("If no one else was around, she would lift one to her face, inhaling Wolf's smell. . . .")[182] And she is nostalgic for *this* moment, for the present. For her life now. She imagines a future when she'll look back at her "time with Wolf" with longing. ("Phoebe felt herself slipping back into the present time . . . tinged now by a certain nostalgia.") They drive to Italy. She presses Wolf for more information. Faith never did "hit it" in the end. A peripheral figure at best, she never does meet Meinhof, her idol. Abandoned by the RAF after a failed mission and desperate to prove her radical credentials, she joins another guerrilla group in Berlin. A bomb she places in a courthouse kills an innocent man. Faith's belief in the "movement" ends on the cliffs of Corniglia, a village above the Ligurian Sea. The place where Phoebe and Wolf are standing now.

Her suicide is a familiar conclusion to bad Sixties narratives. The sister Phoebe had worshiped was not the person she'd imagined. For Faith, politics was not just a matter of moral conviction but a thrilling adventure, the consequences for others be damned. ("She killed us both, Phoebe thought. Killed all of us.") Faith was all energy; she ended up a figure of entropy. ("Faith spent herself. She gave herself away.")

The veil of nostalgia drops from Phoebe's eyes; she appears to be cured of that enervating emotion for good. She returns to San Francisco, enrolls in college. Packing up Faith's room, she discards its faded treasures. Visiting Barry's startup in Silicon Valley, she senses a "mood of manic anticipation," a "promise of extraordinary wealth." The brother's pragmatism trumps the sister's romanticism. In the era of the personal computer Faith's vaporous dreams of revolution seem woefully passé.

"And yet," Egan writes movingly. "And yet." Phoebe's thoughts drift to the past, as they always do. She recalls a childhood game of hide and seek in a park. In this precious memory, Phoebe is the little sister again. She discovers Faith hiding behind a bush. The sister welcomes her, and she sits in Faith's lap "surrounded by her breath and heartbeat and warm long hair." Phoebe clings to this powerful image of Faith's living body, her beating heart—this memory of Faith alive. And she remembers another, a prior self. A Phoebe who traveled around Europe and who had adventures. Who experimented with drugs and took a lover. Who learned the truth about her sister. How bold she was then! How much *like* Faith. But now she feels alienated from this emboldened self, this other Phoebe. A Phoebe who was. "The subject of her memories seemed another person altogether, to be admired, envied, measured against." Phoebe is forever gazing backward at somebody else. She cannot help it. Her nostalgia is without end, or cure.

Just as the Frame of Reference reframed the Frame of Reality (the moment one accepted a Free Meal, or took a Free Ride), the Frame of Reality reframed the Frame of Reference. The Diggers understood acutely the limits of nonconformity. In their broadside "In Search of a Frame" (1966) the anonymous authors critiqued the layout of one of the new "alternative" magazines being published at that moment—the sort of youth-oriented journal that Dave Eggers and his friends revive nostalgically in *A Heartbreaking Work of Staggering Genius*. A photograph of the acid rock band Big Brother and the Holding Company (the lead singer of which was Janis Joplin) appears here for a reason. "Whatever the revolutionary implications of [Big Brother's] band are, none threaten Town Square and Bally and all they stand for. By sponsoring the magazine the merchants simply attached the rock-revolution image to their product."[183] A photo of Joplin and the members of Big Brother—the hottest act at the Avalon Ballroom at that moment—conferred a tinge of radical chic to these menswear labels.

Theorists of the counterculture point to the extraordinary affluence of the West during this period and the unprecedented educational opportunities and leisure time made available to young Boomers then—the material conditions that made resistance to the "System" possible.[184] At the same time, the System that came into place during this period anticipated and profited from the new climate of nonconformity. The appropriation of countercultural forms and values by advertising occurred at the moment of the counterculture's emergence, the Diggers noted. The marketing techniques they described in "In Search of a Frame," now known to us as "hip consumerism," have proven to be extremely resilient.[185]

Earlier I described the Sixties return as both the endurance of Sixties memory in the present and the mnemonic retrieval of Sixties imagery—the "return of" and "return to." These returns have occurred in concert with a repurposing of Sixties countercultural forms and symbols as nostalgic commodities. The nostalgic Sixties evoked by these images and objects obscures the messy Sixties of historical memory. It presents to us a Sixties that "can be sold back to us as this great moment of hope and wonder," as William Ayers has described it.[186] This Sixties is beyond our reach; its unapproachability is its allure. As practices of return suggest. Nelson's *Woodshed* examines our collective longing to have "been there"; Green's *Partially Buried* examines the fashion for "Panther chic" during a period of neoliberal retrenchment; Durant's "Woodstock" works explore the merchandising of Sixties imagery and the memory of the fabled concert to aging Boomers and their children ("Echo Boomers").[187]

And in Dana Spiotta's novel *Eat the Document* (2006) even Smithson has become a prop for selling nostalgic goods. A Millennial couple pay a visit to an "ultrahip" shopping area in downtown Seattle. Josh and Miranda have recently met in a bookstore specializing in countercultural literature. He is an ambitious young entrepreneur; her progressive views are still being formed. The boutiques of the Seattle "postmall" they visit have a staged bohemian quality (Spiotta describes the stores as "quirky and eccentric"). Many of these deceivingly hip stores are owned by corporate chains. There is a tattoo shop and a "DJ" store. Downstairs a gallery shows projected videos and films. A multiplex specializes in independent and foreign cinema. But the main attraction of this shopping center is a large "trendy" store, Suburban Guerrilla. Immersed in this expansive environment of low lighting, pulsing music and a barrage of visual effects, Miranda explores a display of Sixties-nostalgic clothing and accessories:

> They were fake vintage dresses with bohemian patches. Gauze and macramé peasant dresses. Lace-trimmed camisoles next to a poster of Carole King's 1971 *Tapestry* album. Angel sleeves and high-heeled boots. Clogs and granny glasses, but also tube tops, denim short-short cutoffs, roller skates.[188]

Suburban Guerilla (even the name is oxymoronic) mimics the associative logic of the internet, Josh points out admiringly. The store's layout imitates the design of its "hugely successful retail website," a "brilliant" tactic.[189] The chain's marketing theme is the radical guerrilla politics and avant-garde art of the long Sixties. Miranda peruses a "Paris '68" calendar with images of Situationist graffiti and a datebook whose cover depicts Bernardine Dohrn in a miniskirt shaking her fist. Decks of playing cards feature pictures of New Left personalities like Abbie Hoffman and Mark Rudd. A "Movement Rebels, Outlaws and Fugitives" deck depicts the leaders of the Red Brigades and Red Army Faction (Meinhof, Baader), enumerating their biographies and crimes. On the backs of the cards are the logos of these once fearsome cells (five-pointed red stars, rifles, and so on). A selection of art history books on earthworks and a DVD by the second-generation land artist Andy Goldsworthy are stacked nearby. A large poster of *Spiral Jetty* hangs above the merchandise.

Unlikely as it seems, Josh is a student of radical political theory. At the progressive bookstore, owned by an older man named Nash (who, unbeknownst to them, was once a member of a Weathermen-type collective), he buys the prison memoirs of Alexander Berkman, the anarchist lover of Emma Goldman and would-be assassin of Henry Clay Frick. Josh's reading has not been for nothing. In fact, his studies in Marxist theory have proven useful as he fashions himself into a future CEO. As he suggests to Miranda, in this very store, in Suburban Guerilla, the logic of advanced capitalism has triumphed, and has been laid bare. "This is the purity about capitalism," he explains.

> There is no judgment about content.... See, capitalism can exploit your desire and exploit your need to subvert its exploitation of your desire. It revives—it reinforces—itself on the blood of its critics and their critique. It embraces contradictions. It revels in irony.[190]

The long Sixties ended long before they were born. Their memories of that time are secondhand, gleaned from books and music and films. But their perceptions could not be more different. The System "knows" our desires—even our desire to subvert it, Josh opines. The challenges posed by students, radicals, and avant-garde artists then strengthened that system. Capitalism absorbed its critics. And it benefited from their criticism.

Miranda refutes his argument. She still believes. The questions asked by activists and artists were important, she insists. They mattered—and matter still. The scenario Josh describes is "simplistic and reductive." It isn't dialectical, for it contains no contradictions. There is no "irony" embedded in the System. The irony is his—not the System's. "A confused context is the essence of alienation."[191]

In Suburban Guerrilla Miranda finds her voice. And something more. As she looks more closely at the "guerrilla" playing cards, she connects the dots. The face on one of the cards looks familiar. ("She stared at the mouth. That crooked smile. Of course. Of course.") The man who calls himself Nash, who works in the progressive bookstore, is really Bobby Desoto, a founder of the group SAFE (Secret Attack Fear Effort) that planted bombs in the summer homes of CEOs during the Sixties. He remains "at large." She discovers the identity of an actual guerrilla in Suburban Guerrilla, of all places, a store that trades in the imagery and styles of a counterculture that no longer exists. A historical truth reveals itself in a nostalgia emporium, where history has been made agreeable and sexy so that it can be monetized. Miranda discovers what the Diggers learned so many years before. This is her "Death of Hippie" moment. In the store with the ridiculous name she establishes a historical understanding of the Sixties for herself that will have other reverberations. Her visit to the "postmall" with Josh exposes a deep fissure between them. On the ride home they break up.

Nostalgia is a contagious condition, a "social disease."[192] During the seventeenth and eighteenth centuries it was claimed that you could catch this illness simply by listening to another person talk about home or childhood, or even by learning that such a malady exists.[193] For nostalgia is communicable, a disease of communication. Words and images are its vectors of transmission, as are fashion and music. Music is a particularly effective trigger of that emotion. (Rousseau describes music as a "memorative *sign*" causing us to recall another place or time.)[194] Durant's and Green's works are indeed filled with music. Durant blends tracks or plays them backward. Or he reverses the Maysles film twice over, garbling familiar melodies and voices. In both instances he stages the experience of "aural entropy," the decay of familiar sounds. He crosses Altamont with

Woodstock, the Rolling Stones with Neil Young. He mashes Neil Young and Nirvana. He blends the Seventies and the Nineties, folk rock and grunge. And because we don't hear these songs and voices and remarks correctly, they no longer mean what they once meant. They don't trigger the feelings they used to do.

In *Partially Buried* Green invites us to peruse her library of Seventies albums—the music she recalls hearing as a girl. We may also remember these tracks from childhood—Carole King's raspy anthems, the plaintive ballads of Janis Ian, the R&B numbers of Sly and the Family Stone. We may recall these songs fondly, nostalgically, or with a twinge of boredom. Or we may not remember them at all. For memory, and nostalgia too, are generationally and geographically contingent. In Green's video *Übertragen (Transfer)* (1996), the second installment of her *Partially Buried* sequence, Green asks three contemporaries to describe their childhood recollections of the United States. Simin Farkondeh was born in Tehran to German and Iranian parents. Henrietta Schroeter grew up in West Germany in a family of ethnic Germans. Samir Alschausky, of Turkish descent, was born and raised in East Germany. Farkondeh recalls seeing images of the Vietnam War on television as a small child, and the Iranian Revolution she witnessed as a teenager in 1979. She describes how the students in her high school split into pro- and anti-Shah factions and how she attended a massive protest against the "American lackey."[195] Schroeter recalls the shock of seeing "Most Wanted" posters with headshots of RAF members in West Berlin and listening to her parents discuss the group's violent actions.[196] Alschausky remembers his socialist teachers instructing him and his classmates to send "Free Angela!" postcards to the authorities in the United States after Davis was jailed, and the thrill of seeing Davis herself (a "famous black person ... black like me") speak in his hometown after her acquittal.[197]

*Übertragen (Transfer)* enacts a shift of attention from the autobiographical focus of *Partially Buried*, a meditation on the year 1970 recounted from multiple points of view—the accounts of Michener, Tyrrell, Shinn, the Turners, and Green. In the second part of Green's archaeology, Alschausky, Farkhondeh, and Schroeter recall the same period from different points on the Cold War geopolitical map. Their accounts add texture and complexity to the *Partially Buried* trilogy that heretofore had focused on Green's memories of Ohio and the American South.[198] The common impressions that the members of a generation are said to share are strikingly absent. Our memories are locational, and, Green implies, irreducible: your "pre" is *not* mine.

The artworks and writings I have described cause us to perceive the mechanisms of nostalgia, to question its depleting satisfactions. In antinostalgic practices, history—messy, unresolved, polyphonic—fills the void of longing, the fantasy of a time or society seemingly superior to our own situation.[199] The good Sixties is a nostalgic Sixties, a tantalizing image of universal freedom and equality. Antinostalgic artworks remind us that the values articulated then were bitterly fought for and remain bitterly contested, that the battles of that time are still being waged.[200] Some of these practices ask us to keep faith—to remember the good Sixties without succumbing to an unproductive longing. For cynicism and forgetting are the real targets of antinostalgia. Spiotta's character Miranda, named for Prospero's daughter (that indefatigable believer in the goodness of men) is an avatar of Sixties remembrance. It is Miranda who defies Josh's cynicism. Nostalgic fashions and trinkets create a "confused situation," she says; these commodities simplify and obfuscate actual events and conflicts. They cause us to forget. Miranda seeks a historical understanding of a period she didn't experience whose impact she still feels. She remembers the good Sixties long after that time ended, and that era's astonishing dream of social and environmental justice is only partially fulfilled.

## Continuing Smithson

**The existence of the artist in time is worth as much as the finished product.**

Robert Smithson, "A Sedimentation of the Mind: Earth Projects"

Much aesthetic practice since the Nineties has entailed a retrieval and remixing of the most recognizable Sixties and Seventies forms—the vocabularies of Minimalism and Post-Minimalism, of Conceptualism and Pop.[201] What I am calling the Smithson return emerged within this revivalist milieu. It has yielded projects remarkable in number and variety, the majority of which I imagine Smithson might not have supported or liked. What would he have made of Green's revision of his *Partially Buried Woodshed*, of Nelson's uncanny replica buried in sand, of Durant's miniature sheds and dirt mirrors, their bizarre soundtracks? Of Tacita Dean's audiotape *Trying to Find the Spiral Jetty* and Banks Violette's funereal sculptural ensembles coated in Smithson's salt?

Practices of return enlarge the ways we ordinarily speak about influence—how artists impact one another. Influence is a notoriously imprecise notion; influence is hard to talk about. And it is even harder to talk about when the kind of impact I am describing is so deferred that I am compelled to call this a "return." Is there something internal to Smithson's forms and techniques that induces artists to revisit and revise them? What might his untimely death have to do with this?

One of the most incisive critiques of influence is found in Michael Baxandall's *Patterns of Intention*, a seminal text of the methodological discussions known as the New Art History.[202] What is wrong with influence, this "curse of art criticism," as Baxandall calls it? As a way to describe what happens between two artists, influence is both narrow and vague, he notes. The claim that artist X has influenced artist Y is not as self-evident as it seems, for it implies a one-way transmission. Artist Y is a recipient of influence, who has little agency in the matter. She is impacted by X's example—that is all. Worse, the claim that X has "influenced" Y doesn't say very much. It doesn't describe the character or quality of the impact, the ways that a later artist may have responded to a predecessor's work (*draws on*, *misunderstands*, *quotes*, *emulates*, *parodies*: Baxandall lists quite a few).

It is more interesting to consider *how* Y responds to X, the art historian says, and he sets out to do just that. Of the creator of the *Demoiselles d'Avignon* he writes: "Picasso acted on Cézanne quite sharply."[203]

The Cubist's extreme deformation of the body, his shallowing out of pictorial depth into low relief, and his fracturing of the surfaces of things into facets that flow into one other (a technique known as *passage*) suggest that Picasso must have seen Cézanne's works at his exhibitions at the Salons d'Automne of 1906 and 1907, and at the gallery of their mutual dealer, Vollard. Enlisting some of Cézanne's techniques and ignoring others, Picasso transformed how the other artist's work would now be seen.

Influence is retroactive: it takes the follower to perceive what was distinctive in the predecessor. Baxandall arrives at Borges's famous axiom concerning Kafka: "Every writer *creates* his own precursors."[204] One of the questions not examined in his account is how an artist becomes X to another's Y—how it is that certain figures inspire others to act *upon them*. In Baxandall's system, influence is reversed. It remains one-way. An artist *does* something to the prior artist ("Picasso acted on Cézanne . . ."). Cézanne is oddly passive in this description. Tilting the balance of intention the other way, this claim obscures the dialogic nature of such exchanges, why it is that certain artists inspire others to revisit their work, often belatedly. For the revelation of influence is not always immediate. Many artists who emerged during the long Sixties appear significant to us, but there are very few whom we could describe as the instigators of a return—the kind of impact that is felt broadly and urgently decades later, a very different kind of encounter than that of Picasso and Cézanne, with the death of the latter in fall 1906 precipitating the former's completion of the *Demoiselles* the next summer.

In lieu of a creditable theory of influence (as a result of Baxandall's critique and poststructuralist attacks on the premise of "intention" itself), another rubric was advanced. The notion of *effect* was proposed in a critical forum on the extraordinary impact of Duchamp's example on postwar and postmodern artists.[205] Duchamp's famous rejection of painting for an art of strategies, such as the readymade or body cast, upended conventional ideas of medium, unraveling the traditionalist modernism I have described in part 1. The various reprises of Duchampian tactics during the long Sixties and since demanded a new vocabulary, another way of describing the impact of one artist on another.

An effect is a causative relation between two things, a clue that allows us to reconstruct what happened later on, *a posteriori*.[206] In the art history of influence, X develops a personal style that Y absorbs and modifies. X *leads to* Y. In Baxandall's system, Y invents a new style based on X's; this alters how X's work will be seen. In both of these formulas the impact is unidirectional, one way.

Now an art of effects is dialogical (the influence goes both ways) and intermedial: rather than a signature style identified with an artist's hand (a painter's brushstrokes, a sculptor's chisel marks, a draftsman's hand), Duchamp developed a menu of techniques that reveal themselves in the practices of others long afterwards as so many effects.[207]

Smithson had quite a bit to say about Duchamp, none of it complimentary. He objected to the fetish character of the readymade, the industrial object that Duchamp "alienated" from its ordinary circuit of manufacture and use. And he staunchly distanced his nonsite, a presentation of natural materials, from Duchamp's art of nomination—the industrial object redefined as art because Duchamp had declared it such.[208] The French artist's ubiquity then annoyed Smithson particularly. During the long Sixties the Dadaist's impact was inescapable. Where the prewar era had been by dominated by "Matisse and Picasso ... T. S. Eliot and Ezra Pound," Duchamp was the progenitor of an art of pictorialized readymades (Pop) and a "Cartesian" art of mind (Conceptualism).[209] These "postmodernist" forms had trumped the modernism of medium, yet Duchamp was hardly the "model anti-author" art historians imagine him to be. He was the instigator of another tradition, Smithson says—the progenitor of another art history.[210] "The notion of art history is so animated by Duchamp. I would like to step outside this situation."[211]

Did he succeed? Or did the inescapable historicism that lines up artists in a chain of influence, a story of precursors and emulators, contain his polymorphic art, too? Has the "Duchampitis" he decried been replaced by the malady of "Smithsonitis," a "Smithsonian pedigree that authorizes what is contemporary about contemporary art," as the art historian Pamela Lee has asked?[212]

Smithson and his peers assumed a set of permissions granted by Duchamp. Not unlike his contemporaries Andy Warhol and Bruce Nauman, Smithson developed a menu of techniques that others would mine long after he invented them.[213] Just as Duchamp scholars have enumerated the "deferred action" of his innovations in late-twentieth-century practice, I am pointing to the various adaptations and "perversions" of Smithson's nonsite, land interventions, and travelogues in art since the Nineties.[214] The analogy only goes so far: while Duchamp was an active if restrained presence in later years, and participated in his canonization (attending retrospectives, authorizing editions of his readymades, and so on), Smithson did not live long enough to witness his own revival, or to facilitate it. Dying young, and dying needlessly (the streak of good luck he had enjoyed until then running out suddenly), he leaves us with the baleful image of a brilliant career cut short. He inhabits the temporal zone of the "already over," a nebulous "before" that we cannot reach. We imagine all the things he could have made—earthworks never built, films never filmed, essays never composed. There is an absence, an incompleteness, at the core of his practice that draws us in.

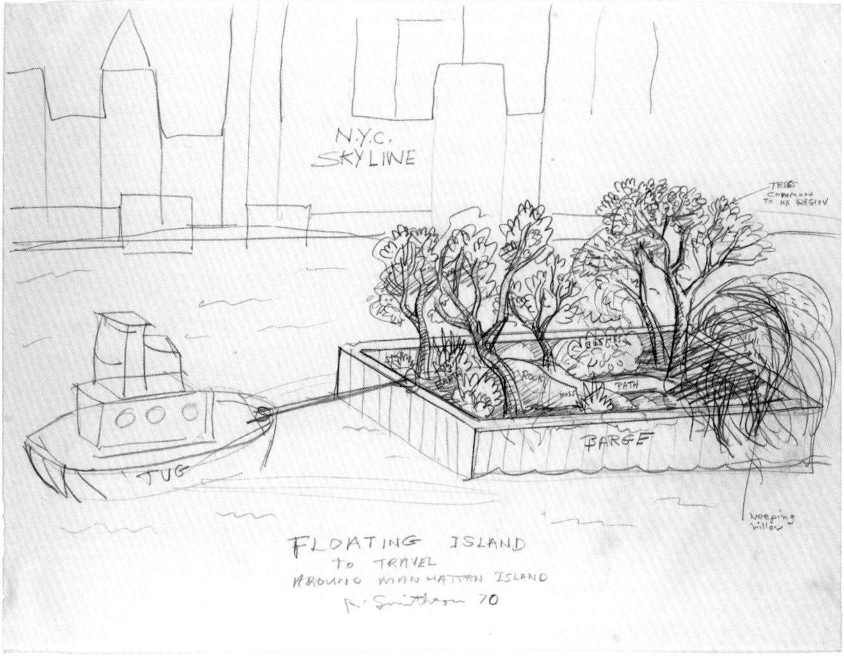


**Fig. 2.34.** Robert Smithson, *Study for Floating Island to Travel around Manhattan Island*, 1970. Pencil on paper. Private Collection. Art © Holt-Smithson Foundation / Licensed by VAGA, New York. Courtesy of James Cohan, New York.

•

The impulse to complete Smithson's works is revealed early, when Holt, Serra, and the dealer Tony Shafrazi returned to Texas that same summer of 1973 to build his unfinished *Amarillo Ramp*.[215] The posthumous history of Smithson's art is marked by such acts of completion, all of them overseen by Holt, who had an intimate knowledge of his working methods and considered these posthumous works bona fide Smithsons. (*Amarillo Ramp* was completed "according to Smithson's specifications," she noted.)[216]

The making of *Floating Island to Travel around Manhattan Island* (1970/2005) is an interesting case. A bewitching drawing of a tugboat pulling a barge of dirt, boulders, trees, and shrubs around the periphery of Manhattan, *Floating Island* is an itinerant nonsite of Central Park, to whose flora and layout it refers (fig. 2.34). One of several proposals for mobile site sculptures that Smithson never got around to making, it had ambiguous specifications.[217] Smithson does not describe the barge's dimensions, the rocks, or the plants. He only mentions a single species of tree (a weeping willow). Nor does he specify for how long and how often the barge would navigate Manhattan's shores.

In 2005, the nonprofit art organization Minetta Brook and other collaborators set out to realize the fantastical work (fig. 2.35). A barge was filled

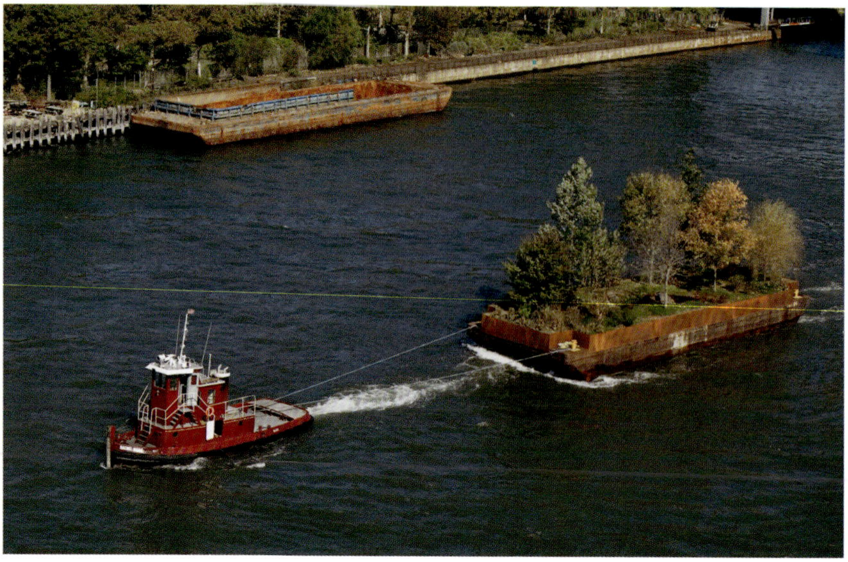

**Fig. 2.35.** Robert Smithson, *Floating Island to Travel around Manhattan Island*, 1970/2005. Produced by Minetta Brook in collaboration with Whitney Museum of American Art, September 17–25, 2005. Photograph: Jane Cohan. Art © Holt-Smithson Foundation/ Licensed by VAGA, New York. Courtesy of James Cohan, New York.

with dirt, boulders, and the requisite flora, and attached to a tugboat. The work traveled around Manhattan for nine days.[218] In projects like *Floating Island* and *Amarillo Ramp*, fidelity to Smithson's intentions (so far as they could be discerned) was paramount. The remark of one of *Floating Island*'s orchestrators—"The only pity about this is that Smithson isn't going to get to see it built"—expressed the belief that Smithson would have recognized the work they made as his own.[219] Yet watching the sentimental film of that project, shot on a perfect day and punctuated by the toots of the tugboat's horn, I am skeptical that Smithson would have fully endorsed the remake and its sunny cinematic depiction. And I am ambivalent: thrilled that *Floating Island could* exist (I have seen a work that I "missed") and keenly aware that even the most faithful realization of the image in his drawing would betray its strange, saturnine sensibility. Smithson's muddy barge was no longer an unrealized fantasy—an uncanny conjunction of land and water moving purposelessly and indefinitely around one of the most densely populated cities on the planet. The realized *Floating Island* was a project of limited duration, a performance. It was not faintly absurd. It had become agreeable.

The practices that interest me are *un*faithful to Smithson's art, troping and undermining the artist's techniques. They bring his site/nonsite system "too far," deplete its dialectical rigor; or they combine his signature formats improperly. But these operations are not smorgasbord samples, casual remixings. What I am calling "return" is a stepchild of postmodernist appropriation, the deliberate, affectively flattened inscription of a found image or object in a new aesthetic framework, an operation that locates agency in the artist who pilfers the source—the Richard Prince who crops and reframes "Marlboro Man" ads or the Sherrie Levine who reproduces totemic works of modernism. Like Baxandall's artist Y, these artists act on their sources strongly.[220] Practices of Smithson return draw on works that anticipate, even foretell, their reprise—that are themselves appropriations and extensions of their sources. As Smithson observed to his interviewer Paul Cummings, "Taking a discarded system and using it ... I guess that has always been my worldview.... The way [Borges] would use leftover fragments."[221]

The critic Craig Owens once described Smithson's project this way: "The work is henceforth defined by the position it occupies in a potentially infinite chain extending from the site itself and the associations it provokes ... to quotations of the work in other works."[222] As Owens noted, the *Spiral Jetty* is not merely the earthwork in the Great Salt Lake, but a film and text composed mainly of citations—Native American myth, the iconography of the spiral, Samuel Beckett's novel *The Unnamable*, and even a *Rolling Stone* article ("Charles Manson: The Incredible Story of the Most Dangerous Man Alive"), to name a few. And so Owens described Smithson's art as allegorical.[223] The allegorical nature of Smithson's project—its layered multiplicity, its incapacity to be contained—affords a sort of permission, a freedom, to interpret his practice at will. Artists inspired by his example cite his artworks and writings promiscuously, even preposterously.[224] Green transforms the *Woodshed* into a narrative of return to the place and period of early memory, an archaeology of her childhood. Durant miniaturizes Smithson's work to Lilliputian proportions and reimagines it as a CD console, a technology that postdates Smithson's lifetime. He presents a *Woodshed* that is both pristine and charred, evoking two moments in the shed's history that precede and postdate Smithson's visit (the day when the farmer built it and the night when it was set ablaze). Nelson remakes a work that Smithson built outdoors inside the white cube it sought to escape—a replica that revels in its uncanny resemblance to the "fresh" *Woodshed* that we only know from pictures.

Then there are practices that complete Smithson's project antithetically, extending and inverting its dialectical structure—the tactic that Harold Bloom refers to as "tesserae" in his celebrated study of influence. As defined by Bloom, "tesserae" is synecdochical and antithetical. Just as a fragment of a pot allows one to combine other fragments into a whole vessel, so a poet "antithetically 'completes' his precursor by so reading the parent-poem as to retain its terms but to mean them in a different sense, *as though the precursor had not gone far enough*."[225] Let us consider Tom Burr's *An American Garden: A View of Central Park, New York, circa*

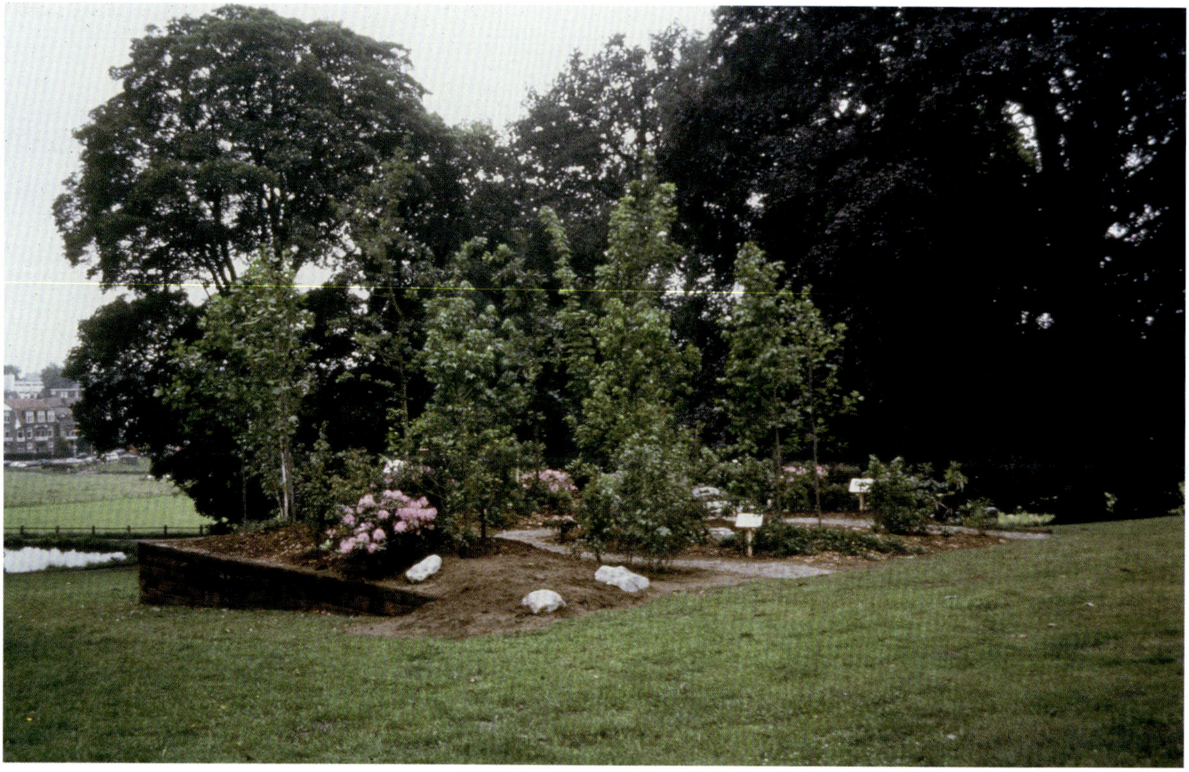

**Fig. 2.36.** Tom Burr, *An American Garden: A View of Central Park, New York, circa 1860*, 1993. Installed in Arnhem, Netherlands. Photograph courtesy of Tom Burr.

*1860*, to my knowledge the earliest work of Smithson return, along these lines. Built for the Sonsbeek exhibition in Arnhem, the Netherlands, in 1993, Burr's earthwork was a miniaturized footprint of the Ramble, the artificially wild section of Central Park discussed in Smithson's late essay "Frederick Law Olmsted and the Dialectical Landscape" (1973). Burr extended Smithson's analysis of Olmsted's masterpiece and aspects of his *Floating Island* drawing in unexpected ways.[226] His displacement of the Ramble to a public park in Holland was a triangular wedge of earth projecting from the side of a hill. The low mounds and paths referenced the Ramble's picturesque topography, while the placards mounted on sticks arranged along the paths presented quotations concerning the Ramble's history (fig. 2.36). The North American shrubbery in this arrangement referenced the types of flora that Olmsted had planted in this part of Central Park and that Smithson, in turn, had proposed to plant in the itinerant *Floating Island*.

In the Ramble Olmsted sought to convey the illusion of naturalness, an artificial wildness, a recollection, itself in miniature, of the primordial forest that covered Manhattan in precolonial times. (Olmsted describes the "sweet-gum, spice-bush, tulip-tree, sassafras, red-maple, black-oak, azalea, andromeda, etc." he discovered at the site of the future forest, a wasteland of overgrown meadows, rocky outcrops, and abandoned shanty towns, and the native shrubs he would plant there.)[227] Siting his work in a park in the Netherlands, Burr established a connection between two places—two nations, two public spaces—and their intertwining histories. His project extended the historical arc of Smithson's dazzling essay, which references the Ice Age, eighteenth-century garden design, and the founding of Nieuw Amsterdam by Dutch merchants—the beginning of the rapacious development of Manhattan Island that Olmsted, by creating Central Park, attempted to stay. But now Burr suffused his earthwork with other histories to which Smithson alludes. The signs he placed amid this "rolling" terrain described the Ramble's users, circa 1973—birdwatchers, sunbathers, muggers, and gay men, who by Smithson's day had transformed Olmsted's Eden into a place of danger and assignations, an "urban jungle" populated by "'hoods, hobos, hustlers, homosexuals'" (Smithson found this description in John Rechy's novel *City of Night* [1963]).[228] And by evoking the Ramble that Smithson knew, the Ramble of the Sixties and Seventies, Burr redirected viewers' attention to the moment of viewing and the actual place where they stood. Pointing downhill to a pond and thicket of trees, his triangular platform (a possible allusion to the Nazi pink triangle and logo of ACT UP, and Amsterdam's triangular *Homomonument*) functioned as a viewing station of Arnhem's gay pickup zone at the park's periphery, a place ordinarily hidden from view (the artist describes the used condoms, empty cigarette packages, beer cans, and tissue paper he discovered there).[229] The placards revealing the Ramble's homoerotic past had a special resonance when Burr exhibited his piece at the nadir of the AIDS epidemic, when outdoor cruising areas and bathhouses were closed by the New York City Health Department and the Ramble was subjected to heightened police surveillance, remaking the outlaw zone celebrated by Rechy and Smithson into Olmsted's sanitized forest.[230]

In the final iteration of *An American Garden*, exhibited at American Fine Arts in New York in 1993, Burr displayed photos of the Arnhem earthwork along with the various citations that had appeared on the signs there inside the gallery (fig. 2.37). Outdoors, at the entrance to the Soho establishment of Colin DeLand, a wooden box filled with soil, a sort of miniaturized, stationary *Floating Island*, displayed a reduced arrangement of the flora that Burr had planted in Arnhem, another reference to the Ramble. And so the New York version of *An American Garden* pointed back to the Arnhem work that pointed back to *Floating Island* and Smithson's essay, and ultimately to Central Park, the starting point of the sequence. Burr "completed" Smithson's project antithetically. Indeed, he

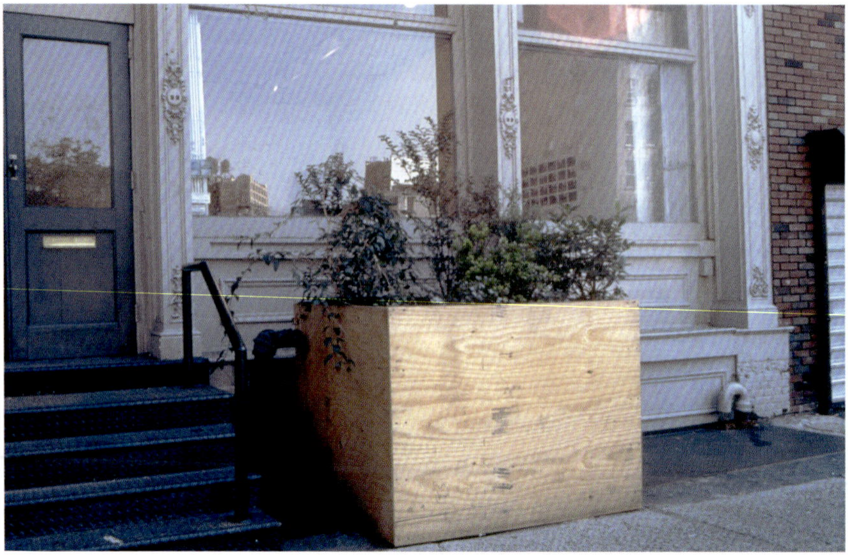

**Fig. 2.37.** Tom Burr, *An American Garden: A View of Central Park, New York, circa 1860*, 1993. Installed at American Fine Arts Co., New York. Photograph courtesy of Tom Burr.

brought it "too far." He extended it, formally and physically, in ways Smithson made imaginable yet never attempted himself. (Burr's conjunction of placard and site has no precedent in Smithson's art.) Smithson's dialectical system was loosened and reimagined as a *loop* of sites and nonsites straddling two continents, the endpoints of which don't meet.

And in *Trying to Find the Spiral Jetty* (1999), Tacita Dean represented the opening sequence of Smithson's film—the drive to and from Rozel Point that Smithson shot from a moving car—as an audio piece devoid of images. Rather than *Spiral Jetty* itself, the journey to Smithson's work is Dean's subject. Smithson's earthwork is both invisible and ever-present during the twenty-seven-minute tape. We listen to the wheels of Dean's rented car spinning on gravel, the same sound that we hear during the opening sequence in Smithson's film. We listen to Dean's conversation with a companion as they find their way through the desert. We hear the clicking sound of Dean taking photos, of her car hitting bumps. We hear things falling, and her companion sneeze. We hear their cries of delight when they finally sight the lake ("And there we have it. Very exciting!"), and their disappointment when, arriving at Rozel Point, they wonder whether the unprepossessing arrangement of rocks below is truly Smithson's masterpiece.

The earthwork that Dean and her companion attempt to locate is the *Spiral Jetty* of 1970. They have traveled to Utah in search of the work depicted in photographs and the eponymous film, the *Jetty* they think they know. Near the end of Smithson's film we look down at the earthwork from a helicopter. We circle around its circumference clockwise and then counterclockwise, and then hover above it, suspended in our imaginary helicopter thousands of feet above the shimmering lake. The *Spiral Jetty* glistens and dissolves in the western sun. We listen to the relentless whir of the propeller as Smithson recites the haunting remarks of Manson Family member Steve "Clem" Grogan outside the Los Angeles County Jail. ("'Spirals,' he whispers. 'Spirals coming away ... circles curling out of the sun.'")[231]

The final frames of *Spiral Jetty* are indeed striking. In the concluding shot filmed in Smithson's studio, the camera closes in on an enlarged black-and-white photo of the newly completed earthwork, pinned to a wall. The film beckons us *into* the picture, entices us there. Is it any wonder that Dean felt compelled to journey to the Great Salt Lake, one of the obligatory pilgrimages of contemporary art tourism, as Kushner's character Reno does, to experience Smithson's earthwork for herself? If Reno's experience of *Spiral Jetty*, fictionally set in 1976, is so transformative she decides, standing on Smithson's boulders, to become an artist, Dean's arrival at the *Jetty* is a letdown. Smithson's work exists; after a challenging trip, Dean finds it.[232] But it is not what she imagined. It no longer resembles the glittering *Spiral Jetty* of the film, the just-completed *Jetty* of the famous photo. Her idea of what Smithson's work *would be* is not borne out by what it *is*:

> **Dean:** Not a lot of people here.... There's a long line of something going out to the water.
> **Companion:** So we walk from here.
> [The wind, their steps, can be heard.]
> **Dean:** I'm not sure this is the *Spiral Jetty....*
> [Crestfallen]:
> It's about the journey.
> [End of tape.][233]

In 1999, the artist Jeremy Millar—a friend of Dean and fellow Smithson enthusiast—purchased an original paperback edition of J. G. Ballard's *The Voices of Time and Other Stories* (1962). Ballard, a British author of entropological fiction, is a key reference for Smithson, and for Millar and Dean as well.[234] In Ballard's story "The Voices of Time," a medical doctor named Powers suffers from a narcoleptic illness that is spreading across the earth, causing its victims to sleep for longer each day until they fall into a coma. Powers is dying, and so is the universe. From a planet in a distant galaxy, NGC 9743, "somewhere in Canes Venatici," a colleague receives messages with numbers on a tape machine. With each message the huge sum grows slightly smaller. Eventually, in the far future, the messages will stop. When zero is reached, "the universe will have ended." Powers packs his books away to send to his brother. The task grows harder as he succumbs to the sleeping disease. ("Spend the time slowly packing away the library; the crates are too heavy to move and lie where they are filled.") Before he is able to finish this task, Powers falls asleep for good. Lying down at the bottom of a pool, he drowns in the river of entropic eternity.[235]

Ballard's book is listed in the inventory of Smithson's library. As he perused this list, Millar learned that he himself owned *The Voices of Time* and other books that Smithson possessed. A proposal for an artwork, *Monument to Entropy (Library)* (1995), took shape. Millar established a single rule as he embarked on this project: he would try to acquire all the books listed in the inventory, but only in the editions that Smithson had owned. The completed work would be a replica of the original library, an exact double.[236]

Millar's project examines one of Smithson's less heralded pursuits. An autodidact who never attended college and an inveterate bibliophile, Smithson built an expansive collection encompassing a range of fields and genres.[237] The inventory of his library assembled after his death, at Holt's instruction, is evidence of his polymath intelligence. There are books of anthropology and archaeology; art, aesthetics, and philosophy; history, political science, and economics; psychology and religion; works of literature, criticism, and linguistics; travel guides and atlases; and glossy magazines and LPs.[238] The inventory lists approximately one thousand entries, and it is plausible that Millar could replicate the library in its entirety. Recall that the fictional Powers fails to pack all his books away, to disassemble his library, before succumbing to the sleeping disease. Is it not likely that Millar will fail at his self-appointed task? Twenty years on, his reconstruction of Smithson's library is far from complete. The books and magazines and LPs that were easy to find during Smithson's lifetime are obscure now, and difficult to acquire. *Monument to Entropy (Library)* recalls a lost world—a downtown Manhattan of cheap bars and cheap rents, of used-book stores and record shops, the Manhattan depicted in Kushner's *The Flamethrowers*, of which there is now scarcely a trace. Perpetually incomplete, Millar's project is the antithesis of Nelson's simulacral tour de force, the *Woodshed* of *Triple Bluff Canyon* that is so "finished" it appears to be a perfect replica. His library is metaphorical, "speculative," deliberately unfinished.[239] It begs questions. Will Millar acquire every one of these dog-eared paperbacks, these crumbling serials, these Golden Oldies, in his lifetime? What would it matter if he did?[240]

The inspiration for another of Millar's projects, *Monument to Entropy (Hotel Palenque)* (1999), is a lecture that Smithson presented at the University of Utah School of Architecture in January 1972. Smithson's

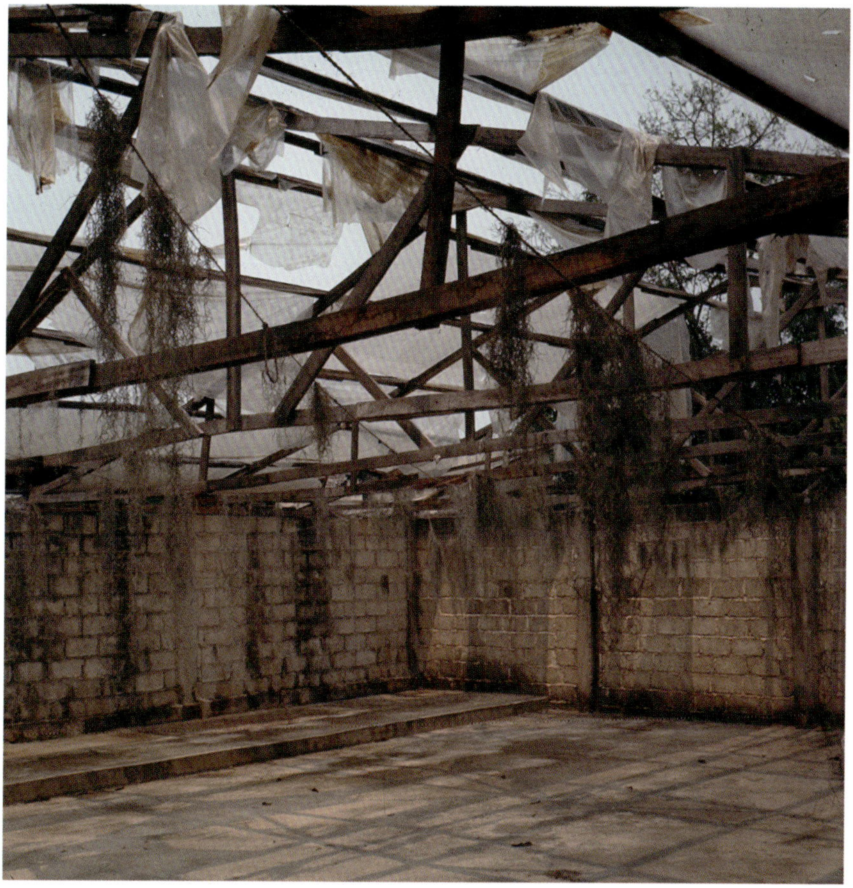

**Fig. 2.38.** Robert Smithson, *Hotel Palenque*, 1969–72. Slide projection of 31 color slides (35 mm; 126 format) and audio recording of lecture by the artist at University of Utah in 1972 (42′57″). Dimensions variable. Detail: The Dance Hall. Solomon R. Guggenheim Museum, New York. Purchased with funds contributed by the International Director's Council and Executive Committee Members: Edythe Broad, Henry Buhl, Elaine Terner Cooper, Linda Fischbach, Ronnie Heyman, Dakis Joannou, Cindy Johnson, Barbara Lane, Linda Macklowe, Brian McIver, Peter Norton, Willem Peppler, Denise Rich, Rachel Rudin, David Teiger, Ginny Williams, and Elliot K. Wolk. 1999 99.5268. Art © Holt-Smithson Foundation / Licensed by VAGA, New York.

work, a slide presentation called *Hotel Palenque*, revisits the artist's 1969 trip to the Yucatán with Holt and Virginia Dwan. Unexpectedly, Smithson avoids Palenque's glorious pyramids and temples, the ordinary fare of an art historical presentation. He instead leads his listeners on an imaginary walk through a run-down motel at the periphery of the archaeological site, a "ruin" as fascinating to the artist as the Mayan citadel. He discusses the hotel's forlorn exterior and its forlorn garden, a courtyard containing stacks of building blocks and broken furniture, and other odd spaces, arriving at a roofless room. Smithson's photo of this space, a would-be dance hall, its naked girders strung up with sheets of plastic and Spanish moss, and his depiction of an empty swimming pool crossed by a suspension bridge leading to nowhere are images as fantastic and strange as Piranesi's *Carceri* (fig. 2.38).[241]

Millar traveled to Palenque exactly thirty years after Smithson's visit. Consulting Smithson's drawing identifying the thirty-one locations he

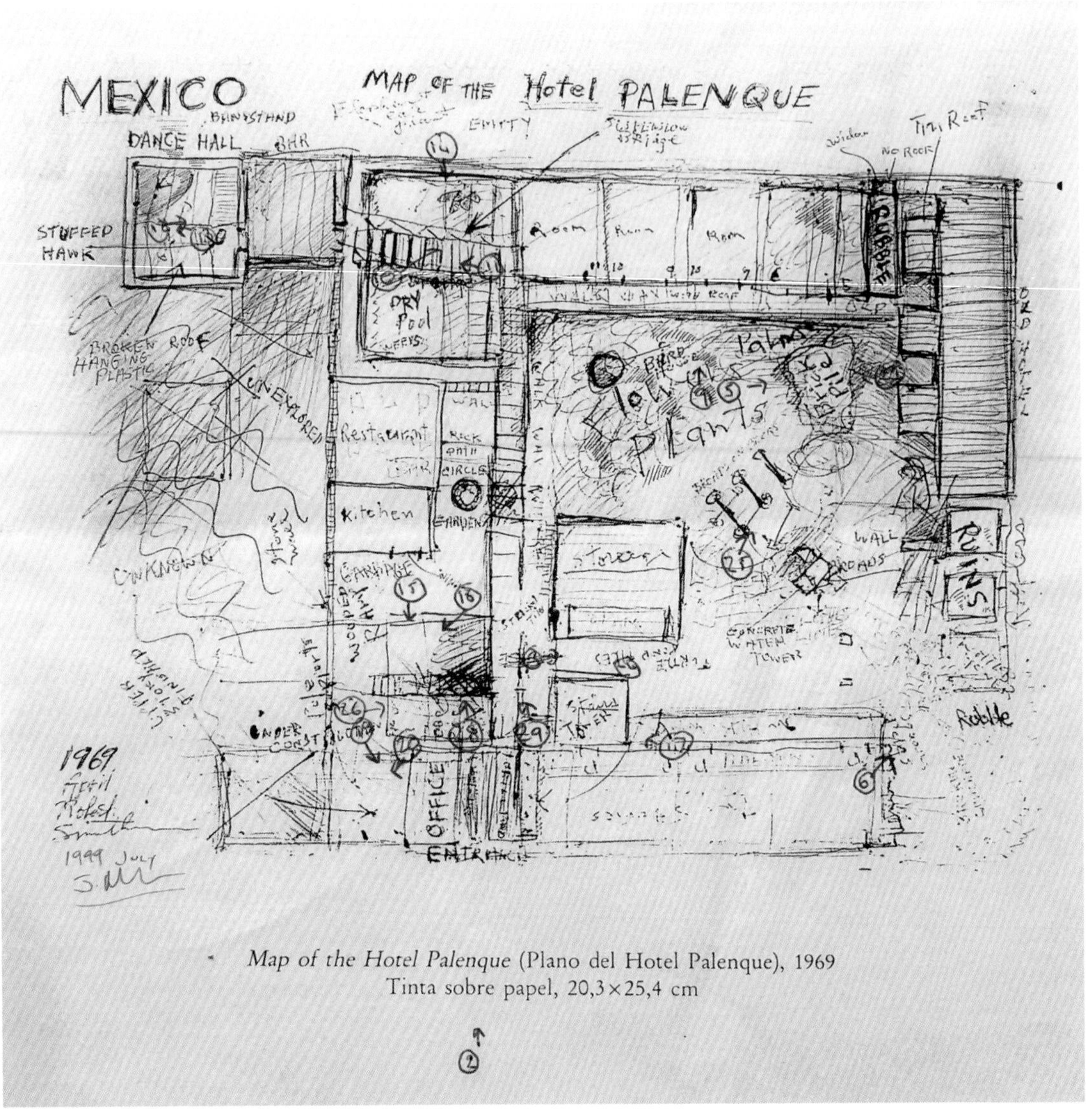


**Fig. 2.39.** Jeremy Millar, *Monument to Entropy (Hotel Palenque Map)*, 1999. Ink on photocopy. Photograph courtesy of Jeremy Millar.

describes in his lecture, Millar meticulously reconstructed the itinerary of *Hotel Palenque*, adding his own notations on top of Smithson's. The resulting drawing is a "collaboration" between the artists, the continuation of one artist's work by another, a palimpsest of their journeys to the same place at different moments in time (fig. 2.39). Millar took two exposures of each location, documenting the motel's present state. He then placed one roll of film in a lockbox behind the front desk and absconded with the key.

Returning to Britain with the key, lockbox receipt, and a second roll of film, he eventually exhibited these artifacts and the photographic contact sheets printed from the negatives (fig. 2.40).[242] Millar's revision of Smithson's project from lecture to installation established a temporal gap between the artists' visits—between the years 1969 and 1999. By the time Millar showed *Monument to Entropy (Hotel Palenque)* at a gallery in Edinburgh in 2007, nearly four decades had passed since Smithson took his exposures. And this made no difference: depicting how much or how little the locations had changed, Millar revealed the unending nature of entropic time, the incontrovertible *fact* of entropy. We rebuild, make things new. These things fall apart. We rebuild again. And they fall apart again eventually.

Millar never did return to Palenque. The roll of film he deposited in the lockbox may remain there, or it may have been removed and destroyed.

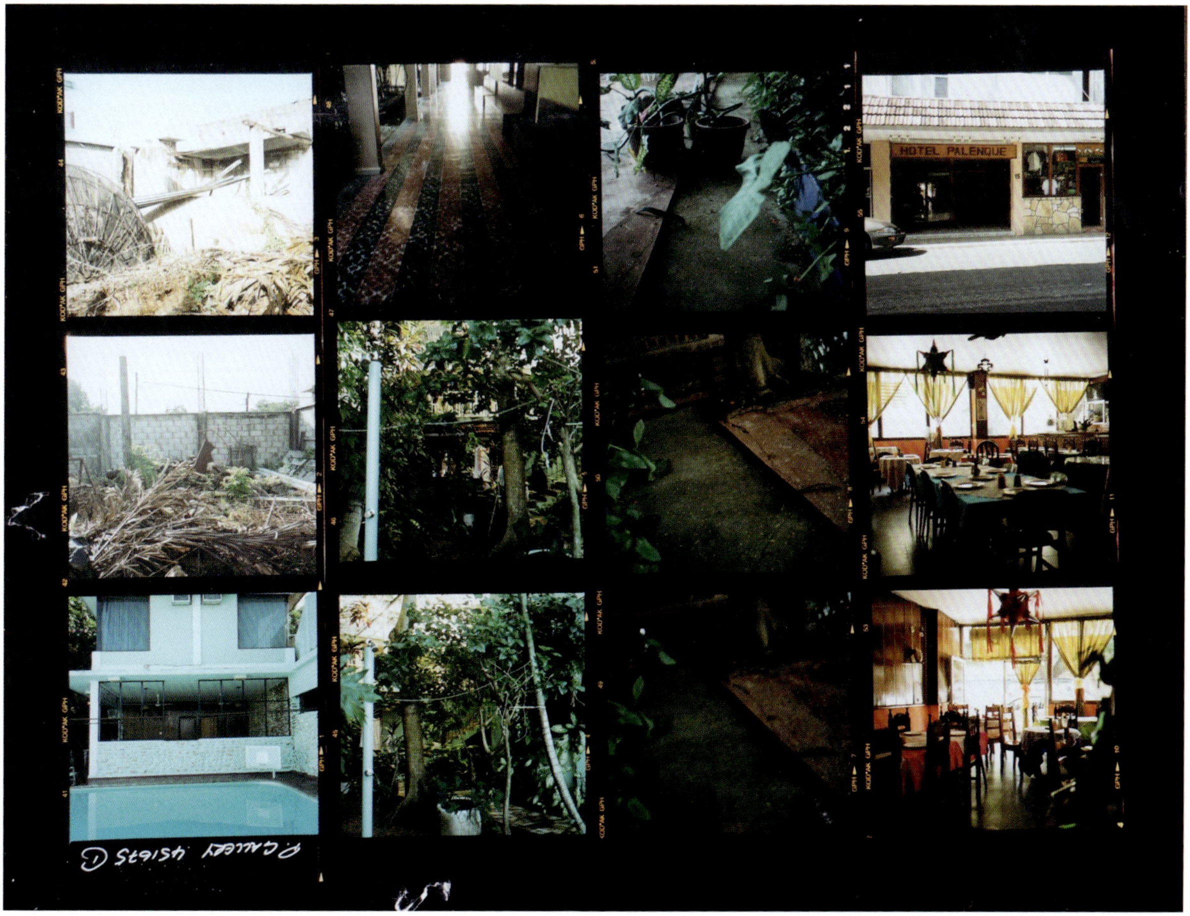


**Fig. 2.40.** Jeremy Millar, *Monument to Entropy (Hotel Palenque)*, 1999. Photographic contact sheets. Photograph courtesy of Jeremy Millar.

Like the works of Dean, Green, Nelson, and Durant I described earlier, his remake of *Hotel Palenque* continues the logic of Smithson's practice in ways that Smithson likely would not have pursued. And like those works, Millar's "return" to Palenque leaves us wondering what Smithson might have made had he lived. Would he have refreshed the *Spiral Jetty* with new boulders and earth? Would he have delayed *Partially Buried Woodshed*'s dismantling, as Holt attempted to do? Would he have extended his dialectic of site and nonsite in unforeseen directions, or transitioned away from the rigorous confines of this system? Practices of return find what is useful and contemporary in Smithson's art, and cause us to speculate about what "might have been." Some of these works reveal the inescapable melancholy that attends these speculations. Millar's remake of *Hotel Palenque*, in particular, teases out the tragic aspect of Smithson's work as we now experience it—the utter strangeness of listening to the artist's disembodied voice describing the slides as they flash before us, and the sound of the architecture students in Salt Lake City breaking into laughter when they finally "get" his quirky humor, and their silence as they consider his claim that a badly built motel is as deserving of their attention as Lord Pakal's pyramids.

The carousel turns, clicks. Another slide falls into place. Smithson discusses another courtyard, another roofless room. We think only of Amarillo.

## An Unintentional Monument

**Her interest was in sites that have become memorials unexpectedly.**

Renée Green, "Partially Buried Continued"

The ephemeral activities of the Sixties and Seventies compel our attention decades after their dispersion. As a thing or building decays, it undergoes a semantic alteration.[243] And indeed *Partially Buried Woodshed*, the emblematic artistic ruin of its time, came to mean something very different after Smithson left the Ohio campus. The painting of the date *May 4 1970* on its façade transformed Smithson's work into a memorial to the students. After Amarillo the *Woodshed* meant something more. It was now a destination, not unlike those sepulchers and tombstones of poets and artists that attract a steady stream of visitors in search of some tangible evidence of the dead. These pilgrims removed the shed's remains—a splinter of wood, a chunk of concrete. They made off with these relics, hastening its decay. The *Woodshed* was now a cenotaph to both Smithson and the students, a monument to those who died too soon.[244] A work by Sam Durant, *What's the Opposite of Entropy?* (1999), explores this double identity of the *Woodshed*, an artwork that came to represent not one tragedy but two (fig. 2.41). Models in bell-bottom jeans and tee shirts lie on one of Durant's miniature scale models. Their eyes are shut, their bodies

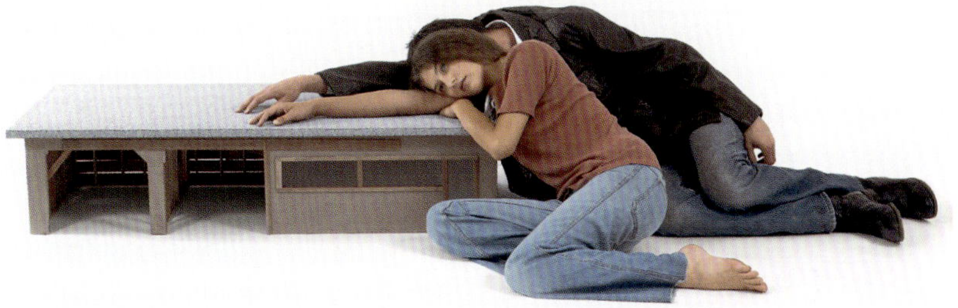

**Fig. 2.41.** Sam Durant, *What's the Opposite of Entropy?* 1999. C-print. Photograph courtesy of Sam Durant.

are limp. We are immediately reminded of those horrifying images of the Kent students dodging the guardsmen's bullets in the Prentice Hall parking lot, of the bodies of the wounded and dead. The long cascade of hair of the female model and the young man's dangling wrist evoke Smithson's earthen spiral, the crucial element that instigated the shed's unraveling.

The histories of *Partially Buried Woodshed* and the May 4 massacre were now inextricably intertwined. Once the *Woodshed* was inscribed with that fateful date it became a memorial to the fallen students; just three years later it became an ad hoc memorial to the young artist. Smithson's "monument" to entropy became an actual monument, entropy's opposite, as the title of Durant's work implies. How may we describe its peculiar monumentality?

In his essay "The Modern Cult of Monuments" (1903), art historian Alois Riegl established a now classic taxonomy of monuments (*Denkmale*).[245] One can hardly do justice to Riegl's magisterial survey of the subject—a compehensive report on the state of historic preservation in the Austro-Hungarian empire at the turn of the last century—here. I want merely to point to the first and fundamental distinction Riegl makes in his essay: his description of monuments as either "intentional" or "unintentional."

An intentional monument is a monument in its oldest sense. It keeps human actions "alive in the minds of future generations." An unintentional monument also recalls the activity of men and women, yet it was not meant to do so. It becomes a monument *after* it has been made. In order for something that was not meant to be a monument originally to be seen as such, there needs to be a present-day consensus or perception that it is one. ("It is not their original purpose . . . that turn[s] these works into monuments, but . . . our modern perception of them.")[246]

Riegl speaks of the viewer who recognizes the intentional monument, and the viewer who attributes a monumental intent where it didn't exist: the *Woodshed* evokes this second notion. It is safe to say that Smithson did not set out to create a monument. We know that he had wanted to bury a building, to rid architecture of its monumental pretensions. He buried the Kent woodshed to fulfill the obligations of a visiting artist's contract. His work only acquired the notoriety it did after it was marked with the date of the massacre. In Green's video *Partially Buried*, Smithson's host during his visit, Brinsley Tyrrell, recalls:

> I guess I always liked the fact that the university never really understood that it got an important piece. Actually nobody building the piece understood that it was going to be an important piece. I don't even think Smithson thought it would be an important piece.[247]

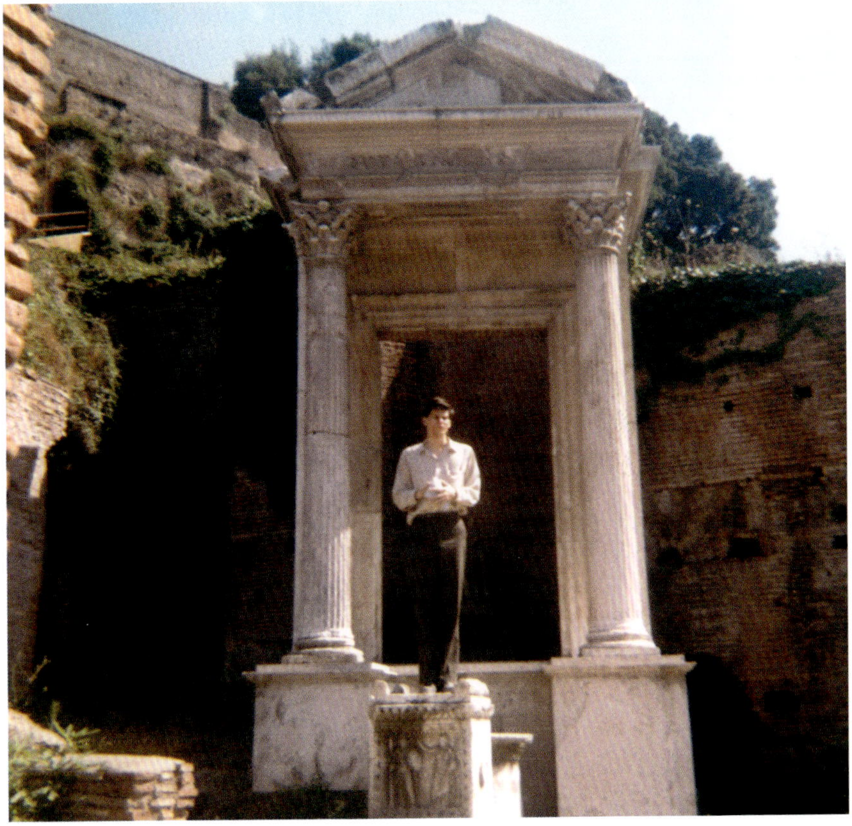

**Fig. 2.42.** Robert Smithson at Juturna Fountain, Roman Forum, Rome, 1961. © Holt-Smithson Foundation / Licensed by VAGA, New York.

Tyrrell describes the *Woodshed* as an unintentional monument. He claims that Smithson didn't think the work would be "important" even though it became so.

Now Smithson was also a theorist of monuments; his interest in the subject was likely triggered during a several-month stay in Rome in 1961, when he toured the city's catacombs, churches, and ruins, a visit recorded in several staged images of the artist posing in front of the House of the Vestals and Fountain of Juturna in the Forum (fig. 2.42).[248] For Riegl, both intentional and unintentional monuments are recognized after they are made. Monuments are links in a vast chain of human actions and events that they ask us to remember. Smithson confounds this anthropocentric timeline, a timeline defined both by the marble (intentional) monuments of Rome and the industrial (unintentional) monuments of Passaic. Entropic time is recursive and infinite. The present is a momentary pause in that vast continuum.[249] In "Entropy and the New Monuments," he describes a new kind of monument purged of human associations:

> Instead of causing us to remember the past like the old monuments, the new monuments seem to cause us to forget the future. Instead of being made of natural materials, such as marble, granite, and other kinds of rock, the new monuments are made of artificial materials, plastic, chrome, and electric light. They are not built for the ages, but rather against the ages.[250]

The "new monuments" are not meant to last; they fail to recall human deeds and events. They cause us not to remember but to forget. The Minimal artworks that inspired Smithson's article were set "against the wheels" of the "linear time clock" of human history. The Perspex boxes of Judd will get scratched, their metal frames will lose their luster. Flavin's fluorescents will flicker out. Such works defy the Abstract Expressionists' agonistic model of history as tragically and eternally human.

If the Minimal object affords Smithson a first definition of the monument, architecture takes center stage in his article on Passaic. Architecture is a most important target for Smithson, as we have seen. The first and most monumental of the arts according to Hegel, architecture is the most prone to anthropocentric projection. (It is not for nothing that most of Riegl's examples are buildings.) Unlike the monuments in the Forum visited by the young artist, the monuments of Passaic do not recall important events. These remnants of early twentieth-century industry and suburban growth—the *Bridge Monument, Sand-Box Monument*, and so on—were not monuments until Smithson declared them such.

Smithson envisions yet another kind of monument in his Passaic text—a monument that further undermines the anthropocentrism of that notion. The "ruin-in-reverse," as he calls it, escapes linear time, evoking a crossed future and past. This ruin-in-reverse is "all the new construction that would eventually be built" along the river's shores, the subdivisions of cheap split-level and Cape Cod homes of the future. Ruins-in-reverse are "the opposite of the 'romantic ruin,'" Smithson writes, "because the buildings don't *fall* into ruin *after* they are built but rather rise into ruin *before* they are built."[251] They reveal entropy's deleterious effects before being constructed. They are neither "intentional" nor "unintentional" so much as anti- or *un*monumental. They announce their entropic fate from the future. They neglect a past they never recalled in the first place. "But the suburbs exist without a rational past and without the 'big events' of history. Oh, maybe there are a few statues, a legend, and a couple of curios, but no past—just what passes for a future."[252]

Unlike the ruin-in-reverse (a practical impossibility, after all), Smithson's *Woodshed* staged its dismantling, its de-architecturization, in human time. It became associated with tragic events. It became a monument unintentionally. ("I don't even think Smithson thought it would be an important piece.") It took on the alluring quality that Riegl calls "historical value," the patina that accrues to things and places that have witnessed momentous events, that were "*there*." Kent State is cluttered with such monuments—the *Woodshed* and all the others. Let us visit the iconic campus one more time.

## The Monuments of Kent (2008)

Return is a private occupation, an individual act. The digger digs alone. But memory, as Benjamin practices it, is a meditation on the spaces, the technologies and social forms, and the persons and things that left these impressions, and that shaped the author's interests and obsessions. And by writing down these fugitive images Benjamin establishes the distance between two moments in time and two selves, deeply connected yet different, the two "Walters" who lived through these moments. A Jew could no longer walk freely in the Tiergarten in 1938, when Benjamin finally published his Berlin memoir, as his younger persona does—the boy who falls in love with his governess as they pass through the flowerbeds beneath the statues of the emperor and empress, and who waits patiently above the otter pool in the zoo to catch sight of this dark creature before it plunges to the deep; who delights at the elaborate depictions of "distant worlds" in the Imperial Panorama (an art form that "died out with the coming of the 20th century") and who attends the annual parade in commemoration of the Prussian victory at Sedan in 1873, the memory of a memory.

Visiting his mother's "Auntie Lehmann" in her apartment at the corner of Steglitzer and Genthiner streets, where she always wore the "same black bonnet and . . . same silk dress" and always sat in the same chair and alcove, and always spoke in a voice "fragile and brittle as glass," he listened as she described the lives of ancestors who had been cattle dealers and grain merchants in the rural counties surrounding Berlin during the last century, and whose children and grandchildren now lived in the capital on streets named for "the little towns they had left behind."[253] And when Benjamin describes departing his grandmother's house on Christmas Day, his arms weighed down with presents, he speaks of horse-drawn carriages and the clinking sound of sleigh bells, of "gaslights coming on, one after another," as if to mark the progress of the lamplighter who "even on this sweet evening, had to shoulder his pole."[254] The most vivid images in *Berlin Childhood around 1900* are of obsolete technologies, of moribund aesthetic and decorative forms, of persons who no longer exist. Recalling these stuffy interiors and streets illuminated by gas lamps, these imperial statues and celebrations, these elderly relations, Benjamin historicizes Benjamin. The present is the unspoken "subject" of these recollections. "But, then, the images of my metropolitan childhood perhaps are capable, at their core, of pre-forming later historical experiences."[255]

•

December 2008. I arrive in Kent in the still of winter. The midwestern sky is unremittingly gray. The cold seeps into my shoes, my feet. I am following the path of Smithson and Michener, of Green and all the others. I have returned to Kent, a place where I have never been. In a certain sense, I have.

A single image remains from that day in 1970, remote but insistent, a memory so faint it almost seems as if I had read it or heard it described—as if it belongs to somebody else. I could well have dreamed it.

The TV is on. I am, I think, sitting at the white Formica-topped table in my mother's kitchen. Or I am sprawled on the linoleum floor looking up at the television. The moment is the delicious hour and a half of repose after school, a time without purpose, a time of indolence and fantasy. The shows I enjoy most—the one about a pretty witch living in a suburban house not unlike our own, the other about a group of comedian-castaways "stranded" on a desert island—are accompanied by laugh tracks. Loud, relentless, these outbursts of engineered mirth instruct a person—a child—how to be amused.

Today there is no laughter. A single image composed of thousands of cathode rays floats in the subtle curvature of the screen. Reporters unseen are talking with animation. Something has just happened—is happening.

The memory is painted in shades of gray. It is all value, no color. Above all, it is *still*. A fixed image on TV is an interruption of business as usual, a sign of emergency. The usual flow of daytime soap operas and commercials and reruns has ground to a halt. A picture on a television: this is my "Kent State." The memory is slender, just an image. This alone endures. It remains. It sticks.

Consider Vic Muniz's *Memory Rendering* of Filo's photo of the massacre, a rendition of the image I remember seeing on TV (fig. 1.35). Muniz's depiction of Mary Ann Vecchio and Jeffrey Miller is multiply filtered, a halftone print of a soft-focus exposure of a drawing of Filo's photograph. Muniz severely redacts the picture he draws from memory, isolating the central figures. He omits the girl in a fringed jacket who stands next to Vecchio in the original photo (Carol Mirman, one of the students who invited Smithson to Kent State). He omits the athletic practice field behind these figures, and the chain-link fence at the border of the field where the guardsmen gathered minutes before. Defining Vecchio and Miller in dense strokes of charcoal, he severs these figures from everyone and everything extraneous. They stand out; they alone matter. And so he emphasizes the girl's cascading hair and her extraordinary pose, and the dead boy's limp passivity. He explores the *effectiveness* of Filo's image, how certain photos stand as synecdoches of events so momentous or gruesome they evade our comprehension, how it is that *this* picture of all the exposures taken at Kent State came to represent the event in its totality, how it became an emblem of the bad Sixties.

In my memory of Filo's photo, the chain-link fence comes forward. It is just behind Vecchio, framing and confining her ample figure. In the actual image Miller's body is front and center. In my memory of the picture Miller is an *implied* presence. He is barely there, or not there, a blank spot, an absence. In my memory there are only Vecchio and the fence, a girl and a pattern of chain links, and the voices of reporters. Could it be that at seven I lacked a sufficient concept of death to connect the grieving teenager and the dead boy? (It may be that I did see the image of Miller's corpse and repressed seeing it.) My memory of that image on TV (of myself staring at this image) remains, in part, because of everything it omits. The memory image is compacted, Benjamin observes. His Berlin memoir is not filled with lengthy anecdotes or remembered conversations. It is a tissue of fragments, a recitation of *details*. Detail after detail. Remembrance is microscopic: the more minute the image, the potentially richer its yield.[256] My recollection of May 4 has lasted so long because it is so reduced, and because I have seen reproductions of Filo's photo repeatedly since then. My memory, my slender memory, is compounded by the memory of those depictions. Suspended in the cathodic ether of the TV set, that image is all there is. This, and the recollection of my befuddlement. The memory that I cannot read Filo's picture. In my memory of May 4 I have no idea what Kent State is or where it is. Why it matters. Why the girl is so upset.

The Kent I discover is no longer the prosperous midwestern city described by Michener—the Kent the radicals set out to "destroy." Kent, in this new century, is a typical Rust Belt town struggling in an era of outsourcing and underemployment. A river, the Cuyahoga, rushes swiftly beneath an old stone bridge next to railroad tracks, holdovers of the city's industrial past. Water Street, where the first riot occurred that weekend, is a strip of fast-food joints and half-occupied storefronts, the ghosts of a once-flourishing retail district denatured by the big-box stores on the highway to Akron. A block from Kent's central intersection, where Water and Main streets cross, I locate a house that looks older than the others. During the late Sixties and early Seventies the Ericksons lived here. Rick and Candy Erickson were among the leading antiwar activists then; their upstairs apartment was a nerve center for the movement. In these "sinister" quarters—the house, Michener claims, was the model for the creepy, crumbling Victorian in Hitchcock's *Psycho*—the Ericksons hosted radicals from around the country, including the future Weathermen. Agitation meetings were held in their living room and in the backyard. The "assault" on the university was plotted here. The house at the top of the hill on Columbus Street (I am standing at the edge of the driveway) scarcely resembles the scary pile depicted in Michener's potboiler. Painted a tasteful gray with green trim and hidden behind overgrown bushes, the former Erickson home is easy to miss.

I reach Commons, the green expanse in the center of the campus. A crust of snow covers the frozen sod. I am standing at the edge of the great lawn at the location where the ROTC building stood. Across the way is an old railroad bell encased in a low structure of yellow brick. A rallying place after football games, the Victory Bell became a contested site during the Sixties and Seventies. The activist Steve Sharoff buried a copy of the U.S. Constitution here, and three days later, the morning of May 4, a thousand young people, Miller and Vecchio among them, gathered in the same spot. A hundred guardsmen carrying rifles and bayonets stood across the lawn, where I am, to defend ROTC's ashen remains. This is where the National Guard commander read the Riot Act through a bullhorn three times, the standard protocol. And when the protesters didn't budge, the soldiers chased them up the hill behind the old bell—Blanket Hill.

I retrace their steps. The brick-and-concrete structure known as Taylor Hall, photographed by Davenport in her *Campus* series, is to my left. Directly in front is an open concrete structure, a student engineering project sited at the hill's summit that came to be known as the Pagoda. When G Troop and A Company reached this position, they marched down to the athletic field where the controversial Gym Annex now stands. Surrounded on three sides by the chain-link fence that ran the field's periphery (the fence that looms in my memory), the guardsmen fended off jeers and rock missiles. They felt trapped. Some of the men conferred in a huddle, as others pointed their guns toward the Prentice Hall parking lot. Suddenly the men retook the hill and gathered around the Pagoda. And without warning they kneeled and fired at the hundreds of kids milling in the parking lot at the base of the hill.

There are monuments everywhere at Kent State, monuments official and unofficial, intended and unintended. Climbing the ridge of Blanket Hill overlooking the great lawn, where the students first faced off against the guardsmen, I discover one of these monuments. An ensemble of granite polyhedrons of progressive length evokes caskets clumsily; the rose granite walls and benches evoke the Eighties corporate lobbies for which the

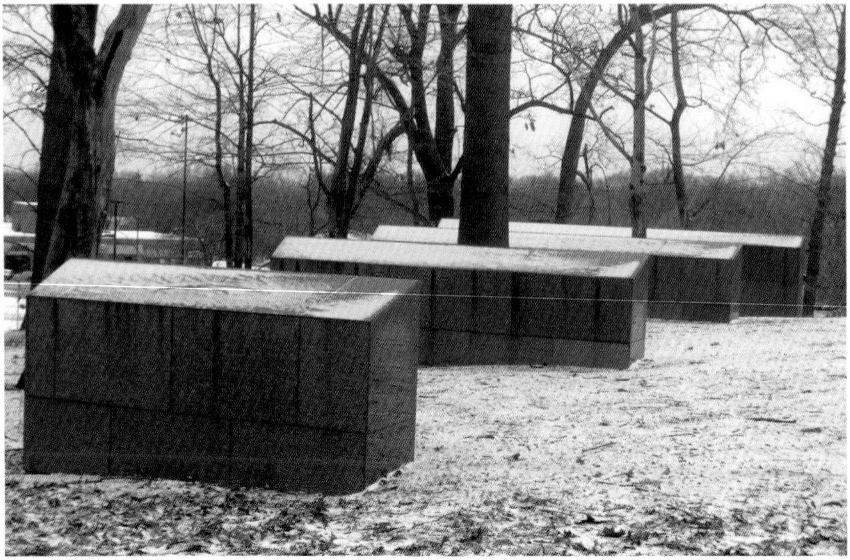

**Fig. 2.43.** Bruno Ast, May 4th Memorial, Kent State University, 1986–90. Photograph by the author.

designer, Bruno Ast, became known (fig. 2.43).[257] In the parking lot itself red granite markers inset in the pavement indicate where the four students fell. The spaces are closed off to cars. I wipe away the snow with my shoe and read the names.[258] Sandy Scheuer was on her way to class when the shootings occurred. She took one of the military-grade bullets in her throat, and her aorta burst. She died minutes later of blood loss at the spot identified by the marker. The athletic Bill Schroeder was also between classes. A framed image in Green's photo frieze shows Schroeder clutching a file folder escaping the approaching guard. Standing not far from Scheuer, he took a round in the back that shattered his ribs and lungs; he died the next day in intensive care.

Allison Krause participated in the protest that morning. Photographs document her and others being chased up Blanket Hill. She then made her way downhill to the parking lot. Standing farthest from the Pagoda of the victims, she dodged behind a car when the shooting started, to no avail. Struck by three rounds in the chest, she was dead on arrival at the hospital.

Jeffrey Miller stood in the access road to the parking lot where the hill flattens out. Minutes earlier he'd yelled epithets at the guardsmen and thrown a canister of tear gas back at them. One of the soldiers pointed his rifle at the foul-mouthed hippie in the bandana. His aim was excellent. A bullet entered Miller's skull just above his mouth and tore up his brain. Blood poured from his skull in a thick stream.

A parking lot is an odd place to mourn. It is not a battlefield or a cemetery, or a civic square. It is not the sort of place where momentous things

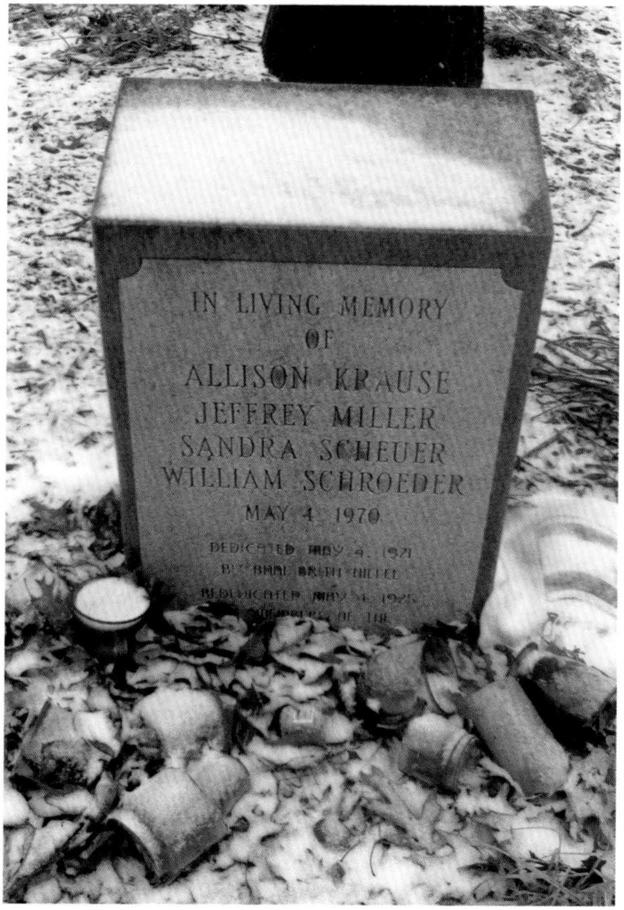


**Fig. 2.44.** Hillel Memorial, Prentice Hall Parking Lot, Kent State University. Photograph by the author.

happen. It is a way station, a place we pass through on our way to other places where we do things—classrooms, offices, libraries. And in fact "Parking Lot R-3" (as the Prentice lot is identified on the campus map) looks ordinary enough with its parked SUVs and sedans, and open spots bordered by white stripes. It isn't. Votive candles and frozen flowers clutter the ground around the Hillel Memorial, oldest of the university's monuments, a simple tombstone engraved with the names of the dead. (See fig. 2.44.) Waist-high lampposts arranged in groups of six surround the student monuments. Visitors leave stones on top of these black lamps as if they were tombs.

Kent State is a monument to that time, a Sixties Gettysburg. There are precious few places where that era's seminal events can be imagined and felt. We "feel" the Sixties at Kelly Ingram Park in Birmingham, where civil rights marchers were attacked by police dogs and knocked down with water hoses wielded by police or fire fighters. We feel it at Dealey Plaza in Dallas. We feel it at Kent State. These sites are imbued with *historia*, the memory of what happened there. Visitors who have made the journey to see these places for themselves are transported imaginatively to the time of the event and to the period the incident came to represent. Unintentional monuments, these sites hold a special status in discussions of Sixties memory. As they age, as they approach the condition of the ruin, they force us to perceive the temporal divide between the Sixties and our moment. As a monument ages, it causes us to perceive that it *has* aged.[259] We perceive its decay as a temporal process. And so we are moved to contemplate time in the abstract sense, time in its inscrutable vastness. The Roman and medieval edifices that occasioned Riegl's analysis were truly ancient; their monumentality was not in doubt. The monuments of Kent inhabit a recent past, a past that is rapidly aging. Taylor Hall, the building at the center of the massacre, is no longer the proud modern edifice admired by Michener during his visit in 1971.[260] Its brick walls and concrete piers have darkened with age; its basement is discolored with water stains; its porch is pitted and cracked. From this lookout crowds of students watched the guardsmen's bellicose progress. And when the men in helmets rushed up the hill and gathered around the Pagoda, and kneeled and fired, the students realized they were not firing blanks but real bullets, and they dodged behind its piers and ran indoors in mortal fear.

Nearby is the most unlikely, the most "unintentional" monument of all (fig. 2.45). *Solar Totem #1* (1967), a work by the Ohio sculptor Don Drumm, was installed in front of Taylor Hall at the time of the building's dedication. A fifteen-foot abstract assemblage of welded Cor-Ten steel, Drumm's sculpture stood directly in the line of fire and took a round in one of its plates. The hole this left is an index of that shattering velocity (fig. 2.46).[261] Peering through this small aperture near the sculpture's base, I mentally trace that volley from the tip of a guardsman's M-1 through Drumm's sculpture to the parking lot downhill. I am excruciatingly aware of what bullets *do*. If a .30 caliber round can rip through steel with such force, what can it do to a body? But why were the guardsmen carrying loaded rifles on a *campus*? Who gave the order to shoot at a crowd of unarmed students at such a distance, where they posed no possible threat? (Was it the grizzled General Canterbury, who threatened to shoot *another* gathering of students who sat down on the Commons after the massacre, a disaster barely prevented by the mediation of three faculty members?) Why were the eight guardsmen who were charged with misconduct never sentenced? Why were the officers never held accountable?[262]

History and memory: nowhere are the definitions of these mnemonic impulses blurrier than here. Unintentional monuments are artifacts. Our

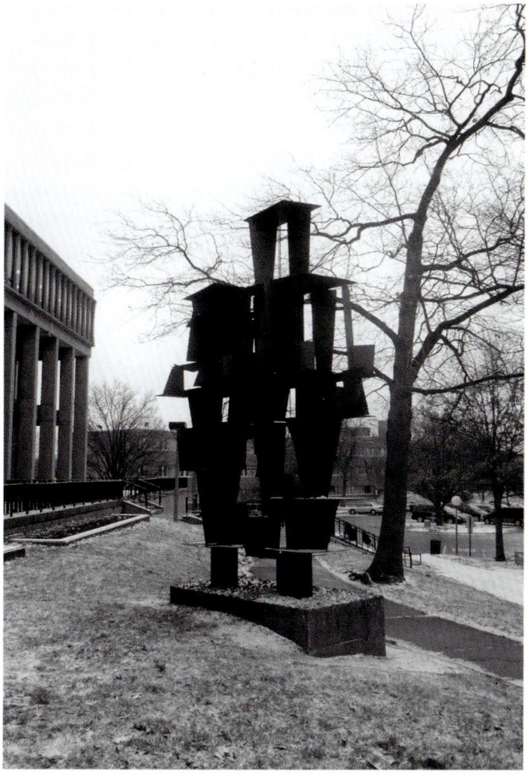

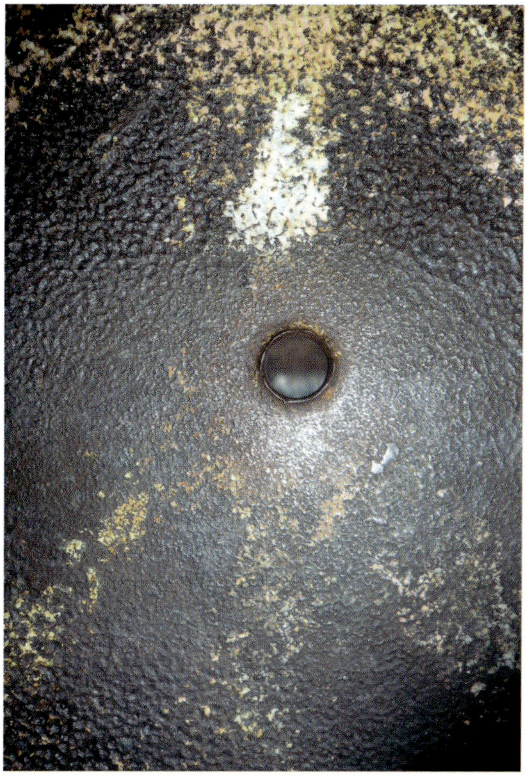

**Fig. 2.45.** Don Drumm, *Solar Totem #1*, 1967. Photograph by the author.

**Fig. 2.46.** Don Drumm, *Solar Totem #1*, 1967. Detail. Photograph by the author.

"modern perception" of these places and things transforms them into monuments, Riegl says. They have come to represent, to stand for, an event or period that appears momentous to us now. They goad us to reconstruct what happened—to arrange a plethora of events into a narrative. They incite us to think as historians do. Mute witnesses of May 4, the monuments of Kent—the Victory Bell, the Pagoda, *Solar Totem #1*, and the like—loom large in historical and journalistic accounts of the massacre. Yet for others these totems are not artifacts of history but containers of memory. For certain visitors to the campus—the number grows smaller—a walk up Blanket Hill is indeed, in every sense, a return:

> *I return here today in body. I remain here in spirit forever.*

Chalk inscriptions cover the rusted plates of Drumm's sculpture. Graffitists draw pointed analogies between the wars in Vietnam and Iraq. Between then and now. For these anonymous authors the difference between "then" and "now" is not so well defined. The bad Sixties are not over, as a matter of fact. They didn't come to an end with Kent State, or Watergate, or the retreat from Saigon. The defense industry didn't close up shop after the troops pulled out of Vietnam. The rationale for invading Iraq was even flimsier than the Gulf of Tonkin Resolution. There is only war and more war. More deaths.

*Over thirty years and we're still fighting an unjust war. How sad!!*

The scathing inscription of one graffitist condemns an America as morally troubled as Hamlet's Denmark:

*Rotten Odious Terrible Cancer*

Interspersed with these jeremiads are gentler inscriptions, epitaphs to May 4's young victims by classmates who are elderly now. They are moving to behold:

*Love you Bill—We also remember you this day!!*

*Pam + Cat*

*Jeff Bill [drawing of a flower]*

I am standing where Jeff Miller was shot.

My memory of that day is just a snapshot. I have come to Ohio to add substance to this image, to fill in the details. And though the events of May 4 are clearer than before (there is nothing as real as a bullet hole), I am even more aware now of that insuperable divide between this moment of presence and that other afternoon when I sighted the crying girl and the chain-link fence, that attenuated recollection that I have managed to hold onto through a kind of mnemonic will. And what I feel (if one can feel such a thing) is nothing less than that great expanse of time, those forty years, that separate the boy who stared at Filo's picture on television uncomprehendingly and the grown man who stands exactly where Filo took his exposure, who dimly recalls that faraway afternoon at that very place.

Up and down the campus street lamps flicker on. One by one the parking lot memorials are illuminated as the sky darkens. Black sentinels, the lampposts light up the death spots and warm the crepuscular air (fig. 2.47). They stamp the windows of nearby SUVs and sedans with impressions of gold. A train whistle, most midwestern of sounds, ripples through the town. The chatter of pedestrians. Students walk where bullets flew.

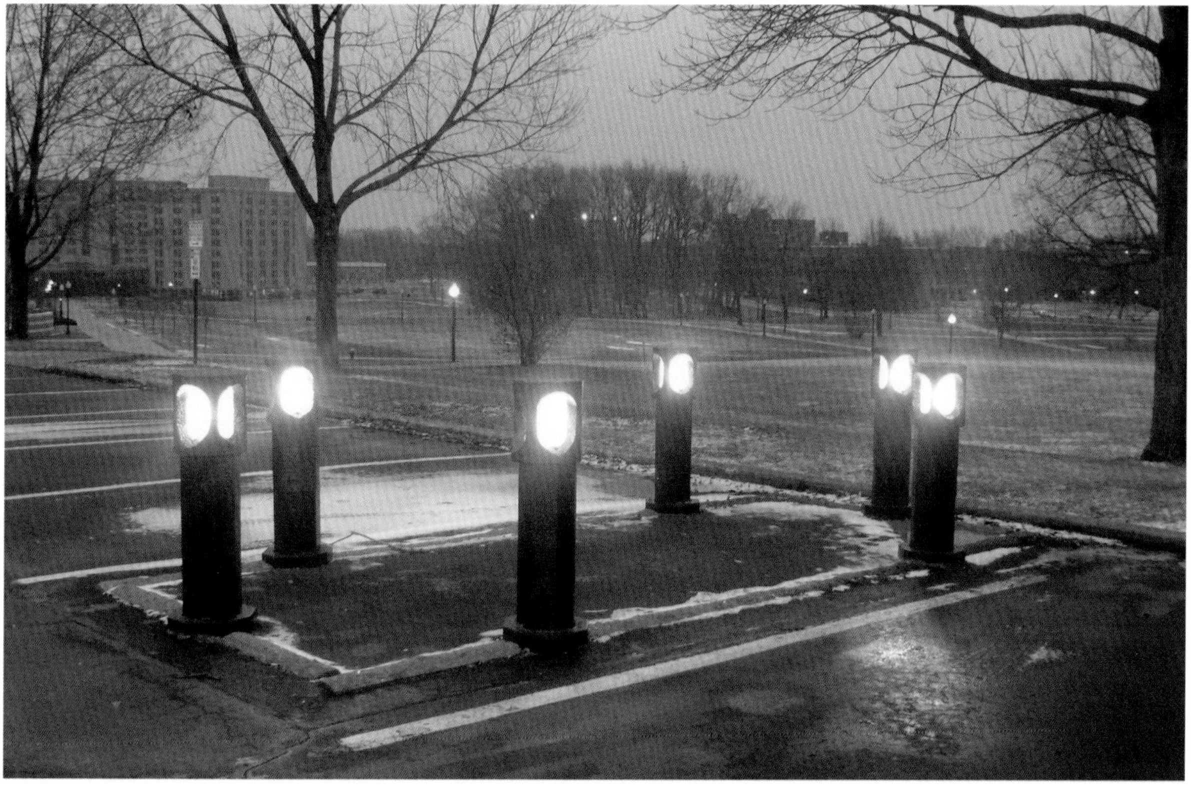

**Fig. 2.47.** May 4th Memorial, Prentice Hall Parking Lot, Kent State University. Photograph by the author.

•

Of Smithson's earthwork there is barely a trace (fig. 2.48). Like the crestfallen Tacita Dean who wonders whether the arrangement of rocks in the Great Salt Lake, the goal of her arduous journey, is indeed *Spiral Jetty*, I had expected more. Smithson defined the site as "open," without boundaries.[263] *Partially Buried Woodshed* has indeed melted into its setting. Ferns and trees grow wildly inside the foundation. A low mound is all that remains of his twenty tons of dirt. Even more drastically than at the sunken *Jetty*, I am forced to adjust my mental image of the "fresh" *Woodshed* with what I see, which is very little. To view the *Woodshed* now is to experience an absence—to remember what it has been, and to experience the site in the present tense. Like those ancient Native American mounds one finds throughout Ohio, such as the Miamisburg earth cone that rises above the plain where it was built, Smithson's earthwork is a platform for viewing. Far more than a thing to see it is a place *for seeing*, as if one were "inside a picture" looking out at everything else.[264] It may be that Smithson did not imagine this, either. (His drawings depict a mix-

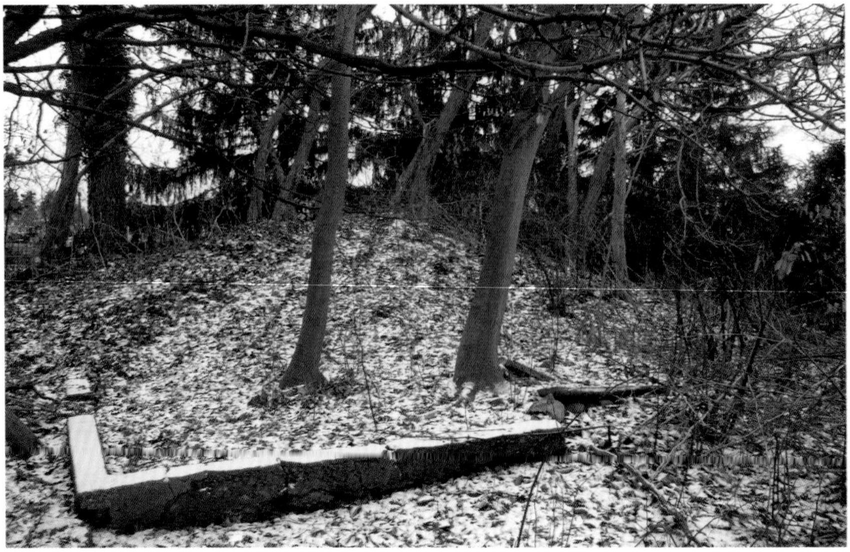

**Fig. 2.48.** Robert Smithson, *Partially Buried Woodshed*, 1970. Photograph by the author, 2008. Art © Holt-Smithson Foundation / Licensed by VAGA, New York.

ing of structure and dirt, not dirt alone.) As his shed unbuilt itself and was unbuilt, the campus architects built up its surroundings. Once located at the university's edge, his ruin stands on a hill at the entrance to a new part of the campus. It is both prominent and invisible, "there" and "not there." (I fantasize that Smithson, had he lived, and were he standing here with me, would approve of his work's liminal state.) Hidden behind the bushes and trees that encircle it, I spy a laboratory, a power plant. In the distance are fields and parking lots, endless parking lots.

Riegl speaks of the point at which a monument cedes that status. When it becomes something else. The more a monument ages, the more profound its "age value." The greater its ruination, the more it expresses its existence *in* time.[265] But this process has limits, the art historian says. A monument that loses its physical integrity completely, that is no longer recognizable, is no longer monumental. It is no longer capable of inspiring the thoughts and emotions that monuments do.[266] Entropy defeats architecture in the end. When it has done its work completely entropy itself becomes invisible. For entropy must be stilled in order to be seen.[267] The "fresh" *Woodshed* was still knowable as "architecture" even (or especially) when it was falling apart. It made entropy visible as a process. The *Woodshed* I encounter is so far gone, the ravages of time so complete, that that process is becoming undetectable. Only by consulting photographs and the drawings that Smithson made am I able to imagine the work that he made that January day, that he intended.

The monuments of Kent are an ensemble now. Together they make up a "May 4th itinerary," officially sanctioned. A brochure published by the university describes the day's events and guides visitors between these intentional and unintentional markers. The *Woodshed* holds a more ambiguous status than the other sites. Though it appears the very cipher of entropy—though it was meant to decay and ultimately disappear—its self-erasure belies its monumentalizing impulse.

Both intentions inform Smithson's art of contradiction. In "The Monuments of Passaic" the artist describes how even the pictures he has taken with his Instamatic may easily be destroyed. ("DO NOT OPEN THIS CARTRIDGE OR YOUR PICTURES MAY BE SPOILED," the package of film warns.) The prints he made of these exposures will fade and crumble to dust, joining the atmosphere they depict. But photography undermines the entropic aims of his practice as well: "Photographs steal away the spirit of the work," he once remarked.[268] They rob the "spirit" of an earthwork or performance by monumentalizing it. They "confe[r] on the event a kind of immortality and importance it would not have otherwise enjoyed," says Susan Sontag.[269] Photography is a unary medium: it gives form to the formless, frames what can't be contained. It proves that the event occurred, that a thing *was*.[270] It remakes an ephemeral occurrence into a static object, a picture. In this way the work that no longer exists remains. It goes on. It has become a monument, despite itself.[271] By photographing these endeavors, Smithson and his contemporaries ensured that their works would be remembered.[272] More precisely, they made works *that were made to be photographed*. Smithson pours the glue, cracks the beam. He leads a tour to a New Jersey quarry or into the depths of the Yucatán. And then he records that event photographically. His works recall a materiality that was, a past presence.[273] They project the memory of the event forward, anticipate its recollection; they cause us to long for an experience we never had.

The dialectic of the transitory and monumental does not begin with Post-Minimalism. The modernist artist or poet gives form to the passing event, we know from Baudelaire, and this aesthetic object, if it succeeds, extends the memory of that impression well beyond that moment. (More than a century and a half after the poet sighted the fascinating woman in black on a noisy Parisian street described in "À une passante," a reader recalls that brief encounter.)[274] The freshly buried *Partially Buried Woodshed* lasted several months, the *Glue Pour* for less than a week. Smithson ensured that these works would be captured photographically, that they would endure as memory. As the *Woodshed* became imbricated with the memory of the massacre, it took on other associations. It became an ad hoc memorial to the fallen students; after Amarillo it became a memorial to the artist. By burying a building until its central beam cracked, Smithson made a work that dismantled architecture's dream of hierarchy, an antimonument that countered the Ozymandian fantasy of eternal memory through its slow erasure. Yet once the *Woodshed*'s lintel was graffitied it became a totemic work of the Vietnam War era, an icon of the bad Sixties and a *paragone* of contemporary art history.

And then the *Woodshed* twists the screw of Smithson's dialectic yet another turn: it foretells its final recovery *by* entropy, its inevitable forgetting. Just as entropy assaults the material integrity of all things, entropic time erases the anthropocentric time of human memory; it causes us to forget. Entropy alone endures. Entropy is "monumental." Smithson's *Woodshed* will reveal its fundamental character after the hot society has precipitated its own destruction, after the earth has become the "vast deposit of bones and stones pulverized into death" imaged in miniature in the *Sand-Box Monument*, a world devoid of all forests and human life, as gray and grim as an Yves Tanguy painting. The cycle of time inaugurated that chilly afternoon in 1970 will come full circle when there is nobody left to recall that day, when there are no more rememberers.

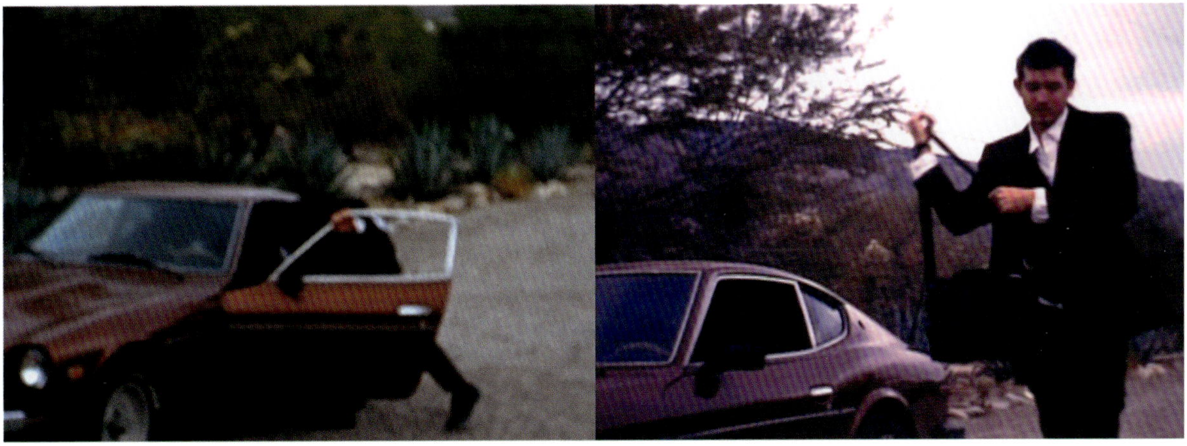

**Fig. 2.49.** Amy Granat and Drew Heitzler, *T.S.O.Y.W.*, 2007. 2-screen, 16 mm film installation, color, sound, 200 minutes, transferred to video. © Amy Granat and Drew Heitzler.

## Entropy and Death

A man drives down a dirt road. The wheels of his sports car kick up dust as the car moves slowly past a stone wall, cactuses, and electric poles. The driver parks and gets out. He is a hipster, a bohemian. He wears a black suit and untucked white shirt.

Shock of dark hair. Five o'clock shadow. His face has the ruddy pallor of youth. We hear explosions, a note played repeatedly. Then the explosions come rapidly, like gunshots. A woman speaks in German. Her voice is harsh, commanding. The words she reads echo and fade. There is a mood of apprehension, a premonition of violence.

So begins the hallucinatory *T.S.O.Y.W.* (2007), a split-screen film projection by Amy Granat and Drew Heitzler.[275] Shot in 16 mm stock with identical Bolex cameras, the films force us to compare them, as doubles do. In Heitzler's film (to the left) the driver emerges from the car at normal speed. The shot is out of focus. In the film at the right, by Granat, the driver exits the car in slow motion. The shot is in focus. In one of the films the driver reaches down in the car to grab his bag; in the other, he bends halfway (fig. 2.49). Granat and Heitzler have filmed not the exact same action but the same action *repeated*. *T.S.O.Y.W.* continues in this way for nearly three and a half hours. As our eyes move ceaselessly from one film to the other, as we watch the same actions captured at altering speeds, with different lenses, and from different points of view, details we miss in one shot become legible in the other. Slowly, we are drawn in.

In the reenactments of Gmelin, Kelly, and Tribe analyzed earlier in this book, the repetition of a historical event exposed a gap between two moments in time, between the Sixties and the contemporary.[276] Despite the obvious resemblance of the depictions, or because of this, a viewer perceived their dissimilarity. Here, the doubled image excites our curiosity. Repeated actions and scenes that occur out of sync cause us to wonder *what* we are seeing. The paired shots animate the driver's story even as they distance us from the narrative. We are seduced—and know we are being seduced.

The best stories want retelling. The narrative of *T.S.O.Y.W.* is familiar. The voice of the woman reading in German is a clue. The title of the work is an English acronym for *The Sorrows of Young Werther*, Goethe's scandalous portrait of an artist whose love for a betrothed young woman is so misguided and so consuming that he ends up shooting himself. Inspired by a remark by Jean Genet, Heitzler and Granat have Werther fall in love with a motorcycle instead of a woman. They retell the Romantic parable of the doomed artist from a slant. Infusing this narrative of infinite variations with an absurd element, they examine the nature of its attraction, the enduring appeal of this archetype.

The scenario loosely follows Goethe's. The driver arrives in a remote village. He watches Fassbinder's film *Querelle* on TV (a reference to Genet, who wrote the screenplay) and saunters in the desert with a camera, just as Werther strolls in the countryside sketching from nature. It is all rather aimless, like those early passages of Goethe's novel where Werther describes his "simple life" in the country and his halfhearted attempts to make art. Just as Werther's story really begins when he meets the beloved, Lotte, the narrative of *T.S.O.Y.W.* takes off when the hipster sights another man's motorbike, which he proceeds to film—and then caress—to the desolate chords of a violin. The men have a beer. A close-up of a bottle reveals the word KLOPSTOCK on the label, a reference to the author of the eighteenth-century "Holy Ode" that Lotte mentions to the deluded Werther, who interprets this as a confirmation of her love.[277] And just as Werther leaves the village for a town to escape this passion, the artist quits the desert for the city. He attends a gallery opening, yet his attempts at socialization do not help—the bustling city cannot distract him from his obsession. Consulting a map, he imagines a great journey and returns to the desert. The opening scene of the car driving in, of the young man getting out, plays again—another repeat. Visiting the motorbike's owner in his trailer, the driver gazes lovingly at the Harley-Davidson parked outside, a bottle of "Klopstock" beer in his hand. He steals the prized motorbike and drives off to the sound of screeching violins.

The second part of *T.S.O.Y.W.* is a road movie, and a meditation on that genre. Granat and Heitzler cross the Werther story with the American literary and cinematic genre of the "open road." The driver's passion for the pilfered bike is a passion for *wandering*. ("It is true," Werther writes, "I am only a wanderer, a pilgrim on this earth!")[278] The lover has no purpose other than to pursue an unrequited love as far as it will go. Until death. In *A Lover's Discourse* Roland Barthes describes the lover's desire as *errance* (errantry). Unlike Odysseus, who finds his way home to Ithaka and the marriage bed, the lover (Werther, the Flying Dutchman) "is doomed to wander until he dies, from love to love."[279] But the driver's journey is not entirely aimless. In *The Sorrows of Young Werther* love defeats art. Once Werther, a dilettante, sights the beloved, he ceases to be an artist. "Nature alone forms the great artist," Goethe's protagonist observes. Once he encounters Lotte in the village his attraction to nature dwindles, and he gives up drawing for good.[280]

In *T.S.O.Y.W.* the great earthworks of the Seventies are objects of desire, amorous destinations. The Harley brings the lover to Turrell's *Roden Crater* (1979 and ongoing) in Coconino County, Nevada; to De Maria's *Lightning Field* (1977) in Quemado, New Mexico; and to Holt's *Sun Tunnels* in western Utah (1973–76) (fig. 2.50).[281] With his beloved motorbike this "Werther" forges a deeper connection to art and nature than he was ever able to with his camera. At the end of a twisting road he arrives at *Spiral Jetty*. Heitzler, in the left screen, films the driver looking down on the *Jetty* from above the lake, and then standing in the center of Smithson's work encircled by the rock rings and sheets of ice, a shot that cannot fail to remind us of Caspar David Friedrich's *Wanderer above a Sea of Fog* (c. 1817), the most iconic image of German Romantic painting (figs. 2.51 and 2.52). In Friedrich's depiction the wanderer stands precariously at the crest of a rocky crag, looking down at mountains submerged in tendrils of mist. His hair is tousled in the wind; he carries a cane indicative of the long trek he has made. His dark suit marks him out against the alpine scenery. The hipster assumes this pose, too—a yellow silhouette in a sea of ice.

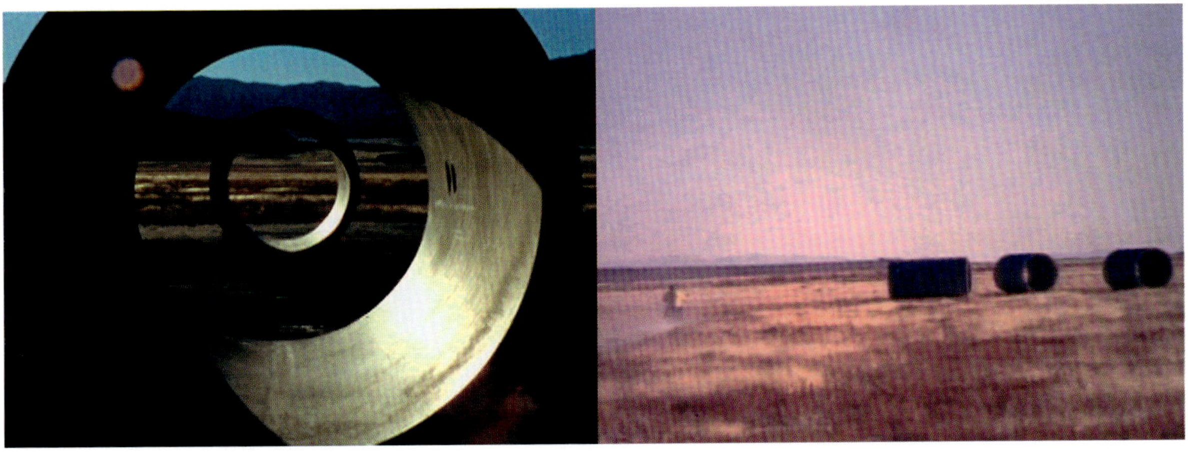

**Fig. 2.50.** Amy Granat and Drew Heitzler, *T.S.O.Y.W.*, 2007. 2-screen, 16mm film installation, color, sound, 200 minutes, transferred to video. © Amy Granat and Drew Heitzler.

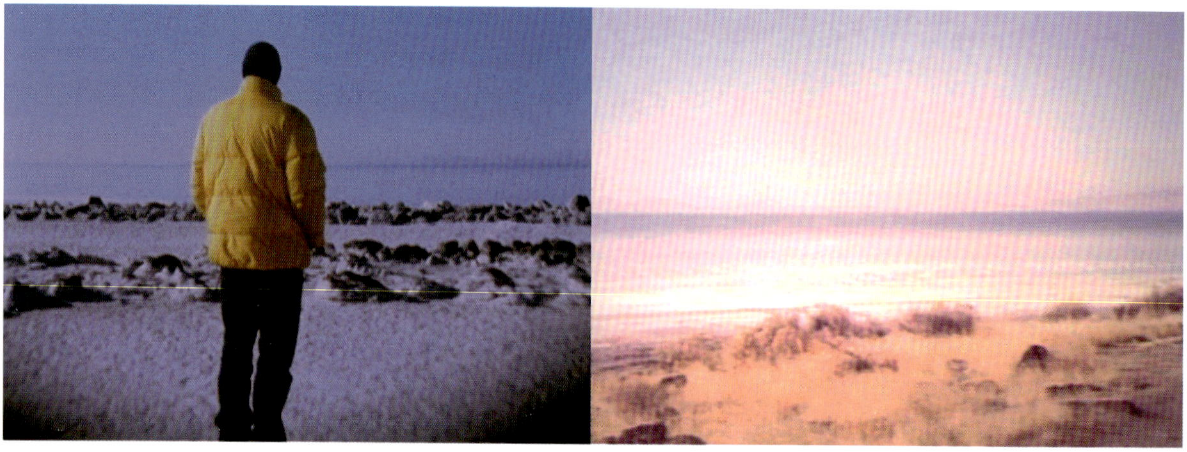

**Fig. 2.51.** Amy Granat and Drew Heitzler, *T.S.O.Y.W.*, 2007. 2-screen, 16 mm film installation, color, sound, 200 minutes, transferred to video. © Amy Granat and Drew Heitzler.

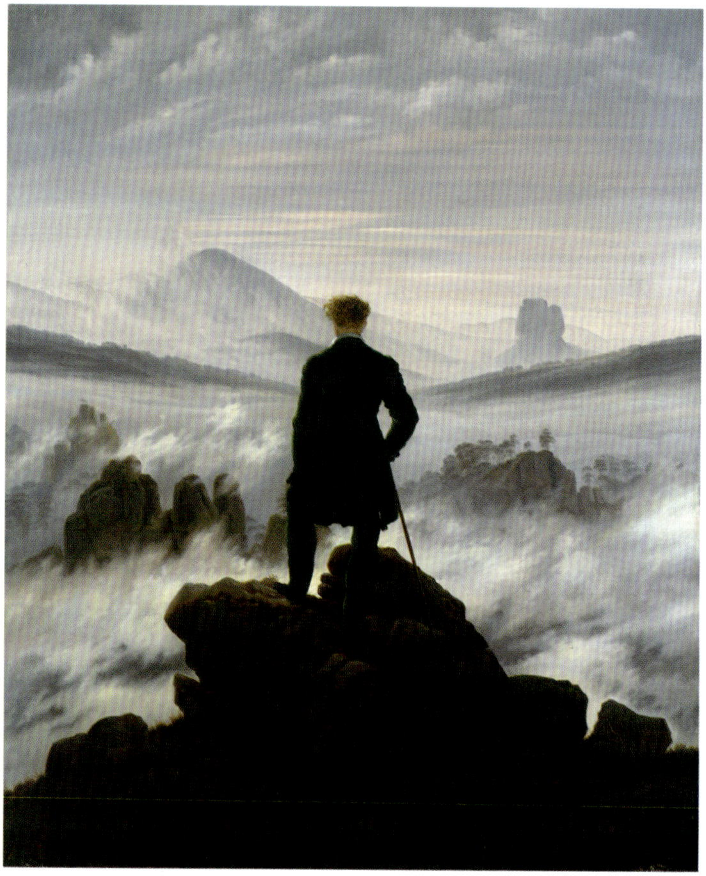

**Fig. 2.52.** Caspar David Friedrich, *Wanderer above a Sea of Fog*, c. 1817. Oil on canvas. On permanent loan from Foundation for the Promotion of the Hamburg Art Collections. Image: Art Resource. Photograph courtesy of bpk Bildagentur / Hamburger Kunsthalle / Elke Walford / Art Resource, New York.

Standing in the bull's eye of Smithson's spiral, he appears to merge with the natural world that has always eluded his grasp, his capacity to depict it.

Arriving in another village, he parks the Harley, grabs a beer, and puts something in his pocket. Close-ups and slow-motion shots reveal this to be a revolver. At the conclusion of Goethe's text the narration undergoes a striking change. The confessional voice of the lover shifts to the "objective" voice of the Editor, who informs us that he must interrupt the story "by direct narration."[282] The Editor describes Werther's final hours: his bitter farewell to Lotte; his request to borrow her husband's pistols; and the gruesome manner of his death. (Werther shoots himself in his right temple, exposing his brain: Goethe does not spare the reader such details.)

Granat and Heitzler conclude *T.S.O.Y.W.* ambiguously. The lover wanders into an industrial zone of oil tanks and desert scrub, a nowhere place. Where is he going? To shoot the beer bottle for target practice, or to shoot himself? He walks away, grows smaller. Trace-images of previous scenes flicker faintly in the empty frames. The yellow jacket dissolves in the blinking whiteness.

Aesthetic practice since the Nineties has witnessed a glamorization of the ephemeral, a fetishizing of the entropic.[283] The project is the testimonial of an action that has already occurred, not unlike the process works of Smithson and his contemporaries, but now the ephemeral work is the expression of a content. "Entropy" is less a physical operation than a *symbol* of entropy, a representation of decay, a fate not unlike that of Bataille's "formless" at the hands of his fellow Surrealist Michel Leiris—the formless that attempts to resist symbolization.[284]

Of a project by the sculptor Kitty Kraus, we read: "As a young artist defining her career at the beginning of the twenty-first century ... Kraus rehearses the trend towards degradation and entropy, finding a mournful beauty in the literal and symbolic failure of form."[285] An incandescent lightbulb is frozen in a block of ink and placed on the floor of the museum (fig. 2.53). Kraus plugs the bulb into an electric socket in the wall. As the ink melts, it drips and dries. The white cube is sullied. The dirty, used-up bulb on the floor is an image of forlorn futility. The process of decay instigated when the bulb was illuminated has ground to a halt. Semiosis has been staunched. A "failure of form" is a symbol of form's "failure." "Entropy" is aestheticized, a "mournful beauty" evoked.

Earlier I described how the ephemeral work inspires a retrospective imagination; it induces a longing to have been present at an event that we have missed. It positions us in the amorphous tense of the present past; it vectors the time of viewing to a previous time.

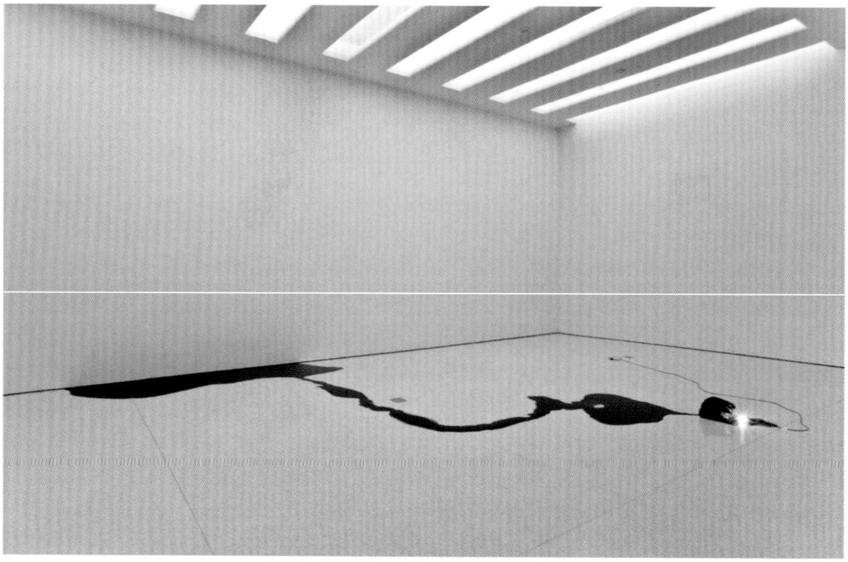

**Fig. 2.53.** Kitty Kraus, *Untitled*, 2006. Exhibited in *Kitty Kraus: Intervals*, Solomon R. Guggenheim Museum, New York, October 9, 2009–January 6, 2010. Photograph: David Heald. © SRGF, New York.

In 2006, Banks Violette invited the drone band SunnO))) and the performer Attila Csihar of the black metal band Mayhem to play the opening of his exhibition at Maureen Paley Gallery in London.[286] As SunnO))) performed in the downstairs space Csihar performed inside a closed coffin in front, unseen by the other musicians. And just as Csihar was both present and absent at that event, the audience was "there" and "not there." The attendees could only hear the amped-up music from the street while the performers remained out of sight. Invited to the gallery's upstairs space afterward, they viewed a replica of the set downstairs. To fabricate this work, *SunnO)))/Repeater (Decay/Coma Mirror)* (fig. 2.54), Violette cast in fiberglass and white resin the keyboard, guitars, amplifiers, speaker cabinets, and platforms the band had just used, and coated these objects in salt. In front, he presented a "repeater" of the coffin in which Csihar performed, painted black and broken up. In the downstairs gallery, which opened the next day, viewers saw the actual set, a negative image of the ensemble upstairs (fig. 2.55). The platforms on which SunnO))) played were all black. The coffin in which Csihar performed was white, slathered with salt, and intact—a reverse image of the shattered coffin they had just seen. Visitors were twice reminded of an event from which they had been barred: the experience of foreclosure, of *not* being present, was precisely what Violette set out to create.

Violette's installations are palimpsests of memory—the memory of an event or of another place, or of those who are no longer here. (By the time a viewer could enter the downstairs gallery, the musicians had long

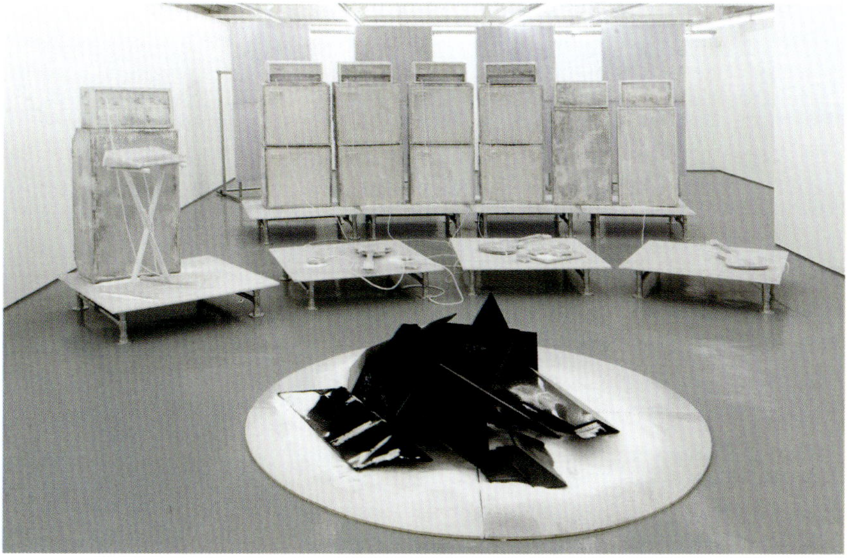

**Fig. 2.54.** Banks Violette, *SunnO))) / (Repeater) Decay / Coma Mirror*, 2006. Steel, hardware, plywood, paint, fiberglass, tinted epoxy, salt, resin; dimensions variable. Exhibition view: Maureen Paley, London, 2006. © Banks Violette. Courtesy of Maureen Paley, London.

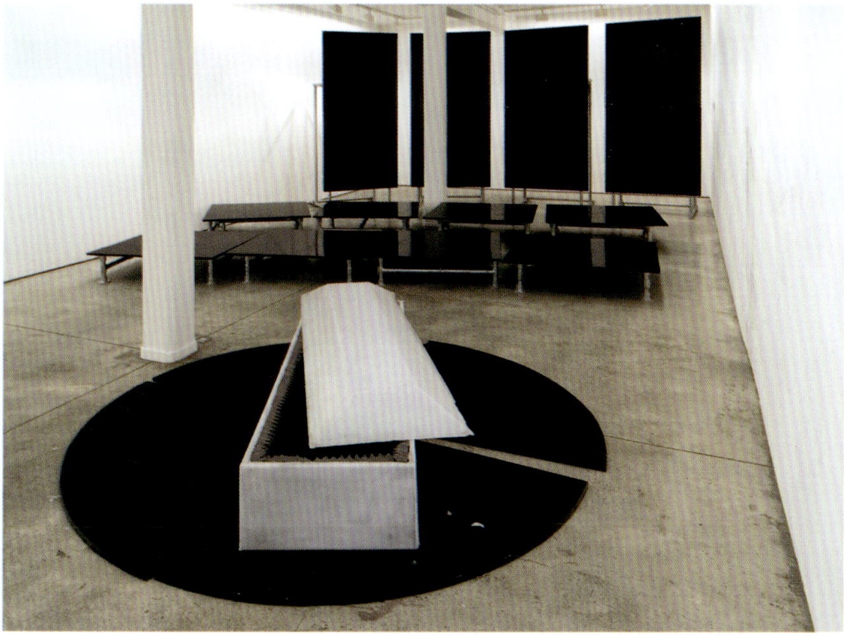

**Fig. 2.55.** Banks Violette, *SunnO))) – (Black Stage/Coma Mirror)*, 2006. Steel hardware, plywood, paint, fiberglass, tinted epoxy; dimensions variable. Exhibition view: Maureen Paley, London, 2006. © Banks Violette. Courtesy of Maureen Paley, London.

departed.) The salt surfaces of these sculptures evoke the Cargill Mine outside of Ithaca, New York, which Smithson visited while preparing his mirror and rock salt nonsites in 1968–69.[287] Born in Ithaca in 1973, Violette often visited the mine as a teenager, where he indulged a serious drug addiction. The salt he applies to his works evokes the memory of Smithson's visit to his hometown four years before his birth, and the recollection of his own experiences of "personal entropy."[288]

Other works of Violette's are memorials to friends who died young, such as *blackouts/blackholes (and all things between)/for DS 7.13.09* (2010), a three-part sculpture of vertical steel beam constructions with mounted plywood flats painted black, exhibited at Gladstone Gallery in New York (fig. 2.56).[289] "Blackout" suggests a state of unconsciousness, a loss of awareness, a fading out (as in "he blacked out"). Or it might suggest the electrical blackouts that Smithson wrote about, the darkening and cooling of the hot society. A black hole is the gravitational collapse, the entropy, of a star. The "DS" to whom Violette dedicated this work—the charismatic artist Dash Snow, whose "Hamster Nests" and other works also explored the theme of "personal entropy"—died of an overdose just short of his twenty-eighth birthday on July 13, 2009.[290] In the elegiac art of Violette one ending points to another. Deaths come in pairs and sequences, death upon death. For within this ensemble also loomed the memory of Steven Parrino, a painter of unshaped monochrome canvases

**Fig. 2.56.** Banks Violette, *blackouts/blackholes (and all things between)/for DS 7.13.09*, 2010. Plywood, aluminum, epoxy, fiberglass, steel, hardware, sandbags, and tape; installation dimensions variable. Exhibition view: Gladstone Gallery, New York, 2010. © Banks Violette. Courtesy of Banks Violette and Gladstone Gallery, New York and Brussels.

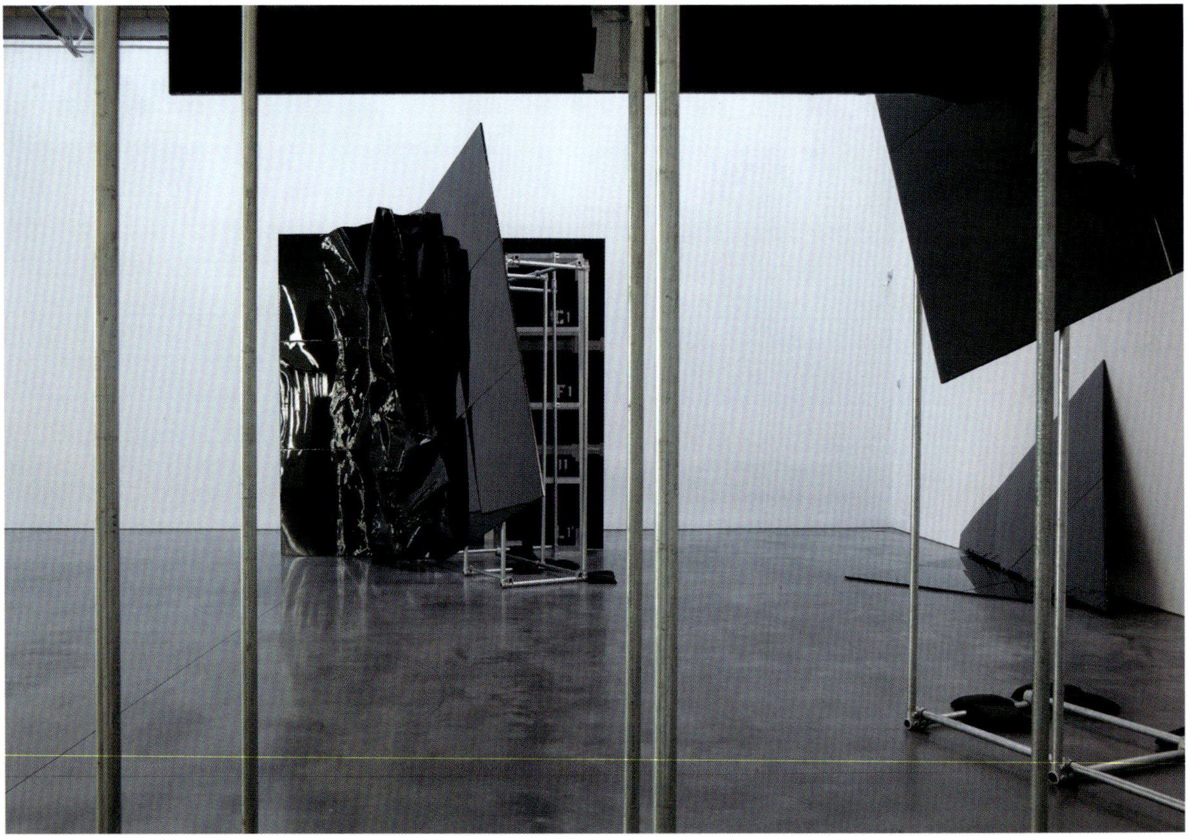

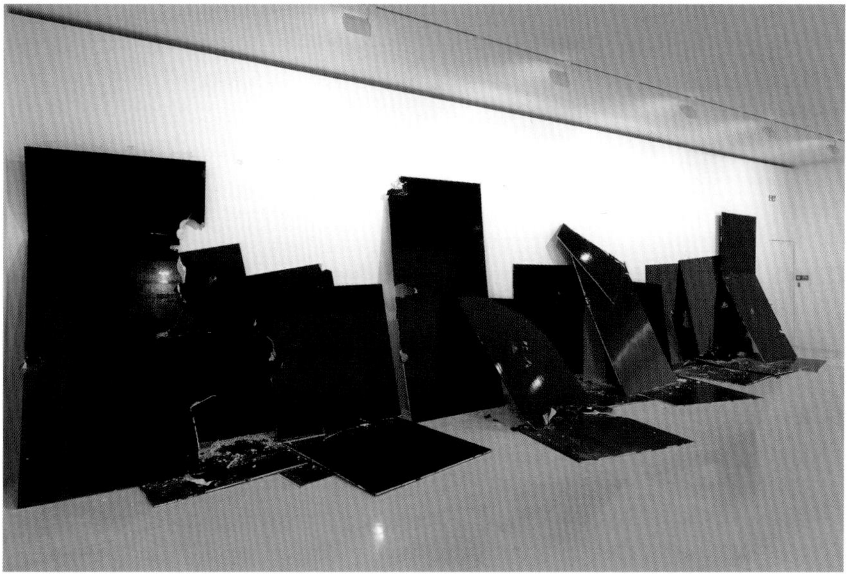

**Fig. 2.57.** Stephen Parrino, *13 Shattered Panels for Joey Ramone,* 2001. 13 standard panels of gypsum plasterboard painted with black industrial lacquer. Dimensions variable (PARRI 2001.0011). © Steven Parrino. Photograph: Zarko Vijatovic. Courtesy of Parrino Family Estate and Gagosian Gallery.

and friend of Granat and Heitzler as well as of Violette. Parrino, who makes a cameo appearance in *T.S.O.Y.W.*, died in a motorcycle accident in the early hours of New Year's Day, 2005. ("He was the original 'Werther,'" Granat recalls.)[291] The rippled black epoxy surfaces of Violette's sculptures recall the crumpled surfaces of Parrino's monochromes, while the striking third element in Violette's presentation, a folded sheet of black-painted plywood wedged between the wall and floor, draws explicitly from Parrino's *13 Shattered Panels for Joey Ramone* (2001), a work completed after Ramone's premature death on April 15, 2001 (fig. 2.57). A work dedicated to Snow is an elegy to Parrino, too. And beneath that reference is Parrino's "shattered" monument to the punk artist.

Goethe writes the lover's story in a galloping present tense that culminates with Werther's suicide. In "The Aspern Papers" James locates the narrator in a present that is permeated with the memory of a more glorious time. Aspern's death from an unnamed natural cause, a fatal disease, is a foregone conclusion when the story begins. The narrator—the unscrupulous scholar—is consumed by a history that precedes him. In his imagination he cultivates an intimacy with the man in the portrait that hangs next to his desk, a person he will never know. Unlike the distracted Werther, Aspern is an artist of genuine, even supreme accomplishment; his premature death appears a transcendental affirmation of a genius so remarkable it has outlived Aspern's mortal self.

*Each life has an ambience*, Smithson says. I take this to mean that our lives are not comparable to the lives of others. Nor do the lives of real artists stand up to these literary inventions. They are considerably messier, less resolved. But these archetypes mediate our perception of those lives; they inflect how we think about artists and writers, and their works. Hesse's tragic death at thirty-four created an atmosphere that altered how her sculpture was seen, Smithson tells us. Even he, her friend and supporter, saw her work differently than before.[292] *Each life has an ambience*. And so the atmosphere surrounding Smithson changed after Amarillo. It has hung about his work ever since.[293] Smithson returns, and returns. And these "returns" are marked by an inescapable melancholy, the memory of his dazzling ascent and his shocking death.

Winter 2013. The elevator door slides open. The corridor is beige, with low ceilings. Outside the patient's room someone asks me to put on a bodysuit made of blue hygienic paper. The bodysuit is thin as tissue. The paper hangs awkwardly on my street clothes. I open a door and walk inside. Wilted bouquets and get-well cards clutter the window sill and radiator. The window looks onto another building as architecturally bland as the one I am in. Between the buildings is the sullen sky of a rainy New York afternoon.

Nancy in patient's gown embraces me lightly and lies down. There are no signs evident in her face or body. I wonder if some mistake has been made. Surely, she will lick this. She has escaped it before, escaped it that day in Amarillo when Smithson invited her to go up in the airplane and she decided not to so she could focus on the maquette of *Sun Tunnels*. Smithson told her she would "be alright," and it was true. Her work had saved her life then, she often said. She would "be alright." And I suffer myself to imagine that the strange twist of luck, the pluck that prevented her from climbing aboard the faulty Beechcraft has not run out.

She has something for me. A paperback just published by a man Smithson befriended when he first moved to New York, who gave the teenage artist his first show.[294] She has brought copies of this memoir to her sickroom as mementos for people like me, a parting gift, I later understood. She points to the cover, a reproduction of one of Smithson's earliest remaining works, a gouache with highlights of ink and pencil (fig. 2.58). The drawing depicts a tortured-looking creature with lost eyes and knobby arms and fingers gnarled like twigs.

"It's Jesus Christ," she says.

Smithson's Jesus is not beautiful in death but grotesque and seen from above. An aerial crucifixion. God the Father looking down at Golgotha. Christ looks up. There is nothing God can or will do. *Lama sabachthani? Why have you forsaken me?*

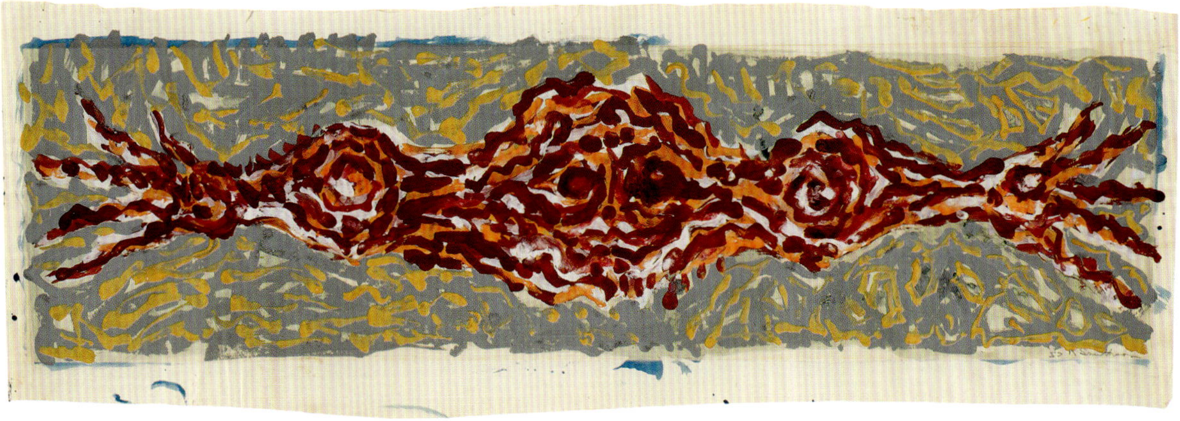

**Fig. 2.58.** Robert Smithson, *Untitled (Monster)*, 1957. Gouache, ink, and graphite on paper. Weatherspoon Art Museum, University of North Carolina at Greensboro. Museum purchase with funds from Lynn Richardson Prickett Acquisition Endowment and Weatherspoon Guild Acquisition Endowment, made possible by the generosity of Alan Brilliant, 2013. Art © Holt-Smithson Foundation / Licensed by VAGA, New York.

"Why would Smithson draw it that way?" My question sounds dim as soon as I ask it. She smiles wanly. The fatigue in her voice betrays something I hadn't seen until this moment.

"He just did things like that."

He had found something to paint that mattered.[295] He was not yet an entropologist, a maker of antimonuments. He had not yet imagined his jetty or buried shed or imagined that pouring glue down a muddy hill could stand as a work of art.

We are talking about Smithson again, yet this time is different. It doesn't feel seemly or even interesting to talk about someone I never knew with someone I *do* know who happens to be sick and who has the good manners not to explain the havoc raging inside her body. How rogue cells are destroying the good ones. How in her film *Revolver* the man with the fatal disease she interviewed had the condition she has now. (She marvels at the coincidence.) How she fell ill in the parking lot at the airport in New Mexico after accepting a Lifetime Achievement Award in New York, another coincidence. How the suitcase she was carrying across the blacktop suddenly felt extremely heavy. How her breath was starting to leave her body with each gulping breath until she was no longer able to breathe.

We discuss the treatments she's embarked on, the furnished apartment she will live in, the cat she has had to leave behind. We discuss the film she is working on in bed, a film about the making of *Amarillo Ramp* with Serra and Shafrazi. And the book I am writing: we discuss this too. The afternoon is fading. Our visit is winding down. There is a great deal to say and too little time to say it. It has always been that way with us. We are not talking, at least not now, about the Sixties. About the Seventies. Our minds are no longer in that time. There is only the present.

# PART 3
# THE END OF THE SIXTIES

**To arrive like this every day for it to be like this to have so many memories and no other memory than these for as long as they can be remembered to remember this.**

Claudia Rankine, *Citizen: An American Lyric*

August 2013. It was a sultry day fifty years ago when Martin Luther King Jr. spoke in this place. In the photos of the original march the Reflecting Pool is a blank spot in the middle of the surging crowd, bordered by giant elms heavy with leaves. King smiles and waves at the thousands of marchers gathered at the solemn temple at the edge of the Potomac.

Fifty years later, the same weather. The air thick with humidity, a constant sun. The marchers sit on blankets and folding chairs or stand on the unforgiving pavement. We mill about on crabgrass and patches of dirt, and crane our necks to catch a glimpse of the podium. We look at one another with curiosity as we listen to the speakers, and we consider our presence in this place.

The organizers of the original march were highly conscious of the twined symbolism of place and time. They held the March on Washington for Jobs and Freedom during the centennial year of the Emancipation Proclamation, held it on the steps of the memorial on whose walls that document is chiseled word for word.[1] Inside, the great marble statue of the slain president looks down the pool of water at the obelisk at the top of the hill: the entire sweep of U.S. history, the nation's unification, fracture, and reunification, its past and future, is embodied in that effigy's impassive gaze.

King was the last of the speakers that day. A century after Lincoln signed his decree, "that great beacon of hope," millions of people were not truly free, he lamented. Black people were barred from whites-only schools and drinking fountains and obstructed from voting. Too many Americans lived "on an island of poverty" in an "ocean of material prosperity."[2] The protesters had gathered to address these galling injustices. And they marched in support of a moral principle:

> We have come to this hallowed spot to remind America of the fierce urgency of now. This is no time to engage in the luxury of cooling off or to take the tranquilizing drug of gradualism. Now is the time to make real the promises of democracy; now is the time to rise from the dark and desolate valley of segregation to the sunlit path of racial justice.[3]

One of King's most enduring phrases, the *fierce urgency of now* is a state of presentness impelled by belief. It suggests being *in* one's moment and taking hold of it—not allowing time to pass us by. *Fierce urgency* is revolutionary time, the time that Arendt calls "impatient," the time of "being new." The year 1963 was "not an end but a beginning," King said. And then the great orator departed from his written remarks and broke into an ecstatic call for freedom. The Georgia preacher's voice soared as he described a time when "freedom would ring" across the nation. A time when young people of all backgrounds and beliefs would join together and "hew out of the mountain of despair a stone of hope."[4]

King's "I Have a Dream" speech is the consummate expression of the good Sixties. Confronting an unacceptable reality, he envisions a utopic future, a perfect union. He imagines an American citizenry bound together by democratic values and mutual respect. King and his fellow activists did have some cause for hope then. The previous May Birmingham's commissioner of public safety, Eugene "Bull" Connor, ordered his men to loose dogs and use water hoses on black children, turning public sympathy in support of the movement. Disgusted by a photo on the front page of the *New York Times* showing a German shepherd mauling a young protester, President Kennedy instigated a report that served as the basis of the Civil Rights Act of 1964.[5] The situation was volatile nonetheless. Three weeks after the protesters went home, a cabal of Klansmen bombed Birmingham's Sixteenth Street Baptist Church, burying four children in the rubble. Kennedy was assassinated in Dallas in November.[6] With the assassinations in 1968 of King and the president's brother, Senator Robert Kennedy, an architect of the Civil Rights Act, the "Dream" shattered. The Gandhian techniques of nonviolence that had proven so effective during the movement's finest hours no longer seemed to work. King's murder triggered the social entropy he preached against. ("We must not allow our creative protest to degenerate into physical violence.")[7] Riots broke out in Chicago, Baltimore, Kansas City, Pittsburgh, Louisville, and many other cities, causing dozens of African Americans to lose their lives. In Washington, DC, people took to the streets. They looted stores and smashed windows. Entire blocks burned on Fourteenth Street. Clouds of smoke darkened the sky above the Capitol.

There are many Sixties endings. The conclusion of the decadal Sixties is one. So are the various endings of the long Sixties.[8] The end of the Sixties is a dividing line, a temporal marker. It suggests the waning of a temporality of imminence ("fierce urgency") and revolutionary ontology ("being new"), and the final and irrevocable decline of futurist modernism, the dream of perpetual newness that the Sixties remembered and still believed in. The end of the long Sixties is a consolidation of the neoliberal order, of unyielding corporate and oligarchical control, and, on the Left, a feeling of powerlessness, of more of the same—a situation critics compare to the period of post-1789 retrenchment known as the Restoration, a time when "a previous language and set of presuppositions for emancipation" had "run into the sand."[9]

Like T. J. Clark, the author of this description, the philosopher Alain Badiou has spoken of an uncanny resemblance between our moment and the postrevolutionary period in France, as if we find ourselves in a time not of Sixties return but of something very different, the reprise of those reactionary moments of history that cause past progressive eras to seem impossibly monumental and distant to those who dare to imagine something better. In the historical scheme of Badiou there are periods of History, when the emancipatory Idea is dominant, and "intervallic" periods, when the Enlightenment values of universal freedom, democracy, and equality have gone into hibernation.[10] The "red years," as Badiou refers to the long Sixties, was the last Historical time of recent memory. Yet intervallic eras matter, too, he insists; they reveal "the possibility of a new situation . . . without for now being in the position to realize that possibility."[11] Badiou, theorist of the Event and witness to the Events of May 1968 in Paris, locates the Sixties at the end of a historical cycle reaching back to the French Revolution (the original "Event.")[12] If History is the full reprise of the emancipatory Idea in Badiou's sense, then what I have called the Sixties return is the reemergence of that imaginative possibility during a reactionary time.

History is hermeneutical, we know from Nietzsche. The central concern of *On the Use and Abuse of History for Life* is how the past operates on us. On the living. "We must know the right time to forget as well as the right time to remember."[13] We need history, *and* we need to "feel unhistorically," the philosopher says. Let us remember—and remember to forget. There is a time for remembering and a time for forgetting.

After the long Sixties ended, another Sixties returned as nostalgia, I have argued. This has not been unproblematic. The memory of the Sixties is the memory of King's idea that we can be in our moment and change our situation for the better. King's famous citation of Theodore Parker's metaphorical remark, "the arc of the moral universe is long, but it bends toward justice," implies that we can intervene in history. We can bend the arc ever so slightly.[14] King incites us to moral action. But if his words are to mean anything to us now, we must not allow ourselves to be weighed down by longing for a time when "fierce urgency" could be imagined and articulated. There is no going back to 1963. If life is impossible without forgetting, as Nietzsche insists, surely the final lesson of the Sixties return is the need to *let go* of Sixties memory after we have returned.[15]

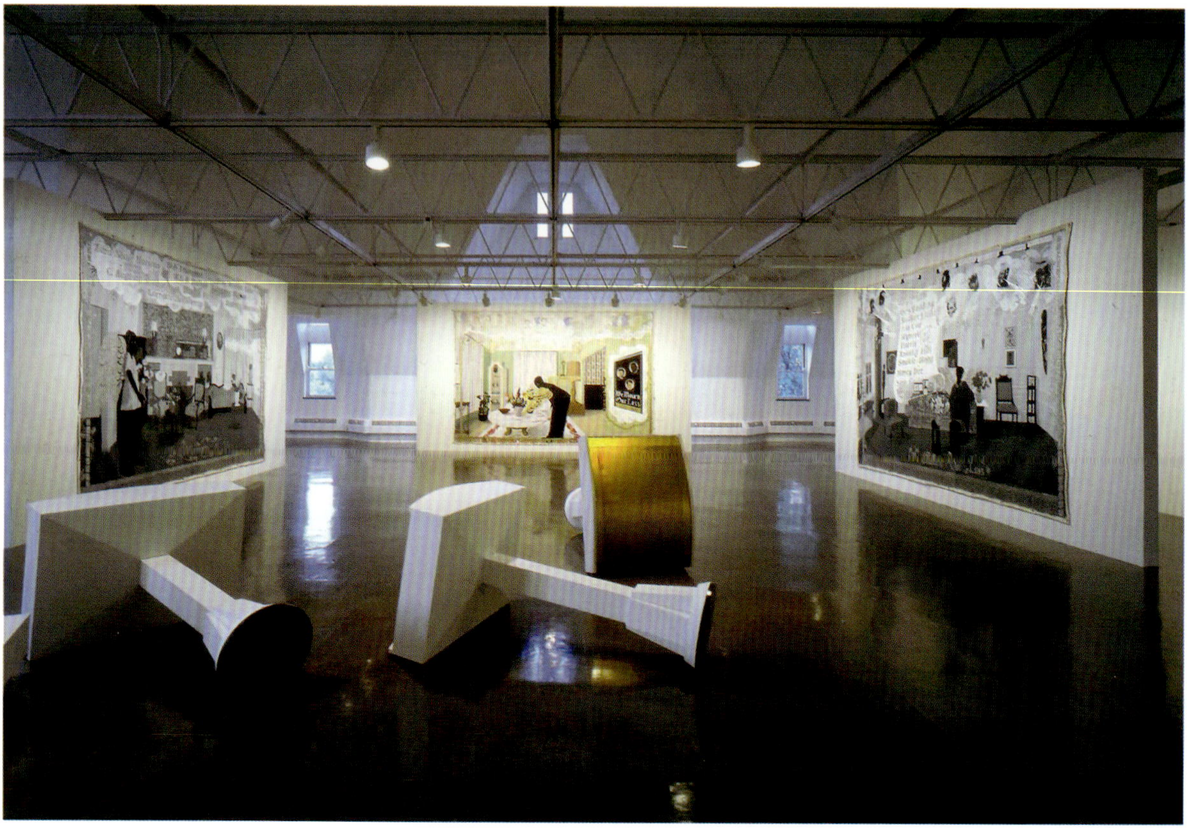

**Fig. 3.1.** Kerry James Marshall, *Mementos,* Renaissance Society of the University of Chicago, May 6, 1998–June 28, 1998. Installation view. © Kerry James Marshall. Courtesy of Kerry James Marshall and Jack Shainman Gallery, New York.

These, at least, are some of the questions explored in *Mementos*, an ensemble of artworks exhibited by Kerry James Marshall at Chicago's Renaissance Society in 1998 (fig. 3.1).[16] The centerpiece of that installation was an arrangement of four oversized (nine-by-thirteen-foot) canvases hung flush on the wall, the *Souvenirs*. A single motif recurs in these works: an angel welcomes us into her living room. Neither white, nor lithe, nor youthful as the angels of Western representation are usually depicted, Marshall's seraphs are middle-aged and elderly black women in contemporary dress. They look like women we know or have known. They just happen to have two enormous wings affixed to their shoulders.

This admixture of the real and unreal, the material and ethereal, is the true conceit of the *Souvenirs*. The paintings straddle two realities, a realm of middle-class domesticity, tangible and contemporary, and a transcendental domain of memory, a "before." Like the angel herself, the living room of *Souvenir I* is deceptively ordinary, with pale green walls and wall-to-wall carpeting, a white curio cabinet lined with figurines and a prized goblet, and a gold-leaf sconce draped with plastic grapes (fig. 3.2). A white sofa wrapped in plastic wards off sitters. The curtains are drawn. No daylight penetrates this airless space.[17] We have arrived at the green parlor at the very moment the angel, who carries a vase of daffodils and roses, approaches a large table with claw-shaped feet. The angel gestures toward a crystal bowl of carnations, tulips, roses, and greenery with one of her wings as she places the vase on the marble tabletop.

A black banner floats in a cloud edged in rays of silver and gold. Depicting the well-known faces of King and the Kennedy brothers, the banner recalls those mass-produced wall hangings that were often seen in African American households during the late Sixties and Seventies along with plates, ashtrays, and pens stamped with images of these men.[18] The phrase "We Mourn Our Loss," written in the Gothic script of the black church, appears beneath their portraits and dates of birth and death. Above it all—above the angel and banner, above the curio cabinet and the strange, sepulchral table—are the faces of many more angels framed by

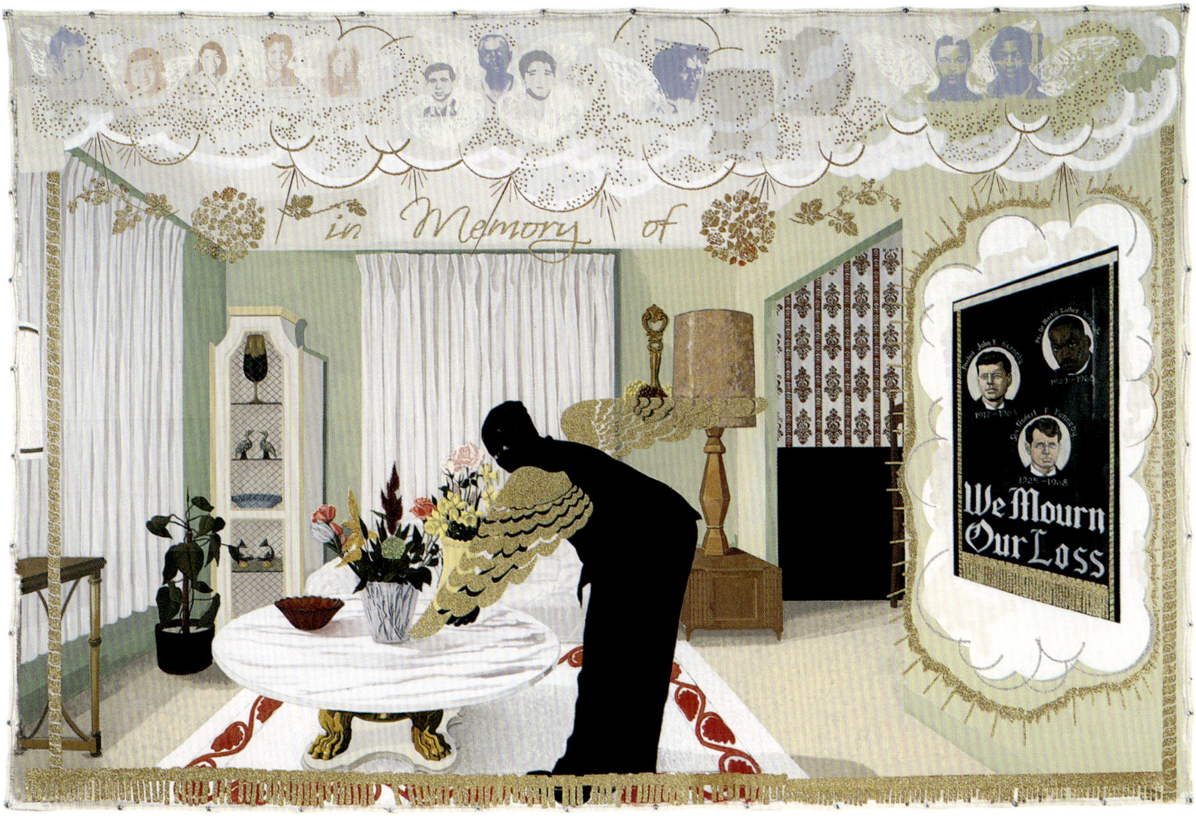


**Fig. 3.2.** Kerry James Marshall, *Souvenir I*, 1997. Acrylic, collage, and glitter on canvas. Museum of Contemporary Art, Chicago, Bernice and Kenneth Newberger Fund. © Kerry James Marshall. Courtesy of Kerry James Marshall and Jack Shainman Gallery, New York.

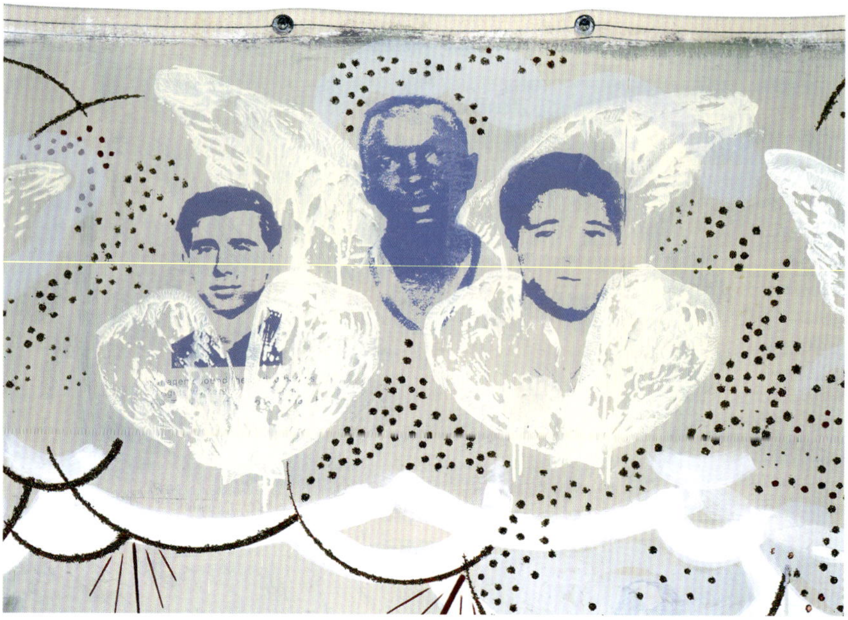

**Fig. 3.3.** Kerry James Marshall, *Souvenir I*, 1997 (detail). Acrylic, collage, and glitter on canvas. Museum of Contemporary Art, Chicago. Bernice and Kenneth Newberger Fund. © Kerry James Marshall. Courtesy of Kerry James Marshall and Jack Shainman Gallery, New York.

little white wings. Circles of gold are suspended in the dewy atmosphere around these cherubim, who float several feet above our heads.[19] And where the portraits of King and the Kennedys are hand-painted in the crude style of the historical banners, the faces and names of these angels are silkscreens of press photos, a medium developed by Andy Warhol during the early Sixties, when many of these individuals lost their lives and articles about their murders and their obituaries featured these portraits.

Ghostlike traces of the dead, these angel-faces appear from left to right in the order of their deaths: the NAACP field organizer Medgar Evers, shot dead on the driveway outside his home in Jackson, Mississippi, in 1963; Addie Mae Collins, Denise McNair, Carole Robertson, and Cynthia Wesley, the young victims of the church bombing;[20] voting volunteers Michael Schwerner, James Chaney, and Andrew Goodman, murdered by Klan members in Philadelphia, Mississippi, during Freedom Summer (fig. 3.3); Malcolm X; and the Black Panthers Fred Hampton and Mark Clark, massacred during a raid of Hampton's apartment by the Chicago Police in 1969. Below this intricate arrangement garlands and rosettes encrusted in gold glitter bracket the inscription "in Memory of," written in the saccharine cursive font of a sympathy card.

*Souvenir I* is knowingly illusionistic. Of all the *Souvenirs* the space is deepest here. The walls and ceiling and dining room entrance recede at acute and oblique angles behind a proscenium of gold fringe and braid.

Prompted by these orthogonals, vision alights on the folds of curtain between the back of the angel's head and the tip of her wing, resting on her penetrating eyes. The carpet with garland borders recedes sharply, causing the marble table and the angel to tilt toward us despite their palpable weight. But Marshall also reminds us of the canvas's physical presence, its flatness—the fact that it is a sailcloth held up by grommets and screws, and that the scene before us rests on a great collage of sheets of paper which, arranged in a grid pattern, interrupt the illusionism that he has carefully established. He wants us to grasp that the other-worldly world of *Souvenir I* cohabits the actual space in which we stand.

Marshall creates volume in order to compress it. The parlor of *Souvenir I* is a stifling place. He draws us into this boxed-in room, inducing sensations of enclosure and containment. He sets up the sort of fiction that Flemish devotional images do: that we have entered a domestic space that is both ordinary and extraordinary, a place where the divine has made itself known and even the most incidental objects—a washing vessel, a vase of flowers, even a mouse trap—are suffused with a peculiar and veiled significance.[21] Just as the interior in Robert Campin's Annunciation scene, the *Mérode Altar*, is both a cozy bedchamber and a setting of divine events, and just as the Virgin could be mistaken for a burgher's daughter of Tournai (fig. 3.4), so too Marshall's angels resemble actual women, I noted.[22] Like the staged reality of Flemish holy scenes, the empathic "realness" of the *Souvenirs* is a rhetorical effect: where the

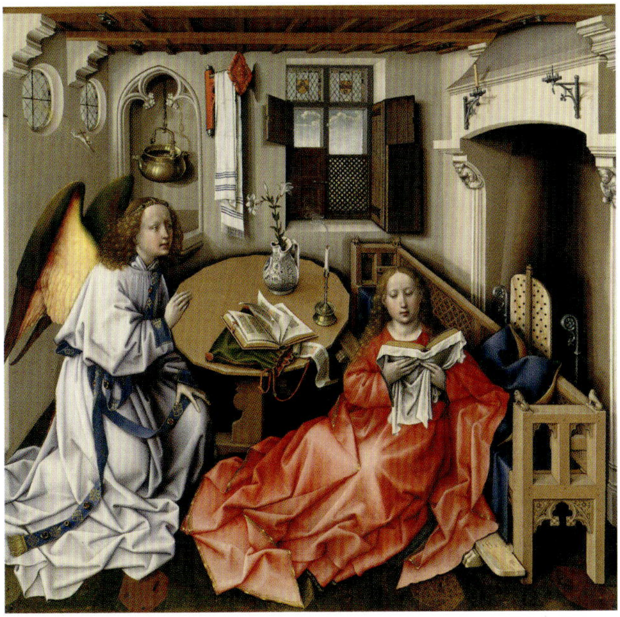

**Fig. 3.4.** Robert Campin (Workshop of), *The Annunciation Triptych (Merode Altarpiece)*, c. 1427–32. Central panel. Oil on wood. The Cloisters Collection, Metropolitan Museum of Art. © The Metropolitan Museum of Art. Image: Art Resource, New York.

masters of Netherlandish art bring us inside domestic interiors to witness the miraculous, Marshall positions us ambiguously in the temporal "no man's land" earlier described as recentness, the unstable mnemonic ground between a monumental past that forces itself into our awareness and a present in which we struggle to make meaning, to carry on.

The angel's eyes fasten on ours. Have we interrupted her in the middle of her devotions—or has she *anticipated* our arrival? What is the purpose of her behest, her invitation?

The woman in black is an angel of memory, who "ask[s] us to remember all the people who are represented there."[23] *Souvenir*, from the Latin *subvenire*, means "to call to mind, to remember." A souvenir is a token of memory, a memento, "a reminder of what is past or gone."[24] All of the works in Marshall's exhibition were mementos. In *Souvenir II*, gold glitter fringe and tassels frame another sacred living room (fig. 3.5). The bowl of carnations, tulips, and greenery sits on a glass-top coffee table. A vase of white roses rests on a stand decorated with gold garlands. And though this angel holds a yellow vase identical to the one carried by her counterpart in *Souvenir I*, the space of this work is shallower and wider. The codes of mourning have loosened somewhat. This angel wears a mourning shirt, yet her skirt is flowery and blue, as are her shoes. Marshall has painted the walls and furniture in warm tones of beige, orange, and rust. A comfortable wingback chair and plush sofa welcome a sitter. A rack of *Ebony* and *Jet* magazines, another familiar sight in black homes of a certain vintage, suggests an ambience of reading and relaxation.

Yet the curtains are drawn here, too, and there is another mourning banner depicting King flanked by the Kennedys. The angel-martyrs of the first *Souvenir* float in a cloud beneath the ceiling. Two more join them: they are Viola Liuzzo and Jimmie Lee Jackson, whose murders in Alabama in 1965, along with the fatal beating of Unitarian minister James Reeb, catalyzed the passage of the Voting Rights Act that summer. We are asked to remember them, too.[25]

**Fig. 3.5.** Kerry James Marshall, *Souvenir II*, 1997. Acrylic, collage, and glitter on unstretched canvas banner. Addison Gallery of American Art, purchased as a gift of the Addison Advisory Council in honor of Jock M. Reynolds's directorship. © Kerry James Marshall. Courtesy of Kerry James Marshall and Jack Shainman Gallery, New York.

The other *Souvenirs* are painted in black, white, and gray in keeping with the somber tonality of mid-twentieth-century newspaper and television imagery. The angel in *Souvenir III* wears a white blouse and black slacks, and carries a bouquet (fig. 3.6). The arrangement of carnations, tulips, and greenery familiar to the beholder of *Souvenir I* and *Souvenir II* rests on an antique table with slipper feet. A Victorian settee draped with a doily, old armchairs, an oval painting of classical temples, a sculpture of a woman carrying a large basket (a Ruth or Rebecca perhaps, or an African slave), and a cabinet filled with crystal goblets establish an atmosphere of refinement and quiet repose. The King-Kennedy mourning banner is less

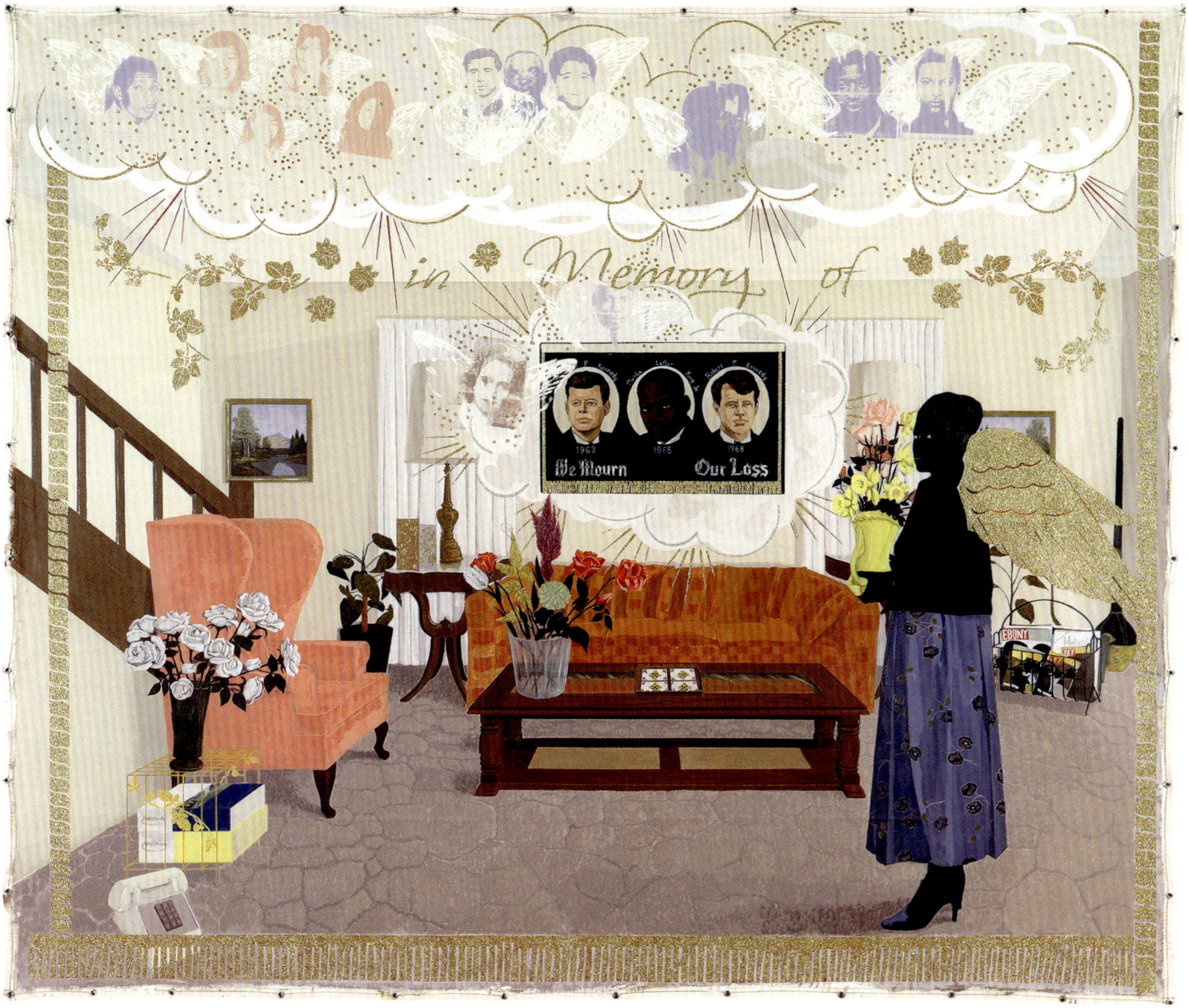


conspicuous, a partial reflection in the mirrored tiles above the mantel, hanging on an imaginary wall behind us. The lamentation "We Mourn Our Loss"—fragmentary, spelled backward—is barely legible. Civil rights history recedes as other histories come into visibility. There are no faces here, only the names of prominent artists, writers, and performers and the dates of their deaths during the decadal Sixties, inscribed in silver glitter, each occupying a cloud of its own: the painter Bob Thompson; the novelist Zora Neale Hurston; the philosopher W. E. B. DuBois; the playwright Lorraine Hansberry; the film star Dorothy Dandridge; the sculptors Augusta Savage, Meta Warrick Fuller, and Marion Perkins, and others are recalled.[26]

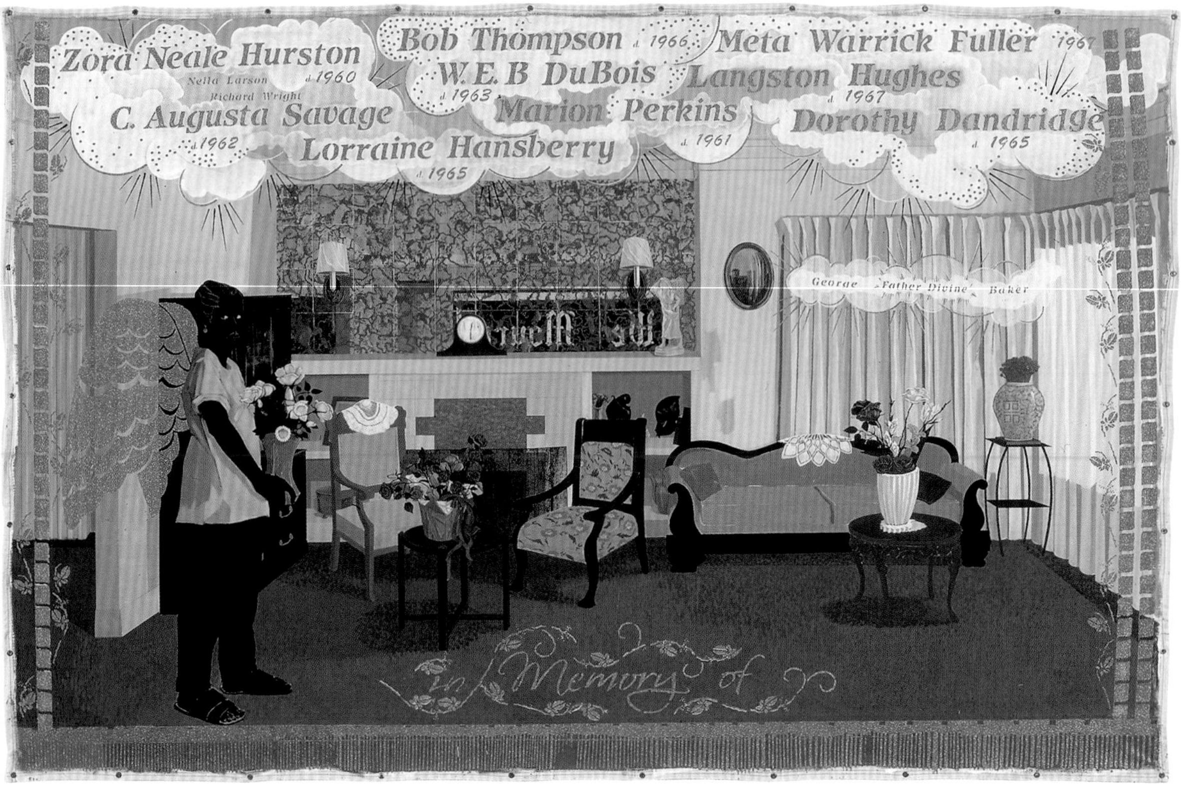


**Fig. 3.6.** Kerry James Marshall, *Souvenir III*, 1998. Acrylic with glitter on unstretched canvas banner. San Francisco Museum of Modern Art. © Kerry James Marshall. Courtesy of Kerry James Marshall and Jack Shainman Gallery, New York.

Names without faces. Names with dates, like tombstones. Everything grisaille. The arc of memory is longer here. We have moved from a period "we" mourn to a farther past, from the Sixties to a time the Sixties remembered. As in Zarina Bhimji's films, which lead from Uganda during the early Seventies to the docks of turn-of-the-century Gujarat, or BLW's *Queen Mother Moore at Greenhaven Federal Prison*, where the respeaker of Moore's words recalls Garvey's 1922 speech at the Longshoremen's Hall, the return to one time brings us to one more distant. The "Sixties" in these works is a way station to another past, to the Twenties and Thirties (when Hurston, Savage, and Perkins were at the height of their reputations) or to the turn of the last century, when Fuller exhibited at the Paris Salon and DuBois published *The Souls of Black Folk* and co-founded the NAACP. The figures named in *Souvenir III* are trailblazers, their accomplishments all the more remarkable for having occurred during the nadir of Jim Crow segregation, intimidation, and violence—yet they are not martyrs.[27]

The abstract paintings and tribal sculptures in *Souvenir IV* evoke a modernist aesthetic vocabulary indebted to African and African Diasporic prototypes (fig. 3.7). The names and faces of twenty-three jazz, blues, rhythm-and-blues, and rock 'n' roll musicians, all of whom died between 1959 and 1970, crowd this space. The most celebrated figures recall others. Billie Holiday (d. 1959) calls out the name of blues singer J. D. Short (d. 1962). Nat King Cole (d. 1965) sings the name of folk performer Vera Hall (d. 1964). Dinah Washington (d. 1963) "remembers" the blues guitarist J. B. Lenoir (d. 1967), who died four years after she did. An oversized scroll inscribed with even more names unfurls above a table stacked with knickknacks and books. The recurring phrase "We Mourn Our Loss" has migrated to the floor, transforming *Souvenir IV* itself from a *scene* of mourning into a great mourning banner, an enormous sympathy card, a collective *declaration* of sorrow.

The angel in this image has collapsed into her settee, her arms folded in her lap. She doesn't even bother to greet us. Pressed behind the elaborate scroll of names, her argent wings almost disappear.

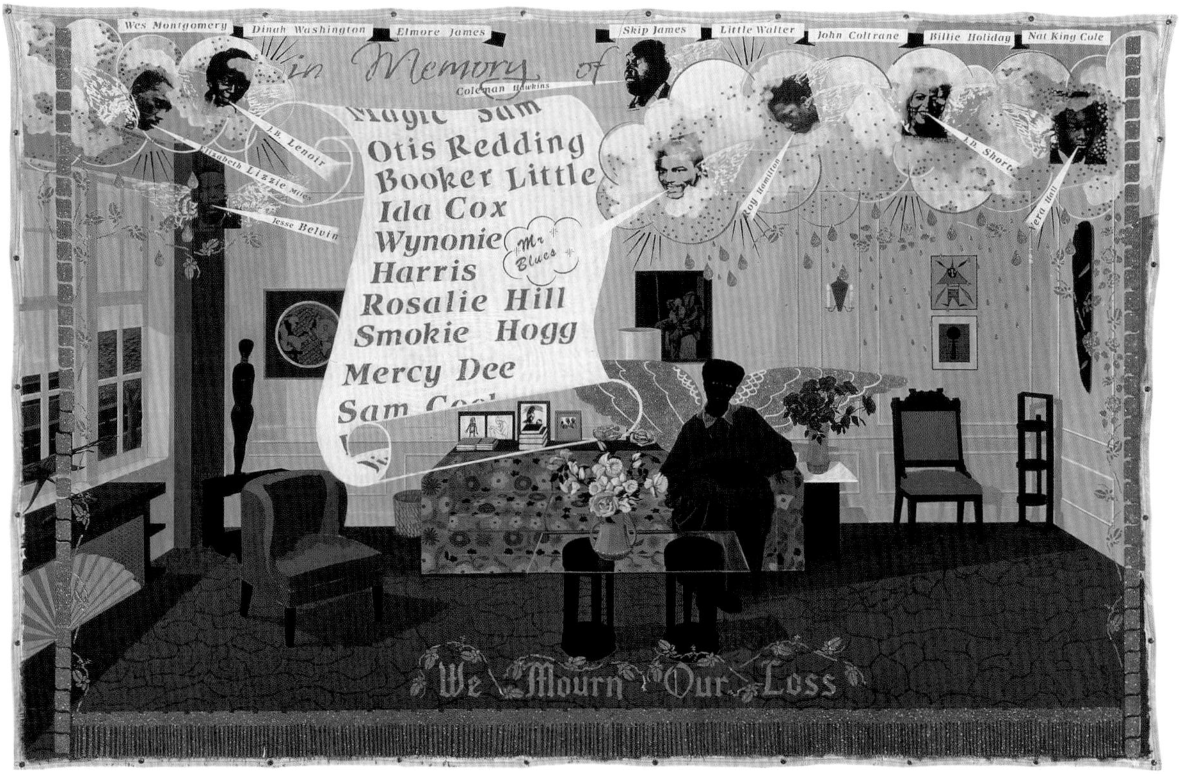


**Fig. 3.7.** Kerry James Marshall, *Souvenir IV*, 1997. Acrylic with glitter on unstretched canvas banner. Whitney Museum of American Art. © Kerry James Marshall. Courtesy of Kerry James Marshall and Jack Shainman Gallery, New York.

We approach a hermetic structure and peer through peepholes cut in the faux-marble walls. Here is another funeral parlor (fig. 3.8).[28] The "deceased" is a pickaninny doll with racist features, his coffin decorated with masses of artificial blossoms. We are reminded of the flower-strewn bier of Emmett Till, the fourteen-year-old Chicago boy who was tortured and lynched in Money, Mississippi, in 1955 after allegedly whistling at a white woman; Till's funeral in Chicago, where his disfigured corpse was displayed in an open coffin at his mother's insistence, jumpstarted the movement. Above the coffin is a projected film. In one sequence black children stand in the cross-fire of gangs as pennies depicting the Illinois-born Lincoln and his memorial spin in the darkness. Another scenario represents a funeral where the mourners worship an ethereal white Christ illuminated by a golden lamp. Speech bubbles erupt from the parishioners' mouths:

> "Jesus," they cry.
> "Jesus. Jesus."

We do not ordinarily think of the Birmingham girls and the all-too-frequent victims of drive-by shootings or police killings in tandem. We think of the former as the intended targets of vicious Klansmen, "martyred heroines of a holy crusade for freedom and human dignity" who "died nobly," as King described them.[29] Others—such as the teenager Hadiya Pendleton, who died in a gang exchange in south Chicago on January 29, 2013, two weeks after participating in President Obama's second inauguration with her high school band—are seen as the unlucky casualties of gang violence; the deaths of these "lost" girls and boys appear random and inexplicable, disconnected from the high ambitions of the civil rights era. In fact, all

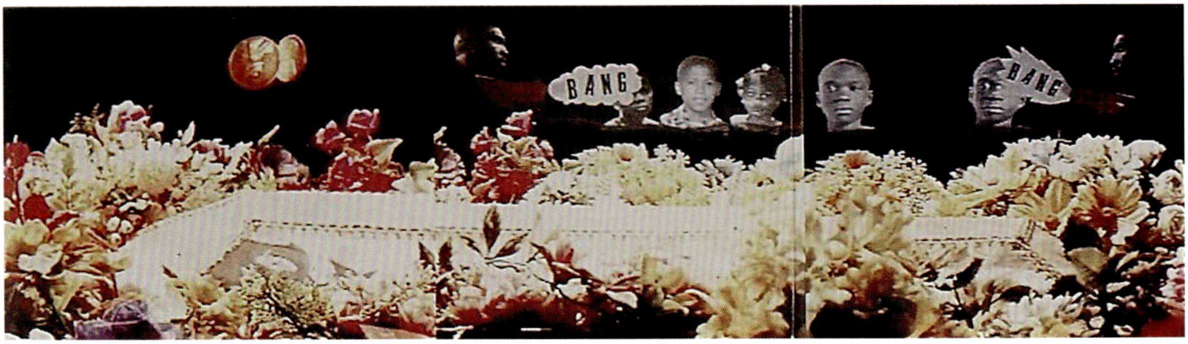


**Fig. 3.8.** Kerry James Marshall, *Laid to Rest*, 1998. 3-channel video installation, 5-minute loop. © Kerry James Marshall. Courtesy of Kerry James Marshall and Jack Shainman Gallery, New York.

of these killings are connected, Marshall implies. No death is "nobler" or more meaningful than any other.[30] Children have died—*are* dying. They die in all kinds of ways. A gang shooting, a "frightened" police officer pulling a trigger: the end is the same. The long history of racial inequity and conflict in the United States has counted too many young victims. Weak gun-control laws abet these tragedies. A half-century on, the economic divisions between whites and blacks that King spoke about persist. Urban ghettos, de facto zones of segregation, remain. If Marshall's great canvases invite us "to remember," his ersatz mausoleum, *Laid to Rest*, locates viewers very much in the present, when the constant, needless killing of African Americans, many of them very young, maintains black life in a state of perpetual mourning.[31] A stark reality intrudes into the reverent memory space of the *Souvenirs*.

Remember, Marshall's angels instruct. Cicerones of memory, these winged women ask us to recall a monumental past. This injunction was the first mode of address of the Renaissance Society show—its explicit subject matter. But now Marshall embedded a reflexive or connotative dimension in these canvases. The angels ask us to join their mourning. To remember. As we gaze at the angelic martyrs' faces, we consider this importunate demand. To whom are the *Souvenirs* addressed? *What* are we supposed to remember? What purpose will memory serve? What are its costs? If we remembered all these names and all these dates, what good would it do? When does memory become the "chain" that Nietzsche warns about, a burden so cumbersome it impedes our ability to live entirely and productively in our own moment?

Marshall transforms middle-class homes into memorials. The black living room is a funeral parlor haunted by spectral visions. Memory, in the *Souvenirs*, is accretive, additive, nominative. With each new painting we are asked to identify more faces and more names. Fourteen martyrs crowd into the parlor in *Souvenir I*. In *Souvenir II* Marshall adds two more. *Souvenirs III* and *IV* retrieve still other names and histories. Musicians cry out the names of other musicians. The dead recall the dead. Something happens when we reach *Souvenir IV*. The process of inscription and remembrance breaks down. The memory scroll is incomplete, the final names have become illegible (the letters *JI* spell only the beginning of Jimi Hendrix's name). The angel does not rise to greet us as her counterparts do. She has put down those daffodils and roses. She appears worn out, ground down. Her hands are clasped in resignation. Has the angel of memory grown weary of her charge?

*Mementos* (1998) depicts a thrift-shop picture frame nailed to a wall (fig. 3.9). The gold-and-silver frame at the center of this image, a C-print,

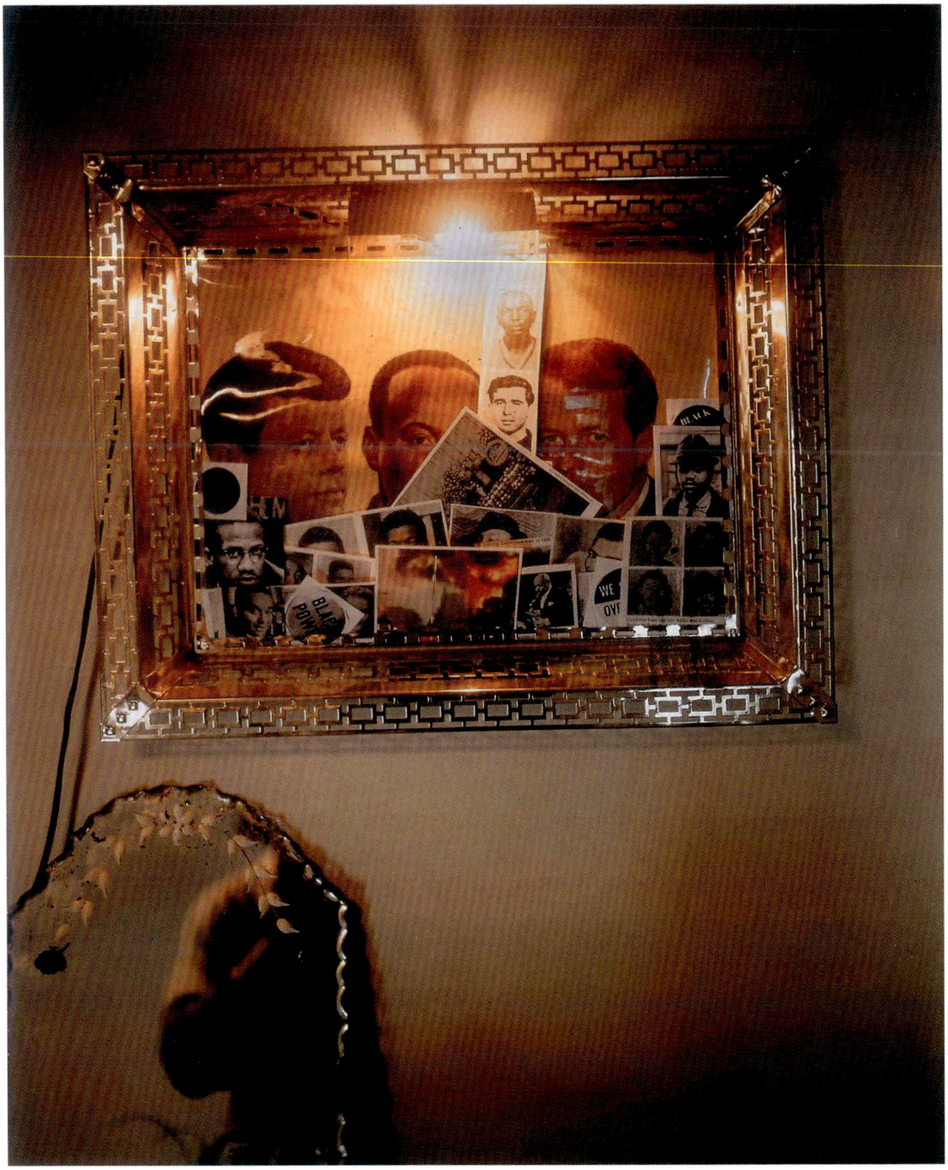


**Fig. 3.9.** Kerry James Marshall, *Mementos*, 1998. C-print. Edition 2. © Kerry James Marshall. Courtesy of Kerry James Marshall and Jack Shainman Gallery, New York.

is stuffed with old photographs of King and the Kennedys; of Malcolm X, Chaney, and Schwerner; Hampton and Clark; Collins, McNair, Robertson, and Wesley; of Coleman Hawkins playing the sax and Zora Neale Hurston in a fashionable hat; movement buttons and decals; a casket smothered in flowers; and a color image of a city in flames, the deadly Detroit riots of July 1967.[32] *Mementos* is the "brain" of the eponymous exhibition, a meditation on Marshall's project and the archival source of its arresting imagery (the portraits of martyrs, artists, and writers in the *Souvenirs*; the bier in *Laid to Rest*).[33] At the top of this image an incandescent lamp casts a warm light. Bathed in the fixture's lambency the photo-archive has been transfigured into a shrine of Sixties recollection. Marshall has propped a mirror on the wall next to the picture-altar. The border of the looking glass is etched in a floral pattern reminiscent of greeting card garlands. In this photo of other photos, the reflexive mode of address of Marshall's project has become explicit. Within the mirror's reflection we make out an arm, an elbow, a wrist, a sliver of shirt. Marshall *pictures himself picturing the Sixties*, a period entirely mediated by its extensive photographic and televisual representation, by these obituaries and portraits and press photos. Marshall is a partial presence at best. His body is fragmentary, his face obscured by the photos stuffed in the gaudy frame: the pictures of movement martyrs and events are more *present* in this image than the artist who gathers them, who remembers.[34]

For Marshall does remember. Born in Birmingham in 1955, he was seven when the Sixteenth Street Baptist Church was bombed and his family immigrated to Los Angeles as part of a larger migration of black people to Southern California, the "land of more of everything."[35] In his painting *Watts 1963* (1995), a work from Marshall's *Housing* series, the artist represents himself and his sister and brother newly arrived in that neighborhood (fig. 3.10). The bright green grass sprinkled with daisies and the sun rising behind the garden apartments evoke a mood of hopeful expectation, while the abstract white splotches and circles of dripping paint disrupt the halcyon image. The introspective feeling evoked by these material intrusions within the world of the painting's sunny illusionism culminates in Marshall's affecting portrayal of his brother, who coils into a fetal position on the thick lawn, impervious to his surroundings.

This is what Marshall remembers.

He remembers the fiery speeches of the Black Panthers, who maintained their headquarters down the street from his family's second home in south-central Los Angeles.

He remembers his "Negro History" teacher Mr. Kowano, a member of the Black Panthers who came to class in army boots and military fatigues.

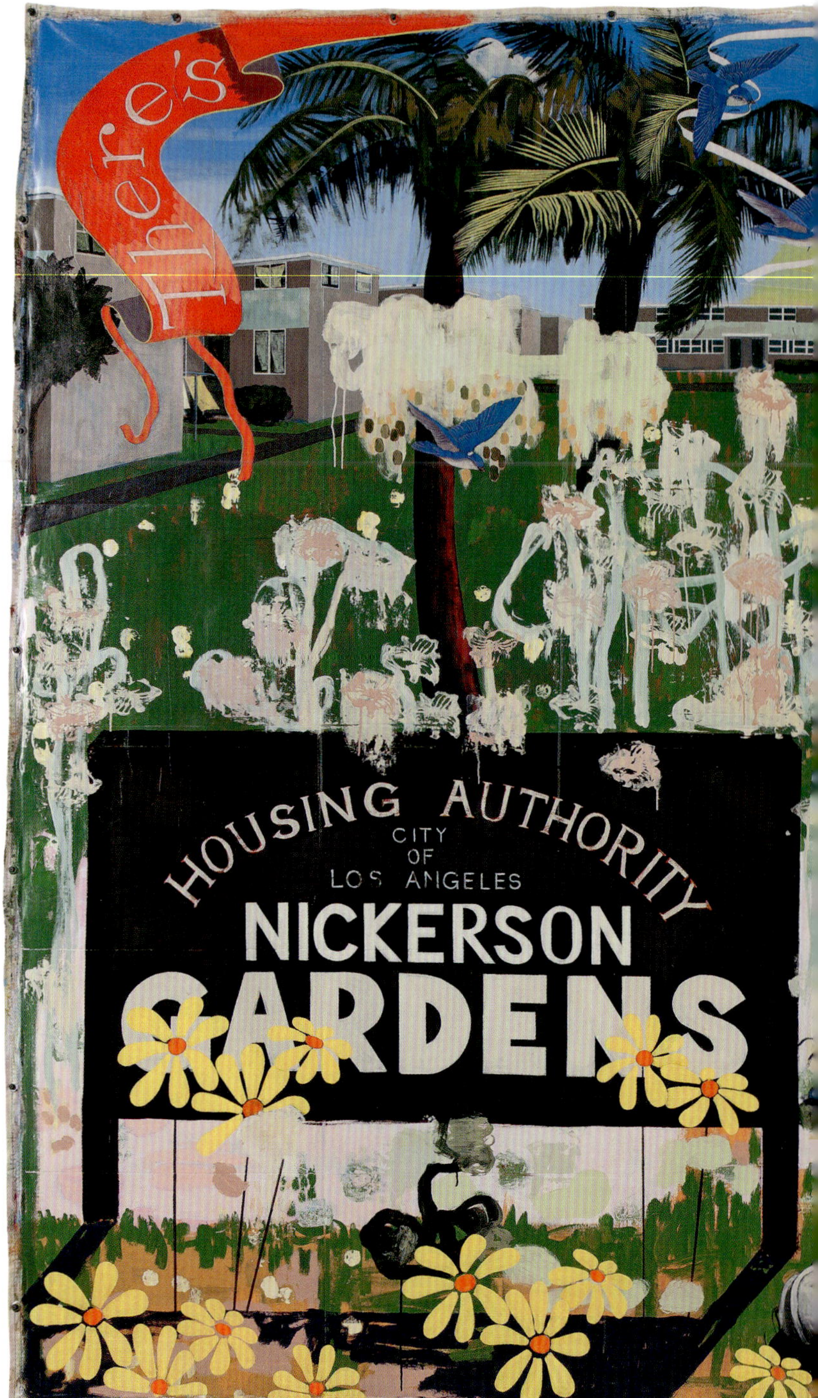


**Fig. 3.10.** Kerry James Marshall, *Watts 1963*, 1995. Acrylic and collage on canvas. Saint Louis Art Museum, Museum Minority Artists Purchase Fund, 190:1995. © Kerry James Marshall. Courtesy of Kerry James Marshall and Jack Shainman Gallery, New York.

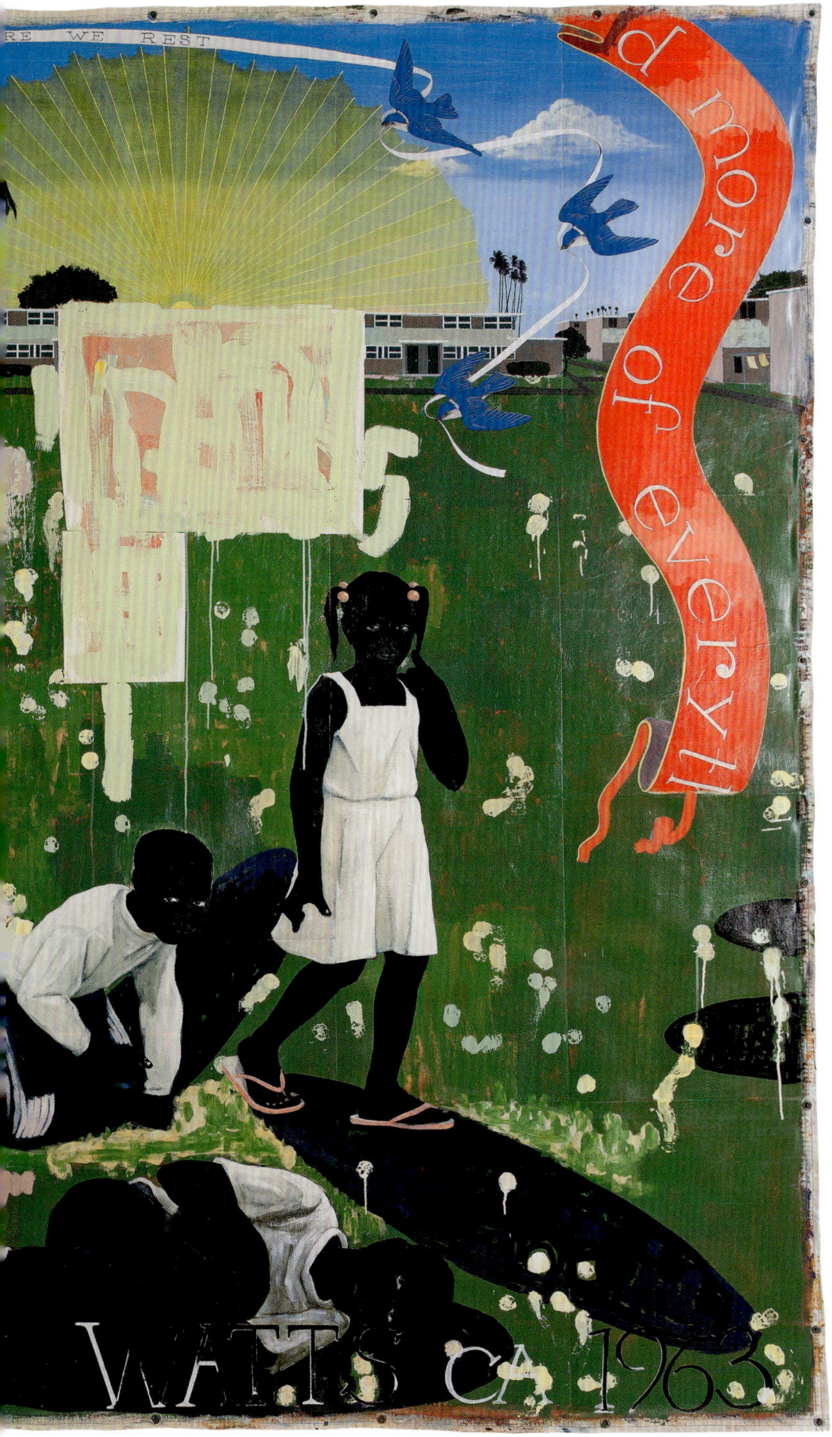

RE WE REST
d more of everyt
WATTS CA 1963

He remembers the protests and strikes that occurred almost daily at his junior high school then.

He remembers, most vividly of all, the summer night in 1965 when he and his brother watched the sky above Watts explode in fire:

> I remember looking out of the second-floor window that night at a wall of flames on Central Avenue. Against that backdrop, about thirty feet above the ground, the logo of this fast-food chain called Jack-in-the-Box (a grinning clown appearing from a box) was rotating slowly atop a pole.... That image is forever seared into my memory. I distinctly remember telling myself: one day I'm going to make a picture of that.[36]

Marshall has described the *Souvenirs* as history paintings. Grand in scale and rhetorically complex, they speak of his stated ambition to revive a highly valorized idiom of Western art that typically excluded black figures and black subject matter.[37] The academic conventions of that genre, codified in the eighteenth-century French and English academies, centered on the depiction of historical and mythological events rich in moral instruction. And so the artist of classical representation condensed complex stories into "pregnant moments" that a viewer could absorb and comprehend. Perhaps because he remembers the long Sixties so acutely Marshall avoids depicting that era's history directly, not unlike the Vik Muniz of the *Memory Renderings* or the An-My Lê of *Viêt Nam* and *Small Wars*. (Marshall never did manage to paint the fast-food clown above a burning Watts.) Or he depicts historical events he never witnessed and historical actors whose lives precede his own.[38] Recent or remote, the black past is ever present in his depictions. Or it never left: history returns unbidden, unconsciously, in the minds of the living. It bubbles up through the earth and from the depths of the sea; it clings to the rooms and buildings he paints, and etches the faces and bodies of his figures. And so different periods often cohabit in the same image.[39] In *Souvenir II*, the buzz cuts and "Mad Men" suits of King and the Kennedys, and the period hairstyles of Liuzzo and the Birmingham girls locate these figures in the early Sixties, while the touch-tone telephone and stack of Ameritech phonebooks date the scene to the period between that company's founding in 1984 and its renaming as AT&T in the 2000s, after the cell phone and internet made the earlier technologies obsolete. Combining signifiers of distinct, if proximate, eras, *Souvenir II* depicts a "present" that already appears dated and increasingly remote twenty years after Marshall completed it.

Who are "we" precisely? Pierre Nora's distinction between *lieux* and *milieux de mémoire* is useful here. The *lieu de mémoire*—the site of official memory, memory sequestered in a memorial—is memory as obligation ("duty memory," Nora calls it). The *milieu de mémoire* is living memory, memory that flourishes in closed communities, such as the oral traditions handed down in rural villages in France. The conservative Nora is nostalgic for these preindustrial memory *milieux*. With urbanization, communities fracture, he claims. Living memory fades. As memory becomes archival, it becomes less personal and authentic. Duty memory trumps the "authentic" memory of the *milieu*.[40]

Marshall's works explore this distinction; they evoke longing for a time imagined to be more momentous than ours—and they defeat that desire. They enjoin us "to remember," and they reflect on the costs of duty-memory, of always gazing backward to an imagined golden age next to which the present is felt to be lacking. The weight of civil rights memory for African Americans is particularly intense. The long Sixties is *the* monumental era of recent black history—a mnemonic burden to those who are constantly reminded of it. Duty-memory transforms daily life into a state of unending recollection. In oppressed communities in particular, "the psychologization of memory has thus given to every individual the sense that his or her salvation ultimately depends on the repayment of an impossible debt."[41] Duty-memory is the mnemonic obligation of communities that carry traumatic recollections, a remembrance that is intertwined with feelings of loss.

Consider the angel in *Souvenir I*. Her skin is coal-black, like the skin of the vast majority of figures in Marshall's black-figure art, a skin so unrelentingly black it evokes not so much a natural skin tone as blackness as a sign within the discursive system we call "race."[42] Not only are her skin and hair black. She wears a black blouse, slacks, and shoes. She is *all* black from head to toe. Only the whites of her eyes interrupt this dominant tonality. Skin and dress intermingle, are one and the same. Together they form a sheath, a single membrane, covering her body. The angel of black history is thus presented as *one who mourns*, whose memory of past sorrows has literally seeped into her skin and burrowed deep into her identity. She mourns a black past that is both tragic and heroic—the movement martyrs and the absence of their kind now. She mourns the loss of a "vocal, powerful, long-departed black self."[43]

The "Reclaim the Dream" March, as this afternoon's event is called, is billed as a "continuation march" not a "commemoration march."[44] It is not enough to remember, the organizers insist. Let us continue the struggle, pick up where the movement left off. Posters and buttons with paired portraits of King and Obama exhort the crowd to "Reclaim the Promise." What does this mean?

Like reenactment, commemoration is a theatrical staging of memory. Though they are very different—today there is no respeaking, only speech—the "Reclaim the Dream" March fosters the dissonant cognition that reenactment does, an uncanny awareness of two eras at once. As we listen to such movement veterans as Myrlie Evers-Williams, or Representative John Lewis, or the Reverend Joseph Lowery, the civil rights era does not feel so far away. The crowd grows silent as Evers-Williams describes the horrible night her husband Medgar was gunned down in the driveway outside their home. Lewis recalls the beatings that he and others endured at the hands of the Alabama police at the bridge at Selma, an event known as Bloody Sunday. Their recollections are searing, their presence induces a feeling of awe—admiration for these individuals and for the history they made, the past that touches down at this gathering and touches every one of us as we listen to their words, to their trembling voices.

No: the Sixties does not seem ancient then. Not when we listen to *them*. Not when Evers-Williams speaks Medgar's name. But as the day wears on, and others take the podium, the heady memories of that time evaporate in the afternoon sun. Phrases like *Reclaim the Promise* ring hollow. In the famous photo of the first march, the Reflecting Pool is an image of serenity and hope. Today, the actual pool is a stagnant brown soup. I walk away from the water's edge to avoid the stench.

The attempt to recharge memory is no simple matter. "Fierce urgency" is not easily retrieved. For there is an undercurrent in these speeches, these proceedings, a sense not of progress but of *déjà vu*, the queasy suspicion that things are moving backward. Return, today, not only suggests the recovery of a past possibility—Benjamin's "time of the now." It also suggests a containment of Sixties energies, the retrenchment that began when the long Sixties ended and that causes that era to appear meaningful as it retreats. The movement's victories are being repealed, the speakers remind us. The U.S. Supreme Court has just gutted key provisions of the Voting Rights Act of 1965, the law that the Selma marchers fought for, that Liuzzo, Jackson, and Reeb died for. State legislatures are passing voter ID laws that make it harder for minorities and the poor to vote. Harsh criminal sentences fall to an inordinate degree on black men, who fill prisons in ever greater numbers. African Americans are targets of racial murders, police profiling, and police abuse.[45]

"In the Fifties there was Emmett Till. Today there is Trayvon Martin."[46] The Reverend Al Sharpton acknowledges the presence of the families of both victims—the northern black boy lynched in Mississippi fifty-eight years ago and the teenager in a hoodie gunned down after leaving a Florida convenience store. His analogy has only grown more pointed since the "Reclaim the Dream" March, as images of riots in Ferguson and Baltimore dredge up memories of Detroit and Watts, and video tapes of unprovoked shootings of African Americans circulate on the internet, and names like Michael Brown, Walter Scott, Sandra Bland, Laquan McDonald, and Tamir Rice have become central references in the Black Lives Matter movement; as nine parishioners are gunned down in yet another black church; as a revived white supremacist movement espouses hatred openly, egged on by an unscrupulous president who openly targets racial, religious, and sexual minorities for political power. The nonagenarian Lowery says it best: "Everything has changed. And nothing has changed."

We end where we began. In 2003 Marshall returned to the theme of the Chicago exhibit. He completed one final painting in the *Souvenirs* sequence; he named this work *Memento V*.

The last of the *Souvenirs* is black, white, and gray. Here is another angel (fig. 3.11). She is dressed in white now, and faces us head on. The deep proscenium space of the first *Souvenir* has been shallowed out. Where in the previous works gold-and-silver glitter borders foster the illusion that we are in front of or inside these interiors, in *Memento V* the silver slats of a Venetian curtain divide the space the angel inhabits from the extremely shallow space in front—the fictive place where we stand. Marshall positions us behind these stripes of stacked lozenges. The angel grasps the curtains, draws them together. (Her hands are in "our" space.) Brilliant and opaque, the glitter blinds attract and repel perception. We peer into a space we have been barred from entering: the chamber of Sixties memory is beyond our reach.

What do we see? Three bowls of flowers, a lamp, a coffee table and matching side tables. A sofa and loveseat upholstered in chintz. A painting of trees frames the angel's face, emphasizing the whites of her eyes and the intensity of her stare. And where earlier works in the series are cluttered with names and faces, with bric-a-brac and furniture, the composition of *Memento V* is austere. The mourning banner has vanished. Just a few martyrs remain. Angels bearing the faces of King and the Kennedys float in the milky atmosphere. A wingless Malcolm hovers opposite. Marshall evokes the great division in Sixties politics between Malcolm's militant black nationalism and King's interracial, nondenominational fellowship—a tension that deepened after the assassinations of these men. Between the silver glitter slats of the curtain we read the cardinal numbers of the decadal Sixties rotated ninety degrees.

Why did Marshall take up this subject five years after the Chicago exhibition? The making of *Memento V* was inspired by the convictions of church bombing conspirators Tommy Blanton and Bobby Frank Cherry in

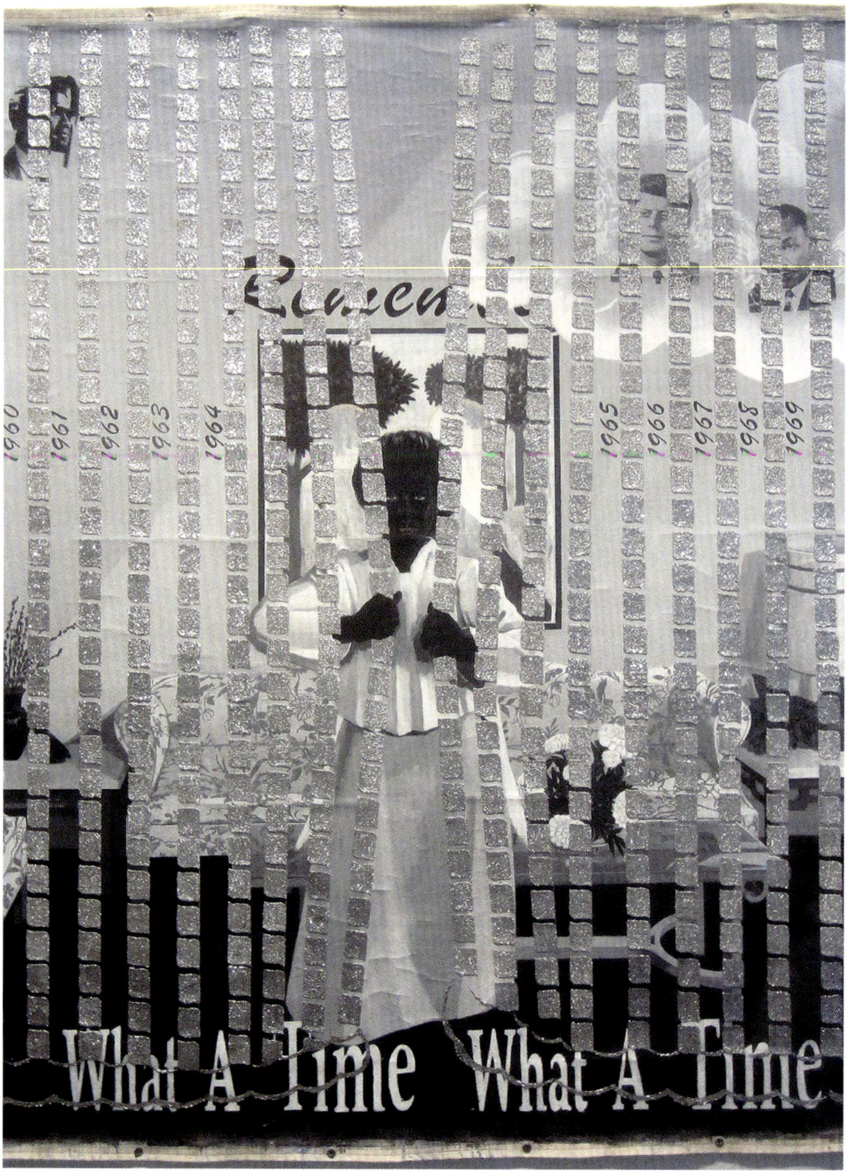


**Fig. 3.11.** Kerry James Marshall, *Memento V*, 2003. Detail. Acrylic and glitter on paper adhered to unstretched canvas banner. © Kerry James Marshall. Courtesy of Kerry James Marshall and Jack Shainman Gallery, New York.

2001–2 after decades of stalling and subterfuge by the local authorities and the FBI.[47] And with the death of Evers's assassin Byron De La Beckwith in a Jackson, Mississippi hospital, also in 2001, and the recent passing of Edgar Ray Killen, who directed the murders of Chaney, Goodman, and Schwerner, at Parchman Farm prison, where the Freedom Riders were once jailed, still other protagonists of the most infamous events of civil rights memory were "laid to rest."[48]

*Memento V* is an image of closure, shutting down. A painting of the end that is still ending, a Sixties that is slipping away. *What a Time/What a Time*, the legend at the bottom reads, a doubled, emphatic expression of Sixties longing. *Remember*, another text states simply. Painted in the same vintage font, this exhortation disappears behind the martyrs' cloud, behind the angelic portraits of King and the Kennedys, who in life dreamed of new frontiers and "beloved" communities, and who in death came to stand for a time that changed everything, that haunts us still.

Let us count the years one more time:

*1960, 1961, 1962, 1963, 1964…*

*1965, 1966, 1967, 1968, 1969…*

Then it is over. There are no more numbers.

The angel retreats, the curtains are drawn, the room fades to darkness. The memory chamber is shuttered. We are no longer asked to remember.

# ACKNOWLEDGMENTS

This book took a lifetime to conceive and realize. Essays commissioned by Richard Francis for Christie's, by Jack Bankowsky and Eric Banks for *Artforum*, and by Okwui Enwezor, Nancy Condee, and Terry Smith for their volume *Antinomies of Art and Culture: Modernity, Postmodernity, Contemporaneity* (Duke University Press, 2009) represent my first attempts to navigate the questions of this book.

I presented this research in courses at Emory University and Johns Hopkins University; my thanks to the students who participated in these classes and whose interest in the subject encouraged my own. Public lectures provided valuable opportunities to test my ideas. Versions of this work were presented at Johns Hopkins University, Stanford University, Rice University, University of Cincinnati, University of Pittsburgh, University of Florida, Ohio State University, University of Michigan, Ontario College of Art and Design, University of Queensland–Brisbane, University of Sydney, Art Gallery of New South Wales, San Francisco Art Institute, Smithsonian American Art Museum, Clark Art Institute, Whitechapel Art Gallery, Los Angeles County Museum of Art, Museo Reina Sofia, Centre Pompidou, College Art Association, and ART Santa Fe; and also at the conferences "Modernity and Contemporaneity," Carnegie Museum of Art; "The Writing of History of Contemporary Art," Tianjin Academy of Fine Arts; and "Dwelling, Walking, Falling: Conference on Experience of Everyday Space," University of Manchester and Whitworth Art Gallery. I thank the many colleagues and students who invited me to present this material.

A number of institutions supported the research and writing of this book and its publication. I developed the project during a fellowship at the Clark Research Institute (my thanks to Mark Haxthausen and Michael Ann Holly for this invitation) and during a yearlong leave at the Smithsonian Institution (thanks to Virginia Mecklenburg, Anne Ellegood, Kristin Hileman, and Amelia Goerlitz; I am especially grateful to the late Cynthia Mills). Research funds associated with the Winship Distinguished Research Professorship at Emory University, endorsed by Robert Paul and

Judith Rohrer, underwrote travel to Kent State and elsewhere. The book was completed in the conducive atmosphere of the National Gallery of Art. My thanks to Franklin Kelly and Elizabeth Pochter for their support for this project. I have also appreciated the interest in my work of my colleagues Molly Donovan, Elizabeth Cropper, Judith Brodie, Sarah Greenough, Mary Morton, Emiko Usui, Lynne Cooke, and Lorenzo Pericolo, and also of Jessica Morgan and David Morehouse of Dia Art Foundation. I drafted the book's final pages during a monthlong stay at a cabin in the mountains of Rappahannock County, Virginia; I am grateful to Sally Nash, Sarah Walton, and Laura Booth for making this possible.

Funding for photo and textual permissions and photo reproductions was provided by the National Gallery of Art. The Andy Warhol Foundation for the Visual Arts provided a generous subvention underwriting the book's publication. I am immensely grateful to Joel Wachs for his interest and support, and to Olga Viso for her advice.

I am grateful, too, to the many artists and writers who provided permission to reproduce their works and, in many instances, spoke or corresponded with me about their practices: Amy Granat, Drew Heitzler, An-My Lê, Cai Guo-Qiang, Sam Durant, Seth Price, Mike Nelson, Matthew Buckingham, Nancy Davenport, Martha Rosler, Mary Kelly, Julie Wyman, Jeremy Millar, Mark Tribe, Kitty Kraus, Felix Gmelin, Renée Green, Mu Chen, Shao Yinong, Tom Burr, Zarina Bhimji, Vik Muniz, Luke Fowler, Richard Serra, John Malpede, Jing Kewen, Anri Sala, Wu Shanzhuan, and Banks Violette.

Sincere thanks to the many librarians, archivists, and gallerists who helped me locate images reproduced in these pages, without which this book would not have been possible: Javier Anguera, Janice Guy, Nicole Klagsbrun, Tamsen Greene, Amy Plumb Oppenheim, Henriëtte Brouwers, Catherine Belloy, Lauren Williamson, Lauren Smith, Miciah Hussey, Kim Bush, Hilary Chassé, Renée Miller, Courtney Willis Blair, Isabelle Hogenkamp, Alessa Rather, Arieh Frosh, Patricia Liu, Isabel Shorney, Andy Avini, Kelsey Tyler, Emma Leach, Alice Culclasure, Tom Martinelli, Tricia McKeever, Julie Schilder, Alan Baglia, Meghan Brown, David Beal, Grant Feichtmeir, Bonita Passarelli, Stephanie F. Reeves, Anthony Yung, Amanda Faehnel, and Rachel Vagts.

Several individuals facilitated my work in important ways. My National Gallery colleagues Kerry Rose, Emily Francisco, and especially Paige Rozanski provided invaluable research assistance. John Long shared his photographic expertise. Cara Gilgenbach, head of Special Collections and Archives at Kent State University Library, provided access to the library's May 4 and Smithson archives and generously guided me through these materials. Gao Minglu and Bingyi have been important guides to the field of contemporary Chinese art, and to China itself; their impact has been significant. So too my Emory colleague Sidney Littlefield Kasfir, who introduced me to the field of African art and to the scholarship on postcolonial East Africa consulted in these pages. Christine Aylward kindly translated Chinese texts and assisted me in photo research at a crucial moment.

Friends and colleagues generously read sections of the book, or the book in its entirety: Suzanne Guerlac, Harry Cooper, Alexander Alberro, Liza Johnson, and two anonymous readers who agreed to review the book for University of Chicago Press. The book benefited considerably from the input of these readers. I cannot thank them enough.

The professionalism of the staff at the University of Chicago Press has been impressive indeed. James Toftness was the book's assistant editor, Tamara Ghattas its production editor, and Mollie McFee and Adrienne Meyers its publicists. Freelance professionals Lys Ann Weiss and Matt Avery also worked with the press as copy editor and designer, respectively. I am especially grateful to the book's commissioning editor at the press, Susan Bielstein, who patiently awaited the manuscript's completion and has made the book a reality. Uniquely and remarkably among editors in her position, Susan read through drafts of the manuscript, lending her fine ear and expert understanding of narrative and pacing to the text in its later stages. The book you hold in your hands bears her meticulous editorial imprint.

The support of friends and colleagues has meant a great deal over the years: Sarah McPhee, Carol Thompson, Mel Bochner, Elise Thoron, Oz Enders, Amy Adler, Eva Usdan, Chris Neville, Sarah Gamble, Andrew Solomon, Brian D'Amato, David Rimanelli, Sally James, Martina Vandenberg, Alan Cooperman, Miriam Peskowitz, Robert Baird, Helena Reckitt, Gregg Bordowitz, Robin Blaetz, Izette Folger, Neil Folger, James Alefantis, Briony Fer, Stephen Campbell, Pam Lee, Marc Gotlieb, Maria Gough, Christine Mehring, Mignon Nixon, Kim Paice, Lisa Freiman, Nora Alter, James Rondeau, Cornelia Grassi, Rex Butler, Sue Best, Toni Ross, Marcia Brennan, Veerle Thielemans, Martine Watson Brownley, Barbara Rose, Constance Caplan, Alexandra Truitt, Carol Brown Goldberg, Virginia Dwan, Anne Kovach, and the late Arthur Danto. Rosalind Lefeber and the late Louis Lefeber have been intellectual role models and inspirations for as long as I can remember. My brothers Fredric and Marc Meyer and my sister-in-law Irene Meyer have been steadfast in their interest and support. Chris Boutlier's belief in this project sustained me during its completion. A special thanks is due to Yve-Alain Bois, without whom this text would not exist. His brilliant teaching and writings have had a profound impact on all of my work, and, unlikely as it may seem, on this book in particular.

Last but not least, I wish to mention two individuals who stood by me during this book's long parturition: my extraordinary mother and greatest advocate, Charlotte Meyer, who has anticipated the book's publication with great interest; and my friend and colleague Harry Cooper, both for his intellectual engagement with this project and for provision of a scholarly ambience in which I could work. This book is dedicated to them.

# NOTES

## Introduction

1. As argued in Thomas Frank, *The Conquest of Cool: Business Culture, Counterculture, and the Rise of Hip Consumerism* (Chicago: University of Chicago Press, 1998).
2. "Election," American Fine Arts Co./Colin De Land Fine Art, October 22–November 18, 2004. Contributors to the show included Carl Andre and Melissa Kretschmer, Alex Bag, Subhankar Banerjee, Christoph Büchel, Tom Burr, Paul Chan, Critical Art Ensemble and Claire Pentecost, Mark Dion, Peter Fend, Andrea Fraser, Hans Haacke, Emily Jacir, Mark Lombardi, Christian Philipp Müller and Jane Johnston, Martha Rosler and John Waters.
3. The Political Action Committee (PAC) took its name from the type of nautical craft operated by John Kerry during his tour in Vietnam.
4. According to Hannah Fischer, *A Guide to U.S. Military Casualty Statistics: Operation Freedom's Sentinel, Operation Inherent Resolve, Operation New Dawn, Operation Iraqi Freedom, and Operation Enduring Freedom* (Washington, DC: Congressional Research Service, 2015), as of 2015, 1,645 soldiers had lost limbs in U.S. operations in Iraq, Afghanistan, and Syria.
5. Jerry Saltz, "Welcome to the Sixties, Yet Again," *New York Magazine*, October 5, 2008. Rosler's work was favorably reviewed in Holland Cotter, "Art in Review: 'Election,'" *New York Times*, October 29, 2004.
6. The literature on the "Baby Boomers"—a reference to the greatly increased birthrate of the post–World War II period—is vast. A distinction is made between an older cohort, born between 1946 and 1955, and a younger generation of late "Boomers," born between 1956 and 1964. "Generation X," the neologism of the author Douglas Coupland, has come to suggest a post-Boomer cohort born approximately between 1961 and 1981. While there is a utility to these definitions, practices by artists and writers born outside Western Europe and the United States confound the Westernism of the Boomer principle described in books like Steve Gillon, *Boomer Nation: The Largest and Richest Generation Ever, and How It Changed America* (New York: Free Press, 2004).
7. I refer to my *Minimalism: Art and Polemics in the Sixties* (New Haven: Yale University Press, 2001).

## Part One

1. T. J. Clark, *Farewell to an Idea: Episodes from a History of Modernism* (New Haven: Yale University Press, 1999), 2–3, 6.
2. Such millenarian claims are hardly fresh. See the classic essay of Charles Maier, "A Surfeit of Memory? Reflections on History, Melancholy, and Denial," *History and Memory* 5, no. 2 (Fall–Winter 1993): 136–52; and, more recently, Slavoj Žižek, *Living in the End Times* (New York: Verso, 2010). Andreas Huyssen reminds us of the importance of "remembering the future" in *Present Pasts: Urban Palimpsests and the Politics of Memory* (Stanford: Stanford University Press, 2003), 6.

3. Matthew Arnold, "The Modern Element in Literature" (1869), in *Essays in Criticism: Third Series* (Boston: The Ball Publishing Company, 1910), 38–40.
4. "The historical sense involves a perception, not only of the pastness of the past, but of its presence." T. S. Eliot, "Tradition and the Individual Talent," in *Selected Essays* (London: Faber & Faber, 1932), 14, 17.
5. "Modernist Painting," in John O'Brian, ed., *Clement Greenberg: The Collected Essays and Criticism*, vol. 4 (Chicago: University of Chicago Press, 1993), 92 (my italics).
6. Rosalind E. Krauss, *The Originality of the Avant-Garde and Other Modernist Myths* (Cambridge, MA: MIT Press, 1985); and Benjamin H. D. Buchloh, "The Primary Colors for the Second Time," *October* 37 (Summer 1986): 41–52.
7. Craig Owens, "The Allegorical Impulse: Toward a Theory of Postmodernism," *October* 12 (Spring 1980): 67–86.
8. Michael Fried, "Art and Objecthood," *Artforum* 5 (June 1967): 12–23.
9. Douglas Crimp, "Pictures," in *Art after Modernism: Rethinking Representation* (New York: New Museum of Contemporary Art, 1984), 185.
10. I am thinking of Fred Wilson's *Mining the Museum* (1992); Renée Green's *Mise-en-Scène* (1992); Kerry James Marshall's *Voyager* (1993) and *Great America* (1994); Matthew Buckingham's *The Spirit and the Letter* (2007); Jeremy Deller's *The Battle of Orgreave* (2001); various works by Edgar Heap of Birds and Yinka Shonibare; and the historical fiction of Hilary Mantel and David Mitchell, among others. See Mark Godfrey, "The Artist as Historian," *October* 120 (Spring 2007): 140–72; Helena Reckitt, *Not Quite How I Remember It* (Toronto: Power Plant, 2008); Nato Thompson, *Ahistoric Occasion* (North Adams, MA: Mass MoCA, 2006); and Chema González, *Así se escribe la historia* (Madrid: Obra Social Caja Madrid, 2008).
11. As Thomas Crow, Lauren Berlant, and Kristen Ross have argued. See Thomas Crow, *The Rise of the Sixties: American and European Art in the Era of Dissent* (New York: Harry Abrams, 1996); Lauren Berlant, "'68 or Something," *Critical Inquiry* 21 (August 1994): 124–55; and Kristin Ross, *May '68 and Its Afterlives* (Chicago: University of Chicago Press, 2002). See also Margaret Iversen's remarks in *October* 123 (Winter 2008): 202.
12. Peter Bürger, *Theory of the Avant-Garde* (Minneapolis: University of Minnesota Press, 1984).
13. Fredric Jameson, "Periodizing the Sixties," in Sohnya Sayres et. al., *The Sixties without Apology* (Minneapolis: University of Minnesota Press, 1984), 207.
14. Fredric Jameson, "Postmodernism, or the Cultural Logic of Late Capitalism," *New Left Review* (1984): 53–92.
15. Jameson, "Periodizing the Sixties," 178–79. The "levels" are philosophy, revolutionary theory and practice, cultural production, and economic developments in France, the United States, and the Third World. For Jameson, homology is not resemblance; what connects the levels is the way each has "broken" with a prior period formation. See *A Singular Modernity: Essay on the Ontology of the Present* (New York: Verso, 2002).
16. Rudi Dutschke quoted in Martin Klimke, *The Other Alliance: Student Protest in West Germany and the United States in the Global Sixties* (Princeton: Princeton University Press, 2010), 92.
17. Jameson, "Periodizing the Sixties," 184, 207.
18. Jameson, "Periodizing the Sixties," 184–85; and Tom Hayden, *The Long Sixties: From 1960 to Barack Obama* (Boulder, CO: Paradigm Press, 2009), 7.
19. Theodore Roszak, "Introduction to the 1995 Edition," in *The Making of a Counter Culture* (Berkeley: University of California Press, 1995), xii (my italics).
20. Some critics periodize the "contemporary" to September 11, 2001, others to 1989 (year of the fall of the Iron Curtain, the end of apartheid, and the seminal art exhibition "Magiciens de la Terre.") See, for example, Nicolas Bourriaud, *Altermodern* (London: Tate Publishing,

2009); and Alexander Alberro, "A Questionnaire on 'The Contemporary': 32 Responses," *October* 130 (Fall 2009): 55–60. Terry Smith narrates a progressive coming-into-being of the new era ("nascent during the Fifties, emergent during the Sixties ... unmistakable since the Eighties") in *What Is Contemporary Art?* (Chicago: University of Chicago Press, 2009), 5.

**21.** See David Horowitz's *mea culpa* in *Radical Son: A Generational Odyssey* (New York: Touchstone, 1998); Ann Burlein, "Countermemory on the Right: The Case of Focus on the Family," in Mieke Bal, Jonathan Crewe, and Leo Spitzer, eds., *Acts of Memory: Cultural Recall in the Present* (Hanover, NH: Dartmouth College Press, 1999), 208–17; and Cheryl Harris, "On Visual Oral History: Meditations on Kerry James Marshall's *Mementos*" in Kerry James Marshall, *Mementos* (Chicago: Renaissance Society, 2000), 13–31, on the Sixties and post-Sixties identities of U.S. Supreme Court Justice Clarence Thomas.

**22.** Saltz, "Welcome to the Sixties, Yet Again."

**23.** See Lauren Berlant, "'68, or Something," 126.

**24.** Mark Tribe and Christina Ulke, "Politics by Other Means," *Journal of Aesthetics and Protest* 5 (September 2007), http://www.joaap.org/5/articles/Tribe/ulketribe.htm.

**25.** "My generation is still defined by the references and ideologies of Sixty-Eight. We have constructed that generation as the monolithic generation, as every generation defines the generation before." João Ribas, spoken remark, in "Generations," CATT (Contemporary Art Think Tank), Washington, DC, April 9, 2010. See also Ribas's remarks in Oliver Wunsch, "Contemporary Knowledge: Interview with João Ribas," *Art 21 Blog*, http://blogart21.org; and the remarks of Pedro Lasch in "In What Ways Have Artists, Academics, and Cultural Institutions Responded to the U.S.-led Invasion and Occupation of Iraq?" *October* 123 (Winter 2008): 151.

**26.** Pierre Nora, "Generation," in *Realms of Memory: Rethinking the French Past*, vol. 1: *Conflicts and Divisions*, trans. Arthur Goldhammer (New York: Columbia University Press, 1996), 507.

**27.** Practitioners relevant to this study include Silvia Kolbowski (artist, b. 1953), Carrie Mae Weems (artist, b. 1953); Penny Siopis (artist, b. 1953); Marcelo Brodsky (photographer, b. 1954); Jiang Ji-Li (author, b. 1954); Gu Wenda (artist, b. 1955); Kerry James Marshall (artist, b. 1955); Xu Bing (artist, b. 1955); Joseph Grigley (artist, b. 1956), Sarah Lewison (artist, b. 1956); Cady Noland (artist, b. 1956); Cai Guo-Qiang (artist, b. 1957); Christian Philipp Müller (artist, b. 1957); Wang Jianwei (artist, b. 1958); Renée Green (artist, b. 1959); Matthew Antezzo (artist, b. 1960); An-My Lê (photographer, b. 1960); Glenn Ligon (artist, b. 1960); Wu Shanzhuan (artist, b. 1960); Sam Durant (artist, b. 1961); Vik Muniz (photographer, b. 1961); Shao Yinong (photographer, b. 1961); Felix Gmelin (artist, b. 1962); Jennifer Egan (novelist, b. 1962); Bettina Röhl (journalist, b. 1962); Zarina Bhimji (film artist, b. 1963); Tom Burr (artist, b. 1963); Matthew Buckingham (artist, b. 1963); Christopher Sorrentino (novelist, b. 1963); Simon Leung (artist, b. 1964); Philippe Parreno (artist, b. 1964); Andrea Bowers (artist, b. 1965); Nancy Davenport (photographer, b. 1965); Tacita Dean (film artist, b. 1965); Andrea Fraser (artist, b. 1965); Jing Kewen (artist, b. 1965); Elisabeth Subrin (filmmaker, b. 1965); Matthew Weiner (TV producer, b. 1965); Nicolás Guagnini (artist, b. 1966); Mark Tribe (artist, b. 1966); Yu Hong (artist, b. 1966); Dana Spiotta (novelist, b. 1966); Rafael Lozano-Hemmer (artist, b. 1967); Mike Nelson (artist, b. 1967); Wang Tong (artist, b. 1967); Dinh Q. Lê (filmmaker, b. 1968); Rachel Kushner (novelist, b. 1968); Zachary Lazar (novelist, b. 1968); Saul Anton (author, b. 1969); Gerard Byrne (film artist, b. 1969); Susan Choi (novelist, b. 1969); Jonathan Monk (artist, b. 1969); Naeem Mohaiemen (artist, b. 1969); Shane O' Sullivan (documentary filmmaker, b. 1969); Kelley Walker (artist, b. 1969); Julie Wyman (artist, b. 1969); Conrad Bakker (artist, b. 1970); Dave Eggers (author, b. 1970); Sharon Hayes (artist, b. 1970); Emily Jacir (artist, b. 1970); Jeremy Millar (artist, b. 1970); Mu Chen (photographer, b. 1970); Rozalinda Borcila (artist, b. 1971); Carol Bove (artist, b. 1971); William Cordova (artist, b. 1971); Viet Thanh Nguyen (novelist and critic, b. 1971); Drew Heitzler (artist, b. 1972);

Kirsten Forkert (artist, b. 1973); Seth Price (artist, b. 1973); Banks Violette (artist, b. 1973); Mark Roeder (artist, b. 1974); Anri Sala (artist, b. 1974); Hank Willis Thomas (artist, b. 1974); Madeleine Thien (novelist, b. 1974); Alejandro Cesarco (artist, b. 1975); James Hoff (artist and publisher, b. 1975); Nathan Hill (novelist, b. 1975); Mario Garcia Torres (artist, b. 1975); Danh Vô (artist, b. 1975); Amy Granat (film artist, b. 1976); Leslie Hewitt (artist, b. 1977); Luke Fowler (artist, b. 1978); Nam Lê (novelist, b. 1978); Miriam Katzeff (publisher, b. 1981); Adam Pendleton (artist, b. 1984); and Emma Cline (novelist, b. 1989). The list goes on.

**28.** In 1971 factionalism tore the ensemble apart. Inspired by the writings of Mao Zedong, Cardew and his colleagues concluded that the orchestra must abandon "bourgeois" techniques of improvisation and individual expression in favor of proletarian music. The remaining members continued to follow Scratch principles. Luke Fowler, "Pilgrimage from Scattered Points," in *Luke Fowler* (Zurich: JRP/Ringier, 2009), 40–41; and Will Bradley, *"Implicit in this Attitude is a Belief in Freedom,"* in *Luke Fowler*, 22–23.

**29.** Hugh Shrapnel, from *25 Years of Scratch* (London: London Musicians' Collective, 1994), quoted in John Tilbury, *Cornelius Cardew: A Life Unfinished* (Matching Tye, Essex, UK: Copula, 2008), 439.

**30.** Cardew's notes, quoted in Tilbury, *Cornelius Cardew*, 366.

**31.** Tilbury, *Cornelius Cardew*, 461.

**32.** Tilbury, *Cornelius Cardew*, 451.

**33.** Cardew asked the six-year-old Horace to appear naked in front of a Maoist "cottage" the orchestra had built during an exhibition at the Alexandra Palace in North London in 1971. The boy refused. Tilbury, *Cornelius Cardew*, 536–37.

**34.** *More about the Language of Love* (1970; *Mera ur kärlekens språk*). Documentary, Sweden.

**35.** The elder Gmelin was the author of *Philosophie des Fernsehens* (1967), *Bankrott der Männerherrschaft* (1967), *Anti-Freud: Von der Psychoanalyse zur Medienwissenschaft* (1978), *Böses kommt aus Kinderbüchern* (1982), and *Mamma ist ein Elefant* (1984).

**36.** All quotes of Sala are from this source.

**37.** Hoxha ran the Albanian Communist Party and the country itself from 1944 to 1985. Purges of political rivals, "revisionist" party members, and dissidents in the church and press and the Sigurimi (secret police) eliminated any opposition to the dictator. Despite his ruthlessness, Hoxha oversaw the rebuilding of a country that had emerged from World War II as "easily the most backward country in Europe." Miranda Vickers, *The Albanians: A Modern History* (New York: I. B. Tauris, 2014), 157. Albania was transformed from an agrarian to an industrial economy, illiteracy was nearly eradicated, and the status of women improved. Alliances with Stalinist Russia and Maoist China financed these initiatives. By the time of Hoxha's death, Albania was in enormous debt, and the Albanian people "had been cowed into a fearful state of submission." Vickers, *The Albanians*, 185, 190, 200.

**38.** After they fell out of favor, the Lubanjas were sentenced to sixteen years in prison. Sala, *Intervista (Finding the Words)*. Harsh sentences based on the flimsiest evidence were common in communist Albania. Prisons and labor camps were overseen by the secret police. In the worst of these camps inmates were tortured, poorly fed, and had little access to medical care. Vickers, *The Albanians*, 181.

**39.** "Love and Honor and Pity and Pride and Compassion and Sacrifice," in Nam Lê, *The Boat* (New York: Alfred A. Knopf, 2008), 3–27. The quotations here are from this source.

**40.** Walter Benjamin, "A Berlin Chronicle," in *Reflections: Essays, Aphorisms, Autobiographical Writings*, trans. Edmund Jephcott, ed. Peter Demetz (New York: Schocken Books, 1986), 26. The original German appears in Walter Benjamin, *Berliner Chronik* (Berlin: Suhrkamp Verlag, 1970), 52.

**41.** Elisabeth Subrin quoted during the panel "After the Revolution? Artists Respond to the Second Wave," P.S. 1, Long Island City, New York, April 12, 2008.

42. See Daniel Mendelsohn, "The Mad Men Account," *New York Review of Books* 58, no. 3 (February 24, 2011): 4–8.
43. Dave Eggers, *A Heartbreaking Work of Staggering Genius* (New York: Vintage Books, 2000), 172.
44. Eggers, *A Heartbreaking Work of Staggering Genius*.
45. Eggers, *A Heartbreaking Work of Staggering Genius*, 175–76.
46. Reinhardt Koselleck, "Author's Preface," in *Futures Past: On the Semantics of Historical Time*, trans. Keith Tribe (New York: Columbia University Press, 2004), 2. Koselleck calls the future of a time its "horizon of expectation." He contrasts this with a future's knowledge of the past, which he calls its "space of experience." See "'Space of Experience' and 'Horizon of Expectation': Two Historical Categories," in *Futures Past*, 255–75. For another account of the past's continued presence "in the here and now" see Eelco Ruina, "Spots of Time," *History and Theory* 45 (October 2006): 305–16.
47. I am thinking of the Iraq War of 2003–4, the Bush-Kerry presidential election of 2004, the 2008 election of President Barack Obama, the fiftieth anniversaries of the great civil rights marches, the rise of the Black Lives Matter movement, and the 2017 Women's March.
48. Leopold von Ranke, "Introduction to the *History of the Latin and Teutonic Nations*" (1824), in Roger Wines, ed., *The Secret of World History: Selected Writings on the Art and Science of History* (New York: Fordham University Press, 1981), 58. My discussion of "proper history" is indebted to Hayden White, "Interpretation in History," in *Tropics of Discourse: Essays in Cultural Criticism* (Baltimore: Johns Hopkins University Press, 1978), 51–80.
49. As Keith Tribe notes, Koselleck's model draws both from Heideggerian theories of time and from the hermeneutical philosophy of Hans-Georg Gadamer and Hans Robert Jauss. See "Translator's Introduction," in *Futures Past*, vii–xx.
50. Arthur C. Danto, *Narration and Knowledge* (New York: Columbia University Press, 1985), xii–xiii.
51. The decade as a method of counting time has grown in importance in the last hundred years. See Jason Scott Smith, "The Strange History of the Decade: Modernity, Nostalgia, and the Perils of Periodization," *Journal of Social History* 32, no. 2 (Winter 1998): 263–85.
52. The more conventional mini-series *The Sixties* (1999) also followed a decadal timeline.
53. Danto, *Narration and Knowledge*, xiii.
54. Thomas Frank, *The Conquest of Cool: Business Culture, Counterculture, and the Rise of Hip Consumerism* (Chicago: University of Chicago Press, 1997), 1–9.
55. The "Sixties" in Jameson's account is "long" (1959–74), as is the "Sixties" of historian Arthur Marwick, inspired by E. J. Hobsbawm's model of periodization. Arthur Marwick, *The Sixties: Cultural Revolution in Britain, France, Italy, and the United States, c. 1958- c. 1974* (New York: Oxford University Press, 1998), 7. The editors of the journal *The Sixties* propose a longer "long Sixties" of "roughly the years 1954–1975." "Time Is an Ocean: The Past and Future of the Sixties," *The Sixties: A Journal of History, Politics and Culture* 1, no. 1 (June 2008): 5. The "long Sixties" of Tom Hayden is a *longue durée* spanning the historical Sixties and early Seventies, and returning in the new century ("the Sixties at fifty.") Hayden, *The Long Sixties*.
56. See the conversation between Lumumba Turner and Renée Green in Renée Green, *Shadows and Signals* (Barcelona: Fundació Antoni Tàpies, 2000), 106.
57. Here I am summarizing a view of the Sixties cherished on the Left. The neoconservative view of the era inverts such claims: the long Sixties is held accountable for every social ill imaginable.
58. On the Sixties and the emergence of a "global consciousness," see George Katsiaficas, *The Imagination of the New Left: A Global Analysis of 1968* (Boston: South End Press, 1987); and Karen Dubinsky et. al., eds., *New World Coming: The Sixties and the Shaping of Global Consciousness* (Toronto: Between the Lines, 2009), 2. The centrality of Sixty-eight has also

been questioned. Recalling his traumatic experience as a child refugee from Nigeria in a resettlement camp in Biafra in 1968, curator Okwui Enwezor notes that the Biafra crisis went largely unnoticed in the West. To these refugees, the protests of students and workers in Europe and the United States felt extremely remote. Enwezor's is an important caveat: in the rush to "globalize" the "Sixties," we risk diminishing local difference, universalizing Western or American periodizations. This point does nothing to diminish the claim of curator Robert Storr (contested by Enwezor) that Sixty-eight saw disruptions of state authority internationally, including in West Africa. In May 1968, Nigerian students demanding the right of assembly closed down the University of Lagos for three weeks, while students in Senegal protesting reductions in scholarships occupied the University of Dakar, leading to the death of one of their classmates and the injury and arrest of many others. Katsiaficas describes unrest in fifteen other African nations as well. Katsiaficas, *The Imagination of the New Left*, 40. For the exchange between Storr and Enwezor, see http://www.youtube.com/watch?v=5TEx1M7JoPI.

**59.** I discuss Alain Badiou's description of the long Sixties as an "event" of historical significance in part 3.

**60.** See Paul Auster, "The Accidental Rebel," *New York Times*, April 23, 2008, A25; Daniel Cohn-Bendit, "An Elusive Legacy: May 1968: Our rebellion was neither the revolution dreamed of by the left nor the root of the modern problems that the right suggests," *Guardian*, May 6, 2008, http://www.guardian.co.uk; Jean-Claude Guillebaud; "France's Bright Shining Lie," *New York Times*, May 24, 2008, A27; and the essays in *Newsweek*, "1968: The Year That Made Us Who We Are" (November 19, 2007), *Artforum* 46, no. 9 (May 2008), and the "1968" issue of *Bookforum* 25, issue 2 (Summer 2018). In 2008, the High Museum, Atlanta, mounted "Road to Freedom: Photographs of the Civil Rights Movement 1956–1968," curated by Julian Cox, and "After 1968: Contemporary Artists and the Civil Rights Legacy," curated by Jeffrey Grove. Various film series were organized around the Sixty-eight theme, including "1968: An International Perspective," organized by Richard Peña, Film Society of Lincoln Center, New York, April 29–May 14, 2008; and "1968: Then and Now," organized by Deborah Willis, Tisch School of the Arts, New York University, September 2–November 22, 2008.

**61.** "Modernity and the Planes of Historicity," in Koselleck, *Futures Past*, 3.

**62.** The Glorious Revolution, which restored Protestant rule to the English throne, typifies this older notion. See Hannah Arendt, *On Revolution* (London: Penguin Books, 1963), 42; and Raymond Williams, *Keywords: A Vocabulary of Culture and Society* (New York: Oxford University Press, 1976), 270. As Williams notes, two words related to the modern notion of revolution, *rebellion* and *revolt*, had entered the English lexicon by the fourteenth and sixteenth centuries, respectively (271).

**63.** Arendt, *On Revolution*, 47–48. Arendt argues that one group of revolutionaries during the English Revolution, the Levellers (also known as the Diggers), called for the kind of sweeping reform symptomatic of the modern concept of revolution (43). I discuss the historical Diggers and their modern-day avatars, the San Francisco Diggers, in part 2.

**64.** Williams, *Keywords*, 273.

**65.** Jean-François Lyotard, *The Postmodern Condition* (Minneapolis: University of Minnesota Press, 1984); and Francis Fukuyama, "The End of History?" *National Interest* (Summer 1989): 3–18.

**66.** "Historical Criteria of the Modern Concept of Revolution" (1969), in Koselleck, *Futures Past*, 44.

**67.** As the idea of revolution became historical, the "grand narratives" of history became ripe for reflection, as the hermeneutical turn in Hayden White's work also confirms. See White,

"Interpretation in History"; and White, *Metahistory: The Historical Imagination in Nineteenth-Century Europe* (Baltimore: Johns Hopkins University Press, 1973).

**68.** Koselleck, *Futures Past*, 56.

**69.** Richard Terdiman, *Present Past: Modernity and the Memory Crisis* (Ithaca: Cornell University Press, 1993).

**70.** Alfred de Musset, *The Confession of a Child of the Century*, trans. Kendall Warren, in John B. Halsted, ed., *Romanticism* (New York: Walker & Company, 1969), 338, 342.

**71.** Nora, "Generation," 513.

**72.** Casimir Pierre Périer, minister to King Louis-Philippe, quoted in "Mémoires Posthumes d'Odilon-Barrot" (1875), *Quarterly Review* 144, no. 287 (July and October, 1877): 329. Périer is describing the replacement of the Bourbon King Charles X with Louis Philippe d'Orléans.

**73.** A propitious scenario for art, however. According to Nora, this sense of belatedness resulted in a strong generational identity and the extraordinary literary and artistic output of figures like Hugo, Delacroix, Balzac, and Musset. Nora, "Generation," 512.

**74.** Musset, *The Confession of a Child of the Century*, 342; and Terdiman, *Present Past*, 82.

**75.** Musset, *The Confession of a Child of the Century*, 341.

**76.** Musset, *The Confession of a Child of the Century*, 347.

**77.** Terdiman's narrative extends from Musset to Baudelaire, Proust, and Freud.

**78.** See the classic account of Karl Mannheim, "The Problem of Generations," in Paul Kecskemeti, ed., *Essays on the Sociology of Knowledge* (New York: Oxford University Press, 1952), 276–322.

**79.** I discuss Dylan's song "The Times They Are a-Changin'" (1964) and Reich's *The Greening of America* (1971) below. See also Margaret Mead, *Culture and Commitment: A Study of the Generation Gap* (New York: Natural History Press, 1970). On the association of youth and regeneration during the Sixties, see Peter Braunstein, "Forever Young: Insurgent Youth and the Sixties Culture of Rejuvenation," in Peter Braunstein and Michael William Doyle, eds., *Imagine Nation: The American Counterculture of the Sixties and Seventies* (New York: Routledge, 2002), 243–73.

**80.** Recent feminist practice has explored this question of generational difference and succession in its examination of the Second Wave. Notable projects include Mary Kelly's works *Love Songs* (2005–7), analyzed below; *Shulie* (1997), Elisabeth Subrin's remake of a 1967 film portrait of Shulamith Firestone; and the recent work of Sharon Hayes. See Elisabeth Subrin, "Trashing *Shulie*: Remnants from an Abandoned Feminist History," in *F is for Phony: Fake Documentary and Truth's Undoing*, ed. Alexandra Juhasz and Jesse Lerner (Minneapolis: University of Minnesota Press, 2006), 59–66; "Feminist Time: A Conversation," *Grey Room* 31 (Spring 2008): 32–68; Catherine Grant, "Fans of Feminism: Re-writing Histories of Second-wave Feminism in Contemporary Art," *Oxford Art Journal* 34, no. 2 (June 2011): 265–86; and Elizabeth Freeman's account of Hayes's and Subrin's practices as "temporal drag" in *Time Binds: Queer Temporalities, Queer Histories* (Durham, NC: Duke University Press, 2010), 59-94.

**81.** The members of a generation occupy "a common location in the historical dimension of the social process." Mannheim, "The Problem of Generations," 290, 299.

**82.** Wilhelm Dilthey, "Über das Studium der Geschichte der Wissenschaften vom Menschen, der Gesellschaft und dem Staat," in *Gesammelte Schriften*, vol. 5 (1875), 37, cited in Hans Jaeger, "Generations in History: Reflections on a Controversial Concept," *History and Theory* 24, no. 3 (October 1985): 276. As Dilthey notes, the leading figures of German Romanticism—Hölderlin, Kleist, Novalis, and the Schlegel brothers, among others—were born during the late 1760s and 1770s, and attended the same *gymnasium* and universities. They emerged as a literary generation at the turn of the century, a phenomenon marked by the Schlegels' publication of the *Athenaeum* in 1798. For an analysis of Dilthey's argument, see Mannheim, "The Problem of Generations," 280–83.

**83.** Mannheim, "The Problem of Generations," 298.

**84.** "We are all conscious of belonging to several generations. . . . We do not necessarily feel that we belong to the generation to which the dates of our birth would consign us." Nora, "Generation," 507.

**85.** Nora, "Generation," 525 (my italics).

**86.** For a dramatization of this question within the context of Paris in 1968, see the remarkable film by Philippe Garrel, *Les amants réguliers* (2005).

**87.** Nora, "Generation," 502–3. According to Nora, the association of the generation with a radical intentionality has outlived its historical possibility. May 1968 was an "enactment of revolutionary memory without a revolutionary opportunity," a degradation of the "Event in its pure state" ( 500–501). For Nora, May is a mere simulation of the authentic Event, even though the institutions of French society were shut down for an entire month. For an excellent analysis and rebuttal of such categorical dismissals of May and its aftereffects, see Ross, *May '68 and Its Afterlives*.

**88.** Charles A. Reich, *The Greening of America* (New York: Random House, 1970), 2–3.

**89.** Reich's countercultural argument valorizing the young above all others affirmed mass cultural narratives arguing essentially the same point. See "Man of the Year: Twenty-Five and Under," *Time Magazine* 89, no. 1 (January 6, 1967): 18.

**90.** Bob Dylan, "The Times They Are A-Changin." Copyright © 1963, 1964 by Warner Bros. Inc.; renewed 1991, 1992 by Special Rider Music. All rights reserved. International copyright secured. Reprinted by permission.

**91.** The themes of *The Greening of America* have lost none of their urgency: (1) *disorder, corruption, hypocrisy* (Reich spoke of the "lawlessness and evasion" of the U.S. government, of the Vietnam War's "indifferent technological cruelty"); (2) *poverty, distorted priorities, and law-making by private power* (an economic structure of extreme poverty and extremely affluence; a tax structure that "subsidizes private wealth"; prioritization of defense spending over domestic needs); (3) *uncontrolled technology and environmental decay*; (4) *decline of democracy and liberty* (power increasingly in the hands of corporations); (5) *the artificiality of work and culture*; (6) *absence of community* (a dissolution of locality in a culture of mobility); (7) *loss of self* (the individual's powerlessness to effect change). Reich, *The Greening of America*, 4–8.

**92.** Irving Howe, "This Age of Conformity," *Partisan Review* 21 (January–February 1954): 1–33.

**93.** The 2010 demonstrations by students in the United Kingdom, Greece, and Italy in response to severe cutbacks in education, the widespread protests of 2011 (the Arab Spring, the Occupy Wall Street movement, the indignado movement in Spain), and the rise of the Black Lives Matter movement and anti-Trumpist politics in the United States suggest a revived politics of resistance, as argued in part 3.

**94.** Roszak, "Preface for the 1995 Edition," in *The Making of a Counter Culture*, xvi; and Susan Buck-Morss, "Response to Questionnaire: In What Ways Have Artists, Academics, and Cultural Institutions Responded to the U.S.-led Invasion and Occupation of Iraq?" *October* 123 (Winter 2008): 27–28.

**95.** Open letter by thirteen members of Harvard College, Class of 1967, to President Drew Gilpin Faust. See Laurence H. M. Holland, "Alums Protest Student Apathy: Grads Criticize 'Docile Behavior of the Student Body,'" *Harvard Crimson*, December 4, 2007. Art historian Benjamin Buchloh enlisted the German term *Untertan*, derived from a novel by Heinrich Mann, to describe the "authoritarian" mentality allegedly prevalent on the contemporary campus. Benjamin Buchloh and Rachel Churner, Introduction to "Response to Questionnaire: In What Ways Have Artists, Academics, and Cultural Institutions Responded to the

U.S.-led Invasion and Occupation of Iraq?" 3. For a critique of such condemnations, see Rosalyn Deutsche, "Response to Questionnaire: In What Ways Have Artists, Academics, and Cultural Institutions Responded to the U.S.-led Invasion and Occupation of Iraq?" 38.

**96.** Demonstrations against the imminent invasion were held in Washington, DC, on January 18, 2003, and in some sixty countries worldwide on February 15–16. An estimated six to ten million protesters participated in these actions. Students for a Democratic Society, "a radical, multi-issue student and youth organization working to build power in our schools and communities," with around one hundred active chapters, was revived in 2006.

**97.** A related discussion concerns a contemporary longing for a moribund Left that Wendy Brown has described as melancholic. Reading Walter Benjamin's 1931 article "Left-Wing Melancholy" through the lens of Freud's "Mourning and Melancholia," Brown describes a contemporary narcissistic longing for "one's past political attachments and identity that exceeds any contemporary investment in political mobilization." Like those Weimar-era admirers of the political hack poet Erich Kästner ("Who cannot see them," writes Benjamin, "their dreamy baby eyes behind horn-rimmed spectacles ... their fatalism in gesture and mode of thought?"), Leftist melancholics long for a Left that was: their attachment to old ideals has become fetishistic, "thing-like and frozen." Wendy Brown, "Resisting Left Melancholy," *boundary 2* 26, no. 3 (1999): 20, 22, 26; and Walter Benjamin, "Left-Wing Melancholy," in Anton Kaes, Martin Jay, and Edward Dimendberg, eds., *The Weimar Republic Sourcebook* (Berkeley: University of California Press, 1994), 304. Brown's productive argument is revisited in Rosalyn Deutsche, "Not Forgetting: Mary Kelly's *Love Songs*," *Grey Room* 24 (Summer 2006): 26–67; and Paige Sarlin, "New Left-Wing Melancholy: Mark Tribe's *The Port Huron Project* and the Politics of Reenactment," http://www.16beavergroup.org/.

**98.** Nathan Hill, *The Nix* (New York: Alfred A. Knopf, 2016).

**99.** Hill, *The Nix*, 393, 407.

**100.** The Democratic Convention protests took place on August 23–28, 1968, before the fall semester began in most universities. Hill acknowledges the literary license he took to construct this narrative, "a blend of historical facts, eyewitness interviews, and the author's imagination, ignorance, and fancy." Hill, *The Nix*, 623.

**101.** The commercial distribution of the Portapak by Sony in 1967 generated the emergence of video art during the late Sixties.

**102.** William F. Pepper, "The Children of Vietnam," *Ramparts* (January 1967): 44-67. The portfolio was introduced by pediatrician Dr. Benjamin Spock. The images preceded by several years the famous photograph of burned children running in terror from Trang Bang, a village bombed with napalm on June 8, 1972.

**103.** "A Time to Break Silence," speech given at Riverside Church, New York City, April 4, 1967, reprinted in James Melvin Washington, ed., *The Essential Writings of Martin Luther King, Jr.* (New York: Harper Collins, 1986), 231–44.

**104.** A herbicide used by American and South Vietnamese forces from 1962 to 1971 to defoliate rural areas of Vietnam, Laos, and Cambodia to starve the enemy of food and cover (some 20 million gallons were dispersed). The chemical is alleged to have caused numerous fatalities, birth defects in hundreds of thousands of children, as well as high rates of cancer among U.S. veterans.

**105.** The protest is described in Tom Wells, *The War Within: America's Battle over Vietnam* (Berkeley: University of California Press, 1994), 193–94; and in David Maraniss, *They Marched into the Sunlight: War and Peace, Vietnam and America, October 1967* (New York: Simon & Schuster, 2003), 348–99. See also *Two Days in October* (2005), a PBS documentary inspired by Maraniss's book, directed by Robert Kenner.

**106.** The student, identified as Jonathan Stielstra, then climbed the roof of the administration building and cut down the American and school flags. Maraniss, *They Marched into the Sunlight: War and Peace Vietnam and America October 1967*, 239, 391-93.

**107.** Paul Soglin, the boy in the sheepskin coat, was brutally attacked. Maraniss, *They Marched into the Sunlight*, 376. As Maraniss describes, Soglin emerged as a leader of the antiwar movement at the university. Eventually elected to the Madison city council, he became the city's mayor six years later.

**108.** Another arm curls around the boy's neck. It would appear that this belongs to the young man with the thick-framed glasses: perhaps we glimpse a circle of close friends rather than a couple.

**109.** The protest was held in front of the White House on April 17, 1965.

**110.** *The Homosexuals* was broadcast on *CBS Reports* on March 7, 1967.

**111.** James Rowan quoted in Kenner, *Two Days in October*. "You didn't think the students would behave like that," said Joseph Kauffman, former dean of students, quoted in the same work.

**112.** Maraniss, *They Marched into the Sunlight*, 397.

**113.** As suggested by the exhibition "ACT UP New York: Activism, Art, and the AIDS Crisis 1987–1993," organized by Helen Molesworth and Claire Grace at the Carpenter Center for the Visual Arts and Harvard Art Museum, October 15–December 23, 2009.

**114.** Mark Godfrey notes a structure of splitting in many works by Buckingham in "The Artist as Historian," 150.

**115.** Departments of Afro-American Studies, American Indian Studies, and Women's Studies were founded in 1970, 1972, and 1975 respectively. The former Commerce Building houses some of these departments.

**116.** A gas spill at Bhopal, India, by the Dow subsidiary Union Carbide in 1984—often described as the worst industrial accident in modern times—led to the death and injury of thousands of people, while in 1988 Dow sold $1.5 million in insecticides to Iraq only months after Saddam Hussein's army murdered the Kurds of Halabja with poison gas. See Michael Dobbs, "U.S. Had Key Role in Iraq Buildup: Trade in Chemical Arms Allowed Despite Their Use on Iranians, Kurds," *Washington Post*, December 30, 2002. For a critical history of Dow's practices see Jack Doyle, *Trespass on Us: Dow Chemical and the Toxic Century* (Monroe, ME: Common Courage Press, 2004).

**117.** Matthew Buckingham, "Archives Are Where You Find Them" (2000), http://www.matthewbuckingham.net.

**118.** See Retort, *Afflicted Powers: Capital and Spectacle in a New Age of War* (New York: Verso, 2005); Jeremy Scahill, *Blackwater: The Rise of the World's Most Powerful Mercenary Army* (New York: Nation Books, 2008); P. W. Singer, *Corporate Warriors: The Rise of the Privatized Military Industry* (Ithaca: Cornell University Press, 2007); and Pratap Chatterjee, *Halliburton's Army: How a Well-Connected Texas Oil Company Revolutionized the Way America Makes War* (New York: Nation Books, 2010).

**119.** Dick Cheney quoted in Maraniss, *They Marched into the Sunlight*, 113.

**120.** Claiming student status, Cheney received repeated deferments. "The protest served as a reminder of a war [Cheney] supported but wished to avoid personally and politically." Matthew Buckingham, Artist's Statement, *Will Someone Please Explain It to Me, I've Just Become a Radical* (2008).

**121.** Paul Potter, "Name the System," reprinted in Mark Tribe, *The Port Huron Project: Reenactments of New Left Protest Speeches* (Milan: Edizioni Charta, 2010), 55.

**122.** The first U.S. Marines arrived in Vietnam on March 8, 1965. The Gulf of Tonkin Resolution, passed by Congress on August 7, 1964, authorized intervention after an American destroyer exchanged fire with North Vietnamese torpedo boats during a covert operation. The protest at which Potter spoke was held on April 17, 1965.

**123.** The performance took place in Washington, DC, on July 26, 2007. Tribe named the series for the "Port Huron Statement," a 1960 text that is considered the founding manifesto of the antiwar movement. Other reenactments included speeches by Stokely Carmichael, César Chavez, Angela Davis, Coretta Scott King, and Howard Zinn, presented between 1965 and 1971. The project includes a webpage, accessed under the artist's personal URL (http://www.marktribe.net/), containing a description of the project, films of each performance, installation shots, and press clippings.

**124.** Notable examples of the genre include Pierre Huyghe's two-channel video *The Third Memory* (1999), a restaging of the bank robbery fictionalized in Sidney Lumet's film *Dog Day Afternoon* (1975); Jeremy Deller's *The Battle of Orgreave* (2001), a re-creation of a 1984 British miners' strike; Francis Alÿs's *Reenactments* (2000), in which the artist restages his own arrest the day before for brandishing a gun; and Andrea Fraser's "Kunst muß hängen" ("Art Must Hang," 2001), the recitation of a speech by the Cologne-based artist Martin Kippenberger in the original German. For an account of this genre, see Sven Lütticken, *Life, Once More: Forms of Reenactment in Contemporary Art* (Amsterdam: Witte de With, 2005); and the special issue of *Journal of Aesthetics & Protest* 5 (September 2007).

**125.** In addition to the projects of Tribe, Malpede, and BLW discussed here, other significant Sixties and Seventies reenactments include Sharon Hayes's *Symbionese Liberation Army (SLA) Screeds #13, 16, 20 & 29* (2001–3), respeakings of four audio tapes of the kidnapped Patty Hearst addressing her parents; Kirsten Forkert's *Art Workers Coalition (Revisited)*, 2006 ongoing, a respeaking of an Art Workers Coalition Open Hearing of 1969; and Philippe Parreno's film *June 8, 1968* (2009), inspired by Paul Fusco's photographs of Robert Kennedy's funeral train. See Julia Bryan-Wilson, "Sounding the Fury," *Artforum* 46, no. 5 (January 2008): 95–96; "We Have a Future: An Interview with Sharon Hayes," *Grey Room* 37 (Fall 2009), 78–79; and Michael Fried, "*Sonnenuntergang*: On Philippe Parreno's *June 8, 1968*," http://nonsite.org/issue-1/sonnenuntergang-on-philippe-parreno's-june-8-1968.

**126.** "In language there are only differences without positive terms." Ferdinand de Saussure, *Course in General Linguistics*, trans. Wade Baskin (New York: Philosophical Library, 1959), 120.

**127.** Claude Lévi-Strauss, *The Raw and the Cooked*, trans. J. and D. Weightman (New York: Harper & Row, 1970), 339–40.

**128.** Roman Jakobson, "Why 'Mama' and 'Papa'?" in Linda R. Waugh and Monique Monville-Burston, eds., *On Language* (Cambridge, MA: Harvard University Press, 1990), 309. Jakobson suggests that the mastery of *mama* comes after that of *papa*. During this transitional period the word for "father," the more "distant" of the parents, is more readily cited than the word for "mother," which signals the desire for a "fulfillment of some need or for the absent fulfiller of childish needs" (310).

**129.** Lévi-Strauss, *The Raw and the Cooked*, 340 (my italics).

**130.** Roland Barthes, "The Structuralist Activity," in *Critical Essays*, trans. Richard Howard (Evanston, IL: Northwestern University Press, 1972), 215.

**131.** Lévi-Strauss, *The Raw and the Cooked*, 341.

**132.** On this point see Jennifer Allen, "'Einmal ist keinmal'—Observations on Reenactment," in Lütticken, *Life, Once More*, 185.

**133.** Jacques Derrida, "Différance," in *Margins of Philosophy*, trans. Alan Bass (Chicago: University of Chicago Press, 1982), 1–27.

**134.** Rosalind E. Krauss, "The Photographic Conditions of Surrealism," in *The Originality of the Avant-Garde and Other Modernist Myths* (Cambridge, MA: MIT Press, 1985), 109. See also Craig Owens, "Photography *en abyme*" (1977), in Scott Bryson, Barbara Kruger, Lynne Tillman, and Jane Weinstock, eds., *Beyond Recognition: Representation, Power, and Culture* (Berkeley: University of California Press, 1992), 16–30.

**135.** John Cage, "On Robert Rauschenberg, Artist, and His Work," in *Silence* (Middletown, CT:

Wesleyan University Press, 1961), 102. Cage is describing Rauschenberg's *Factum I* and *Factum II* (1957). For a further discussion of these works see Branden W. Joseph, *Random Order: Robert Rauschenberg and the Neo-Avant-Garde* (Cambridge, MA: MIT Press,2003), 191–205.

**136.** As she prepared *WLM Remix*, Kelly did not ask the women who posed for the photo to come in period dress. They showed up that way: the "look" of the earlier moment had become fashionable again. "Body Politic: Mary Kelly Interviewed by Ian White," *Frieze* 107 (May 2007): 133.

**137.** Kelly inserts a clue distinguishing the versions. The placard in the 1970 image reads UNITE FOR WOMEN'S EMANCIPATION. It is replaced by the sign in Kelly's 2005 reenactment that reads FROM STONE TO CLOUD, an excerpt from Sylvia Plath's 1960 poem "Love Letter," a Sixties allusion, until the 1970 sign bleeds in.

**138.** Gilles Deleuze, *Difference and Repetition*, trans. Paul Patton (New York: Columbia University Press, 1994), 69.

**139.** *Womanhouse* was a collaborative art project organized by Judy Chicago and Miriam Schapiro in a soon-to-be-demolished house in Los Angeles from January 30 to February 28, 1972.

**140.** Kelly's *Interim, Part III: Historia* (1989), an installation of four pedestals surmounted by shapes resembling open books, points to the theme of sculpture-as-book explored in *Multi-Story House*.

**141.** As I describe in "The Minimal Unconscious," *October* 130 (Fall 2009): 141–76.

**142.** As marked by another work in the *Love Songs* sequence, *Flashing Nipple Remix* (2005), a reenactment of a 1971 protest performance staged outside the Miss World Contest in London. Kelly and the other performers attached lights to their shirts at their nipples and to the crotches of their pants. A dance of choreographed movements illuminated and animated these anatomical parts, while obscuring the performer's faces and the rest of their bodies.

**143.** Kelly's students during the 2000s, these women inspired the making of *Love Songs*. "Body Politic: Mary Kelly Interviewed by Ian White," 133.

**144.** Grant, "Fans of Feminism," 283.

**145.** A future we are arguably now in. The anticipatory aspect of *Love Songs* was borne out by the Women's March of January 21, 2017, immediately following the inauguration of President Donald Trump. Attracting millions of protesters internationally, the event promised a new "wave" of feminist politics in the process of defining itself.

**146.** Respeaking is thus a form of "spectropoetics," defined by T. J. Demos as an aesthetic attention to "the haunting memories and ghostly presences that refuse to rest in peace and cannot be firmly situated within representation." T. J. Demos, *Return to the Postcolony: Specters of Colonialism in Contemporary Art* (Berlin: Sternberg Press, 2013), 8.

**147.** Freud speaks of the uncanniness of the double, the unfamiliarity of a thing that resembles another thing, a form of resemblance and differentiation that he and Otto Rank relate to the narcissistic fantasy of immortality and its inverse, death. Sigmund Freud, "The 'Uncanny,'" in *The Standard Edition of the Complete Psychological Works of Sigmund Freud*, trans. James Strachey (London: Hogarth Press, 1955), 236. On the uncanny and reenactment, see the brief remarks in Arne, "History Will Repeat Itself," 53–55.

**148.** The speech was delivered on April 15, 1967, as part of the Spring Mobe (Mobilization to End the War in Vietnam) protest. Unable to secure permission to hold the event at the original site, Tribe staged the event in nearby Tudor City on September 7, 2008.

**149.** Photographs indicate that Carmichael wore a jacket, tie, and trench coat.

**150.** https://www.marktribe.net/port-huron-project/let-another-world-be-born-stokley-carmichael-1967-2008/. Tribe put up online only the first of the two performances. Ultimately, the "time" of contemporary reenactment is more fractured and multiply layered than my account of temporal juxtaposition, or doubling, implies. See Rebecca Schneider, "Now and Again," in Tribe, *The Port Huron Project*, 21–25. Schneider examines the temporalities of reenactment in depth in *Performance Remains: Art and War in Times of Theatrical Reenactment* (New York: Routledge, 2011).

**151.** Stokely Carmichael, "Let Another World Be Born" (1967), in Tribe, *The Port Huron Project*, 31.

**152.** President Nixon ended the draft in 1973 to quell antiwar dissent. The percentage of African American soldiers in the U.S. military increased after this decision from 17 percent to a high of 24 percent during the Eighties. U.S. Department of Defense, http://www.defense.gov/home/features/2007/blackhistorymonth/ timeline.html. After September 11, 2001, black enrollment declined due to low approval ratings for the Bush administration in the African American community. Joseph Williams and Kevin Baron, "Military Sees Decline in Black Enlistees: Iraq War Cited in 58% Drop since 2000," *Boston Globe*, October 7, 2007.

**153.** Tribe, *The Port Huron Project*, 52, 54.

**154.** President George W. Bush, Speech at the Veterans of Foreign Wars Convention, Kansas City, Missouri, *New York Times*, August 22, 2007, http://www.nytimes.com/2007/08/22/washington/ w23policytext.html. Equating the destruction of the Twin Towers with Pearl Harbor, Bush made a spurious connection between the Iraq War and the Allied invasion of Normandy: Omaha Beach then, Baghdad now.

**155.** Antonio Negri and Michael Hardt, *Empire* (Cambridge, MA: Harvard University Press, 2000), 169.

**156.** Kennedy visited Kentucky on February 13–14, 1968. His "Poverty Tours" brought him to the Mississippi Delta, a Navajo reservation in New Mexico, urban neighborhoods in Brooklyn and San Francisco, and California's Central Valley.

**157.** Prior to the 2004 reenactment Malpede spent several years in eastern Kentucky retracing Kennedy's itinerary in local archives and conducting interviews with individuals who participated in the historic tour. The project remains ongoing in the form of a webpage: http://rfkineky.org/project/about.htm.

**158.** Kennedy's former assistant Peter Edelman shared his recollections of the tour, which he organized.

**159.** Queen Mother Moore quoted in BLW, "I am going to tell you something no one else can tell you who wasn't there . . . ," *Journal of Aesthetics and Protest* 5 (September 2007), http://www.joaap.org/5/articles/BLW/BLW.htm. Henceforth, Garvey's speeches were greeted by audiences with the command "Speak, Garvey, speak!" Colin Grant, *Negro with a Hat: The Rise and Fall of Marcus Garvey and His Dream of Mother Africa* (New York: Oxford University Press, 2008), 357.

**160.** *RKY in EKY Times*, September 8–11, 2004, pdf handout. http://rfkineky.org/project/about.htm.

**161.** BLW, "I am going to tell you something no one else can tell you who wasn't there . . ." (my italics).

**162.** As Rebecca Schneider argues in *Performing Remains*, 182.

**163.** BLW's collaboration with the City Studio Youth Art Education Project in San Francisco occurred on March 18, 2008. See http://citystudio-pic.blogspot.com/2008/03/saturday-performance-workshop-with-blw.html.

**164.** On the uses of the shadow and other indices as mnemonic traces, see Lisa Saltzman, *Making Memory Matter: Strategies of Remembrance in Contemporary Art* (Chicago: University of Chicago Press, 2006).

**165.** The present study follows the claim of structuralist epistemology that history is synchronic, and thus discontinuous, in opposition to historicism's view that history unfolds linearly and continuously. Theorized by such philosophers of knowledge as Alexandre Koyré and Georges Canguilhem, this premise is most famously espoused by Michel Foucault.

**166.** Walter Benjamin, "Theses on the Philosophy of History," in *Illuminations*, ed. Hannah Arendt (New York: Schocken Books, 1969), 262.

**167.** Benjamin, "Theses on the Philosophy of History," 256.

**168.** Benjamin, "Theses on the Philosophy of History," 261. Benjamin's translator Harry Zohn relates Benjamin's term to the mystical *nunc stans* of Thomas Aquinas (the "eternal now").

**169.** As Susan Buck-Morss notes, the "Theses" rephrases the Enlightenment dream of universal freedom and equality in the prophetic language of the Kabbalah as interpreted by Benjamin's friend and colleague Gershom Scholem. Susan Buck-Morss, *The Dialectics of Seeing: Walter Benjamin and the Arcades Project* (Cambridge, MA: MIT Press, 1989), 231, 233.

**170.** My remarks are inspired by the distinction between passive and active memory in Renée Green, *Between and Including* (Vienna: Secession, 1999), 66, 180.

**171.** Benjamin, "Theses on the Philosophy of History," 261 (my italics).

**172.** Benjamin, "Theses on the Philosophy of History," 257, 263. Describing memory as digging, Benjamin characterizes the work of the historian in a metaphor drawn from atomic physics: "I set forth how this project—as in the method of smashing an atom—releases the enormous energy of history that lies bound in the 'once upon a time' of classical historical narrative." Quoted in Buck-Morss, *The Dialectics of Seeing*, 250.

**173.** Walter Benjamin, *The Arcades Project*, trans. Howard Eiland and Kevin McLaughlin (Cambridge, MA: Belknap Press of Harvard University Press, 1999), 470. The statement appears in Konvolut (File) N, the section of Benjamin's research on historical method that informed the writing of the "Theses."

**174.** Benjamin, "Theses on the Philosophy of History," 263.

**175.** Benjamin, *The Arcades Project*, 462; Benjamin, "Theses on the Philosophy of History," 263.

**176.** E. J. Hobsbawm, *The Age of Empire, 1875–1914* (London: Pantheon Books, 1987), 3. See also Saul Friedländer, *Memory, History, and the Extermination of the Jews of Europe* (Bloomington: Indiana University Press, 1993), viii.

**177.** On the historians' controversy see Friedländer, *Memory, History, and the Extermination of the Jews of Europe*, 64–101. For a helpful survey of the "memory boom," see Gavriel D. Rosenfeld, "A Looming Crash or a Soft Landing? Forecasting the Future of the Memory 'Industry,'" *Journal of Modern History* 81 (March 2009): 122–58.

**178.** Charles Meier, "A Surfeit of Memory? Reflections on History, Melancholy, and Denial," *History and Memory* (Fall–Winter 1993): 147. A similar argument appears in Andreas Huyssen, *Twilight Memories: Marking Time in a Culture of Amnesia* (New York: Routledge, 1995).

**179.** For another account of aesthetic "returns" to sites of traumatic memory see Demos, *Return to the Postcolony*. As the author notes, Bhimji and other artists in this study "are of a generation born during the Sixties and Seventies, and are thus considering the colonial history of their parents' and grandparents' generations" (10).

**180.** The signing of the Buganda Agreement in 1900, named for the kingdom of Buganda (where the capital, Kampala, is located), defined the territory of Uganda as a British Protectorate. Under this definition Uganda was subject to "indirect rule," a form of domination that accrued wealth to the British empire but did not entail large-scale settlement of English subjects on appropriated lands. Some control was retained by the kabaka (king) of Buganda and other local authorities. On the distinction between direct and indirect rule, see Mahmood Mamdani, *Citizen and Subject: Contemporary Africa and the Legacy of Late Colonialism* (Princeton: Princeton University Press, 1996.)

**181.** Historians trace the depredations of postcolonial Uganda to the country's colonial and precolonial origins. During the late eighteenth and early nineteenth centuries, the Baganda kings (kabakas) established a pattern of cruel behavior later adopted by British governors who favored the kingdom of Buganda in the south over other kingdoms to the north and west, and the Baganda over other ethnic groups. See A. B. K. Kasozi, *The Social Origins of Violence in Uganda, 1964–1985* (Montreal: McGill-Queen's University Press, 1994); and Phares Mutibwa, *Uganda since Independence: A Story of Unfulfilled Hopes* (Tenafly, NJ: Africa World Press, 1992).

**182.** Sidney Littlefield Kasfir, "Up Close and Far Away: Renarrating Buganda's Troubled Past," *African Arts* 45, no. 32 (Autumn 2012): 57.

**183.** Chika Okeke-Agulu, "Conversation with Zarina Bhimji," *Art Journal* (Winter 2010): 74.

**184.** Idi Amin quoted in *Uganda Argus*, August 10, 1972, reprinted in Okeke-Agulu, "Conversation with Zarina Bhimji," 73.

**185.** Riots had already broken out against Asian businesspeople during the Forties. In 1968 Obote established a committee on the "Africanization of Commerce and Industry" to explore the illegal appropriation of Asian property. Mutibwa, *Uganda since Independence*, 8.

**186.** The expulsion of the Asians followed that of thirty thousand Kenyan workers in 1969, and of Uganda's small Israeli population earlier in 1972, as Amin shifted his alliance from Israel to Gaddafi's Libya and other Islamic nations. Kasozi, *The Social Origins of Violence in Uganda*, 120; and Mutibwa, *Uganda since Independence*, 89–92.

**187.** An estimated 6 billion to 7 billion shillings were stolen. These assets and Asian-owned property were distributed to Amin's military cronies and the black middle class and peasantry, who showed little sympathy for the Asians' plight. Mutibwa, *Uganda since Independence*, 95. From an economic standpoint, the expulsion was a disaster: it destroyed the country's tax base, caused a shortage of skilled workers, and ruined Amin's efforts to attract foreign investments. Kasozi, *The Social Origins of Violence in Uganda*, 119–20.

**188.** Mahmood Mamdani, *From Citizen to Refugee: Uganda Asians Come to Britain* (London: Frances Pinter Ltd., 1973), 19.

**189.** "Flight of the Asians," *Time Magazine*, September 11, 1972, 24, 27–28.

**190.** Mamdani, *From Citizen to Refugee*, 65–66.

**191.** Bhimji titled this project *Love* (1998–2006).

**192.** The airport was the destination of an Air France plane hijacked by Palestinian guerrillas from Tel Aviv on July 4, 1976, the day of the U.S. Bicentennial, and the site of the successful rescue operation by Israeli forces.

**193.** Mamdani, *From Citizen to Refugee*, 27–28. On British quotas for refugees of color and nativist responses to the arrival of the Ugandan Asians, see Mamdani, *From Citizen to Refugee*, 73–127; and "Flight of the Asians," 27.

**194.** *Out of Blue* was commissioned for documenta XI by exhibition director Okwui Enwezor.

**195.** See T. J. Demos's excellent study of Bhimji's cinematic technique in "Ghostly Affect: Zarina Bhimji's Yellow Patch," in *Return to the Postcolony*, 72.

**196.** Marcel Proust, *The Captive*, trans. C. K. Scott Moncrieff, Terence Kilmartin, and Andreas Mayor (New York: Vintage Books, 1982), 185. Bhimji's interest in the "yellow patch" was inspired by a lecture she attended by the novelist Doris Lessing, who grew up in colonial Rhodesia (Zimbabwe) and authored the semi-autobiographical *Children of Violence*. Email to the author, April 26, 2017.

**197.** For Proust, the yellow patch represents not only a kind of aesthetic transcendence, but the asymptotical goal of aesthetic perfection. Proust's character, the elderly novelist Bergotte, goes to see *View of Delft* in the middle of an illness. As he looks at Vermeer's painting, his thoughts turn to his own art. He worries that his recent books were "too dry," lacking the rich color of the Dutch master; he ponders the sacrifices he has made in his life in his attempt to achieve aesthetic mastery. As Bergotte contemplates these questions, he collapses and dies, in front of the Vermeer.

**198.** Okeke-Agulu, "Conversation with Zarina Bhimji," 69.

199. Okeke-Agulu, "Conversation with Zarina Bhimji," 69.
200. Sigmund Freud, "Beyond the Pleasure Principle," in *The Freud Reader*, ed. Peter Gay (New York: W. W. Norton, 1989), 607.
201. Cathy Caruth, ed., *Trauma and Memory* (Baltimore: Johns Hopkins University Press, 1995), 5.
202. Bessel A. van der Kolk, "Trauma and Memory," in Bessel A. van der Kolk, Alexander C. McFarlane, and Lars Weisaeth, eds., *Traumatic Stress: The Effects of Overwhelming Experience on Mind, Body, and Society* (New York: Guilford Press, 1996), 287, 289, 296.
203. See Demos, "Ghostly Affect"; and Bhimji's remarks in "Interview with Sonia Boyce" in Zarina Bhimji, *I Will Always Be Here* (Birmingham, UK: Ikon, 1991), without pagination.
204. Bhimji's father first traveled to Uganda as a boy in the 1910s, and returned there in the 1920s.
205. In a nuanced reading of *Love Songs* inspired by Alain Badiou's notion of the "event," Rosalyn Deutsche describes feminism as a cross-generational "haunting" extending beyond and before the two moments represented by the work (1970/2005). As Deutsche notes, the 1970 march was itself a repetition of turn-of-the-century suffragist marches. Deutsche, "Not Forgetting: Mary Kelly's *Love Songs*," 33.
206. Achille Mbembe, *On the Postcolony* (Berkeley: University of California Press, 2001), 14.
207. *Jangbar* depicts the stations at Mackinnon Road, Molo, Kikuyu, Makindu, and Tsavo, Kenya. Some twenty-five hundred railroad builders died from the effects of malaria, heat exhaustion, and starvation, and the attacks of man-eating lions at the Tsavo River, as described in Charles Miller, *The Lunatic Express: An Entertainment in Imperialism* (New York: Macmillan, 1971), 289–392.
208. An-My Lê, "Interview with Hilton Als," in *Small Wars* (New York: Aperture, 2005), 123.
209. Lê, "Interview with Hilton Als," 121.
210. Lê worked for the Compagnons du Devoir du Tour de France after receiving her graduate degree in photography from Yale. Lê, "Interview with Hilton Als," 120.
211. The year 1970 witnessed the Kent State shootings, revolts on army bases, and the rise of Vietnam Veterans against the War, a group that staged Operation RAW (Rapid American Withdrawal), a mock four-day, search-and-destroy "mission" between Morristown, New Jersey, and Valley Forge, Pennsylvania, to "bring the war home" to American civilians. Wells, *The War Within*, 454–55.
212. Lê recalls: "I certainly wanted to avoid doing a project on the role the war played in my exploration of the Vietnamese landscape when I was able to return there in the mid-1990s. At the same time, it is difficult to ignore the complicated history of the country when you look at the landscape." Email to the author, June 25, 2012.
213. Anonymous woman quoted in Dinh Q. Lê, *The Farmers and the Helicopters* (2006), three-channel video.
214. See Rebecca Schneider's dissection of "high/low" hierarchies of reenactment in *Performance Remains*, 1–31.
215. Viet Thanh Nguyen, *Nothing Ever Dies: Vietnam and the Memory of War* (Cambridge, MA: Harvard University Press, 2016), 64.
216. "We were all artists trying to make sense of our own personal baggage." Lê, "Interview with Hilton Als," 121–22. Many of the participants had memories of the war connected to older siblings or fathers who had served in Vietnam.
217. See, for example, Hal Foster, "The Return of the Real," in *The Return of the Real: The Avant-Garde at the End of the Century* (Cambridge, MA: MIT Press, 1996), 127–70.
218. Sigmund Freud, "Remembering, Repeating, and Working-Through," in *The Standard Edition of the Complete Psychological Works of Sigmund Freud*, vol. 12, trans. James Strachey (London: Hogarth Press, 1950), 145–57. Laplanche and J.-B. Pontalis define "working through"

as "a sort of psychical work which allows the subject to accept certain repressed elements and to free himself from the grip of mechanisms of repetition." In a successful working-through, the patient is able to bring to the surface latent feelings of victimhood or violation. *The Language of Psychoanalysis* (New York: W. W. Norton, 1973), 488. For an elaboration of Freud's concept within the context of Holocaust testimony, see Dominick LaCapra, *History and Memory after Auschwitz* (Ithaca: Cornell University Press, 1998), 180–210.

**219.** The transgenerational trauma or "phantom" is examined in Nicolas Abraham and Maria Torok, *The Shell and the Kernel* (Chicago: University of Chicago Press, 1994), 165–206.

**220.** My focus in this study is on works of individual acts of return that disinter episodes of recent history for present-day use. Other works of Sixties or Seventies memory speak in a public voice. (Maya Lin's *Vietnam Veterans Memorial* [1983] on the Mall in Washington, DC, is the most celebrated work of this type.) A project of particular interest to the present study is Rafael Lozano-Hemmer's *Voz Alta* ("Loud Voice"; 2008), a commissioned work that took place in the Plaza de las Tres Culturas in Mexico City, the location of the Tlateloco massacre on the fortieth anniversary of the event. Invited to speak into a megaphone, individuals shared first- and secondhand memories of the massacre. A spotlight focused on the former Ministry of Foreign Affairs triggered three other spotlights that pointed in different directions: to due north; to the Zócalo square in the southeast; and to the Monument to the Revolution in the southwest. The searchlight flashed on and off and increased in intensity as each participant spoke. A local radio station broadcasted the event to listeners beyond the plaza. See http://www.lozano-hemmer.com/voz_alta.php.

**221.** As argued passionately within the context of contemporary France in Ross, *May '68 and Its Afterlives*, 1–3. On trauma and Holocaust narration, see Shoshana Felman and Dori Laub, *Testimony: Crises of Witnessing in Literature, Psychoanalysis, and History* (New York: Routledge, 1992); on the dominance of traumatic memory in recent theory, see Huyssen, *Present Pasts*, 8–9.

**222.** The writings of Marshall McLuhan, including *Understanding Media: The Extensions of Man* (1964), have been particularly influential. For a critical analysis of media's depiction of contemporary events during the Sixties, see Todd Gitlin, *The Whole World Is Watching: Mass Media in the Making and Unmaking of the New Left* (Berkeley: University of California Press, 1980).

**223.** Aristotle, "On Memory and Reminiscence," trans. J. I. Beare, in *The Basic Works of Aristotle*, ed. Richard McKeon (New York: Modern Library, 2001), 609–10.

**224.** "The Best of Life," in Vik Muniz, *Seeing Is Believing* (New York: International Center for Photography, 1998), without pagination.

**225.** *Reflex: A Vik Muniz Primer* (New York: Aperture, 2005), 31.

**226.** See Joan Wallach Scott's important critique of the idea that subjective experience confers authenticity on an account, "The Evidence of Experience," *Critical Inquiry* 17, no. 4 (Summer 1991): 773–97.

**227.** "Introduction," in Sohnya Sayres et al., *The Sixties without Apology* (Minneapolis: University of Minnesota Press, 1984), 8.

**228.** *The Sixties without Apology* was published by the *Social Text* collective (founded in 1979). As Jameson noted, the concept of generation was as significant to this cohort as to "the Russians of the late 19th century." "Periodizing the Sixties," in Sayres et al., *The Sixties without Apology*, 178.

**229.** See "Who Owns the Sixties? The Opening of a Scholarly Generation Gap," *Lingua Franca* (May–June 1996).

**230.** Gerard J. DeGroot, *The Sixties Unplugged: A Kaleidoscopic View of a Disorderly Decade* (Cambridge, MA: Harvard University Press, 2008), 2.

**231.** Nora, "Generation," 525 (my italics).

**232.** "Time Is an Ocean: The Past and Future of the Sixties," *The Sixties: A Journal of History, Politics and Culture* 1, no. 1 (June 2008): 1.

**233.** "Narrative in the strictest sense is distinguished by the exclusive use of the third person and of such strict forms as the preterit and the pluperfect." Gérard Genette, "Boundaries of Narrative," *New Literary History* 8, no. 1 (Autumn 1976): 11.

**234.** My aim is not to diminish the archival turn in contemporary art history—a tendency I identify with and strongly support. As scholars grounded their interpretations in rigorous research, the art practices of the long Sixties have been historicized formally, discursively, and politically. But this necessitated a suppression of the critic's voice and personal memory, when, this book argues, a mnemonic and nostalgic fascination with the time of childhood or what precedes it impels many of these accounts.

**235.** Otto F. Gmelin committed suicide in 1995, a detail I explore later in this essay.

**236.** The milieu of DFFB students in this period is described in Nora M. Alter, *Projecting History: German Nonfiction Cinema 1967–2000* (Ann Arbor: University of Michigan Press, 2002), 50n19 and 77–80.

**237.** For a fine account of Gmelin's project, see David Rimanelli, "Revolutionary Time Warp: Felix Gmelin's *Farbtest, Die Rote Fahne II*," in *Felix Gmelin: The Aging Revolution* (Frankfurt: Portikus, 2005), without pagination.

**238.** For a survey of these writings (Günter Grass, Peter Schneider, Bernward Vesper, Uwe Timm, and Leander Scholz), see Ingo Cornils, "Writing the Revolution: The Literary Representation of the German Student Movement as Counter-Culture," in Steve Giles and Maike Oergel, eds., *Counter-Cultures in Germany and Central Europe: From Sturm und Drang to Baader-Meinhof* (Oxford: Peter Lang, 2003), 295–314. As Cornils argues, the sequence of events I recount is rehearsed in most of these texts.

**239.** Fritz Teufel quoted in William Grimes, "Fritz Teufel, a German Protester in the '60s, Dies at 67." *New York Times*, August 8, 2010.

**240.** Harun Farocki quoted in "Risking His Life: Images of Holger Meins," in *Nachdruck/Imprint: Texts/Writings* (New York: Lukas & Sternberg, 2001), 278. See also Farocki's recollections in Antje Ehmann and Koduro Eshon, eds., *Against What? Against Whom?* (London: Raven Row, 2010), 221–22.

**241.** The cause of the deaths of Meinhof, Raspe, Ensslin, and Baader is much contested. The sole survivor of October 18, 1977, Irmgard Möhler, insisted no suicide pact had been made. For a discussion of this controversy, see Leith Passmore, *Ulrike Meinhof and the Red Army Faction: Performing Terrorism* (London: Palgrave Macmillan, 2011), 103–17.

**242.** The coalition was an alliance of the CDU (Christian Democratic Union) and SD (Social Democratic) parties. The German student Leftist organization, Sozialistischer Deutscher Studentenbund, had the same acronym as Students for a Democratic Society in the United States.

**243.** Kiesinger, a former Nazi party member, had overseen the international radio propaganda program of the Foreign Ministry under Goebbels. Nick Thomas, *Protest Movements in Sixties West Germany: A Social History of Dissent and Democracy* (New York: Berg, 2003), 93. Hans Globke, a director of the Federal Chancellory, had co-authored the original Emergency Laws that brought Hitler to power and the Reich Citizenship Law that revoked citizenship of German Jews, among other anti-Semitic regulations. Werner Heyde, an administrator of the Nazi "euthanasia" program, worked as a psychiatrist and civil servant after the war under an alias under the protection of prominent judges and physicians. Theodor Oberländer, minister of displaced persons under Chancellor Adenauer and a member of the Reichstag, had been actively involved in "ethnic cleansing" programs in the East. The president of

West Germany from 1959 to 1969, Heinrich Lübke, had worked as an engineer for Albert Speer.

**244.** Thomas, *Protest Movements in Sixties West Germany*, 72–74. On the West German student Left in 1966–68 see also Stefan Aust, *The Baader-Meinhof Group: The Inside Story of a Phenomenon*, trans. Anthea Bell (London: Bodley Head, 2008); and Jeremy Varon, *Bringing the War Home: The Weather Underground, the Red Army Faction, and Revolutionary Violence in the Sixties and Seventies* (Berkeley: University of California Press, 2004).

**245.** The plot was foiled, the hippie plotters arrested. The irony was not lost on Meinhof, who noted that a pie thrown in Humphrey's face was considered a crime; dropping napalm on civilians was not. See "Napalm and Pudding" (1967) in Ulrike Meinhof, *Everybody Talks about the Weather... We Don't: The Writings of Ulrike Meinhof*, ed. Karin Bauer (New York: Seven Stories Press, 2007), 229–33. See also Aust, *The Baader-Meinhof Group*, 19–22.

**246.** "Open Letter to Farah Diba" (1967) in Meinhof, *Everybody Talks about the Weather... We Don't*, 171–77. The Shah was restored to the throne in 1953 during a U.S.-led coup after the democratically elected prime minister, Mohammed Mossadegh, proposed to nationalize the Iranian oil fields. Known as Operation Ajax, the coup was instigated by CIA director Allan Dulles and Kermit Roosevelt, Jr., a grandson of President Theodore Roosevelt. On the visit of the Pahlavis to Berlin, see Thomas, *Protest Movements in Sixties West Germany*, 107–23.

**247.** Thomas, *Protest Movements in Sixties West Germany*, 108–10. See also Jillian Becker, *Hitler's Children: The Story of the Baader-Meinhof Gang* (London: Michael Joseph, 1977), 36 and following.

**248.** Erich Duensing quoted in Thomas, *Protest Movements in Sixties West Germany*, 115.

**249.** Thomas, *Protest Movements in Sixties West Germany*, 112. Ohnesorg's killer, Karl-Heinz Kurras, an agent of the East German Stasi, was twice acquitted for the crime.

**250.** Gudrun Ensslin, June 3, 1967, quoted in Tom Vague, *Televisionaries: The Red Army Faction Story 1963–1993* (San Francisco: AK Press, 1994), 10.

**251.** Varon, *Bringing the War Home*, 39.

**252.** The congress was held at the Free University on February 17–18, 1968. An estimated 5,000 activists attended. Thomas, *Protest Movements in Sixties West Germany*, 56–60.

**253.** Dutschke quoted in Klimke, *The Other Alliance*, 92.

**254.** On the participation of Smith and Robinson in the Vietnam Congress, see Klimke, *The Other Alliance*, 93.

**255.** Gudrun Ensslin cited in Aust, *The Baader-Meinhof Group*, 37.

**256.** "From Protest to Resistance" (1968) in Meinhof, *Everybody Talks about the Weather... We Don't*, 240.

**257.** The pretext of Meinhof's meeting with Baader was a phony interview conducted by the journalist at the German Central Institute for Social Questions in Berlin on May 14, 1970.

**258.** Jones and Stasinski, "Felix Gmelin Interview, December 13, 2003," without pagination. Conradt was one of many Sixties artists and filmmakers engaged with Muybridge's art. See Mel Bochner, "The Serial Attitude," *Artforum* 6, no. 4 (December 1967): 28–33; and Hollis Frampton, "Eadweard Muybridge: Fragments of a Tesseract," *Artforum* 11, no. 7 (March 1973): 43–52.

**259.** I am indebted to Gregg Bordowitz's discussion of Raymond Williams's "structure of feeling" in "The AIDS Crisis Is Ridiculous," in James Meyer, ed., *The AIDS Crisis Is Ridiculous and Other Writings 1986–2003* (Cambridge, MA: MIT Press, 2004), 43–68.

**260.** As Harum Farocki remarked to the author at a conference at the University of Florida, Gainesville, March 2006. According to the entry for *Der Rote Fahne* on the webpage of IMDB, Farocki was a co-director of the film, as were Holger Meins, Helke Sander, and Wolfgang Petersen, the future director of such commercial films as *Das Boot*, *Troy*, and

*The Perfect Storm*. Conradt was the cinematographer of Farocki's *Inextinguishable Fire*. Many of these students were enrolled in the seminar of the cinematographer Michael Ballhaus.

**261.** Varon, *Bringing the War Home*, 39–40; and Felix Gmelin, email to the author, March 9, 2006.

**262.** A period of liberalization in Czechoslovakia, followed by the invasion of that country by Warsaw Pact countries on August 20–21, 1968.

**263.** Richard Wolin, *The Wind from the East: French Intellectuals, the Cultural Revolution, and the Legacy of the Sixties* (Princeton: Princeton University Press, 2010).

**264.** China's break with the Soviet Union occurred in response to Khrushchev's alleged softened stance to imperialism and his repudiation of Stalin, as suggested by Roderick MacFarquhar and Michael Schoenhal, *Mao's Last Revolution* (Cambridge, MA: Belknap Press, 2006).

**265.** Sabine von Dirke, *"All Power to the Imagination!": The West German Counterculture from the Student Movement to the Greens* (Lincoln: University of Nebraska Press, 1997), 44.

**266.** Gao Minglu, *Total Modernity and the Avant-Garde in Twentieth Century Chinese Art* (Cambridge, MA: MIT Press, 2011), 34–35. As Gao explains, the principle of *wenhua yishi* draws from both Confucian and Chinese avant-gardist traditions, as well as Marxist-Leninist aesthetics, which it also critiques. It also draws from the Romantic conception of culture as a "way of life ... whether of a people, a period, a group," which Raymond Williams traces to philosopher Johann Gottfried Herder, among others. Williams, "Culture," in *Keywords*, 87–93.

**267.** *Quotations from Chairman Mao Tsetung* (Peking [Beijing]: Foreign Languages Press, 1972), 266.

**268.** "Mao Tsetung" is the transliteration in use at that time, while "Mao Zedong" is the current transliteration of the name. As Mao observed, "The fundamental cause of the development of a thing is not external but internal. It lies within the contradictoriness within the thing." Mao Tsetung, "On Contradiction," in *Five Essays on Philosophy* (Peking [Beijing]: Foreign Languages Press, 1977), 26.

**269.** *Quotations from Chairman Mao Tsetung*, 14–15.

**270.** Wolin, *The Wind from the East*, 124.

**271.** Harun Farocki, Interview, in Gerd Conradt, *Starbuck Holger Meins* (film), 2001. Farocki is describing his film *Die Worte des Vorsitzenden* (*The Words of the Chairman*; 1967).

**272.** The activities of the Tel Quel group, which published two double issues on Maoism in 1972 and visited China in 1974, exemplify this phantasmatic Maoism. Even an observer as well informed as scholar John K. Fairbank described the Cultural Revolution as "the best thing that happened to the Chinese people in centuries." Quoted in Wolin, *The Wind from the East*, 126. For some, the translation of Maoist ideas to Western life proved to be extremely generative. Rather counterintuitively, the Maoist critique of culture confirmed the critique of everyday life already under way in Situationist circles (and taken up by the French feminist and gay rights movements), while the chairman's analysis of bureaucracy and expertise found sympathetic ears among the May 1968 protesters and those followers of Foucault and Althusser who developed a localized politics centered on the *enquête* of institutions. For many others, though, the effort to "be Chinese" proved less fruitful. The "poetical" readings of Maoist maxims calcified into doctrinaire interpretations. The "criticism/self-criticism" (CSC) interrogations conducted by the Weathermen, also known as "Weatherfries," where members charged one another with allegations of racism, sexism, individualism, and revisionist sentiments for hours on end, were nearly as emotionally abusive as the struggle sessions being conducted inside China. This blind devotion to Maoist principles led to more dramatic acts of violence by the Weathermen and RAF.

**273.** Edward Said, *Orientalism* (New York: Vintage Books, 1978), 7. For a critique of Third World exoticism in the German context, see Bahman Nirumand, "Sehnsuchtsräume: Warum die

Revolution ausblieb," in Daniel Cohn-Bendit and Rüdiger Dammann, eds., *1968: Die Revolte* (Frankfurt: S. Fischer Verlag, 2007), 223–34. Gmelin explores this theme in greater depth in *Two Films Exchanging Soundtracks* (2004), a two-channel projection that crosses Michael Makritsch's *Traktat* (1967), which explores the idea of personal liberation through hashish, and Cecilia Linqvist's *Revolutionens Barn* (*Children of the Revolution*; 1974), which compares the educational systems in socialist Sweden and China.

**274.** The protest occurred outside Moabit Prison on November 28, 1967. For images of red flags in Sixties protest, see Becker, *Hitler's Children*, 205; and Astrid Proll, ed., *Baader-Meinhof/Pictures on the Run 67–77* (Zurich: Scalo, 1998), 52.

**275.** On the RAF's identification with the characters of *Moby-Dick* and their battle against the BRD with Ahab's quixotic pursuit of the white whale, see Aust, *The Baader-Meinhof Group*, 192–95. On Meins as "Starbuck" see Varon, *Bringing the War Home*, 220; and Conradt, *Starbuck Holger Meins*.

**276.** See Ulrike Meinhof's description of that experience, "From the Dead Tract," http://www.germanguerilla.com/red-army-faction/documents/72-73-meinhof.html.

**277.** The first hunger strike was instigated by Baader on January 17, 1973; the second on May 8, 1973; the third by Meinhof on September 13, 1974. Meins died on the fifty-fourth day of the final strike. Scores of strikers participated in each action (Varon, *Bringing the War Home*, 218–19). For an excellent account of the strikes and their significance, see Leith Passmore, "The Art of Hunger: Self-Starvation in the Red Army Faction," *German History* 27, no. 1 (January 1, 2009): 32–59. For a description by one of the participants, see Margrit Schiller, *Remembering the Armed Struggle: Life in Baader-Meinhof* (London: Zidane Press, 2009), 138 and following.

**278.** Meins's final days are described in Aust, *The Baader-Meinhof Group*, 206–9.

**279.** The image is reproduced in the photo gallery in Aust, *The Baader-Meinhof Group*. On Meins's funeral see Aust, *The Baader-Meinhof Group*, 210–12; Varon, *Bringing the War Home*, 220; and Schiller, *Remembering the Armed Struggle*, 142–43.

**280.** "The Germans even forbade us to use the words 'corpse' or 'victim.' The dead were blocks of wood, shit, with absolutely no importance. . . . [They] made us refer to the bodies as *Figuren*, that is, as puppets, as dolls." Itzhak Dugin, survivor of Vilna, in Claude Lanzmann, ed., *Shoah: An Oral History of the Holocaust* (New York: Pantheon, 1985), 12–13.

**281.** As argued in Passmore, "The Art of Hunger," 53.

**282.** Even Meins's funeral took the form of a protest, culminating in a famous remark by Dutschke at his friend's graveside ("Holger, the struggle will continue"). The charge of extrajudicial murder remains open to question. As Meins's supporters noted, the daily caloric intake of 600–800 calories administered by the Wittlich doctors was well below the 1,200–1,600 calories needed for survival.

**283.** Beate Sturm, a friend of Meins, recalled seeing him with several volumes of the works of Chairman Mao. "He had underlined the great man's pithy sayings on every page." Aust, *The Baader-Meinhof Group*, 89. An anonymous female figure quoted in Conradt's film *Starbuck Holger Meins* (possibly Sturm) reiterates this point.

**284.** Gmelin recalls having "only a vague idea" of his father's political activities then (Otto's participation in the Easter protests, his appearance in *Die Rote Fahne* and other underground films). Felix Gmelin, conversation with the author, Williamstown, Massachusetts, February 23, 2007.

**285.** Born in Heidelberg in 1962, Gmelin followed his parents to several cities in West Germany and to southern Spain before they lived in Berlin from 1967 to 1969 and settled in Gothenburg, Sweden, in 1969.

**286.** "Felix Gmelin: Interview with Ronald Jones and Robert Stasinski," without pagination.

287. Benjamin, "A Berlin Chronicle," 26.
288. Buck-Morss, *The Dialectics of Seeing*, 39.
289. "In the year 1932, as I was abroad, it began to be clear to me that I soon would have to take leave of the city in which I was born, perhaps permanently. I had experienced the procedure of immunization several times in my life as healing; I adhered to it again in this situation and called forth in myself those images that in exile are wont to awaken homesickness most strongly, those of childhood. The feeling of nostalgia was not allowed to dominate my spirit anymore." Envelope No. 1, Benjamin Papers, Georges Bataille Archive, Bibliothèque Nationale, Paris, quoted in Buck-Morss, *The Dialectics of Seeing*, 390n84. Benjamin's attempts to "self-immunize" himself against homesickness may possibly explain his excision in the 1938 version of several sections of a more personal nature from the 1932 and 1932–34 versions as he attempted to achieve a more strictly materialist analysis. See Howard Eiland, "Translator's Foreword," in Walter Benjamin, *Berlin Childhood around 1900*, trans. Howard Eiland (Cambridge, MA: Belknap Press of Harvard University Press, 2006), x–xi.
290. Benjamin drafted the first version, "A Berlin Chronicle," in Ibiza and Poveromo, Italy, in 1932 under contract to a Berlin weekly, *Die literarische Welt*. He reworked this draft into several different versions (renamed *Berlin Childhood around 1900*) between 1932 and 1938. Despite repeated attempts, Benjamin was never able to publish the text in its entirety. On the history of the writing and publication of his Berlin text, see Eiland, "Translator's Foreword," vii–xvi.
291. "Berlin Childhood around 1900: 1934 Version," in Walter Benjamin, *Selected Writings, 1935–1938*, vol. 3, trans. Edmund Jephcott, Howard Eiland, and others (Cambridge, MA: Belknap Press of Harvard University Press, 2002), 394–95.
292. Benjamin, "A Berlin Chronicle," 26, 28.
293. Benjamin, "Berlin Childhood around 1900: 1934 Version," 392.
294. On Benjamin's identity as the scion of well-to-do Jewish forebears, see Hannah Arendt, "Introduction: Walter Benjamin: 1892–1940," in *Illuminations: Essays and Reflections*, 1–55.
295. Benjamin, "A Berlin Chronicle," 37, 46; and "From *Berlin Childhood around 1900*, 1932–1934 Version," in Benjamin, *Berlin Childhood around 1900*, 159. Benjamin's mother, Pauline Schönflies, died in 1930, two years before he began his text.
296. Dana Spiotta, *Eat the Document* (New York: Scribner, 2006).
297. See Gregory Bateson, *Steps to an Ecology of Mind: Collected Essays in Anthropology, Psychiatry, Evolution, and Epistemology* (Chicago: University of Chicago Press, 1972).
298. As argued in the important study by Alexander and Margarete Mitscherlich, *The Inability to Mourn: Principles of Collective Behavior* (New York: Grove Press, 1975).
299. Michael Schneider, "Fathers and Sons Retrospectively: The Damaged Relationship between Two Generations," trans. Jamie Owen Daniel, *New German Critique* 31 (Winter 1984): 5, 8–9.
300. Schneider, "Fathers and Sons Retrospectively," 9–10.
301. Examples of the genre include Christoph Meckel, *Suchbild: Über Meinen Vater* (Picture Puzzle: About My Father), and Sigfrid Gauch, *Vaterspuren* (Traces of Father), among other texts.
302. Schneider, "Fathers and Sons Retrospectively," 34.
303. Ulrike Meinhof, "Hitler within You" (1960), in *Everybody Talks about the Weather... We Don't*, 138–43.
304. Otto Franz Gmelin (1886–1940), the author of numerous neo-Romantic novels, belonged to the Bamberger Dichterkreis (1936–43), the consortium of National Socialist authors. According to Felix Gmelin, Otto Franz was "probably" his father's uncle. The younger Otto referred to him as "the Nazi." Email to the author, March 8, 2012.
305. On the "third" generation see Eric Santner, *Stranded Objects: Mourning, Memory and Film in Postwar Germany* (Ithaca: Cornell University Press, 1990), 46.

306. Aust, *The Baader-Meinhof Group*, 55.

307. Left as an infant with his father Bernward Vesper (son of Nazi writer Will Vesper and author of the *Vaterliteratur* text *Die Reise* (*The Journey*), Felix Ensslin became an orphan after Vesper killed himself in 1971 and his mother died during the German Autumn. In 2005 Ensslin co-curated the exhibition "Zur Vorstellung des Terrors: Die RAF" in collaboration with Klaus Biesenbach at Kunst Werken Berlin. For a fine discussion of this history and the representation of Ensslin in Alexander Kluge's film *Deutschland im Herbst (German in Autumn)*, see Alter, *Projecting History*, 71–75.

308. Brought to a hippie settlement in Sicily, the girls never made it to the refugee camp, which was bombed by the Israelis before they arrived. They were eventually located by the writer Stefan Aust and reunited with their father, as described in Aust, *The Baader-Meinhof Group*, 75–78.

309. Ulrike Meinhof, from a filmed interview of 1969, reproduced in Shane O'Sullivan, *Children of the Revolution* (film; 2011). O'Sullivan's film also explores the history of Fusako Shigenobu, founder of the Japanese Red Army in 1971, and her daughter Mei Shigenobu. On the construction of Meinhof's mental illness, a condition attributed to a brain operation in 1962, see Passmore, "The Art of Hunger," 46–48.

310. Bettina Röhl, from an interview in O'Sullivan, *Children of the Revolution*. For more on this history see Bauer, "In Search of Ulrike Meinhof," 72.

311. Röhl, from an interview in O'Sullivan, *Children of the Revolution*.

312. Bettina Röhl, "Unsere Mutter—'Staatsfiend No. 1,'" *Der Spiegel* 29 (1995): 88–109; "Icon of the Left, Propagandist, and Communist," in Bauer, *Everybody Talks about the Weather... We Don't*, 256–63.

313. Röhl, from an interview in O'Sullivan, *Children of the Revolution*.

314. Bettina Röhl, *So macht Kommunismus Spass! Ulrike Meinhof, Klaus Rainer Röhl und die Akte Konkret* (Hamburg: EuropSische VA, 2006).

315. The posthumous reputation of Meinhof is also explored in Silvia Kolbowski's video *A Few Howls Again?* (2008–9). Kolbowski depicts a model in profile lying on the floor in a blue prison shirt, a pose based on a famous photo of Meinhof's corpse in her cell at Stammheim. Her face is pale, and her neck is ribboned with a red scar from hanging. Statements written in the first person from the imaginary point of view of Meinhof allow her to "speak" after more than three decades—to describe the controversy around the circumstances of her death and to protest her mythification (as Röhl has done). "Meinhof" rises up briefly, and then, lying down, falls back into silence.

316. Röhl, "Icon of the Left, Propagandist, and Communist," 259.

317. Röhl, "Icon of the Left, Propagandist, and Communist," 261.

318. The work is a revision of Gmelin's previous work, *Film Stills* (2004).

319. "Felix Gmelin: Interview with Ronald Jones and Robert Stasinski," without pagination.

320. Genesis 9:24 (King James Version).

321. Otto Gmelin's intentions in making the tape are unknown. A committed feminist, Otto may have conceived the tape as a critique of the performances of Otto Meuhl, who enlisted naked female models as mere "materials," or to explore the concept of "bankrupt masculinity" theorized in his book *Bankrott der Männerherrschaft* (The Bankruptcy of Masculine Power: Studies in Women's Emancipation; 1969), co-authored with Helen Saussure. In a previous film, a *tableau vivant* of *Déjeuner sur l'herbe*, Otto presents a naked young man surrounded by clothed female companions, inverting the traditional gendering of Manet's work.

322. Otto Gmelin died by his own hand in 1995, on Felix's wedding day. Email to the author, March 31, 2006.

323. Friedrich Nietzsche, *The Use and Abuse of History*, trans. Adrian Collins (Indianapolis: Liberal Arts Press, 1949), 4. My invocation of Nietzsche is indebted to a suggestive essay

by Yve-Alain Bois, *Susan Smith's Archaeology*, exhibition catalogue (New York: Margarete Roeder Gallery, 1989).

**324.** Nietzsche, *The Use and Abuse of History*, 5. Already Nietzsche has begun to advance the concept of eternal recurrence that would haunt his later work: the nagging suspicion that what has come before "will return again, and that whatever there is, *is* a return of itself, that it has all happened before, and will happen again exactly in the same way each time, forever." Arthur C. Danto, *Nietzsche as Philosopher* (New York: Columbia University Press, 2005), 183–84.

**325.** Danto, *Nietzsche as Philosopher*, 8.

**326.** Monumental history is indebted to Winckelmann, who describes antiquity as an incomparable model of emulation. Yet as Hayden White suggests, monumental history is equally futuristic (and thus modernist): the contemplation of prior deeds "points men toward the future on the basis of respect for past greatness." In this regard, Nietzsche's model suggests an important departure from a merely emulative conception of pastness. See Hayden White, *Metahistory: The Historical Imagination in Nineteenth Century Europe* (Baltimore: Johns Hopkins University Press, 1973), 350.

**327.** "Equal importance is given to everything, and ... too much to anything." Nietzsche, *The Use and Abuse of History*, 19.

**328.** Benjamin, "Theses on the Philosophy of History," 256.

**329.** Nietzsche, *The Use and Abuse of History*, 21.

**330.** Nietzsche, *The Use and Abuse of History*, 21.

**331.** See Huyssen, *Twilight Memories*, 6–7.

**332.** Nietzsche, *The Use and Abuse of History*, 5.

**333.** Nietzsche, *The Use and Abuse of History*, 21.

**334.** Nietzsche, *The Use and Abuse of History*, 9.

**335.** "It is impossible to shake off this chain." Nietzsche, *The Use and Abuse of History*, 9.

**336.** As argued in my essay "The Return of the Sixties in Contemporary Art and Criticism," in Okwui Enwezor, Nancy Condee, and Terry Smith, eds., *Antinomies of Art and Culture: Modernity, Postmodernity, Contemporaneity* (Durham, NC: Duke University Press, 2009), 324–32.

**337.** On the archival tendency in contemporary art, at once a staging of research and metacritical reflection on archival probity, see Hal Foster, "An Archival Impulse," *October* 110 (Fall 2004): 3–22.

**338.** Conradt has made a film composite of all of the versions entitled *Farbtest—Colourtest, 1968–2008* (2010).

**339.** As Felix Gmelin's projection *Manifesto* (2010) suggests. This work also revisits Otto Gmelin's participation in Makritsch's *Traktat*. Where in the original film Otto ventriloquizes the speech and gestures of German authority, in this work—a sequence of slides of stills from *Traktat*—Otto is robbed of his voice. The subtitles are quotations from the graphic designer and Canadian chief officer of design, Bruce Mau. Accompanied by the clicking sounds of a now obsolete carousel slide projector, a technology introduced by Kodak in 1962 and widely used during the Sixties, Otto "speaks" Mau's "theories" of "innovation," including aleatory procedures and other once avant-garde techniques.

**340.** On the spectacularization of Sixties and Seventies performance (exemplified by the problematic Marina Abramović retrospective at the Museum of Modern Art, "The Artist Is Present," 2010), see Carrie Lambert-Beatty, "Against Performance Art," *Artforum* 48, no. 9 (May 2010): 208–13.

**341.** See George Katsiaficas, *The Imagination of the New Left: A Global Analysis of 1968* (Boston: South End Press, 1987); David Caute, *The Year of the Barricades: A Journey through 1968* (New York: Harper & Row, 1988); Jeremi Suri, *Power and Protest: Global Revolution and the Rise of Détente* (Cambridge, MA: Harvard University Press, 2003); Gerard J. DeGroot, *The*

*Sixties Unplugged: A Kaleidoscopic History of a Disorderly Decade* (Cambridge, MA: Harvard University Press, 2008); Karen Dubinsky et al., eds., *New World Coming: The Sixties and the Shaping of Global Consciousness* (Toronto: Between the Lines Press, 2009); "The International 1968, Part I and Part II," *American Historical Review* 114, no. 1 (February 2009): 42–135 and (April 2009): 329–404; and "1968: Memories and Legacies of a Global Revolt," in Philipp Gassert and Martin Klimke, eds., *Bulletin of the German Historical Institute*, suppl. 6 (2009), 5–24.

**342.** A turn announced by the *Xingxing meizhan* ("First Exhibition of the Stars"), organized in the park next to the National Gallery in Beijing on September 27, 1979, concludes with the "China/Avant-Garde" exhibition held at the National Gallery in February 1989 and the Tiananmen Square events of that June.

**343.** On the circumstances that occasioned the emergence of the '85 movement, see Norman Bryson, "Something to Do with Freedom," in *Wu Shanzhuan: Red Humor International* (Hong Kong: Asia Art Archive, 2005), without pagination; and Gao, *Total Modernity and the Avant-Garde in Twentieth Century Chinese Art*, 4–9. Where Bryson observes that the '85 movement "emerges *from* the state," insofar as it was legitimated by party initiatives to foster economic growth, Gao Minglu argues that Chinese avant-gardism must be understood with a longer history of Chinese modernity, a modernity conceived from the beginning as an overcoming or rejection of the opposition of "art" and "life" constitutive of Western theories of modernism and avant-gardism.

**344.** Gao, *Total Modernity and the Avant-Garde in Twentieth Century Chinese Art*, 1.

**345.** Wu Hung, "The Cultural Revolution Revisited," in Wu Hung, ed., *Chinese Art at the Crossroads: Between Past and Future, East and West* (London: Institute of International Visual Arts, 2001), 14. According to Wu Hung, Political Pop "brought post–Cultural Revolution art to an end" (15). See also Wu Hung, "Ruins, Fragmentation, and the Chinese Modern/Postmodern," in Gao Minglu, ed., *Inside Out: New Chinese Art* (San Francisco: San Francisco Museum of Modern Art and Asia Society Galleries, 1998), 59–66. Of the practices I discuss, only Wu Shanzhuan's *Red Humor–Red Characters* (1987) conforms to this periodization. To my thinking, the practices of Jing Kewen, Shao Yinong and Mu Chen, Cai Guo-Ciang, and others suggest a more durational and recursive understanding of the idea of "post–Cultural Revolution" art, in which the vivid and traumatic memories of that time are perpetually and continually manifest.

**346.** Mannheim distinguishes the generation *tout court* from the "close circle" or "generation-unit." Dilthey's Romantics fall in the latter category. "The Problem of Generations," 303. Alan Spitzer argues that persons born in different places and into markedly distinct classes are not part of the same generation at all. Alan B. Spitzer, "The Historical Problem of Generations," *American Historical Review* 78, no. 5 (December 1973): 1355.

**347.** Jiang Ji-Li, *Red Scarf Girl: A Memoir of the Culture Revolution* (New York: Harper Collins, 1997), 28.

**348.** The red flag has also been described in sanguinary terms: "A (rectangular) piece of solidified 'blood.'" Wu Shanzhuan, "On the Space of Performance, Installation and Object," in *Wu Shanzhaun: Red Humor International*, Artist's Writings, 11.

**349.** Shao Yinong and Mu Chen, "It Is Not Merely a Memory," in Jiang Jiehong, ed., *Burden or Legacy: From the Chinese Culture Revolution to Contemporary Art* (Hong Kong: Hong Kong University Press, 2007), 91.

**350.** Jiang, *Red Scarf Girl*, 28.

**351.** Jiang, *Red Scarf Girl*, 107.

**352.** Yue Minjun (b. 1962), Geng Jianyi (b. 1962), and Fang Lijun (b. 1963).

**353.** The artist's nostalgic discourse ("I just want to paint the best condition of China of my time") is less engaging than his work. Jing Kewen quoted in Feng Boyi, "Memories,

Imagination, and 'Revolutionary Red,'" in *Memory Glory Dream: Paintings of Jing Kewen 1990–2007* (Beijing: Timezone 8 Limited, 2007), 30.

**354.** Jiang, *Red Scarf Girl*, 22–23.

**355.** Jiang, *Red Scarf Girl*, 30–31.

**356.** Moying Li, *Snow Falling in Spring: Coming of Age in China during the Cultural Revolution* (New York: Farrar, Straus & Giroux, 2008); Da Chen, *China's Son: Growing Up in the Cultural Revolution* (New York: Delacorte Press, 2001). Like the various genres of post–Cultural Revolution art, the Cultural Revolution memoir has undergone different phases, including the "scar literature" of the late Seventies, the accounts of such established literary figures as Yang Jiang (*Six Chapters of Life in a Cadre School*, 1981/1986) and Yue Daiyun (*To the Storm*, 1985), and (my concern here) the memoirs of those who endured the Cultural Revolution as children. Most of these texts were written in exile outside the reach of governmental scrutiny. For a study of this genre see Zhihui Geng, "Cultural Revolution Written and Read in English: Image Formation, Reception, and Counternarrative," Ph.D. diss., University of Minnesota, 2008. On the Cultural Revolution memoir as a literary form with roots in classical Chinese literature, see Margo Gewurtz, "The Afterlife of Memory in China: Yang Jian's Cultural Revolution Memoir," *ARIEL: Life Writing in International Contexts* 39, nos. 1–2 (January–April 2008): 29–45.

**357.** Gao, *Total Modernity and the Avant-Garde in Twentieth Century Chinese Art*, 223.

**358.** As Gao Minglu explains, the phrase "This afternoon: no water" was talismanic for Wu. A sign stating this made no sense when Wu discovered there was water after all. Washing his hands while reading this message, he perceived a profound disconnect between the act of reading and lived experience. Gao, *Total Modernity and the Avant-Garde in Twentieth Century Chinese Art*, 223–24.

**359.** Norman Bryson, "The Post-Ideological Avant-Garde," in Gao, *Inside Out*, 55–56.

**360.** I am grateful to Christine (Ju) Aylward for this translation. According to Aylward, the phrase *hushuobadao* is the grammatically correct way to spell "nonsense" in Mandarin. Writing the first of these characters *wu*, Wu Shanzhuan spelled this phrase *wushuobadao* "incorrectly" in a southern idiom, perhaps to appeal to the local audience in Zhoushan and possibly referring to his own name. The characters *badao*, which signify "eight ways," could also allude ironically to the eight phases of or ways to Taoist immortality.

**361.** Gao, *Total Modernity and the Avant-Garde in Twentieth Century Chinese Art*, 221.

**362.** See Martina Köppel-Yang, "*Zaofan Youli*/Revolt Is Reasonable: Remanifestations of the Cultural Revolution in Chinese Contemporary Art of the Eighties and Nineties," *Yishu: Journal of Contemporary Chinese Art* 1, no. 2 (August 2002): 66–75.

**363.** Gao, *Total Modernity and the Avant-Garde in Twentieth Century Chinese Art*, 224.

**364.** Wu Shanzhuan, "The Starting Point for the Red Character/ Deficit Word" (1986), in *Wu Shanzhuan: Red Humor International*, Artist's Writings, 4 (my italics).

**365.** According to Jiang Jiehong, character simplification remained a priority for several years after Mao's death during the tenure of his successor Hua Guofeng (1976–81). Jiang, *Burden or Legacy*, 13.

**366.** Wu Shanzhuan, "Silent Ocean, Blind Ocean, Genderless Ocean" (1986), in *Wu Shanzhuan: Red Humor International*, Artist's Writings, 2.

**367.** Gao, *Total Modernity and the Avant-Garde in Twentieth Century Chinese Art*, 223.

**368.** Wu Shanzhuan, "On Our Painting" (1987), in *Wu Shanzhuan: Red Humor International*, Artist's Writings, 8.

**369.** Jiang, *Red Scarf Girl*, 39.

**370.** Shao and Mu, "It Is Not Merely a Memory," 75.

**371.** Wu decorated porcelain and even organic materials, including cabbages, with red characters.

372. Jiang, *Red Scarf Girl*, 38.

373. The first known *dazibao* was displayed on May 25, 1966, by members of the department of philosophy at Beijing University; it denounced Song Shuo, the vice minister of the Higher Education Beijing Municipal Committee. On the semantic violence of the *dazibao*, see Francesca Del Lago, "Images, Words and Violence: Cultural Revolutionary Influences on Chinese Avant-Grade Art," in Wu, *Chinese Art at the Crossroads*, 32–39.

374. Xu Bing quoted in Jiang, *Burden or Legacy*, 14.

375. Jiang, *Red Scarf Girl*, 49.

376. MacFarquhar and Schoenhals, *Mao's Last Revolution*, chaps. 6 and 7.

377. Gao, *Total Modernity and the Avant-Garde in Twentieth Century Chinese Art*, 225.

378. *Inside Out: New Chinese Art* was organized by Gao Minglu and traveled to the Asia Society in New York, the San Francisco Asia Art Museum, and other venues in 1998–2000. The San Francisco presentation was on display February 26–June 1, 1999.

379. The curator, Gao Minglu, notes: "Wu kept some part of the '*dazibao*' and brought it with him when he moved to Iceland. When I was organizing *Inside Out*, Wu mounted the fragments into the scrolls for us to hang in the museum. He also asked us to put in some porcelain since he was not present in the process of the installation." Email to the author, April 3, 2013.

380. Shao and Mu, "It Is Not Merely a Memory," 75.

381. The series is divided into six parts, the first five of which depict assembly halls. The final group pictures pilgrimage sites associated with the Long March and the People's Revolution.

382. Shao and Mu, "It Is Not Merely a Memory," 88.

383. Mu recalls more ambivalent images, too, such as the "ugly" wall in the middle of town plastered with "harsh bloody red" *dazibao* she passed on the way to school. When she wrote an essay criticizing the aesthetically displeasing wall, her teacher gave her a poor grade. In contrast, the teacher praised a subsequent essay by Mu eulogizing a stone in a road built by the government. "From then on I didn't trust the teacher anymore." Email to the author, February 10, 2013.

384. Shao and Mu, "It Is Not Merely a Memory," 89.

385. *Rent Collection Courtyard: A Revolution in Sculpture*, supplement to *China Reconstructs* (Beijing, 1967), 4–5. For a detailed presentation of the sculpture, see *Rent Collection Courtyard: Sculptures of Oppression and Revolt* (Peking [Beijing]: Foreign Languages Press, 1970).

386. A *mu* is a little less than two-tenths of an acre.

387. In the years since the work's creation Liu's family members have contested the version of the events it depicts and what they perceive to be an inaccurate portrait of the landlord, whose "water dungeon" never existed. Vanessa Piao, "Grandson of China's Most-Hated Landlord Challenges Communist Lore," *New York Times*, July 26, 2016.

388. The Sichuan version was first exhibited on October 1, 1965, the anniversary of the founding of the People's Republic of China on October 1, 1949 (National Day). The version produced for the Forbidden City was installed in autumn 1966. Completed only months after the Cultural Revolution was announced, it differed from the Sichuan set in several ways. Utilizing metal armatures, a technique favored by Soviet-trained artists at the Central Academy of Fine Arts (CAFA), who joined the original group of Sichuan artists, the Beijing set had more figures, and concluded with triumphant images of soldiers and a cowering Liu—a fictional scene, as it turned out, as Liu Wencai had died on October 17, 1949, before the People's Liberation Army entered Sichuan. Interview with Cai Guo-Qiang, Washington, DC, November 28, 2012; and Piao,"Grandson of China's Most-Hated Landlord Challenges Communist Lore." Cai's versions of *Rent Collection Courtyard* combine the wooden and metal armatures of the Sichuan and Beijing sets.

389. As director of the exhibition *documenta V* (1972), Szeemann had attempted to show a copy of the original *Rent Collection Courtyard* at Kassel, a commission that came to naught. The memory of this unrealized commission was a subtext of Cai's project.
390. Cai Guo-Qiang, *Venice's Rent Collection Courtyard* (Vancouver: Annie Wong Art Foundation, 1999), without pagination.
391. Cai's father, a scholar-poet, bookseller, and antiquarian, continued to paint and practice calligraphy, yet burned certain books and hid examples of Tang and Song calligraphy and stone rubbings for fear of their discovery. Memories of the shooting of the artist's dog and a classmate's brother by marauding Red Guards also remain. Interview with Cai Guo-Qiang.
392. Alexandra Munroe, "Cai-Guo-Qiang: I Want to Believe," in Thomas Krens and Alexandra Munroe, *Cai Guo-Qiang: I Want to Believe* (New York: Guggenheim Museum, 2008), 26.
393. Munroe, "Cai-Guo-Qiang: I Want to Believe," 27. Cai's well-known works involving gunpowder-induced explosions exemplify this claim.
394. As the great success of *Venice's Rent Collection Courtyard* abroad and its controversial reception at home would reveal. Awarded the Biennale's Golden Lion Award, *Venice's Rent Collection Courtyard* incurred the wrath of the Sichuan Art Institute, which threatened to sue Cai for infringement of copyright. The case was eventually dropped.
395. The students were familiar with the Soviet clay sculpture techniques used to build the 1966 Beijing set which were still being taught at CAFA. Interview with Cai Guo-Qiang.
396. Cai reduced the number of figures and simplified the *tableaus*. *Venice's Rent Collection Courtyard* presented 108 figures out of the original 119. Later iterations were more severely reduced. Interview with Cai Guo-Qiang.
397. As David Joselit suggests in "Image Explosion: Global Readymades," in Thomas Krens and Alexandra Munroe, *Cai Guo-Qiang: I Want to Believe*, 50–60.
398. The photos of the Bilbao and Dayi sets turned slowly, while the image of the New York work spun too quickly for a viewer to see. David Joselit describes the different speeds of Cai's practice as "slow," "medium," and "fast," attributing different functions to these velocities. Joselit, "Image Explosion: Global Readymades," 55–58.
399. See James Meyer, "The Functional Site, or The Transformation of Site-Specificity," in Erika Suderburg, ed., *Space, Site, Intervention: Situating Installation Art* (Minneapolis: University of Minnesota Press, 2000), 23–37.

## Part Two

1. The artists Bas Jan Ader, Andre Cadere, and Christopher D'Arcangelo also died young during the long Sixties.
2. Michael Kimmelman, "The Dia Generation," *New York Times Magazine*, April 6, 2003.
3. Henry James, "The Aspern Papers," in *The Turn of the Screw and Other Short Novels* (New York: New American Library, 1962), 155–56.
4. Aspern was "one of the most brilliant minds of his day (and in those years . . . there were, as everyone knows, many)." James, "The Aspern Papers,"155.
5. I am thinking of such artists as Sol LeWitt, Mel Bochner, and Donald Judd.
6. The occupants of the plane were pilot Gale Ray Rogers, photographer Robert Curtin, and Robert Smithson. Nancy Holt, *The Making of Amarillo Ramp (1973–2013)* (film; 2014). See Mel Bochner's eloquent account of Smithson's death in Bruce Conley and Joe Amrhein, eds., *Robert Smithson: A Collection of Writings on Robert Smithson on the Occasion of the Exhibition of Dead Tree at Pierogi 2000* (Brooklyn: Pierogi 2000, 1997), without pagination.
7. An allusion to a Native American myth of an underwater whirlpool connecting the Great

Salt Lake to the Pacific Ocean. Robert Smithson, "The Spiral Jetty," in Jack Flam, ed., *Robert Smithson: The Collected Writings* (Berkeley: University of California Press, 1996), 146.

8. Smithson, "The Spiral Jetty," 147. For a fine description of *Spiral Jetty*'s scale, see Erin Hogan, *Spiral Jetta: A Road Trip through the Land Art of the American West* (Chicago: University of Chicago Press, 2008), 20–21.
9. Maurice Merleau-Ponty, *Phenomenology of Perception*, trans. Colin Smith (London: Routledge & Kegan Paul, 1962), 203.
10. Smithson, "The Spiral Jetty," 147.
11. "Four Conversations between Dennis Wheeler and Robert Smithson," ed. Eva Schmidt, in Flam, ed., *Robert Smithson: The Collected Writings*, 199. Smithson appropriated this term from mathematics and phonetics. A "surd" number is an irrational number, a "surd" sound, a voiceless consonant. The English "surd" is also a pun on the French "sourd," which means "deaf" or "deaf person," derived from the Latin *surdus* ("deaf, silent, stupid").
12. Rosalind Krauss describes a viewer's experience of *Spiral Jetty* as a "moment-to-moment passage through space and time." See Rosalind E. Krauss, *Passages in Modern Sculpture* (Cambridge, MA: MIT Press, 1977), 282.
13. The Smithson "return" was instigated by such shows as "Robert Smithson Unearthed: Works on Paper, 1957–73," Miriam and Ira D. Wallach Art Gallery, Columbia University, New York, 1991; "Robert Smithson, el paisaje entrópico: Una retrospectiva, 1960–73," IVAM Centro Julio González, Valencia, 1993; "Robert Smithson: Photo Works," Los Angeles County Museum of Art, Los Angeles, 1993; "Robert Smithson: Retrospective 1955–73," National Museum of Contemporary Art, Oslo, 1999; and "L'informe: Mode d'emploi," Musée national d'art moderne, Paris, 1996. Smithson's work was also discussed at length in Caroline Jones, *Machine in the Studio: Constructing the Postwar American Artist* (Chicago: University of Chicago Press, 1996).
14. The early years of the new millennium brought a major retrospective ("Robert Smithson," Museum of Contemporary Art, Los Angeles, Whitney Museum of American Art, Dallas Museum of Art); two major monographs (Ann Reynolds, *Robert Smithson: Learning from New Jersey and Elsewhere* [Cambridge, MA: MIT Press, 2003]; and Jennifer L. Roberts, *Mirror-Travels: Robert Smithson and History* [New Haven: Yale University Press, 2004]). There were also a variety of other projects, including Lynne Cooke and Karen Kelly with Bettina Funcke and Barbara Schröder, eds., *Robert Smithson: The Spiral Jetty: True Fictions, False Realities* (New York: Dia Art Foundation, 2005); Grant Arnold, ed., *Robert Smithson in Vancouver: A Fragment of a Greater Fragmentation* (Vancouver: Vancouver Art Gallery, 2003); and Chrissie Iles, Shamim M. Momin, and Debra Singer, "Introduction," and Debra Singer, "The Way Things Never Were: Nostalgia's Possibilities and the Unpredictable Past," in *Whitney Biennial 2004* (New York: Whitney Museum of American Art, 2004), 14–17 and 22–33. The exhibition "The Smithson Effect," organized by the Utah Museum of Fine Arts in 2011, explored Smithson's relevance for twenty-two contemporary artists, including Green, Durant, Dean, Burr, Mark Dion, Simon Leung, and Conrad Bakker.
15. Works associated with the antiwar movement of the Sixties and Seventies, such as *Partially Buried Woodshed*, assume a special interest in an era of "permanent" war in which resistance has little traction, and conflicts such as the Iraq invasion seem both to "repeat" Vietnam and to suggest a new era of dispersed, transnational conflicts. For a discussion of art practices responsive to these conditions, see T. J. Demos, *Zones of Conflict* (New York: Pratt Manhattan Gallery, 2008).
16. The U.S.-led invasion of Iraq was launched on March 20, 2003. Reports of the Abu Ghraib tortures appeared in the U.S. mainstream press in April–May 2004. Hurricane Katrina occurred on August 23–31, 2005.

17. Carl Andre, "Robert Smithson: He Always Reminded Us of the Questions We Should Have Asked Ourselves." *Arts Magazine*, September 1978, 102.
18. Smithson, "The Artist and Politics: A Symposium" (1970), in Flam, ed., *Robert Smithson: The Collected Writings*, 134. For an introduction to Smithson's entropology see James Lingwood, "The Entropologist," *Robert Smithson, el paisaje entrópico: Una retrospectiva, 1960-73* (Valencia: IVAM Centro Julio González, 1993), without pagination.
19. The Smithson/Warhol conjuncture is evocatively explored in Saul Anton, *Warhol's Dream* (Dijon: Les presses du réel, 2007). The authors J. G. Ballard and Thomas Pynchon also foretell the entropic future envisioned by Smithson.
20. Smithson, "Entropy and the New Monuments," in Flam, ed., *Robert Smithson: The Collected Writings*, 11.
21. Smithson, "Entropy and the New Monuments," 11. The Blackout of November 9, 1965, resulted in a loss of electricity in the northeastern states of the United States and parts of Ontario. More than thirty million people were left without power.
22. Thomas Pynchon recalled the "somber glee ... at any idea of mass destruction or decline" felt by some intellectuals during this period. Thomas Pynchon, *Slow Learner: Early Stories* (Boston: Little, Brown, 1984), 13.
23. "Entropy and the New Monuments," 11.
24. "'... The Earth, Subject to Cataclysms, Is a Cruel Master': Interview with Grégoire Müller," in Flam, ed., *Robert Smithson: The Collected Writings*, 257. Smithson is referring to a passage in Claude Lévi-Strauss, *Tristes Tropiques*, trans. John and Doreen Weightman, (London: Penguin Books, 1992), 413–14.
25. See Claude Lévi-Strauss, "Clocks and Steam-Engines," in Georges Charbonnier, ed., *Conversations with Claude Lévi-Strauss* (London: Jonathan Cape, 1969), 33; and Lévi-Strauss's elaboration of this distinction in *The Savage Mind* (London: Weidenfeld & Nicholson, 1966). Both books, as well as *Tristes Tropiques*, are in the inventory of Smithson's library (see Eugenie Tsai and Cornelia Butler, *Robert Smithson* [Los Angeles: Museum of Contemporary Art, 2004], 249). On Smithson's interest in Lévi-Strauss's analogy, see Flam, ed., *Robert Smithson: The Collected Writings*, 207, 240–41; and Reynolds, *Robert Smithson: Learning from New Jersey and Elsewhere*, 185–87.
26. For a history of entropy theory see Max Jammer, "Entropy," in Philip Wiener, *Dictionary of the History of Ideas* (New York: Scribner's, 1973), vol. 2, 112–20; and P. W. Bridgman, *The Nature of Thermodynamics* (New York: Harper & Row, 1941), a book that is listed in the inventory of Smithson's library.
27. As Derrida notes in a well-known commentary on this argument, the invention of writing is essential to the evolution of "hot" societies. The members of a "cold" system exist in a state of prelapsarian bliss unpolluted by writing. According to Derrida, Lévi-Strauss's hot/cold binary reinforces the Rousseauvian opposition of "nature" and "culture," and thus a primitivizing alterity. See Jacques Derrida, "The Violence of the Letter: From Lévi-Strauss to Rousseau," in *Of Grammatology*, trans. Gayatri Chakravorty Spivak (Baltimore: Johns Hopkins University Press, 1974), 101–40.
28. Lévi-Strauss, "Clocks and Steam-Engines," 33–34.
29. As claimed by Kelvin and Helmholtz in 1852 and 1854, respectively. Jammer, "Entropy," 113–15.
30. Liza Bear and Willoughby Sharp, "Discussions with Heizer, Oppenheim, Smithson" (1970), in Flam, ed., *Robert Smithson: The Collected Writings*, 250–51. At the same time that Smithson envisions an entropic future, he points to the prehistoric past. *Spiral Jetty* depicts the dinosaur halls of the American Museum of Natural History, while Smithson's "Strata: A Geophotographic Fiction" leaps backward from the Jurassic era to the Precambrian age.

Robert Smithson, "Strata: A Geophotographic Fiction" (1970), in Flam, ed., *Robert Smithson: The Collected Writings*, 77.

**31.** See Alexander Dumbadze, *Bas Jan Ader: Death Is Elsewhere* (Chicago: University of Chicago Press, 2013).

**32.** Robert Smithson quoted in "Out of the Past: A Conversation on Eva Hesse," *Artforum* 46, no. 6 (February 2008): 249.

**33.** Rudolph Clausius, *The Mechanical Theory of Heat with Its Applications to the Steam Engine and to the Physical Properties of Bodies* (1867), quoted in Jammer, "Entropy," 114.

**34.** Denoted by the letter "S" (possibly derived from "Sadi"), Clausius's neologism derives from the Greek *en + tropein* ("change," "turn," "the transformation").

**35.** Gordon Matta-Clark, *Splitting* (1972); Dennis Oppenheim, *Annual Rings* (1968).

**36.** On prolepsis as an aesthetic form, see Michael Ann Holly, *Past Looking: Historical Imagination and the Rhetoric of the Image* (Ithaca: Cornell University Press, 1996). The mnemonic endurance of ephemeral artworks is discussed in Schneider, *Performance Remains*, 87–110.

**37.** Writing on Georges Bataille's heterology (his "science" of the radically other) in relation to Smithson's work, Yve-Alain Bois distinguishes *scission*, a pairing of incommensurate terms, from *synthesis*, a reconciliation of opposites (Hegel's *Aufhebung*). Yve-Alain Bois and Rosalind E. Krauss, *Formless: A User's Guide* (New York: Zone books, 1997), 67–73.

**38.** Enantiomorphy, a subfield of crystallography, is the study of molecular structures that are symmetrical and reversed. In *Enantiomorphic Chambers* (1965), Smithson's demonstration of this idea, two mirrors face one another obliquely. A viewer who stands between them sees the other mirror's reflection rather than her own body image as she would expect: each chamber is the other's mirror.

**39.** For a history of the emergence of the "two Americas," see Rick Perlstein, *Nixonland: The Rise of a President and the Fracturing of America* (New York: Scribner, 2008). The "good" and "bad" Sixties is also discussed in Bernard von Bothmer, *Framing the Sixties: The Use and Abuse of a Decade from Reagan to George W. Bush* (Amherst: University of Massachusetts Press, 2010), 11–27.

**40.** Bill Clinton quoted in John Campbell McMillian, "Locating the New Left," *Reviews in American History* 34, no. 4 (December 2006): 551.

**41.** On the Sixties and the university, see Robert Bork, *Slouching toward Gomorrah* (New York: HarperCollins, 1996), chaps. 1 and 2; and Allan Bloom, *The Closing of the American Mind* (New York: Simon & Schuster, 1987), "The Sixties," 313–35. On the Sixties and "moral decline," see Gertrude Himmelfarb, *One Nation, Two Cultures* (New York: Knopf, 1999); and Frank Rich, "Gingrich Family Values," *New York Times*, May 14, 1995, sec. 4, p. 15. On the Sixties and "cultural decline," see Hilton Kramer, "A Note on The New Criterion," *New Criterion* 1, no. 1 (September 1982): 1–2; and Roger Kimball, *The Long March: How the Cultural Revolution of the Sixties Changed America* (New York: Encounter Books, 2001). For a summary of these views, see Edward P. Morgan, *What Really Happened to the Sixties: How Mass Media Culture Failed American Democracy* (Lawrence: University Press of Kansas, 2010).

**42.** Frank, *The Conquest of Cool*. Examples of this "declension narrative" include Allen K. Matusow, *The Unraveling of America: A History of Liberalism in the Sixties* (New York: Harper & Row, 1984); and William L. O' Neill, *Coming Apart: An Informal History of America in the Sixties* (New York: Quadrangle, 1971). For a fictional account of the "bad Sixties," see Zachary Lazar, *Sway* (Boston: Back Bay Books, 2007).

**43.** See Todd Gitlin's seminal memoir *The Sixties: Years of Hope, Days of Rage* (New York: Bantam Books, 1987); and Joan Morrison and Robert K. Morrison, eds., *From Camelot to Kent State: The Sixties Experience in the Words of Those Who Lived It* (New York: Times Books, 1987).

44. Barack Obama, *The Audacity of Hope: Thoughts on Reclaiming the American Dream* (New York: Crown, 2006), 29.
45. Obama's Democratic Convention acceptance speech was held on August 28, 2008, the forty-fifth anniversary of King's "I Have a Dream" speech.
46. Obama, *The Audacity of Hope*, 30.
47. Obama, *The Audacity of Hope*, 28.
48. Obama, *The Audacity of Hope*, 36.
49. Benjamin, *The Arcades Project*, 458.
50. *Glue Pour* (Vancouver, December 1969). Smithson made two related works that fall, *Asphalt Rundown* (Rome, October 1969) and *Concrete Pour* (Chicago, November 1969). He had attempted to pour mud elsewhere, to no avail.
51. Robert Hobbs, *Robert Smithson: Sculpture* (Ithaca, NY: Cornell University Press, 1981), 182–83.
52. Sue Zimmerman, "Breakability Fascinates Smithson," *Daily Kent Stater*, January 20, 1970. Robert Smithson/Nancy Holt Archives, Archives of American Art, Smithsonian Institution, Roll 3835, Frame 1051. Another art professor present at Kent at the time, Craig Lucas, recalled that Smithson had intended to pour asphalt rather than mud and could not find an appropriate hill for a pouring work. See Jane Crawford's film *Sheds* (Persistent Pictures, 2004).
53. "Entropy Made Visible: Interview with Alison Sky" and "Incidents of Mirror-Travel in the Yucatan," in Flam, ed., *Robert Smithson: The Collected Writings*, 305–7 and 127.
54. National Gallery of Art, Washington, DC, Accession no. 1998.116.1.a–f. A pair of related sketches are in the collection of the Wexner Center for the Arts, Ohio State University. A drawing in black ink of the finished work is in the Kramarsky Collection, New York.
55. A reference to Robert Morris's *Untitled (Corner Piece)* (1964) and revision of Smithson's *Red Sandstone Corner* (1968) and *Corner Mirror with Coral* (1969) into a site-specific intervention.
56. Lewis Carroll, *Through the Looking Glass* (Mineola, NY: Dover Publications, 1999), 54. Smithson discusses Humpty Dumpty as a figure of entropy in "Entropy Made Visible: Interview with Alison Sky," in Flam, ed., *Robert Smithson: The Collected Writings*, 301.
57. Arthur C. Danto, *The Transfiguration of the Commonplace* (Cambridge, MA: Harvard University Press, 1981), 5.
58. Reynolds, *Robert Smithson: Learning from New Jersey and Elsewhere*, 197.
59. Hobbs, *Robert Smithson: Sculpture*, 191n56. Smithson's estimation of the work is cited in Nancy Holt, Letter to Alex Gildzen, May 4, 1975, quoted in Hobbs, *Robert Smithson: Sculpture*, 191n 57; and Dorothy Shinn, "Buried Shed Rises in Esteem of Earth Artists," *Akron Beacon Journal*, May 5, 1995, E5. Holt spoke of a "parallel" between Smithson's work and the May massacre in Dorothy Shinn, *Robert Smithson's Partially Buried Woodshed* (Kent, OH: Kent State University School of Art Gallery, 1990), 5, an interpretation I pursue here.
60. The artist was "devastated" by the student murders, Holt recalled. Shinn, "Buried Shed Rises in Esteem of Earth Artists."
61. Interview with Al Elkins, former student at Kent State University, Washington, DC, March 15, 2010. In 1968 the Black Student Union staged a protest in response to the presence of recruiters from the Oakland police. The previous April, antiwar activists had occupied the university's Music and Speech Building. For an account of student activism at Kent State during this period, see "After May 4: 'Kent State Still Haunts You': An Interview with Ruth Gibson," in Scott L. Bills, ed., *Kent State/May 4: Echoes through a Decade* (Kent, OH: Kent State University Press, 1982), 82–91.
62. Wells, *The War Within*, 371 and 390–94.
63. Laird conceived Vietnamization as a technique to placate a restless Congress and the anti-

war movement. He was also allegedly concerned with his own career: after leaving the Pentagon he ran as a moderate for a U.S. Senate seat, and won. Wells, *The War Within*, 287–88.

**64.** Nixon initiated the bombings, also known as Operation Menu, shortly after taking office in 1969. Wells, *The War Within*, 290–91, 415. On Nixon's efforts to scuttle peace negotiations by the Johnson administration in order to win the presidency in November 1968, see Peter Baker, "Nixon Tried to Spoil Johnson's Vietnam Peace Talks in '68, Notes Show," *New York Times*, January 2, 2017.

**65.** Wells, *The War Within*, 403.

**66.** According to Laird, the misinformation was inserted into Nixon's speech at the suggestion of National Security Advisor Henry Kissinger. Wells, *The War Within*, 421.

**67.** "The action I have taken tonight is indispensible for the continuing success of the withdrawal program." "President Richard Nixon's Cambodia Address," Richard Nixon Foundation, https://www.youtube.com/watch?v=3cAAnoqmksg.

**68.** Agnew called the massacre "predictable." Wells, *The War Within*, 426; and Rowland Evans, Jr., and Robert D. Novak, *Nixon in the White House: The Frustration of Power* (New York: Vintage Books, 1971), 277.

**69.** *On Strike… Shut it Down: A Report on the First National Strike in U.S. History May, 1970* (Chicago: Urban Research Corporation, 1970), 1, 9. See Richard E. Peterson and John A. Bilorusky, *May 1970: The Campus Aftermath of Cambodia and Kent State* (Berkeley: Carnegie Foundation, 1971); Wells, *The War Within*, 424–30; David Barber, *A Hard Rain Fell: SDS and Why It Failed* (Jackson: University Press of Mississippi, 2008), 222–25; and Perlstein, *Nixonland*, 490–91. Another police shooting occurred at South Carolina State University at Orangeburg, South Carolina, on February 8, 1968. Three African American students died in the conflict.

**70.** "King Lear, Act VI," was how one adviser described the ambience in the West Wing during the week after the Kent State shootings. See Wells, *The War Within*, 439–41; and Perlstein, *Nixonland*, 497.

**71.** Wells, *The War Within*, 429.

**72.** On May 8, 1970, teams of construction workers affiliated with the AFL-CIO set upon antiwar protesters in downtown Manhattan, an event known as the Hard Hat Riot.

**73.** A Gallup Poll indicated that 58 percent of the U.S. population "blamed" the students for their deaths. Rumors circulated that Jeff Miller was a "dirty hippie." Allison Krause was smeared for cohabiting with her boyfriend, a calumny associated with FBI director J. Edgar Hoover. Perlstein, *Nixonland*, 489 and 493–95; and Wells, *The War Within*, 424. For local responses to the massacre, see James A. Michener, *Kent State: What Happened and Why* (New York: Random House, 1971), 434–46.

**74.** John Lindsay, mayor of New York; John Gardner, former Secretary of HEW; and Henry Kissinger quoted in Wells, *The War Within*, 428, 430. The quotation from the SUNY Buffalo publication *The Spectrum* appears in *On Strike … Shut it Down: A Report on the First National Strike in U.S. History May, 1970*, 10.

**75.** Smithson did not participate in the Art Workers Coalition's Mobe action of October 15, 1969, and Art Strike of May 22, 1970. For his views on the ecology movement, see "Art through the Camera's Eye," Flam, ed., *Robert Smithson: The Collected Writings*, 375.

**76.** Entropy is a "concomitant factor of progress." Charbonnier, ed., *Conversations with Claude Lévi-Strauss*, 40–41.

**77.** Carol Mirman interviewed by Sandra Perlman Halem, April 1, 2000, Kent State Oral Histories Collection, Kent State Library.

**78.** The festival took place January 19–23, 1970. The invited guests were John Ashbery, Allan Kaprow, Alan Rich, Robert Smithson, and John Vaccaro. The choreographer Louis Falco performed with his company. They presented lectures, participated in panel discussions, and led workshops. Advertisement, *Daily Kent Stater*, January 16, 1970, 9; and Carol Mirman, Undated Letter to Robert Smithson, Robert Smithson/Nancy Holt Archives, Archives of American Art, Smithsonian Institution, Roll 3833, Frame 53. Smithson was invited by several undergraduates, including Robert Swick and Carol Mirman, in consultation with sculpture professor Brinsley Tyrrell. His visit is discussed in Hobbs, *Robert Smithson Sculpture*, 188; and Alex Gildzen, "*Partially Buried Woodshed*: A Robert Smithson Log," *Arts Magazine* 52, no. 9 (May 1978): 118–20.

**79.** In previous years, more established figures had attended the festival, such as the Abstract Expressionist artist Grace Hartigan and the Realist painter Fairfield Porter in 1966 and 1967, respectively.

**80.** "Creative Arts Festival, January 17–23," advertisement, *Daily Kent Stater*, January 21, 1970, 10.

**81.** Hoffman staged the action on August 24, 1967.

**82.** Alan Rich, Keynote Address, Kent State Creative Arts Festival, January 19, 1970. Robert Smithson Papers, Special Collections, Kent State University Library.

**83.** Holt, Letter to Alex Gildzen, May 4, 1975, quoted in Hobbs, *Robert Smithson: Sculpture*, 191n57.

**84.** "Students on approximately 10 percent of [U.S.] campuses . . . focused some part of their protest on campus buildings. Occupying a building or part of one was the most frequently used tactic, and the two most frequently chosen objects were the ROTC building and the administration building." *On Strike . . . Shut It Down: A Report on the First National Strike in U.S. History May, 1970*, 14. In early May 1970, before and after the Kent State massacre, ROTC buildings were firebombed at Yale, Princeton, University of Maryland, Hobart, Rutgers, and Michigan State. Christopher Hewitt, *Political Violence and Terrorism in Modern America: A Chronology* (Westport, CT: Praeger, 2005), 60. Similar actions took place at Case Western Reserve University, University of Kentucky, University of Cincinnati, Ohio State, Ohio University, Miami University of Ohio, Tulane, Washington University, and St. Louis University. Perlstein, *Nixonland*, 490.

**85.** Bois, "Threshole," in *Formless*, 187.

**86.** Denis Hollier, *Against Architecture: The Writings of Georges Bataille* (Cambridge, MA: MIT Press, 1989), 33, 46. My discussion here is indebted to Hollier's brilliant text.

**87.** Georges Bataille, "Architecture" (1929), quoted in Hollier, *Against Architecture*, 47.

**88.** Originally titled *La prise de la Concorde*, Hollier's *Against Architecture*, one of the texts responsible for Bataille's revival, was first published in 1974.

**89.** "Aussi bien nul bâtiment, sauf à se réduire à la baraque, ne peut-il se passer de cet ordre qui l'apparente au discours." ("No building, unless reduced to a shack, can do without this order allying it with discourse.") Jacques Lacan, "À la mémoire d'Ernest Jones: Sur sa théorie de la symbolisme," in *Écrits* (Paris: Seuil, 1966), 698.

**90.** In 1971 the first official monument to May 4th, the Hillel Memorial, was placed in the Prentice Hall parking lot by the national Jewish affairs organization B'nai B'rith (three of the murdered students were Jewish). The original aluminum plate was later replaced by the granite headstone I describe below.

**91.** The arson occurred on March 28, 1975. A half-empty bottle of kerosene was found at the site. See "Sculpture Damaged," *Daily Kent Stater*, April 3, 1975, 3; and William Bierman, "Burn the Woodshed! Spare the Woodshed!" *Beacon: The Sunday Magazine of the Akron Beacon Journal*, July 25, 1975, 4–7, 14–15, 18. These materials and other archival sources relating to Smithson's work were found in Robert Smithson Papers, Special Collections, Kent State Library.

**92.** Smithson ascribed a market value of $10,000 to *Partially Buried Woodshed* in his deed of gift to the university, yet this protective measure did not prevent the *Woodshed*'s dismantling. See Hobbs, *Robert Smithson: Sculpture*, 191.

**93.** Hobbs, *Robert Smithson: Sculpture*, 6. The Committee on Campus Physical and Natural Environment, chaired by architecture professor Foster Armstrong and campus planner Gae Russo, argued for the work's demolition. Only a letter campaign and visit by Holt to Kent in 1975 prevented their designs until the final "clean up" of the shed's remains by a grounds crew in 1984.

**94.** Kate Mosher, "KSU Art Settles in Place as Earth Claims *Woodshed*," *Ravenna-Kent Record Courier*, September 8, 1982, 2.

**95.** KSU President Michael Schwartz quoted in John C. Kuehner, "Artful Vanishing Act? 'Shed' Gone, Valued at $250,000," *Ravenna-Kent Record-Courier*, February 27, 1984. For other responses to the removal, see Susie Cobbledick, Letter to the Editor, *Daily Kent Stater*, March 8, 1984; and the editorial in *Kent-Ravenna Record Courier*, May 2, 1984, 4. On its local re-estimation, see Shinn, "Buried Shed Rises in Esteem of Earth Artists."

**96.** The Hearn work was the first installment of Green's *Partially Buried in Three Parts* (1996–97), which includes *Partially Buried*, *Übertragen (Transfer)*, and *Partially Buried Continued*. Green's project has been exhibited in several versions since its debut at Pat Hearn in 1996: at the Museum of Contemporary Art, Chicago (1997), Gwangju Biennale (1997), Vienna Secession (1999), Fundació Antoni Tàpies (2000), and Musée cantonal des beaux-arts Lausanne (2009–10).

**97.** According to Michener, two boys broke a window and threw lit railroad flares inside. Other witnesses have speculated that a government agent provocateur may have been involved. James A. Michener, *Kent State: What Happened and Why* (New York: Random House, 1971), 194.

**98.** The tent city protest led to the founding of the May 4th Coalition, a group dedicated to preserving the memory of the murdered students and the antiwar movement at Kent State. See Scott L. Bills, ed., *Kent State/May 4: Echoes through a Decade* (Kent, OH: Kent State University Press, 1982), 212–30.

**99.** Michener, *Kent State: What Happened and Why*, viii. For a different account of May 4th see *The Middle of the Country: The Events of May 4th as Seen by Students & Faculty at Kent State University*, ed. Bill Warren (New York: Avon, 1970), and the report commissioned by President Nixon on the shootings chaired by William W. Scranton, The President's Commission on Campus Unrest, *Special Report: The Kent State Tragedy* (October 1970). Alternative narratives include William A. Gordon, *The Fourth of May* (Buffalo: Prometheus Books, 1990), I.F. Stone, *The Killings at Kent State: How Murder Went Unpunished* (New York: Vintage Books, 1971), and Joseph Kelner and James Munves, *The Kent State Coverup* (New York: Harper & Row, 1980).

**100.** President Richard Nixon introduced the expression "Silent Majority" in a speech of November 3, 1969.

**101.** Michener, *Kent State: What Happened and Why*, 18.

**102.** Michener, *Kent State: What Happened and Why*, 339–40.

**103.** Michener, *Kent State: What Happened and Why*, 552.

**104.** Michener, *Kent State: What Happened and Why*, 99–115.

**105.** Michener, *Kent State: What Happened and Why*, 544.

**106.** The "no particular order" is a kind of order, maintained from one version of *Partially Buried* to another and adapted for each installation. Javier Anguera, email to the author, January 2, 2018.

**107.** Smithson, "A Tour of the Monuments of Passaic, New Jersey" in Flam, ed., *Robert Smithson: The Collected Writings*, 70--72.

**108.** On August 7, 1970, a seventeen-year-old named Jonathan Jackson attempted to kidnap a judge, a deputy district attorney, and three jury members in a misguided attempt to release his older brother and other prisoners held at California's Soledad Prison who became known as the "Soledad Brothers." Judge Harold Haley, two San Quentin convicts, and Jackson himself died in the shootout. Davis was captured two months later, and was tried and eventually acquitted.

**109.** Davis moved to Germany to study with Adorno's colleague Herbert Marcuse, whom she met as a student at Brandeis. The image of Davis and Adorno in *Partially Buried, 1992 Cologne*, alluded to a prior work of Green's, *Import/Export Funk Office* (1992), a work that examined exchanges between German and African American culture during the Sixties and Nineties and that centered on Davis, Adorno, and the critic Dietrich Dietrichsen.

**110.** See Davis's sharp analysis of a fashion spread "reenacting" her 1970 arrest. Angela Y. Davis, "Afro Images: Politics, Fashion and Nostalgia," *Critical Inquiry* 21, no. 1 (Autumn 1994): 39; and Carrie Mae Weems's sardonic video *Afro Chic* (2009), in which Weems and other women in natural wigs put on a mock fashion show in front of historical photos of Davis and Huey Newton.

**111.** The first version of *Partially Buried* offered the albums to viewers to play on an old record player or DVD player. In the most recent iteration of the work, displayed at Green's 2010 retrospective at the Musée cantonal des beaux-arts, Lausanne, the record player was presented as an object; a boom box played a selection of "oldies."

**112.** The corollary of the Super 8 footage in *Partially Buried* is the slide show in the third section of Green's triptych, *Partially Buried Continued*—a medium promoted by Kodak for familial self-representation during this period. See Monica McTighe, "The Family Slide Show as Critical History in Renée Green's *Partially Buried Continued*," *Third Text* 21, no. 4 (2007): 441–50.

**113.** Per Lynne Tillman's remarks in Renée Green, *Between and Including* (Vienna: Secession, 2001), 139. On the artist's accretive approach, see the detailed analysis of Alexander Alberro, "The Fragment and the Flow: Sampling the Work of Renée Green," in Renée Green, *Shadows and Signals* (Barcelona: Fundació Antoni Tàpies, 2000), 20–43.

**114.** Shinn, *Robert Smithson's Partially Buried Woodshed*.

**115.** The riots occurred over the course of six nights in July 1966 in Hough, a predominantly African American neighborhood of Cleveland. Four residents were killed and thirty injured in exchanges with the police and National Guard.

**116.** "Partially Buried. Transcript 2 (1996)," in Green, *Shadows and Signals*, 109.

**117.** "Partially Buried (1999). Version B: Reading Script," in Green, *Shadows and Signals*, 69.

**118.** William Ayers, Bernardine Dohrn, and Jeff Jones, respectively, quoted in Emile De Antonio, Mary Lampson, and Haskell Wexler, *Underground* (1976).

**119.** Barry Mann and Cynthia Weil, "New World Coming" (1970).

**120.** Other examples of the genre include Cornelia Parker's installation of a blown-up shed, *Cold Dark Matter* (1991); Tacita Dean's video *From Columbus, Ohio to the Partially Buried Woodshed* (1999); and Charlesworth, Lewandowski, and Mann's *Partially Shed (May 4 Kent 1970)* (2005), a "reconstruction" of the upper portion of Smithson's sculpture exhibited in the Deptford X Festival, Greenwich, England. For another account of some of these projects, see Alex Coles, "Revisiting Robert Smithson in Ohio: Tacita Dean, Sam Durant and Renée Green," *Parachute* 104 (November–December 2001): 128–37.

**121.** *Mirror Displacement (Cayuga Salt Mine Project)*, "Earth Art," Andrew Dickson White Museum, Cornell University, February 11–March 16, 1969.

**122.** Matusow, *The Unraveling of America*, 304.

**123.** "Altamont," Blum & Poe, Santa Monica, 1999. The show is discussed in Michael Darling, "Sam Durant's Riddling Zones," in *Sam Durant* (Los Angeles: Museum of Contemporary Art, 2003), 18–25. The exhibition included Durant's *Proposal for Monument at Altamont Raceway, Tracy, CA* (1999), a platform of polyurethane ooze evoking Linda Benglis's work of the Sixties and Altamont's hilly topography, and a row of mirrors and strips of gray felt spelling *altamont* in reverse, reminiscent of works by Smithson and Morris.

**124.** Nils Plath, "Rewinding Histories, Artful Disassembling: View of Works by Sam Durant," in *Sam Durant: Entropy in Reverse* (New Plymouth, NZ: Govett Brewster Art Gallery, 2004), 9–24.

**125.** Gitlin, *The Sixties: Years of Hope, Days of Rage*, 406; John Burks, "Rock & Roll's Worst Day: The Aftermath of Altamont," *Rolling Stone*, February 7, 1970; and Joel Selvin, *Summer of Love: The Inside Story of LSD, Rock & Roll, Free Love and High Times in the Wild West* (New York: Dutton, 1994), 241–50.

**126.** "The Rolling Stones Disaster at Altamont: Let It Bleed," *Rolling Stone*, January 21, 1970; and Burks, "Rock & Roll's Worst Day: The Aftermath of Altamont."

**127.** Kersting, "Interview with Sam Durant," 59. The "Altamont" show staged a logic of "impurity" pervasive throughout Durant's practice, first marked in the artist's drawing *3 Rules of Plumbing* (1992). Rather than privilege one term or the other—the pure or the impure—Durant explores the constitutive relationship of these notions, the collapse of one into the other.

**128.** "The Monuments of Passaic, New Jersey," in Flam, ed., *Robert Smithson: The Collected Writings*, 71. In the example of entropy of J. W. Gibbs ("Gibbs's Paradox") that inspired Smithson's *Sand-Box Monument*, a box contains two gases separated by a divider. When the partition is opened, the gases mix into a unified state. The paradox discovered by Gibbs is that entropy is eventually stilled; an "order" is reinstated. Ultimately, the mixture of white and black sand of the *Sand-Box Monument* can become no grayer. For a discussion of Gibbs's proposition, see Bridgman, *The Nature of Thermodynamics*, 168–70. Another work influenced by Gibbs, Thomas Pynchon's short story "Entropy" (1960), narrates the collapse of two discrete social and climatological systems into a single environment. "Entropy," in Pynchon, *Slow Learner: Early Stories*, 81–99.

**129.** See the descriptions of Nelson's work in Rachel Withers, "Mike Nelson: Modern Art Oxford," *Artforum* 43, no. 3 (November 2004): 238; Dan Fox, "Mike Nelson," *Frieze* 85 (September 2004): 118; and especially Jeremy Millar, "Ordo Ab Chao," in Mike Nelson, *Triple Bluff Canyon* (Oxford: Modern Art Oxford, 2004), without pagination.

**130.** The U.S. Congress passed the Patriot Act on October 26, 2001. Maxwell presented his lecture on January 30, 1993.

**131.** Jordan Maxwell, quoted in Nelson, *Triple Bluff Canyon*.

**132.** The work was inspired by the 1970 color photograph by Alex Gildzen published on the cover of the May 1978 issue of *Arts Magazine*, dedicated to Smithson.

**133.** The interior was the actual volume of Smithson's shed. Mike Nelson, email to the author, April 16, 2007.

**134.** "Cultural Confinement" (1972), in Flam, ed., *Robert Smithson: The Collected Writings*, 154.

**135.** http://en.wikipedia.org/wiki/British_fatalities_during_Operation_Telic.

**136.** On the Iraq War and collapse of dissent during the 2000s, see Retort, *Afflicted Powers: Capital and Spectacle in a New Age of War*.

**137.** The classic account is Robert Morris, "Anti Form," *Artforum* 6, no. 8 (April 1968): 33–35. Morris's installation *Continuous Project Altered Daily* (1970), a work that changed daily, gave form to this idea of an art of process unfolding in "real time."

**138.** "Four Conversations between Dennis Wheeler and Robert Smithson," 1969–70, original manuscript, quoted in Reynolds, *Robert Smithson: Learning from New Jersey and Elsewhere*, 117–18.

**139.** William Wordsworth, "Lines Composed a Few Miles above Tintern Abbey, On Revisiting the Banks of the Wye During a Tour, July 13, 1798," in *The Complete Poetical Works of William Wordsworth*, vol. I (Cambridge, MA: Houghton Mifflin, 1910), 16.

**140.** Paul Cummings, "Interview with Robert Smithson for the Archives of American Art/Smithsonian Institution," in Flam, ed., *Robert Smithson: The Collected Writings*, 271.

**141.** Smithson, "The Monuments of Passaic, New Jersey," 74.

**142.** Green, "Partially Buried," 69.

**143.** Jean Starobinski defines nostalgia as "an emotional upheaval which is related to the workings of memory." Jean Starobinski, "The Idea of Nostalgia," *Diogenes* 54 (Summer 1966): 89–90.

**144.** See Rosalind E. Krauss, "Sculpture in the Expanded Field," in *The Originality of the Avant-Garde and Other Modernist Myths* (Cambridge, MA: MIT Press, 1985), 277–90.

**145.** As noted in Tim Griffin, "The Personal Effects of Seth Price," *Artforum* 47, no. 10 (Summer 2009): 288. Price has since explored this theme in his sculptures, reliefs, and clothing lined with patterns derived from security envelopes and shipping containers.

**146.** Holt oversaw the making of Smithson's *Amarillo Ramp* with Serra and collaborated on Serra's video *Boomerang* (1974). Jonas and Peter Campus videotaped Smithson and Holt's *East Coast/West Coast* (1969). Jonas assisted Serra in mapping out *Shift* (1972).

**147.** Only Barbara Helman speaks to her husband in the final seconds of the tape.

**148.** Michael Heizer, *Circular Surface Planar Displacement Drawing*, Jean Dry Lake, Nevada, 1970.

**149.** Rachel Kushner, *The Flame Throwers* (New York: Scribner, 2013), 8.

**150.** Kushner, *The Flame Throwers*, 68.

**151.** "Rachel Kushner, *The Flame Throwers*," *Paris Review* online (August 8, 2013).

**152.** Starobinski, "The Idea of Nostalgia," 84.

**153.** Starobinski, "The Idea of Nostalgia," 94.

**154.** J. J. Rousseau, *Dictionary of Music*, trans. W. Waring and J. French (London, 1778), quoted in Starobinski, "The Idea of Nostalgia," 93. Starobinski notes the relative antiquity of "love melancholia" in comparison with nostalgia (84).

**155.** Susan Stewart, *On Longing: Narratives of the Miniature, the Gigantic, the Souvenir, the Collection* (Durham, NC: Duke University Press, 1993), 23.

**156.** Starobinski, "The Idea of Nostalgia," 93.

**157.** Arendt, *On Revolution*, 46.

**158.** A subject beyond the compass of this study, Sixties nostalgia took many forms, ranging from the fashion for Victorian and Edwardian clothing and "granny" glasses in the Haight-Ashbury and on Carnaby Street to the Twenties and Thirties revivalism associated with the films *Bonnie and Clyde* (1967) and *The Great Gatsby* (1974).

**159.** The founding members of the Diggers included the performers Emmett Grogan, Peter Coyote, and Peter Berg. On the Digger Feeds see Emmett Grogan, *Ringolevio: A Life Played for Keeps* (New York: New York Review of Books, 1990), 249–50; and Charles Perry, *The Haight-Ashbury: A History* (New York: Rolling Stone Press, 1984), 97–99. The Digger concept of "Free" in its many applications is explored in Bradford D. Martin, *The Theater Is the Street* (Amherst: University of Massachusetts Press, 2004), 92–106.

**160.** Rirkrit Tiravanija's *Free* (1993) and other distributions of food and Superflex's *Free Shop: Anything the Customer Wants to Purchase Is Free* (2008) are contemporary expressions of this Digger principle.

**161.** Nietzsche, *The Use and Abuse of History*, 6.

**162.** Nietzsche, *The Use and Abuse of History*, 4.

**163.** Nietzsche, *The Use and Abuse of History*, 7, 9 (my italics).

**164.** Helen Swick Perry compared the counterculture to Fruitlands, the communistic community established by Alcott in 1843, in *The Human Be-In* (New York: Basic Books, 1970), 7. The analogy to Morris's Arcadia appears in Theodore Roszak, *The Making of a Counterculture*, xxxiii.

**165.** George Metesky, "The Ideology of Failure," *Berkeley Barb*, November 18, 1966, reprinted in Jesse Kornbluth, ed., *Notes from the New Underground* (New York: Viking, 1968), 52.

"George Metesky" is a pseudonym. The actual Metesky, known as the Mad Bomber, set off bombs in New York City during the 1940s and 1950s and was eventually institutionalized.

**166.** Metesky, "The Ideology of Failure," in Kornbluth, *Notes from the New Underground*, 51. In *No Future* (Durham, NC: Duke University Press, 2004), Lee Edelman denounces the figure of the child in whose name a hetero-normative future is proclaimed and secured. Edelman posits "queerness" as a limit and antagonism of this "reproductive futurism."

**167.** Allen Ginsberg spoke of a community of individuals "naked in forests seeking natural vision and meditation." Allen Ginsberg, "Renaissance or Die" (1967), in Kornbluth, *Notes from the New Underground*, 55.

**168.** Perry, *The Haight-Ashbury*, 98.

**169.** The newpaper's publishers organized the event. The press conference was attended by poet Gary Snyder and Yippie leader Jerry Rubin.

**170.** See Allen Cohen, "The Gathering of the Tribes," *San Francisco Oracle* 5 (January 1967): 2; and Grogan, *Ringolevio*, 274–75.

**171.** For more detailed descriptions of the event, see Perry, *The Human Be-In*; Matusow, *The Unraveling of America*, 275–77; and Perry, *The Haight-Ashbury*, 120–27.

**172.** Perry, *The Human Be-In*, 87, 89.

**173.** Cohen, "The Gathering of the Tribes," 2.

**174.** Cohen, "The Gathering of the Tribes," 86.

**175.** The San Francisco Be-In inspired an article in *Newsweek* and a cover issue of *Time Magazine* on "The Hippies" (July 16, 1967).

**176.** See David Joselit's insightful analysis of media's tendency to "replay" these events in *Feedback: Television against Democracy* (Cambridge, MA: MIT Press, 2007), 78.

**177.** "The Death of Hippie," Broadside distributed in Haight-Ashbury, Fall 1967, reprinted in Kornbluth, *Notes from the New Underground*, 266. On the Death of Hippie parade see Martin, *The Theater Is the Street*, 120–21.

**178.** Jennifer Egan, *The Invisible Circus* (New York: Picador, 1995), 1–2. All of the citations in this discussion are from this source.

**179.** The melancholic pines for a lost loved one, the nostalgic for a place or time that he or she has missed. Starobinski, "The Idea of Nostalgia," 84–85.

**180.** Orchestrated by the Diggers and the Art Liberation Front, the Invisible Circus occurred at the Glide Memorial Church in San Francisco's Tenderloin on February 24, 1967. See Grogan, *Ringolevio*, 280–86; and Perry, *The Haight-Ashbury*, 185–87.

**181.** Phoebe visits an unsavory drug dealer in Amsterdam who claims to have met her sister. After they smoke pot with the addict who has enticed her there, the dealer attempts to assault her and takes her money.

**182.** Egan, *The Invisible Circus*, 189.

**183.** "In Search of a Frame," *Berkeley Barb*, November 23, 1966, 6. www.diggers.org.

**184.** See Jameson, "Periodizing the Sixties"; and Roszak, *The Making of a Counterculture*, xii.

**185.** As Thomas Frank has noted, the widespread embrace of the VW Bug and microbus by the counterculture was the result of a hugely successful ad campaign. Frank, *The Conquest of Cool*. On the assimilation of youthful imagery and ideas during the Sixties, see Braunstein, "Forever Young," in Braunstein and Doyle, eds., *Imagine Nation*, 243–73.

**186.** William Ayers quoted in Jenny Turner, "Whoosh," *London Review of Books* 29, no. 11 (June 7, 2007): 26. Julie Taymor's movie musical *Across the Universe* (2007) is a case in point. Marketed to a teen audience, the film showcased a new generation of young actors performing stereotypical "Sixties" roles to an all-Beatles cover soundtrack. Among the characters are a Vietnam soldier, an antiwar activist, a McCartney-esque Liverpudlian, a Hendrix-esque guitarist and a Joplin-esque blues singer. An Asian lesbian is the only disruption in this stereotypical lineup. For a fine critical analysis of the film, see Jeremy Varon, "Long Live Lennon! Lennon is Dead! The Affirmative Character of Post-Sixties Idealism," *The Sixties* 1, no. 1 (June 2008): 69–75.

**187.** Woodstock '89 was held in the same location as the original concert. Woodstock '94 took place ten miles from the original site, and included contemporary rock and rave acts and several of the original participants. Woodstock '99 was staged far from the original site, included none of the original acts, and turned violent. A "Heroes of Woodstock" tour was staged in 2009 and included several Sixties acts. A fiftieth anniversary event is proposed for 2019.

**188.** Dana Spiotta, *Eat the Document* (New York: Scribner, 2006), 256.

**189.** Spiotta, *Eat the Document*, 257.

**190.** Spiotta, *Eat the Document*, 258.

**191.** Spiotta, *Eat the Document*, 258.

**192.** Stewart, *On Longing*, ix.

**193.** Starobinski, "The Idea of Nostalgia," 85–86.

**194.** Rousseau, *Dictionary of Music*, quoted in Starobinski, "The Idea of Nostalgia," 92 (my italics).

**195.** "Übertragen/Transfer I" (1996), in Green, *Shadows and Signals*, 91–92.

**196.** "Übertragen/Transfer I" (1996), in Green, *Shadows and Signals*, 88.

**197.** "Übertragen/Transfer I" (1996), in Green, *Shadows and Signals*, 86.

**198.** The second installment of *Partially Buried in Three Parts* is a hinge between the first and third parts, one that opens up the global optic of *Partially Buried Continued*, a symmetrical composition to *Partially Buried*. In contrast to the maternal/Vietnam War/Smithson theme of *Partially Buried*, the points of reference are Green's father, Friendly Green, a GI in South Korea during the Fifties; the Gwangju Massacre of 1980; and the writings of the Korean American author Teresa Hak Kyung Cha, a murder victim who also died young.

**199.** In *The Future of Nostalgia* (New York: Basic Books, 2001), Svetlana Boym redeems nostalgia from its usual meaning as melancholia, as disease. Her particular concern is the alliance of nostalgia and neo-nationalistic feeling, a nostalgia she calls "restorative." A positive, "reflective" nostalgia is both a form of longing and a meditation on that longing (xviii, 41–55), a conclusion Boym draws from Susan Stewart's work different from my antinostalgic reading of *On Longing*. Where "restorative" nostalgia establishes a monocular interpretation of the past, "reflective" nostalgia unleashes the "non-teleological possibilities" of a past time (50). Sixties nostalgia is neither restorative nor reflective but a melancholic longing. The concern of this book is how nostalgia can mystify and calcify our perception of periods of radical imagination. Boym would perhaps describe the practices I am considering here as reflectively nostalgic, and indeed her position has been adapted in Singer, "The Way Things Never Were."

**200.** The U.S. Supreme Court's 2013 repeal of Sections 4 and 5 of the Voting Rights Act of 1965; voter ID initiatives in Kansas, North Carolina, Texas, and other states; and the Voting Fraud Commission formed by the Trump administration are concerted efforts of minority disenfranchisement. Assaults by the Trump White House on the Clean Air Acts of 1963 and 1970, the Clean Water Act of 1972, and other environmentalist policies established during the Johnson and Nixon administrations are further efforts to repeal the progressive policies of the Sixties and Seventies.

**201.** See Lynn Zelevansky, *Sense and Sensibility: Women Artists and Minimalism in the Nineties* (New York: Museum of Modern Art, 1994); "Pop after Pop," *Artforum* 43, no. 2 (October 2004); Simon Leung, ed., "Contemporary Returns to Conceptual Art: Renée Green, Silvia Kolbowski, and Stephen Prina," *Art Journal* 60, no. 2 (Summer 2001): 54–71.

202. Michael Baxandall, *Patterns of Intention: On the Historical Explanation of Pictures* (New Haven: Yale University Press, 1985), 60.

203. Baxandall, *Patterns of Intention*, 61. Baxandall compares the aesthetic field at a given moment to a billiard table without pockets. The agent of influence—the cue ball—in this instance is not X but Y, the interpreter not the precursor. Every time Y collides with X the game is rearranged. Y and X are repositioned, but so are all the other artists.

204. Jorge Luis Borges, "Kafka and His Precursors," in *Labyrinths: Selected Stores and Other Writings*, ed. Donald A. Yates and James E. Irby (New York: New Directions, 1964), 201.

205. Martha Buskirk and Mignon Nixon, eds., *The Duchamp Effect*, *October* 70 (Fall 1994).

206. An effect is "something that is produced by an agency or cause." Jess Stein, ed., *The Random House Dictionary of the English Language* (New York: Random House, 1973), 454–55.

207. See, for example, Rosalind E. Krauss, "Notes on the Index: Seventies Art in America," *October* 3 (Spring 1977): 68–81; and Martha Buskirk, "Thoroughly Modern Marcel," in Buskirk and Nixon, eds., *The Duchamp Effect*, 191–204. As Buskirk suggests, the miniature reproductions of Duchamp's early works in *Box in a Valise*, the notes of his *Green Box*, and the later editions of his readymades kept these works in circulation for decades. In a nuanced reading of Freud's notion of *Nachträglichkeit*, Hal Foster inscribes Duchamp's impact in a broader narrative of avant-garde recurrence, a periodic return of the repressed. Hal Foster, "What's Neo about the Neo Avant-Garde" in Buskirk and Nixon, eds., *The Duchamp Effect*, 5–32.

208. "Robert Smithson on Duchamp: Interview with Moira Roth" (1973), in Flam, ed., *Robert Smithson: The Collected Writings*, 311–12.

209. "Robert Smithson on Duchamp: Interview with Moira Roth" (1973), 310.

210. As the critic Gene Swenson argued at the time in his exhibition catalogue *The Other Tradition* (Philadelphia: Institute of Contemporary Art, 1965).

211. "Robert Smithson on Duchamp: Interview with Moira Roth" (1973), 310.

212. Pamela M. Lee, *New Games: Postmodernism after Contemporary Art* (New York: Routledge, 2013), 70. Lee's genealogy of Smithson's precedence focuses on his impact on postmodernist theory in the pivotal writings of Craig Owens that mediated the current Smithson return.

213. Tacita Dean put it this way: "Smithson has become an important figure in my working life not because I depend on him in any way, but because his work allows me a conceptual space in which to reside." Tacita Dean, "Trying to Find the Spiral Jetty" (1997), artist's statement, unpublished.

214. See Brian Wallis, "Excavating the Seventies," *Art in America* 85, no. 9 (September 1997): 96–99, 122; and Cornelia Butler, "A Lurid Presence: Smithson's Legacy and Post-Studio Art," in Tsai and Butler, *Robert Smithson*, 224–43.

215. Smithson died on July 20, 1973. Holt, Serra, and Shafrazi completed *Amarillo Ramp* between August 3 and September 1.

216. Nancy Holt, *The Making of Amarillo Ramp* (2013).

217. *Floating Island* and related projects are described in Hobbs, *Robert Smithson: Sculpture*, 199–204.

218. See Randy Kennedy, "It's Not Easy Making Art That Floats," *New York Times*, September 16, 2005. The project involved the collaboration of Holt, Minetta Brook, Whitney Museum of American Art, and the Estate of Robert Smithson. It is documented in the film *Floating Island to Travel around Manhattan Island by Robert Smithson* (Minetta Brook and Whitney Museum of American Art; 2005).

219. Diane Shamash quoted in Kennedy, "It's Not Easy Making Art That Floats."

220. Once described as subversive of modernist models of originality, appropriation is nothing but intentional: a calculated decision to borrow or "steal" a found image or thing.

**221.** Cummings, "Interview with Robert Smithson for the Archives of American Art/Smithsonian Institution," in Flam, ed., *Robert Smithson: The Collected Writings*, 294.

**222.** "Earthwords," in Owens, *Beyond Recognition*, 47.

**223.** In postmodernist allegory "one text is doubled by another" or "*read through another*," like a palimpsest. Allegory is temporalized—"a symbol introduced in continuous series, the temporal extension of metaphor"—and thus opposed to the Romantic symbol, the timeless expression of an "inner essence" or truth. "Earthwords," in Owens, *Beyond Recognition*, 48; and "The Allegorical Impulse: Toward a Theory of Postmodernism" in Owens, *Beyond Recognition*, 53–54, 62. The Benjaminian theme of allegory is particularly apposite in a discussion of *Partially Buried Woodshed*. If the ruin is the "emblem" of allegory, a rhetorical mode that Benjamin associates with fragmentation and death, the *Woodshed* is the emblematic allegorical object of Smithson's oeuvre: the work that has inspired the greatest citation by artists is a memorial to the dead. On the ruin as allegorical emblem see Buck-Morss, *The Dialectics of Seeing*, 159–201.

**224.** For an account of "preposterous" citation in contemporary art, see Mieke Bal, *Quoting Caravaggio: Contemporary Art, Preposterous History* (Chicago: University of Chicago Press, 1999).

**225.** Harold Bloom, *The Anxiety of Influence: A Theory of Poetry* (New York: Oxford University Press, 1973), 14 (my italics). The practices of Burr and Millar discussed here invite Bloom's analogy yet are not reducible to it. Rather than a psychoanalytic model of misprision (the Bloomian poet competes with and misreads the precursor), the extension of Smithson's practice, inspired by postmodernist appropriation techniques, is consciously citational.

**226.** "Frederick Law Olmsted and the Dialectical Landscape," in Flam, ed., *Robert Smithson: The Collected Writings*, 157–71.

**227.** Frederick Law Olmsted, "The Greensward Plan" (1858), proposal for Central Park, quoted in Tom Burr, "Catalogue Entry," in Jan Brand, Catelijne de Muynck, and Valerie Smith, eds., *Sonsbeek 1993* (Arnhem: Snoeck-Ducaju & Zoon 1993), 202.

**228.** "Frederick Law Olmsted and the Dialectical Landscape," in Flam, ed., *Robert Smithson: The Collected Writings*, 169.

**229.** Burr, "Catalogue Entry," 202.

**230.** Burr, "Catalogue Entry," 202. The citations were drawn from *The Ramble in Central Park: An Historic Landscape Master Plan* (New York, 1982). For a comparable work see Burr's *Circa 1977* and its accompanying text, "Trash," in Bernhard Bürgi, ed., *Platzwechsel: Ursula Biemann, Tom Burr, Mark Dion, Christian Philipp Müller* (Zürich: Kunsthalle Zürich, 1995), 69–89.

**231.** Robert Smithson, *The Spiral Jetty* (1970, film). The citation appears in David Dalton and David Felton, "Charles Manson: The Incredible Story of the Most Dangerous Man Alive," *Rolling Stone*, June 25, 1970.

**232.** A companion work, the video *From Columbus, Ohio to Partially Buried Woodshed* (1999) documents Dean's journey to Kent to view *Partially Buried Woodshed*. Where in *Trying to Find the Spiral Jetty* Dean reaches Smithson's work, she never locates the *Woodshed*.

**233.** Tacita Dean, *Trying to Find the Spiral Jetty* (1997, audiotape).

**234.** See "The Crystal Land," a text inspired by Ballard's novel *The Crystal World* (1966), and "The Artist as Site-Seer: Or, a Dintorphic Essay" in Flam, ed., *Robert Smithson: The Collected Writings*, 7–9 and 340–45; and Tacita Dean's film *J.G.* (2013).

**235.** J. G. Ballard, "The Voices of Time," in *The Best Short Stories of J. G. Ballard* (New York: Picador USA, 1995), 87, 93, 98.

**236.** The artist Conrad Bakker has embarked on a similar project. *Untitled Project: Robert Smithson Library & Book Club* (2014 ongoing) is a re-creation of Smithson's library as a work of sculpture in two parts: a "complete" set of the books that Smithson owned (exhibited at the Utah Museum of Fine Arts, September 12, 2014–February 8, 2015), and an ongoing project of individual carved and painted "books" commissioned by members of a mail order "Book

Club." The completion of Millar's library falls on Millar alone, that of Bakker on the principle of consumer desire. See Whitney Tassie, *Salt 10: Conrad Bakker*, exhibition pamphlet (Salt Lake City: Utah Museum of Fine Arts, 2014), without pagination.

**237.** Smithson worked for a time at the Eighth Street Bookshop in Greenwich Village in 1956 and visited the store often during his daily walks. See Eugenie Tsai, *Robert Smithson Unearthed: Drawings, Collages, Writings* (New York: Columbia University Press, 1991).

**238.** See Tsai and Butler, *Robert Smithson*, 249–63. For an analysis of the library's contents, see Alexander Alberro, "The Catalogue of Robert Smithson's Library" in Tsai and Butler, *Robert Smithson*, 244–48.

**239.** Email to the author, July 11, 2014.

**240.** A comparable work is Stephen Prina's *Exquisite Corpse: The Complete Works of Manet* (begun 1988). Beginning with Manet's first painting, Prina has "remade" every work completed by the Impressionist in a white monochrome format the same size as the original, accompanied by a poster documenting the project as a whole. The series is ongoing.

**241.** Hobbs, *Robert Smithson: Sculpture*, 164–65.

**242.** Millar exhibited the works at sleeper, Edinburgh, in November–December 2007. He presented the receipt in a frame and the key in a vitrine. The contact sheets (rephotographs of Smithson's photographs) were installed beneath the pedestal.

**243.** "The image of the ruin is always ambivalent and open to manifold interpretations." Paul Zucker, *Fascination of Decay—Ruins: Relic-Symbol-Ornament* (Ridgewood, NJ: Gregg Press, 1968), 2.

**244.** On the double identity of the *Woodshed* as artwork and memorial, see Nora Alter, "Beyond the Frame: Renée Green's Video Practice," in Green, *Shadows and Signals*, 161.

**245.** Alois Riegl, "The Modern Cult of Monuments: Its Character and Its Origin," trans. Kurt W. Forster and Diane Ghirardo, *Oppositions* 25 (1982): 21–51.

**246.** Riegl, "The Modern Cult of Monuments," 23.

**247.** Brinsley Tyrrell quoted in Green, *Shadows and Signals*, 71. Brian Wallis describes the *Woodshed* as an "inadvertent memorial" in "Excavating the Seventies," 97.

**248.** It is intriguing to consider that Smithson had himself photographed in front of the House of the Vestals and Juturna Fountain, also associated with the Vestals and an iconography of purity—the state of existence destroyed by entropy—in addition to the Colosseum. (My thanks to Eric Varner for identifying these monuments.) Organized around a show at Galleria George Lester, Smithson's trip is documented in his letters in the Robert Smithson/Nancy Holt Papers, Archives of American Art, Smithsonian Institution, Roll 3832, Frames 744–47 and 784–87; and in Cummings, "Interview with Robert Smithson for the Archives of American Art/Smithsonian Institution," in Flam, ed., *Robert Smithson: The Collected Writings*, 286, 293. As Reynolds notes, Smithson's thinking on this subject was also prompted by such exhibitions as "Monuments, Trophies, and Tombstones" (Museum of Contemporary Crafts, New York, 1967) and "Sculpture in Environment" (New York, 1967). See Reynolds, *Robert Smithson: Learning from New Jersey and Elsewhere*, 267n116.

**249.** See Pamela M. Lee, *Chronophobia: On Time in the Art of the Sixties* (Cambridge, MA: MIT Press, 2004), 154–256; and Roberts, *Mirror-Travels*, 36–59. Where Lee teases out the dynamism of Smithson's recursive model, Roberts stresses the crystalline stasis that is the "end result" of entropic time.

**250.** "Entropy and the New Monuments," in Flam, ed., *Robert Smithson: The Collected Writings*, 11.

**251.** "The Monuments of Passaic, New Jersey," in Flam, ed., *Robert Smithson: The Collected Writings*, 72.

**252.** "The Monuments of Passaic, New Jersey," in Flam, ed., *Robert Smithson: The Collected Writings*, 72.

**253.** Benjamin, "Berlin Childhood around 1900, Final Version," 64.

**254.** Benjamin, "Berlin Childhood around 1900, Final Version," 92.

**255.** Benjamin, "Berlin Childhood around 1900, Final Version," 38.

**256.** "Remembrance advances from small to smallest details, from the smallest to the infinitesimal, while that which it encounters in these microcosms grows ever mightier." Benjamin, "A Berlin Chronicle," 6.

**257.** The May 4th Memorial, designed by Bruno Ast in 1986 and completed in 1990, was the result of a national competition after a work by George Segal, *In Memory of May 4 1970, Kent State: Abraham and Isaac*, was rejected. (The Segal is now at Princeton.) Ast's design was much reduced from his original plan for budgetary reasons. The KSU art professor Brinsley Tyrrell was then asked to design another memorial at the same location. Tyrrell planted 58,175 daffodil bulbs (in memory of the number of American casualties in Vietnam), which were intended to bloom annually during the anniversary of the May 4 massacre. Other memorials include an abstract sculpture by the art professor Alistair Granville-Jackson, *The Kent Four* (1973), located on the commons, and the May 4th Reading Room in the university library (1974). On the history of May 4 monuments on the campus, see James E. Dalton, ed., *Kent State May 4 Memorial Design Competition* (Kent: Kent State University, 1988); Sterling Victor Fleischer, "Public Sculpture, Public Debate and the Politics of Commemoration: The George Segal Controversy and the Memorialization of May 4, 1970, at Kent State University," M.A. thesis, Kent State University, 2000; and John Fitzgerald O'Hara, "Kent State/May 4 and Postwar Memory," *American Quarterly* 58, no. 2 (June 2006): 301–28.

**258.** The parking lot monuments were installed in 1999 after members of the May 4th Task Force complained that the locations where the murdered students lay were still being used, quite inappropriately, as parking spaces.

**259.** Riegl calls the monument's capacity to project its existence in time "age value." See Riegl, "The Modern Cult of Monuments," 207.

**260.** Michener, *Kent State: What Happened and Why*, 10. Taylor Hall was completed in 1966–67, four years before Michener's visit.

**261.** The bullet hole in the sculpture served as evidence during the various investigations of the shootings.

**262.** The faculty members included geology professor Glenn Frank. In 2012, the U.S. Department of Justice decided not to reopen the case despite the repeated efforts of survivors and victims' families.

**263.** "The Spiral Jetty," in Flam, ed., *Robert Smithson: The Collected Writings*, 152. In order to suggest this absence of boundaries Smithson established them in this instance, dictating as part of the terms of his gift of the work that the project would encompass the shed's footprint to a circumference of forty-five feet.

**264.** "Ohio, 1949," in *Barnett Newman: Selected Writings and Interviews*, ed. John P. O'Neill (New York: Alfred A. Knopf, 1990), 175.

**265.** Where the monuments Riegl speaks of evoke a faraway time, *Partially Buried Woodshed* expresses an accelerated or artificial "age value." Nelson also aged his "shed" deliberately, "Frankensteining" the work from other destroyed woodsheds and agricultural buildings whose lathing had "aged appropriately." Mike Nelson, email to the author, April 16, 2007.

**266.** Riegl, "The Modern Cult of Monuments," 33.

**267.** Bois, "Threshole," 188. As Bois notes, in the case of the *Woodshed* Smithson drew up a contract that spelled out its financial and artistic value, and the university's obligation to preserve the work as Smithson intended (which, of course, it did not do).

**268.** "Discussions with Heizer, Oppenheim, Smithson," in Flam, *Robert Smithson: The Collected Writings*, 251.

**269.** Susan Sontag, *On Photography* (New York: Picador, 1973), 11.

270. Roland Barthes, *Camera Lucida: Reflections on Photography*, trans. Richard Howard (New York: Farrar, Straus, Giroux, 1981), 77.

271. See Lawrence Alloway, "Artists and Photographs," *Studio International* 179, no. 921 (April 1970): 162–64; and Ron Horning, "In Time: Earthworks, Photodocuments, and Robert Smithson's Buried Shed," *Aperture* 106 (Spring 1987): 74–77.

272. "The work is nothing unless it is recorded." Richard Long, "Heaven and Earth" (documentary, Channel 4, dir. Nico Wasserman, Tate Media, 2009). At the same time, this proliferation of images and descriptions is an entropic effect. "The more information you have the higher degree of entropy, so that one piece of information tends to cancel out the other." Smithson, "Entropy Made Visible: Interview with Alison Sky," 302.

273. On this point see Darsie Alexander, "Reluctant Witness: Photography and the Documentation of Sixties and Seventies Art," in Helen Molesworth, *Work Ethic* (Baltimore: Baltimore Museum of Art, 2003), 53–64; and Miwon Kwon, "Bloody Valentines: Afterimages by Ana Mendieta," in M. Catherine de Zegher, ed., *Inside the Invisible* (Cambridge, MA: MIT Press, 1996), 165–71.

274. To the Baudelaire of "À une passante" Andreas Huyssen opposes the Éluard of the expression "le dur désir du durer," the desire to achieve an enduring art. Huyssen, *Present Pasts*, 37. For a related comparison see Alex Potts, "Introduction," in Jon Wood, David Hulks, and Alex Potts, eds., *The Modern Sculpture Reader* (Leeds, UK: Henry Moore Institute, 2007), xlv.

275. The soundtrack of *T.S.O.Y.W.* was composed by Amy Granat, Jutta Koether, and Stefan Tcherepnin. The lover is played by Skylar Haskard.

276. A "contemporary" circa 2007. In one scene, the driver reads the *New York Times*. A back shot reveals the headline of the article he reads: James Glanz, "American Faces Charge of Graft for Work in Iraq," *New York Times*, November 17, 2005. In a later shot, the driver reads an article with the headline "Torture."

277. Friedrich Gottlieb Klopstock (1724–1803).

278. Johann Wolfgang von Goethe, *The Sorrows of Young Werther*, trans. Elizabeth Mayer and Louise Brogan (New York: Modern Library, 1993), 99.

279. "The Ghost Ship," in Roland Barthes, *A Lover's Discourse: Fragments*, trans. Richard Howard (New York: Farrar, Straus & Giroux, 1978), 101.

280. Goethe, *The Sorrows of Young Werther*, 14. "Since you are so concerned that I should not neglect my drawing, I would rather skip that subject than confess that I have not done much lately" (49).

281. The lover also visits Sarah Vanderlip's *CA Truckhead* (2004) in the High Desert Test Sites near Twenty-nine Palms and Joshua Tree, California.

282. Goethe, *The Sorrows of Young Werther*, 125.

283. The appeal of "entropic" procedures in the current art market is undeniable: "This material instability functions as a collector purity test. Because while [Terence] Koh's rocketing market invites speculation, only a fool buys perishable work. . . . Such fragility attracts collectors who pride themselves on supporting 'avant-garde' art." Marc Spiegler, "Is Terence Koh's Sperm Worth $100,000?" *New York Magazine*, January 15, 2007, 67.

284. Pointing to Michel Leiris's description of spit as "the very symbol of the formless," Yve-Alain Bois observes that Leiris "gives consistency to the inconsistency of spit, and he gives it symbolic value (which is exactly what Bataille avoids doing)." Bois and Krauss, *Formless: A User's Guide*, 18.

285. "Guggenheim Presents Work by Kitty Kraus for the Second Exhibition in New Intervals Series Exhibition: *Intervals: Kitty Kraus*, October 9, 2009–January 6, 2010." Press Release, Guggenheim Museum. http://www.guggenheim.org/new-york/press-room/press-releases/3056-kitty-krausrelease.

**286.** "Banks Violette," Maureen Paley Gallery, London, June 2–July 23, 2006. For a description of the show, see Alex Needham, "Kill to Get the Money," *i-D* 2, no. 19 (September 2006): 188–91.

**287.** Smithson made these works for the "Earth Art" show curated by Willoughby Sharp at Andrew Dickson White Museum of Art, Cornell University, February 1969.

**288.** Banks Violette quoted in Karen Rosenberg, "Renouncing the Dark Arts," *New York Magazine*, June 2–9, 2007, 106. See Violette's discussion of Smithson's Cayuga project in "Banks Violette," *Art World*, October–November 2008, 76.

**289.** "Banks Violette," Gladstone Gallery, New York, February 12–April 17, 2010.

**290.** Snow's best-known work, *Nest*, was an event and installation co-organized with Dan Colen at Deitch Projects in New York, July 26–August 18, 2007. Snow and Colen's "hamster nest" was created from twenty-five hundred New York phone books shredded and scattered about Deitch's space. The artists and invited guests proceeded to deface and pollute the gallery for five nights. They listened to a band, drank, and got high, covered the walls with graffiti, made body prints, and hurled paint-soaked paper rags on the walls that resembled clumps of vomit. A corner of the gallery served as a *pissoir*. Ordinary visitors were invited to view the mess during the day and in the weeks that followed. See Jessica Slaven, "Sculpture in the Expended Field," *Paper Monument* 2 (Fall 2008): 20; and *Nest: Dash Snow Dan Colen* (New York: Deitch Projects, 2008).

**291.** Amy Granat, email to the author, October 24, 2014.

**292.** As the biographical fixation surrounding the work of Eva Hesse suggests. The construction of Hesse as tragic "victim" has been particularly pernicious, dating to the release of her diaries shortly after her death, on which see the excellent studies by Anne M. Wagner, "Another Hesse," *October* 69 (Summer 1994): 49–84; and Briony Fer, "Bordering on Blank: Eva Hesse and Minimalism," in *On Abstract Art* (New Haven: Yale University Press, 2000), 109–30.

**293.** See the hagiographic "Introduction" by Philip Leider in Holt, *The Writings of Robert Smithson*, 3.

**294.** Alan Brilliant, *Smithson* (Greensboro, NC: Unicorn Press, 2013).

**295.** A theme that Smithson explored again in 1960–61. On the religious iconography of Smithson's youthful work and its bearing on his later practice, see Thomas Crow, "Cosmic Exile: Prophetic Turns in the Life and Art of Robert Smithson," in Tsai and Butler, *Robert Smithson*, 33–56.

## Part Three

**1.** The March on Washington for Jobs and Freedom was held on August 28, 1963. On the march and its orchestration, see Taylor Branch, *Parting the Waters: The King Years 1954–63* (New York: Simon & Schuster, 1988), 846–87.

**2.** Martin Luther King Jr., "I Have a Dream," in James M. Washington, ed., *A Testament of Hope: The Essential Writings and Speeches of Martin Luther King, Jr.* (New York: Harper Collins, 1991), 217.

**3.** King, "I Have a Dream," 218.

**4.** King, "I Have a Dream," 219–20.

**5.** Kennedy's reaction to Bill Hudson's famous photo of Walter Gadsen being attacked is described in Branch, *Parting the Waters: The King Years 1954–63*, 764. Kennedy issued his "Report to the American People on Civil Rights," the template for the Civil Rights Act of 1964 banning discrimination in public accommodations, transportation, and schools, on June 11, 1963.

**6.** The assassination of President Kennedy was a major setback for the movement, yet one that emboldened King and his colleagues to carry on with a renewed sense of purpose. Branch, *Parting the Waters*, 922.

7. King, "I Have a Dream," 218.
8. The Watergate scandal (1973); the resignation of President Nixon (1974); the fall of Saigon (1975); the fall of the Gang of Four and the celebration of the U.S. Bicentennial (1976); the German Autumn (1978); and the election of Margaret Thatcher and Ronald Reagan (1979). For another account of this periodization, see Christopher Connery, "The End of the Sixties," *boundary 2* 36, no. 1 (Spring 2009): 183–210.
9. T. J. Clark, "For a Left with No Future," *New Left Review* 74 (March–April, 2012): 55–56. On "restoration" as a historical phenomeon, see Thomas Crow, *Restoration: The Fall of Napoleon in the Course of European Art, 1812–1820*, The Andrew W. Mellon Lectures in the Fine Arts (Princeton: Princeton University Press, 2018).
10. During intervallic periods "an open, shared universally practicable idea of emancipation is wanting." Alain Badiou, *The Rebirth of History: Times of Riots and Uprisings*, trans. Gregory Elliott (London: Verso, 2012), 38–39.
11. Badiou describes the antiauthoritarian protests of the Arab Spring, the antiausterity (Indignados) protests in Spain, the *banlieue* riots in France, prodemocracy demonstrations in Hong Kong, and the "occupy Wall Street" protests as Events—proleptic eruptions whose lasting impacts are impossible to predict. Badiou, *The Rebirth of History*, 27.
12. There is a marked disagreement between the positions of Clark and Badiou. Where Clark advocates a "truly present-centered, non-prophetic, disenchanted" politics, Badiou embraces an avant-gardist ontology of imminence: the Event is prophetic and futuristic. Clark, "For a Left with No Future," 57; and Badiou, *The Rebirth of History*, 109.
13. Nietzsche, *The Use and Abuse of History for Life*, 8.
14. Martin Luther King Jr., "Where Do We Go from Here," in Washington, ed., *A Testament of Hope*, 252.
15. King, "Where Do We Go from Here," 7.
16. Kerry James Marshall, "Mementos," Renaissance Society, University of Chicago, May 6–June 28, 1998. The exhibition traveled to the Brooklyn Museum of Art, the San Francisco Museum of Modern Art, the Institute of Contemporary Art, Boston, the Santa Monica Museum, and the Boise Art Museum.
17. A reproduction of the charcoal presentation drawing for *Souvenir I* reveals the artist's thinking as he developed the series. The curtains, though drawn, are translucent. Daylight pours into the room. On the opposite wall a curtain partially covers a monochromatic black rectangle. Marshall has not yet articulated the mourning banner with portraits inset in a cloud of glitter. The drawing is reproduced in *Kerry James Marshall* (New York: Harry N. Abrams, 2000), 96.
18. Richard Powell traces a tradition of such imagery to the chromolith portraits of Frederick Douglass, Booker T. Washington, and President Lincoln found in African American households in the late nineteenth and early twentieth centuries. Richard Powell, "Lamentations from the 'Hood," in *Kerry James Marshall: Mementos* (Chicago: Renaissance Society of University of Chicago, 1998), 33.
19. The angels' wings are linoleum block prints.
20. The bombing is described in Joe Campbell and Jimmy Bryan, "This Time There Was No Phone Threat, Warning," *Birmingham News*, September 16, 1963; and Diane McWhorter, *Carry Me Home—Birmingham, Alabama: The Climactic Battle of the Civil Rights Revolution* (New York: Touchstone, 2002), 525.
21. On Campin's synthesis of verism and supernaturalism—a naturalism rooted in the Aquinian belief that physical things are "corporeal metaphors of things spiritual," see Erwin

Panofsky, *Early Netherlandish Painting: Its Origins and Character* (New York: Icon Editions, 1971), 142–43. Panofsky's observation that Campin combines a deeply recessive space with markers of flatness in a disjunctive manner is also germane in a discussion of the *Souvenirs* (166–67).

**22.** The angels are portraits of relatives and a family friend, drawn from life in their own homes. Kerry James Marshall, "Notes on Career and Work," in *Kerry James Marshall*, 122.

**23.** Marshall, "Notes on Career and Work," in *Kerry James Marshall*, 122.

**24.** *The American College Dictionary* (New York: Random House, 1966), 759.

**25.** Jimmie Lee Jackson, a civil rights activist from Marion, Alabama, was shot dead trying to protect his mother from a vicious assault by state troopers after a voting rights march on February 26, 1965. Viola Liuzzo, a mother of five and civil rights advocate from Detroit affiliated with the Unitarian Universalist Church, was murdered by Klan night riders while driving a black marcher to Selma from Montgomery on March 25, 1965. Where the murder of Jackson was largely ignored, the shooting of Liuzzo and murder of white UU minister James Reeb in Selma on March 11, 1965, brought national attention to the cause. The omission of Reeb in *Souvenir II* was pointed out to me by Annie Storr and Sean McCormally.

**26.** The names of novelists Nella Larsen and Richard Wright (d. 1960) and the charismatic preacher George "Father Divine" Baker (d. 1965), written in a smaller font, also appear in this work.

**27.** Fuller exhibited at the Paris Salon in 1903; DuBois published *The Souls of Black Folk* in 1903 and co-founded the NAACP in 1909. Dandridge was the first actress to be nominated for an Academy Award in a leading role. Hansberry was the first female black playwright to have a show produced on Broadway. DuBois was the first African American to receive a Ph.D. from Harvard. Savage was an important teacher and mentor for generations of younger black artists.

**28.** *Mementos* was a multimedia installation of many parts. It included *Untitled (16th Street Baptist Church Sign with Flowers)* (1998), a replica of the cruciform sign of the Birmingham church festooned with wax flowers; five framed civil rights–era slogans (*We Shall Overcome*, *Black Power*, *Black Is Beautiful*, *Burn Baby Burn*, *By Any Means Necessary*) made with the large stamps and printer's pads displayed in the show; *Untitled (Sculpture Installation: 5 Stamps and 3 Pads)* (1998); a second C-print, *Untitled* (1998); and five paintings inspired by the mourning banner entitled *We Mourn Our Loss #1–5* (1997).

**29.** Martin Luther King Jr., "Eulogy for the Martyred Children," in Washington, ed., *A Testament of Hope*, 221.

**30.** Marshall first treated the theme of ghetto violence in his *Lost Boys* series (1993).

**31.** Claudia Rankine, "The Condition of Black Life Is One of Mourning," *New York Times*, June 22, 2015. Unfortunately, *Laid to Rest* is as relevant now as when Marshall exhibited it: the "present" invoked by his work is ongoing.

**32.** The Detroit riots occurred in the 12th Street neighborhood on July 23–25, 1967. The event left forty-three people dead, thirty-three of whom were African American. Some seven thousand individuals were arrested, and thirteen hundred buildings were destroyed. Marwick, *The Sixties*, 579.

**33.** Marshall, "Notes on Career and Work," 121.

**34.** Marshall is himself a collector of Sixties souvenirs and artifacts, including the front door to the apartment in West Chicago where Hampton and Clark were murdered on December 4, 1969, currently on loan to the DuSable Museum of African American History. The incident has inspired another work of Sixties return, William Cordova's installation "House That *Frank Lloyd Wright* Built 4 Fred Hampton and Mark Clark" (2006), a full-scale reconstruction of the floor plan of Hampton's home.

35. See Kellie Jones, *Now Dig This! Art & Black Los Angeles, 1960–1980* (New York: DelMonico Books/Prestel, 2011).
36. See "An Argument for Something Else: Dieter Roelstraete in Conversation with Kerry James Marshall, Chicago 2012," in *Kerry James Marshall: Painting and Other Stuff* (Antwerp: M HKA, 2013), 16–18.
37. Marshall, "Notes on Career and Work," 123.
38. Among such works I would point to *Nat Turner with the Head of His Master* (2011), a reconstruction of Turner's beheading of his master drawing upon Old Master images of liberation, and *Scipio Moorhead, Portrait of Himself, 1776* (2007), a depiction of a colonial-era enslaved artist whose engraving of Phillis Wheatley is the sole representation of that poet.
39. In Marshall's painting *Great America* (1994) an amusement park Tunnel of Love boat ride evokes the brutal transatlantic transport of black slaves during the colonial and antebellum periods, a temporal and geographical "nowhere" at the core of black diasporic memory. Other details summon a past that remains uncannily present. A head bobs in the water, implying a man has fallen or was pushed overboard. Sheet-like apparitions evoke ghosts and Klansmen. Intricate designs drawn in pencil resemble *veves* (voodoo symbols) of Yoruba origin, recalling the African religious traditions suppressed and creolized during enslavement. See Marshall's remarks on this work and his approach in *In the Tower: Kerry James Marshall* (Washington, DC: National Gallery of Art, 2013), without pagination.
40. Nora, "Between Memory and History," 7–24.
41. Nora, "Between Memory and History," 16. Nora is referring to Jewish memory.
42. Jeff Wall, "Introduction," in *Kerry James Marshall* (Vancouver: Vancouver Art Gallery, 2010), 15. Upon reading Ralph Ellison's *Invisible Man* as a teenager, Marshall decided to paint black figures exclusively so as to introduce images of people of African descent to the walls of the world's museums, which had historically excluded them. The crucial work from this phase is Marshall's black-on-black *Invisible Man* (1986).
43. Powell, "Lamentations from the 'Hood," in *Kerry James Marshall: Mementos*, 37, 42.
44. Press Release, National Action Network Reclaim the Dream March, July 8, 2013. The event was co-organized by the Rev. Al Sharpton and Martin Luther King III.
45. Jim Rutenberg, "A Dream Undone: Inside the 50 Year Campaign to Repeal the Voting Rights Act," *New York Times Magazine*, July 29, 2015; and Michelle Alexander, *The New Jim Crow: Mass Incarceration in the Age of Colorblindness* (New York: New Press, 2012).
46. Rev. Al Sharpton, National Action Network March on Washington 50th Anniversary Celebration, Washington, DC, August 24, 2013.
47. Rick Bragg, "38 Years Later, Last of Suspects Is Convicted in Church Bombing," *New York Times*, May 23, 2002. On the prosecutions of the conspirators and the FBI's problematic role in this history, see McWhorter, *Carry Me Home—Birmingham, Alabama*, 571–602. The case was prosecuted by U.S. Attorney Doug Jones, who was elected the Democratic senator from Alabama in an upset election against Republican candidate Roy Moore on December 12, 2017.
48. De La Beckwith died in Jackson on January 21, 2001. Edgar Ray Killen died in the Mississippi State Penitentiary, known as Parchman Farm, on January 11, 2018.

# INDEX

Page numbers in **bold** refer to images.